The Art and Science of C

A Library-Based Introduction to Computer Science

The Art and Science of *C*

A Library-Based Introduction to Computer Science

ERIC S. ROBERTS
Stanford University

 Addison-Wesley Publishing Company

Reading, Massachusetts ▪ Menlo Park, California ▪ New York ▪ Don Mills, Ontario
Wokingham, England ▪ Amsterdam ▪ Bonn ▪ Sydney ▪ Singapore ▪ Tokyo
Madrid ▪ San Jose ▪ Milan ▪ Paris

Sponsoring Editor, Lynne Doran Cote
Senior Production Supervisor, Jim Rigney
Associate Production Supervisor, Amy Willcutt
Production Technology Supervisor, Laurie Petrycki
Electronic Production Specialist, Tricia Deforge
Electronic Production Administrator, Sally Simpson
Special Projects Editor, Sue Gleason
Development Editors, Lauren Rusk and Laura Michaels
Copy Editor, Karen Stone
Text Designer, Catherine Hawkes
Cover Design, Diana Coe
Senior Manufacturing Manager, Roy Logan

About the cover

The cover photograph of the New York Public Library reflects the library-based approach used in this text. It is particularly appropriate that the lion guarding the entrance is named "Patience," because patience is an essential quality for successful programmers.

Photo Credits

Front cover photo by Jose Pouso.

Photo A on page 5 is reproduced with the consent of Unisys Corporation.

Photos B, C, and D on page 5 are reproduced courtesy of International Business Machines Corporation.

Photo of Eric Roberts by Reneé Burgard.

Library of Congress Cataloging-in-Publication Data
Roberts, Eric S.
 The art and science of C : a library-based introduction to computer science /
Eric S. Roberts.
  p. cm.
 Includes index.
 ISBN 0-201-54322-2
 1. C (Computer program language) I. Title
QA76.73.C15R62 1995
005.13'3—dc20   94-16744
                                                                CIP

1 2 3 4 5 6 7 8 9 10—MA—9897969594

In loving memory of Grace E. Bloom
(1924–1994) for helping me appreciate
the value of ideas and the importance
of writing clearly about them.

About the Author

I first began teaching introductory computer science more than 20 years ago while I was still a student at Harvard. Since receiving my Ph.D. in 1980, I have taught computer science at Harvard, Wellesley, and Stanford, where I am Associate Chair of the Computer Science Department. In that capacity, I am responsible for the undergraduate program in computer science. Although I have taught advanced courses in computer science and have also worked in the research industry, my greatest joy comes from opening up the enormous power of computers to students who are just beginning to learn about them. In their excitement, my own love for computer science is constantly renewed.

In addition to my teaching at Stanford, I have served since 1990 as the president of Computer Professionals for Social Responsibility, a public-interest association of computer professionals with 2000 members in 22 chapters throughout the United States. Computers affect our society in many different ways. Just as it is important to learn about the technology, it is critical that we also take the responsibility to ensure that computers are used for the benefit of all. If you have suggestions as to how I might make the presentation more clear, or you encounter errors in this text, please let me know. You can reach me by electronic mail at ericr@aw.com.

Eric S. Roberts
Department of Computer Science
Stanford University

To the Student

Welcome! By picking up this book, you have taken a step into the world of computer science—a field of study that has grown from almost nothing half a century ago to become one of the most vibrant and active disciplines of our time.

Over that time, the computer has opened up extraordinary possibilities in almost every area of human endeavor. Business leaders today are able to manage global enterprises on an unprecedented scale because computers enable them to transfer information anywhere in a fraction of a second. Scientists can now solve problems that were beyond their reach until the computer made the necessary calculations possible. Filmmakers use computers to generate dramatic visual effects that are impossible to achieve without them. Doctors can determine much more accurately what is going on inside a patient because computers have enabled a massive transformation in the practice of medicine.

Computers are a profoundly empowering technology. The advances we have seen up to now are small compared to what we will see in the next century. Computers will play a major role in shaping that century, just as they have the last 50 years. Those of you who are students today will soon inherit the responsibility of guiding that progress. As you do so, knowing how to use computers can only help.

Like most skills that are worth knowing, learning how computers work and how to control their enormous power takes time. You will not understand it all at once. But you must start somewhere. Twenty-five centuries ago, the Chinese philosopher Lao-tzu observed that the longest journey begins with a single step. This book can be your beginning.

For many of you, however, the first step can be the hardest to take. Many students find computers overwhelming and imagine that computer science is beyond their reach. Learning the basics of programming, however, does not require advanced mathematics or a detailed understanding of electronics. What matters in programming is whether you can progress from the statement of a problem to its solution. To do so, you must be able to think logically. You must have the necessary discipline to express your logic in a form that the computer can understand. Perhaps most importantly, you must be able to see the task through to its completion without getting discouraged by difficulties and setbacks. If you stick with the process, you will discover that reaching the solution is so exhilarating that it more than makes up for any frustrations you encounter along the way.

This book is designed to teach you the fundamentals of programming and the basics of C, which is the dominant programming language in the computing industry today. It treats the *whys* of programming as well as the *hows,* to give you a feel for the programming process as a whole. It also includes several features that will help you focus on the essential points and avoid errors that slow you down. The next few pages summarize these features and explain how to use this book effectively as you begin your journey into the exciting world of computer science.

For Chapter Review

Each chapter includes easily accessible material to guide your study
and facilitate review of the central topics.

C H A P T E R   4

Statement Forms

The statements was interesting but tough.

— Mark Twain, *Adventures of Huckleberry Finn*, 1884

The list of **objectives** previews the key topics covered by the chapter. Because each objective identifies a concrete skill, the chapter objectives help you to assess your mastery of the essential material.

Objectives

- To understand the relationship between statements and expressions.
- To recognize that the equal sign used for assignment is treated as a binary operator in C.
- To understand that statements can be collected into blocks.
- To recognize that control statements fall into two classes: conditional and iterative.
- To learn how to manipulate Boolean data and to appreciate its importance.
- To increase your familiarity with the relational operators: $=$, $!=$, $<$, $<=$, $>$, and $>=$.
- To understand the behavior of the &&, ||, and ! operators.
- To master the details of the if, switch, while, and for statements.

99

To make the best possible use of this textbook for learning the C language,
be sure to take advantage of the tools it provides.

Summary

In Chapter 3, you looked at the process of programming from a holistic perspective that emphasized problem solving. Along the way, you learned about several control statements in an informal way. In this chapter, you were able to investigate how those statements work in more detail. You were also introduced to a new type of data called *Boolean data*. Although this data type contains only two values—TRUE and FALSE—being able to use Boolean data effectively is extremely important to successful programming and is well worth a little extra practice.

This chapter also introduced several new operators, and at this point it is helpful to review the precedence relationships for all the operators you have seen so far. That information is summarized in Table 4-1 the operators are listed from highest to lowest precedence.

The important points introduced in this chapter include:

- *Simple statements* consist of an expression followed by a semicolon.
- The = used to specify assignment is an operator in C. Assignments are therefore legal expressions, which makes it possible to write *embedded* and *multiple assignments*.
- Individual statements can be collected into *compound statements*, more commonly called *blocks*.
- Control statements fall into two classes: *conditional* and *iterative*.
- The genlib library defines a data type called bool that is used to represent Boolean data. The type bool has only two values: TRUE and FALSE.
- You can generate Boolean values using the *relational operators* (<, <=, >, >=, ==, and !=) and combine them using the *logical operators* (&&, ||, and !).
- The logical operators && and || are evaluated in left-to-right order in such a way that the evaluation stops as soon as the program can determine the result. This behavior is called *short-circuit evaluation*.

Operator					Associativity
unary -	++	--	!	*(type cast)*	right-to-left
*	/	%			left-to-right
+	-				left-to-right
<	<=	>	>=		left-to-right
==	!=				left-to-right
&&					left-to-right
||					left-to-right
?:					right-to-left
=	*op=*				right-to-left

TABLE 4-1

Precedence table for operators used through Chapter 4

The **Summary** describes, in more detail, what you should have learned in connection with the Objectives.

Learning to Program

Programming is both a science and an art. Learning to program well requires much more than memorizing a set of rules. You must learn through experience and by reading other programs. This text includes several features to aid in this process.

The final character in the string is a special character called *newline,* indicated by the sequence \n. When the printf function reaches the period at the end of the sentence, the cursor is sitting at the end of the text, just after the period. If you wanted to extend this program so that it wrote out more messages, you would probably want to start each new message on a new screen line. The **newline** character, defined for all modern computer systems, makes this possible. When the printf function processes the newline character, the cursor on the screen moves to the beginning of the next line, just as if you hit the Return key on the keyboard (this key is labeled Enter on some computers). In C, programs must include the newline character to mark the end of each screen line, or all the output will run together without any line breaks.

2.2 A program to add two numbers

To get a better picture of how a C program works, you need to consider a slightly more sophisticated example. The program add2.c shown in Figure 2-2 asks the user to enter two numbers, adds those numbers together, and then displays the sum.

The add2.c program incorporates several new programming concepts that were not part of hello.c. First, add2.c uses a new library called simpio, simplified

The text includes a large number of **program examples** that illustrate how individual C constructs are used to create complete programs. These examples also serve as models for your own programs; in many cases, you can solve a new programming problem by making simple modifications to a program from the text.

FIGURE 2-2 add2.c

```
/*
 * File: add2.c
 * ------------
 * This program reads in two numbers, adds them together,
 * and prints their sum.
 */

#include <stdio.h>
#include "genlib.h"
#include "simpio.h"

main()
{
    int n1, n2, total;

    printf("This program adds two numbers.\n");
    printf("1st number? ");
    n1 = GetInteger();
    printf("2nd number? ");
    n2 = GetInteger();
    total = n1 + n2;
    printf("The total is %d.\n", total);
}
```

The `printf` function can display any number of data values as part of the output. For each integer value you want to appear as part of the output, you need to include the code `%d` in the string that is used as the first argument in the `printf` call. The actual values to be displayed are given as additional arguments to `printf`, listed in the order in which they should appear. For example, if you changed the last line of the `add2.c` program to

```
printf("%d + %d = %d\n", n1, n2, total);
```

the value of `n1` would be substituted in place of the first `%d`, the value of `n2` would appear in place of the second `%d`, and the value of `total` would appear in place of the third `%d`. The final image on the computer screen would be

```
This program adds two numbers.
1st number? 2⏎
2nd number? 3⏎
2 + 3 = 5
```

The `printf` function is discussed in more detail in Chapter 3.

Sample output appears in consistent, predictable format, with rounded corners to emulate the computer screen. Your input appears in color.

Cascading `if` statements

The syntax box on the right illustrates an important special case of the `if` statement that is useful for applications in which the number of possible cases is larger than two. The characteristic form is that the `else` part of a condition consists of yet another test to check for an alternative condition. Such statements are called **cascading if statements** and may involve any number of `else if` lines. For example, the program `signtest.c` in Figure 4-3 uses the cascading `if` statement to report whether a number is positive, zero, or negative. Note that there is no need to check explicitly for the `n < 0` condition. If the program reaches that last `else` clause, there is no other possibility, since the earlier tests have eliminated the positive and zero cases.

In many situations, the process of choosing between a set of independent cases can be handled more efficiently using the `switch` statement, which is described in a separate section later in this chapter.

> **SYNTAX** for *cascading `if` statements*
>
> ```
> if (condition₁) {
>     statements₁
> } else if (condition₂) {
>     statements₂
> } else if (condition₃) {
>     statements₃
> } else {
>     statementsₙₒₙₑ
> }
> ```
> *any number may appear*
>
> where:
>   each *conditionᵢ* is a Boolean expression
>   each *statementsᵢ* is a block of statements to be executed
>   if *conditionᵢ* is TRUE
>   *statementsₙₒₙₑ* is the block of statements to be executed
>   if every *conditionᵢ* is FALSE

The `?:` operator (optional)

The C programming language provides another, more compact mechanism for ~~ing conditional execution~~ that can be extr~~emely~~ ~~~~ ~~~~ ~~ator. (This~~

Syntax boxes summarize key rules of C syntax, for an at-a-glance review of key programming concepts.

To Avoid Errors

All programmers, even the best ones, make mistakes. Finding these mistakes, or bugs, in your programs is a critically important skill. The following features will help you to build this skill.

To help you learn to recognize and correct bugs, this text includes several buggy programs that illustrate typical errors. To make sure you do not use these programs as models, such incorrect programs are marked with a superimposed image of a bug.

== Equal
!= Not equal

When you write programs that test for equality, be very careful to use the == operator, which is composed of two equal signs. A single equal sign is the assignment operator. Since the double equal sign violates conventional mathematical usage, replacing it with a single equal sign is a particularly common mistake. This mistake can also be very difficult to track down because the C compiler does not usually catch it as an error. A single equal sign usually turns the expression into an embedded assignment, which is perfectly legal in C; it just isn't at all what you want. For example, if you wanted to test whether the value of the variable x were equal to 0 and wrote the following conditional expression

```
if (x    0) . . .                          This is incorrect.
```

Common Pitfalls provide handy reminders about mistakes all beginning programmers are likely to make, and how to avoid them. Faulty lines of code are highlighted with a bug image and annotated in color.

the results would be confusing. This statement would not check to see if x were equal to 0. It would instead insist on this condition by assigning the value 0 to x, which C would then interpret (for reasons too arcane to describe at this point) as indicating a test result of FALSE. The correct test to determine whether the value of the variable x is equal to 0 is

```
if (x == 0) . . .
```

Be careful to avoid this error. A little extra care in entering your program can save a lot of debugging time later on.

After the Chapter

Learning to program requires considerable practice. To make sure that you get the necessary experience, each chapter includes an extensive set of exercises and questions that test your mastery of the material.

REVIEW QUESTIONS

1. Is the construction

    ```
    17;
    ```

    a legal statement in C? Is it useful?

2. Describe the effect of the following statement, assuming that i, j, and k are declared as integer variables:

    ```
    i = (j = 4) * (k = 16);
    ```

3. What single statement would you write to set both x and y (which you may assume are declared to be type double) to 1.0?

4. What is meant by the term *associativity?* What is unusual about the associativity of assignment with respect to that of the other operators you have seen?

5. What is a block? What important fact about blocks is conveyed by the term *compound statement,* which is another name for the same concept?

6. What are the two classes of control statements?

7. What does it mean to say that two control statements are nested?

8. What are the two values of the data type bool?

9. What happens when a programmer tries to use the mathe... equality in a conditional expression?

10. What restriction does C place on the types of values that ca... the relational operators?

11. How would you write a Boolean expression to test whet...

Each chapter concludes with a wealth of **Review Questions,** which require brief answers to chapter content questions, code adaptions, or debugging exercises.

PROGRAMMING EXERCISES

1. Although this chapter has focused on mathematical algorithms, the Greeks were fascinated with algorithms of other kinds as well. In Greek mythology, for example, Theseus of Athens escapes from the Minotaur's labyrinth by taking in a ball of string, unwinding it as he goes along, and then following the path of string back to the exit. Theseus's strategy represents an algorithm for escaping from a maze, but it is not the only algorithm he could have used to solve this problem. For example, if a maze has no internal loops, you can always escape by following the *right-hand rule,* in which you always keep your right hand against the wall. This approach may lead you to backtrack from time to time, but it does ensure that you will eventually find the opening to the outside.

    For example, imagine that Theseus is in the maze shown below at the position marked by the Greek letter theta (Θ):

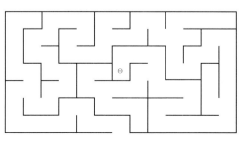

Programming Exercises call for you to try your hand at more extensive programming projects.

To the Instructor

In 1991–92, Stanford decided to restructure its introductory computer science curriculum to use ANSI C instead of Pascal. We chose to adopt ANSI C in our introductory courses for the following reasons:

- Students demanded a more practical language. Future employers want students to have more direct experience with the tools industry uses, which today are principally C and C++. With few employment opportunities listed for Pascal programmers in the newspaper employment section, our students began to question the relevance of their education.
- Our Pascal-based curriculum taught students to program in a language that they would never again use. We discovered that many of those students, when they abandoned Pascal for more modern languages, often forgot everything they had learned about programming style and the discipline of software engineering. Having now taught these skills in the context of a language that the students continue to use, we have found that they end up writing much better programs.
- Many of our advanced computer science courses, particularly in the systems area, require students to program in C. Working with C from the beginning gives students much more experience by the time they reach the advanced courses.
- Learning C early paves the way to learning C++ and the object-oriented paradigm. Because our students have a strong background in C programming after their first year of study, we have been able to offer our course on object-oriented system design much earlier in the curriculum.
- C makes it possible to cover several important topics, such as modular development and abstract data types, that are hard to teach in a Pascal environment.
- In the last five years, C has made significant headway toward replacing Fortran as the lingua franca of programming for the engineering sciences.

Given our experience over the last three years, I am convinced that the choice was a good one and that our program is stronger because of the change.

At the same time, it is important to recognize that teaching C in the first programming course is not always easy. C was designed for programmers, not introductory students. Many of its features make sense only when understood in terms of a larger conceptual framework that new students do not recognize. In many respects, C is a complex language. To teach it at the introductory level, we must find a way to control its complexity.

The library-based approach

One of the central goals of this text is to enable teachers to manage C's inherent complexity. Managing complexity, however, is precisely what we do as programmers. When we are faced with a problem that is too complex for immediate solution, we divide it into smaller pieces and consider each one independently. Moreover, when the complexity of one of those pieces crosses a certain threshold, it makes sense to isolate that complexity by defining a separate abstraction that has a simple interface. The interface protects clients from the underlying details of the abstraction, thereby simplifying the conceptual structure.

The same approach works for teaching programming. To make the material easier for students to learn, this text adopts a library-based approach that emphasizes the principle of abstraction. The essential character of that approach is reflected in the following two features that set this book apart from other introductory texts:

1. Libraries and modular development—essential concepts in modern programming—are covered in considerable detail early in the presentation. Part II focuses entirely on the topics of libraries, interfaces, abstractions, and modular development. Students learn how to use these techniques effectively before they learn about arrays.
2. The text demonstrates the power of libraries by using them. It is one thing to tell students that libraries make it possible to hide complexity. It is quite another to demonstrate that concept. This text introduces several new libraries that hide details from the students until they are ready to assimilate them. The libraries give students the power to write useful programs that they could not develop on their own. Later chapters reveal the implementation of those libraries, thereby allowing students to appreciate the power of abstraction.

In 1992, I attempted to teach the introductory course using only the ANSI libraries. The results were not encouraging. Each new topic required that the student understand so much about the rest of C that there was no effective way to present the material. For example, students had to understand the mechanics of arrays, pointers, and allocation before they could use string data in any interesting way, even though string manipulation is simpler conceptually. My best students managed to understand what was going on by the end of the quarter. Most, however, did not. Since we introduced the library-based approach in early 1993, students have assimilated the material more easily and learned much more about computer science.

The library interfaces and associated implementations used in this text are reprinted in Appendix B, which also gives instructions for obtaining the source code electronically through anonymous FTP (File Transfer Protocol).

The order of presentation

This book presents topics in the same order as Stanford's introductory course, except for the material in Chapter 17, which we cover in the second course. Depending on your audience and the goals of your course, you may want to vary the order of presentation. The following notes provide an overview of the chapters and indicate some of the more important dependencies.

Chapter 1 traces the history of computing and describes the programming process. The chapter requires no programming per se but provides the contextual background for the rest of the text.

I have designed Chapters 2 and 3 for students with little or no background in programming. These chapters are conceptual in their approach and focus on problem solving rather than on the details of the C language. When new students are faced with detailed rules of syntax and structure, they concentrate on learning the rules instead of the underlying concepts, which are vastly more important at this stage. If your students already know some programming, you could move much more quickly through this material.

Chapters 2 and 3 are informal in their approach and concentrate on developing the student's problem-solving skills. Along the way, they introduce several basic statement forms and control structures, but only as idioms to accomplish a specific task. Chapter 4 adds formal structure to this topic by describing each statement form in turn, detailing its syntax and semantics. The chapter also includes an extensive discussion of Boolean data.

Chapter 5 introduces functions and procedures. It begins with simple examples of functions and then continues with increasingly sophisticated examples. The mechanics of parameter passing are discussed in a separate section that includes many diagrams to help students follow the flow of data from one function to another. The chapter ends with a significant programming example that illustrates the concept of stepwise refinement.

The algorithmic concepts presented in Chapter 6 are fundamental to computer science but may not be required for all students. If your audience consists of engineers or potential computer science majors, the material will prove extremely valuable. For less technical audiences, however, you can eliminate much of this material without disturbing the flow of the presentation.

I have found that integrating graphics in the introductory course is a great way to increase student interest in the material. Chapter 7 exists for that reason. At this stage, students have learned the mechanics of functions but have no burning need to write them. Letting students draw complex pictures on the screen gives them that incentive. The graphics library is implemented for several of the major programming environments and can therefore be used in most institutions.

Chapter 8 has two themes, which are in some sense separable. The first part of the chapter discusses design criteria for interfaces and is essential for anyone who needs to understand how modern programming works. The second part of the chapter applies those principles to build a random number library. The `random.h` interface itself is less important than the general principles, although use of the random number library is required for a few of the exercises later in the text.

Chapter 9 introduces strings as an abstract type and represents, to a certain extent, the cornerstone of the library-based approach. By using a dynamic string library, students can easily write programs that perform sophisticated string manipulation, even though they do not yet understand the underlying representation, which is covered in Chapter 14. Introducing strings at this point in the presentation enables students to write much more exciting programs than they could otherwise.

On a first reading, it is easy to miss the purpose of Chapter 10, which appears to be an extension of the discussion of strings begun in Chapter 9. The fundamental value of Chapter 10 does not lie in the Pig Latin program, which is more fun than it is practical. The entire reason for the example is that it provides the motivation to build the scanner interface used to separate words on the input line. The scanner module proves its usefulness over and over again, not only in the first course but in subsequent courses as well. It is the most practical tool students create in the course and therefore serves as a compelling example of the value of modularity.

Chapters 11 through 16 introduce the fundamental compound structures—arrays, pointers, files, and records—in an order that has worked well in practice. Because the base language is C, it is important to present pointers as soon as possible after introducing arrays so that you can emphasize the connections between them. Moreover, having established these concepts, it is then possible in Chapter 14 to consider string data more closely, thereby revealing the underlying representation that was concealed by the abstract definition. Chapter 16 integrates the fundamental data structures with the construction of a data-driven teaching machine, which is the most sophisticated example of programming presented in the text.

Chapter 17 includes three important topics that often appear in the first programming course: recursion, abstract data types, and analysis of algorithms. At Stanford, which is on the quarter system, we teach all these topics in the second course. If you decide to teach recursion in the first course, I strongly recommend that you do so early enough to allow students time to assimilate the material. One possibility is to discuss recursive functions immediately after Chapter 5 and recursive algorithms after Chapter 6. Another approach is to cover recursion and analysis of algorithms together at the end of Chapter 12.

Instructor's Manual

The Instructor's Manual contains supplemental materials including a course syllabus, suggestions for lecture design, sample assignments and examinations, and solutions to all programming exercises. In addition to the printed manual, instructors who adopt this text can retrieve electronic copies of solution sets and related materials. For details on obtaining solutions, please contact your local Addison-Wesley representative. All other supplemental material is available on-line. For explicit instructions see Appendix B.

Acknowledgments

The text has come a long way from its initial stages as class notes, in large measure because of suggestions from people who have worked with the text in one capacity or another. I am particularly grateful to the Stanford lecturers—Jon Becker, Katie Capps, Stephen Clausing, Todd Feldman, Allison Hansen, Margaret Johnson, Jim Kent, Andrew Kosoresow, Mehran Sahami, and Julie Zelenski—who have taught this material in 14 different sections of the introductory course over the past three years. I am also indebted to all the section leaders and teaching assistants as well as the coordinators of the student-teaching program—Felix Baker, John Lilly, Sandy Nguyen, Bryan Rollins, and Scott Wiltamuth—who provided much needed logistical support.

Many of the best ideas for the text came from a seminar on teaching introductory computer science that I conducted beginning in 1992–93. It provided a forum for thrashing out the hard issues and made a significant difference in the text. I want to thank everyone who participated: Perry Arnold, Jon Becker, Tom Bogart, Karl Brown, Bryan Busse, Katie Capps, Peter Chang, Scott Cohen, Stacey Doerr, Jeff Forbes, Stephen Freund, Jon Goldberg, Tague Griffith, Matt Harad, Lindsay Lack, Christine Lee, Tricia Lee, John Lilly, Albert Lin, Mara Mather, Hugh McGuire, Jeffrey Oldham, David O'Keefe, Bryan Rollins, Samir Saxena, Nikhyl Singhal, Eric Tucker, Garner Weng, Howard Wong-Toi, and John Yong.

I also want to thank all the students who have used and critiqued the draft version of the text: Adjo Amekudzi, Eric Anderson, Andrew Arnold, Kevin Berk, Kevin Carbajal, Ajit Chaudhari, Alida Cheung, Hye-won Choi, Elisabeth Christensen, Ralph Davis, Joel Firehammer, Peter Frelinghuysen, Trevor Gattis, Teddy Harris, Heather Heal, Enoch Huang, Ann Lee, Ted Lee, Daphne Lichtensztajn, Lisa Maddock, Allan Marcus, Brad McGoran, Forrest Melton, Adrienne Osborn, Masatoshi Saito, Anne Stern, Ricardo Urena, and Nichole Wilson.

In 1993–94, several faculty members at other universities tested this material in draft form and made several valuable suggestions. I especially want to thank Margo Seltzer at Harvard University, Rob Langsner at the University of Nevada (Reno), Richard Chang at the University of Maryland (Baltimore County), Jane Turk at La Salle University, and Kim Kihlstrom at Westmont College for helping to refine the text from its early stages.

I am also indebted to my reviewers:

Stephen Allan
Utah State University

Don Goelman
Villanova University

Stan Kolasa
Rutgers University

Harry R. Lewis
Harvard University

Bill Muellner
Elmhurst College

Rayno Niemi
Rochester Institute of Technology

Robert G. Plantz
Sonoma State University

David Rosenthal
Seton Hall

James Schmolze
Tufts University

Michael Skolnick
Rensselaer Polytechnic

Jeffrey A. Slomka
Southwest Texas State University

Kevin Smith
Emory University

Phil Tromovitch
SUNY- Stony Brook

John A. Trono
St. Michaels' College

Robert Walker
Rensselaer Polytechnic

Richard Weinand
Wayne State University

In addition, I have received useful advice along the way from several friends and colleagues, including Josh Barnes, Pavel Curtis, Kathleen Kells, James Finn, and Steve Lewin-Berlin.

The final version of this text owes much to my editors at Addison-Wesley, who have been helpful throughout the process. In particular, I thank Lynne Doran Cote, Sue Gleason, Peter Gordon, Laura Michaels, Jim Rigney, Karen Stone, and Amy Willcutt for all their work. And I am extremely fortunate to have Lauren Rusk as both my developmental editor and my partner; without her, nothing would ever come out as well as it should.

Contents

PART THREE
Compound Data Types 373

CHAPTER 1

Introduction

Objectives

- To understand the distinction between hardware and software.

- To recognize that problem solving is an essential component of computer science.

- To understand the meaning of the term *algorithm.*

- To appreciate the role of the compiler as a translator between a higher-level programming language and the lower-level machine language.

- To recognize the principal types of programming errors.

- To appreciate the importance of software maintenance and the use of good software engineering practice.

As we approach the end of the twentieth century, it is hard to believe that computers did not even exist as recently as 1940. Computers are everywhere today, and it is the popular wisdom, at least among headline writers, to say that we live in the computer age.

1.1 A brief history of computing

In a certain sense, however, computing has been around since ancient times. Much of early mathematics was devoted to solving computational problems of practical importance, such as monitoring the number of animals in a herd, calculating the area of a plot of land, or recording a commercial transaction. These activities required people to develop new computational techniques and, in some cases, to invent calculating machines to help in the process. For example, the abacus, a simple counting device consisting of beads that slide along rods, has been used in Asia for thousands of years, possibly since 2000 B.C.

Throughout most of its history, computing has progressed relatively slowly. In 1623, a German scientist named Wilhelm Schickard invented the first known mechanical calculator, capable of performing simple arithmetical computations automatically. Although Schickard's device was lost to history through the ravages of the Thirty Years' War (1618–1648), the French philosopher Blaise Pascal used similar techniques to construct a mechanical adding machine in the 1640s, a copy of which remains on display in the Conservatoire des Arts et Métiers in Paris. In 1673, the German mathematician Gottfried Leibniz developed a considerably more sophisticated device, capable of multiplication and division as well as addition and subtraction. All these devices were purely mechanical and contained no engines or other source of power. The operator would enter numbers by setting metal wheels to a particular position; the act of turning those wheels set other parts of the machine in motion and changed the output display.

During the Industrial Revolution, the rapid growth in technology made it possible to consider new approaches to mechanical computation. The steam engine already provided the power needed to run factories and railroads. In that context, it was reasonable to ask whether one could use steam engines to drive more sophisticated computing machines, machines that would be capable of carrying out significant calculations under their own power. Before progress could be made, however, someone had to ask that question and set out to find an answer. The necessary spark of insight came from a British mathematician named Charles Babbage, who is one of the most interesting figures in the history of computing.

During his lifetime, Babbage designed two different computing machines, which he called the Difference Engine and the Analytical Engine; each represented a considerable advance over the calculating machines available at the time. The tragedy of his life is that he was unable to complete either of these projects. The Difference Engine, which he designed to produce tables of mathematical functions, was eventually built by a Swedish inventor in 1854—30 years after its original design. The Analytical Engine was Babbage's lifelong dream, but it remained incomplete when Babbage died in 1871. Even so, its design contained many of the essential features found in modern computers. Most importantly, Babbage conceived of the Analytical Engine as a general-purpose machine, capable of performing many different functions depending upon how it was *programmed*. In Babbage's design, the operation of the Analytical Engine was controlled by a pattern of holes punched on a card that the machine could read. By changing the pattern of holes, one could change the behavior of the machine so that it performed a different set of calculations.

Much of what we know of Babbage's work comes from the writings of Augusta Ada Byron, the only daughter of the poet Lord Byron and his wife Annabella. More than most of her contemporaries, Ada appreciated the potential of the Analytical Engine and became its champion. She designed several sophisticated programs for the machine, thereby becoming the first programmer. In the 1970s, the U.S. Department of Defense named its own programming language Ada in honor of her contribution.

Some aspects of Babbage's design did influence the later history of computation, such as the use of punched cards to control computation—an idea that had first been introduced by the French inventor Joseph Marie Jacquard as part of a device to automate the process of weaving fabric on a loom. In 1890, Herman Hollerith used punched cards to automate data tabulation for the U.S. Census. To market this technology, Hollerith went on to found a company that later became the International Business Machines (IBM) corporation, which has dominated the computer industry for most of the twentieth century.

Babbage's vision of a programmable computer did not become a reality until the 1940s, when the advent of electronics made it possible to move beyond the mechanical devices that had dominated computing up to that time. A prototype of the first electronic computer was assembled in late 1939 by John Atanasoff and his student, Clifford Barry, at Iowa State College. They completed a full-scale implementation containing 300 vacuum tubes in May 1942. The computer was capable of solving small systems of linear equations. With some design modifications, the Atanasoff-Barry computer could have performed more intricate calculations, but work on the project was interrupted by World War II.

The first large-scale electronic computer was the ENIAC, an acronym for *electronic numerical integrator and computer*. Completed in 1946 under the direction of J. Presper Eckert and John Mauchly at the Moore School of the University of Pennsylvania, the ENIAC contained more than 18,000 vacuum tubes and occupied a 30-by-50 foot room. The ENIAC was programmed by plugging wires into a pegboardlike device called a **patch panel.** By connecting different sockets on the patch panel with wires, the operators could control ENIAC's behavior. This type of programming required an intimate knowledge of the internal workings of the machine and proved to be much more difficult than the inventors of the ENIAC had imagined.

Perhaps the greatest breakthrough in modern computing occurred in 1946, when John von Neumann at the Institute for Advanced Study in Princeton proposed that programs and data could be represented in a similar way and stored in the same internal memory. This concept, which simplifies the programming process enormously, is the basis of almost all modern computers. Because of this aspect of their design, modern computers are said to use **von Neumann architecture.**

Since the completion of ENIAC and the development of von Neumann's stored-programming concept, computing has evolved at a furious pace. New systems and new concepts have been introduced in such rapid succession that it would be pointless to list them all. Most historians divide the development of modern computers into the following four generations, based on the underlying technology.

- *First generation.* The first generation of electronic computers used vacuum tubes as the basis for their internal circuitry. This period of computing begins with the Atanasoff-Barry prototype in 1939.
- *Second generation.* The invention of the transistor in 1947 ushered in a new generation of computers. Transistors perform the same functions as vacuum tubes but are much smaller and require a fraction of the electrical power. The first computer to use transistors was the IBM 7090, introduced in 1958.
- *Third generation.* Even though transistors are tiny in comparison to vacuum tubes, a computer containing 100,000 or 1,000,000 individual transistors requires a large amount of space. The third generation of computing was enabled by the development in 1959 of the **integrated circuit** or **chip,** a small wafer of silicon that has been photographically imprinted to contain a large number of transistors connected together. The first computer to use integrated circuits in its construction was the IBM 360, which appeared in 1964.
- *Fourth generation.* The fourth generation of computing began in 1975, when the technology for building integrated circuits made it possible to put the entire processing unit of a computer on a single chip of silicon. The fabrication technology is called **large-scale integration.** Computer processors that consist of a single chip are called **microprocessors** and are used in most computers today.

The early machines of the first and second generations are historically important as the antecedents of modern computers, but they would hardly seem interesting or useful today. They were the dinosaurs of computer science: gigantic, lumbering beasts with small mental capacities, soon to become extinct. The late Robert Noyce, one of the inventors of the integrated circuit and founder of Intel Corporation, observed that, compared to the ENIAC, the typical modern computer chip "is twenty times faster, has a larger memory, is thousands of times more reliable, consumes the power of a light bulb rather than that of a locomotive, occupies 1/30,000 the volume, and costs 1/10,000 as much." Computers have certainly come of age.

1.2 What is computer science?

Growing up in the modern world has probably given you some idea of what a computer is. This text, however, is less concerned with computers as physical devices than with computer science. At first glance, the words *computer* and *science* seem

By processing data electronically, the ENIAC reduced U.S. census tabulation time from twelve years to three. The complexity, cost, and physical proportions of this machine limited its accessibility and appeal.

A step ahead of the first generation, computers like the IBM 7090 were programmed using punched cards.

The integrated circuit reduced the size of computers and increased their power. With the introduction of the IBM 360, the number of computers purchased for business grew substantially.

Like the telephone and television, the computer is fast becoming an indispensible tool giving users access, from their living rooms, to databases and on-line information centers around the world.

an incongruous pair. In its classical usage, *science* refers to the study of natural phenomena; when people talk about *biological science* or *physical science,* we understand and feel comfortable with that usage. Computer science doesn't seem the same sort of thing. The fact that computers are human-made artifacts makes us reticent to classify the study of computers as a science. After all, modern technology has also produced cars, but we don't talk about "car science." Instead, we refer to "automotive engineering" or "automobile technology." Why should computers be any different?

To answer this question, it is important to recognize that the computer itself is only part of the story. The physical machine that you can buy today at your local computer store is an example of computer **hardware.** It is tangible. You can pick it up, take it home, and put it on your desk. If need be, you could use it as a doorstop, albeit a rather expensive one. But if there were nothing there besides the hardware, if a machine came to you exactly as it rolled off the assembly line, serving as a doorstop would be one of the few jobs it could do. A modern computer is a general-purpose machine, with the potential to perform a wide variety of tasks. To achieve that potential, however, the computer must be **programmed.** The act of programming a computer consists of providing it with a set of instructions—a program—that specifies all the steps necessary to solve the problem to which it is assigned. These programs are generically known as **software,** and it is the software, together with the hardware, that makes computation possible.

In contrast to hardware, software is an abstract, intangible entity. It is a sequence of simple steps and operations, stated in a precise language that the hardware can interpret. When we talk about computer science, we are concerned primarily with the domain of computer software and, more importantly, with the even more abstract domain of problem solving. Problem solving turns out to be a highly challenging activity that requires creativity, skill, and discipline. For the most part, computer science is best thought of as the science of problem solving in which the solutions happen to involve a computer.

This is not to say that the computer itself is unimportant. Before computers, people could solve only relatively simple computational problems. Over the last 50 years, the existence of computers has made it possible to solve increasingly difficult and sophisticated problems in a timely and cost-effective way. As the problems we attempt to solve become more complex, so does the task of finding effective solution techniques. The science of problem solving has thus been forced to advance along with the technology of computing.

1.3 A brief tour of computer hardware

This text focuses almost exclusively on software and the activity of solving problems by computer that is the essence of computer science. Even so, it is important to spend some time in this chapter talking about the structure of computer hardware at a very general level of detail. The reason is simple. Programming is a learn-by-doing discipline. You will not become a programmer just by reading this book, even if you solve all the exercises on paper. Learning to program is hands-on work and requires you to use a computer.

In order to use a computer, you need to become acquainted with its hardware. You have to know how to turn the computer on, how to use the keyboard to type in a program, and how to execute that program once you've written it. Unfortunately, the steps you must follow in order to perform these operations differ significantly from one computer system to another. As someone who is writing a general text-book, I cannot tell you how your own particular system works and must instead concentrate on general principles that are common to any computer you might be using. As you read this section, you should look at the computer you have and see how the general discussion applies to that machine.

Most computer systems today consist of the components shown in Figure 1-1. Each of the components in the diagram is connected by a communication channel called a **bus,** which allows data to flow between the separate units. The individual components are described in the sections that follow.

The CPU

The **central processing unit** or **CPU** is the "brain" of the computer. It performs the actual computation and controls the activity of the entire computer. The actions of the CPU are determined by a program consisting of a sequence of coded instructions stored in the memory system. One instruction, for example, might direct the computer to add a pair of numbers. Another might make a character appear on the computer screen. By executing the appropriate sequence of simple instructions, the computer can be made to perform complex tasks.

In a modern computer, the CPU consists of an **integrated circuit**—a tiny chip of silicon that has been imprinted with millions of microscopic transistors connected to form larger circuits capable of carrying out simple arithmetic and logical operations.

Memory

When a computer executes a program, it must have some way to store both the program itself and the data involved in the computation. In general, any piece of

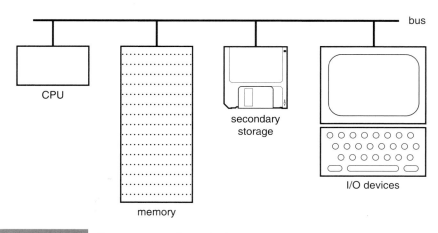

FIGURE 1-1 Components of a typical computer

computer hardware capable of storing and retrieving information is a storage device. The storage devices that are used while a program is actively running constitute its **primary storage,** which is more often called its **memory.** Since John von Neumann first suggested the idea in 1946, computers have used the same memory to store both the individual instructions that compose the program and the data used during computation.

Memory systems are engineered to be very efficient so that they can provide the CPU with extremely fast access to their contents. In today's computers, memory is usually built out of a special integrated-circuit chip called a **RAM,** which stands for *random-access memory.* Random-access memory allows the program to use the contents of any memory cell at any time. Chapter 11 discusses the structure of the memory system in more detail.

Secondary storage

Although computers usually keep active data in memory whenever a program is running, most primary storage devices have the disadvantage that they function only when the computer is turned on. When you turn off your computer, any information that was stored in primary memory is lost. To store permanent data, you need to use a storage device that does not require electrical power to maintain its information. Such devices constitute **secondary storage.**

The most common secondary storage devices used in computers today are **disks,** which consist of circular spinning platters coated with magnetic material used to record data. In a modern personal computer, disks come in two forms: **hard disks,** which are built into the computer system, and **floppy disks,** which are removable. When you compose and edit your program, you will usually do so on a hard disk, if one is available. When you want to move the program to another computer or make a backup copy for safekeeping, you will typically transfer the program to a floppy disk.

I/O devices

For the computer to be useful, it must have some way to communicate with users in the outside world. Computer input usually consists of characters typed on a keyboard. Output from the computer typically appears on the computer screen or on a printer. Collectively, hardware devices that perform input and output operations are called **I/O devices,** where I/O stands for *input/output.*

I/O devices vary significantly from machine to machine. Outside of the standard alphabetic keys, computer keyboards have different arrangements and even use different names for some of the important keys. For example, the key used to indicate the end of a line is labeled Return on some keyboards and Enter on others. On some computer systems, you make changes to a program by using special **function keys** on the top or side of the keyboard that provide simple editing operations. On other systems, you can accomplish the same task by using a hand-held pointing device called a **mouse** to select program text that you wish to change. In either case, the computer keeps track of the current typing position, which is usually indicated on the screen by flashing line or rectangle called the **cursor.**

In this text, computer input and output are illustrated using an inset box with rounded corners. In most cases, the contents of the box indicate what appears on the screen when you execute your program and is called a **sample run.** For example, the following sample run illustrates what will appear on the screen after you execute the add2.c program introduced in Chapter 2.

```
This program adds two numbers.
1st number? 2↵
2nd number? 2↵
The total is 4.
```

Input from the user is shown in color to distinguish it from the output generated by the program. To make the user actions more clear, the diagram also uses the ↵ symbol to indicate that the user has pressed the Return or Enter key, signifying the end of the input line, although this symbol does not actually appear on the screen.

 ## 1.4 Algorithms

Now that you have a sense of the basic structure of a computer system, let's turn to computer science. Because computer science is the discipline of solving problems with the assistance of a computer, you need to understand a concept that is fundamental to both computer science and the abstract discipline of problem solving—the concept of an **algorithm.**[1] Informally, you can think of an algorithm as a strategy for solving a problem. To appreciate how computer scientists use the term, however, it is necessary to formalize that intuitive understanding and tighten up the definition.

To be an algorithm, a solution technique must fulfill three basic requirements. First of all, an algorithm must be presented in a clear, unambiguous form so that it is possible to understand what steps are involved. Second, the steps within an algorithm must be effective, in the sense that it is possible to carry them out in practice. A technique, for example, that includes the operation "multiply r by the exact value of π" is not effective, since it is not possible to compute the exact value of π. Third, an algorithm must not run on forever but must deliver its answer in a finite amount of time. In summary, an algorithm must be

1. *Clearly and unambiguously defined.*
2. *Effective,* in the sense that its steps are executable.
3. *Finite,* in the sense that it terminates after a bounded number of steps.

---

[1] The word *algorithm* comes to us from the name of the ninth-century Arabic mathematician Abu Ja'far Mohammed ibn Mûsâ al-Khowârizmî, who wrote a treatise on mathematics entitled *Kitab al jabr w'al-muqabala* (which itself gave rise to the English word *algebra*).

These properties will turn out to be more important later on when you begin to work with complex algorithms. For the moment, it is sufficient to think of algorithms as abstract solution strategies—strategies that will eventually become the core of the programs you write.

As you will soon discover, algorithms—like the problems they are intended to solve—vary significantly in complexity. Some problems are so simple that an appropriate algorithm springs immediately to mind, and you can write the programs to solve such problems without too much trouble. As the problems become more complex, however, the algorithms needed to solve them begin to require more thought. In most cases, several different algorithms are available to solve a particular problem, and you need to consider a variety of potential solution techniques before writing the final program. You will have a chance to revisit this topic in Chapter 6, which addresses how to decide which algorithm is best for a given problem.

1.5 Programming languages and compilation

Solving a problem by computer consists of two conceptually distinct steps. First, you need to develop an algorithm, or choose an existing one, that solves the problem. This part of the process is called **algorithmic design.** The second step is to express that algorithm as a computer program in a programming language. This process is called **coding.**

As you begin to learn about programming, the process of coding—translating your algorithm into a functioning C program—will seem to be the more difficult phase of the process. As a new programmer, you will, after all, be starting with simple problems just as you would when learning any new skill. Simple problems tend to have simple solutions, and the algorithmic design phase will not seem particularly challenging. Because the language and its rules are entirely new and unfamiliar, however, coding may at times seem difficult and arbitrary. I hope it is reassuring to say that coding will rapidly become easier as you learn more about the programming process. At the same time, however, algorithmic design will get harder as the problems you are asked to solve increase in complexity.

When new algorithms are introduced in this text, they will usually be expressed initially in English. Although it is often less precise than one would like, English is a reasonable language in which to express solution strategies as long as the communication is entirely between people who speak English. Obviously, if you wanted to present your algorithm to someone who spoke only Russian, English would no longer be an appropriate choice. English is likewise an inappropriate choice for presenting an algorithm to a computer. Although computer scientists have been working on this problem for decades, understanding English or Russian or any other human language continues to lie beyond the boundaries of current technology. The computer would be completely unable to interpret your algorithm if it were expressed in human language. To make an algorithm accessible to the computer, you need to translate it into a programming language. There are many programming languages in the world, including Fortran, BASIC, Pascal, Lisp, and a host of others. In this text, you will learn how to use the programming language C—the language that has become the *de facto* standard in the computing industry over the last several years.

The programming languages listed above, including C, are examples of what computer scientists call **higher-level languages.** Such languages are designed to be independent of the particular characteristics that differentiate computers and to work instead with general algorithmic concepts that can be implemented on any computer system. Internally, each computer system understands a low-level language that is specific to that type of hardware. For example, the Apple Macintosh computer and the IBM PC use different underlying machine languages, even though both of them can execute programs written in a higher-level language such as C.

To make it possible for a program written in a higher-level language to run on different computer systems, the program must first be translated into the low-level machine language appropriate to the computer on which the program will run. For example, if you are writing C programs for a Macintosh, you will need to run a special program that translates C into machine language for the Macintosh. If you are using the IBM PC to run the same program, you need to use a different translator. Programs that perform the translation between a higher-level language and machine language are called **compilers.**

Before you can run a program on most computer systems, it is necessary to enter the text of the program and store it in a **file,** which is the generic name for any collection of information stored in the computer's secondary storage. Every file must have a name, which is usually divided into two parts separated by a period, as in myprog.c. When you create a file, you choose the **root name,** which is the part of the name preceding the period, and use it to tell yourself what the file contains. The portion of the filename following the period indicates what the file is used for and is called the **extension.** Certain extensions have preassigned meanings. For example, the extension .c indicates a program file written in the C language. A file containing program text is called a **source file.**

The general process of entering or changing the contents of a file is called **editing** that file. The editing process differs significantly between individual computer systems, so it is not possible to describe it in a way that works for every type of hardware. When you work on a particular computer system, you will need to learn how to create new files and to edit existing ones. You can find this information in the computer manual or the documentation for the C compiler you are using.

Once you have a source file, the next step in the process is to use the compiler to translate the source file into a format the computer can understand directly. Once again, this process varies somewhat from machine to machine. In most cases, however, the compiler translates the source file into a second file, called an **object file,** that contains the actual instructions appropriate for that computer system. This object file is then combined together with other object files to produce an **executable file** that can be run on the system. These other object files typically include predefined object files, called **libraries,** that contain the machine-language instructions for various operations commonly required by programs.

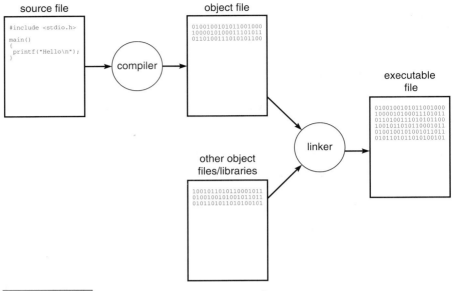

FIGURE 1-2 The compilation process

The process of combining all the individual object files into an executable file is called **linking.** The entire process is illustrated by the diagram shown in Figure 1-2.

In some computers, the individual steps shown in the diagram occur without any action on your part. You indicate that you want to run the program, and all of the necessary steps are carried out automatically. On other computers, you may have to perform the compiling and linking steps individually.

In any case, the only file that contains something humans can read is the source file. The other files contain information intended solely for the machine. As a programmer, all your work takes place in the context of the source file. You edit it and then give it to the compiler for translating.

1.6 Programming errors and debugging

Besides translation, compilers perform another important function. Like human languages, programming languages have their own vocabulary and their own set of grammatical rules. These rules make it possible to determine that certain statements are properly constructed and that others are not. For example, in English, it is not appropriate to say "we goes" because the subject and verb do not agree in number. Rules that determine whether a statement is legally constructed are called **syntax rules.** Programming languages have their own syntax, which determines how the elements of a program can be put together. When you compile a program, the compiler first checks to see whether your program is syntactically correct. If you have violated the syntactic rules, the compiler displays an error message. Errors that result from breaking these rules are called **syntax errors.** Whenever you get a message from the compiler indicating a syntax error, you must go back and edit the program to correct it.

Syntax errors can be frustrating, particularly for new programmers. They will not, however, be your biggest source of frustration. More often than not, the programs you write will fail to operate correctly not because you wrote a program that contained syntactic errors but because your perfectly legal program somehow comes up with incorrect answers or fails to produce answers at all. You look at the program and discover that you have made a mistake in the logic of the program—the type of mistake programmers call a **bug.** The process of finding and correcting such mistakes is called **debugging** and is an important part of the programming process.

Bugs can be extremely insidious and frustrating. You will be absolutely certain that your algorithm is correct and then discover that it fails to handle some case you had previously overlooked. Or perhaps you will think about a special condition at one point in your program only to forget it later on. Or you might make a mistake that seems so silly you cannot believe anyone could possibly have blundered so badly.

Relax. You're in excellent company. Even the best programmers have shared this experience. The truth is that programmers—all programmers—make logic errors. In particular, *you* will make logic errors. Algorithms are tricky things, and you will often discover that you haven't really gotten it right.

In many respects, discovering your own fallibility is an important rite of passage for you as a programmer. Describing his experiences as a programmer in the early 1960s, the pioneering computer scientist Maurice Wilkes wrote:

> Somehow, at the Moore School and afterwards, one had always assumed there would be no particular difficulty in getting programs right. I can remember the exact instant in time at which it dawned on me that a great part of my future life would be spent in finding mistakes in my own programs.

What differentiates good programmers from the rest of their colleagues is not that they manage to avoid bugs altogether but that they take pains to minimize the number of bugs that persist in the finished code. When you design an algorithm and translate it into a syntactically legal program, it is critical to understand that your job is not finished. Almost certainly, your program has a bug in it somewhere. Your job as a programmer is to find that bug and fix it. Once that is done, you should find the next bug and fix that. Always be skeptical of your own programs and test them as thoroughly as you can.

 ## 1.7 Software maintenance

One of the more surprising aspects of software development is that programs require maintenance. In fact, studies of software development indicate that, for most programs, paying programmers to maintain the software after it has been released constitutes between 80 and 90 percent of the total cost. In the context of software, however, it is a little hard to imagine precisely what maintenance means. At first hearing, the idea sounds rather bizarre. If you think in terms of a car or a bridge, maintenance occurs when something has broken—some of the metal has rusted away, a piece of some mechanical linkage has worn out from overuse, or something has gotten smashed up in an accident. None of these situations apply to software. The code itself doesn't rust. Using the same program over and over again does not in any way diminish its functioning. Accidental misuse can certainly have dangerous consequences but does not usually damage the program itself; even if it does, the program can often be restored from a backup copy. What does maintenance mean in such an environment?

Software requires maintenance for two principal reasons. First, even after considerable testing and, in some cases, years of field use, bugs can still survive in the original code. Then, when some unusual situation arises or a previously unanticipated load occurs, the bug, previously dormant, causes the program to fail. Thus, debugging is an essential part of program maintenance. It is not, however, the most important part. Far more consequential, especially in terms of how much it contributes to the overall cost of program maintenance, is what might be called *feature enhancement*. Programs are written to be used; they perform, usually faster and less expensively than other methods, a task the customer needs done. At the same time, the programs probably don't do everything the customer wants. After working with a program for a while, the customer decides it would be wonderful if the program also did something else, or did something differently, or presented its data in a more useful way, or ran a little faster, or had an expanded capacity, or just had a few more simple but attractive features (often called *bells and whistles* in the trade). Since software is extremely flexible, suppliers have the option of responding to such requests. In either case—whether one wants to repair a bug or add a feature—someone has to go in, look at the program, figure out what's going on, make the necessary changes, verify that those changes work, and then release a new version. This process is difficult, time-consuming, expensive, and prone to error.

■■■■ 1.8 The importance of software engineering

Part of the reason program maintenance is so difficult is that most programmers do not write their programs for the long haul. To them it seems sufficient to get the program working and then move on to something else.[2] The discipline of writing programs so that they can be understood and maintained by others is called **software engineering.** In this text, you are encouraged to write programs that demonstrate good engineering style.

As you write your programs, try to imagine how someone else might feel if called upon to look at them two years later. Would your program make sense? Would the program itself indicate to the new reader what you were trying to do? Would it be easy to change, particularly along some dimension where you could

---

[2] In defense of these programmers, it is important to note that they are often pressed to do just that since the company has tight cost and deadline constraints. Unfortunately, this kind of a rush to market often constitutes a false economy because the company ends up paying much more down the road in added maintenance costs.

reasonably expect change? Or would it seem obscure and convoluted? If you put yourself in the place of the future maintainer (and as a new programmer in most companies, you will probably be given that role), it will help you to appreciate why good style is critical.

Many novice programmers are disturbed to learn that there is no precise set of rules you can follow to ensure good programming style. Good software engineering is not a cookbook sort of process. Instead it is a skill blended with more than a little bit of artistry. Practice is critical. One learns to write good programs by writing them, and by reading others, much as one learns to be a novelist. Good programming requires discipline—the discipline not to cut corners or to forget about that future maintainer in the rush to complete a project. And good programming style requires developing an aesthetic sense—a sense of what it means for a program to be readable and well presented.

1.9 Some thoughts on the C programming language

As noted in an earlier section, the language that will serve as the basis for this text is the programming language C, in the form that has now been accepted by the American National Standards Institute as ANSI C. The C language was originally developed by Dennis Ritchie in the early 1970s. In the two decades since its invention, C has become one of the most widely used languages in the world. At all levels of the software industry, more and more programs are written in C—programs that are used by millions of people throughout the world. More than many other languages, C was designed to unlock the power of the computer and offers programmers considerable control over the programs they write. It is precisely this power that has contributed to the widespread use of the language.

But power has a down side. For one thing, C tends to be a bit more difficult to learn than other languages, in part because the language makes visible many of the low-level constructs one needs to take full advantage of the machine. For another, programmers can misuse the power of C—and many do, perhaps because they are careless, or because they think it is somehow a badge of honor to have accomplished a task in the most intricate and obscure way, or because they have never learned good programming methodology. It's as if we can apply to programming the oft-repeated aphorism that "power corrupts and absolute power corrupts absolutely." Judging from the C code that exists in the world, there are more than a few absolutely corrupted programmers out there.

Fortunately, there is hope. First of all, C is not really so different from other programming languages in this regard. In one of the most important observations ever made about programming, Larry Flon of Carnegie Mellon University (later at UCLA) said, "There does not now, nor will there ever, exist a programming language in which it is the least bit hard to write bad programs." The important factors are care and discipline, not the structure of the language. Second, it may be reassuring to know that the aphorism about power from the preceding paragraph is in fact a misquote. What Lord Acton actually wrote in 1887 begins with "power *tends* to corrupt." The additional qualifying verb is critically important. If you learn to use the power of C well, it is possible to avoid power's corrupting influence and instead write extremely good programs that stand as models of programming style and elegance.

SUMMARY

The purpose of this chapter is to set the stage for learning about computer science and programming, a process that you will begin in earnest in Chapter 2. In this chapter, you have focused on what the programming process involves and how it relates to the larger domain of computer science.

The important points introduced in this chapter include:

- The physical components of a computer system—the parts you can see and touch—constitute *hardware.* Before computer hardware is useful, however, you must specify a sequence of instructions, or *program,* that tells the hardware what to do. Such programs are called *software.*

- Computer science is not so much the science of computers as it is the science of solving problems using computers.

- Strategies for solving problems on a computer are known as *algorithms.* To be an algorithm, the strategy must be clearly and unambiguously defined, effective, and finite.

- Programs are typically written using a *higher-level language* that is then translated by a *compiler* into the lower-level machine language of a specific computer system.

- To run a program, you must first create a *source file* containing the text of the program. The compiler translates the source file into an *object file,* which is then linked with other object files to create the executable program.

- Programming languages have a set of *syntax rules* that determine whether a program is properly constructed. The compiler checks your program against these syntax rules and reports a *syntax error* whenever the rules are violated.

- The most serious type of programming error is one that is syntactically correct but that nonetheless causes the program to produce incorrect results or no results at all. This type of error, in which your program does not correctly solve a problem because of a mistake in your logic, is called a *bug.* The process of finding and fixing bugs is called *debugging.*

- Most programs must be updated periodically to correct bugs or to respond to changes in the demands of the application. This process is called *software maintenance.* Designing a program so that it is easier to maintain is an essential part of *software engineering.*

- This text uses the programming language C to illustrate the programming process. Although C programs are often written with too little regard for software engineering principles, it is possible to write programs in C that are models of good programming style.

REVIEW QUESTIONS

1. What new concept in computing was introduced in the design of Babbage's Analytical Engine?

2. Who is generally regarded as the first programmer?

3. What concept lies at the heart of von Neumann architecture?

4. What is the difference between hardware and software?

5. Traditional science is concerned with abstract theories or the nature of the universe—not human-made artifacts. What abstract concept forms the core of computer science?

6. What are the three criteria an algorithm must satisfy?

7. What is the distinction between algorithmic design and coding? Which of these activities is usually harder?

8. What is meant by the term *higher-level language?* What higher-level language is used as the basis of this text?

9. Why is it necessary to use different compilers when you run your programs on computers made by different manufacturers?

10. What is the relationship between a source file and an object file? As a programmer, which of these files do you work with directly?

11. What is the difference between a syntax error and a bug?

12. True or false: Good programmers never introduce bugs into their programs.

13. True or false: The major expense of writing a program comes from the development of that program; once the program is put into practice, programming costs are negligible.

14. What is meant by the term *software maintenance?*

15. Why is it important to apply good software engineering principles when you write your programs?

The Basics of C Programming

Overview

Learning C, or any programming language, is in many respects like learning to communicate in a foreign language. You need to acquire a vocabulary to know what the words mean. You need to study syntax so that you can assemble those words into sentences. And you must come to recognize common idioms so that you can understand what people actually say. Therefore, Part One introduces you to the vocabulary, syntax, and idiomatic structure of C. But mastering these conventions is not enough. As in any language, you must have something to say. The essence of programming is solving problems. While knowing how to express them is important, learning how to find solutions is the greater challenge. Thus, Part One focuses on strategies for problem solving, to enable you not just to *write* but to *think* like a programmer.

CHAPTER 2

Learning by Example

Tigers are easy to find, but I needed adult wisdom to know dragons. "You have to infer the whole dragon from the parts you can see and touch," the old people would say. Unlike tigers, dragons are so immense, I would never see one in its entirety. But I could explore the mountains, which are the top of its head. "These mountains are also *like* the tops of *other* dragons' heads," the old people would tell me.

— Maxine Hong Kingston, *The Woman Warrior*, 1975

Objectives

- To get a feel for the structure of C programs by reading through simple examples in their entirety.

- To appreciate the importance of libraries as toolboxes that simplify the programming process and to be able to use library functions for simple input and output.

- To recognize that many simple programs are composed of three phases: input, computation, and output.

- To understand the role of variables in a program as placeholders for data values.

- To recognize the existence of different data types, including `int`, `double`, and `string`.

- To be able to specify simple computation through the use of arithmetic expressions.

- To understand the process of numeric conversion.

- To be able to write new programs by making simple modifications to existing programs.

The purpose of this book is to teach you the fundamentals of programming. Along the way, you will become quite familiar with a particular programming language called C, but the details of that language are not the main point. Programming is the science of solving problems by computer, and most of what you learn from this text will be independent of the specific details of C. Even so, you will have to master many of those details eventually so that your programs can take maximum advantage of the tools that C provides.

From your position as a new student of programming, the need to understand both the abstract concepts of programming and the concrete details of a specific programming language leads to a dilemma: there is no obvious place to start. To learn about programming, you need to write some fairly complex programs. To write those programs in C, you must know enough about the language to use the appropriate tools. But if you spend all your energy learning about C, you will probably not learn as much as you should about more general programming issues. Moreover, C was not designed for beginning programmers. There are many details that just get in the way if you try to master C without first understanding something about programming, and you end up being unable to see the forest because you're distracted by all the trees.

Because it's important for you to get a feel for what programming is before you master its intricacies, this chapter begins by presenting a few simple programs in their entirety. Try to understand what is happening in them generally without being concerned about details just yet. You will learn about those details in Chapter 4. The main purpose of this chapter and the one that follows is to help build your intuition about programming and problem solving, which is far more important in the long run.

2.1 The "Hello world" program

In honor of the designers of C, our first programming example comes from the book that has served as C's defining document, *The C Programming Language,* by Brian Kernighan and Dennis Ritchie. That example is called the "Hello world" program and has become part of the heritage shared by all C programmers—a community that you are poised to enter. The text of the program is shown in Figure 2-1.

The program itself is stored as a file in the permanent storage of the computer system you are using. The name of the file is `hello.c`, where the `.c` identifies the file as a C program.

As Figure 2-1 indicates, the `hello.c` program is divided into three sections: a *program comment,* a list of *library inclusions,* and the *main program.* Although its structure is extremely simple, the `hello.c` program is typical of the programs you will see in the next few chapters, and you should use it as a model of how C programs should be organized.

Comments

The first section of `hello.c` is simply an English-language *comment* describing what the program does. In C, a **comment** is any text that is enclosed between the

FIGURE 2-1 hello.c

```
/*
 * File: hello.c
 * -------------
 * This program prints the message "Hello, world."
 * on the screen.  The program is taken from the
 * classic C reference text "The C Programming
 * Language" by Brian Kernighan and Dennis Ritchie.
 */

#include <stdio.h>
#include "genlib.h"

main()
{
    printf("Hello, world.\n");
}
```

program
comment

library
inclusions

main
program

markers /* and */. Comments may continue for several lines. In the hello.c program, the comment begins with the /* on the first line and ends with the */ eight lines later.

Comments are written for human beings, not for the computer. They are intended to convey information about the program to other programmers. When the C compiler translates a program into a form that can be executed by the machine, it ignores the comments entirely.

In this text, every program begins with a special comment called the **program comment** that describes the operation of the program as a whole. It includes the name of the program file and a message that describes the operation of the program. In this case, the program comment also indicates the original source of the program. Comments might also describe any particularly intricate parts of the program, indicate who might use it, offer suggestions on how to change the program behavior, and the like. For a program this simple, extensive comments are usually not necessary. As your programs become more complicated, however, you will discover that good comments are one of the best ways for you to make them understandable to someone else.

Library inclusions

The second section of the program consists of the lines

```
#include <stdio.h>
#include "genlib.h"
```

These lines indicate that the program uses two *libraries*. A **library** is a collection of tools written by other programmers that perform specific operations. The libraries used by the hello.c program are a standard input/output library (stdio) that is supplied along with ANSI C and a <u>gen</u>eral <u>lib</u>rary (`genlib`) designed specifically for use with this book. Every program in this book will include both of these libraries, which means that these lines will appear in every program immediately after the program comment. Some programs may need to use additional libraries as well. Those programs must contain an `#include` line for each library that is used.

When you write your own programs, you can use the tools provided by these libraries, which saves you the trouble of writing them yourself. Libraries are critical to programming, and you will quickly come to depend on several important libraries as you begin to write more sophisticated programs.

To use a library, however, your program must specify enough information for the C compiler to know what facilities are available as part of that library. In most cases, that information is provided in the form of a **header file,** a file that contains a description for the compiler of the tools provided by that library. For example, `stdio.h` is the name of a header file that defines the contents of the standard input/output library. Similarly, `genlib.h` is the name of a header file that defines the contents of the general library. The `.h` in each of these file names indicates a header file, just as the `.c` in `hello.c` indicates a C program. The contents of header files are discussed more thoroughly in Chapters 7 and 8.

Notice that the punctuation differs in the two `#include` lines:

```
#include <stdio.h>
#include "genlib.h"
```

The library `stdio` is part of the standard set of libraries that are always available when you use ANSI C. Standard libraries are marked with angle brackets so that you can include `stdio` by writing

```
#include <stdio.h>
```

Personal libraries that you write yourself and the extended libraries that accompany this book are specified using quotation marks. Because the `genlib` library is one of these extended libraries, the `#include` line is written as

```
#include "genlib.h"
```

As this text introduces each new library, the corresponding `#include` line will be shown with the appropriate punctuation so you'll know how to gain access to that library.

The main program

The last section of the `hello.c` file shown in Figure 2-1 is the program itself, which consists of the lines

```
main()
{
    printf("Hello, world.\n");
}
```

These four lines represent the first example of a *function* in C. A **function** is a sequence of individual program steps that have been collected together and given a name. The name of this function, as given on the first line, is main. The steps the function performs are listed between the curly braces and are called **statements.** Collectively, the statements constitute the **body** of the function. The function main shown in the hello.c example contains only one statement, but it is common for functions to contain several statements that are performed sequentially.

Whenever you run a C program, the computer executes the statements enclosed in the body of the function named main, which must exist in every complete C program. In the hello.c example, the body of main consists of the single statement

```
printf("Hello, world.\n");
```

This statement uses the library function printf, which is one of the facilities in the standard input/output library that became available when the programmer included the line

```
#include <stdio.h>
```

earlier in the program.

But what does printf do? Like main, printf is a function, which means that the name printf corresponds to a sequence of operations. When you want to invoke those operations, you can simply refer to them collectively by using the function name. In programming, the act of invoking a function by using its name is referred to as **calling** that function. Thus the statement

```
printf("Hello, world.\n");
```

in the hello.c program represents a **call** to the printf function.

When you call a function, you often need to provide additional information. In C, for example, printf is a function that displays data on the screen. But what data should it display? This additional information is indicated using a list of *arguments* enclosed in parentheses after the function name. An **argument** is information that the caller of a particular function makes available to the function itself. Here, printf has been given one argument, the sequence of characters, or **string**, enclosed in quotation marks, as follows:

```
"Hello, world.\n"
```

This string is your first example of *data* in a programming language. There are many different types of data in C, and you will devote a great deal of your attention to the question of how to use data. For the moment, however, you can consider **data** to be the information manipulated by the program: any messages displayed, input requested from the user, values delivered as the result of computation, or intermediate results generated along the way.

In this program, the single statement in main tells the printf library function to display all the characters that make up the string passed to printf as an argument. The printf function dutifully responds by displaying the H, the e, the l, and so on, until the entire message appears on the screen as shown:

```
Hello, world.
```

The final character in the string is a special character called *newline,* indicated by the sequence \n. When the printf function reaches the period at the end of the sentence, the cursor is sitting at the end of the text, just after the period. If you wanted to extend this program so that it wrote out more messages, you would probably want to start each new message on a new screen line. The **newline** character, defined for all modern computer systems, makes this possible. When the printf function processes the newline character, the cursor on the screen moves to the beginning of the next line, just as if you hit the Return key on the keyboard (this key is labeled Enter on some computers). In C, programs must include the newline character to mark the end of each screen line, or all the output will run together without any line breaks.

2.2 A program to add two numbers

To get a better picture of how a C program works, you need to consider a slightly more sophisticated example. The program add2.c shown in Figure 2-2 asks the user to enter two numbers, adds those numbers together, and then displays the sum.

The add2.c program incorporates several new programming concepts that were not part of hello.c. First, add2.c uses a new library called simpio, simplified

---

FIGURE 2-2 add2.c

```
/*
 * File: add2.c
 * ------------
 * This program reads in two numbers, adds them together,
 * and prints their sum.
 */

#include <stdio.h>
#include "genlib.h"
#include "simpio.h"

main()
{
    int n1, n2, total;

    printf("This program adds two numbers.\n");
    printf("1st number? ");
    n1 = GetInteger();
    printf("2nd number? ");
    n2 = GetInteger();
    total = n1 + n2;
    printf("The total is %d.\n", total);
}
```

input/output. This library is an extension used in this text, so the `#include` line uses quotation marks, just as it did in the case of `genlib`:

```
#include "simpio.h"
```

Another new programming feature that deserves special attention appears as the first line of the function `main`

```
int n1, n2, total;
```

This line is the first example of a *variable declaration.* Within a program, a **variable** is a placeholder for some piece of data whose value is unknown when the program is written. For example, when you write a program to add two numbers, you don't yet know what numbers the user will want to add. The user will enter those numbers when the program runs. So that you can refer to these as-yet-unspecified values in your program, you create a variable to hold each value you need to remember, give it a name, and then use its name whenever you want to refer to the value it contains. Variable names are usually chosen so that programmers who read the program in the future can easily tell how each variable is used. In the `add2.c` program, the variables `n1` and `n2` represent the numbers to be added, and the variable `total` represents the sum.

Before you use a variable in C, you must *declare* that variable. **Declaring** a variable tells the C compiler that you are introducing a new variable name and specifies the type of data that variable can hold. For example, in `add2.c` the line

```
int n1, n2, total;
```

declares all three of the variable names—`n1`, `n2`, and `total`—and indicates to the compiler that each holds a value of type `int`. The type name `int` stands for **integer,** a number without fractional parts. Variables and declarations are discussed in more detail in the section on "Variables" later in this chapter.

As with any program, the computer runs the `add2.c` program by executing each of the statements in the body of `main`. The first statement in `add2.c` is similar to the statement that formed the entire body of the earlier `hello.c` example:

```
printf("This program adds two numbers.\n");
```

When this statement is executed, the computer simply displays the message

```
This program adds two numbers.
|
```

on the screen and returns the cursor, represented by the vertical line, to the beginning of the following line. The purpose of the message is to tell the user what the program does.

After displaying the introductory message, the strategy for the rest of the program can be divided into three phases:

1. The **input** phase, in which the program asks the user to enter the two numbers to be added
2. The **computation** phase, in which the program computes the sum
3. The **output** phase, in which the program displays the results of the computation on the computer screen

The input phase

In the input phase, the program must ask the user to enter each of the two numbers and then store those numbers in the variables `n1` and `n2`, respectively. For each number, the input process consists of two steps. First, the program needs to display a message on the screen so that the user knows what is expected; this type of message is generally called a **prompt.** As with other messages to the user, you can use `printf` to display the prompt, as follows:

```
printf("1st number? ");
```

Note that this time there is no newline character at the end of the argument string given to `printf`. Leaving out the newline character means that the cursor will remain at the end of the displayed text, right after the space following the question mark, as the following sample run shows:

```
This program adds two numbers.
1st number? |
```

The cursor at the end of the line tells the user that an input value is required, and the prompt message indicates what value is required. In most cases, you will include the newline character in `printf` calls that are used to display output data but not in those that are used to display prompts for input data.

To read the number itself, the program uses the statement

```
n1 = GetInteger();
```

This statement is the first example of an extremely important programming construct called an *assignment statement.* In C, an **assignment statement** stores a value written to the right of an equal sign in a variable written to the left of that equal sign. In this case, the right-hand side of the assignment statement is a call to the function `GetInteger`; the left-hand side of the assignment statement is the variable `n1`.

The function `GetInteger` is part of the `simpio` library and is used to read integer values from the user. When `GetInteger` is called, the program waits for the user to enter a whole number using the keyboard. When the user has finished typing the number and has pressed the Return key, that value is then passed back to the main program as the result of the `GetInteger` function. In programming terminology, we say that `GetInteger` **returns** the value the user typed. The effect

of the assignment statement as a whole is to call the `GetInteger` function, let
the user enter a value, and finally store the value returned by `GetInteger` in the
variable `n1`.

It is useful to review in more detail the execution of the statements

```
printf("1st number? ");
n1 = GetInteger();
```

The first statement simply displays the specified prompt on the screen, leaving the
cursor at the end of the line. The computer then goes on to execute the statement

```
n1 = GetInteger();
```

As part of the call to `GetInteger`, the program waits for the user to enter a
numeric value, which is interpreted as an integer. For example, the user might
enter the number 2. The screen now looks like the following sample run. (To make
the user actions more clear, the diagram uses the ⏎ symbol to indicate that the user
has pressed the Return or Enter key signifying the end of the input line. That symbol does not actually appear on the screen. In this book, the user's input is shown
in color to distinguish it from the text generated by the program.)

```
This program adds two numbers.
1st number? 2⏎
```

The value 2 is then stored in the variable `n1`.

When tracing through the operation of a program on paper, programmers often
use a simple box diagram to indicate that a variable has been given a particular
value. Each variable corresponds to a box in the diagram. Each box has a name,
which is fixed throughout the time the function runs, and a value, which changes
as new values are stored in that variable. Thus, to illustrate that the assignment
statement has stored the value 2 in the variable `n1`, you draw a box, name the box
`n1`, and then indicate its value by writing a 2 inside the box, as follows:

After reading in the first number, the program reads in the second by repeating the
same basic steps:

```
printf("2nd number? ");
n2 = GetInteger();
```

For example, if the user's second number were 3, the screen would look like

```
This program adds two numbers.
1st number? 2↵
2nd number? 3↵
```

You can now diagram the values for the two variables this way:

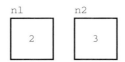

The computation phase

The computation phase of the program consists of calculating the sum of these two numbers. In programming, computation is specified by writing an *expression* that indicates the necessary operations. The result of the expression is then stored in a variable using an assignment statement so that the result can be used in subsequent parts of the program. The structure of expressions is defined more formally later in this chapter. Even without a complete definition, however, it is usually easy to understand how C expressions work because they look very much like expressions in traditional mathematics.

In the add2.c program, you want to add the values stored in the variables n1 and n2. To do so, you use the + operator, which is familiar from basic arithmetic. To keep track of the result, you store it in the variable total, which you declared for precisely this purpose. The assignment statement that performs these operations is

```
total = n1 + n2;
```

As is the case with any assignment statement in C, the computer calculates the value represented by the expression on the right-hand side of the equal sign and then stores it in the variable written on the left-hand side. Here, the effect of the assignment statement is to add the values stored in the variables n1 and n2 and then to assign that result to the variable total.

The output phase

The output phase of the program consists of displaying the computed result. As with other output operations, displaying the result is accomplished using the printf function. This time, however, there's a new twist. The last statement in the add2.c program is

```
printf("The total is %d.\n", total);
```

As before, printf displays each of the characters in the argument string on the screen. When it gets to the percent sign (%), however, printf does something special. The % and the letter that follows it are called a **format code.** Here, for example, the format code is %d. A format code in a printf string acts as a place-holder for a value, which is inserted at that point in the output. The letter that appears in the format code is used to specify the output format. In this case, the %d format code means that the output should be displayed as a _decimal integer. Thus, the program at this point is going to display a message that looks like

```
The total is ____.
```

where the underlined area is replaced with a decimal integer value.

To know what integer to display, printf takes the value from the next argument in the call, which in this case is the variable total. That value is displayed on the screen, and the newline character causes the cursor to move to the next line. Combining this last line with the messages already on the screen shows the complete sample run for the add2.c program:

```
This program adds two numbers.
1st number? 2↵
2nd number? 3↵
The total is 5.
```

The printf function can display any number of data values as part of the output. For each integer value you want to appear as part of the output, you need to include the code %d in the string that is used as the first argument in the printf call. The actual values to be displayed are given as additional arguments to printf, listed in the order in which they should appear. For example, if you changed the last line of the add2.c program to

```
printf("%d + %d = %d\n", n1, n2, total);
```

the value of n1 would be substituted in place of the first %d, the value of n2 would appear in place of the second %d, and the value of total would appear in place of the third %d. The final image on the computer screen would be

```
This program adds two numbers.
1st number? 2↵
2nd number? 3↵
2 + 3 = 5
```

The printf function is discussed in more detail in Chapter 3.

▓▓▓ 2.3 Perspectives on the programming process

Section 2.2 analyzed the add2.c program in detail, taking each statement in the program and describing its specific function. To become a successful programmer, you need to learn what the different statements available in C do and how to use them. At times, you will certainly find yourself going through your own programs statement by statement, particularly when you are searching for a bug that keeps your program from operating correctly. But this detailed view is not the only way to look at programs. Sometimes it helps to stand back and look at the program as a whole.

Look at the main program for the add2.c program again and try to express in one sentence what it does:

```
main()
{
    int n1, n2, total;

    printf("This program adds two numbers.\n");
    printf("1st number? ");
    n1 = GetInteger();
    printf("2nd number? ");
    n2 = GetInteger();
    total = n1 + n2;
    printf("The total is %d.\n", total);
}
```

Even if the first call to printf were not a dead giveaway, the odds are good that you could figure out what this program does without having read the explanations from the previous section and without understanding how any of the different kinds of statements works in detail. The program adds two numbers and displays the result.

What is perhaps more important is that you can also modify the add2.c program to do something a little different. For example, changing the program so that it adds three numbers would not be difficult at all. Recognizing large-scale patterns and building new programs from existing models are essential strategies for programming.

When you look at a program like add2.c, you can choose to perceive it in either of two ways. If you go through the program line by line, as in Section 2.2, you develop an understanding of the program from the perspective of its individual parts—a *reductionistic* approach. But you can also look at a program from a more global perspective—as a complete entity whose operation as a whole is of primary concern. This *holistic* perspective allows you to see the program in a different light—one that is critical to successful programming.

Reductionism is the philosophical principle that the whole of an object can best be understood by understanding the parts that make it up. Its antithesis is **holism,** which recognizes that the whole is often more than the sum of its parts. As you learn how to write programs, you must learn to see the process from each of these perspectives. If you concentrate only on the big picture, you will end up not understanding the tools you need for solving problems. However, if you focus exclusively on details, you will miss the forest for the trees.

In learning about programming, the best approach is usually to alternate between these two perspectives. Taking the holistic view helps sharpen your intuition about the programming process and enables you to stand back from a program and say, "I understand what this program does." On the other hand, to practice writing programs, you have to adopt enough of the reductionistic perspective to know how those programs are put together.

For the rest of this chapter, we will take the reductionistic approach and delve more deeply into two concepts that were introduced in the context of the add2.c program: data types and expressions. You will learn enough about those concepts to begin writing some interesting programs. In Chapter 3, however, we return to the holistic approach and focus on the abstract process of solving problems.

 ## 2.4 Data types

To be useful in a wide variety of applications, programs must be able to store many different types of data. The add2.c program works with integers, but they are only one of many kinds of data available in C. In many applications, you need to work with numbers that are not integers but instead have fractional parts, such as 1.5 or 3.1415926. When you use a word-processing program, the individual data values are characters, which are then assembled into larger units, such as words, sentences, and paragraphs. As your programs get more complicated, you will begin to work with large collections of information structured in a variety of ways. All these different classes of information constitute **data.**

Whenever you work with some piece of data—an integer or a number with a fractional part or a character—the C compiler needs to know its *data type.* Holistically speaking, a **data type** is defined by two properties: a set of values, or **domain,** and a set of operations. For data types, the domain is simply the set of values that are elements of that type. For example, the domain of the type int includes all integers (. . . −2, −1, 0, 1, 2 . . .) up to the limits established by the hardware of the machine. For character data, the domain is the set of symbols that appear on the keyboard or that can be displayed on the terminal screen. The set of operations comprises the tools you have to manipulate values of that type. For example, given two integers, you might add them together or divide one by another. Given text data, on the other hand, it is hard to imagine what an operation like multiplication might mean. You would instead expect to use operations such as comparing two words to see if they are in alphabetic order or displaying a message on the screen. Thus, the operations must be appropriate to the elements of the domain, and the two components together—the domain and the operations—define the data type. The next two sections introduce two new types—double and string—so that you get used to the idea that data comes in different forms.

Floating-point data

Many applications require the use of numbers that can include fractional parts. For example, if you wanted to write a program that dealt with distances, it would certainly be limiting if you were forced to deal only with whole numbers. A measurement might come out to be exactly 1 inch or exactly 3 inches, but it could just as well be 2.5 inches or 0.73 inches. Programs that work with such measurements must be able to represent these nonintegral values as well.

In most programming languages, numbers that include a decimal fraction are called **floating-point numbers,** which are used to approximate real numbers in mathematics. The most common type of floating-point number in C is the type double, which is short for double-precision floating-point.[1] If you need to store floating-point values in a program, you must declare variables of type double, just as you had to declare variables of type int in add2.c.

To write a complete program that works with floating-point values, you also must be able to read in and display numbers of type double. As with integers, reading in floating-point numbers is accomplished using a function from the simpio library. To read in a floating-point number, you call the function GetReal, which is identical in operation to the GetInteger function described in the section on "The input phase" earlier in this chapter, except that it returns a value of type double. To display a floating-point value on the screen, you again use the function printf. This time, however, instead of using %d to indicate a decimal integer, you use a different format code. There are several format codes that apply to floating-point numbers, but the easiest one to use is %g, which stands for the general floating-point format.

The programming example in Figure 2-3 shows how easy it is to change the entire add2.c program into one that adds two floating-point numbers. The only differences are the change in the types of the variables, the use of GetReal in the place of GetInteger, and the use of %g in place of %d in the printf line.

String data

Although the first computers were designed primarily to solve numeric problems (and computers are still sometimes called "number crunchers" as a result), modern computers spend less of their time working with numbers than they do with text. Because the operations on numbers are so simple, the programming examples in the first few chapters of this book concentrate on numeric data. In practice, however, it is very important to be able to manipulate text data as well.

The most primitive elements of text data are individual characters. Characters, however, are most useful when they are collected together into sequential units. In programming, a sequence of characters is called a *string*. Strings make it possible to display informational messages on the screen. You have already seen several

---

[1] This particular type is called *double-precision* because it offers twice as much accuracy as the floating-point type float, which was much more commonly used when C was first developed. Today, most programmers tend to use the type double for all floating-point values.

FIGURE 2-3 add2f.c

```
/*
 * File: add2f.c
 * -------------
 * This program reads in two floating-point numbers, adds them
 * together, and prints their sum.
 */

#include <stdio.h>
#include "genlib.h"
#include "simpio.h"

main()
{
    double n1, n2, total;

    printf("This program adds two floating-point numbers.\n");
    printf("1st number? ");
    n1 = GetReal();
    printf("2nd number? ");
    n2 = GetReal();
    total = n1 + n2;
    printf("The total is %g\n", total);
}
```

examples of strings in the example programs, beginning with hello.c. It is important, however, to recognize that strings are data and that they can be manipulated and stored in much the same way that numbers can.

When considered in detail, strings turn out to be a complicated data type for which a full treatment lies well beyond the scope of this chapter. Even so, it is useful to know a little about strings at this point for two reasons. First, strings provide an example of a data type that is quite different from either int or double. Because they both refer to numbers and use the same basic set of arithmetic operations, the types int and double are in fact quite similar. Strings are used in very different ways. Second, strings make it possible to write more interesting programs, even if you do not yet know how to manipulate them in a very sophisticated way.

To use string data at all, you need a way to name the data type. Although the designers of C provided several operations that work with strings in the libraries associated with the language, they did not define an explicit string type. This omission poses a problem for the student programmer. To make up for this deficiency, however, the type string is defined in the header file genlib.h.

The details of the definition for string are not important at this point, provided you know how objects of type string behave. Moreover, it doesn't matter whether string is defined as part of the language or as part of a library. Types defined in libraries simply become part of the repertoire of data types and are used just as built-in types are. In your programming, you should think of the type string as if it were an integral part of C, even though you know it is actually defined by the genlib library.

You can declare variables of type string in the same way that you declared variables of type int or double in earlier programs. For example, if you want to keep track of someone's name, which consists of a sequence of characters and is therefore a string, you could write the declaration

```
string name;
```

at the beginning of your program.

For the moment, we will not define any operations on strings other than the ones necessary to read them from the keyboard and display them on the screen. Reading in a string is handled in much the same way as reading in a number. The simpio library contains a function GetLine that reads in an entire line and returns it as a string. Given a value of type string, you can use printf to display it on the screen, just as you do with numeric data. The only difference is that you need to use the format code %s instead of the %d or %g you use for numeric types. These two string operations, by themselves, provide you with a great deal of additional power. For example, you can make a small extension to the "Hello world" program so that it offers a more personal welcome than the generic greeting provided by hello.c. The new version is shown in Figure 2-4.

FIGURE 2-4   greeting.c

```
/*
 * File: greeting.c
 * ----------------
 * This program prints a more personal greeting than did
 * the original "Hello, world." program by reading in the
 * name of the user.
 */

#include <stdio.h>
#include "genlib.h"
#include "simpio.h"

main()
{
    string user;

    printf("What is your name? ");
    user = GetLine();
    printf("Hello, %s.\n", user);
}
```

If you run this program using my first name, you would get the following sample run:

```
What is your name? Eric↵
Hello, Eric.
```

Strings are so important to programming that this book devotes several chapters to them. You will have a chance to learn more about strings beginning in Chapter 9.

2.5 Expressions

Whenever you want a program to perform calculations, you write an *expression* that specifies the necessary operations in a form similar to that used for expressions in mathematics. For example, to add the values in the variables n1 and n2 in the add2.c program, the appropriate expression is

```
n1 + n2
```

In C, an **expression** is composed of *terms* and *operators*. A **term**, such as n1 and n2 in the previous expression, represents a single data value. An **operator,** such as the + sign, is a character (or sometimes a short sequence of characters) that indicates a computational operation. In an expression, a term must be one of the following:

- *A constant.* Any data value that appears as part of the program and does not change with the data is called a **constant.** Numbers such as 0 or 3.14159 are examples of constants.
- *A variable.* Variables serve as placeholders for data that can change during the execution of a program.
- *A function call.* Values are often generated by calling other functions, possibly in libraries, that return data values to the original expression. In the add2.c program, the function GetInteger is used to read in each of the input values; the function call GetInteger() is therefore an example of a term. Function calls are discussed further in Chapter 5.
- *An expression in parentheses.* Parentheses may be used in an expression to indicate the order of operations, in the same way they are used in mathematics. From the compiler's point of view, the expression in parentheses becomes a term that must be handled as a unit before computation can proceed.

When a program is run, the process of performing each of the specified operations in an expression is called **evaluation.** When an expression is evaluated, each operator is applied to the data values represented by the surrounding terms. After all the operators have been evaluated, what remains is a single data value that indicates the result of the computation. For example, given the expression

```
n1 + n2
```

the evaluation process consists of taking the values in the variables n1 and n2 and adding them together, and the result of the evaluation is whatever that sum happens to be.

Constants

When you write a formula in mathematics, some symbols in the formula typically represent unknown values while other symbols represent constants whose values are known. Consider, for example, the mathematical formula for computing the circumference (C) of a circle given its radius (r):

$$C = 2\pi r$$

To translate this formula into a program statement, you would use variables to record the radius and circumference. These variables change depending on the data. The values 2 and π, however, are constants—explicit values that never change. The value 2 is an integer constant, and the value π is a real number constant, which would be represented in a program by a floating-point approximation, such as 3.14159. Because constants are an important building block for constructing expressions, it is important to be able to write constant values for each of the basic data types.

1. *Integer constants.* To write an integer constant as part of a program or as input data, you simply write the digits that make up the number. If the integer is negative, you write a minus sign before the number, just as in mathematics. Commas are never used. Thus, the value one million must be written as 1000000 and not as 1,000,000.

2. *Floating-point constants.* Floating-point constants in C are written with a decimal point. Thus, if `2.0` appears in a program, the number is represented internally as a floating-point value; if the programmer had written `2`, this value would be an integer. Floating-point values can also be written in a special programmer's style of scientific notation, in which the value is represented a floating-point number multiplied by a integral power of 10. To write a number using this style, you write a floating-point number in standard notation, followed immediately by the letter E and an integer exponent, optionally preceded by a + or - sign. For example, the speed of light in meters per second is approximately

   $$2.9979 \times 10^8$$

   which can be written in C as

   ```
   2.9979E+8
   ```

   where the E stands for the words *times 10 to the power.*

3. *String constants.* You write a string constant in C by enclosing the characters that comprise the string in double quotation marks. For example, the very first example of data used in this text was the string

   ```
   "Hello, world.\n"
   ```

   in the `hello.c` program. This string consists of the characters shown between the quotation marks, including the letters, the space, the punctuation symbols, and the special newline character. The quotation marks are not part of the string but serve only to mark its beginning and end.

Variables

A **variable** is a placeholder for a value and has three important attributes: a *name,* a *value,* and a *type.* To understand the relationship of these attributes, think of a variable as a box with a label attached to the outside. The name of the variable appears on the label and is used tell the different boxes apart. If you have three boxes (or variables), you can refer to a particular one using its name. The value of the variable corresponds to the contents of the box. The name on the label of the box never changes, but you can take values out of a box and put new values in as often as you like. The type of the variable indicates what kind of data values can be stored in the box. For example, if you have a box designed to hold values of type int, you cannot put values of type string into that box.

Variable names in C are constructed according to the following rules:

1. The name must start with a letter or the underscore character (_). In C, upper-case and lowercase letters appearing in a variable name are considered to be different, so the names ABC, Abc, and abc refer to three separate variables.
2. All other characters in the name must be letters, digits, or the underscore. No spaces or other special characters are permitted in names.
3. The name must not be one of the following **keywords,** which are names that C defines for a specific purpose:

auto	double	int	struct
break	else	long	switch
case	enum	register	typedef
char	extern	return	union
const	float	short	unsigned
continue	for	signed	void
default	goto	sizeof	volatile
do	if	static	while

4. Variable names can be of any length, but C compilers are required to con-sider only the first 31 characters as significant.[2] Thus, if two variable names have the same first 31 characters, subsequent differences may not be recog-nized by some compilers. For example, the variable name

   anExtremelyLongVariableNameWith43Characters

   may be treated as identical to

   anExtremelyLongVariableNameWithADifferentEnding

   because the two names are exactly the same through the first 31 characters. As a general rule to guard against such mix-ups, it is usually best to avoid using names with more than 31 characters.

---

[2] Variable names that are shared between separate program files often consider even fewer characters to be significant. To be safe, it is best to make sure that any names that are shared between files can be distinguished by considering their first eight characters.

5. The variable name should make it obvious to the reader what value is being stored. Although names of friends, expletives, and the like may be legal according to the other rules, they do absolutely nothing to improve the readability of your programs.

As noted in the discussion of the add2.c program, you must explicitly specify the data type of every variable before you use it in a program. This process is known as declaring the variable. Variables are usually declared at the beginning of a function. (So far in this text, the only function in which variables have been declared is the function main, but it is legal to declare variables in any function.) The declaration itself consists of a type name, followed by a list of variables to be declared as instances of that type. For example, the add2.c program declares three variables with the line

```
int n1, n2, total;
```

The names of these variables are n1, n2, and total, all of which are of type int. Thus, using the box analogy for variables, the effect of this declaration is to create the following three boxes, with the names n1, n2, and total:

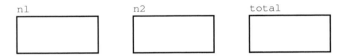

The initial value of each variable is undefined, and you should not make any assumptions about what values these boxes hold when the program begins. The variable n1 might contain 73 or any other random value; you won't know what value is there until you put one there yourself.

If you need to declare values of a different type, you can use additional declaration statements at the beginning of the function. For example, you could declare the variable msg to be of type string by writing the declaration

```
string msg;
```

Once again, the effect of this declaration in terms of the box analogy is to create a new box with the name msg:

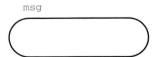

In this diagram, I have chosen a different shape for the box to emphasize that the type of the variable msg is different from that of the variables n1, n2, and total. The variable n1, for example, is of type int and can hold only integer data; the

variable `msg` is of type `string` and can hold only string data. Trying to put the wrong type of data into one of these variables is the computational equivalent of attempting to put a square peg into a round hole and will be caught by the compiler as an error.

Assignment statements

As illustrated in the `add2.c` program earlier in this chapter, variables are given values through the use of assignment statements. In C, an assignment statement has the following form:

>   *variable* = *expression*;

As you will learn in Chapter 3, the line above is an example of a *programming paradigm.* The words in italics represent items you fill in with anything that fits the indicated class. In writing an assignment statement, you can use any variable name on the left-hand side of the equal sign and any expression on the right-hand side. The remainder of the paradigm—in this case the equal sign and the semicolon—is fixed. Thus, in order to write an assignment statement, you start with a variable name, followed by an equal sign, an expression, and a semicolon, in that order.

When new statements are introduced in this text, they will be accompanied by a *syntax box* like the one to the right. Syntax boxes contain a capsule summary of the grammatical structure for a particular statement type and serve as a handy reference.

> **SYNTAX** for assignment **statements**
>
> >   *variable* = *expression*;
> > where:
> >   *variable* is the variable you wish to set
> >   *expression* specifies the value

As noted in the preceding section, jotting down box diagrams can help you visualize the roles of variables in a program. Whenever a variable is declared as part of a function definition, you can draw a new box to hold its value and label the box with the variable name. For example, if a function begins with the declarations

```
int n1, n2;
string msg;
```

you can represent the variables in that function graphically by drawing a box for each variable, as follows.

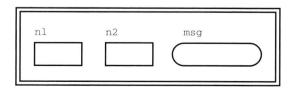

In this text, the double-line border surrounding all the variables is used to indicate that those variables are all defined within the same function.

In box diagrams of this sort, the boxes are initially empty, which indicates that you have not yet assigned values to the variables. If the program executes the statement

```
n1 = 42;
```

you can represent this assignment in the diagram by writing 42 inside the box named n1:

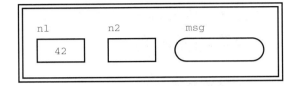

Similarly, you can indicate the effect of the statement

```
msg = "Welcome!";
```

as follows:

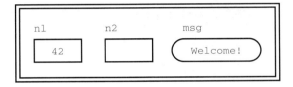

Again, a variable can only hold a value of the appropriate type. If, for instance, you were to write the statement

```
msg = 173;
```

in your program, the C compiler would mark this statement as an error because the variable msg has been declared as a string.

The most important property illustrated by the diagram is that each variable holds precisely one value. Once you have assigned a value to a variable, the variable maintains that value until you assign it a new one. The value of one variable does not disappear if you assign its value to another variable. Thus the assignment

```
n2 = n1;
```

changes n2 but leaves n1 undisturbed:

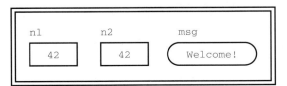

Assigning a new value to a variable erases its previous contents. Thus, the statement

```
msg = "Aloha!";
```

changes the picture to

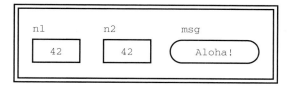

The previous value of the variable `msg` is lost.

Operators and operands

In an expression, the actual computational steps are indicated by symbolic operators that connect the individual terms. The simplest operators to define are those used for arithmetic expressions, which use the standard operators from arithmetic. The arithmetic operators that apply to all numeric data types are:

+   Addition
–   Subtraction (or negation, if written with no value to its left)
*   Multiplication
/   Division

Each of these operators forms a new expression by connecting two smaller expressions, one to the left and one to right of the operator. These subsidiary expressions (or **subexpressions**) to which the operator is applied are called the **operands** for that operator. For example, in the expression

```
x + 3
```

the operands for the + operator are the subexpressions x and 3. Operands are often individual terms, but they can also be more complicated expressions. For example, in the expression

```
(2 * x) + (3 * y)
```

the operands to + are the subexpressions `(2 * x)` and `(3 * y)`.

As in conventional mathematics, the operator – can be used in two forms. When it is positioned between two operands, it indicates subtraction, as in x - y. When used with no operand to its left, it indicates negation, so -x denotes the negative of whatever value x has. When used in this way, the – operator is called a **unary operator** because it applies to a single operand. The other operators (including – when it denotes subtraction) are called **binary operators** because they apply to a pair of operands.

These new operators make it possible to write programs that compute much more interesting and useful results than the sum of two numbers. For example, suppose you want to write a program to convert a length given in inches to its metric counterpart in centimeters. All you really need to know is that 1 inch equals 2.54 centimeters; you can construct the rest of the program just by adapting lines from the add2f.c example and putting them back together in the appropriate way. The final result is shown in Figure 2-5.

Combining integers and floating-point numbers

In C, values of type int and double can be freely combined. If you use a binary operator with two values of type int, the result is of type int. If either or both operands are of type double, however, the result is always of type double. Thus, the value of the expression

```
n + 1
```

is of type int, if the variable n is declared as type int. On the other hand, the expression

```
n + 1.5
```

is always of type double. This convention ensures that the result of the computation is as accurate as possible. In the case of the expression n + 1.5, for example, there would be no way to represent the .5 if the result were computed using integer arithmetic.

FIGURE 2-5   inchtocm.c

```
/*
 * File: inchtocm.c
 * ----------------
 * This program reads in a length given in inches and converts it
 * to its metric equivalent in centimeters.
 */

#include <stdio.h>
#include "genlib.h"
#include "simpio.h"

main()
{
    double inch, cm;

    printf("This program converts inches to centimeters.\n");
    printf("Length in inches? ");
    inch = GetReal();
    cm = inch * 2.54;
    printf("%g in = %g cm\n", inch, cm);
}
```

Integer division and the remainder operator

The fact that applying a binary operator to two integer operands always results in an integer leads to an interesting situation with respect to the division operator. If you write an expression like

```
9 / 4
```

C's rules specify that the result of this operation must be an integer because both operands are of type `int`. When the program evaluates this expression, it divides 9 by 4 and throws away any remainder. Thus, the value of the expression is 2, not 2.25. If you want to compute the mathematically correct result, at least one of the operands must be a floating-point number. For example, the three expressions

```
9.0 / 4
9 / 4.0
9.0 / 4.0
```

each produce the floating-point value 2.25. The remainder is thrown away only if both operands are of type `int`.

There is an additional arithmetic operator that computes a remainder, which is indicated in C by the percent sign (`%`). The `%` operator requires that both operands be of type `int`. It returns the remainder when the first operand is divided by the second. For example, the value of

```
9 % 4
```

is 1, since 4 goes into 9 twice, with 1 left over. The following are some other examples of the `%` operator:

```
0 % 4 = 0              19 % 4 = 3
1 % 4 = 1              20 % 4 = 0
4 % 4 = 0            2001 % 4 = 1
```

The `/` and `%` operators turn out to be extremely useful in a wide variety of programming applications. The `%` operator, for example, is often used to test whether one number is divisible by another. For example, to determine whether an integer `n` is divisible by 3, you just check whether the result of the expression `n % 3` is 0.

C behaves in a confusing way when one or both of the operands to `%` are negative. In fact, different implementations of C can behave differently in such cases. If you rely on one particular behavior, you might be surprised if you move your program to another computer. To ensure that your programs will work the same way on all machines, you should avoid using `%` with negative operands.

Precedence

If an expression has more than one operator, the order in which those operators are applied becomes an important issue. In C, you can always specify the order by putting parentheses around individual subexpressions. For example, the parentheses in the expression

```
(2 * x) + (3 * y)
```

indicate that C should perform each of the multiplication operations before the addition. But what happens if the parentheses are missing? Suppose that the expression is simply

```
2 * x + 3 * y
```

How does the C compiler decide the order in which to apply the individual operations?

In C, as in most programming languages, that decision is dictated by a set of ordering rules chosen to conform to standard mathematical usage. They are called **rules of precedence.** For arithmetic expressions, the rules are:

1. The C compiler first applies any unary minus operators (a minus sign with no operand to its left).
2. The compiler then applies the multiplicative operators (*, /, and %). If two of these operators apply to the same operand, the leftmost one is performed first.
3. It then applies the additive operators (+ and -). Once again, if two operators at this level of precedence apply to the same operand, C starts with the leftmost one.

Thus, in the expression

```
2 * x + 3 * y
```

the multiplication operations are performed first, even when the parentheses are missing. Using parentheses may make the order clearer, but in this case their use is not required because the intended order of operations matches the precedence assumptions of traditional mathematics. If you instead want the addition to be performed first, you must indicate that fact explicitly by using parentheses, as in

```
2 * (x + 3) * y
```

The rules of precedence apply only when two operators compete for a single operand. For instance, in the expression

```
2 * x + 3 * y
```

the operators * and + compete for the operand x. The rules of precedence dictate that the * is performed first because multiplication has higher precedence than addition. Similarly, looking at the two operators next to the value 3, you can again determine that the * is performed first, for precisely the same reason. Note, however, that the rules of precedence do not specify which of the two multiplications is performed first. These subexpressions are entirely independent, and the C compiler is free to evaluate them in either order. The left-to-right rule applies only when two operators at the same precedence level compete for the same operand. For example, precedence rules make a big difference in the evaluation of the expression

```
10 - 5 - 2
```

Because the precedence rules dictate that the leftmost - be performed first, the computation is carried out as if the expression had been written

```
(10 - 5) - 2
```

which yields the value 3. If you want the subtractions performed in the other order, you must use explicit parentheses:

```
10 - (5 - 2)
```

In this case, the result would be 7.

There are many situations in which parentheses are required to achieve the desired result. For example, suppose that, instead of adding two floating-point numbers the way add2f.c does, you wanted them averaged instead. The program is almost the same, as shown in Figure 2-6.

Note that the parentheses are necessary in the statement

```
average = (n1 + n2) / 2;
```

to ensure that the addition is performed before the division. If the parentheses were missing, C's precedence rules would dictate that the division be performed first, and the result would be the mathematical expression

$$n1 + \frac{n2}{2}$$

FIGURE 2-6 ave2f.c

```
/*
 * File: ave2f.c
 * -------------
 * This program reads in two floating-point numbers and
 * computes their average.
 */

#include <stdio.h>
#include "genlib.h"
#include "simpio.h"

main()
{
    double n1, n2, average;

    printf("This program averages two floating-point numbers.\n");
    printf("1st number? ");
    n1 = GetReal();
    printf("2nd number? ");
    n2 = GetReal();
    average = (n1 + n2) / 2;
    printf("The average is %g\n", average);
}
```

instead of the intended

$$\frac{n1 + n2}{2}$$

Applying precedence rules

To illustrate precedence rules in action, let's consider the expression

```
8 * (7 - 6 + 5) % (4 + 3 / 2) - 1
```

Put yourself in the place of the computer. How would you go about evaluating this expression?

Your first step is to evaluate the parenthesized subexpressions, and you might as well start with the first one: `(7 - 6 + 5)`.[3] To compute the value of this expression, you subtract 6 from 7 to get 1 and then add 5 to get 6. Thus, after evaluating the first subexpression, you are left with

```
8 * 6 % (4 + 3 / 2) - 1
```

where the box indicates that the value is the result of a previously evaluated subexpression.

In the second parenthesized subexpression, you must do the division first, since division and multiplication take precedence over addition. Thus, your first step is to divide 3 by 2, which results in the value 1 (remember that integer division throws away the remainder). You then add the 4 and 1 to get 5. At this point, you are left with the following expression:

```
8 * 6 % 5 - 1
```

From here, C's precedence rules dictate that you perform the multiplication and remainder operations, in that order, before the subtraction: 6 times 8 is 48, and the remainder of 48 divided by 5 is 3. Your last step is to subtract 1, leaving 2 as the value of the complete expression.

Type conversion

You have already learned that it is possible to combine values of different numeric types within a C program. When you do so, C handles the situation by using **automatic type conversion,** a process by which values of one type are converted into another compatible type as an implicit part of the computation process. For example, whenever an integer and a floating-point value are combined using an arithmetic operator, the integer is automatically converted into the mathematically equivalent `double` before the operation is applied. Thus, if you write the expression

```
1 + 2.3
```

---

[3] The C compiler is actually free to evaluate the parenthesized subexpressions in either order depending on what is most convenient for the machine, but the final answer is the same in either case. In writing your programs, it is important to avoid situations in which the evaluation order might make a difference.

the integer 1 is converted internally into the floating-point number 1.0 before the addition is performed.

In C, automatic type conversions are also performed whenever an assignment is made. Thus, if the variable `total` is declared to be of type `double`, and you write the assignment statement

```
total = 0;
```

the integer 0 is converted into a `double` as part of making the assignment. Some programming languages (and some programmers) insist on writing this statement as

```
total = 0.0;
```

which has the same effect. On the other hand, the values 0 and 0.0 mean different things mathematically, so it is logical to use the form that is most appropriate to the sense of the application. Writing the value 0 indicates that the value is precisely 0, because integers are exact. When 0.0 appears in a statistical or mathematical context, however, the usual interpretation is that it represents a number close to zero, but one whose accuracy is known only to one significant digit after the decimal point. To avoid ambiguity, this text uses integers to indicate exactness, even in floating-point contexts.

Assigning a value of type `double` to a variable of type `int` also triggers an automatic conversion, which consists of dropping any fraction. Thus, if n is declared to be of type `int`, the assignment

```
n = 1.9999;
```

has the somewhat surprising effect of setting n to 1. The operation of throwing away the decimal fraction (which happens both here and in integer division) is called **truncation.**

Suppose that you have been asked to write a program that translates a metric distance in centimeters back into English units—the inverse of the `inchtocm.c` program in Figure 2-5. If all you need is the number of inches, the body of the program looks pretty much the same as before:

```
main()
{
    double inch, cm;

    printf("This program converts centimeters to inches.\n");
    printf("Length in centimeters? ");
    cm = GetReal();
    inch = cm / 2.54;
    printf("%g cm = %g in\n", cm, inch);
}
```

The only real difference is that you divide by the conversion factor 2.54 instead of multiplying.

Suppose, however, that your employer wants you to display the answer not simply as the total number of inches, but as an integral number of feet plus the number of leftover inches. To compute the whole number of feet, you can divide the total number of inches by 12 and throw away any remainder. To calculate the number of inches left over, you can multiply the number of feet by 12 and subtract that quantity from the total number of inches. The entire program is shown in Figure 2-7.

The assignment statement

```
feet = totalInches / 12;
```

throws away the remainder because `feet` is declared to be an integer variable.

There are also cases in which you need to specify a type conversion even though the rules for automatic conversion do not apply. Suppose, for example, you have declared two integer variables, `num` and `den`, and you want to compute their mathematical quotient (including the fraction) and assign it to the `double` variable `quotient`. You can't simply write

```
quotient = num / den;
```

because both `num` and `den` are integers. When the division operator is applied to two integers, it throws away the fraction. To avoid this problem, you have to convert at least one of the values to `double` before the division is performed.

FIGURE 2-7   cmtofeet.c

```c
/*
 * File: cmtofeet.c
 * ----------------
 * This program reads in a length given in centimeters and converts
 * it to its English equivalent in feet and inches.
 */

#include <stdio.h>
#include "genlib.h"
#include "simpio.h"

main()
{
    double totalInches, cm, inch;
    int feet;

    printf("This program converts centimeters to feet and inches.\n");
    printf("Length in centimeters? ");
    cm = GetReal();
    totalInches = cm / 2.54;
    feet = totalInches / 12;
    inch = totalInches - feet * 12;
    printf("%g cm = %d ft %g in\n", cm, feet, inch);
}
```

In C, you can specify explicit conversion by using what is called a **type cast,** a unary operator that consists of the desired type in parentheses followed by the value you wish to convert. For example, you can convert the denominator of the fraction by writing

```
quotient = num / (double) den;
```

Since the denominator is now of type double, the division is carried out using floating-point arithmetic and the fraction is retained. Equivalently, you can convert the numerator by writing

```
quotient = (double) num / den;
```

This statement has the same effect, but only because the precedence of a type cast is higher than that of division, which means that the expression is evaluated as if it had been written

```
quotient = ((double) num) / den;
```

If the precedence of the type cast were lower than division, C would divide one integer by the other, throw away the fraction, and then convert the integer result back to a double, which would not give the mathematically correct answer.

 ## Summary

In this chapter, you have had the opportunity to look at several complete C programs to get an idea of their general structure and how they work. Your principal objective has been to focus on the programming process itself by adopting a holistic view. By building on the programming examples provided here, you should be ready at this point to write simple programs that involve only the following operations:

- Reading in numeric values supplied by the user
- Displaying text and data on the screen
- Computing new results by applying arithmetic operations to existing data

Important points about programming introduced in this chapter are:

- Well-written programs contain *comments* that explain in English what the program is doing.
- Most programs use *libraries* that provide tools the programmer need not recreate from scratch. Every program in this textbook uses two libraries— stdio and genlib—and may use additional libraries as well.
- You gain access to libraries by adding at the top of the program a #include line that specifies a *header file*. As shown in the sample programs, header files for system libraries (such as stdio.h) are enclosed in angle brackets; header files for personal libraries and those designed for use with this text (such as genlib.h and simpio.h) are enclosed in quotation marks.
- Every complete C program contains a function main. When the program is run, the statements in the body of main are executed in order.

- Many programs are composed of the following three phases: *input, computation,* and *output.*
- To accept input typed by the user, you use the functions `GetInteger`, `GetReal`, and `GetLine` from the `simpio` library, depending on the type of data.
- To display messages and data values on the computer screen, you use the function `printf` from the `stdio` library.
- Data values come in many different types, each of which is defined by a *domain* and a *set of operations.*
- *Constants* are used to specify values that do not change within a program.
- *Variables* have three attributes: a name, a value, and a type. All variables used in a C program must be *declared,* which establishes the name and type of the variable.
- Variables are given values through the use of *assignment statements.* Each variable can hold only one value at a time; when a variable is assigned a new value, any previous value is lost.
- Expressions are composed of individual *terms* connected by *operators.* The subexpressions to which an operator applies are called its *operands.*
- When an operator is applied to two operands of type `int`, the result is also of type `int`. If either or both operands are of type `double`, so is the result.
- If the / operator is applied to two integers, the result is the integer obtained by dividing the first operand by the second and then throwing the remainder away. The remainder can be obtained by using the % operator.
- The order of operations in an expression is determined by *rules of precedence.* The operators introduced so far fall into three precedence classes:

unary −	(type cast)	(highest)
* /	%	
+ −		(lowest)

For the binary operators introduced so far, whenever two operators from the same precedence class compete for the same operand, those operators are applied in left-to-right order.

- Automatic conversion between numeric types occurs when values of different types are combined in an expression or when an assignment is performed.
- Explicit conversion between numeric types can be indicated by using a type cast.

REVIEW QUESTIONS

1. What is the purpose of the comments shown at the beginning of each program in this chapter?

2. What is the purpose of a programming library?

3. ANSI C defines a library called math, which provides several trigonometric and algebraic functions. Even though you do not yet know what these functions are, what line would you need to add to your program to gain access to them?

4. In Chapter 7, you will learn about a specialized library called graphics that provides some simple functions for drawing pictures on the screen and was designed specifically for use with this text. What line would you need to add to your program to gain access to the facilities provided by that library? Why is the punctuation for this line different from that used in the answer to the preceding question?

5. What is the name of the function that must be defined in every C program?

6. What is the purpose of the special character \n that appears at the end of most strings passed to printf? Why is this special character not ordinarily used when displaying a prompt for user input?

7. What does the word *argument* refer to in programming? What purpose do arguments serve?

8. What declarations would you need to write to introduce two integer variables named voteCount1 and voteCount2? What declarations would you write to introduce three floating-point variables named x, y, and z?

9. What are the three phases that comprise the simple programs presented in this chapter?

10. What is the purpose of the GetInteger function? How would you use it in a program?

11. What is the significance of %d and %g when they appear in a printf string? What is the difference between the two?

12. Describe the difference between the philosophical terms *holism* and *reductionism*. Why are these concepts important to programming?

13. What are the two attributes that define a data type?

14. What is the #include line for the genlib library used in conjunction with all programs throughout the remainder of this text?

15. Identify which of the following are legal constants in C. For the ones that are legal, indicate whether they are integers or floating-point constants.
   a. 42   g. 1,000,000
   b. -17   h. 3.1415926
   c. 2+3   i. 123456789
   d. -2.3   j. 0.000001
   e. 20   k. 1.1E+11
   f. 2.0   l. 1.1X+11

16. Rewrite the following floating-point constants in C's form for scientific notation:

a. 6.02252×10^{23}
b. `29979250000.0`
c. `0.00000000529167`
d. `3.1415926535`

(Each of these constants represents an approximation of an important value from chemistry, physics, or mathematics: (a) Avogadro's number, (b) the speed of light in centimeters per second, (c) the Bohr radius in centimeters, and (d) the mathematical constant π. In the case of π, there is no advantage in using the scientific notation form, but it is nonetheless possible and you should know how to do so.)

17. Indicate which of the following are legal variable names in C:

a. `x`
b. `formula1`
c. `average_rainfall`
d. `%correct`
e. `short`
f. `tiny`
g. `total output`
h. `aReasonablyLongVariableName`
i. `12MonthTotal`
j. `marginal-cost`
k. `b4hand`
l. `_stk_depth`

18. What can you assume about the value of a variable before it is assigned a value in a program?

19. Indicate the values and types of the following expressions:

a. `2 + 3`
b. `19 / 5`
c. `19.0 / 5`
d. `3 * 6.0`
e. `19 % 5`
f. `2 % 7`

20. If the variable `k` is declared to be of type `int`, what value does `k` contain after the program executes the assignment statement

```
k = 3.14159;
```

What value would `k` contain after the assignment statement

```
k = 2.71828;
```

21. What is the difference between the unary minus operator and the binary subtraction operator?

22. By applying the appropriate precedence rules, calculate the result of each of the following expressions:

a. `6 + 5 / 4 - 3`
b. `2 + 2 * (2 * 2 - 2) % 2 / 2`
c. `10 + 9 * ((8 + 7) % 6) + 5 * 4 % 3 * 2 + 1`
d. `1 + 2 + (3 + 4) * ((5 * 6 % 7 * 8) - 9) - 10`

23. In C, how do you specify conversion between numeric types?

PROGRAMMING EXERCISES

1. Type in the `hello.c` program exactly as it appears in this chapter and get it working.

2. The following program was written without comments or instructions to the user, except for a few input prompts:

```
#include <stdio.h>
#include "simpio.h"

main()
{
    double b, h, a;

    printf("Enter b: ");
    b = GetReal();
    printf("Enter h: ");
    h = GetReal();
    a = (b * h) / 2;
    printf("a = %g\n", a);
}
```

   Read through the program and figure out what it is doing. What result is it calculating? Rewrite this program so it is easier to understand, both for the user and for the programmer who must modify the program in the future.

3. Extend the `inchtocm.c` program given in Figure 2-5 so that it reads in two input values: the number of feet, followed on a separate line by the number of inches. Here is a sample run of the program:

```
This program converts from feet and inches to
centimeters.
Number of feet? 5↵
Number of inches? 11↵
The corresponding length is 180.34 cm.
```

4. Write a program that reads in two numbers: an account balance and an annual interest rate expressed as a percentage. Your program should then display the new balance after a year. There are no deposits or withdrawals—just the interest

payment. Your program should be able to reproduce the following sample run:

```
Interest calculation program.
Starting balance? 6000↵
Annual interest rate percentage? 4.25↵
Balance after one year: 6255
```

5. Extend the program you wrote in Exercise 4 so that it also displays the balance after two years have elapsed, as shown in the following sample run:

```
Interest calculation program.
Starting balance? 6000↵
Annual interest rate percentage? 4.25↵
Balance after one year: 6255
Balance after two years: 6520.84
```

Note that the interest used in this example is compounded annually, which means the interest from the first year is added back to the bank balance and is therefore itself subject to interest in the second year. In the first year, the $6,000 earns 4.25 percent interest, or $255. In the second year, the account earns 4.25 percent interest on the entire $6,255.

6. Write a program that asks the user for the radius of a circle and then computes the area of that circle (A) using the formula

$$A = \pi\, r^2$$

where π is approximately 3.14159. Note that there is no "raise to a power" operator in C. Given the arithmetic operators you know C has, how can you write an expression that achieves the desired result?

7. Write a program that reads in a temperature in degrees Fahrenheit and returns the corresponding temperature in degrees Celsius. The conversion formula is

$$C = \frac{5}{9}(F - 32)$$

The following is a sample run of the program:

```
Program to convert Fahrenheit to Celsius.
Fahrenheit temperature? 212↵
Celsius equivalent: 100
```

If you write this program carelessly, the answer always comes out 0. What bug causes this behavior?

8. In Norton Juster's children's story *The Phantom Tollbooth,* the Mathemagician gives Milo the following problem to solve:

    ```
    4 + 9 – 2 * 16 + 1 / 3 * 6 – 67 + 8 * 2 – 3 + 26 – 1 / 34 + 3 / 7 + 2 – 5
    ```

    According to Milo's calculations, which are corroborated by the Mathemagician, this expression "all works out to zero." If you do the calculation, however, the expression comes out to zero only if you start at the beginning and apply all the operators in strict left-to-right order. What would the answer be if the Mathemagician's expression were evaluated using C's precedence rules? Write a program to verify your calculation.

9. Write a program that converts a metric weight in kilograms to the corresponding English weight in pounds and ounces. The conversion factors you need are

    1 kilogram = 2.2 pounds
    1 pound = 16 ounces

10. Write a program that computes the average of four integers.

11. There's an old nursery rhyme that goes like this:

    As I was going to St. Ives,
    I met a man with seven wives,
    Each wife had seven sacks,
    Each sack had seven cats,
    Each cat had seven kits:
    Kits, cats, sacks, and wives,
    How many were going to St. Ives?

    The last line turns out to be a trick question: only the speaker is going *to* St. Ives; everyone else is presumably heading in the opposite direction. Suppose, however, that you want to find out how many representatives of the assembled multitude—kits, cats, sacks, and wives—were coming *from* St. Ives. Write a C program to calculate and display this result. Try to make your program follow the structure of the problem so that anyone reading your program would understand what value it is calculating.

CHAPTER 3

Problem Solving

Objectives

- To appreciate that problem solving is an important conceptual skill that requires more than learning the mechanics of a programming language.

- To discover that many interesting problems can be solved by applying a few simple tools called programming idioms.

- To be able to recognize and use C's shorthand assignment forms.

- To be able to use the `for` statement, the `while` statement, and the `if` statement in simple idiomatic forms.

- To recognize how easy it is to introduce errors into a program and therefore to appreciate the need for thorough testing and a disciplined approach to program development.

- To understand how to use the formatting features of `printf`.

- To appreciate the importance of designing programs so that they can be understood by other programmers.

Chapter 2 introduced several simple C programs to give you a general sense of their structure and how they work. This chapter focuses on what makes programming interesting: the process of solving problems. Once you come up with a solution strategy, the process of coding the program—transforming the strategy into a working program—is relatively straightforward, usually much easier than designing the strategy itself.

This chapter shows you how to write several new programs that build on the add2.c example in Chapter 2. Here, however, the main focus is not on the C programs themselves but rather on the general process of designing solutions. As you read, you should try to maintain a holistic perspective and concentrate on understanding the big picture. Don't worry if the syntactic rules seem a bit confusing or if you're not sure how a particular statement works, as long as you have a sense of what the program is doing as a whole. You will have the opportunity to learn the syntactic rules and various other details of the coding process in Chapter 4.

3.1 Programming idioms and paradigms

Before the invention of writing, history and religion passed from generation to generation as part of an oral tradition. *The Iliad* and *The Odyssey* of Homer, the Vedic literature of India, the Old Norse mythologies, the sermons and songs that kept African traditions alive through centuries of slavery—all are examples of an oral tradition. These works are characterized by the patterned repetition of phrases, which make it easier for singers, preachers, and storytellers to remember them. These repeated patterns, called **formulas,** provide the memory cues that make it possible to remember and make variations on a long and detailed story.

In its entirety, C is itself a long and detailed story with many rules and techniques to remember. Even so, as you write your programs, you will notice many patterns that come up repeatedly, like formulas from oral tradition. If you learn to recognize these patterns and think of them as conceptual units, you will soon discover that there is less to remember about programming in C than you might have thought. Programmers call these common patterns **programming idioms,** which refers to a statement or group of statements in C for which much of the structure is fixed but which nonetheless allow you to change individual aspects of the pattern to fit a particular situation. To write effective programs, you must learn how to apply these programming idioms to the task at hand. Eventually, you should be able to do so without devoting any conscious attention to the process. A general idea will come into your mind as part of a solution strategy, and you will automatically translate that idea into the appropriate idiom as you compose the program.

As an example of a programming idiom, consider the add2.c program in Chapter 2. As part of the input phase of the program, the user was asked to supply an integer value. On each occasion, the add2.c program accomplished this task using the following statements:

1. A call to printf to display a prompt
2. A call to GetInteger to read in the integer

These statements represent a programming idiom—the **read-an-integer idiom**—that has the form

```
printf("prompt string");
variable = GetInteger();
```

These two lines are an example of a programming **paradigm,** a fragment of C code that shows the syntactic structure of a particular statement or idiom. Within a paradigm, italics indicate the parts you need to replace with something of the indicated category. In this paradigm, for example, you can fill in any prompt string or variable name in the spaces provided. By substituting "1st number? " in place of *prompt string* and n1 in place of *variable,* you get the statements from add2.c that request the first input value.

```
printf("1st number? ");
n1 = GetInteger();
```

By using "2nd number? " and n2 instead, you get the statements that request the second input value.

```
printf("2nd number? ");
n2 = GetInteger();
```

You can substitute any string for *prompt string* and any variable name for *variable.* By doing so, you can use the same basic idiom to request any integer value.

Shorthand assignment idioms

Some idioms in C exist principally to provide convenient shorthand forms for common operations. Of these, the most important are *shorthand assignment* operations, which are extremely common in C.

Before shorthand assignment operations are defined formally, it is useful to understand the situations in which they occur. Suppose that the variable balance contains your bank balance and that you want to deposit an amount whose value is stored in the variable deposit. The new balance is given by the expression balance + deposit. You might therefore write an assignment statement like

```
newbalance = balance + deposit;
```

In most cases, however, you don't want to use a new variable to store this result. The point of making a deposit is that it changes the bank balance, and it therefore makes sense to change the value stored in the variable balance to account for the additional funds. Instead of storing the result of the expression in a new variable such as newbalance, it would be more useful to add balance and deposit together and then store the result back in the variable balance, using the following assignment statement:

```
balance = balance + deposit;
```

To understand what this assignment is doing, you cannot think of the equal sign in the assignment as a mathematical expression of equality. As a mathematical equation, the formula

$$x = x + y$$

is solvable only if y is equal to 0. Otherwise, there is no way that x can equal $x + y$. An assignment statement is an active operation that explicitly stores the value of the expression on the right in the variable on the left. Thus, the assignment statement

```
balance = balance + deposit;
```

is not an assertion that `balance` is equal to `balance + deposit`. It is a command to change the value of `balance` so that it is equal to the sum of its previous value and the value of `deposit`.

Although the statement

```
balance = balance + deposit;
```

has the desired effect—adding `deposit` to `balance` and leaving the result in `balance`—it is not the statement that a C programmer would usually write. Statements that perform some operation on a variable and then store the result back in that same variable occur so frequently in programming that the designers of C included an idiomatic shorthand for it. For any binary operator *op,* the statement

   variable = variable op expression;

can be replaced by

   variable op= expression;

The combination of an operator with the = used for assignment form is called a **shorthand assignment operator.**

Using the shorthand assignment operator for addition, the more common form of the statement

```
balance = balance + deposit;
```

is therefore

```
balance += deposit;
```

which means, in English, "add `deposit` to `balance`."

Because this same shorthand applies to any binary operator in C, you can subtract the value of `surcharge` from `balance` by writing

```
balance -= surcharge;
```

divide the value of `x` by 10 using

```
x /= 10;
```

or double the value of `salary` by using

```
salary *= 2;
```

Increment and decrement operators

Beyond the shorthand assignment operators, C offers a further level of abbreviation for two particularly common programming operations—adding or subtracting 1 from a variable. Adding 1 to a variable is called **incrementing** that variable;

subtracting 1 is called **decrementing** that variable. To indicate these operations in an extremely compact form, C uses the operators ++ and -- For example, the statement

```
x++;
```

in C has the same ultimate effect as

```
x += 1;
```

which is itself short for

```
x = x + 1;
```

Similarly,

```
y--;
```

has the same effect as

```
y -= 1;
```

or

```
y = y - 1;
```

The ++ and -- operators occur all the time in C programs.[1] As you will discover in Chapter 13, however, these operators are both more complicated and more useful than this section suggests.

3.2 Solving problems on a larger scale

Programming idioms and paradigmatic forms act as building blocks from which you can construct programs. When faced with a problem, your job as a programmer is to assemble these building blocks into a coherent program that solves it. The rest of this chapter introduces several new programming idioms in the context of specific enhancements to the add2.c program from Chapter 2.

The add2.c program presented in Figure 2-2 reads in two numbers, adds them together, and prints their sum. Adding two numbers, however, is not a very challenging task. If all problems were that simple, we wouldn't need computers. One of the main advantages of computers is their ability to process considerable amounts of data very quickly. The interesting problem from a practical perspective is not how to add two numbers, but how to perform addition on a much larger scale.

Suppose you want to modify add2.c to add 10 or 100 or even 1000 numbers. Would you choose the same strategy? Probably not. For 10 numbers, the same

---

[1] The ++ and -- operators are in many ways the most readily identifiable features of C. Nothing else so clearly jumps out at you and declares that a particular program is a C program and not one written in another language. As an indication of how pervasive these operators have become, the successor language to C, which was developed to take advantage of a set of techniques known as object-oriented programming, is called C++, because that name means "the successor to C" in the iconography of the C programming language.

strategy would certainly work, but the idea of declaring 100 variables and then reading them in using separate statements is more than a little daunting. If there were 1000 input values, the strategy used in add2.c would result in an extremely repetitive program over 50 pages long.

Let's consider the problem of finding the sum of 10 numbers. How can you get around having to declare 10 variables? Solving problems like this one is what makes computer programming hard; it is also what makes it interesting and fun. Think about the problem for a minute. Imagine that you are adding up 10 numbers—without a computer—and that I start calling those numbers out to you: 7, 4, 6, and so on. What would you do? You could write down the numbers and then add them at the end. This strategy is analogous to the one used in the add2.c program. It's effective, but it won't win any prizes for speed or cleverness. Alternatively, you could try adding the numbers as you go: 7 plus 4 is 11, 11 plus 6 is 17, and so on. You don't have to keep track of each individual number, just the current total. When you hear the last number, you're all set to announce the answer.

The fact that you don't have to remember each individual number should help answer the question of how to add 10 numbers without declaring 10 variables. With this new strategy, you should be able to write a new add10.c program using only two variables: one for each number as it comes in and one for the current total. Each time you read in a new number, you simply add it to the variable that holds the total of all the numbers so far. At that point, you can use the same variable to hold the next number, which is treated in precisely the same way.

This insight should enable you to begin the task of coding a program that uses the new strategy. Knowing that you need to declare two variables—a current value and a running total—you could begin the program with the following declaration:

```
int value, total;
```

You also know that you must execute the following steps for each input value:

1. Request an integer value from the user and store it in the variable value.
2. Add value to the running sum stored in the variable total.

You already know how to code the first step; it is a perfect example of the request-an-integer idiom introduced in the preceding section and therefore looks like this:

```
printf(" ? ");
value = GetInteger();
```

You also know how to code the second step. Adding value to total is an instance of the shorthand assignment idioms introduced earlier in this chapter. To add value to total, the idiom is

```
total += value;
```

The two idioms—one for reading in an integer and one for adding that integer to a running total—give you everything you need to code the operations that must occur for each input value in the add10.c program. For each of the 10 input values, the program must execute the following statements:

```
printf(" ? ");
value = GetInteger();
total += value;
```

At this point, all you need to do is find some way to make the program execute this set of statements 10 times. As it happens, there is a simple idiom for achieving this goal. Before introducing that idiom, however, it is useful to consider how such an idiom differs from those you have encountered so far.

 ## 3.3 Control statements

In every program in Chapter 2, all the statements have some direct effect: they read in numbers, compute results, or display data on the screen. Moreover, the statements in these programs are always executed sequentially, beginning with the first statement in the function main and ending with the last. As you begin to solve more sophisticated problems, however, you will discover that strictly sequential execution is not enough. To complete the add10.c program, for example, you must be able to execute a set of statements over and over again—10 times, to be exact. To specify that repetition, you need to use a **control statement,** which is a statement that affects how other statements are executed.

In this chapter, control statements are introduced only in the context of particular idioms used to accomplish common tasks. Chapter 4 covers the same control statements from a more general perspective, which will enable you to apply them to a wider class of programming problems.

The repeat-N-times idiom

Before discussing control statements as a general class, it is useful to consider a specific example. In the evolving add10.c program, you already have a set of statements that read in a value and add it to a running total. To complete the process, you need to repeat that set of statements 10 times.

To repeat an operation a specified number of times, the standard approach in C is to use the for statement, which is an example of a control statement. The details of the for statement are explained in Chapter 4. For now, you will use it in the following form, which represents the **repeat-N-times idiom:**

```
for (i = 0; i < N; i++) {
    statements to be repeated
}
```

In the repeat-N-times idiom, the value N indicates the number of repetitions you want.[2] For example, if you replace N with 5, the statements enclosed within the braces will be executed five times. To use this idiom in the add10.c program, you need to replace N by 10. The statements enclosed in the braces are the three statements that (1) print a prompt, (2) read an integer into value, and (3) add that value

---

[2] The variable i used in this idiomatic pattern is called an *index variable* and can actually be any integer variable.

to `total`. If you make these substitutions in the paradigm, you get the following code:

```
for (i = 0; i < 10; i++) {
    printf(" ? ");
    value = GetInteger();
    total += value;
}
```

The `for` statement idiom provides a concrete example of how control statements are written in C. Control statements in C consist of two distinct parts:

1. *The control line.* The first line of a control statement is called the **control line.** It begins with a keyword that identifies the statement type and typically contains additional information that defines the control operation as a whole. In the case of the `for` statement idiom, the control line is

   ```
   for (i = 0; i < N; i++)
   ```

   The control line in the `for` statement is used to control the number of times the statements enclosed within the curly braces should be executed.
2. *The body.* The statements enclosed within the curly braces constitute the **body** of the control statement. In the case of the `for` statement, these statements are repeated the number of times indicated by the control line. By convention, each statement within the body is written on a separate line. Moreover, each statement within the body is indented four spaces with respect to the control line so that the range of statements affected by the control statement is easy to see.

The control line and the body are conceptually independent. Once you have written the control line for a control statement, you can put any statements you want inside the body. Thus the `for` statement can be used to repeat any operation. For example, if you execute the statements

```
for (i = 0; i < 2; i++) {
    printf("a rose is ");
}
printf("a rose.\n");
```

you get one of Gertrude Stein's most familiar lines:

```
a rose is a rose is a rose.
```

The fact that the `for` statement can be applied to any set of statements makes it an enormously powerful tool.

Iteration and loops

In programming, the process of repeating an operation is called **iteration.** Iteration is essential to the solution strategy for many problems, particularly those that involve large amounts of data. Typically, programs to solve such problems need to execute the same operations for each data value. For example, the add10.c program repeats the process of reading a value and adding it to the running total for each of the 10 input values.

Programmers generally use the term **loop** to refer to any portion of the program that is repeated through the action of a control statement such as the for statement. The origin of the word *loop* lies in the early days of computing, when programs were fed into computing machines in the form of punched paper tape. To repeat the same set of operations over and over, programmers connected the ends of a short segment of tape, so that the tape formed a physical loop. Instructions on the tape passed through the tape reader and then came back around to be executed again and again as needed.

When a for loop runs, the computer executes each instruction in the body in sequential order. When the last statement has been executed, the program returns to the beginning of the loop and checks to see if the desired number of repetitions have been completed. If so, the program exits from the entire loop and continues with the statements that follow the closing brace at the end of the for statement. If more repetitions are required, the computer starts again with the first statement in the loop body and then goes on to each subsequent statement in turn. A complete execution of the statements within the loop is called a **cycle.**

Index variables

In the control line of the for statement

```
for (i = 0; i < N; i++)
```

the variable i is called the **index variable.** Although you can use any integer variable, using i follows a strong historical tradition. When programmers see the variable i in a for loop, they assume that it is keeping track of the number of cycles and don't pay much attention to it.

Regardless of whether you use i or some other variable, that variable name must be declared at the beginning of the function just like any other variable. Thus, the program to add 10 numbers must include a declaration of i. Since the program already declares two other integer variables—value and total—you can add the declaration of i to the same line:

```
int value, total, i;
```

Inside the for loop, the variable i keeps track of how many cycles have been executed. On the first cycle, the value of i is 0. On the next cycle, i has the value 1. On each subsequent cycle, the value of i increases by one, until, on the last cycle, it has the value N-1, where N is the limit specified in the for control line. Thus, over the entire execution of the loop, the variable i counts from 0 to N-1. For this reason, for loops are sometimes called **counting loops.**

Although most `for` loops you will encounter in C programs start counting at 0, it is possible to modify the `for` loop idiom so that the counting begins with any other number. The new idiom is

```
for (i = first; i <= last; i++) {
    statements to be repeated
}
```

When using this idiom, the value of the index variable `i` begins with the value *first* and counts upward until it reaches the value *last*. Note that this new idiom uses the `<=` operator (less than or equal to) instead of the operator `<` (less than) used in the original idiom.

The major advantage of the revised `for` loop idiom is that it allows you to begin counting with 1, which is more customary in the real world than starting with 0. For example, the program `count10.c` shown in Figure 3-1 counts from 1 to 10, displaying each number as it goes. As you will see in Chapter 11, however, C programmers often have good reasons for starting counts from 0. If all you need to do is repeat an operation *N* times, it is usually best to conform to traditional C practice and use the `for` control line

```
for (i = 0; i < N; i++)
```

even though the following line would also work:

```
for (i = 1; i <= N; i++)
```

The second version should be used only when you need the value of `i`, as in the `count10.c` program in Figure 3-1.

FIGURE 3-1 count10.c

```
/*
 * File: count10.c
 * ---------------
 * This program counts from 1 to 10, displaying each number
 * on the screen.
 */

#include <stdio.h>
#include "genlib.h"

main()
{
    int i;

    for (i = 1; i <= 10; i++) {
        printf("%d\n", i);
    }
}
```

The importance of initialization

The `for` loop provides you with almost everything you need to write the `add10.c` program, but there is still one important detail to consider. The heart of the `add10.c` program is the `for` loop

```
for (i = 0; i < 10; i++) {
    printf(" ? ");
    value = GetInteger();
    total += value;
}
```

which repeats the operations required for each individual number for each of the input values. As each new input value is read in, the program adds it to the variable `total`, which serves to keep track of the total so far.

This strategy works perfectly once the program is underway. For example, if `total` is 123 and the user enters the value 17, the program simply adds 17 to the contents of `total` to give it a new value of 140. But what about the first time through? The very first number is read into the variable `value` and added into `total` using the line

```
total += value;
```

You know that this idiom instructs the computer to take `value` and add it to the previous contents of `total`, leaving the result in `total`. But what are the previous contents of `total`? On the first cycle of the loop, you don't know the answer to this question. Until you assign a value to a variable within a function, its value is undefined.

Even so, you know what its value ought to be. For the program to work correctly, the value of `total` must be 0 before the first cycle of the `for` loop so that its value will be correct after the first value is added in. To ensure that `total` has the correct initial value, you need to set it to 0 explicitly *before* the loop begins. Thus, you need to write the following statement at the beginning of the program:

```
total = 0;
```

Using an assignment statement to ensure that a variable has its proper initial value is called **initialization.** Failure to initialize variables is a common source of error.

You now have all the pieces you need to complete the `add10.c` program. The complete program is shown in Figure 3-2.

The read-until-sentinel idiom

The `add10.c` program is a useful illustration of how to use the `for` statement, but in its present form it is unlikely to meet the needs of any significant number of users. The program always adds precisely 10 values; to use the program with a different number of values would require an explicit, albeit minor, change in the program. What you really need is a more general program that can add any number of input values.

If you wanted to convert the `add10.c` program into one that solves this more general problem, there is one approach that requires only a minor programming

FIGURE 3-2 add10.c

```
/*
 * File: add10.c
 * -------------
 * This program adds a list of ten numbers, printing
 * the total at the end.  Instead of reading the numbers
 * into separate variables, this program reads in each
 * number and adds it to a running total.
 */

#include <stdio.h>
#include "genlib.h"
#include "simpio.h"

main()
{
    int i, value, total;

    printf("This program adds a list of ten numbers.\n");
    total = 0;
    for (i = 0; i < 10; i++) {
        printf(" ? ");
        value = GetInteger();
        total += value;
    }
    printf("The total is %d\n", total);
}
```

change. Instead of using a constant value like 10 in the for statement control line, you could ask the user to enter the number of data values at the beginning and store that number in a variable. Assuming that n has been declared as an integer, the first few lines of the program would then change to

```
printf("This program adds a list of numbers.\n");
printf("How many numbers in the list? ");
n = GetInteger();
total = 0;
for (i = 0; i < n; i++) {
    . . .
```

The only problem with this strategy is that the user will almost certainly hate it. If you want your computer to add a column of figures, you probably won't be happy about having to count those numbers first. You need to take a different approach.

From the user's point of view, the best approach is to define a special input value and let the user enter that value to signal the end of the input list. A special value used to terminate a loop is called a **sentinel.** The choice of an appropriate value to use as a sentinel depends on the nature of the input data. The value chosen as a sentinel should not be a legitimate data value; that is, it should not be a value that the user would ever need to enter as normal data. For example, when adding a list of integers, the value 0 is an appropriate sentinel. There might be some 0s in a column of figures, but the user can always ignore them because they don't affect the final total. Note that the situation would be different if you were writing a program to average exam scores. Averaging in a 0 score does change the result, and some students have been known to get 0 scores from time to time. In this situation, 0 is a legitimate data value. To allow the user of the program to enter 0 as a score, it is necessary to chose a different sentinel value that does not represent an actual score. On most exams, it is impossible to have a negative score, so it would make sense to choose some value like –1 as the sentinel for that application.

To extend `add10.c` into the new `addlist.c` program, the only change you need to make is in the loop structure. The `for` loop, which is most commonly used to execute a set of operations a predetermined number of times, is no longer appropriate. You need a new idiom that reads data until the special input sentinel is found. That idiom is the **read-until-sentinel idiom** and has the following form:

```
while (TRUE) {
    prompt user and read in a value
    if (value == sentinel) break;
    rest of body
}
```

This new idiom for a sentinel-based loop enables you to complete the `addlist.c` program, which is shown in Figure 3-3.

In Chapter 4, you will learn much more about the control statements out of which the read-until-sentinel idiom is formed. You will find the idiom very useful, even before you understand the details. I realize that setting aside your curiosity and relying on an idiom you don't really understand can be difficult. As you learn more about programming, however, you will discover that this situation happens frequently, even for expert programmers. In fact, one of the marks of an expert programmer is being able to use a library or a piece of code *without* understanding all its details. As programs become more complex, the ability to use tools that you understand only at the holistic level is an increasingly important skill.

Building a more practical application

A program to add a column of figures is not likely to sell a million copies or turn you into the next software billionaire. Who needs a program to add lists of numbers anyway?

The answer, of course, is that most people need to add lists of numbers once in a while, but they rarely think about the problem in this abstract form. Most people think in terms of more specific day-to-day activities, for which adding a list of numbers may be essential. For example, most of us spend some time each month balancing our checkbooks—an activity that consists of little more than adding and subtracting numbers. If you wanted to solve this more practical problem, it might make sense to repackage the `addlist.c` program as a checkbook balancer.

FIGURE 3-3   addlist.c

```
/*
 * File: addlist.c
 * ---------------
 * This program adds a list of numbers.  The end of the
 * input is indicated by entering 0 as a sentinel value.
 */

#include <stdio.h>
#include "genlib.h"
#include "simpio.h"

main()
{
    int value, total;

    printf("This program adds a list of numbers.\n");
    printf("Signal end of list with a 0.\n");
    total = 0;
    while (TRUE) {
        printf(" ? ");
        value = GetInteger();
        if (value == 0) break;
        total += value;
    }
    printf("The total is %d\n", total);
}
```

How would the program change if you were to rewrite it as a checkbook balancer? The answer depends largely on how fancy you want it to be. For an initial version, you might simply make the following alterations:

1. Change the comments at the beginning of the program so that future readers understand the program's purpose.
2. Change the variable names to make them more appropriate to the problem.
3. Provide more explicit instructions to the user.
4. Change the program to use floating-point numbers so that the user can enter both dollars and cents.
5. Allow the user to enter an initial balance.
6. Enable the program to display the current balance on each cycle of the loop, so that the user can track the account through every transaction.

A program that incorporates this first set of changes is the balance.c program shown in Figure 3-4. To make this program work without changing the basic

FIGURE 3-4   balance1.c (initial version)

```
/*
 * File: balance1.c
 * ----------------
 * This file contains the first version of a program to
 * balance a checkbook.  The user enters checks and deposits
 * throughout the month (checks are entered as negative
 * numbers).  The end of the input is indicated by entering
 * 0 as a sentinel value.
 */

#include <stdio.h>
#include "genlib.h"
#include "simpio.h"

main()
{
    double entry, balance;

    printf("This program helps you balance your checkbook.\n");
    printf("Enter each check and deposit during the month.\n");
    printf("To indicate a check, use a minus sign.\n");
    printf("Signal the end of the month with a 0 value.\n");
    printf("Enter the initial balance: ");
    balance = GetReal();
    while (TRUE) {
        printf("Enter check (-) or deposit: ");
        entry = GetReal();
        if (entry == 0) break;
        balance += entry;
        printf("Current balance = %g\n", balance);
    }
    printf("Final balance = %g\n", balance);
}
```

structure, you must rely on the user to indicate checks by entering them as negative values. Adding the negative value to the running total corresponds to subtracting the value of the check. The convention also makes reasonable intuitive sense, and the user should be able to follow that convention as long as the program provides the necessary instructions.

If you run the program, it might produce the following sample run showing an initial balance of $100 against which the user has written four checks (for $50, $35, $10, and $25) and to which the user has made a single deposit of $50, resulting in a final balance of $30.

```
This program helps you balance your checkbook.
Enter each check and deposit during the month.
To indicate a check, use a minus sign.
Signal the end of the month with a 0 value.
Enter the initial balance: 100↵
Enter check (-) or deposit: -50↵
Current balance = 50
Enter check (-) or deposit: -35↵
Current balance = 15
Enter check (-) or deposit: -10↵
Current balance = 5
Enter check (-) or deposit: 50↵
Current balance = 55
Enter check (-) or deposit: -25↵
Current balance = 30
Enter check (-) or deposit: 0↵
Final balance = 30
```

Although the program is still not as versatile or fancy as you might like, it is now able to perform a function that potential users might regard as valuable.

Conditional execution and the `if` statement

Suppose you want to extend this program by adding some additional features. For example, you might want it to detect when the user has bounced a check. To add such a feature, you must first learn how to write programs that can make decisions. When writing a program, you often encounter situations in which you want the program to execute a statement only if some condition applies or to choose between two alternative courses of action depending on the result of some test. This style of operation within a program is called **conditional execution.**

The simplest way to express conditional execution in C is with the `if` statement, which can be used in either of two basic forms:

```
if (conditional-test) {
  . . . statements executed if the test is true . . .
}
```

or

```
if (conditional-test) {
  . . . statements executed if the test is true . . .
} else {
  . . . statements executed if the test is false . . .
}
```

The first form of the `if` statement is used when your solution strategy calls for a set of statements to be executed only in a particular circumstance. If that circumstance does not apply, those statements are skipped. The second form is used when the solution strategy calls for two distinct contingencies: if some condition holds, the program executes one set of statements; if not, it executes another set of statements.

The *conditional-test* component shown in these paradigms is a special type of expression that asks a question. You will learn a great deal more about this sort of expression in Chapter 4, but for now, you can get by with a very simple class of conditional tests formed by using C's **relational operators.** The six relational operators defined in C are given in the following list, along with their more conventional mathematical equivalents in parentheses. Because some of the mathematical forms (≠, ≤, and ≥) do not exist on a standard keyboard, C uses a combination of two symbols to suggest the mathematical form.

```
==  Equal (=)
!=  Not equal (≠)
>   Greater than (>)
<   Less than (<)
>=  Greater than or equal to (≥)
<=  Less than or equal to (≤)
```

Each of these operators is used to compare two values, one on each side. For example, to test whether the value of the variable x is greater than or equal to 0, you would write the following conditional test:

```
x >= 0
```

Conditional tests make it possible to implement the proposed change in the checkbook balancing program: determining whether a check has bounced. If the user enters a check that exceeds the current balance, you can make the program do two things:

1. Print out a message to the user indicating that a check has bounced.
2. Deduct the service charge assessed by the bank as a bounced-check penalty, which we will assume for the moment is $10.

To make this extension to the program, you need to include a conditional test to check whether the user has exceeded the current balance. An approach that seems particularly inviting is simply to check whether there is a negative balance at the end of the operation, as shown in Figure 3-5. Note the bug symbol on the program example, which indicates that the program contains an as-yet-undiscovered bug. To make sure that you don't copy incorrect code, I have marked all buggy examples in this book with such symbols.

The only change from the previous version of this program is that the following if statement has been added to the end of the while loop:

```
if (balance < 0) {
    printf("This check bounces.  $10 fee deducted.\n");
    balance -= 10;
}
```

In English, this statement says that if the balance is less than 0, the program prints out a message to that effect and makes the appropriate charge against the balance. The last line within the body of the if statement is

---

FIGURE 3-5   balance2.c (buggy version)

```
/*
 * File: balance2.c
 * ------------------
 * This file contains a buggy second attempt at a program to
 * balance a checkbook.
 */

#include <stdio.h>
#include "genlib.h"
#include "simpio.h"

main()
{
    double entry, balance;

    printf("This program helps you balance your checkbook.\n");
    printf("Enter each check and deposit during the month.\n");
    printf("To indicate a check, use a minus sign.\n");
    printf("Signal the end of the month with a 0 value.\n");
    printf("Enter the initial balance: ");
    balance = GetReal();
    while (TRUE) {
        printf("Enter check (-) or deposit: ");
        entry = GetReal();
        if (entry == 0) break;
        balance += entry;
        if (balance < 0) {
            printf("This check bounces.  $10 fee deducted.\n");
            balance -= 10;
        }
        printf("Current balance = %g\n", balance);
    }
    printf("Final balance = %g\n", balance);
}
```

```
    balance -= 10;
```

which is a shorthand for the longer

```
    balance = balance - 10;
```

3.4 An exercise in debugging

This change in the checkbook-balancing program seems so simple that it hardly merits a second thought. All too often, programmers make changes that appear small and innocuous without bothering to test the resulting program thoroughly. Failure to test code is a very serious error. A more important error, however, is the failure to recognize that all code, no matter how simple it seems, needs testing. The program shown in Figure 3-5 contains a subtle bug. Finding the bug is complicated by the fact that the program seems to work if you test it superficially. For example, the following sample run makes it seem as if the program is functioning correctly:

```
This program helps you balance your checkbook.
Enter each check and deposit during the month.
To indicate a check, use a minus sign.
Signal the end of the month with a 0 value.
Enter the initial balance: 100↵
Enter check (-) or deposit:  -50↵
Current balance = 50
Enter check (-) or deposit:  -60↵
This check bounces. $10 fee deducted.
Current balance = -20
Enter check (-) or deposit:  50↵
Current balance = 30
Enter check (-) or deposit:
```

When the user enters the $60 check, the program correctly determines that this amount is more than there is in the account because the value of balance becomes negative. To let the user know about this state of affairs, the program writes out a message and deducts the $10 charge, as instructed. So far, so good.

If you decided to end your testing here, you would never discover the bug in this program. Let's try a different set of input data, which is the same except that the last deposit is $10, not $50. This time the sample run looks like this:

```
This program helps you balance your checkbook.
Enter each check and deposit during the month.
To indicate a check, use a minus sign.
Signal the end of the month with a 0 value.
Enter the initial balance: 100↵
Enter check (-) or deposit:  -50↵
Current balance = 50
Enter check (-) or deposit:  -60↵
This check bounces. $10 fee deducted.
Current balance = -20
Enter check (-) or deposit:  10↵
This check bounces. $10 fee deducted.
Current balance = -20
Enter check (-) or deposit:
```

The sample run reveals a serious problem: when the user makes the $10 deposit, trying to move the account back into the black, the program decides that user has bounced a *check* and promptly charges another $10 fee.

After you discover the symptoms of the failure, the problem is easy to identify. For a check to bounce, two things must be true. First, the user must have just written a check. Second, the act of writing that check must have resulted in a negative balance. Your program tests only the second condition. To correct the error, you must include both of these conditions in your test. In particular, the program must determine whether a check was written before looking to see whether that check might have bounced. To test for both conditions, you use the `&&` operator, which is C's way of spelling "and":

```
if (entry < 0 && balance < 0) {
    printf("This check bounces.  $10 fee deducted.\n");
    balance -= 10;
}
```

Making this change in the program results in the corrected checkbook-balancing program shown in Figure 3-6.

Are you finished with the program? Probably not. All you've done so far is discover and fix one bug. To be confident that your program works, you should test it more thoroughly. In particular, you should see if it works correctly on the example for which it failed before. Running the same set of data through the `balance.c` program yields the following sample run:

```
This program helps you balance your checkbook.
Enter each check and deposit during the month.
To indicate a check, use a minus sign.
Signal the end of the month with a 0 value.
Enter the initial balance: 100↵
Enter check (-) or deposit: -50↵
Current balance = 50
Enter check (-) or deposit: -60↵
This check bounces. $10 fee deducted.
Current balance = -20
Enter check (-) or deposit: 10↵
Current balance = -10
Enter check (-) or deposit:
```

So far, so good. The $10 deposit is handled correctly, indicating that the bug you sought to fix is indeed gone. But what about other bugs? When you are writing a program, how can you be sure that you have found all the problems?

The short answer is: you can't. Many programs that have gone through years and years of testing without any apparent problems suddenly fail when a previously

FIGURE 3-6   balance3.c (corrected version)

```
/*
 * File: balance3.c
 * ----------------
 * This file contains a corrected version of a program to
 * balance a checkbook, including a working bounced-check
 * feature.
 */

#include <stdio.h>
#include "genlib.h"
#include "simpio.h"

main()
{
    double entry, balance;

    printf("This program helps you balance your checkbook.\n");
    printf("Enter each check and deposit during the month.\n");
    printf("To indicate a check, use a minus sign.\n");
    printf("Signal the end of the month with a 0 value.\n");
    printf("Enter the initial balance: ");
    balance = GetReal();
    while (TRUE) {
        printf("Enter check (-) or deposit: ");
        entry = GetReal();
        if (entry == 0) break;
        balance += entry;
        if (balance < 0 && entry < 0) {
            printf("This check bounces.  $10 fee deducted.\n");
            balance -= 10;
        }
        printf("Current balance = %g\n", balance);
    }
    printf("Final balance = %g\n", balance);
}
```

untested condition occurs. The best you can do with a program is to be as thorough as possible in your testing so that the chance of leaving in one of these lingering bugs is minimized.

In the case of the checkbook balancer, it certainly pays to attempt some additional tests. So far, all the numbers used in the examples have been integers. To test it properly, you need to run the program using values that include cents. Suppose, for example, that, after again starting from an initial balance of $100, the user writes checks for $49.95 and $19.95. The following sample run shows the balance after these two checks.

```
This program helps you balance your checkbook.
Enter each check and deposit during the month.
To indicate a check, use a minus sign.
Signal the end of the month with a 0 value.
Enter the initial balance: 100.00↵
Enter check (-) or deposit: -49.95↵
Current balance = 50.05
Enter check (-) or deposit: -19.95↵
Current balance = 30.1
Enter check (-) or deposit:
```

The last balance display seems a little odd at first glance. The balance in the account after the two checks is 30 dollars and 10 cents, and it is somewhat disconcerting to see that value displayed as 30.1 instead of 30.10. When working with dollars and cents, it is customary to write out exactly two digits after the decimal point. Unfortunately, the `%g` specification in `printf`, which is used here to display the floating-point values, always shows the result in the shortest possible form. Numerically, 30.1 and 30.10 are equivalent, and `printf` chooses the first one, even though it is not appropriate to the application.

The fact that the `balance.c` program displays 30.1 instead of 30.10 might not be a bug in the technical sense. The answer is, after all, mathematically correct. On the other hand, it is almost certainly not what the user wants to see. To satisfy the user, you need to correct this deficiency.

Fortunately, changing the program to display two digits after the decimal point is easy. All you need to do is replace the `%g` in the two `printf` calls with `%.2f`. This format code tells `printf` to display floating-point output with two digits to the right of the decimal point. Thus, the final statement in the program should look like this:

```
printf("Final balance = %.2f\n", balance);
```

But what do the characters in the `%.2f` specification mean? What other options exist for controlling the format of the output data? These questions are important if you want to design programs that will satisfy your users, who often have exacting requirements concerning how output is displayed. The next section answers these questions by looking more closely at `printf` and its operation.

 ## 3.5 Formatted output

The `printf` function is one of C's most distinctive features and has been part of the standard library since early in the history of the language. It provides a powerful and convenient mechanism for displaying information. So far in this book, you have used `printf` to display integers, real numbers, and strings, but you have only scratched the surface of its capabilities. To write programs that are more sophisticated in the way they display output data, you will need to take a more in-depth look at what `printf` has to offer.

A call to the `printf` function has the following paradigmatic form:

```
printf("control string", expression₁, expression₂, ...);
```

The number of expressions passed as arguments depends on the number of data values that need to be displayed. There may be no values, in which case the call is simply

```
printf("control string");
```

or there may be a long list. As you learned in Chapter 2, `printf` operates by moving through the control string, character by character, displaying each one on the terminal screen. Thus, in the statement

```
printf("Hello, world.\n");
```

the call to `printf` prints the H, the e, the l, and so on, up to the period and the newline character at the end of the string.

If `printf` encounters a percent sign (%) as it goes through the characters in the control string, it responds in a special way. As noted earlier in this chapter, `printf` treats the percent sign and the letter that follows it as a placeholder for a value that should be printed in that position. That value is supplied by the first unused expression in the `printf` argument list. The first percent sign in the control string goes with the first expression after the control string, the second percent sign goes with the second expression, and so on, until all the arguments and percent signs have been used up. For example, in the statement

```
printf("%d + %d = %d\n", n1, n2, total);
```

the first `%d` is used to print the value of `n1`, the second `%d` is used to print the value of `n2`, and the third `%d` is used to print the value of `total`. If the values of `n1`, `n2`, and `total` were 2, 3, and 5, respectively, the `printf` statement above would generate the following output:

```
2 + 3 = 5
```

As a programmer, it is your responsibility to ensure that the number of percent sign substitutions in the control string precisely matches the number of expressions beyond the control string that are passed as arguments to `printf`. Unfortunately, the C compiler has no way to check whether this rule is obeyed. If you write a call to `printf` in which the number of substitution slots does not match the number of values, your program will generate unpredictable output, if it continues to run at all.

Format codes for `printf`

The real power of the `printf` function comes from the fact that it can display values in a variety of formats (the `f` at the end of `printf` stands for *formatted*). In order to determine precisely how a value should be displayed, the percent sign in the control string is followed by a key letter that specifies an output format. The combination of the percent sign and the key letter is called a **format code.** In the example from the preceding section, the format code is `%d`, which specifies a decimal integer. In addition to the `%d` format code, you have already seen examples of the `%g` and `%s` format codes, which stand for floating-point and string output, respectively. Note that each of these format codes requires its corresponding expression to be of a particular data type. When you use the `%d` format, you must make sure that the expression you provide is of type `int`. Similarly, the `%g` format requires a floating-point expression, and the `%s` format requires a string. Unfortunately, the C compiler is unable to check whether these types match, and it is therefore important to exercise extra caution to make sure that the format codes are appropriate for their arguments.

The most common format codes for `printf` are listed below, arranged by the data type to which they apply. A complete listing of the format codes available for use with `printf` appears in Appendix A.

COMMON PITFALLS

When using the `printf` function, be certain that the number of arguments matches the number of percent sign substitutions in the control string. Moreover, be sure that the type of each argument is consistent with the corresponding format code.

`%d` *Decimal integer.* In `%d` format, the value is displayed as a string of digits in standard base-10 (decimal) notation. If the number is negative, the value is preceded by a minus sign.

`%f` *Floating-point.* In `%f` format, the value is displayed as a string of digits with a decimal point in the appropriate place.

`%e` *Exponential.* In `%e` format, the value is displayed in scientific notation using the standard programming language representation

$$d.dddde\pm xx$$

which corresponds to the mathematical quantity

$$d.ddddd \times 10^{xx}$$

If you use the format code `%E` instead of `%e`, the output is exactly the same except that the letter `E` used to indicate the exponent appears in upper case in the output.

`%g` *General.* In this format, the value is displayed using either `%f` or `%e` format, whichever is shorter. If you use the format code `%G` instead of `%g`, any output appearing in scientific notation will use an uppercase `E`. The `%g` format is probably the best format to use if you have no way to predict in advance how large the values will be.

`%s` *String.* In `%s` format, the corresponding expression must be a string, which is displayed on the terminal screen, character by character. Percent signs appearing within this string have no special effect.

`%%` *Percent sign.* The `%%` specification is not really a format but instead provides a way for printing a percent sign as part of the output.

Controlling spacing, alignment, and precision

When Charles Babbage first envisioned the automatic computer in the middle of the nineteenth century, a large part of his motivation to create one was to generate tables of mathematical functions that would no longer be subject to the enormous rate of error associated with tables generated by hand. Today, computers still produce a great deal of tabular data. Thus, the ability to generate tables and reports organized in columns remains an important facet of practical programming.

One of the most important features in the printed version of a table is that the information is lined up vertically in columns. Suppose, for example, that you had been commissioned to generate, as part of an environmental study, a table showing the total area, forested area, and percentage of forestation for each state in the United States.[3] Ideally, the first few lines of your table would look something like this:

```
State               Area    Forest    Percent
Alabama            50750     33945     66.9%
Alaska            591000    201632     34.1%
Arizona           114000     30287     26.6%
Arkansas           53187     26542     49.9%
California        158706     61532     38.8%
Colorado          104000     33340     32.1%
```

In tables of this sort, it is important that the values for each entry line up vertically in such a way that whoever reads the table can tell what each value means. Given the tools you have learned about so far, it would be impossible to generate a table in this form. If you were limited to the `printf` format codes alone, the best you could do would be to use a `printf` statement like

```
printf("%s %d %d %f%%\n", state, totalArea, forestArea, percent);
```

Unfortunately, this call would run all of the data together and the output would come out looking like this:

```
State Area Forest Percent
Alabama 50750 33945 66.8867%
Alaska 591000 201632 34.1171%
Arizona 114000 30287 26.5675%
Arkansas 53187 26542 49.9032%
California 158706 61532 38.7711%
Colorado 104000 33340 32.0577%
```

In this version of the table, the columns swim across the screen and are almost impossible to read.

[3] Data source: *The World Almanac and Book of Facts*, New York: Pharos Books, 1992.

In order to generate a table in the more readable columnar form shown earlier, you need to be able to control several properties of the output format. First of all, the vertical columns are created by making sure that each data entry occupies a certain amount of space. The number of character positions allocated to the entries in a particular column is called the **field width.** In the nicely formatted version of the table, the name of the state is printed in a field 14 characters wide, and the two areas (total area and forested area) are each printed in a field six characters wide. The field widths are chosen so that they can hold the largest data item that might legitimately appear in that column. The longest state name (North or South Carolina) is 14 characters long, so a 14-character field is adequate, at least for the present. As the largest state, Alaska determines the field width necessary to hold the area information, and you can see from the data (Alaska's area is 591,000 square miles) that a six-digit field is sufficient. As a software engineering strategy, it often pays to leave room for some expansion in such fields, though the example is easier to understand if the amount of extra space is minimized.

The second formatting property that you need to consider is **alignment.** When numbers are displayed in a table, the standard approach is to line the numbers up so they all end at the same position because doing so makes them much easier to read. This style of alignment is called **right alignment** because all the data entries line up on the right. On the other hand, you would like the names of the states to line up at the left margin. This style of alignment is called **left alignment** and is the most common style for nonnumeric data.

Finally, it is extremely useful to be able to control the numeric **precision** at which the data values are displayed. In the ugly version of the table, the percentage of forested area for Alabama is shown as 66.8867% because

$$\frac{33945 \times 100}{50750} = 66.8867$$

when calculated to the limits of precision used with %g format output. While this value is indeed what the formula gives, displaying it with all those digits is silly and misleading. Given the likely accuracy of the input data, you can have no confidence whatever that the percentage of forested area is 66.8867 rather than 66.8868 or even 66.887. After all, you don't really know that the area is exactly 50,750 square miles and not 50,751 square miles, which would result in a slightly different forested percentage. Moreover, the last few digits in the percentage are almost certainly not significant for the study. In the first version of the table, the percentage of forested area for Alabama is listed as 66.9%, which is probably as much precision as you need. By specifying that you want only one digit to appear after the decimal point, you can ensure that the table does not include extra digits that are unlikely to be correct.[4]

---

[4] Unfortunately, many people who come across this sort of data in a table assume that all of the digits are accurate; after all, they came out of a computer. The truth is that the output data can never be more precise than the input data, and displaying too many digits creates a false impression of accuracy that is impossible to justify on statistical grounds. To avoid creating that sort of misimpression, you should make sure that data values are never printed with extra digits beyond those you know to be correct.

The `printf` function gives you the opportunity to control the width, alignment, and precision of the output data by including additional formatting information as part of the format code. This additional information, written between the percent sign and the key letter, looks like a floating-point number but is actually composed of the following parts, each of which is optional:

- A minus sign, which indicates that the data in this field should be left aligned. If the minus sign does not appear, the data will be aligned on the right.
- A numeric field width, which specifies the minimum number of characters to be used for the output field. If you attempt to display a value that would otherwise take less space than is indicated by the field width, the field will be **padded** with extra blank space until it reaches the appropriate size. If no minus sign precedes the field width, the extra space is added on the left so that the fields are right aligned; if a minus sign is present, the extra space is added on the right, after the value. Note that the field width indicates a minimum width. If a value is too large to fit into a field of the specified size, the field is simply expanded to include the complete value, even though doing so will disturb the column alignment. If the field width does not appear, the data value is displayed using exactly the number of character positions required, with no padding on either side.
- A decimal point followed by a specification of numeric precision. The interpretation of this specification depends on the format code. For the `%e` and `%f` formats, the precision specification indicates the number of digits that should follow the decimal point; for the `%g` format, the precision specifies the maximum number of significant digits. For the `%s` format, the precision specifies the maximum number of characters to display from the string, which makes it possible to avoid having a longer-than-expected string adversely affect the column widths. If the precision specification is missing, `printf` displays the value in its entirety.

You already used the precision specification earlier in this chapter to improve the output of the checkbook-balancing program. Since checkbooks deal with amounts of money expressed in dollars and cents, it is conventional to specify that exactly two digits be shown after the decimal point. This goal is easily accomplished by using the format specification

```
%.2f
```

which indicates that the value should be printed with exactly two digits after the decimal point.

These new formatting specifications make it possible to develop the `printf` call to display the forestation data in the columnar table presented earlier in this section. To make the state appear at the left edge of a 14-character string field, you need to use the format specification

```
%-14s
```

The minus sign specifies left alignment; the 14 indicates the width of the field. If you also wanted to ensure that a new state with an even longer name didn't extend past the column boundary, you could include a precision specification indicating that only the first 14 characters should be printed. That complete format specification would look like this:

```
%-14.14s
```

Using this format, if `printf` were given the string `"District of Columbia"`, only the first 14 characters would appear:

```
District of Co
```

Without the precision specification, the string `"District of Columbia"` would appear in full, and all of the other fields on that line would be shifted six characters to the right.

For each of the two areas—total and forested—you need a right-aligned numeric field six digits wide, so the appropriate format specification would be

```
%6d
```

For the percentage of forestation, the field width is four: two digits before the decimal point, the decimal point itself, and one digit after the decimal point. Moreover, since you only want to display a single digit after the decimal point, the format specification for the percentage of forested land is

```
%4.1f
```

By putting all these specifications together, you can write the `printf` statement necessary to produce the properly formatted table:

```
printf("%-14.14s   %6d   %6d   %4.1f%%\n",
         state, totalArea, forestArea, percent);
```

3.6 Crafting a program

In any program, no matter how polished and complete it seems, the odds are good that someone—the original programmer or someone who inherits the project—will want to change something about it later. There may be bugs to fix or new capabilities that need to be added. Part of our job as programmers is to realize that all programs will someday need to be changed, and it is also our responsibility to make life easier for those who have to make the changes.

Programming style

An important way you can help simplify the task of maintaining programs you write is to make your programs easy to read. One of the fundamental truths about software development is that programs are read more often than they are written. Moreover, the most crucial readers of a program are not machines but people—the other programmers who will work on that program over its lifetime. Getting your program into a state the compiler can accept is only part of the programming process. Good programmers spend most of their time on aspects of the program that the compiler ignores entirely, such as the comments. When the compiler sees the `/*` symbol that indicates the beginning of a comment, it stops paying any attention to characters until it sees the closing `*/`. If your human readers do the same, your comments are not doing their job. Good style and program readability are critical for program maintenance. Writing good comments and ensuring that your code makes sense to human readers may take some extra time initially, but that investment will end up saving considerable time when the program is later revised.

What constitutes good programming style? How do you achieve it? From a stylistic point of view, what are the criteria that determine whether a particular program is well written or badly written? Unfortunately, it is difficult to provide precise answers to these questions, just as it is difficult to provide rules for maintaining good writing style in English. This book presents some guidelines and strategies for achieving good programming style, but the real proof lies in whether your programs are in fact easy for other people to read. As an experiment, take a look at one of your programs and ask yourself how easy it would be to understand if you were seeing it for the first time.

There are, however, several stylistic guidelines that you can follow to help you write better programs. The following are some of the most important ones:

- *Use comments to tell your readers what they need to know.* Explain anything that you think is complicated or that might be difficult for someone to understand simply by reading the program itself. If you anticipate that someone might want to modify a program, indicate briefly how you might go about doing so. On the other hand, don't cloud the issue by talking at length about obvious aspects of the program. For example, some programmers insist on writing comments like

  ```
  total += value; /* Add value to total */
  ```

  Anyone who needs this comment should not be working on the program in the first place. Finally, and perhaps most importantly, make sure the comments you write correctly reflect the current state of the program. When you make changes, be sure to update the comments as well.
- *Use indentation to mark the various levels of program control.* Careful use of indentation to highlight the bodies of functions, loops, and conditionals is critical to readability and makes the program structure much clearer. Indentation rules for each of the control statements will be discussed in Chapter 4.
- *Use meaningful names.* For example, in the checkbook program, the variable name `balance` indicates clearly to the reader the value that variable contains. Using just the single character `b` would make your program shorter and easier to type, but it would not be nearly as useful to the reader.
- *Develop a convention for variable names that helps readers identify their function.* In this text, names of variables and data types always begin with a lowercase letter, such as `n1`, `total`, or `string`. By contrast, function names

(such as `GetInteger`) usually begin with an uppercase letter. Moreover, whenever a name consists of several English words run together, as in `GetInteger`, the first letter in each of those words is capitalized to make the name easier to read.

- *Use standard idioms and conventions when appropriate.* Many software companies publish local rules about style or program structure, some of which may be at odds with the practice suggested in this book. Following the old adage, "when in Rome, do as the Romans do," you should adhere to local standards when they exist so that other programmers will have an easier time understanding the programs you write. On the whole, programming prospers when a community can agree on a common set of basic conventions.
- *Avoid unnecessary complexity.* It is often worth sacrificing some efficiency in the interest of readability.

The bottom line is that you want your programs to be easy to read. To make sure that they are, you should proofread your own programs for style, just as a writer would proofread an article. Start each programming assignment early enough that you can put it away for a day. Then take it out and look at it from a fresh perspective. How easy is the program for you to understand? How easy would it be for someone else to maintain the program in the future? If you discover that your program doesn't make sense or is somehow difficult to read, you should take the time to revise it.

Designing for change

You can also make programs easier to modify by designing them to accommodate change. Because programmers know that programs are more likely to change in certain areas than in others, you can usually make an educated guess about which aspects of a program should be made as flexible as possible.

Think back to the `balance.c` program presented earlier in this chapter. What aspects of that program are programmers most likely to want to change? If nothing else, it is almost certain that the charge assessed for bouncing a check will change over time. How easy would it be for a programmer to alter that value? As the program is written now, that programmer would have to ferret around in the details of the program to discover exactly where the $10 figure appears in the program. The programmer would then need to make two changes. The most obvious one is in the line

```
balance -= 10;
```

However, it is equally important to update the `printf` statement on the previous line as follows:

```
printf("This check bounces. $10 fee deducted.\n");
```

Considering this problem from the perspective of those who will make future changes, you really want to be able to make a single edit that then propagates its effect throughout the entire program. By doing so, you are programming defensively. No one can come along and break the program by changing something in one place but not in another.

The #define mechanism

The best tool available in C for centralizing editing changes is the #define construct. In its simplest form, #define has the following paradigmatic form:

```
#define symbol value
```

In this paradigm, *symbol* represents a name that follows the same rules used for variables and *value* represents a C constant. Whenever the symbol appears anywhere in the program after #define is introduced, the specified value is substituted in place of the symbol. For example, if you put the line

```
#define BouncedCheckFee 10.00
```

at the beginning of the checkbook program, you could then rewrite the if statement as follows to take advantage of the definition:

```
if (entry < 0 && balance < 0) {
    printf("This check bounces.   $%.2f fee deducted.\n",
            BouncedCheckFee);
    balance -= BouncedCheckFee;
}
```

To change the bounced-check fee in the future, the programmer who inherits this program would only have to change the #define statement at the top of the program.

The final version of the checkbook-balancing program, which includes both the change in the printf format specification and the definition of the BouncedCheckFee constant, is shown in Figure 3-7. Note that the program also includes additional comments to help new programmers understand how to change BouncedCheckFee to some different value.

Using #define to set values of constants that are likely to change is an important part of good software engineering. You will see many additional examples of this technique throughout the text.

 ## Summary

In Chapter 2, you learned how to write simple programs that accept input data, calculate results, and generate output. Chapter 3 has sought to extend your knowledge by introducing the concept of *control statements*. By using control statements, you can make your programs solve much more sophisticated problems, such as those that involve testing to see whether a condition holds or those that require repetition of a certain operation.

This chapter encourages you to approach control statements by thinking about the kinds of problems they can solve. Each statement is a tool appropriate to a particular situation, and you have seen how to apply particular tools through the use

FIGURE 3-7 balance4.c (final version)

```c
/*
 * File: balance4.c
 * ----------------
 * This file contains the final version of a program to
 * balance a checkbook.
 */

#include <stdio.h>
#include "genlib.h"
#include "simpio.h"

/*
 * Constant: BouncedCheckFee
 * -------------------------
 * To change the charge assessed for bounced checks, change
 * the definition of this constant.  The constant must be a
 * floating-point value (i.e., must contain a decimal point).
 */

#define BouncedCheckFee 10.00

/* Main program */

main()
{
    double entry, balance;

    printf("This program helps you balance your checkbook.\n");
    printf("Enter each check and deposit during the month.\n");
    printf("To indicate a check, use a minus sign.\n");
    printf("Signal the end of the month with a 0 value.\n");
    printf("Enter the initial balance: ");
    balance = GetReal();
    while (TRUE) {
        printf("Enter check (-) or deposit: ");
        entry = GetReal();
        if (entry == 0) break;
        balance += entry;
        if (entry < 0 && balance < 0) {
            printf("This check bounces.  $%.2f fee deducted.\n",
                    BouncedCheckFee);
            balance -= BouncedCheckFee;
        }
        printf("Current balance = %.2f\n", balance);
    }
    printf("Final balance = %.2f\n", balance);
}
```

of simple *idioms* and *paradigms*. Chapter 4 looks at control statements in more detail.

Beyond becoming familiar with control statements, you also had the opportunity—primarily through the evolution of the `balance.c` example—to discover that writing programs to solve problems is not as easy as it might appear. Particularly if you think too quickly about your modifications to a program or fail to test programs thoroughly, it is easy to introduce subtle bugs into your programs that keep them from working as you intend. To some extent, such bugs are an unavoidable part of the programming process, but you can save yourself considerable time and aggravation by using good programming discipline. To help you develop that discipline, this chapter includes several useful guidelines and conventions to improve your programming skills.

Important points about programming introduced in this chapter are:

- Common operations within a program can be represented as *programming idioms*, which permit you to learn one simple pattern that is applicable to a variety of programming problems.
- C defines several *shorthand assignment* operators that make it easier for you to specify certain common operations.
- Strategies that work for two or three data values are often not appropriate as the scale of the problem grows.
- The `for` statement can be used to repeat a set of statements a specified number of times.
- When used in the particular idiomatic form given in this chapter, the `while` statement can be used to repeat a set of statements until a designated *sentinel* value is entered.
- The `if` statement is used to specify that a particular set of statements should be executed only if a certain condition applies. The condition itself is ordinarily expressed by using relational operators to compare two data values.
- Seemingly innocuous changes can introduce serious bugs. You should always be suspicious of your programs and test them as thoroughly as you can.
- The `printf` function provides considerable control over output formatting.
- Programs should be written so that they can be understood easily by other programmers. It is important for you to write your programs with future readers in mind.

REVIEW QUESTIONS

1. Explain the concept of a programming idiom. What role do such idioms play in the process of learning to program?

2. What is the idiom that corresponds to the English command "request an integer value from the user and store it in a variable"?

3. What idiom would you use to multiply the value of the variable `cellCount` by 2?

4. What is the most common way in C to write a statement that has the same effect as

   ```
   x = x + 1;
   ```

5. What idiom would you use to repeat a set of commands 15 times?

6. Define the following terms: *loop, control line, cycle, body,* and *index variable.*

7. What `for` control line would you use to count from 15 to 25?

8. In the `add10.c` program, the statement

   ```
   total = 0;
   ```

   appears before the `for` loop. Why is this statement important? On the other hand, why is it not necessary to include the following statement as well?

   ```
   value = 0;
   ```

   Explain how the different use of these variables makes it necessary to initialize `total` but not `value`.

9. What is a sentinel? What considerations are involved in choosing a sentinel value for a particular application?

10. What is the idiom presented in this chapter for repeating an operation on a list of input values until a sentinel value appears?

11. What statement is used in this chapter to specify conditional execution, and what are its two forms?

12. What are the six relational operators that exist in C, and what are the corresponding mathematical symbols?

13. Why is it important to test programs thoroughly, even after making simple, seemingly innocuous changes?

14. In the `balance.c` program, what is the reason for using the format specification `%.2f` in the `printf` calls?

15. How would you write a `printf` statement to display the string value stored in the variable `name`, so that the resulting output was left justified in a 20-character field? How would you ensure that names longer than 20 characters would not affect the alignment of other items in a table?

16. How would you write a `printf` statement to display the floating-point value stored in the variable `distance` so that exactly three digits appear to the right of the decimal point?

17. What factors should you consider when choosing variable names for your programs?

18. What is the advantage of the `#define` construct in terms of program maintenance?

19. How would you use `#define` to introduce a constant named `Pi` with the value 3.14159?

20. In the `balance.4` program (Figure 3-7), the comment associated with the definition of `BouncedCheckFee` indicates that the constant value must be a floating-point number. What statement in the program would fail to operate correctly if `BouncedCheckFee` were defined as an integer in violation of this rule? How could you change the program to eliminate this restriction?

21. As a programmer, you must be able to put yourself in the position of a user. From this perspective, consider the `balance.c` program presented in this chapter. Is the program easy to use? Does it provide the capabilities you want? What changes would you make in the behavior of the program?

22. In any form of writing, it is important to consider your audience. If your audience misses the point, the text has not accomplished its purpose. In writing a program, who is your most important audience?

PROGRAMMING EXERCISES

1. As noted in the section on "The read-until-sentinel idiom," one strategy for generalizing the `add10.c` program is to allow the user to enter the number of values to be added when the program is run. As outlined in the text, make the modifications necessary to change the `add10.c` program so that it reads in the number of values first, followed by the actual numbers to be added.

2. Write a program that displays the message

```
Hello, world.
```

10 times on separate lines.

3. Using the Gertrude Stein "a rose is a rose is a rose" example as an model, write the `for` loop that displays the repeated parts of Macbeth's lament

```
Tomorrow and tomorrow and tomorrow.
```

4. Modify the add10.c program so that instead of adding integers, it adds 10 floating-point numbers.

5. Write a program that prints out the squares of the numbers from 1 to 10, using the format shown in the following sample run:

```
1 squared is 1
2 squared is 4
3 squared is 9
4 squared is 16
5 squared is 25
6 squared is 36
7 squared is 49
8 squared is 64
9 squared is 81
10 squared is 100
```

Design your program so that the limits 1 and 10 are easy to change.

6. According to legend, the German mathematician Karl Friedrich Gauss (1777–1855) began to show his mathematical talent at a very early age. When he was in elementary school, Gauss was asked by his teacher to compute the sum of the numbers between 1 and 100. Gauss·is said to have given the answer instantly: 5050. Write a program that computes the answer to the question Gauss's teacher posed.

7. Write a program that reads in five integers from the user and then displays their average, as illustrated by the following sample run:

```
This program averages a list of 5 integers.
? 95↵
? 100↵
? 89↵
? 91↵
? 97↵
The average is 94.4
```

Note that even though all the input values are integers, the average may have a decimal fraction. Also, remember to design your program so that it is easy to change the number of input values to some number other than five.

8. Modify the program you wrote in exercise 7 so that the program begins by

asking the user for the number of values, like this:

```
This program averages a list of integers.
How many values are there in the list? 5↵
? 95↵
? 100↵
? 89↵
? 91↵
? 97↵
The average is 94.4
```

9. Using the addlist.c example as a model, write a program that reads in a list of integers until the user enters the value −1 as a sentinel. At that point, the program should display the average of the values entered so far. Your program should be able to duplicate the following sample run:

```
This program averages a list of integers.
Enter -1 to signal the end of the list.
? 95↵
? 100↵
? 89↵
? 91↵
? 97↵
? -1↵
The average is 94.4
```

Writing this program requires more thought than writing the addlist.c program in the text and is a good test of your problem-solving abilities.

10. The section on "The repeat-N-times idiom" uses the following code to display one of Gertrude Stein's familiar lines:

```
for (i = 0; i < 2; i++) {
    printf("a rose is ");
}
printf("a rose.\n");
```

Rewrite this program so that the word *rose* appears only once. Your new program should generate exactly the same output as the original, including the period and the newline character.

11. In the program you wrote for exercise 5, the output was not formatted into columns, which makes the result more difficult to read. Change the program so

that it prints a tabular version of both the squares and cubes of the numbers from 1 to 10, as follows:

```
Number   Square    Cube
  1         1         1
  2         4         8
  3         9        27
  4        16        64
  5        25       125
  6        36       216
  7        49       343
  8        64       512
  9        81       729
 10       100      1000
```

12. Suppose you are writing a program to display a table of vote totals for candidates at a convention. When your program is ready to display the output data, the name of the candidate is stored in the string variable `candidate`, and the votes for that candidate are stored in the integer variable `votes`. How would you write a `printf` statement to display the name and vote count so that the names line up on the left and the numbers line up on the right, as illustrated by the following table, which shows the delegate tallies from the Democratic Party convention of 1992:

```
Clinton          3372
Brown             596
Tsongas           209
Other              74
```

In writing this `printf` statement, display the name of each candidate in a 15-character field; if the name is longer than that, only the first 15 characters should appear. You may assume that there are fewer than 10,000 delegates at the convention and therefore that the number of votes never requires more than four digits to represent.

Remember that you need not write a program to generate the entire table—just the one `printf` statement. Even so, try to think of a way to test your `printf` statement to be sure it works in the desired way.

13. In exercise 4 in Chapter 2, you wrote a program to calculate compound interest over two years. Rewrite the program so that it displays the accumulated balance after each of N years, where N is a number entered by the user.

14. Write a program that reads in a list of integers from the user until the user enters the value 0 as a sentinel. When the sentinel appears, your program

should display the largest value in the list, as illustrated in the following sample run:

```
This program finds the largest integer in a list.
Enter 0 to signal the end of the list.
 ? 17↵
 ? 42↵
 ? 11↵
 ? 19↵
 ? 35↵
 ? 0↵
The largest value is 42
```

Think about the problem before you start to write the program. What strategy do you plan to use?

Figuring out how to find the largest number in a list is by far the most conceptually important exercise in this chapter. Once you understand how to solve the fundamental problem—not the problem of how to write the necessary statements in C but rather of how to design the algorithmic strategy—you are ready to go on and learn more about the details of programming.

C H A P T E R   4

Statement Forms

The statements was interesting but tough.

— Mark Twain, *Adventures of Huckleberry Finn*, 1884

Objectives

- To understand the relationship between statements and expressions.
- To recognize that the equal sign used for assignment is treated as a binary operator in C.
- To understand that statements can be collected into blocks.
- To recognize that control statements fall into two classes: conditional and iterative.
- To learn how to manipulate Boolean data and to appreciate its importance.
- To increase your familiarity with the relational operators: `=`, `!=`, `<`, `<=`, `>`, and `>=`.
- To understand the behavior of the `&&`, `||`, and `!` operators.
- To master the details of the `if`, `switch`, `while`, and `for` statements.

In Chapter 2, you learned that a C program operates by executing the statements contained within the body of a function called `main`. This chapter covers the different statement types available in C and, in the process, extends the set of tools you have for solving problems.

As in most programming languages, statements in C fall into one of two principal classifications: **simple statements,** which perform some action, and **control statements,** which affect the way in which other statements are executed. You have already seen a variety of simple statements in C, such as assignments and calls to the `printf` function. You have also encountered various control statements. The `for` statement makes it possible to repeat a set of program steps a given number of times, the `while` statement allows you to specify repetition until some condition occurs, and the `if` statement makes it possible to choose different paths through a program depending on some conditional test. Up to now, however, you have studied these statements in an informal, idiomatic way. To use the full power these statements provide, you need a more detailed understanding of how each type of statement works and how it can be applied as part of your problem-solving repertoire.

 4.1 Simple statements

In the programs in Chapters 2 and 3, you saw simple statements used to accomplish a variety of tasks. In particular, there were statements that read in data from the user, such as

```
n1 = GetInteger();
```

statements that compute new values, such as

```
total = n1 + n2;
```

and statements that display information, such as

```
printf("The total is %d.\n", total);
```

Informally, it makes sense to think of each of these statement types as a separate tool and to use them idiomatically. If you need to read an integer, all you need to do is remember that there is an idiom for that purpose, which you can then write down. If you need to display a value, you know that you should use the `printf` function along with the special facilities for `printf` formatting described in the section on "Formatted output" in Chapter 3. Viewed formally, however, these simple statements all have a unified structure that makes it easy for the C compiler to recognize a legal statement in a program. In C, all simple statements—regardless of their function—fit the following rule

| SIMPLE STATEMENT RULE | A simple statement consists of an expression followed by a semicolon. |

Thus, the paradigm for a simple statement is simply this:

expression;

Adding the semicolon after the expression turns the expression into a legal statement form.

Even though any expression followed by a semicolon is a *legal* statement in C, it is not true that every such combination represents a *useful* statement. To be useful, a statement must have some discernible effect. The statement

```
n1 + n2;
```

consists of the expression `n1 + n2` followed by a semicolon and is therefore a legal statement. It is, however, an entirely useless one because nothing is ever done with the answer; the statement adds the variables `n1` and `n2` together and then throws the result away.[1] Simple statements in C are typically assignments (including the shorthand assignments and increment/decrement operators) or calls to functions, such as `printf`, that perform some useful operation.

It is easy to see that program lines such as

```
printf("Hello, world.\n");
```

are legal statements according to the Simple Statement Rule. In the definition of expression given in Chapter 2, function calls are legal expressions, so that the function call part of the above line—everything except the semicolon—is a legal expression. Putting the semicolon at the end of the line turns that expression into a simple statement.

But what about assignments? If a line like

```
total = 0;
```

is to fit the Simple Statement Rule, it must be the case that

```
total = 0
```

is itself an expression.

In C, the equal sign used for assignment is simply a binary operator, just like `+` or `/`. The `=` operator takes two operands, one on the left and one on the right. For our present purposes, the left operand must be a variable name, although that restriction is relaxed in Chapter 11. When the assignment operator is executed, the expression on the right-hand side is evaluated, and the resulting value is then stored in the variable that appears on the left-hand side. Because the equal sign used for assignment is an operator,

```
total = 0
```

is indeed an expression, and the line

```
total = 0;
```

is therefore a simple statement.

---

[1] Some C compilers are clever enough to issue a warning for useless statements of this sort.

Embedded assignments

The description of assignment in the previous section should seem familiar because it is equivalent in effect to the earlier, less formal definition given in the section on "Assignment statements" in Chapter 2. Now comes the interesting wrinkle. If an assignment is an expression, then that expression must itself have a value. Moreover, if an assignment produces a value, it must also be possible to embed that assignment in some more complicated expression.

When an assignment is used as part of some larger expression, the value for the assignment subexpression is the value assigned. For example, if the expression

```
x = 6
```

appears as an operand to another operator, the value of that assignment as an expression is the value assigned to the variable x, which is 6. Thus, the expression

```
(x = 6) + (y = 7)
```

has the effect of setting x to 6 and y to 7, which makes the value of the expression as a whole 13. The parentheses are required in this example because the = operator has a lower precedence than +. Assignments that are written as part of larger expressions are called **embedded assignments.**

Although they have some important and extremely convenient uses, embedded assignments often make programs more difficult to read because they tend to hide the fact that the values of variables are changing somewhere in the middle of a more complicated expression. For this reason, this text limits the use of embedded assignments to a few special circumstances where they seem to make the most sense.

Multiple assignments

Of these special circumstances in which embedded assignments are used, the easiest one to describe occurs when you want to set several variables to the same value. Instead of writing separate assignment statements, C's definition of assignment makes it possible to write a single statement like

```
n1 = n2 = n3 = 0;
```

which has the effect of setting all three variables to 0. This statement has the desired result because C evaluates assignment operators from right to left. The entire statement is therefore equivalent to

```
n1 = (n2 = (n3 = 0));
```

The expression n3 = 0 is evaluated, which sets n3 to 0 and then passes 0 along as the value of the assignment expression. That value is assigned to n2, and the result is then assigned to n1. Statements of this sort are called **multiple assignments**.

When writing multiple assignments, it is good practice to ensure that all the variables are of the same type to avoid the possibility that automatic conversion will lead to unintended results. To illustrate the type of problem that can occur, suppose that the variable d has been declared as a `double` and the variable i has been declared as an `int`. What is the effect of the following statement?

```
d = i = 1.5;                           This statement is likely to confuse the reader.
```

When this expression is evaluated, the value 1.5 is truncated to an integer before it is assigned to i, so i gets the value 1. The value of the embedded assignment expression is the value assigned, so it is the integer 1, not the floating-point value 1.5, that is assigned to d. This assignment triggers a second conversion, and the final result is that d is assigned the value 1.0.

In C's precedence hierarchy, assignment operators, including the shorthand assignment operators like += and *=, are evaluated *after* the arithmetic operators. If two assignments compete for the same operand, the assignments are applied from right to left. This rule runs counter to the rule used for the other operators, which are applied from left to right. The direction in which operators of the same precedence class are evaluated is called the **associativity** of that class. Traditional operators like + and – are evaluated from left to right and are therefore called **left associative.** The assignment operators are evaluated from right to left and are called **right associative.** A table showing the precedence and associativity for all the operators introduced through Chapter 4 appears in the Summary at the end of this chapter, and a complete precedence table for all the operators in C is provided in Appendix A.

Blocks

Simple statements allow programmers to specify actions. Except for the `hello.c` program in Chapter 2, however, every program you have seen so far requires more than one simple statement to do the job. For most programs, the solution strategy requires a coordinated action consisting of several sequential steps. The `add2.c` program, for example, had to first get one number, then get a second, then add the two together, and finally display the result. Translating this sequence of actions into actual program steps required the use of several individual statements that all became part of the main program body.

To specify that a sequence of statements is part of a coherent unit, you can assemble those statements into a **block,** which is a collection of statements enclosed in curly braces, as follows:

```
{
     statement₁
     statement₂
     statement₃
      . . .
     statementₙ
}
```

You have already seen blocks in several of the programming examples from the previous chapters. The body of each main program is a block, as are all the control statement bodies in the programs in Chapter 3.

As discussed in the section on "Programming style" in Chapter 3, the statements in the interior of a block are usually indented relative to the enclosing context. The compiler ignores the indentation, but the visual effect is extremely helpful to the human reader because it makes the structure of the program jump out at you from the format of the page. Empirical research has shown that using either three or four spaces at each new level makes the program structure easiest to see; the programs in this text use four spaces for each new level. Indentation is critical to good programming, so you should strive to develop a consistent indentation style in your programs.

The only aspect of blocks that tends to cause any confusion for new students is the role of the semicolon. In C, the semicolon is part of the syntax of a simple statement; it acts as a statement *terminator* rather than as a statement *separator*. While this rule is perfectly consistent, it can cause trouble for people who have previously been exposed to the language Pascal, which uses a different rule. In practical terms, the differences are:

1. There is always a semicolon at the end of the last simple statement in a block in C. In Pascal, the semicolon is usually not present, although most compilers allow it as an option.
2. There is never a semicolon after the closing brace of a statement block in C. In Pascal, a semicolon may or may not follow the END keyword depending on the context.

The convention for using semicolons in C has advantages for program maintenance and should not cause any problem once you are used to it.

When the C compiler encounters a block, it treats the entire block as a single statement. Thus, whenever the notation *statement* appears in an idiom or a paradigm, you can substitute for it either a single statement or a block. To emphasize that they are statements as far as the compiler is concerned, blocks are sometimes referred to as **compound statements.**

4.2 Control statements

In the absence of any directives to the contrary, statements in a C program are executed one at a time in the order in which they appear. For most applications, however, this strictly top-to-bottom ordering is not sufficient. Solution strategies for real-world problems tend to involve such operations as repeating a set of steps or choosing between alternative sets of actions. Statements that affect the way in which other statements are executed are called *control statements.*

Control statements in C fall into two basic classes:

1. *Conditionals.* In solving problems, you will often need to choose between two or more independent paths in a program, depending on the result of some conditional test. For example, you might be asked to write a program that behaves one way if a certain value is negative and some different way

otherwise. The type of control statement needed to make decisions is called a **conditional.** In C, there are two conditional statement forms: the `if` statement introduced in Chapter 3 and the `switch` statement introduced later in this chapter.

2. *Iteration.* Particularly as you start to work with problems that involve more than a few data items, your programs will often need to repeat an operation a specified number of times or as long as a certain condition holds. In programming, such repetition is called **iteration.** In C, the control statements used as the basis for most iteration are the `while` statement and the `for` statement, which were introduced in Chapter 3.

Each control statement in C consists of two parts: the *control line,* which specifies the nature of the repetition or condition, and the *body,* which consists of the statements that are affected by the control line. In the case of conditional statements, the body may be divided into separate parts, where one set of statements is executed in certain cases and another set of statements is executed in others.

The body of each control statement consists of other statements. The effect of the control statement itself—no matter whether it specifies repetition or conditional execution—is applied to each of the statements in the body. Those statements, moreover, can be of any type. They may be simple statements, they may be compound statements, or they may themselves be control statements, which in turn contain other statements. When a control statement is used within the body of another control statement, it is said to be **nested.** The ability to nest control statements, one inside another, is one of the most important characteristics of modern programming languages.

 ## 4.3 Boolean data

In the course of solving a problem, it is often necessary to have the program test a particular condition that affects the subsequent behavior of the program. For example, the final version of the `balance.c` program in Chapter 3 uses an `if` statement involving a conditional test to determine whether a check has bounced. The `if` statement, along with many of the other facilities that control the execution of a program, use expressions whose values are either true or false. This type of data—for which the only legal values are true and false—is called **Boolean data,** after the mathematician George Boole, who developed an algebraic approach for working with such values.

Most modern programming languages define a special Boolean type whose domain consists of precisely these two values. C does not define such a type—a deficiency that makes understanding the nature of logical decisions much more difficult for new programmers. To correct this shortcoming, the `genlib` library defines a special type called `bool`. It also defines the constant names `TRUE` and `FALSE`, both of which must be written entirely in upper case. You can declare variables of type `bool` and manipulate them in the same way as other data objects.

C defines several operators that work with Boolean values. These operators comprise two major classes, *relational operators* and *logical operators,* which are discussed in the next two sections.

Relational operators

The **relational operators** are used to compare two values. C defines six relational operators, which actually fall into two precedence classes. The operators that test the ordering relationship between two quantities are

> Greater than
< Less than
>= Greater than or equal to
<= Less than or equal to

These operators appear in the precedence hierarchy below the arithmetic operators + and – and are followed in the hierarchy by the following operators, which test for equality and inequality:

== Equal
!= Not equal

When you write programs that test for equality, be very careful to use the == operator, which is composed of two equal signs. A single equal sign is the assignment operator. Since the double equal sign violates conventional mathematical usage, replacing it with a single equal sign is a particularly common mistake. This mistake can also be very difficult to track down because the C compiler does not usually catch it as an error. A single equal sign usually turns the expression into an embedded assignment, which is perfectly legal in C; it just isn't at all what you want. For example, if you wanted to test whether the value of the variable x were equal to 0 and wrote the following conditional expression

if (x = 0) . . .   This is incorrect.

the results would be confusing. This statement would not check to see if x were equal to 0. It would instead insist on this condition by assigning the value 0 to x, which C would then interpret (for reasons too arcane to describe at this point) as indicating a test result of FALSE. The correct test to determine whether the value of the variable x is equal to 0 is

if (x == 0) . . .

Be careful to avoid this error. A little extra care in entering your program can save a lot of debugging time later on.

The relational operators can only be used to compare **atomic data** values—data values that are not built up from smaller component parts. For example, integers, floating-point numbers, Boolean values, and characters (which are introduced in Chapter 9) constitute atomic data because they cannot be decomposed into smaller pieces. Strings, on the other hand, are not atomic because they are composed of individual characters. Thus, you can use relational operators to compare two values of the types int, double, or bool, but you cannot use them to compare two values of type string. A mechanism by which to compare strings will be introduced in Chapter 5.

Logical operators

In addition to the relational operators, which take atomic values of any type and produce Boolean results, C defines three operators that take Boolean operands and combine them to form other Boolean values:

!	Logical not (TRUE if the following operand is FALSE)
&&	Logical and (TRUE if both operands are TRUE)
||	Logical or (TRUE if either or both operands are TRUE)

These operators are called **logical operators** and are listed in decreasing order of precedence.

The operators &&, || and ! closely resemble the English words *and, or,* and *not.* Even so, it is important to remember that English can be somewhat imprecise when it comes to logic. To avoid that imprecision, it is often helpful to think of these operators in a more formal, mathematical way. Logicians define these operators using **truth tables,** which show how the value of a Boolean expression changes as the values of its operands change. For example, the truth table for the && operator, given Boolean values p and q, is

p	q	p&&q
FALSE	FALSE	FALSE
FALSE	TRUE	FALSE
TRUE	FALSE	FALSE
TRUE	TRUE	TRUE

The last column of the table indicates the value of the Boolean expression p && q given individual values of the Boolean variables p and q shown in the first two columns. Thus, the first line in the truth table shows that when p is FALSE and q is FALSE, the value of the expression p && q is also FALSE.

The truth table for || is

p	q	p||q
FALSE	FALSE	FALSE
FALSE	TRUE	TRUE
TRUE	FALSE	TRUE
TRUE	TRUE	TRUE

Note that the || operator does not indicate *one or the other,* as it often does in English, but instead indicates *either or both,* which is its mathematical meaning.

The ! operator has the following simple truth table:

p	!p
FALSE	TRUE
TRUE	FALSE

If you need to determine how a more complex logical expression operates, you can break it down into these primitive operations and build up a truth table for the individual pieces of the expression.

In most cases, logical expressions are not so complicated that you need a truth table to figure them out. The only common case that seems to cause confusion is when the ! or != operator comes up in conjunction with && or ||. When talking about situations that are not true (as is the case when working with the ! and != operators), conventional English is sometimes at odds with mathematical logic, and you should use some extra care to avoid errors. For example, suppose you wanted to express the idea "x is not equal to either 2 or 3" as part of a program. Just reading from the English version of this conditional test, new programmers are very likely to write

```
if (x != 2 || x != 3) . . .
```
                                                          This test is incorrect!

If you look at this conditional test from the mathematical point of view, you can see that the expression within the if test is TRUE if either (a) x is not equal to 2 or (b) x is not equal to 3. No matter what value x has, one of the statements must be TRUE, since, if x is 2, it cannot also be equal to 3, and vice versa. Thus, the if test as written above would always succeed.

To fix this problem, you need to refine your understanding of the English expression so that it states the condition more precisely. That is, you want the test in the if statement to succeed whenever "it is not the case that either x is 2 or x is 3." You could translate this statement directly to C by writing

```
if (!(x == 2 || x == 3)) . . .
```

but the resulting statement is a bit ungainly. The question you really want to ask is whether *both* of the following conditions are TRUE:

- x is not equal to 2, *and*
- x is not equal to 3.

If you think about the question in this form, you could write the test as

```
if (x != 2 && x != 3) . . .
```

This simplification is a specific illustration of the following more general relationship from mathematical logic:

!(p || q) *is equivalent to* !p && !q

for any logical expressions p and q. This transformation rule and its symmetric counterpart

!(p && q) *is equivalent to* !p || !q

are called **De Morgan's laws.** Forgetting to apply these rules and relying instead on the English style of logic is a common source of programming errors.

Another common mistake comes from forgetting to use the appropriate logical connective when combining several relational tests. In mathematics, one often sees an expression of the form

```
0  <  x  <  10
```

While this expression makes sense in mathematics, it is not meaningful in C. In order to test that x is both greater than 0 and less than 10, you need to indicate both conditions explicitly, as follows:

```
0 < x && x < 10
```

Short-circuit evaluation

C interprets the && and || operators in a way that differs from the interpretation used in many other programming languages. In Pascal, for example, evaluating these operators (which are written as AND and OR) requires evaluating both halves of the condition, even when the result can be determined halfway through the process. The designers of C took a different approach that is often more convenient for programmers.

Whenever a C program evaluates any expression of the form

exp1 && *exp2*

or

exp1 || *exp2*

the individual subexpressions are always evaluated from left to right, and evaluation ends as soon as the answer can be determined. For example, if *exp1* is FALSE in the expression involving &&, there is no need to evaluate *exp2* since the final answer will always be FALSE. Similarly, in the example using ||, there is no need to evaluate the second operand if the first operand is TRUE. This style of evaluation, which stops as soon as the answer is known, is called **short-circuit evaluation.**

A primary advantage of short-circuit evaluation is that it allows one condition to control the execution of a second one. In many situations, the second part of a compound condition is meaningful only if the first part comes out a certain way. For example, suppose you want to express the combined condition that (1) the value of the integer x is nonzero and (2) x divides evenly into y. You can express this conditional test in C as

```
(x != 0) && (y % x == 0)
```

because the expression y % x is evaluated only if x is nonzero. The corresponding expression in Pascal fails to generate the desired result, because both parts of the Pascal condition will always be evaluated. Thus, if x is 0, a Pascal program containing this expression will end up dividing by 0 even though it appears to have a

COMMON PITFALLS

To test whether a number is in a particular range, it is not sufficient to combine relational operators, as is conventional in mathematics. The two parts of the condition must be written explicitly using &&, as in

```
(0 < x) && (x < 10)
```

conditional test to check for that case. Conditions that protect against evaluation errors in subsequent parts of a compound condition, such as the conditional test

```
(x != 0)
```

in the preceding example, are called **guards.**

Flags

Variables of type `bool` are so important that they have a special name: **flags.** For example, if you declare a Boolean variable using the declaration

```
bool done;
```

the variable `done` becomes a flag, which you can use in your program to record whether or not you are finished with some phase of the operation. You can assign new values to flags just as you can to any other variable. For example, you can write

```
done = TRUE;
```

or

```
done = FALSE;
```

More importantly, you can assign any expression that has a Boolean value to a Boolean variable. For example, suppose the logic of your program indicates that you are finished with some phase of the operation as soon as the value of the variable `itemsRemaining` becomes 0. To set `done` to the appropriate value, you can simply write

```
done = (itemsRemaining == 0);
```

The parentheses in this expression are not necessary but are often used to emphasize the fact that you are assigning the result of a conditional test to a variable. The statement above says, "Calculate the value of (`itemsRemaining == 0`), which will be either TRUE or FALSE, and store that result in the variable `done`."

Avoiding redundancy in Boolean expressions

Even though the statement

```
done = (itemsRemaining == 0);
```

is sufficient to store the correct Boolean value in the variable `done`, this type of statement seems difficult for people to learn. New programmers have a tendency to achieve the same effect with the following, much longer `if` statement:

```
if (itemsRemaining == 0) {
    done = TRUE;
} else {
    done = FALSE;
}
```

These lines are a highly inefficient way to achieve the desired result.

Although these lines have the desired effect, they do not have the efficiency or the elegance you should seek to achieve in your programs. The second version requires five lines to do the work of one and will make your programs much longer than they need to be. As you work with Boolean data, it is important to remember that you can assign Boolean values just like any other values and that explicit tests are not necessary.

A similar problem occurs when you use a flag as part of a conditional test. To test whether done has the value TRUE, an experienced programmer writes

```
if (done) . . .
```

and not

```
if (done == TRUE) . . .
```
                                                    The == TRUE is redundant

Even though this second expression also works, the equality test is redundant. The value of done is already guaranteed to be either TRUE or FALSE, which is precisely the sort of value the if statement wants. You don't need to ask whether done is equal to TRUE, since the extra test provides no new information.

An example of Boolean calculation

As astronomers have known for centuries, the earth takes a little more than 365 days to make a complete revolution around the sun. Because it takes about a quarter of a day more than 365 days for it to complete its annual cycle, an extra day builds up every four years, which must then be added to the calendar, creating a leap year. This adjustment helps keep the calendar in sync with the sun's orbit, but it is still off by a slight amount. To ensure that the beginning of the year does not slowly drift through the seasons, the actual rule used for leap years is slightly more complicated. Leap years come every four years, except for years ending in 00, which are leap years only if they are divisible by 400. Thus, 1900 was not a leap year even though 1900 is divisible by 4. The year 2000, on the other hand, is a leap year because it is divisible by 400.

Suppose you have been asked to write a program that reads in a year and determines whether that year is a leap year. How would you write the Boolean expression necessary to answer that question? In order to be a leap year, one of the following conditions must hold:

- The year is divisible by 4 but not divisible by 100, or
- The year is divisible by 400.

If the year is contained in the variable y, the following Boolean expression has the correct result:

```
((y % 4 == 0) && (y % 100 != 0)) || (y % 400 == 0)
```

Given C's rules of precedence, none of the parentheses in this expression are actually required, but using parentheses makes long Boolean expressions easier to read. If you take the result of this expression and store it in a flag called isLeapYear, you can then test the flag at other points in the program to determine whether the isLeapYear condition is true. A program that performs the leap-year calculation is shown in Figure 4-1.

COMMON PITFALLS

Be careful to avoid redundancy when using Boolean data. Standard warning signs include the comparison of a Boolean value against the constant TRUE and the use of an if statement to produce a Boolean result that was already available as a conditional expression.

FIGURE 4-1 Main program from leapyear.c

```
main()
{
    int year;
    bool isLeapYear;

    printf("Program to determine whether a year is a leap year.\n");
    printf("What year? ");
    year = GetInteger();
    isLeapYear = ((year % 4 == 0) && (year % 100 != 0))
                   || (year % 400 == 0);
    if (isLeapYear) {
        printf("%d is a leap year.\n", year);
    } else {
        printf("%d is not a leap year.\n", year);
    }
}
```

4.4 The `if` statements

The simplest way to express conditional execution in C is by using the `if` statement, which comes in two forms:

> `if` (*condition*) *statement*
> `if` (*condition*) *statement* `else` *statement*

The *condition* component of this paradigm is a Boolean-valued expression. The statements can be either simple statements or blocks.

You use the first form of the `if` statement when your solution strategy calls for a set of statements to be executed only if a particular condition applies. If that condition does not apply, the statements that form the body of the `if` statement are simply skipped. For example, in the balance.c example in Chapter 3, the statement

```
if (entry < 0 && balance < 0) {
    printf("This check bounces.  $10 fee deducted.\n");
    balance -= 10;
}
```

fits into this category: either a check bounces or it doesn't, and the program needs to take action only in the bounced-check case.

You use the second form of the `if` statement for situations in which the program must choose between two independent sets of actions based on the result of a test. This statement form is illustrated by the oddeven.c program given in Figure 4-2, in which the program reads in a number and classifies it as either even or odd. The conditional expression used to determine the answer is

```
n % 2 == 0
```

FIGURE 4-2 Main program from **oddeven.c**

```
main()
{
    int n;

    printf("Program to classify a number as even or odd.\n");
    printf("n = ? ");
    n = GetInteger();
    if (n % 2 == 0) {
        printf("That number is even.\n");
    } else {
        printf("That number is odd.\n");
    }
}
```

This expression first calculates the remainder of n divided by 2 and then checks to see if it is 0, which would indicate that n is an even number. If so, the statement immediately after the `if` line is executed, which reports that the number is indeed even. If the remainder is not 0, n must be odd, and the statement following the `else` line reports that fact. The block of statements executed when the conditional expression is TRUE is called the **then clause** of the `if` statement. The block of statements executed when the condition is FALSE is called the **else clause.**

The fact that the `else` clause is optional in the `if` statement sometimes creates an ambiguity, which is called the **dangling-else problem.** If you write several `if` statements nested one within another, some of which have `else` clauses and some of which don't, it can be difficult to tell which `else` goes with which `if`. When faced with this situation, the C compiler follows the simple rule that each `else` clause is paired with the most recent `if` statement that does not already have an `else` clause. While this rule is simple for the compiler, it can still be hard for human readers to recognize quickly where each `else` clause belongs. By adopting a more disciplined programming style than C requires, it is possible to get rid of dangling-else ambiguities. The following rule governing how to use blocks within `if` statements eliminates the problem:

IF/ELSE BLOCKING RULE	For any `if` statement that (1) requires more than a single line or (2) requires an `else` clause, always use curly braces to enclose in a separate block the statements under the control of the `if` statement.

Because this text uses the If/Else Blocking Rule, the `if` statement appears only in one of the following four forms:

1. A single-line `if` statement used for extremely short conditions
2. A multiline `if` statement in which the statements are enclosed in a block

3. An if-else statement that *always* uses blocks to enclose the statements controlled by the if statement, even if they consist of a single statement
4. A *cascading* if statement, used for expressing a series of conditional tests

Each of these forms is discussed in more detail in the sections that follow.

S Y N T A X   for single-line if statements

```
    if (condition) statement;
where:
    condition is the Boolean value being tested
    statement is a single statement to be executed if
        condition is TRUE
```

S Y N T A X   for multiline if statements

```
    if (condition) {
        statements;
    }
where:
    condition is the Boolean value being tested
    statements is a block of statements to be executed if the
        condition is TRUE
```

S Y N T A X   for if-else statements

```
    if (condition) {
        statements_T
    } else {
        statements_F
    }
where:
    condition is the Boolean value being tested
    statements_T is a block of statements to be executed if
        condition is TRUE
    statements_F is a block of statements to be executed if
        condition is FALSE
```

Single-line if statements

The simple one-line format shown in the syntax box on the left is used only for those if statements in which there is no else clause and in which the body is a single statement short enough to fit on the same line as the if. In this type of situation, using braces and extending the if statement from one to three lines would make the program longer and more difficult to read. The only example so far of this style is the statement

```
    if (value == Sentinel) break;
```

presented in the section on "Sentinel-based loops" in Chapter 3.

Multiline if statements

Whenever the body of an if statement consists of multiple statements or a single statement that is too long for a single line, the statements are enclosed in a block, as shown in the syntax box on the left. In this form, the statements are executed if the condition is TRUE. If the condition is FALSE, the program takes no action at all and continues with the statement following the if.

The if-else statement

To avoid the dangling-else problem, the bodies of if statements that have else-clauses are always enclosed within blocks, as shown in the syntax box on the left. Technically, the curly braces that surround the block are necessary only if there is more than one statement governed by that condition. By systematically using those braces, however, you can minimize the possibility of confusion and make your programs easier to maintain.

Cascading if statements

The syntax box on the right illustrates an important special case of the if statement that is useful for applications in which the number of possible cases is larger than two. The characteristic form is that the else part of a condition consists of yet another test to check for an alternative condition. Such statements are called **cascading if statements** and may involve any number of else if lines. For example, the program signtest.c in Figure 4-3 uses the cascading if statement to report whether a number is positive, zero, or negative. Note that there is no need to check explicitly for the n < 0 condition. If the program reaches that last else clause, there is no other possibility, since the earlier tests have eliminated the positive and zero cases.

In many situations, the process of choosing between a set of independent cases can be handled more efficiently using the switch statement, which is described in a separate section later in this chapter.

SYNTAX for *cascading* if **statements**

```
if (condition₁) {
    statements₁
} else if (condition₂) {            any
    statements₂                     number
} else if (condition₃) {            may
    statements₃                     appear
} else {
    statements_none
}
```

where:
  each *condition_i* is a Boolean expression
  each *statements_i* is a block of statements to be executed
      if *condition_i* is TRUE
  statements_none is the block of statements to be executed
      if every *condition_i* is FALSE

The ?: operator (optional)

The C programming language provides another, more compact mechanism for expressing conditional execution that can be extremely useful in certain situations: the ?: operator. (This operator is referred to as *question-mark colon*, even though

---

FIGURE 4-3   Main program from **signtest.c**

```
main()
{
    int n;

    printf("Program to classify a number by its sign.\n");
    printf("n = ? ");
    n = GetInteger();
    if (n > 0) {
        printf("That number is positive.\n");
    } else if (n == 0) {
        printf("That number is zero.\n");
    } else {
        printf("That number is negative.\n");
    }
}
```

the two characters do not actually appear adjacent to one another.) Unlike any other operator in C, `?:` is written in two parts and requires three operands. The general form of the operation is

> (*condition*) ? *expression₁* : *expression₂*

The parentheses around the condition are not technically required, but most C programmers include them to emphasize the boundaries of the conditional test.

When a C program encounters the `?:` operator, it first evaluates the condition. If the condition turns out to be TRUE, *expression₁* is evaluated and used as the value of the entire expression; if the condition is FALSE, the value is the result of evaluating *expression₂*. The `?:` operator is therefore a shorthand form of the `if` statement

```
if (condition) {
    value = expression₁;
} else {
    value = expression₂;
}
```

where the value of the `?:` expression as a whole is whatever would have been stored in `value` in the expanded, `if`-statement form.

For example, you can use the `?:` operator to assign to `max` either the value of `x` or the value of `y`, whichever is greater, as follows:

```
max = (x > y) ? x : y;
```

One of the most common situations in which the `?:` operator makes sense is in calls to `printf` where the output you want differs slightly depending on some condition. For example, suppose that you are writing a program that counts the number of some item and that, after doing all the counting, stores the number of items in the variable `nItems`. How would you report this value to the user? The obvious way is just to call `printf` using a statement like

```
printf("%d items found.\n", nItems);
```

But if you are a language purist, you might be a little chagrined to read the output

```
1 items found
```

when `nItems` happens to have the value 1. You could, however, correct the English by enclosing the `printf` line in the following `if` statement:

```
if (nItems > 1) {
    printf("%d items found.\n", nItems);
} else {
    printf("%d item found.\n", nItems);
}
```

The only problem is that this solution strategy requires a five-line statement to express a relatively simple idea. As an alternative, you could use the `?:` operator as follows:

```
printf("%d item%s found.\n", nItems, (nItems > 1) ? "s" : "");
```

The string `"item"` in the output would then be followed by the string `"s"` if `nItems` is greater than one and an empty string otherwise.

As another example, you can use `?:` to print out the value of a Boolean variable in a readable way. Remember that the type `bool` is not actually part of the C language, and there is therefore no built-in mechanism for printing values of that type. Even so, you can easily use `printf` and `?:` to display the value of the Boolean variable `errorFlag` as follows:

```
printf("errorFlag = %s\n", (errorFlag) ? "TRUE" : "FALSE");
```

In C, it is possible to overuse the `?:` operator. If an essential part of the decision-making structure with a program is hidden away in the `?:` operator, those decision-making operations can easily get lost in the rest of the code. On the other hand, if using `?:` makes it possible to handle some small detail without writing a complicated `if` statement, this operator can simplify the program structure considerably.

4.5 The `switch` **statement**

The `if` statement is ideal for those applications in which the program logic calls for a two-way decision point: some condition is either TRUE or FALSE, and the program acts accordingly. Some applications, however, call for more complicated decision structures involving more than two choices, where those choices can be divided into a set of mutually exclusive cases: in one case, the program should do x; in another case, it should do y; in a third, it should do z; and so forth. In many applications, the most appropriate statement to use for such situations is the `switch` statement, which is outlined in the syntax box on the right.

The header line of the `switch` statement is

```
switch (e)
```

where e is an expression called the **control expression.** The body of the `switch` statement is divided into individual groups of statements introduced with one of two keywords: `case` or `default`. A `case` line and all the statements that follow it up to the next instance of either of these keywords

---

SYNTAX   for the `switch` **statement**

```
switch (e) {
    case c₁:
        statements₁
        break;
    case c₂:
        statements₂
        break;
    ... more case clauses ...
    default:
        statements_def
        break;
}
```

where:
   e is the control expression, which is used to choose what statements are executed
   each c_i is a constant value
   each $statements_i$ is a sequence of statements to be executed if c_i is equal to e
   $statements_{def}$ is a sequence of statements to be executed if none of the c_i values match the expression e

are called a **case clause**; the `default` line and its associated statements are called the **default clause**. For example, in the paradigm shown in the syntax box, the range of statements

```
case c₁:
    statements₁
    break;
```

constitutes the first `case` clause.

When the program executes a `switch` statement, the control expression e is evaluated and compared against the values c_1, c_2, and so forth, each of which must be an integer constant (or, as you will see in Chapter 9, any value that behaves like an integer, such as a character). If one of the constants matches the value of the control expression, the statements in the associated `case` clause are executed. When the program reaches the `break` statement at the end of the clause, the operations specified by that clause are complete, and the program continues with the statement following the entire `switch` statement. If none of the case constants match the value of the control expression, the statements in the `default` clause are executed.

The paradigm shown in the syntax box deliberately suggests that the `break` statements are a required part of the syntax. I encourage you to think of the `switch` syntax in precisely that form. C is defined so that if the `break` statement is missing, the program starts executing statements from the next clause after it finishes the selected one. While this design can be useful in some cases, it tends to cause more problems than it solves. To reinforce the importance of remembering to include the `break` statement, every `case` clause in this text ends with an explicit `break` statement (or sometimes with a `return` statement, as discussed in Chapter 5).

The one exception to this rule is that multiple `case` lines specifying different constants can appear together, one after another, before the same statement group. For example, a `switch` statement might include the following code:

```
case 1:
case 2:
    statements
    break;
```

which indicates that the specified statements should be executed if the `select` expression is either 1 or 2. The C compiler treats this construction as two `case` clauses, the first of which is empty. Because the empty clause contains no `break` statement, a program that selects that path simply continues on with the second clause. From a conceptual point of view, however, you are probably better off to think of this construction as a single `case` clause representing two possibilities.

The `default` clause is optional in the `switch` statement. If none of the cases match and there is no `default` clause, the program simply continues on with the next statement after the `switch` statement without taking any action at all. To avoid the possibility that the program might ignore an unexpected case, it is good programming practice to include a `default` clause in every `switch` statement unless you are certain you have enumerated all the possibilities.

COMMON PITFALLS

It is good programming practice to include a `break` statement at the end of every `case` clause within a `switch` statement. Doing so will help you to avoid programming errors that can be extremely difficult to find. It is also good practice to include a default clause unless you are sure you have covered all the cases.

FIGURE 4-4 Main program from `cardrank.c`

```
main()
{
    int n;

    printf("What is the rank of the card (1-13)? ");
    n = GetInteger();
    switch (n) {
      case  1: printf("Ace\n"); break;
      case 11: printf("Jack\n"); break;
      case 12: printf("Queen\n"); break;
      case 13: printf("King\n"); break;
      default: printf("%d\n", n); break;
    }
}
```

Because the `switch` statement can be rather long, programs are easier to read if the `case` clauses themselves are short. If there is room to do so, it also helps to put the `case` identifier, the statements forming the body of the clause, and the `break` statement all together on the same line. This style is illustrated in the `cardrank.c` program in Figure 4-4, which shows an example of a `switch` statement that might prove useful in writing a program to play a card game. In this game, the cards within each suit are represented by the numbers 1 to 13. Displaying the number of the card is fine for the cards between 2 and 10, but this style of output is not particularly satisfying for the values 1, 11, 12, and 13, which should properly be represented using the names Ace, Jack, Queen, and King. The `cardrank.c` program uses the `switch` statement to display the correct symbol for each card.

The fact that the `switch` statement can only be used to choose between cases identified by an integer (or integer-like) constant does place some restrictions on its use. You will encounter situations in which you want to choose between several cases based on the value of a string variable or in which the values you want to use as case indicators are not constants. Since the `switch` statement cannot be used in such cases, you will instead need to rely on cascading `if` statements. In situations that allow the use of the `switch` statement, using it can make your program both more readable and more efficient.

4.6 The `while` statement

The simplest iterative construct is the `while` statement, which repeatedly executes a simple statement or block until the conditional expression becomes FALSE. The paradigm for the `while` statement is shown in the syntax box. As with the `if` statement, the C compiler allows you to eliminate the curly braces surrounding the body if the body consists of a single statement. For the `while` loops used in this text, the body is always enclosed in braces to improve readability.

SYNTAX **for the `while` statement**

```
while (condition) {
     statements
}
```
where:

condition is the conditional test used to determine whether the loop should continue for another cycle

statements are the statements to be repeated

The entire statement, including both the `while` control line itself and the statements enclosed within the body, constitutes a **while loop.** When the program executes a `while` statement, it first evaluates the conditional expression to see if it is TRUE or FALSE. If it is FALSE, the loop **terminates** and the program continues with the next statement after the entire loop. If the condition is TRUE, the entire body is executed, after which the program goes back to the top to check the condition again. A single pass through the statements in the body constitutes a **cycle** of the loop.

There are two important principles to observe about the operation of a `while` loop:

1. The conditional test is performed before every cycle of the loop, including the first. If the test is FALSE initially, the body of the loop is not executed at all.
2. The conditional test is performed only at the *beginning* of a loop cycle. If that condition happens to become FALSE at some point during the loop, the program doesn't notice that fact until a complete cycle has been executed. At that point, the program evaluates the test condition again. If it is still FALSE, the loop terminates.

Using the `while` loop

You have already seen examples of the `while` statement, beginning with the section on "Sentinel-based loops" in Chapter 3. That particular style of using `while` was designed for sentinel detection and represents a somewhat special case. To illustrate the use of the `while` statement in its more traditional form, it is useful to pose a problem for which the conditional test falls most naturally at the beginning of the loop.

Suppose that you have been asked to write a program that adds up the digits in a positive integer. A sample run for this program might then be

```
This program sums the digits in an integer.
Enter a positive integer: 1729↵
The sum of the digits is 19
```

where the result of 19 comes from adding $1 + 7 + 2 + 9$. How would you go about writing such a program?

You have already seen several programs that keep a running total, and the same basic strategy applies here. You need to declare a variable for the sum, initialize it to 0, go through a loop adding in digits, and finally display the sum at the end. That much of the structure, with the rest of the problem left written in English, is shown below:

```
main()
{
    int n, dsum;

    printf("This program sums the digits in an integer.\n");
    printf("Enter a positive integer: ");
    n = GetInteger();
    dsum = 0;
    For each digit in the number, add that digit to dsum.
    printf("The sum of the digits is %d\n", dsum);
}
```

The sentence

   For each digit in the number, add that digit to dsum.

clearly specifies a loop structure of some sort, since there is an operation that needs to be repeated for each digit in the number. If it were easy to determine how many digits a number contained, you might choose to use a for loop and count up to the number of digits. Unfortunately, finding out how many digits there are in an integer is just as hard as adding them up in the first place. The best way to write this program is just to keep adding in digits until you discover that you have added the last one. Loops that run until some condition occurs are most often coded using the while statement.

   The essence of this problem lies in determining how to break up a number into its component digits. The key insight is that the arithmetic operators / and % are sufficient to accomplish the task. The last digit of an integer n is simply the remainder left over when n is divided by 10, which is the result of the expression n % 10. The rest of the number—the integer that consists of all digits *except* for the last one—is given by n / 10. For example, if n has the value 1729, the / and % operators can be used to break that number into two parts, 172 and 9, as shown in the following diagram:

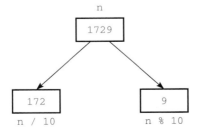

Thus, in order to add up the digits in the number, all you need to do is add the value n % 10 to the variable dsum on each cycle of the loop and then divide the number n by 10. The next cycle will add in the second-to-last digit from the original number, and so on, until the entire number has been processed in this way.

But how do you know when to stop? Eventually, as you divide n by 10 in each cycle, you will reach the point at which n becomes 0. At that point, you've processed all the digits in the number and can exit from the loop. In other words, as long as the value of n is greater than 0, you should keep going. Thus, the while loop needed for the problem is

```
while (n > 0) {
    dsum += n % 10;
    n /= 10;
}
```

The entire digitsum.c program is shown in Figure 4-5.

Infinite loops

When you use a while loop in a program, it is important to make sure that the condition used to control the loop will eventually become FALSE, so that the loop can exit. If the condition in the while control line always evaluates to TRUE, the computer will keep executing cycle after cycle without stopping. This situation is called an **infinite loop.**

As an example, suppose that you had carelessly written the while loop in the digitsum.c program with a >= operator in the control line instead of the correct > operator, as shown below:

```
while (n >= 0) {
    dsum += n % 10;          This loop will never stop running.
    n /= 10;
}
```

The loop no longer stops when n is reduced to 0, as it does in the correctly coded example. Instead, the computer keeps executing the body over and over and over again, with n equal to 0 every time.

FIGURE 4-5 Main program from **digitsum.c**

```
main()
{
    int n, dsum;

    printf("This program sums the digits in an integer.\n");
    printf("Enter a positive integer: ");
    n = GetInteger();
    dsum = 0;
    while (n > 0) {
        dsum += n % 10;
        n /= 10;
    }
    printf("The sum of the digits is %d\n", dsum);
}
```

To stop an infinite loop, you must type a special command sequence on the keyboard to interrupt the program and forcibly cause it to quit. This command sequence differs from machine to machine, and you should be sure to learn what command to use on your own computer.

Solving the loop-and-a-half problem

The while loop is designed for situations in which there is some test condition that can be applied at the beginning of a repeated operation, before any of the statements in the body of the loop are executed. If the problem you are trying to solve fits this structure, the while loop is the perfect tool. Unfortunately, many programming problems do not fit easily into the standard while loop paradigm. Instead of allowing a convenient test at the beginning of the operation, some problems are structured in such a way that the test you would like to write to determine if the loop is complete falls most naturally somewhere in the middle of the loop.

Consider for example, the problem of reading input data until a sentinel value appears, which was discussed in the section on "Sentinel-based loops" in Chapter 3. When expressed in English, the structure of the sentinel-based loop consists of repeating the following steps:

1. Read in a value.
2. If the value is equal to the sentinel, exit from the loop.
3. Perform whatever processing is required for that value.

Unfortunately, there is no test you can perform at the very beginning of the loop to determine whether the loop is finished. The termination condition for the loop is reached when the input value is equal to the sentinel; in order to check this condition, the program must have first read in some value. If the program has not yet read in a value, the termination condition doesn't make sense. Before the program can make any meaningful test, it must have executed the part of the loop that reads in the input value. When a loop contains some operations that must be performed before testing for completion, it represents an instance of what programmers call the **loop-and-a-half problem.**

One way to solve the loop-and-a-half problem in C is to use the break statement, which, in addition to its use in the switch statement, has the effect of immediately terminating the innermost enclosing loop. By using break, it is possible to code the loop structure for the sentinel problem in a form that follows the natural structure of the problem:

```
while (TRUE) {
    prompt user and read in a value
    if (value == sentinel) break;
    process the data value
}
```

The initial line

```
while (TRUE)
```

needs some explanation. The while loop is defined so that it continues until the condition in parentheses becomes FALSE. The symbol TRUE is a constant, so it can never become FALSE. Thus, as far as the while statement itself is concerned, the loop will never terminate. The only way this program can exit from the loop is by executing the break statement inside it.

It is possible to code this sort of loop without using the while (TRUE) control line or the break statement. To do so, however, you must change the order of operations within the loop and request input data in two places: once before the loop begins and then again inside the loop body. When structured in this way, the paradigm for the sentinel-based loop is

> *prompt user and read in the first value*
> while (*value* != *sentinel*) {
>   *process the data value*
>   *prompt user and read in a new value*
> }

Figure 4-6 shows how this paradigm can be used to implement the addlist.c program presented in Chapter 3 without using a break statement.

Unfortunately, there are two drawbacks to using this strategy. First, the order of operations in the loop is not what most people would expect. In any English explanation of the solution strategy, the first step is to get a number and the second is to add it to the total. The while loop paradigm used in Figure 4-6 reverses the order of the statements within the loop and makes the program more difficult to follow. The second problem is that this paradigm requires two copies of the statements that read in a number. Duplication of code presents a serious maintenance problem because subsequent edits to one set of statements might be made in the other. Empirical studies have shown that students who learn to solve the loop-and-a-half

---

FIGURE 4-6 Revised main program from addlist.c

```
main()
{
    int value, total;

    printf("This program adds a list of numbers.\n");
    printf("Signal end of list with a 0.\n");
    total = 0;
    printf(" ? ");
    value = GetInteger();
    while (value != 0) {
        total += value;
        printf(" ? ");
        value = GetInteger();
    }
    printf("The total is %d\n", total);
}
```

problem using the `break` statement form are more likely to write correct programs than those who don't.[2]

Despite the disadvantages, some instructors dislike using `break` to solve the loop-and-a-half problem. The principal reason for doing so is that it is easy to overuse the `break` statement in C. One way to guard against the overuse of the `break` statement is disallow its use entirely. To me, such an approach seems overly draconian. In this text, I use the `break` statement within a `while` loop only to solve the loop-and-a-half problem and not in other, more complex situations where its use is likely to obscure the program's structure.

 ## 4.7 The `for` statement

One of the most important control statements in C is the `for` statement, which is most often used in situations in which you want to repeat an operation a particular number of times. The general form of the `for` statement is shown in the syntax box to the right.

The operation of the `for` loop is determined by the three italicized expressions on the `for` control line: *init*, *test*, and *step*. The *init* expression indicates how the `for` loop should be initialized and usually sets the initial value of the index variable. For example, if you write

```
for (i = 0; . . .
```

the loop will begin by setting the index variable `i` to 0. If the loop begins

```
for (i = -7; . . .
```

the variable `i` will start as `-7`, and so on.

> **S Y N T A X for the `for` statement**
>
> ```
> for (init; test; step) {
>     statements
> }
> ```
>
> where:
> *init* is an expression evaluated to initialize the loop
> *test* is a conditional test used to determine whether the loop should continue, just as in the `while` statement
> *step* is an expression used to prepare for the next loop cycle
> *statements* are the statements to be repeated

The *test* expression is a conditional test written in exactly like the test in a `while` statement. As long as the test expression is TRUE, the loop continues. Thus, in the loop that has served as our canonical example up to now

```
for (i = 0; i < n; i++)
```

the loop begins with `i` equal to 0 and continues as long as `i` is less than `n`, which turns out to represent a total of `n` cycles, with `i` taking on the values 0, 1, 2, and so forth, up to the final value `n−1`. The loop

```
for (i = 1; i <= n; i++)
```

---

[2] The best known study corroborating this finding is "Cognitive strategies and looping constructs: an empirical study" by Elliot Soloway, Jeffrey Bonar, and Kate Ehrlich (*Communications of the ACM*, November 1983).

begins with i equal to 1 and continues as long as i is less than or equal to n. This loop also runs for n cycles, with i taking on the values 1, 2, and so forth, up to n.

The *step* expression indicates how the value of the index variable changes from cycle to cycle. The most common form of step specification is to increment the index variable using the ++ operator used in the for loops throughout Chapter 3, but this is not the only possibility. For example, one can count backward by using the -- operator or count by twos by using += 2 instead of ++.

As an illustration of counting in the reverse direction, the program liftoff.c in Figure 4-7 counts down from 10 to 0.

When liftoff.c is run, it generates the following sample run:

```
10
 9
 8
 7
 6
 5
 4
 3
 2
 1
 0
Liftoff!
```

The liftoff.c program demonstrates that any variable can be used as an index variable. In this case, the variable is called t, presumably because that is the traditional variable for a rocket countdown, as in "T minus 10 seconds and counting." In any case, the index variable must be declared at the beginning of the program, just like any other variable.

The expressions *init, test,* and *step* are each optional, but the semicolons must appear. If *init* is missing, no initialization is performed. If *test* is missing, it is assumed to be TRUE. If *step* is missing, no action occurs between loop cycles. Thus the control line

```
for (;;)
```

is identical in operation to

```
while (TRUE)
```

Nested for loops

As your programs become more complicated, you will often need to nest one for statement inside another. In this case, the inner for loop is then executed through its entire set of cycles for each iteration of the outer for loop. Each for loop must have its own index variable so that the variables do not interfere with one another.

FIGURE 4-7 liftoff.c

```
/*
 * File: liftoff.c
 * ---------------
 * Simulates a countdown for a rocket launch.
 */

#include <stdio.h>
#include "genlib.h"

/*
 * Constant: StartingCount
 * -----------------------
 * Change this constant to use a different starting value
 * for the countdown.
 */

#define StartingCount 10

/* Main program */

main()
{
    int t;

    for (t = StartingCount; t >= 0; t--) {
        printf("%2d\n", t);
    }
    printf("Liftoff!\n");
}
```

As an example of nested for loops, consider the timestab.c program in Figure 4-8.

The timestab.c program displays the following 10×10 multiplication table:

```
 1    2    3    4    5    6    7    8    9   10
 2    4    6    8   10   12   14   16   18   20
 3    6    9   12   15   18   21   24   27   30
 4    8   12   16   20   24   28   32   36   40
 5   10   15   20   25   30   35   40   45   50
 6   12   18   24   30   36   42   48   54   60
 7   14   21   28   35   42   49   56   63   70
 8   16   24   32   40   48   56   64   72   80
 9   18   27   36   45   54   63   72   81   90
10   20   30   40   50   60   70   80   90  100
```

FIGURE 4-8 timestab.c

```
/*
 * File: timestab.c
 * ----------------
 * Generates a multiplication table where each axis
 * runs from LowerLimit to UpperLimit.
 */

#include <stdio.h>
#include "genlib.h"

/*
 * Constants
 * ---------
 * LowerLimit -- Starting value for the table
 * UpperLimit -- Final value for the table
 */

#define LowerLimit  1
#define UpperLimit 10

/* Main program */

main()
{
    int i, j;

    for (i = LowerLimit; i <= UpperLimit; i++) {
        for (j = LowerLimit; j <= UpperLimit; j++) {
            printf(" %4d", i * j);
        }
        printf("\n");
    }
}
```

The outer for loop, which uses i as its index variable, runs through each row of the table. For each row, the inner for loop runs through each column in that row, displaying the individual entry, which is the value of i * j (the row number times the column number). Note that the printf("\n") call that advances the cursor to the next line appears in the outer loop, because this statement should only be executed once at the end of each row, and not after every value in the row.

The relationship between `for` and `while`

As it happens, the `for` statement

```
for (init; test; step) {
    statements;
}
```

is identical in operation to the `while` statement

```
init;
while (test) {
    statements;
    step;
}
```

Even though the `for` statement can easily be rewritten using `while`, there are considerable advantages to using the `for` statement when it makes sense to do so. With a `for` statement, all the information you need to understand exactly which cycles will be executed is contained in the header line of the statement. For example, whenever you see the statement

```
for (i = 0; i < 10; i++) {
    . . . body . . .
}
```

in a program, you know that the statements in the body of the loop will be executed 10 times, once for each of the values of i between 0 and 9. In the equivalent `while` loop form

```
i = 0;
while (i < 10) {
    . . . body . . .
    i++;
}
```

the increment operation at the bottom of the loop can easily get lost if the body is large.

Using `for` with floating-point data

Because the *init, test,* and *step* components of the `for` loop can be arbitrary expressions, there is no obvious reason why the loop index in a `for` loop has to be an integer. The fact that it is possible to count from 0 to 10 by twos using the `for` loop

```
for (i = 0; i <= 10; i += 2) . . .
```

suggests that it might also be possible to count for 1.0 to 2.0 in increments of 0.1 by declaring x as a `double` and then using

```
for (x = 1.0; x <= 2.0; x += 0.1) . . .        This test may fail.
```

On some machines, this statement has the desired effect. On others, it might fail to include the last value. For example, when the `for` loop

```
for (x = 1.0; x <= 2.0; x += 0.1) {
    printf("%.1f\n", x);          This loop might not include the value 2.0.
}
```

is run on the computer system I used to produce this text, it generates the following output:

```
1.0
1.1
1.2
1.3
1.4
1.5
1.6
1.7
1.8
1.9
```

Notice that the value 2.0, which you would expect to see from looking at the loop control line, is missing.

The problem here is that floating-point numbers are not exact. The value 0.1 is very close to the mathematical fraction $1/10$ but is almost certainly not precisely equal to it. As 0.1 is added to the index variable x, the inaccuracy can accumulate to the point that, when x is tested against 2.0 to determine whether the loop is finished, its value may be 2.000000001 or something similar, which is not less than or equal to 2.0. The condition in the `for` loop is therefore not satisfied, and the loop terminates after running for what seems to be one too few cycles. The best way to fix this problem is to restrict yourself to using integers as index variables in `for` loops. Because integers are exact, the problem never arises.

If you really want to count from 1.0 to 2.0 by increments of 0.1, you could count from 10 to 20 and then divide the index by 10:

```
for (i = 10; i <= 20; i++) {
    x = i / 10.0;
    printf("%.1f\n", x);
}
```

This `for` loop correctly produces the 11 values in the sequence 1.0, 1.1, 1.2, . . . , 2.0.

The same warning about comparing floating-point numbers for equality applies in many other circumstances besides the `for` loop. Numbers that seem as if they should be exactly equal might not be, given the limitations on the accuracy of floating-point numbers stored in a particular machine.

COMMON PITFALLS

Be very careful when testing floating-point numbers for equality. Because floating-point numbers are only approximations, they might not behave in the same way as real numbers in mathematics. In general, it is best to avoid using a floating-point variable as a `for` loop index.

 # Summary

In Chapter 3, you looked at the process of programming from a holistic perspective that emphasized problem solving. Along the way, you learned about several control statements in an informal way. In this chapter, you were able to investigate how those statements work in more detail. You were also introduced to a new type of data called *Boolean data.* Although this data type contains only two values—TRUE and FALSE—being able to use Boolean data effectively is extremely important to successful programming and is well worth a little extra practice.

This chapter also introduced several new operators, and at this point it is helpful to review the precedence relationships for all the operators you have seen so far. That information is summarized in Table 4-1 the operators are listed from highest to lowest precedence.

The important points introduced in this chapter include:

- *Simple statements* consist of an expression followed by a semicolon.
- The = used to specify assignment is an operator in C. Assignments are therefore legal expressions, which makes it possible to write *embedded* and *multiple assignments.*
- Individual statements can be collected into *compound statements*, more commonly called *blocks.*
- Control statements fall into two classes: *conditional* and *iterative.*
- The `genlib` library defines a data type called `bool` that is used to represent Boolean data. The type `bool` has only two values: TRUE and FALSE.
- You can generate Boolean values using the *relational operators* (<, <=, >, >=, ==, and !=) and combine them using the *logical operators* (&&, ||, and !).
- The logical operators && and || are evaluated in left-to-right order in such a way that the evaluation stops as soon as the program can determine the result. This behavior is called *short-circuit evaluation.*

Operator					Associativity
unary –	++	––	!	(*type cast*)	right-to-left
*	/	%			left-to-right
+	–				left-to-right
<	<=	>	>=		left-to-right
==	!=				left-to-right
&&					left-to-right
||					left-to-right
?:					right-to-left
=	*op*=				right-to-left

TABLE 4-1

Precedence table for operators used through Chapter 4

- The `if` statement is used to express conditional execution when a section of code should be executed only in certain cases or when the program needs to choose between two alternate paths.
- The `switch` statement is used to express conditional execution when a problem has the following structure: in case 1, do this; in case 2, do that; and so forth.
- The `while` statement specifies repetition that occurs as long as some condition is met.
- The `for` statement specifies repetition in which some action is needed on each cycle in order to update the value of an index variable.

REVIEW QUESTIONS

1. Is the construction

    ```
    17;
    ```

    a legal statement in C? Is it useful?

2. Describe the effect of the following statement, assuming that i, j, and k are declared as integer variables:

    ```
    i = (j = 4) * (k = 16);
    ```

3. What single statement would you write to set both x and y (which you may assume are declared to be type `double`) to 1.0?

4. What is meant by the term *associativity?* What is unusual about the associativity of assignment with respect to that of the other operators you have seen?

5. What is a block? What important fact about blocks is conveyed by the term *compound statement,* which is another name for the same concept?

6. What are the two classes of control statements?

7. What does it mean to say that two control statements are nested?

8. What are the two values of the data type `bool`?

9. What happens when a programmer tries to use the mathematical symbol for equality in a conditional expression?

10. What restriction does C place on the types of values that can be compared using the relational operators?

11. How would you write a Boolean expression to test whether the value of the integer variable n was in the range 0 to 9, inclusive?

12. Describe in English what the following conditional expression means:

```
(x != 4) || (x != 17)
```

For what values of x is this condition TRUE?

13. What does the term *short-circuit evaluation* mean?

14. Assuming that `myFlag` is declared as a Boolean variable, what is the problem with writing the following `if` statement?

```
if (myFlag == TRUE) . . .
```

15. What are the four different formats of the `if` statement used in this text?

16. Describe in English the general operation of the `switch` statement.

17. Suppose the body of a `while` loop contains a statement that, when executed, causes the condition for that `while` loop to become FALSE. Does the loop terminate immediately at that point or does it complete the current cycle?

18. Why is it important for the `digitsum.c` program in Figure 4-5 to specify that the integer is positive?

19. What is the loop-and-a-half problem? What two strategies are presented in the text for solving it?

20. What is the purpose of each of the three expressions that appear in the control line of a `for` statement?

21. What `for` loop control line would you use in each of the following situations:
a) Counting from 1 to 100.
b) Counting by sevens starting at 0 until the number has more than two digits.
c) Counting backward by twos from 100 to 0.

22. Why is it best to avoid using a floating-point variable as the index variable in a `for` loop?

PROGRAMMING EXERCISES

1. As a way to pass the time on long bus trips, young people growing up in the United States have been known to sing the following rather repetitive song:

> 99 bottles of beer on the wall.
> 99 bottles of beer.
> You take one down, pass it around.
> 98 bottles of beer on the wall.
>
> 98 bottles of beer on the wall. . . .

Anyway, you get the idea. Write a C program to generate the lyrics to this song. (Since you probably never actually finished singing this song, you should decide how you want it to end.) In testing your program, it would make sense to use some constant other than 99 as the initial number of bottles.

2. While we're on the subject of silly songs, another old standby is "This Old Man," for which the first verse is

> This old man, he played 1.
> He played knick-knack on my thumb.
> With a knick-knack, paddy-whack,
> Give your dog a bone.
> This old man came rolling home.

Each subsequent verse is the same, except for the number and the rhyming word at the end of the second line, which gets replaced as follows:

2—shoe	5—hive	8—pate
3—knee	6—sticks	9—spine
4—door	7—heaven	10—shin

Write a program to display all 10 verses of this song.

3. Write a program that reads in a positive integer N and then calculates and displays the sum of the first N odd integers. For example, if N is 4, your program should display the value 16, which is $1 + 3 + 5 + 7$.

4. *Why is everything either at sixes or at sevens?*

> — Gilbert and Sullivan, *H.M.S. Pinafore,* 1878

Write a program that displays the integers between 1 and 100 that are divisible by either 6 or 7.

5. Repeat exercise 4, but this time have your program display only those numbers that are divisible by 6 or 7 but not both.

6. Rewrite the `liftoff.c` program given in Figure 4-7 so that it uses a `while` loop instead of a `for` loop.

7. Rewrite the `digitsum.c` program given in Figure 4-5 so that instead of adding the digits in the number, it generates the number that has the same digits in the reverse order, as illustrated by this sample run:

```
This program reverses the digits in an integer.
Enter a positive integer: 1729⏎
The reversed number is 9271
```

8. In mathematics, there is a famous sequence of numbers called the Fibonacci sequence after the thirteenth-century Italian mathematician Leonardo Fibonacci. The first two terms in this sequence are 0 and 1, and every subsequent term is the sum of the preceding two. Thus the first several numbers in the Fibonacci sequence are as follows:

$$
\begin{aligned}
F_0 &= 0 \\
F_1 &= 1 \\
F_2 &= 1 \quad (0 + 1) \\
F_3 &= 2 \quad (1 + 1) \\
F_4 &= 3 \quad (1 + 2) \\
F_5 &= 5 \quad (2 + 3) \\
F_6 &= 8 \quad (3 + 5)
\end{aligned}
$$

Write a program to display the values in this sequence from F_0 through F_{15}. Make sure the values line up as shown in the following sample run:

```
This program lists the Fibonacci sequence.
 F(0)  =    0
 F(1)  =    1
 F(2)  =    1
 F(3)  =    2
 F(4)  =    3
 F(5)  =    5
 F(6)  =    8
 F(7)  =   13
 F(8)  =   21
 F(9)  =   34
F(10)  =   55
F(11)  =   89
F(12)  =  144
F(13)  =  233
F(14)  =  377
F(15)  =  610
```

9. Modify the program in the preceding exercise so that instead of specifying the index of the final term, the program displays those terms in the Fibonacci sequence that are less than 10,000.

10. Write a program to display the following diagram on the screen. The number of rows in the figure should be a #define constant, which has the value 8 for this sample run:

```
*
**
***
****
*****
******
*******
********
```

11. Modify the program you wrote in exercise 10 so that it generates a different triangle. In this triangle, each line contains two more points than the previous line does, and the point of the triangle faces upward, as follows:

```
              *
            ***
          *****
        *******
      *********
    ***********
  *************
***************
```

CHAPTER 5

Functions

To live is to function. That is all there is in living.

— Oliver Wendell Holmes, Jr., radio address, 1931

Objectives

- To appreciate the importance of functions as a tool for simplifying program structure.

- To understand the concept of calling a function and the reason for supplying arguments as part of the call.

- To understand function prototypes and how to write them.

- To be able to implement simple functions containing statements used in the previous chapters.

- To be able to use the `return` statement to specify the result of a function.

- To understand the concept of predicate functions and how to use them effectively.

- To understand the relationship between formal parameters in a function and arguments in its caller.

- To appreciate how the computer uses stack frames to keep track of local variables and return addresses for each function call.

- To understand the meaning of the term *procedure.*

- To be able to apply stepwise refinement as a problem-solving strategy.

This chapter examines in more detail the concept of a function, which was first introduced in Chapter 2. A *function* is a set of statements that have been collected together and given a name. By allowing the programmer to signify the entire set of operations with a single name, programs become much shorter and much simpler. Without functions, simple programs would become unmanageable as they increased in size and sophistication.

In order to appreciate how functions reduce the conceptual complexity of programs, you need to understand the concept in two ways. From the reductionistic perspective, you need to understand how functions work in an operational sense so you can predict their behavior. At the same time, you must be able to take a step backward and look at functions holistically, so that you can also understand why they are important and how to use them effectively.

 ## 5.1 Using library functions

You have been working with functions in this text ever since the very first program—the "Hello world" program from Chapter 2. That program contained just one statement, which was a call to the `printf` function:

```
printf("Hello, world.\n");
```

A function, such as `printf`, represents a set of programming steps used to perform a useful operation. In this respect, a function is similar to a complete program. Indeed, the programs you have seen up to now have been written as a function, which happens to have the name `main`.

The difference in concept between a function and a program lies primarily in who or what makes use of it. When, as a user, you sit down in front of your computer and start up an application, you are running a program that performs some action on your behalf. Thus, programs are invoked by and serve the needs of an external *user*. Functions, on the other hand, provide a mechanism by which a *program* can invoke a set of previously defined operations on its behalf. The operation of a function is thus entirely internal to the program domain.

As a user of the "Hello world" program, you have no idea that the program calls the `printf` function as part of its operation; you know only that the words "Hello world" appear on the screen. The programmer who wrote the `hello.c` program, however, recognized that `printf` provides a useful service that makes it possible to display messages on the screen with very little difficulty. Most of the hard work was done by the system programmer who wrote the program steps necessary to implement the `printf` function itself. Since that work has already been done, other programmers like yourself can use the `printf` function without having to write all the steps that make it work. You don't even have to know what those steps are.

In order to consider functions more concretely, it helps to review some of the basic terminology for functions that was introduced in Chapter 2. First of all, a **function** consists of a set of statements that have been collected together and given a name. The act of executing the set of statements associated with a function is known as **calling** that function. To indicate a function call in C, you write the name of the function, followed by a list of expressions enclosed in parentheses. These expressions are called **arguments** and allow the calling program to pass information to the function. In `hello.c`, the `printf` function knows what to display because the main program provided the necessary data as part of the function call. If a function requires no information from its caller, it need not have any arguments, but an empty set of parentheses must still appear in the function call.

Once called, the function takes the data supplied as arguments, does its work, and then returns to the program step from which the call was made. Remembering what the calling program was doing and being able to get back precisely to that point is one of the defining characteristics of the function-calling mechanism. The operation of going back to the calling program is called **returning** from the function. As part of the return operation, functions can also send results back to the calling program, as illustrated by the function `GetInteger` in the statement

```
n1 = GetInteger();
```

After the `GetInteger` function performs its task of reading in an integer from the user, it passes that integer back to the calling program as the value of the `GetInteger()` call. This operation is called **returning a value.**

In a sense, arguments provide input to functions and the return values provide output back to their callers. Despite the conceptual similarity, it is critically important to make a sharp distinction between input operations, such as `GetInteger`, and the use of arguments in the function domain. A function like `GetInteger` provides a mechanism for getting input from the user; when `GetInteger` needs an input value, whoever is sitting in front of the terminal must physically enter that value on the keyboard. Arguments to a function, on the other hand, provide a means for a function to receive input from its caller, which is another part of the program and not the human user. Data passed in the form of arguments may have been entered by the user at an earlier point in the program, but could just as easily have been calculated as part of the program operation. You should also be careful to differentiate the use of output operations, such as `printf`, from the technique of returning a result. When you use `printf`, the output appears on the terminal screen. When a function returns a result, that information goes back to the calling program, which is free to use it in whatever way makes sense for the program. New programmers have a tendency to use input/output operations within functions when the logic of the situation calls for using arguments and results.

To understand how functions fit into the framework of C, you need to recognize that a function call is simply an expression and can be used in any context in which an expression can appear. Moreover, the arguments to a function are also expressions, which can themselves contain function calls or any other operations that would be legal in an expression.

To illustrate that functions and their arguments are expressions, it is useful to introduce several standard functions from the `math` system library. This library includes many of the standard mathematical functions you learned in high-school algebra and trigonometry. For example, the `math` library contains the function `sqrt` for taking the square root of its argument, as well as `sin` and `cos` for trigonometric sines and

COMMON PITFALLS

Be careful to differentiate in your mind the ideas of input and output in the program domain and the related concepts of arguments and results in the function domain. Input and output allow communication between a *program* and its *user.* Arguments and results allow communication between a *function* and its *caller.*

cosines. Each of these functions takes a `double` as an argument and returns a result, also of type `double`. You can use these functions in simple statements, such as

```
root3 = sqrt(3.0);
```

or in more complicated ones. For example, you can compute the distance from the origin to the point (x, y) using the standard distance formula for points in a plane:

$$distance = \sqrt{x^2 + y^2}$$

In C, this formula corresponds to the statement

```
distance = sqrt(x * x + y * y);
```

Similarly, you can compute a tangent using the trigonometric identity

$$\tan\theta = \frac{\sin\theta}{\cos\theta}$$

which can be written in C as

```
tangent = sin(theta) / cos(theta);
```

A list of the important functions available in the `math` library is included in Appendix A.

5.2 Function declarations

In ANSI C, all functions must be declared before they are used. Function declarations are analogous to variable declarations, which you have already seen in the section on "Variables" in Chapter 2. A variable declaration tells the compiler the name of a variable and the type of value it contains. A function declaration works similarly, but specifies more details. In C, a function declaration defines

- the name of the function
- the type of each argument to the function and, in most cases, a descriptive name for the argument
- the type of value the function returns

A function declaration in C is called a **function prototype** and has the following form:

$$result\text{-}type\ name\ (argument\text{-}specifiers)\ ;$$

The *result-type* field indicates the type of the function result, the *name* field indicates the function name, and the *argument-specifiers* field indicates the names and types of the arguments to be passed to this function. The format for this field is simply a list, separated by commas, of the type of each argument. As discussed later in this section, each type name in the argument specifications may be followed by a variable name that provides additional information to human readers.

SYNTAX for function prototypes

result-type name(argument-specifiers);

where:
   result-type is the type of value the function returns.
   name is the function name.
   argument-specifiers is a list, separated by commas, of individual specifications for the argument types.
      An argument specification consists of a type, optionally followed by a descriptive variable name.

For example, the `math` library contains the following prototype for the `sqrt` function:

```
double sqrt(double);
```

The prototype tells you that the function `sqrt` takes one argument, which is a `double`, and returns a `double` as well.

Note that the prototype specifies only the types of the values that pass back and forth between the caller and the function itself. The prototype says nothing about the actual statements that define the function or even about what the function does. To use the `sqrt` function, you need to understand that the result is the square root of its argument. The C compiler, however, does not need this information. All it needs to know is that `sqrt` takes a `double` and returns a `double`. The precise effect of the function is communicated to programmers by the function name and the associated documentation.

Another way to provide useful information to programmers is to include, along with each of the argument specifications, a descriptive name that identifies the nature of that particular argument. This name does not affect the program in any substantive way, although it provides important information to the programmer who wants to use that function. For example, `sin` is declared in `math.h` as

```
double sin(double);
```

which specifies only the type of the argument. Programmers who need to use this function might prefer to see the prototype written as

```
double sin(double angleInRadians);
```

A prototype written in this form provides useful new information: that `sin` takes one argument of type `double`, representing an angle measured in radians. In your own functions, you should always include descriptive names for the expected arguments and use these names when you talk about the operation of that function in the associated comments.

If a function does not take arguments, C uses the special keyword `void` as the argument specification. For example, the function `GetInteger` from the `simpio` library takes no arguments from its caller and returns a value of type `int`. The prototype for this function is therefore

```
int GetInteger(void);
```

 ## 5.3 Writing your own functions

The functions introduced so far in this chapter have all been part of some programming library. Library functions are interesting in their own right, but they do not tell the whole story of functions. As a programmer, you will often be content to use library functions without knowing any of the internal details. But you will also want to use functions that are not part of any library. In those cases, you have no choice but to define the functions yourself.

For example, suppose that you have been assigned the task of writing a program that converts temperatures from the Celsius scale used in most countries to the

Fahrenheit scale used in the United States. You will probably want to define a simple conversion function that you can then use in other parts of the program. The computation is relatively easy, because the process of converting one temperature scale to another is simply a matter of applying the formula

$$F = \frac{9}{5}C + 32$$

Adding a new function to a C program consists of two distinct steps:

1. You need to specify the function prototype, which is usually done near the top of the entire program, after the `#include` lines.
2. At some later point in the program, you need to provide the implementation of that function, which specifies the actual steps involved.

The prototype is short and indicates only the argument and result types. The implementation is longer and provides the details.

In writing a function, it is usually best to start with the prototype. In this example, you are writing a function that converts from Celsius to Fahrenheit. You may choose any name for that function, using the same rules as those given for naming variables in Chapter 2. The name should make it easy for anyone reading the program to determine what the function does. For example, the following name is not easily open to misinterpretation:

```
double CelsiusToFahrenheit(double c);
```

The implementation for a function is written by starting with its prototype, taking away the semicolon at the end of the line, and then adding the body of the function. A **function body** is always a block and therefore consists of statements enclosed in curly braces. The statements in the block may be preceded with variable declarations such as the ones used in the function `main` for most of the programs presented so far.

The `return` statement

If a function returns a result, the statements in the function body must include at least one **return statement**, which specifies the value to be returned. The paradigmatic form for the `return` statement is shown in the syntax box to the left.

In most cases, the `return` statement includes a parenthesized expression that indicates the value of the result.[1] However, it can also be used for functions that have no

---

SYNTAX **for the `return` statement**

    return (*expression*);

where:
    expression is the value to be returned.

If the function has no result, the syntax is:

    return;

---

[1] The parentheses in the paradigm for the `return` statement are optional, but C programmers often use them to improve readability.

results. Such functions are discussed in the section on "Procedures" later in this chapter. When it is used in the

```
return (expression);
```

form, the return statement causes the function to return the indicated value immediately. As such, the return statement encompasses both of the following English ideas: "I'm done now" and "Here is the answer." In some programming languages, such as Pascal and Fortran, indicating that the execution of a function is complete and specifying its result are separate operations. If you have had experience with such languages, it may take some time to get used to the return statement in C.

The return statement completes the list of tools you need to write the implementation of CelsiusToFahrenheit:

```
double CelsiusToFahrenheit(double c)
{
    return (9.0 / 5.0 * c + 32);
}
```

The function calculates the value of the appropriate expression and returns the result as the value of the function.

Putting functions together with main programs

By itself, the function CelsiusToFahrenheit does not constitute a complete program. Every complete program also has a function named main, which is called when the program starts up. To test your CelsiusToFahrenheit function, you might want to implement a version of main that used CelsiusToFahrenheit to generate a temperature conversion table. The complete program to do so is shown in Figure 5-1.

The main program consists of the for loop that you used in Chapter 4 to generate tables. Each line in the temperature conversion table is generated by the statement

```
printf("%3d %3g\n", c, CelsiusToFahrenheit(c));
```

This statement calls the CelsiusToFahrenheit function to compute the Fahrenheit equivalent of the Celsius temperature c.[2] That value is then passed as an argument to printf, which goes on to display the value.

Note that the program in Figure 5-1 has many more comments than most of the programs presented so far. Each function should have its own descriptive comment so that readers of the program can understand each function as a unit. In my experience, one of the most helpful comments you can write for a function is one that gives an example of how the function is used. Hereafter in this text, the comments for a function include a "Usage" line that provides such an example.

---

[2] In the for loop, the index variable c is declared to be an int, even though CelsiusToFahrenheit is defined to take a double. As noted in the section on "Using for with floating-point data" in Chapter 4, integers are exact, and the program is therefore certain to run the correct number of times. When CelsiusToFahrenheit is called with the argument c, an automatic conversion is performed to change the value to type double.

FIGURE 5-1 c2ftable.c

```
/*
 * File: c2ftable.c
 * -----------------
 * This program illustrates the use of functions by generating
 * a table of Celsius to Fahrenheit conversions.
 */

#include <stdio.h>
#include "genlib.h"

/*
 * Constants
 * ---------
 * LowerLimit -- Starting value for temperature table
 * UpperLimit -- Final value for temperature table
 * StepSize   -- Step size between table entries
 */

#define LowerLimit   0
#define UpperLimit 100
#define StepSize     5

/* Function prototypes */

double CelsiusToFahrenheit(double c);

/* Main program */

main()
{
    int c;

    printf("Celsius to Fahrenheit table.\n");
    printf("  C    F\n");
    for (c = LowerLimit; c <= UpperLimit; c += StepSize) {
        printf("%3d  %3g\n", c, CelsiusToFahrenheit(c));
    }
}

/*
 * Function: CelsiusToFahrenheit
 * Usage: f = CelsiusToFahrenheit(c);
 * ----------------------------------
 * This function returns the Fahrenheit equivalent of the Celsius
 * temperature c.
 */
```

```
double CelsiusToFahrenheit(double c)
{
    return (9.0 / 5.0 * c + 32);
}
```

Functions involving internal control structures

Functions are not usually as simple as CelsiusToFahrenheit is. In many cases, calculating a function requires making some tests or writing a loop. Such details add to the complexity of the implementation but do not change its basic form. For example, the library function abs computes the absolute value of its integer argument and has the prototype

```
int abs(int n);
```

The abs function is defined in the ANSI standard library stdlib. Suppose, however, that you had to write it yourself. How would you write its implementation? The definition of absolute value indicates that if the argument is negative, the function should return its negation, which is a positive number. If the argument is positive or zero, the function should simply return the argument value unchanged. Thus, you can implement the abs function as follows:

```
int abs(int n)
{
    if (n < 0) {
        return (-n);
    } else {
        return (n);
    }
}
```

As this implementation shows, a return statement can occur anywhere in the function body.

Similarly, you can define a function MinF to return the smaller of two floating-point arguments as follows:

```
double MinF(double x, double y)
{
    if (x < y) {
        return (x);
    } else {
        return (y);
    }
}
```

The control structure used within a function can be much more complex than the simple examples above. Suppose you want to define a function called Factorial that takes an integer n and returns the product of the integers between 1 and n. The first several factorials are shown in the following list:

```
Factorial(0)    =       1              (by definition)
Factorial(1)    =       1       =      1
Factorial(2)    =       2       =      1 × 2
Factorial(3)    =       6       =      1 × 2 × 3
Factorial(4)    =      24       =      1 × 2 × 3 × 4
Factorial(5)    =     120       =      1 × 2 × 3 × 4 × 5
Factorial(6)    =     720       =      1 × 2 × 3 × 4 × 5 × 6
```

Factorials are usually designated in mathematics using an exclamation point, as in $n!$, and have extensive applications in statistics, combinatorial mathematics, and computer science. A function to compute factorials is a useful tool for solving problems in those domains.

The `Factorial` function takes an integer and returns an integer, so its prototype looks like this:

```
int Factorial(int n);
```

Implementing `Factorial`, however, requires some work. As a programming problem, the task of computing a factorial is similar in many respects to adding a list of numbers, which you learned about in Chapter 3. In the `addlist.c` program, a variable called `total` is declared to keep track of the running total. At the beginning of the program, `total` is initialized to 0. As each new value comes in, it is added to `total` so that `total` continues to reflect the sum of the numbers entered so far. In the current problem, the situation is much the same, except that you have to keep track of a product rather than a sum. To do so, you can:

1. Declare a variable called `product`.
2. Initialize it to 1.
3. Multiply it by each of the integers between 1 and n.
4. Return the final value of `product` as the result of the function.

To cycle through each of the integers required in step 3, you need a `for` loop, which begins at 1 and continues until it reaches n. The `for` loop will require an index variable, for which the traditional choice of i seems quite appropriate. Thus, you need to declare two variables at the beginning of `Factorial` by writing

```
int product, i;
```

The variable `product` holds the running product, and i holds the index.

The implementation of `Factorial`, shown in Figure 5-2, is short enough to present all at once without explaining the details step by step.

Functions that return nonnumeric values

The examples of functions presented so far in this section all return numeric results, and the historical association of the word *function* with mathematics often makes numeric functions seem the most natural. However, functions in C can return values of any data type. For example, if you were writing a program to work with dates, it might be useful to have a function to convert a numeric month between 1 and 12 into the `string` that indicates the corresponding month name

---

FIGURE 5-2 Factorial function

```
int Factorial(int n)
{
    int product, i;

    product = 1;
    for (i = 1; i <= n; i++) {
        product *= i;
    }
    return (product);
}
```

---

between January and December. While the numeric values are easier to work with internally (if, for example, you needed to compare two dates to see which came earlier), the output display may be more readable with the traditional English names. To solve this problem, you could define the function `MonthName` as shown in Figure 5-3.

To use this function, you would call `MonthName` from some other part of the program and then use `printf` to display the result. For example, if the integer variables `month`, `day`, and `year` contain the values 7, 20, and 1969 (the date of the Apollo 11 landing on the moon), the statement

```
printf("%s %d, %d\n", MonthName(month), day, year);
```

FIGURE 5-3 MonthName function

```
string MonthName(int month)
{
    switch (month) {
      case  1: return ("January");
      case  2: return ("February");
      case  3: return ("March");
      case  4: return ("April");
      case  5: return ("May");
      case  6: return ("June");
      case  7: return ("July");
      case  8: return ("August");
      case  9: return ("September");
      case 10: return ("October");
      case 11: return ("November");
      case 12: return ("December");
      default: return ("Illegal month");
    }
}
```

would generate the output

```
July 20, 1969
```

In the `switch` statement within the `MonthName` function, the `return` statements in each `case` clause automatically exit from the entire function and make an explicit `break` statement unnecessary. As indicated in the section on the `switch` statement in Chapter 4, you can avoid a lot of pain in the debugging process if you design your programs so that every `case` clause ends with either a `break` or a `return` statement.

Predicate functions

The examples in the preceding section illustrate that functions can return values of different data types. The function `Factorial`, for example, returns a value of type `int`, and the function `MonthName` returns a value of type `string`. Although functions in C can return values of any type, there is one result type that deserves special attention. That type is the data type `bool`, which was introduced in Chapter 4 and is defined by including the `genlib` library. Functions that return values of type `bool` are called **predicate functions** and play an important role in modern programming.

Recall that there are only two values of type `bool`: TRUE and FALSE. Thus a predicate function—no matter how many arguments it takes or how complicated its internal processing may be—must eventually return one of these two values. The process of calling a predicate function is therefore analogous to asking a yes/no question and getting an answer.

Consider the following function definition, which, given an integer n, answers the question "is n an even number?":

```
bool IsEven(int n)
{
    return (n % 2 == 0);
}
```

A number is even if there is no remainder when that number is divided by two. If n is even, the expression

```
n % 2 == 0
```

therefore has the value TRUE, which is returned as the result of the `IsEven` function. If n is odd, the function returns FALSE. Because `IsEven` returns a Boolean result, you can use it directly in a conditional context. For example, the following main program uses `IsEven` to list all the even numbers between 1 and 10:

```
main()
{
    int i;

    for (i = 1; i <= 10; i++) {
        if (IsEven(i)) printf("%2d\n", i);
    }
}
```

When new programmers use predicate functions, they often make the errors described in the section on "Avoiding redundancy in Boolean expressions" in Chapter 4. Until you get more experience with Boolean data and predicate functions, you may find yourself tempted to put an `if` statement inside the implementation of `IsEven` or to make unnecessary comparisons against `TRUE`, such as

```
if (IsEven(i) == TRUE) . . .          The == TRUE is redundant.
```

If you find yourself making such errors, you may want to review the discussion of Boolean data in Chapter 4.

As another example of a predicate function, you could write one that tests whether a given year is a leap year, as follows:

```
bool IsLeapYear(int year)
{
    return ( ((year % 4 == 0) && (year % 100 != 0))
            || (year % 400 == 0) );
}
```

You encountered the Boolean expression to determine whether `year` is a leap year in Chapter 4. By taking this expression and putting it into a function, you no longer have to include the entire calculation explicitly to make this test. Once the function is defined, the rest of the program can simply use statements of the form:

```
if (IsLeapYear(year)) . . .
```

A predicate function to test for string equality

Until now, your ability to work with string data has been limited to a few extremely simple operations: you know how to use `GetLine` to read in a string and how to use `printf` to display one on the screen. In Chapter 9, you will learn about an entire library of string functions that enable you to manipulate string data in a variety of ways. Meanwhile, it makes sense to introduce you to one of its functions. That function is `StringEqual`, which you can use to tell whether two strings contain exactly the same characters.

There are two principal reasons for introducing the `StringEqual` function at this point in the text. First, having `StringEqual` in your repertoire of programming idioms will allow you to use strings in much more creative ways, which will in turn make it possible for you to write more interesting programs. Second, `StringEqual` is a predicate function and helps to illustrate the importance of these functions in programming applications.

The prototype for the `StringEqual` function is

```
bool StringEqual(string s1, string s2);
```

which indicates that `StringEqual` takes two strings as arguments and returns a Boolean value. That value is TRUE if the two strings, `s1` and `s2`, are precisely equal, character for character. If there are any differences between the strings, `StringEqual` returns FALSE. The following examples illustrate this behavior:

```
StringEqual("abc", "abc")       returns TRUE
StringEqual("abc", "def")       returns FALSE
StringEqual("abc", "abcd")      returns FALSE
StringEqual("abc", "ABC")       returns FALSE
```

Note that the characters in the string must match exactly; if there are extra characters in one string or if the case of the characters differs in the two strings, `StringEqual` returns FALSE.

You can use `StringEqual` whenever you want to ask the user a question and then take some action based on the response. For example, suppose you have written a program that plays a game with the user and you want to offer the user a chance to play again. You can ask the user a question by displaying an appropriate prompt and then get a response by calling `GetLine`:

```
printf("Would you like to play again? ");
answer = GetLine();
```

The `StringEqual` function makes it possible for the program to do something with the answer. For example, you can write a main program that looks like this:

```
main()
{
    string answer;

    while (TRUE) {
        PlayOneGame();
        printf("Would you like to play again? ");
        answer = GetLine();
        if (StringEqual(answer, "no")) break;
    }
}
```

If the user enters the word `no`, the program exits from the `while` loop. If the user gives any other response, the program plays another game. A program that checks the user's response more carefully is discussed in exercise 11.

5.4 Mechanics of the function-calling process

So far in this chapter, we have considered functions from the holistic perspective. Thinking about functions in this way helps you understand how they are used and what they provide as a programming resource. To develop confidence that the functions you write will work as they should, however, you also need to develop an understanding of how functions operate internally.

As a first step toward understanding the mechanics of functions, consider the program shown in Figure 5-4, which includes both the `Factorial` function presented earlier in this chapter and a main program that displays a factorial table.

The `fact.c` program makes good sense if you look at it as two separate pieces. The main program simply counts from `LowerLimit` to `UpperLimit`. On each cycle, it calls `Factorial` on the index `i` and then displays the result. By this point, you are accustomed to using the name `i` to indicate an otherwise unremarkable index variable used to count cycles in a `for` loop. No surprises here. The `Factorial` function is likewise straightforward. There is a little more going on than in the main program, but not much more. You can easily understand what this function is doing. In particular, you should recognize that `n` is the number whose factorial we're computing, that `product` holds the accumulating product on each cycle, and that `i` is once again an unremarkable index variable used to track the progress of the `for` loop. Thus, each piece of the program makes sense in and of itself.

For new students, confusion arises only when looking at the program as a whole. If you do that without understanding how to think about functions, you can run into some interesting problems. First, there are two variables named `i`, one in the main program and one in the `Factorial` function. Each variable is used as a loop index, but the two variables will have different values. Second and equally confusing is the fact that there are other parts of the program in which two different names are used to refer to the same value. In the main program, the number whose factorial we are seeking to compute is stored in the loop index `i`. In the `Factorial` function, that same value is called `n`. How do you make sense out of all this confusion?

Even if the program is confusing as a whole, it is important to remember that the functions make sense when you look at them one at a time. As long as you look only at `main` or only at `Factorial`, none of these points of confusion exist. Each function definition makes sense by itself. That fact—as commonplace as it might seem—is of fundamental importance. As programs grow, there is no way you can comprehend them as a whole. Your only hope of making sense of a large program is to break it down into pieces, each of which is small enough to make sense by itself. In the `fact.c` program, the problem of making a list of factorials has been separated into two easy-to-understand pieces.

Parameter passing

To understand how the two pieces of the program work together, you will find it helpful to develop a sense of how C itself handles the confusion. That it manages to do so is important for us as programmers and enables us to think about the individual functions separately. How does C make sense of the facts that the same name may be used for different values and that a single conceptual value may be represented by different names? To help you understand the answer to this question, it is useful to introduce a semantic distinction between argument values in the caller and the variables used to hold those values in the context of a function.

When the main program calls `Factorial` (which itself appears as one of the arguments to the function `printf`), the argument is the expression `i`. When this

FIGURE 5-4 fact.c

```c
/*
 * File: fact.c
 * ------------
 * This program includes the Factorial function and a test
 * program that prints the factorials of the numbers between
 * the limits LowerLimit and UpperLimit, inclusive.
 */

#include <stdio.h>
#include "genlib.h"

/*
 * Constants
 * ---------
 * LowerLimit -- Starting value for factorial table
 * UpperLimit -- Final value for factorial table
 */

#define LowerLimit 0
#define UpperLimit 7

/* Function prototypes */

int Factorial(int n);

/* Main program */

main()
{
    int i;

    for (i = LowerLimit; i <= UpperLimit; i++) {
        printf("%d! = %5d\n", i, Factorial(i));
    }
}

/*
 * Function: Factorial
 * Usage: f = Factorial(n);
 * -----------------------
 * Returns the factorial of the argument n, where factorial
 * is defined as the product of all integers from 1 up to n.
 */
```

```
int Factorial(int n)
{
    int product, i;

    product = 1;
    for (i = 1; i <= n; i++) {
        product *= i;
    }
    return (product);
}
```

statement is executed, the effect is to look up the current value of i and pass it to the function Factorial, which has the prototype

```
int Factorial(int n);
```

The prototype declares a variable named n of type int—a variable whose purpose is to serve as a placeholder for the actual argument. A variable defined in a function header that serves as a placeholder is called a **formal parameter.**

When a function is called, the following steps are taken:

1. The values of each argument are computed as part of the operation of the calling program. Because the arguments are expressions, this computation can involve operators and other functions, all of which are evaluated before the new function is actually called.
2. The value of each argument is copied into the corresponding formal parameter variable. If there is more than one argument, the arguments are copied into the parameters in order; the first argument is copied to the first parameter, and so forth. If necessary, automatic type conversions are performed between the argument values and the formal parameters as in an assignment statement. For example, if a value of type int is passed to a function where the parameter is declared as a double, the integer is converted into the equivalent floating-point value before it is copied into the parameter variable.
3. The statements in the function body are evaluated until a return statement appears.
4. The value of the return expression is evaluated and converted, if necessary, to the result type specified for the function.
5. The calling program continues, with the returned value substituted in place of the call.

Every call to a function results in the creation of a separate set of variables. When variables were represented graphically in Chapter 2 as boxes, all the boxes were enclosed within a larger box representing the function main, which was the only function in the program. If you want to follow the computer's operation for a larger program with more than one function, you need to draw a new set of variable boxes each time one function calls another. As was true in the case of the function main, there must be one box for every variable that function declares, including the formal parameters. These variables are meaningful only within the program that declares them and are therefore called **local variables.**

For example, when the main program runs in the fact.c example, you first need to create space for the variables in the function main. The function main declares only one variable—the loop index i—so that the variables for main can be represented as follows:

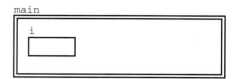

The double lines around the variable boxes are used to enclose all the variables associated with a particular function call. This collection of variables is called the **frame**—or, for reasons that will soon be apparent, the **stack frame**—for that function.

Assume that LowerLimit is defined to be 0 as it was in the program listing. In this case, on the first cycle through the for loop, i has the value 0. As before, you can represent this condition in the frame by noting the value inside the box for that variable.

The main program then calls printf and, as part of evaluating the arguments to printf, computes the result of the expression

    Factorial(i)

To represent the computer's actions in the frame diagram, you begin by looking up the value of i in the current frame, where you discover that the value is 0. You must then create a new frame for Factorial, for which the value 0 is the first (and only) argument. The Factorial function has three variables: the formal parameter n and the local variables product and i. Your frame for Factorial therefore needs three variable cells:

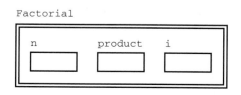

The first thing that happens is that the formal parameter n is initialized with the

value of the argument, which was 0. The contents of the frame then look like this:

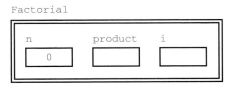

When you create the frame for Factorial, the frame for main does not go away entirely. Instead that frame is set aside temporarily until the operation of Factorial is complete. To indicate this situation in the conceptual model represented by the box diagram, the best technique is to draw each new frame diagram on an index card and then to place the new card on top of the card for the previous frame, thereby covering it up. For example, when you call the function Factorial, the index card representing the Factorial frame goes on top of the frame for main.

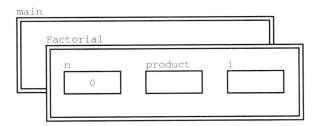

As the diagram shows, the entire set of frames forms a stack with the most recent frame on top, which is the origin of the term *stack frame*. The frame for main is still there; you just can't see any of it as long as the function Factorial is active. In particular, the name i no longer refers to the variable declared in main but to the variable named i in Factorial.

The next step in the process is to execute the body of Factorial by running through each of its steps in the current frame. The variable product is initialized to 1, and the program reaches the for loop. In the for loop, the variable i is initialized to 1, but since the value is already larger than n, the body of the for loop is not executed at all. Thus, when the program reaches the return statement, the frame looks like this:

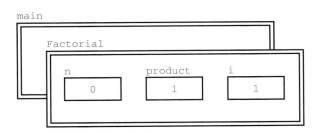

When `Factorial` returns, the value of `product` is passed back to the caller as the result of the function. Returning from a function also implies throwing away its frame, exposing once again the variables in `main`:

```
main

    i
   ┌─────────┐
   │    0    │
   └─────────┘
```

The result, 1, is then passed to the `printf` function. The `printf` function goes through the same process; the details of that operation, however, are hidden from you because you don't know how `printf` works internally. Eventually, `printf` displays the value 1 on the screen and then returns, after which the function `main` goes on to execute the next `for` loop cycle.

Calling functions from within other functions

Much of the power of functions comes from the fact that once a function has been defined, you can use it not only in the context of a main program, but also as a tool to implement other functions that can be used as more sophisticated tools. These functions can then be called from other functions, and so on, creating an arbitrarily complex hierarchy.

Suppose you have a group of n distinct objects on a table in front of you. From that group of objects, you would like to select k objects. The question you want to answer is: How many different ways are there to select k objects out of the original collection of n distinct objects?

To make the problem concrete, suppose that the objects on the table are the five U.S. coins: a penny, a nickel, a dime, a quarter, and a half-dollar. You want to know how many different ways there are to take, for example, two coins from the table. You could take the penny and the nickel, the penny and the dime, the nickel and the quarter, or any of several other combinations. If you list all the possibilities, you discover that there are 10 different combinations, as follows:

penny + nickel	nickel + quarter
penny + dime	nickel + half-dollar
penny + quarter	dime + quarter
penny + half-dollar	dime + half-dollar
nickel + dime	quarter + half-dollar

In this example, n is 5 and k is 2. The solution can be expressed as a function of the values n and k. That function comes up frequently in probability and statistics and is called the **combinations function,** which is often written in mathematics as

$$\binom{n}{k}$$

or, in functional notation, as

C(*n*, *k*)

As it turns out, the combinations function has a simple definition in terms of factorials:

$$C(n, k) = \frac{n!}{k! \times (n-k)!}$$

For example, you can verify that C(5, 2) is indeed 10 by working out the mathematics step by step:

$$C(5, 2) = \frac{5!}{2! \times 3!}$$
$$= \frac{120}{2 \times 6}$$
$$= 10$$

If you want to implement this function in C, it would probably be best to use a longer name than the single letter C used in mathematics. The one-character name might well cause confusion, if for no other reason than that the function and the language in which it is implemented would have the same name. As a general rule, function names used in this text tend to be longer and more expressive than variable names. Function calls often appear in parts of the program that are far removed from the point at which those functions are defined. Since the definition may be hard to locate in a large program, it is best to choose a function name that conveys enough information about the function so that the reader does not need to look up the definition. Local variables, on the other hand, are used only within the body of a single function, and it is therefore easier to keep track of what they mean. In the interest of having the name of the combinations function make sense immediately when anyone looks at it, we will use the name Combinations as the function name, rather than the letter C.

To implement the Combinations function using the definition based on factorials, you can take advantage of the fact that you already have an implementation of Factorial. Given Factorial, the implementation of Combinations is a straightforward translation of its mathematical definition:[3]

```
int Combinations(int n, int k)
{
    return (Factorial(n) / (Factorial(k) * Factorial(n - k)));
}
```

---

[3] The mathematical definition based on factorials does not lead to a particularly efficient implementation of the Combinations function, and you would almost certainly choose a different implementation strategy in practice. Nonetheless, this definition is easy to read and provides a useful opportunity to illustrate the mechanics of one function calling another.

You can then write a simple main program to test the `Combinations` function as follows:

```
main()
{
    int n, k;

    printf("Enter number of objects in the set (n)? ");
    n = GetInteger();
    printf("Enter number to be chosen (k)? ");
    k = GetInteger();
    printf("C(%d, %d) = %d\n", n, k, Combinations(n, k));
}
```

The complete program, `combine.c`, is shown in Figure 5-5.

FIGURE 5-5 combine.c

```
/*
 * File: combine.c
 * ---------------
 * This program tests a function to compute the mathematical
 * combination function Combinations(n, k), which gives the
 * number of ways to choose a subset of k objects from a set
 * of n distinct objects.
 */

#include <stdio.h>
#include "genlib.h"
#include "simpio.h"

/* Function prototypes */

int Combinations(int n, int k);
int Factorial(int n);

/* Main program */

main()
{
    int n, k;

    printf("Enter number of objects in the set (n)? ");
    n = GetInteger();
    printf("Enter number to be chosen (k)? ");
    k = GetInteger();
    printf("C(%d, %d) = %d\n", n, k, Combinations(n, k));
}
```

```
/*
 * Function: Combinations
 * Usage: ways = Combinations(n, k);
 * ------------------------------------
 * Implements the Combinations function, which returns the number
 * of distinct ways of choosing k objects from a set of n objects.
 * In mathematics, this function is often written as C(n,k), but a
 * function called C is not very self-descriptive, particularly in
 * a language which has precisely the same name.
 */

int Combinations(int n, int k)
{
    return (Factorial(n) / (Factorial(k) * Factorial(n - k)));
}

/*
 * Function: Factorial
 * Usage: f = Factorial(n);
 * ------------------------
 * Returns the factorial of the argument n, where factorial
 * is defined as the product of all integers from 1 up to n.
 */

int Factorial(int n)
{
    int product, i;

    product = 1;
    for (i = 1; i <= n; i++) {
        product *= i;
    }
    return (product);
}
```

The following output illustrates one possible sample run of the `combine.c` program:

```
Enter number of objects in the set (n)? 5↵
Enter number to be chosen (k)? 2↵
C(5, 2) = 10
```

What happens inside the computer when this program runs? Just as in the factorial example, a frame is created for the function `main`, which now declares two variables, n and k. After the user enters the two values and the program reaches the printf statement, the variables in the frame have the following values:

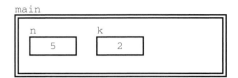

To execute the printf statement, the computer must evaluate the call to the Combinations function, which results in the creation of a new frame that overlays the previous one:

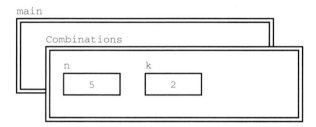

In this example, which has more function calls than the factorial example does, each new frame must record precisely what the program was doing before it made the call. Here, for example, the call to Combinations comes from the last line in main, as indicated by the tag M_1 in the program text that follows:

```
main()
{
     int n, k;

     printf("Enter number of objects in the set (n)? ");
     n = GetInteger();
     printf("Enter number to be chosen (k)? ");
     k = GetInteger();
     printf("C(%d, %d) = %d\n", n, k, Combinations(n, k));
}
```

M_1

When the computer executes a new function call, it keeps track of where execution should continue in the calling program once this call is completed. The point at which execution should continue is called the **return address,** which is represented in these diagrams using a circled tag. To help you remember where you are in the execution of the program, you need to record in the frame diagram the point from which the call was made, like this:

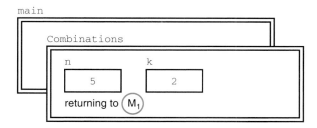

Once the new frame has been created, the program begins to execute the body of the `Combinations` function, which is reprinted with each call to `Factorial` noted with a tag as follows:

```
int Combinations(int n, int k)
{
    return (Factorial(n) / (Factorial(k) * Factorial(n - k)));
}
```

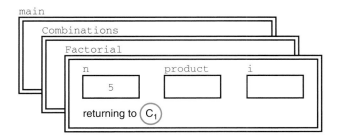

To execute this statement, the computer must make the three indicated calls to the function `Factorial`. According to the rules specified by ANSI C, the compiler may make these calls in any order. In this case, let us arbitrarily choose to evaluate them from left to right. The first call requests the computer to calculate `Factorial(n)` and results in the creation of the following frame:

The `Factorial` function runs through its operation just as it did before and returns the value 120 to the point in its caller indicated by the tag C_1. The frame for the `Factorial` function disappears, and you are left in the frame for `Combinations` ready to go on to the next phase of the computation. You can illustrate the current state of things by going back and filling in the returned value in place of the original call like this:

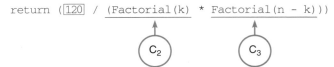

The box around 120 in the diagram indicates that the enclosed value is not part of the program but the result of some previous computation.

From this point, the computer goes on to evaluate the second call to `Factorial`, where the argument is `k`. Since `k` has the value 2, this call causes the following frame to be created:

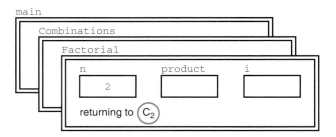

Once again, the `Factorial` function completes its operation without making further calls, and the function returns to point C_2 with the value of 2!, which is 2. Inserting this value into the expression that records the result so far shows the computation in the following state:

There is now only one more call to make, which begins by evaluating the argument expression `n - k`. Given the values of `n` and `k` in the `Combinations` frame, the argument expression has the value 3, which leads to the creation of another frame:

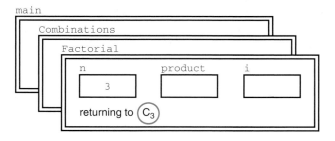

From this point, `Factorial` calculates the value of 3! and returns the value 6 to position C₃ in the caller, resulting in the following position:

```
return ( 120 / ( 2 * 6 ) );
```

The `Combinations` function now has all the values it needs to calculate the result, which is 10. To find out what to do with this result, you need to consult the `Combinations` frame, which is once again the top frame on the stack:

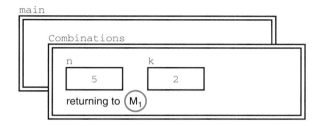

The frame indicates that the program should take the return value and substitute it in place of the call at M_1 in the function `main`. If you take 10 and substitute it for the call to `Combinations` in `printf` statement, you get the following state:

```
printf("C(%d, %d) = %d\n", n, k, 10 );
```

Given this result, `printf` can happily generate the output line

```
C(5, 2) = 10
```

which is the last operation in the program.

This exercise of going through all the internal details is intended to help you understand the function-calling mechanism in C. You might find it helpful to trace through your own programs once or twice at this level of detail, but you should not make a habit of it. Instead, you should learn to think about functions more informally and try to develop an intuitive sense of how they work. When a program calls a function, the function performs its operation and the program then continues from the point at which the call was made. If the function returns a result, the calling program is free to use that result in subsequent computation. As a programmer, you need to get to the point where you feel comfortable thinking about the process without worrying about the details. The computer, after all, is taking care of them for you.

5.5 Procedures

So far, the functions presented in this chapter have all returned some kind of value to their caller. In programming, it is quite common to call a function not for the result it returns but rather for the effect it produces. For example, when you call the printf function in a statement such as

```
printf("Hello, world.\n");
```

you are not trying to get printf to come back with some value. What you care about is displaying the message on the screen.

A function that does not return a value and is instead executed for its effect is called a **procedure.** Many programming languages, including Pascal and Fortran, provide completely separate mechanisms for defining functions and procedures. In those languages, functions and procedures are distinct conceptual entities. In C, these two concepts are merged, and most books about C use the term *function* to refer to both procedures and functions. For the most part, I follow that convention in this book. But it is important to recognize that some functions will return no result. Thus, when it is important to emphasize that a particular function has no result, I will sometimes use the word *procedure.*

In C, a procedure is identified by using the keyword void in the function prototype in place of the result type. For example, the prototype

```
void GiveInstructions(void);
```

declares a function that takes no arguments and returns no result. As with any function, the prototype appears near the beginning of the program; the implementation of GiveInstructions appears separately later in the program. A generic implementation of such a procedure might be

```
void GiveInstructions(void)
{
    printf("This program performs some important calculation\n");
    printf("for the user.  This function, or one very much\n");
    printf("like it, can be used to give the user whatever\n");
    printf("instructions are required to use the program,\n");
    printf("such as the format for input data and the like.\n");
}
```

As is true with most procedures, GiveInstructions does not include a return statement but instead simply "falls off the end," which C interprets as indicating that the execution of the procedure is complete. Procedures can, however, use a return statement to force an immediate return from the procedure. When return is used within a procedure, no expression may follow the word return.

Once the GiveInstructions procedure is defined, all the main program has to do in order to display the instructions on the screen is call that procedure. Thus the main program would presumably begin as follows:

```
main()
{
    GiveInstructions();
    rest of main program
}
```

By making these `printf` statements into a separate procedure, you can improve the structure of the program and make it easier to read. When someone is reading through the main program, the single line

```
GiveInstructions();
```

tells the reader everything that is likely to be important. A reader interested in what happens in the rest of the program can easily read past this line, since it is not necessary to read through an entire series of `printf` calls. On the other hand, anyone interested in the details of the instructions can find the implementation of the `GiveInstructions` procedure and focus on that part of the program.

 ## 5.6 Stepwise refinement

As suggested by the `GiveInstructions` example in the preceding section, procedures and functions enable you to divide a large programming problem into smaller pieces that are individually easy to understand. The process of dividing up a problem into manageable pieces is called **decomposition** and represents a fundamental programming strategy. Finding the right decomposition, however, turns out to be a difficult task that requires considerable practice. If you choose the individual pieces well, each one will have conceptual integrity as a unit and make the program as a whole much simpler to understand. If you choose poorly, however, the decomposition can end up getting in the way. Although this chapter and several of those that follow present some useful guidelines, there are no hard-and-fast rules for selecting a particular decomposition; you will learn how to apply this process through experience.

When you are faced with the task of writing a program, the best strategy is usually to start with the main program. From the perspective of the main program, you think about the problem as a whole and then try to identify the major pieces of the entire task. Once you figure out what the big pieces of the program are, you can then subdivide the entire problem into individual components along these lines. Since some of these components might themselves be complicated, it is often appropriate to break them down into still smaller pieces. You can then continue this process until every piece of the problem is simple enough to be solved on its own. This process is called **top-down design,** or **stepwise refinement.**

To illustrate this process, the rest of this chapter is devoted to developing a program to generate a calendar display. The calendar runs through an entire year, displaying each month in a format that looks like this:

```
        February 1992
    Su  Mo  Tu  We  Th  Fr  Sa
                             1
     2   3   4   5   6   7   8
     9  10  11  12  13  14  15
    16  17  18  19  20  21  22
    23  24  25  26  27  28  29
```

The implementation has to be clever enough to know, for example, that February 1 fell on a Saturday in 1992 and that February has 29 days in a leap year. Moreover, the program must be able to display the data in a form in which everything lines up correctly on the screen. There is quite a lot to do.

This program is many times longer and considerably more complicated than any program or function you have seen so far in this text. If, however, you break the program into pieces so that no individual piece is either long or complicated, the program as a whole becomes manageable.

Starting at the top

Start by thinking about the main program. What does it have to do? At a very general level, the calendar program must read in a year from the user and then display a calendar for that year. It might also be good to provide the user with some instructions, particularly if the program ends up having special cases or restrictions of which the user should be aware. The principle of stepwise refinement indicates that once you have the general description for a program, you should stop there and write it down, using calls to procedures and functions to take care of those parts of the program that have yet to be written. If you adopt this approach, the main program might look like this:

```
main()
{
    int year;

    GiveInstructions();
    year = GetYearFromUser();
    PrintCalendar(year);
}
```

The first statement is a call to a GiveInstructions procedure, which will turn out to be quite similar in its implementation to the GiveInstructions procedure that appeared in the section on "Procedures" earlier in this chapter. The second statement is a call to a function GetYearFromUser, which you will use to handle the process of reading in a year. The implementation of GetYearFromUser might be as simple as displaying a prompt and calling GetInteger, but you might want to include other operations as well, such as checking to see if the user has entered a valid year. The last line of the main program calls the function PrintCalendar, passing it the desired year as an argument. Implementing this last function will involve most of the work required to solve the entire problem, but the problem is now slightly simpler because the main program has taken care of all the user interaction.

At the level of detail shown in the implementation of main, the program makes complete sense. As long as GiveInstructions, GetYearFromUser, and PrintCalendar do their jobs, the program will work just fine. Of course, you haven't yet written implementations for any of those functions, so it might seem premature to depend on them. Doing so, however, is the key to successful decomposition. As you go along, you invent new procedures and functions that solve useful pieces of the task and then implement each level in the solution hierarchy in terms of those pieces.

Implementing `PrintCalendar`

After writing the main program, you are left with three functions to write. Although you could choose to start with any of them, let's go right to the heart of the problem and implement `PrintCalendar`. Judging from the call in the main program, the prototype for `PrintCalendar` is

```
void PrintCalendar(int year);
```

What does its implementation look like?

Consider the `PrintCalendar` function at the abstract level and think about what it does. It displays a complete calendar by printing out 12 individual monthly calendars. This insight is sufficient to write an implementation of the function that is appropriate to this level of the decomposition. The body of `PrintCalendar` is simply a loop that calls another function to display each individual month and then prints a newline character so that each month is separated from the next one by a blank line:

```
void PrintCalendar(int year)
{
    int month;

    for (month = 1; month <= 12; month++) {
        PrintCalendarMonth(month, year);
        printf("\n");
    }
}
```

The `PrintCalendarMonth` function takes two arguments—the month and the year—since it requires both pieces of information. The argument `month` is required so that the function knows which month to display; `year` is required because the calendar for a particular month varies from year to year.

Implementing `PrintCalendarMonth`

Implementing `PrintCalendarMonth` is a little more difficult. The problem is to display a single month in a format that looks like this:

```
     February 1992
    Su Mo Tu We Th Fr Sa
                       1
     2  3  4  5  6  7  8
     9 10 11 12 13 14 15
    16 17 18 19 20 21 22
    23 24 25 26 27 28 29
```

The first two lines of output are reasonably easy to handle. The only part that might seem hard is taking the numeric value `month` and translating it into its conventional name. This operation, however, turns out to be very easy for a reason that is well worth noting: you already have seen a function that performs precisely this operation. The function MonthName presented in the section on "Functions that return nonnumeric values" earlier in this chapter is just what you need. Given MonthName, you can display the two header lines of the calendar using the statements:

```
printf("    %s %d\n", MonthName(month), year);
printf(" Su Mo Tu We Th Fr Sa\n");
```

Now comes the interesting part. The rest of the monthly calendar consists of the integers between 1 and the number of days in the month. A for loop can handle this aspect of the task. The catch is that the formatting is tricky. For one thing, the month has to start on the correct day of the week. For another, after each Saturday, the output has to continue at the beginning of the next line.

To solve the formatting problems, you will need to keep track of both the day of the week and the day of the month. How should the days of the week be represented? One approach is simply to number them. The most convenient numbering scheme, given the calendar layout, is to define Sunday to be 0, Monday to be 1, and so forth, up to Saturday, which is numbered 6. So that you could refer to the names of these days in the program, you might choose to define them as constants, as follows:

```
#define  Sunday     0
#define  Monday     1
#define  Tuesday    2
#define  Wednesday  3
#define  Thursday   4
#define  Friday     5
#define  Saturday   6
```

There is an advantage to starting the weekday numbering with 0: doing so means that you can implement the operation of cycling past the end of one week by using the remainder operator. If the variable weekday contains the integer corresponding to the current day of the week, the expression

```
(weekday + k) % 7
```

indicates the day of the week that occurs k days later on. For example, if today is a Friday (when weekday has the value 5), 10 days from today is a Monday, because the expression

```
(5 + 10) % 7
```

comes out to be 1. In particular, you can apply this formula to write the following statement, which corresponds to the idea of moving ahead to the next weekday:

```
weekday = (weekday + 1) % 7;
```

The more familiar expression

```
weekday++;
```
                                        The ++ operator will count past 6

is not appropriate here because weekday would eventually become 7, 8, 9, and so forth, which do not correspond to weekdays. By dividing by 7 and taking the remainder, you can ensure that the result is always between 0 and 6. When you use the remainder operation to confine the result of a calculation to a small cyclical range by taking a remainder, you are using a process that mathematicians call **modular arithmetic.** Modular arithmetic is extremely useful in programming; you will see several additional examples of its use throughout the text.

If you keep track of the weekday, writing the main loop inside the PrintCalendarMonth function is not difficult. The following code does the job:

```
for (day = 1; day <= nDays; day++) {
    printf(" %2d", day);
    if (weekday == Saturday) printf("\n");
    weekday = (weekday + 1) % 7;
}
```

This loop displays each number, keeps track of the weekday, and puts in the newline after each Saturday. The last line of the calendar must end with a newline, so the loop should be followed by the following statement:

```
if (weekday != Sunday) printf("\n");
```

which ensures that a newline character follows the last line even if that week did not complete the cycle back to Sunday.

At this point, only three tasks remain:

1. Figuring out the number of days in the month
2. Determining on what day of the week the beginning of the month falls
3. Indenting the first line of the calendar so that the first day appears in the correct position

The strategy of stepwise refinement suggests that you should not try to solve these problems at this level of the decomposition. Instead, you can turn these three operations into calls to functions that you implement later. Applying this strategy enables you to write a complete implementation of PrintCalendarMonth:

```
void PrintCalendarMonth(int month, int year)
{
    int weekday, nDays, day;

    printf("    %s %d\n", MonthName(month), year);
    printf(" Su Mo Tu We Th Fr Sa\n");
    nDays = MonthDays(month, year);
    weekday = FirstDayOfMonth(month, year);
    IndentFirstLine(weekday);
    for (day = 1; day <= nDays; day++) {
        printf(" %2d", day);
        if (weekday == Saturday) printf("\n");
        weekday = (weekday + 1) % 7;
    }
    if (weekday != Sunday) printf("\n");
}
```

Using stepwise refinement to implement `PrintCalendarMonth` means that writing the implementations for three of the functions used within it—`MonthDays`, `FirstDayOfMonth`, and `IndentFirstLine`—was deferred until later. When you go back to fill in these missing pieces, you can implement the functions in any order, but you must complete them all before you can execute the program.

The easiest function to implement is the last one in the list: `IndentFirstLine`. This function is intended to take the day of the week supplied by `FirstDayOfMonth` and make sure that the first line of the calendar starts with enough blank spaces so that the first day appears at the correct position. If the month begins on a Sunday, the calendar should start immediately at the beginning of the first line. If it begins on a Monday, the program needs to print out one day's worth of spaces to account for the missing Sunday. Because each calendar entry takes up three spaces, the implementation of `IndentFirstLine` is simply a loop that prints out three spaces for every missing day, counting from the beginning of the week. The following implementation accomplishes the task:

```
void IndentFirstLine(int weekday)
{
    int i;

    for (i = 0; i < weekday; i++) {
        printf("   ");
    }
}
```

Of the two remaining functions, `MonthDays` is considerably simpler and requires nothing more than implementing the following rhyme:

> Thirty days hath September,
> April, June, and November,
> All the rest have thirty-one,
> Except February alone,
> Which has twenty-eight, in fine,
> And each leap year, twenty-nine.

The verse lists several independent cases, which suggest the use of a `switch` statement. The complete implementation of the function follows:

```
int MonthDays(int month, int year)
{
    switch (month) {
      case 2:
        if (IsLeapYear(year)) return (29);
        return (28);
      case 4: case 6: case 9: case 11:
        return (30);
      default:
        return (31);
    }
}
```

You already have an implementation of IsLeapYear from the section on "Predicate functions" earlier in this chapter, and you should simply use it. It is almost always better to use existing code than to rewrite it from scratch.

The FirstDayOfMonth function could be hard to implement, but only if you try to be too clever. A simple, workable strategy is to pick some day in history and count forward from there. Computers are, after all, quite fast; the user won't notice any delay. For example, January 1, 1900, fell on a Monday. For every year since then, you need to add 365 or 366 days, depending on whether the year was a leap year. For each month of the current year preceding the one in question, you need to add the number of days in that month. By performing these calculations using modular arithmetic and taking the remainder after dividing by 7, the program can compute the weekday for the beginning of any month since 1900 using the following implementation:

```
int FirstDayOfMonth(int month, int year)
{
    int weekday, i;

    weekday = Monday;
    for (i = 1900; i < year; i++) {
        weekday = (weekday + 365) % 7;
        if (IsLeapYear(i)) weekday = (weekday + 1) % 7;
    }
    for (i = 1; i < month; i++) {
        weekday = (weekday + MonthDays(i, year)) % 7;
    }
    return (weekday);
}
```

Completing the final pieces

Finishing the program is just a matter of filling in some of the details. For example, you need to implement the functions GiveInstructions and GetYearFromUser. Because the definition of FirstDayOfMonth requires that the year not be earlier than 1900, it would be good for these functions to mention that restriction and to enforce it. For example, the following implementation of GetYearFromUser checks to see if the year meets that condition; if not, the user is given a chance to retry.

```
int GetYearFromUser(void)
{
    int year;

    while (TRUE) {
        printf("Which year? ");
        year = GetInteger();
        if (year >= 1900) return (year);
        printf("The year must be at least 1900.\n");
    }
}
```

The rest of the process consists of copying the implementations of IsLeapYear and MonthName from earlier in the chapter, making sure all the function prototypes are included, writing comments, and, finally, compiling and testing the program. The complete implementation is shown in Figure 5-6.

FIGURE 5-6   calendar.c

```
/*
 * File: calendar.c
 * -----------------
 * This program is used to generate a calendar for a year
 * entered by the user.
 */

#include <stdio.h>
#include "genlib.h"
#include "simpio.h"

/*
 * Constants:
 * ----------
 * Days of the week are represented by the integers 0-6.
 * Months of the year are identified by the integers 1-12;
 * because this numeric representation for months is in
 * common use, no special constants are defined.
 */

#define Sunday     0
#define Monday     1
#define Tuesday    2
#define Wednesday  3
#define Thursday   4
#define Friday     5
#define Saturday   6

/* Function prototypes */

void GiveInstructions(void);
int GetYearFromUser(void);
void PrintCalendar(int year);
void PrintCalendarMonth(int month, int year);
void IndentFirstLine(int weekday);
int MonthDays(int month, int year);
int FirstDayOfMonth(int month, int year);
string MonthName(int month);
bool IsLeapYear(int year);
```

```
/* Main program */

main()
{
    int year;

    GiveInstructions();
    year = GetYearFromUser();
    PrintCalendar(year);
}

/*
 * Function: GiveInstructions
 * Usage: GiveInstructions();
 * --------------------------
 * This procedure prints out instructions to the user.
 */

void GiveInstructions(void)
{
    printf("This program displays a calendar for a full\n");
    printf("year.  The year must not be before 1900.\n");
}

/*
 * Function: GetYearFromUser
 * Usage: year = GetYearFromUser();
 * --------------------------------
 * This function reads in a year from the user and returns
 * that value.  If the user enters a year before 1900, the
 * function gives the user another chance.
 */

int GetYearFromUser(void)
{
    int year;

    while (TRUE) {
        printf("Which year? ");
        year = GetInteger();
        if (year >= 1900) return (year);
        printf("The year must be at least 1900.\n");
    }
}
```

```
/*
 * Function: PrintCalendar
 * Usage: PrintCalendar(year);
 * --------------------------
 * This procedure prints a calendar for an entire year.
 */

void PrintCalendar(int year)
{
    int month;

    for (month = 1; month <= 12; month++) {
        PrintCalendarMonth(month, year);
        printf("\n");
    }
}

/*
 * Function: PrintCalendarMonth
 * Usage: PrintCalendarMonth(month, year);
 * ---------------------------------------
 * This procedure prints a calendar for the given month
 * and year.
 */

void PrintCalendarMonth(int month, int year)
{
    int weekday, nDays, day;

    printf("    %s %d\n", MonthName(month), year);
    printf(" Su Mo Tu We Th Fr Sa\n");
    nDays = MonthDays(month, year);
    weekday = FirstDayOfMonth(month, year);
    IndentFirstLine(weekday);
    for (day = 1; day <= nDays; day++) {
        printf(" %2d", day);
        if (weekday == Saturday) printf("\n");
        weekday = (weekday + 1) % 7;
    }
    if (weekday != Sunday) printf("\n");
}

/*
 * Function: IndentFirstLine
 * Usage: IndentFirstLine(weekday);
 * --------------------------------
 * This procedure indents the first line of the calendar
 * by printing enough blank spaces to get to the position
 * on the line corresponding to weekday.
 */
```

```
void IndentFirstLine(int weekday)
{
    int i;

    for (i = 0; i < weekday; i++) {
        printf("   ");
    }
}

/*
 * Function: MonthDays
 * Usage: ndays = MonthDays(month, year);
 * -------------------------------------
 * MonthDays returns the number of days in the indicated
 * month and year.  The year is required to handle leap years.
 */

int MonthDays(int month, int year)
{
    switch (month) {
      case 2:
        if (IsLeapYear(year)) return (29);
        return (28);
      case 4: case 6: case 9: case 11:
        return (30);
      default:
        return (31);
    }
}

/*
 * Function: FirstDayOfMonth
 * Usage: weekday = FirstDayOfMonth(month, year);
 * ----------------------------------------------
 * This function returns the day of the week on which the
 * indicated month begins.  This program simply counts
 * forward from January 1, 1900, which was a Monday.
 */

int FirstDayOfMonth(int month, int year)
{
    int weekday, i;

    weekday = Monday;
    for (i = 1900; i < year; i++) {
        weekday = (weekday + 365) % 7;
        if (IsLeapYear(i)) weekday = (weekday + 1) % 7;
    }
    for (i = 1; i < month; i++) {
        weekday = (weekday + MonthDays(i, year)) % 7;
    }
    return (weekday);
}
```

```
/*
 * Function: MonthName
 * Usage: name = MonthName(month);
 * --------------------------------
 * MonthName converts a numeric month in the range 1-12
 * into the string name for that month.
 */

string MonthName(int month)
{
    switch (month) {
        case  1: return ("January");
        case  2: return ("February");
        case  3: return ("March");
        case  4: return ("April");
        case  5: return ("May");
        case  6: return ("June");
        case  7: return ("July");
        case  8: return ("August");
        case  9: return ("September");
        case 10: return ("October");
        case 11: return ("November");
        case 12: return ("December");
        default: return ("Illegal month");
    }
}

/*
 * Function: IsLeapYear
 * Usage: if (IsLeapYear(year)) . . .
 * ----------------------------------
 * This function returns TRUE if year is a leap year.
 */

bool IsLeapYear(int year)
{
    return ( ((year % 4 == 0) && (year % 100 != 0))
            || (year % 400 == 0) );
}
```

Summary

In this chapter, you learned about *functions,* which enable you to refer to an entire set of operations by using a simple name. By allowing the programmer to ignore the internal details and concentrate only on the effect of a function as a whole, functions provide a critical tool for reducing the conceptual complexity of programs.

This chapter also provided you with an essential programming technique—the strategy of *stepwise refinement.* By starting with a general outline of the program and successively refining each piece of the outline by dividing it into successively simpler steps, you can solve a complex problem by writing a collection of functions that are individually quite simple.

The important points introduced in this chapter include:

- A *function* consists of a set of program statements that have been collected together and given a name. Other parts of the program can then *call* that function, possibly passing it information in the form of *arguments* and receiving a result *returned* by that function.
- Every function must be declared before it is used. A function declaration is called a *prototype.*
- In addition to the prototype, functions have an *implementation,* which specifies the individual steps that function contains.
- A function that returns a value must have a `return` statement that specifies the result. Functions may return values of any type.
- Functions that return Boolean values are called *predicate functions* and play an important role in programming.
- The `strlib` library includes the predicate function `StringEqual`, which compares two strings for equality.
- Within the body of a function, the variables that act as placeholders for the argument values are called *formal parameters.*
- Variables declared with a function are *local* to that function and cannot be used outside of it. Internally, all the variables declared within a function, including the parameters, are stored together in a *stack frame.*
- When a function returns, it continues from precisely the point at which the call was made. The computer refers to this point as the *return address* and keeps track of it in the stack frame.
- A function that returns no result and is executed only for its effect is called a *procedure.*
- To apply *stepwise refinement,* you begin coding at the level of the main program. You decompose the main program into separate functions that implement some piece of the total solution. Once the main program is complete, you apply the same strategy to each of the functions it calls, continuing the process until you have implemented every function.

REVIEW QUESTIONS

1. Explain in your own words the difference between a function and a program.

2. Define the following terms as they apply to functions: *call, argument, return.*

3. What is the difference between passing information to a function by using arguments and reading input data using functions like `GetInteger`? When would each action be appropriate?

4. What is the prototype of the function `sqrt` in the `math` library?

5. The `math` library contains a function with the following prototype:

    ```
    double atan2(double, double);
    ```

    Even if you have no idea what this function does, what information does the prototype give you about using this function?

6. What is the purpose of including names along with the argument types in function prototypes?

7. When writing a prototype, how do you indicate that a function takes no arguments?

8. How do you specify the result of a function in C?

9. Can there be more than one `return` statement in the body of a function?

10. Why was it unnecessary to include a `break` statement at the end of each `case` clause in the `MonthName` function shown in Figure 5-3?

11. What is a predicate function?

12. What function would you use to determine whether two strings were equal? In what library is that function defined?

13. What is the relationship between arguments and formal parameters?

14. Variables declared within a function are said to be local variables. What is the significance of the word *local* in this context?

15. What does the term *return address* mean?

16. What is a procedure?

17. In your own words, describe the strategy of stepwise refinement.

PROGRAMMING EXERCISES

1. Write a program that displays the value of the mathematical constant

$$\phi = \frac{1 + \sqrt{5}}{2}$$

   This constant ϕ is called the *golden ratio*. Classical mathematicians believed that this number represented the most aesthetically pleasing ratio for the dimensions of a rectangle, but it also turns up in computational mathematics.

2. In high-school algebra, you learned that the standard quadratic equation

$$ax^2 + bx + c = 0$$

has two solutions given by the formula

$$x = \frac{-b \pm \sqrt{b^2 - 4ac}}{2a}$$

The first solution is obtained by using + in place of ±; the second is obtained by using – in place of ±.

Write a C program that accepts values for a, b, and c, and then calculates the two solutions. If the quantity under the square root sign is negative, the equation has no real solutions, and your program should display a message to that effect. You may assume that the value for a is nonzero. Your program should be able to duplicate the following sample run:

```
Enter coefficients for the quadratic equation:
a: 1↵
b: -5↵
c: 6↵
The first solution is 3
The second solution is 2
```

3. Modify the c2ftable.c program shown in Figure 5-1 so it displays a conversion table that translates temperatures in the opposite direction: from Fahrenheit to Celsius. Your program should be divided into a main program and a conversion function, just as the c2ftable.c program is. The main program should generate a table of Celsius equivalents, shown with one digit after the decimal point, for each Fahrenheit temperature between 32 and 100, counting in steps of two degrees. Thus your table should have the basic format shown in the condensed sample run that follows:

```
Fahrenheit to Celsius table.
   F      C
  32     0.0
  34     1.1
       . . .
  98    36.7
 100    37.8
```

4. The Fibonacci sequence, in which each new term is the sum of the preceding two, was introduced in Chapter 4, exercise 8. Rewrite the program requested in that exercise, changing the implementation so that your main program calls a

function `Fib(n)` to calculate the nth Fibonacci number. In terms of the number of mathematical calculations required, is your new implementation more or less efficient that the one you used in Chapter 4?

5. Write a function `RaiseIntToPower` that takes two integers, n and k, and returns n^k. Use your function to display a table of values of 2^k for all values of k from 0 to 10.

6. Write a function `RaiseRealToPower` that takes a floating-point value x and an integer k and returns x^k. Implement your function so that it can correctly calculate the result when k is negative, using the relationship

$$x^{-k} = \frac{1}{x^k}$$

Use your function to display a table of values of 10^k for all values of k from –4 to 4, as shown in this sample run:

```
                   k
    k            10
  --------------------
   -4           0.0001
   -3           0.001
   -2           0.01
   -1           0.1
    0           1.0
    1          10.0
    2         100.0
    3        1000.0
    4       10000.0
```

Note: There is no single `printf` format code that will correctly display each of the output lines in this table. To write a main program that produces precisely this output, you need to use a different format specification when the value of k is negative.

7. Write a function `NDigits(n)` that returns the number of digits in the integer n, which you may assume is positive. Design a main program to test your function. For hints about how to write this program, you might want to look back at the `digitsum.c` program that was given in Figure 4-5.

8. When a floating-point number is converted to an integer in C, the floating-point value is truncated by throwing away any fraction. Thus, when 4.99999 is converted to an integer, the result is 4. In many cases, it would be useful to have the option of *rounding* a floating-point value to the nearest integer. For a positive floating-point number x, the rounding operation can be achieved by adding 0.5 to x and then truncating the result to an integer. If the decimal fraction of x is less than .5, the truncated value will be the integer less than x; if the fraction is .5 or more, the truncated value will be the next larger integer. Because truncation always moves toward zero, negative numbers must be rounded by subtracting 0.5 and truncating, instead of adding 0.5.

Write a function `Round(x)` that rounds a floating-point number `x` to the nearest integer. Demonstrate that your function works by designing a suitable main program to test it.

9. Write a predicate function `IsPerfectSquare(n)` that returns `TRUE` if the integer `n` is a perfect square. Remember that the function `sqrt` returns a floating-point result, which is therefore only an approximation of the actual square root.

10. Write a predicate function `ApproximatelyEqual(x, y)` that returns `TRUE` if the two floating-point numbers `x` and `y` are approximately equal in the sense that the absolute value of the difference between the two numbers divided by the smaller of their absolute values is less than some constant ε. In mathematical terms, the property you are seeking to verify is

$$\frac{|x-y|}{\min(|x|,|y|)} < \varepsilon$$

In the program, you should use the line

```
#define Epsilon 0.000001
```

to define the constant ε. Using `#define` makes it easy to change the desired accuracy. You may also use the function `fabs` in the `math` library to take the absolute value of a floating-point value.

The `ApproximatelyEqual` function is useful in avoiding precision problems that arise when comparing floating-point numbers for equality. To illustrate this principle, use `ApproximatelyEqual` to construct a correct test condition for the `for` loop

```
for (x = 1.0; x <= 2.0; x += 0.1) {
    printf("%.1f\n", x);
}
```

so that the loop correctly displays the values 1.0, 1.1, 1.2, and so on, up to and including 2.0. As noted in the section on "Using `for` with floating-point data" in Chapter 4, this loop will not include the value 2.0 on some machines because of limitations in floating-point accuracy.

11. In the section entitled "A predicate function to test for string equality," the following loop was used to give the user the opportunity to play another game (the game itself was unspecified):

```
while (TRUE) {
    PlayOneGame();
    printf("Would you like to play again? ");
    answer = GetLine();
    if (StringEqual(answer, "no")) break;
}
```

The major problem with this approach is that the loop exits only if the user enters the answer no; the program interprets any other response, such as NO or Absolutely not, as positive, and plays another game. From the perspective of program design, it would be much better to compare the user's response against both yes and no. If the user gives either of these responses, the program would act accordingly. If the user gives any other response, the program could ask the question again.

Write a predicate function GetYesNoResponse that takes a prompt string as its argument and displays that prompt as a question to the user. If the user responds with the word yes, GetYesNoResponse should return TRUE. If the user responds with no, GetYesNoResponse should return FALSE. If the user gives any other response, the function should display a message informing the user of the legal responses and then ask the question again.

Given the GetYesNoResponse function, you could then change the game-playing loop to

```
while (TRUE) {
    PlayOneGame();
    if (!GetYesOrNo("Would you like to play again? ")) break;
}
```

which might then generate the following sample run:

```
. . . play the game . . .
Would you like to play again? yes↵
. . . play the game . . .
Would you like to play again? maybe↵
Please answer yes or no.
Would you like to play again? yes↵
. . . play the game . . .
Would you like to play again? no↵
```

12. The values of the Combinations function used in the text are often displayed in the form of a triangle using the following arrangement:

$$C(0,0)$$

$$C(1,0) \quad C(1,1)$$

$$C(2,0) \quad C(2,1) \quad C(2,2)$$

$$C(3,0) \quad C(3,1) \quad C(3,2) \quad C(3,3)$$

$$C(4,0) \quad C(4,1) \quad C(4,2) \quad C(4,3) \quad C(4,4)$$

and so on. This figure is called Pascal's Triangle after the seventeenth-century French mathematician Blaise Pascal, who invented it. Pascal's Triangle has the interesting property that every interior entry is the sum of the two entries above it.

Write a C program to display the first eight rows of Pascal's Triangle like this:

```
                    1
                 1     1
              1     2     1
           1     3     3     1
        1     4     6     4     1
     1     5    10    10     5     1
  1     6    15    20    15     6     1
1     7    21    35    35    21     7     1
```

13. Modify the calendar program from Figure 5-6 so that the year can be entered using only two digits, in which case the year is assumed to be in the twentieth century. Thus, if the user entered 94, the program would generate a calendar for 1994.

14. The restriction in the calendar program that limits its use to years since 1900 could be something of an annoyance. To fix this problem, change the implementation of the `FirstDayOfMonth` function so that for years prior to 1900, it counts backward to find the appropriate day of the week. What other parts of the program must you change after you remove this restriction?

## CHAPTER 6

Algorithms

People like definite decisions,
Tidy answers, all the little ravellings
Snipped off, the lint removed. . . .

— Gwendolyn Brooks, *Annie Allen*, 1949

Objectives

- To acquire a better sense of the process of algorithm development by investigating several algorithms from classical mathematics.

- To recognize that most problems can be solved using any of several different algorithms.

- To understand the considerations involved in choosing between alternative algorithms.

- To gain a sense of how to establish that an algorithm is correct.

- To understand and be able to apply the concept of a brute-force algorithm.

- To be able to write programs that use the technique of successive approximation.

- To learn how to use the `Error` function to report error conditions to the user.

- To be able to write programs that perform series expansions.

Functions are important to programming in part because they provide a basis for the implementation of algorithms. The algorithm itself is the abstract strategy and is often expressed in English. The function is the concrete realization of that algorithm in the context of a programming language. When you want to implement an algorithm as part of a program, you will usually write a function—which may in turn call other functions to handle part of its work—to carry out that algorithm.

You have seen several simple algorithms implemented in the context of the sample programs, but you have not had a chance to focus on the nature of the algorithmic process itself. Most of the programming problems you have seen so far are simple enough that the appropriate solution technique springs immediately to mind. As problems become more complex, however, the solution strategies require more thought, and you will need to consider more than one strategy before writing the final program.

This chapter illustrates how algorithmic strategies take shape by solving several problems from classical mathematics, each of which can be approached in a variety of ways. By looking at more than one solution to each problem, you can get a sense of how to compare different strategies and choose among them.

6.1 Testing for primality

The first mathematicians in Western recorded history were temple priests in Egypt nearly 4000 years ago. From that time, mathematics continued to develop and reached a golden age in ancient Greece, which produced such mathematicians as Euclid, Pythagoras, Thales, Archimedes, and Hypatia. Greek mathematicians were fascinated with many different areas of mathematics but seemed to have a particular fondness for studying the properties of the nonnegative integers—a field of mathematics now known as **number theory.**

A central problem in number theory—both for Greek mathematicians and for their counterparts today—is the problem of determining whether a given number is *prime.* A positive integer n is **prime** if it has exactly two positive divisors, which are always itself and 1. For example, 23 is prime because there are no numbers except 1 and 23 that divide it evenly. The number 35, on the other hand, is not prime because, in addition to the factors 1 and 35, it can also be divided evenly by 7 and 5. It is important to notice that, according to this definition, the integer 1 is *not* prime, because it has only one divisor.

Prime numbers are important today because they play a central role in many forms of **cryptography,** the study of codes. In the world of modern electronic communications, computers are often used to perform encoding and decoding operations. Several of the best coding techniques available are based on prime numbers. The details of encryption are beyond the scope of this text, but it is interesting to know that prime numbers do have practical applications.

As a programmer, how could you design a function to determine whether an integer n is prime? If you work directly from the definition, the most obvious approach would be to count the number of divisors and see if there are exactly two. Common sense indicates that any divisors of n must be less than or equal to n, so if you check all the numbers between 1 and n, you will find all the possible divisors.

This observation suggests that you can determine whether n is prime by following these steps:

1. Check each number between 1 and *n* to see whether it divides evenly into *n*.
2. Add 1 to a running count each time you encounter a new divisor.
3. Check to see whether the divisor count is 2 after all numbers have been tested.

A simple version of IsPrime

You can use this strategy as the basis for the implementation of a function, IsPrime, that tests whether a number is prime, as shown in Figure 6-1. As the prototype for the function indicates, IsPrime takes an integer n and returns a Boolean value, making it a predicate function. The implementation uses the variable divisors to keep track of the number of divisors found so far. At the beginning of the program, divisors is set to 0 and is incremented every time a new divisor is found. The number n is prime if the count of the divisors is exactly two after all numbers between 1 and n have been tested. The test is written using the Boolean expression divisors == 2, and the function simply returns that value as its result.

Verifying that a strategy represents an algorithm

The strategy used in this implementation of IsPrime is not particularly clever or efficient, but it does have one highly desirable property. It works. The IsPrime function represents an algorithm for determining whether a number is prime. To demonstrate that IsPrime is indeed an algorithm, it helps to recall the requirements imposed on algorithms, as they were presented in Chapter 1. An algorithm must be:

1. *Clear and unambiguous* in its definition.
2. *Effective,* in the sense that its steps are executable.
3. *Finite,* in the sense that it terminates after a bounded number of steps.

Does the IsPrime function meet each of these conditions?

FIGURE 6-1   Simple implementation of IsPrime

```
bool IsPrime(int n)
{
    int divisors, i;

    divisors = 0;
    for (i = 1; i <= n; i++) {
        if (n % i == 0) divisors++;
    }
    return (divisors == 2);
}
```

First, is the definition of `IsPrime` clear and unambiguous? For algorithms expressed in English, this condition is often difficult to meet. Like all other human languages, English can be fuzzy. When you try to express an algorithm in English, you are likely to leave out a step or gloss over some critical detail. When you express an algorithm in a programming language, however, the language definition specifies a precise interpretation. Although a human reader might misunderstand some aspect of the program, a correctly functioning compiler will interpret the statements in exactly one way. The assignment of meaning to the syntactic forms in a programming language is called the **semantics** of the language. Because the semantics of programming languages are much more rigid than the semantics of human languages, it is easier to meet the first condition when the algorithm is presented in program form.

Second, are the steps in `IsPrime` effective in the sense that it is possible to carry them out? Once again, the fact that the algorithm has been presented in the form of a program helps to meet this criterion. The semantics of the C programming language assign meaning to each of the constructs in the program, and the compiler generates the necessary instructions for the machine to execute.

Third, does `IsPrime` terminate after a finite amount of time? You can answer this question by looking at the program structure. The only long-running component of the function is the `for` loop. From the control line, you know that the loop will go through exactly n cycles each time the function `IsPrime` is called. If n is very large, the function may take a long time, but it must return eventually.

Because it meets each of the three required conditions, the function `IsPrime` given in Figure 6-1 is indeed an algorithm.

Demonstrating the correctness of the `IsPrime` algorithm

In addition to establishing that the implementation is an algorithm, it is also important to determine whether that algorithm is correct. Does it give the right answer for every possible value of n? Proving that an algorithm is correct is very hard to do in any formal way, and most of the techniques for generating such proofs lie well beyond the scope of this text. Even so, it is possible to outline the general direction of such a proof in the case of the `IsPrime` implementation.

Think about the meaning assigned to the variable `divisors` in the program. In each cycle of the `for` loop, `divisors` records the number of divisors encountered up to that point. Before the `for` loop begins, no divisors have been found, and it is therefore appropriate to initialize `divisors` to 0. In each cycle of the loop, the program adds 1 to `divisors` each time it finds a new divisor. Thus, at the end of ith loop cycle, `divisors` holds the number of divisors between 1 and i. Since this property is true for every value of i, it must be true that at the end of the nth cycle, the variable `divisors` contains the number of divisors between 1 and n. If the number of divisors is 2, then n must be prime.

A property that is true at the initial entry to a loop and that continues to be true at the end of each loop cycle is called a **loop invariant.** For certain simple programs, you can most easily establish the correctness of the program by demonstrating that the appropriate loop invariant is maintained. For more complicated programs, proving correctness can be quite difficult. In those cases, you will have to rely on less formal methods to determine whether your program is in fact delivering the correct answers.

In general, there are two methods you can adopt to increase your confidence in the correctness of a program. First, you can go through the code step by step and convince yourself that it behaves as you intended it to behave. This process is called **desk-checking.** Learning to perform desk-checking with a properly skeptical eye and acquiring good skills for reasoning about programs require practice and discipline. The second approach is **testing,** in which you run your program on as many test cases as you can to check that it performs correctly for each of those cases. For example, if you write a main program that calls IsPrime on each number between 1 and 1000 and you then check the output to make sure all the numbers are correctly classified, your confidence in the correctness of this algorithm will certainly increase.

It is important, however, to remember that completely rigorous testing is almost certainly impossible. There are just too many cases to test. Edsger Dijkstra, one of the leading computer scientists of our time, has observed that "testing can reveal the presence of errors, but never their absence." It is essential that you keep this principle in mind as you begin to write larger and more sophisticated programs.

Improving algorithmic efficiency

As with most programming problems, determining whether a number is prime can be solved in a variety of ways. The strategy used in Figure 6-1 has certain weaknesses. In particular, the algorithm is inefficient and is not practical if the numbers you want to check are large. For example, if you called IsPrime on the number 1,000,000, the function would actually check each of the million values between 1 and 1,000,000 to see whether they are divisors. Testing all these numbers is silly because 1,000,000 is obviously not prime; if nothing else, it is divisible by 2. Surely there must be a better approach that determines the answer without going through all the steps.

There are several ways in which you could increase the efficiency of the IsPrime implementation by changing the underlying algorithm. For example, each of the following three changes can have a significant effect on the number of steps IsPrime performs:

1. As the example of 1,000,000 makes clear, IsPrime does not have to check all the divisors. As soon as it finds *any* divisor greater than 1 and less than n, it can stop right there and report that n is not prime. You should therefore change the program structure so that the function returns as soon as a divisor is found.

2. Once the program has checked to see whether the number is divisible by 2, it doesn't need to check whether it is divisible by the other even numbers. If n is divisible by 2, the program can stop right there and report that n is not prime. If n is not divisible by 2, however, then it can't possibly be divisible

by 4 or 6 or any other even number. Thus, once 2 has been eliminated as a possibility, `IsPrime` needs to check only the odd numbers.

3. The program does not need to check for potential divisors all the way up to n. For example, it could clearly stop at the halfway point because any value that is larger than n/2 can't possibly divide evenly into n. With a little more thought, however, you can prove to yourself that the program doesn't need to try any divisors larger than the square root of n. To understand why, suppose that n is evenly divisible by some integer d_1. By the definition of divisibility, n / d_1 is therefore an integer, which we'll call d_2. What can you say about the size of d_1 and d_2? Because n is equal to $d_1 \times d_2$, if either of those factors is larger than the square root of n, the other one must be smaller. Thus, if n has any divisors, there must be one that is smaller than its square root. This insight means that the `for` loop in the program needs to run only as long as

$$i \leq \sqrt{n}$$

If you combine these three strategies, you can write a much more efficient implementation of the `IsPrime` function. The trick, however, is that you must be careful as you write the program to ensure that the function still works correctly. An attempt that looks as if it's heading in the desired direction is shown in Figure 6-2.

Unfortunately, as the bug symbol indicates, this implementation has some serious problems. The most glaring error is that the function returns the wrong answer for the argument values 1 and 2. According to the mathematical definition of primality, the number 1 is *not* a prime. This function incorrectly reports that it is, because the `for` loop does not find any divisors. Moreover, in trying to avoid checking for even divisors later on, the function uses the statement

```
if (n % 2 == 0) return (FALSE);
```

This statement fails to take account of the fact that there is one even prime number—the number 2 itself. By checking to see whether n is even without also checking to see whether it is 2, `IsPrime` gets the wrong answer in this case as well.

FIGURE 6-2 An attempt at a more efficient **IsPrime**

```
bool IsPrime(int n)
{
    int i;

    if (n % 2 == 0) return (FALSE);
    for (i = 3; i <= sqrt(n); i += 2) {
        if (n % i == 0) return (FALSE);
    }
    return (TRUE);
}
```

This program contains several serious errors.

To fix these bugs, the easiest approach is simply to check for 0 and 1 explicitly by inserting the following lines at the beginning of the program:

```
if (n <= 1) return (FALSE);
if (n == 2) return (TRUE);
```

Such statements, which check for special cases prior to beginning an algorithmic process, are quite common in programming. The tests themselves are usually quite simple, as illustrated by the preceding `if` statements. The hard part is noticing that special cases exist in the first place.

A more surprising problem is that the new implementation of `IsPrime`, which was designed to be more efficient, sometimes takes longer to run than the old one did. How can this be? The new implementation employs several clever insights to improve the efficiency of the algorithm, but somehow the changes aren't effective.

The problem in this case is subtle and lies in the `for` loop control line:

```
for (i = 3; i <= sqrt(n); i += 2)
```

As you will see later in this chapter, modern computers can calculate a square root in a surprisingly short time. Even so, it still takes much longer to compute a square root than it does to perform such simple arithmetic operations as multiplication and division. As written, `IsPrime` calls the `sqrt` function on every cycle of the `for` loop, even though the answer it returns is the same on every iteration. Because the value of `n` doesn't change inside the loop, the value of `sqrt(n)` does not change either. To avoid calling `sqrt` over and over again just to get the same answer, you should calculate `sqrt(n)` once before the loop begins and store that answer in a variable. For example, you could introduce a `double` variable called `limit` and then replace the `for` loop control line with the following two statements:

```
limit = sqrt(n);
for (i = 3; i <= limit; i += 2)
```

This simple change increases the efficiency of the `IsPrime` implementation significantly.

The implementation has another problem that is even harder to see. Finding this bug is complicated by the fact that it may not show up in testing. You could call this function on thousands of input values and get the correct answer every time. But someone might still come along with a previously untested case for which the function fails. Even more disturbing is the fact that this implementation of `IsPrime` might give the correct answer on one machine and the wrong answer on a different one.

To understand the problem, you may want to review the discussion of "Using `for` with floating-point data" in Chapter 4. In that section, you learned that it is dangerous to depend on tests for strict equality involving floating-point numbers. Suppose the number `n` is the square of a prime number. For example, suppose `n` is 49, which is the square of 7. What value does `sqrt` return when it is called on 49? In the world of exact mathematics, the square root is exactly 7, but the computer is not operating in that world. Floating-point numbers are only approximations,

COMMON PITFALLS

When you design a general algorithm, it is important to consider whether there are any special cases in which the general algorithm might fail. If there are, you must be sure to handle these cases explicitly in the program.

COMMON PITFALLS

When you use a loop within a program, check to see if there are any calculations within the loop that could just as well be performed before the loop begins. If there are, you can increase the efficiency of the program by calculating the result once, storing the result in a variable, and then using that variable inside the loop.

and it is possible that `sqrt(49)` returns 6.999999999999 instead. Although this number is barely less than 7.0, the difference may be enough to affect the outcome of the test `i <= limit`. As written, the conditional test requires perfect mathematical accuracy, which is not guaranteed with floating-point numbers. If `i` is 7 and `limit` is 6.999999999999, the last cycle of the loop will not be executed, and the program will never check whether n is divisible by 7. Because 7 is the only factor of 49, failure to check 7 as a divisor means that 49 will be incorrectly classified as a prime. On the other hand, if `sqrt(49)` returns 7.0 or 7.000000000001, the `IsPrime` function will give the right answer. The correctness of the implementation therefore depends on the how the hardware performs floating-point arithmetic.

Having the correctness of an implementation depend on the characteristics of the computer on which it runs is a serious failing. In this case, it is easy to modify the program so that the accuracy of the machine does not matter. If the square root of n might be too small a limit, the function can always check an extra possible divisor, just to make sure. Testing one extra divisor doesn't hurt and is a small price to pay for ensuring that the answer is correct. Thus, to correct the program, all you need to do is change the assignment to `limit` to

```
limit = sqrt(n) + 1;
```

It would also be good programming practice to declare `limit` as an `int`, thereby ensuring that all values used in the `for` loop control line are integers.

The final version of `IsPrime` that incorporates these corrections is shown in Figure 6-3.

Choosing between alternative implementations

What are the relative advantages of the original implementation of `IsPrime` and this new version? The final version is considerably more efficient, and this efficiency will likely be of significant interest to anyone who needs to use this

FIGURE 6-3   Corrected implementation of IsPrime

```
bool IsPrime(int n)
{
    int i, limit;

    if (n <= 1) return (FALSE);
    if (n == 2) return (TRUE);
    if (n % 2 == 0) return (FALSE);
    limit = sqrt(n) + 1;
    for (i = 3; i <= limit; i += 2) {
        if (n % i == 0) return (FALSE);
    }
    return (TRUE);
}
```

function as part of a larger application. On the other hand, you should recognize that the original version has advantages too. In particular, the first version of the program is much more readable, and it is much easier to see that the results produced by that implementation will conform to the definition of prime numbers. The extra complexity of the final version is reflected in the fact that it was much harder to get it working.

When you are faced with choosing an algorithm for a particular problem, your primary concern is *correctness*. Striving to make a program more efficient is an admirable goal, but you should never pursue efficiency to the point that your program starts giving the wrong answers.

After correctness, several other factors are also important to successful programming, including *efficiency, clarity,* and *maintainability.* For many practical applications, efficiency is extremely important. A program that runs too slowly may not be usable in applications where quick action is required. An air traffic control system that takes five minutes to detect that two planes are on a collision course is probably useless; a system that can issue the same warning in a second might save lives. In an environment in which several programmers collaborate on the same program, clarity must be a high-priority concern. Other programmers must be able to make sense out of your code, so you should strive to make their jobs as easy as you can. And for programs that are expected to be in use for a long time, maintainability is essential. A program consciously designed to accommodate change will be easier to maintain than one whose author failed to anticipate the direction of its development.

You need to learn that even though one algorithm may be "better" than another according to some measure, it is often the case that no algorithm is "best" from all perspectives. For example, an algorithm that is quite efficient in terms of the amount of time it requires to run may be very difficult to understand—a failing that often makes it hard for someone other than the author to use that program. Conversely, the clearest algorithms are often not particularly efficient. Which algorithm to use depends on the requirements of the application. Such considerations are known as **tradeoffs,** and it is important to strike the correct balance between the competing factors.

6.2 Computing the greatest common divisor

Other problems provide even more striking demonstrations of how the choice of algorithm can affect efficiency. One particularly good example—again from classical mathematics—is the problem of finding a greatest common divisor. Given two numbers, x and y, the greatest common divisor (or GCD for short) is the largest number that divides evenly into both. For example, the GCD of 49 and 35 is 7, the GCD of 6 and 18 is 6, and the GCD of 32 and 33 is 1. Suppose that your task is to write a function that accepts the integers x and y as input and returns their GCD. From the caller's point of view, what you want is a function that takes two integers and returns another integer that is their greatest common divisor. The prototype for this function is therefore

```
int GCD(int x, int y);
```

As with the primality testing algorithm, several solution strategies are available for this problem.

Brute-force algorithms

One simple approach to calculating the GCD is based on a more general strategy that is often called the **brute-force method.** This method consists of trying every possibility. To start, you simply "guess" that GCD(x, y) is x—it can't be larger than x and still divide evenly into x—and then check this supposition by dividing your guess into both x and y and seeing if it works. If it does, you have the answer; if not, you subtract 1 from the guess and try again.

A function that implements this strategy for calculating the GCD is shown in Figure 6-4.

Once again, you must ask yourself several questions about the implementation. Will the brute-force implementation of GCD always give the correct answer? Will it always terminate, or might the function continue forever?

To see that the program gives the correct answer, you need to look at the condition in the while loop

```
x % g != 0 || y % g != 0
```

As always, the while condition indicates under what circumstances the loop will continue. To find out what condition causes the loop to terminate, you have to negate the while condition. Negating a condition involving && or || can be accomplished by applying De Morgan's law, which was introduced in the section on "Logical operators" in Chapter 4. De Morgan's law indicates that the following condition must hold when the while loop exits:

```
x % g == 0 && y % g == 0
```

From this condition, you can see immediately that the final value of g is certainly a common divisor. To recognize that it is in fact the greatest common divisor, you have to think about the strategy embodied in the while loop. The critical factor to

---

FIGURE 6-4 Brute-force implementation of GCD

```
int GCD(int x, int y)
{
    int g;

    g = x;
    while (x % g != 0 || y % g != 0) {
        g--;
    }
    return (g);
}
```

notice in the strategy is that the program counts *backward* through all the possibilities. The GCD can never be larger than x (or y, for that matter), and the brute-force search therefore begins with that value. If the program ever gets out of the while loop, it must have already tried each value between x and the current value of g. Thus, if there were a larger value that divided evenly into both x and y, the program would already have found it in an earlier iteration of the while loop.

To demonstrate that the function terminates, you must first recognize that the value of g must eventually reach 1, even if no larger common divisor is found. At this point, the while loop will surely terminate, because 1 will divide evenly into both x and y, no matter what values those variables have.

Euclid's algorithm

Brute force is not, however, the only effective strategy. In fact, the brute-force algorithm used in the GCD implementation presented in the preceding section is a poor choice if you are at all concerned with efficiency. Consider what happens, for example, if you call the function with the numbers 1,000,005 and 1,000,000. The brute-force algorithm will run through the body of the while loop one million times before it comes up with 5—an answer that you can easily determine just by thinking about the two numbers.

What you need to find is an algorithm that is guaranteed to terminate with the correct answer but that requires fewer steps than the brute-force approach. This is where cleverness and a clear understanding of the problem pay off. Fortunately, the necessary creative insight has already been supplied by the Greek mathematician Euclid, whose *Elements* (book 7, proposition II) contains an elegant solution to this problem. In modern English, we can describe Euclid's algorithm as follows:

1. Divide x by y and compute the remainder; call that remainder r.
2. If r is zero, the procedure is complete, and the answer is y.
3. If r is not zero, set x equal to the old value of y, set y equal to r, and repeat the entire process.

You can translate this algorithm into an implementation of the GCD function, as shown in Figure 6-5.

This implementation of the GCD function also correctly finds the greatest common divisor of two numbers. It differs from the brute-force implementation in two respects. On the one hand, it computes the result much more quickly. On the other, it is more difficult to prove correct.

Defending the correctness of Euclid's algorithm (optional)

Although it is difficult to present a formal proof of correctness for Euclid's algorithm, this section sketches the outline of such a proof by invoking the mental model of mathematics the Greeks used. In Greek mathematics, geometry held center stage, and numbers were thought of as distances. For example, when Euclid set out to find the greatest common divisor of two numbers, such as 55 and 15, he framed the problem as one of finding the longest measuring stick that could be used to mark off each of the two distances involved. Thus, we can visualize the

FIGURE 6-5 Euclid's algorithm for GCD

```
int GCD(int x, int y)
{
    int r;

    while (TRUE) {
        r = x % y;
        if (r == 0) break;
        x = y;
        y = r;
    }
    return (y);
}
```

specific problem by starting out with two sticks, one 55 units long and one 15 units long, as follows:

x

y

The problem is to find a new measuring stick that you can lay end to end on top of each of these sticks so that it precisely covers each of the distances, x and y.

Euclid's algorithm begins by marking off the large stick in units of the shorter one:

x

y

Unless the smaller number is an exact divisor of the larger one, there is some remainder, as indicated by the shaded section of the upper stick. In this case, 15 goes into 55 three times with 10 left over, which means that the shaded region is 10 units long. The fundamental insight that Euclid had is that the greatest common divisor for the original two distances must also be the greatest common divisor of the length of the shorter stick and the distance represented by the shaded region in the diagram.

Given this observation, you can solve the original problem by reducing it to a simpler problem involving smaller numbers. Here, the new numbers are 15 and 10, and you can find their GCD by reapplying Euclid's algorithm. You start by representing the new values, x' and y', as measuring sticks of the appropriate length. You then mark off the larger stick in units of the smaller one.

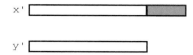

Once again, this process results in a leftover region, which this time has length 5. If you then repeat the process one more time, you discover that the shaded region of length 5 is itself the common divisor of x' and y' and, therefore, by Euclid's proposition, of the original numbers x and y. That this new value is indeed a common divisor of the original numbers is demonstrated by the following diagram:

Euclid supplies a complete proof of his proposition in the *Elements*. If you are intrigued by how mathematicians thought about such problems over 2000 years ago, you may find it interesting to look up this reference.

Comparing the efficiency of the GCD algorithms

To illustrate the difference in efficiency of the two algorithmic strategies, consider the numbers 1,000,005 and 1,000,000. To find the GCD of these two numbers, the brute-force algorithm requires a million steps; Euclid's algorithm requires only two. At the beginning of Euclid's algorithm, x is 1000005, y is 1000000, and r is set to 5 during the first cycle of the loop. Since the value of r is not 0, the program sets x to 1000000, sets y to 5, and starts again. On the second cycle, the new value of r is 0, so the program exits from the `while` loop and reports that the answer is 5.

In each of the two examples presented so far in this chapter—testing primality and calculating greatest common divisors—the choice of algorithm has a profound effect on the efficiency of the solution. In Chapter 17, you will learn how to quantify differences in algorithmic efficiency.

▰▰ 6.3 Numerical algorithms

In the modern world, computers are useful in a wide range of applications. As a result, computer programmers are called on to write many different kinds of programs that involve a variety of computational operations. Some programmers may have no use for anything as mathematical as a square root and can therefore be content with knowing nothing at all about the `math` library. Even for those programmers who do use square roots, most are satisfied just to use the `sqrt` function without thinking about its internal operation. What makes it possible for them to do so, however, is that, somewhere along the line, a programmer took the time and trouble to write the `sqrt` function in the first place. The techniques used by computers to implement mathematical functions like `sqrt` are called **numerical algorithms** and represent an important area of computer science.

Because square roots occur frequently in geometry, mathematicians have been interested for over 2000 years in the problem of how to calculate them, and they have developed a variety of algorithmic strategies for solving that problem. To illustrate those solution techniques—and to consider more general properties of numerical algorithms at the same time—the next section, on "Successive approximation," and a later one, on "Series expansion," present two different approaches to the problem of calculating the square root function.

Successive approximation

One of the most important general strategies for solving numerical problems is the technique of successive approximation. **Successive approximation** is a general strategy for finding an approximate answer that consists of the following steps:

1. Start by making a guess at the answer.
2. Once you have made a guess, you then use that guess to generate an even better one. For example, suppose that you test your guess and discover it is too large. You can make it a little smaller and use the smaller value as a new guess. Conversely, if your original guess is too small, you can choose a larger value as the next guess.
3. If you can somehow guarantee that your guess is getting closer and closer to the real answer on each cycle, repeating the process will eventually result in a guess that is close enough to satisfy the needs of any application.

The difficult part of the successive approximation technique consists of choosing new guesses in step 2 so that they satisfy the condition expressed at the beginning of step 3. Your strategy for choosing new guesses must take into account some knowledge of the problem. What you need to find is a sequence of guesses in which each guess is closer to the actual answer than the preceding one, approaching it arbitrarily closely as the sequence proceeds. Whenever a sequence of values approaches a limit as you calculate more and more terms, the sequence is said to **converge.**

The strategy for using successive approximation to calculate the square root function was devised in the seventeenth century by Isaac Newton. Newton's method for calculating a square root is best illustrated by an example. Suppose that you want to find the square root of the number 16. You start by making a wild guess. The answer has to be less than 16. You might start by trying 8. Is your guess too big or too small? Well, if 8 were the square root, then 8 times 8 would have to be 16. It's not. Because 8 times 8 is 64, the value 8 is too large to be the square root of 16. You need to try a smaller number. But how much smaller? Is there any way to use the characteristics of the problem to select the next guess?

Newton's insight was that the actual square root must lie between your current guess and the value that results when you divide the original number by that guess. In this case, your guess is 8, and 16 divided by 8 is 2. Just as 8 is too large, 2 is too small. To generate a more accurate guess, you can average those two values, which are known to lie on opposite sides of the correct answer. The result will be closer to the square root of 16, although it is still an approximation. In this example, averaging the values 8 and 2 gives 5 as your new guess.

From this point, you simply repeat the process. Dividing 16 by 5 gives 3.2. Averaging 5 and 3.2 then produces the next guess, 4.1, which is much closer to the correct answer. If you continue this process, the next two guesses are 4.001219512 and 4.00000018584. By the fourth guess, Newton's method has already produced a value that is extremely close to right answer. This process will never generate the exact answer, but you can continue to apply the technique until you get an approximation that is as close as you want it to be.

If you never get the exact answer, how do you know when to stop? The most straightforward approach is to continue the process until the answer is "close enough," in the sense that the difference between the computed result and the actual one becomes so small that it is no longer considered meaningful. If you have been keeping up with the exercises, this strategy has another significant advantage, because the solution to exercise 10 in Chapter 5 provides just the tool you need to determine whether the process is complete. In that exercise, you implemented a function `ApproximatelyEqual` that returns `TRUE` if two floating-point numbers are equal within an accuracy specified by `Epsilon`, which is defined as part of the program. If you copy the `ApproximatelyEqual` function into your square root program, you can stop as soon as the square of your guess is approximately equal to the original number.

This informal process can be restructured into a more formal English algorithm as follows:

1. To compute the square root of a number x, begin by making an arbitrary guess g. One possibility is just to start with g equal to x, although you can use any positive value.
2. If the guess g is close enough to the actual square root, the algorithm is complete, and the function can return g as the result.
3. If g is not sufficiently accurate, generate a new guess by averaging the values g and x/g. Because one of these values will be less than the actual square root and the other will be larger, choosing the average allows you to pick a value that is closer to the correct answer.
4. Store the new guess in the variable g, and repeat the process from step 2.

A function that implements this algorithm is shown in Figure 6-6. In this implementation, the function is called `Sqrt` with a upper case `S` to avoid interfering with the `sqrt` function defined in the math library.

The first two statements in the implementation of `Sqrt` are included to account for two important situations. The first statement

```
if (x == 0) return (0);
```

FIGURE 6-6 Newton's algorithm for **Sqrt**

```
double Sqrt(double x)
{
    double g;

    if (x == 0) return (0);
    if (x < 0) Error("Sqrt called with negative argument %g", x);
    g = x;
    while (!ApproximatelyEqual(x, g * g)) {
        g = (g + x / g) / 2;
    }
    return (g);
}
```

is necessary for the Sqrt function to compute correctly the square root of 0. If this statement is not used, Newton's method ends up trying to divide by 0 when it computes x/g in the first cycle of the loop. Dividing by 0 is meaningless as a mathematical concept, and the behavior of the program is unpredictable if you attempt to do so. Fortunately, it is a simple matter to check for 0 first and return the correct answer immediately.

The second statement in the function

```
if (x < 0) Error("Sqrt called with negative argument %g", x);
```

is used to handle the case in which the Sqrt function is passed a negative argument. Although the square root function is undefined for negative values of x, the Sqrt function should be prepared for the possibility that someone might call it with a negative value. If nothing else, the function must report the error so that its caller can know that it occurred.

Reporting errors

There are many different ways in which a program can respond to error conditions that come up during its execution. The programs in this text use the Error function, which is defined in the genlib library, to report error conditions to the user. The Error function takes a control string followed by additional arguments, just as printf does. When Error is called, it displays the string "Error: " followed by the control string, substituting values in place of format codes in the same way that printf does. At the end of the line, Error automatically includes a newline character to move the cursor to the beginning of the next line.

The main difference between Error and printf is that Error does not return to its caller. Once the error message has been displayed, the entire program terminates, just as if it had finished executing all the statements in the main program.

Thus, if `Sqrt` were called on the value –1, the following output would appear on the screen:

```
Error: Sqrt called with negative argument -1
```

As soon as the error message appears, the program stops running without executing any more statements.

The process of responding to an error within a program is called **error handling.** Having a program write out an error message and stop is not a particularly sophisticated error-handling strategy. In the context of a library function such as `sqrt`, it would be much better to provide some mechanism by which the caller could take corrective action. Unfortunately, the best error-handling strategies are beyond the scope of this text. It is nevertheless critically important that the program do something when an error condition occurs. If you do not check for the situation, the program may give incorrect answers or fail to produce an answer at all. For example, if the `Sqrt` function did not test for negative arguments, the function would go into an infinite loop trying to approximate an answer that does not exist. Having the program report the error and stop is a much more useful response than having it run forever.

 ## 6.4 Series expansion

While Newton's method is a reasonable approach to the problem of calculating square roots, there are many alternative algorithms that are just as effective, some of which are easier to apply in other contexts. One of the most widely used methods is **series expansion,** in which the value of a function is approximated by adding together terms in a mathematical series. If the addition of each new term brings the total closer to the desired value, the series converges, and you can use that series to approximate the result.

Zeno's paradox

To illustrate the idea of series expansion, this section once again explores a problem arising from Greek mathematics. In the fifth century B.C., the philosopher Zeno of Elea invented a paradox that seems to suggest that motion is impossible. Imagine that you are trying to move across a room. To do so, you must first go halfway across it. From there, you must go half of the remainder, which means covering another quarter of the original distance. From there, you must again reach the next halfway point by going an additional eighth of the total, and so on. Since the remaining distance is always a quantity that can be halved, Zeno argued, the process must continue on forever, and you can never actually reach your goal. This argument is known as **Zeno's paradox.**

In Zeno's paradox, each step in the process of crossing the room consists of going half the remaining distance. If you translate Zeno's problem into a more mathematical form, the total fraction of the distance covered can be expressed as the following sum:

$$\frac{1}{2} + \frac{1}{4} + \frac{1}{8} + \frac{1}{16} + \frac{1}{32} + \frac{1}{64} + \frac{1}{128} + \cdots$$

Zeno was correct in observing that there are an infinite number of terms in this series.[1] What Zeno did not realize in the fifth century B.C. is that an infinite series can have a finite sum—a fact that does, after all, seem somewhat paradoxical.

What is the sum of Zeno's series? There are several ways to figure it out. From the mathematical point of view, you can start by letting s be the unknown sum of the series:

$$s = \frac{1}{2} + \frac{1}{4} + \frac{1}{8} + \frac{1}{16} + \frac{1}{32} + \frac{1}{64} + \frac{1}{128} + \cdots$$

If you then multiply each side of the equation by 2, the resulting equation is

$$2s = 1 + \frac{1}{2} + \frac{1}{4} + \frac{1}{8} + \frac{1}{16} + \frac{1}{32} + \frac{1}{64} + \frac{1}{128} + \cdots$$

The right-hand side of the equation is interesting. After the first term, the infinite series contains exactly the same terms as the original series does. You can therefore substitute s in place of all those terms, which yields the much simpler equation

$$2s = 1 + s$$

Subtracting s from each side gives you

$$s = 1$$

You could also write a program to compute an approximation to the series

$$\frac{1}{2} + \frac{1}{4} + \frac{1}{8} + \frac{1}{16} + \frac{1}{32} + \frac{1}{64} + \frac{1}{128} + \cdots$$

simply by adding up the terms. If you number each term starting from 1, the ith term in the sum has the form

$$\frac{1}{2^i}$$

A mathematical series in which the ith term involves raising some quantity to the ith power is called a **power series.** Power series calculations play an extremely important role in computational mathematics.

Because you now have a formula that allows you to calculate the value of each term from the term number, you can easily write a program that uses this formula

---

[1] In a mathematical series, each value that is added to form the total is called a *term*. Since terms in a series can themselves involve mathematical operations—such as the fraction bar in every term used to represent Zeno's calculation—the definition of *term* as it applies to a series is slightly different from the one used in the discussion of expressions in Chapter 2.

to calculate each term and then add that term to a running total. For most power series, however, there is an even easier approach. Rather than calculate each term from scratch, calculating each term from the previous one saves a lot of computation. In Zeno's series, the first term is $1/2$, and every subsequent term is half of the previous one. Thus, if you keep track of the current term as well as the sum, your program can use the following structure to find the sum of the series:

```
sum = 0.0;
term = 0.5;
while (TRUE) {
    sum += term;
    term /= 2;
}
```

This program fragment contains an infinite loop.

The only practical difficulty with this program is that it never stops. There is no exit condition for the `while` statement, and the program is therefore caught in an infinite loop. How can you change the program so as to avoid this problem?

When you write programs that perform series expansions, the fact that floating-point numbers are only approximations of real numbers turns out to be extremely useful. As the series expansion continues, the value of `term` becomes smaller and smaller. At some point, the value of `term` will become so small that the exact value of `sum + term` can no longer be represented with the limited precision used by the machine. Suppose, for example, that `sum` has the value 2.3 and that `term` has the value 0.0000000000000000001. Mathematically, of course, the value of `sum + term` should be 2.3000000000000000001, but the computer is probably unable to represent floating-point numbers with 20 digits of accuracy. Using floating-point arithmetic, the answer is probably just 2.3. The fact that the value of `term` will eventually become insignificant leads to an effective strategy for stopping the `while` loop. If you replace the `while` control line in the infinite loop with

```
while (sum != sum + term)
```

the loop will continue as long as adding `term` to `sum` produces some noticeable effect.

A complete main program for calculating the sum of Zeno's series is shown in Figure 6-7.

Using a series expansion for the square root function

Like many mathematical functions, the square root function has an associated power series that makes it possible to use the summation technique presented in the preceding section to generate approximate results. Unfortunately, finding out what that power series is requires some familiarity with calculus. Once the formula for the series has been derived, writing the program isn't all that difficult.

If you haven't had any calculus, feel free to skip the entire next section and start again with the section on "Implementing the Taylor series approximation." If you take calculus later, you then may want to read this section to see how computational mathematicians come up with the techniques used to implement the functions in the mathematical libraries.

FIGURE 6-7 Main program to sum Zeno's series

```
main()
{
    double sum, term;

    sum = 0.0;
    term = 0.5;
    while (sum != sum + term) {
        sum += term;
        term /= 2;
    }
    printf("The sum of Zeno's series is %g\n", sum);
}
```

The Taylor series expansion for approximating a square root (optional)

One of the most useful forms of power series is the Taylor series, which you would ordinarily learn about at some point during the first year of college-level calculus. The eighteenth-century mathematician Brook Taylor discovered that, at least for argument values within a certain range, functions that can be repeatedly differentiated can be approximated using the following formula:

$$f(x) \cong f(a) + f'(a)(x-a) + f''(a)\frac{(x-a)^2}{2!} + f'''(a)\frac{(x-a)^3}{3!} + \cdots + f^{(n)}(a)\frac{(x-a)^n}{n!}$$

In this formula, which is called **Taylor's formula** after its discoverer, the symbol a represents a constant, and the notations f', f'', and f''' represent the first, second, and third derivatives of the function f, and so on.

Consider the case in which f is the square root function. In mathematics, taking the square root of a number x is the same as raising x to the power $1/2$, so that $f(x)$ is defined as

$$f(x) = x^{\frac{1}{2}}$$

To find f', all you need to do is use the general formula that the derivative of x^c for any constant c is

$$c\,x^{c-1}$$

In the case of the square root function, c is $1/2$, so the first derivative is

$$f'(x) = \frac{1}{2}x^{-\frac{1}{2}}$$

From this point, you apply the same rule to generate additional derivatives. In every case, the previous coefficient gets multiplied by the previous exponent, and the exponent is reduced by 1. Thus, the next few derivatives of the square root function are the following:

$$f''(x) \ = \ -\frac{1}{4}x^{-\frac{3}{2}}$$

$$f'''(x) \ = \ \frac{3}{8}x^{-\frac{5}{2}}$$

$$f''''(x) \ = \ -\frac{15}{16}x^{-\frac{7}{2}}$$

In Taylor's formula, these derivatives are evaluated only on the constant a, so it makes sense to choose a value of a that makes these derivatives easy to calculate. If you let a be equal to 1, for example, raising a to any power always gives the answer 1, leaving only the coefficients, as follows:

$$f(1) \ = \ 1$$

$$f'(1) \ = \ \frac{1}{2}$$

$$f''(1) \ = -\frac{1}{4}$$

$$f'''(1) \ = \ \frac{3}{8}$$

$$f''''(1) \ = -\frac{15}{16}$$

By inserting these values into Taylor's formula, you discover that the following power series gives an approximation to the square root function:

$$\sqrt{x} \cong 1 + \frac{1}{2}(x-1) - \frac{1}{4}\frac{(x-1)^2}{2!} + \frac{3}{8}\frac{(x-1)^3}{3!} - \frac{15}{16}\frac{(x-1)^4}{4!} + \cdots$$

As long as a simple condition applies—which we will get to in the section on "Staying within the radius of convergence" later in this chapter—the more terms in this series you evaluate, the closer the answer will be.

Implementing the Taylor series approximation

At this point, you need to write a function that approximates the square root by evaluating its power series expansion:

$$\sqrt{x} \cong 1 + \frac{1}{2}(x-1) - \frac{1}{4}\frac{(x-1)^2}{2!} + \frac{3}{8}\frac{(x-1)^3}{3!} - \frac{15}{16}\frac{(x-1)^4}{4!} + \cdots$$

As illustrated in the section on "Zeno's paradox" earlier in this chapter, the most effective strategy for computing the sum of a power series is to find a way to compute each new term from the preceding term. To see how this principle applies to the Taylor series expansion for approximating a square root, let's start by numbering the terms as follows:

$$t_0 = 1$$

$$t_1 = \frac{1}{2}(x-1)$$

$$t_2 = -\frac{1}{4}\frac{(x-1)^2}{2!}$$

$$t_3 = \frac{3}{8}\frac{(x-1)^3}{3!}$$

$$t_4 = -\frac{15}{16}\frac{(x-1)^4}{4!}$$

How does each term differ from the preceding one? To answer this question, think of each term as having these three separate components:

$$\texttt{coeff}\frac{\texttt{xpower}}{\texttt{factorial}}$$

For example, for t_3, the `coeff` component is 3/8, the `xpower` component is $(x-1)^3$, and the `factorial` component is 3!. The question then becomes how each of these components changes from term to term.

Consider the `xpower` component, for example. Starting with the current `xpower` component, all you have to do to get the next one is multiply by $x - 1$. By storing the current `xpower` value in a variable, you can make sure that it maintains the correct value with one multiplication inside each loop cycle.

What about the `factorial` component? This component always has the value $i!$ for term i. Factorials have the useful property that the factorial of any number i is just i times the factorial of the next smaller number. This property can be easily demonstrated by expanding the computation of factorial by replacing $(i + 1)!$ with its definition, as follows:

$$(i + 1)! \;=\; (i + 1) \times i \times (i - 1) \times (i - 2) \times \cdots \times 2 \times 1$$
$$=\; (i + 1) \times i!$$

Thus, to prepare for the $(i+1)^{st}$ cycle of the loop, all you need to do is multiply the current `factorial` component by $i+1$.

The only component left to compute is `coeff`. It turns out to be a running product, just like the others.[2] In general, to get the value of `coeff` for the $(i+1)^{st}$ cycle, you simply multiply the current value in the ith cycle by

$$\frac{1}{2} - i$$

---

[2] Understanding in detail how the coefficient changes from term to term requires knowing how these terms were originally computed using Taylor's formula. If you read the preceding discussion on "The Taylor Series expansion," you know that the coefficients come from the derivatives of the square root function. Even if you skipped that section, however, the formula is easy enough to apply.

You can use these formulas to compute the components for the next term by using the components of the current one. If the variables `coeff`, `xpower`, and `factorial` contain the components of the current term, all you have to do to calculate those components for the next term is to execute the statements

```
coeff *= (0.5 - i);
xpower *= (x - 1);
factorial *= (i + 1);
```

as the main loop within the function. Just as in the program to compute the sum of Zeno's series, the main loop must be executed until adding in the value of a term doesn't change the sum. Writing a loop that tests for this condition and initializing all the variables gives rise to the function `TSqrt` shown in Figure 6-8.

Staying within the radius of convergence

Unfortunately, the `TSqrt` function is not as general as it should be. As a Taylor series expansion, the formula for the square root function is effective only when the argument falls within a limited range that allows the calculation to converge. That range is called the **radius of convergence.** For the square root function calculated using $a = 1$, the Taylor series formula requires that x be in the range

$$0 < x < 2$$

If x falls outside of the radius of convergence, the terms in the expansion keep getting bigger, and the Taylor series just gets farther and farther from the answer. This restriction makes the `TSqrt` function less useful, although it is still effective inside that range.

FIGURE 6-8   Taylor series expansion for TSqrt

```
double TSqrt(double x)
{
    double sum, factorial, coeff, term, xpower;
    int i;

    factorial = coeff = xpower = 1;
    sum = 0;
    term = 1;
    for (i = 0; sum != sum + term; i++) {
        sum += term;
        coeff *= (0.5 - i);
        xpower *= (x - 1);
        factorial *= (i + 1);
        term = coeff * xpower / factorial;      This function fails
    }                                           if x ≥ 2
    return (sum);
}
```

When faced with restrictions of this sort, you should think about ways to transform the general problem into a specific one that fits the requirements of the solution you have at hand. Thus, you need to find a way to express the square root of a large number that falls outside the legal range in terms of a square root that falls inside that range.

To accomplish this transformation of the problem, it is useful to remember that

$$\sqrt{4\,x} = \sqrt{4}\,\sqrt{x} = 2\,\sqrt{x}$$

A factor of 4 inside the square root sign can be turned into a factor of 2 outside the square root sign.

This observation provides you with the tools you need to complete the solution. If you have a number that is too large, you can always divide it by 4, use TSqrt to take the square root of what remains, and then multiply that result by 2. If a single division by 4 is not sufficient to bring the number into the desired range, you can divide by 4 several times before calling TSqrt, as long as you remember to multiply the result by 2 just as many times.

The easiest way to handle this new piece of the solution strategy is to separate the square root function into two pieces. You already have a TSqrt that calculates square roots within a limited range. Without changing that function, you can write a Sqrt function that performs all the divisions necessary to bring the number within range and all the multiplications necessary to fix up the answer at the end. The Sqrt function is also an appropriate place to include the special case checks for 0 and for negative values of x that were used in the Sqrt implementation in Figure 6-6.

The complete implementation of Sqrt using the Taylor series formula, including both the functions Sqrt and TSqrt with their associated comments, is shown in Figure 6-9.

FIGURE 6-9 Code for Taylor series version of **Sqrt**

```
/*
 * Function: Sqrt
 * Usage: root = Sqrt(x);
 * ------------------------
 * Returns the square root of x, calculated using a
 * Taylor series expansion, as described in the text.
 * The Sqrt function is actually implemented as two
 * functions.  The job of the outer Sqrt function is to
 * divide the argument repeatedly by 4 until it is in
 * the range 0 < x < 2, where the Taylor series converges.
 * It then calls TSqrt to perform the actual Taylor series
 * calculation.  When finished, Sqrt adjusts the answer by
 * multiplying the result by 2 for each time it needed to
 * be divided by 4 to bring it in range.
 */
```

```
double Sqrt(double x)
{
    double result, correction;

    if (x == 0) return (0);
    if (x < 0) Error("Sqrt called with negative argument %g", x);
    correction = 1;
    while (x >= 2) {
        x /= 4;
        correction *= 2;
    }
    return (TSqrt(x) * correction);
}


/*
 * Function: TSqrt
 * Usage: root = TSqrt(x);
 * -----------------------
 * Returns the square root of x, calculated by expanding
 * the Taylor series around a = 1, as described in the
 * text.  The function is effective only if x is in the
 * range 0 < x < 2.  Term i in the summation has the form
 *
 *                     xpower
 *         coeff   *   ---------
 *                     factorial
 *
 * where coeff comes from ith derivative of the function,
 * factorial is i!, and xpower is the ith power of (x - a).
 * Each of these components is computed from its previous
 * value.
 */

double TSqrt(double x)
{
    double sum, factorial, coeff, term, xpower;
    int i;

    factorial = coeff = xpower = 1;
    sum = 0;
    term = 1;
    for (i = 0; sum != sum + term; i++) {
        sum += term;
        coeff *= (0.5 - i);
        xpower *= (x - 1);
        factorial *= (i + 1);
        term = coeff * xpower / factorial;
    }
    return (sum);
}
```

6.5 Specifying the size of numeric types

When you are working on numerical applications such as those in this chapter, it is often important to be able to exercise some control over the range and precision of the numeric data types. To some extent, these characteristics are determined by the hardware, since all data values within a computer are stored electronically in its memory system. Depending on the type of computer, the individual units into which memory is divided can be of different sizes. From the programmer's point of view, the major impact of these variations in internal structure is that the numeric data types may be subject to different limitations on different machines, making it more difficult to write programs that are portable. A **portable** program is one that can be run successfully on many different computer systems in exactly the same form.

To make it easier for programmers to write portable programs and to ensure that numerical calculations are as precise as they need to be, ANSI C includes several distinct integer and floating-point types. Although `int` and `double` are sufficient for a wide variety of applications and are used throughout this text as the only numeric types, it is sometimes preferable to use one of the other numeric types to make sure that the compiler will reserve enough space to hold a certain piece of data on the widest possible variety of computer systems. The next three sections describe the numeric types available in C other than `int` and `double` and give some suggestions about when it is appropriate to use these types.

Integer types

Data values of type `int` are stored internally inside the computer's memory in individual storage units that have a limited capacity. They therefore have a maximum size, which depends on the machine and the C compiler being used. On many personal computers, the maximum value of type `int` is 32,767, which is rather small by computational standards. If you wanted, for example, to perform a calculation involving the number of seconds in a year, you could not use type `int` on those machines, because that value (31,536,000) is considerably larger than the largest available value of type `int`.

To get around this problem, C defines several integer types, distinguished from each other by the size of their domains. The three principal types are `int`, `long`, and `short`, although each of them can be modified by the keyword `unsigned`, as described in the next section.

The data type `int` represents the standard integer type for a particular machine. ANSI C ensures that values of type `int` can always be at least as large as 32,767, but otherwise places no restrictions on the compiler designers. On some computer systems, the type `int` may have a considerably larger range, and it is common to find systems on which the upper limit for type `int` is 2,147,483,647.[3]

---

[3] The numbers used as the limits on integer sizes are not really as random as they appear to be. Computers store numbers internally using the binary system, and each of these limits is one less than a power of two.

The designers of ANSI C could have chosen to define the allowable range of type int more precisely. For example, they could have declared that the maximum value of type int would be 2,147,483,647 on every machine. Had they done so, it would be easier to move a program from one system to another and have it behave in the same way. The problem with establishing such a rule for every machine is that doing so may force some machines to sacrifice efficiency just to ensure that they are following the rule. If a particular computer can implement small integers efficiently but must perform extra operations to work with large integers, forcing that machine to use large integers has a cost. To avoid that cost, C allows compilers to represent values of type int in the size that is most convenient for that machine.

Because the only guarantee that C makes about values of type int is that they can be at least as large as 32,767, you should use type int only if you are certain that the value of a variable or expression can never exceed that limit. If a value might conceivably be larger than 32,767, it is best to use the data type long, which indicates to the compiler that a larger integer domain is required. ANSI C specifies that variables of type long must be able to hold values at least as large as 2,147,483,647, but some compilers may allow even larger values.

The data type short is defined so that the programmer can explicitly choose to use less storage for a particular variable than the compiler might reserve if that variable were declared as an int. The type short is retained in the language mostly for historical reasons and is not used much in modern programming.

If you combine integer data of different sizes in a single expression, the type of the result will be that of the longest type involved in the calculation. For example, if you were to add a variable of type int to one of type long, the result would be of type long. This rule ensures that the result type has as large a domain as its operands do.

When using data of type short or long, you must use different printf format codes. To display a value of type long, you must precede the letter d in the %d conversion specification with the letter l (note that this is the letter *ell* and not the digit *one*) to specify that the value is a long. Similarly, if you are printing a value of type short, you must precede the d with the letter h for *half* because short integers were originally half the size of integers in the early versions of C.

Unsigned types

In C, each of the integer types int, long, and short may be preceded by the keyword unsigned. Adding unsigned specifies a new data type in which only non-negative values are allowed. Because unsigned variables do not need to represent negative values, declaring a variable to be one of the unsigned types allows it to hold twice as many positive values. For example, if the maximum value of type int is 32,767, the maximum value of type unsigned int will be 65,535. C allows the type unsigned int to be abbreviated to unsigned, and most programmers who use this type tend to follow this practice.

Values of type unsigned int can be displayed by specifying the %u conversion in a printf call. To display values of type unsigned long or unsigned short, you must use the specifications %lu and %hu, respectively.

For the most part, you will not need to use unsigned types unless you are writing programs that require you to maintain extremely tight control over the internal representation used by the machine. Unsigned types are included in this text primarily for completeness and are otherwise not used at all.

Floating-point types

Like integers, floating-point numbers are represented in a fixed amount of internal memory and therefore have size limitations. For floating-point numbers, however, the limitation on memory affects the precision of the data (how many significant digits are available) as well as the range. Because precision is a function of the hardware, the precision of a floating-point number may differ from machine to machine. On one machine, for example, floating-point numbers might be limited to 10 significant digits. On that machine, the values 1.0 and 1.00000000001 will appear to be the same because the computer cannot represent the latter number exactly.

As with integers, C provides three types of floating-point numbers. The type `float` is the least precise, but takes up less memory than the type `double`. Over the last decade, however, computer memory has gotten cheaper, and most C programmers now tend to use the more precise type `double` for all floating-point data—a practice followed in this text. All calculations involving values of type `float` or `double` are performed in C as if they had been declared as type `double`; the data type affects only how the values are stored.

For certain extremely exacting numerical computations, however, the type `double` may not be sufficiently precise. For applications that require extremely high precision, the ANSI standard also includes a type called `long double`, although this type is rarely necessary in practice.

 Summary

In this chapter, you learned several general strategies for designing algorithms. The examples presented were chosen from classical mathematics, mostly because mathematics provides an interesting set of problems that you can solve without knowing about data types other than numbers. As you learn about other data types in later chapters, you will discover that the algorithmic techniques presented here can be applied to other sorts of problems as well.

Important points introduced in this chapter include:

- There are often many different algorithms that can solve a particular problem. Choosing the algorithm that best fits the application is an important part of your task as a programmer.
- When choosing between different algorithms, you need to consider many different factors, including *efficiency, maintainability,* and *clarity.* Choosing a particular algorithm will often involve evaluating *tradeoffs* between these qualities.

- You should never sacrifice correctness as you work to improve other aspects of your program.
- Proving that a program is correct is an extremely difficult task. In most cases, thorough testing is necessary to increase your confidence that a particular solution is correct. Even with good testing, however, subtle errors may remain.
- *Brute-force algorithms* are those that check every possibility without trying to be clever. Such algorithms are usually easy to understand but are likely to be extremely inefficient.
- *Successive approximation* often provides a mechanism by which guesses can be transformed into solutions by continually improving the accuracy of the guess.
- Error conditions that occur during a program can be reported to the user by calling the `Error` function, which is defined in the `genlib` library.
- Many mathematical functions can be approximated using the technique of *series expansion.*

REVIEW QUESTIONS

1. What are the three properties that are required for a strategy to be considered an algorithm?

2. What is a loop invariant?

3. Explain in your own words why it is unnecessary to consider factors greater than $\sqrt{n}$ when you are testing to see if *n* is a prime.

4. One of the common pitfalls boxes in this chapter makes a suggestion for improving the efficiency of loops. What method does it suggest?

5. What are some of the factors you would consider in choosing between alternative algorithms for solving a particular problem?

6. In the examples that use Euclid's algorithm to calculate the GCD of x and y, x is always larger than y. Does this matter? What happens if x is smaller than y?

7. When you have written a program that converges toward a solution, how do you know when to stop?

8. In what ways does the `Error` function differ in its behavior from `printf`?

9. What is Zeno's paradox?

10. In evaluating a power series, is it better to compute each new term directly or by using the preceding term? Why?

11. The control line for the `while` loops used to calculate the sum of each power series looks like this:

    ```
    while (sum != sum + term)
    ```

    At first glance, this test seems unusual. Mathematically, it should be possible to simplify this test to

    ```
    while (term != 0)
    ```

    Programs that use this second test require much longer to run. Why?

12. Why is it necessary to include the special case test for 0 in the Taylor series implementation of `Sqrt`?

PROGRAMMING EXERCISES

1. Although this chapter has focused on mathematical algorithms, the Greeks were fascinated with algorithms of other kinds as well. In Greek mythology, for example, Theseus of Athens escapes from the Minotaur's labyrinth by taking in a ball of string, unwinding it as he goes along, and then following the path of string back to the exit. Theseus's strategy represents an algorithm for escaping from a maze, but it is not the only algorithm he could have used to solve this problem. For example, if a maze has no internal loops, you can always escape by following the *right-hand rule,* in which you always keep your right hand against the wall. This approach may lead you to backtrack from time to time, but it does ensure that you will eventually find the opening to the outside.

    For example, imagine that Theseus is in the maze shown below at the position marked by the Greek letter theta (Θ):

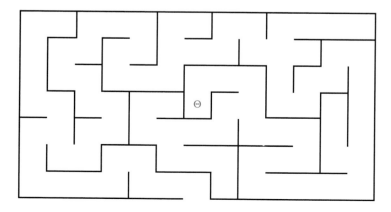

To get out, Theseus walks along the path shown by the dotted line in the next diagram, which he can do without taking his right hand off the wall.

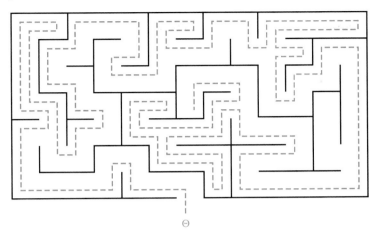

Suppose you have been asked to write a program for a robot named Theseus to implement the right-hand rule. You have access to a library that contains these functions:

```
void MoveForward(void);   /* Move forward to the next square  */
void TurnRight(void);     /* Turn right without moving        */
void TurnLeft(void);      /* Turn left without moving         */
bool IfFacingWall(void);  /* TRUE if Theseus is facing a wall */
bool IfOutside(void);     /* TRUE if Theseus has escaped       */
```

Use the functions to write a procedure `EscapeFromMaze` that implements the algorithm suggested by the right-hand rule.

2. In many cases, it is not enough to know whether a number is prime; sometimes, you need to know its factors. Every positive integer greater than 1 can be expressed as a product of prime numbers. This factorization is unique and is called the **prime factorization.** For example, the number 60 can be decomposed into the factors $2 \times 2 \times 3 \times 5$, each of which is prime. Note that the same prime can appear more than once in the factorization.

   Write a program to display the prime factorization of a number *n*. The following is a sample run of the program:

   ```
   Enter number to be factored: 60↵
   2 * 2 * 3 * 5
   ```

3. Greek mathematicians took a special interest in numbers that are equal to the sum of their proper divisors (a proper divisor of *n* is any divisor less than *n*

itself). They called such numbers **perfect numbers.** For example, 6 is a perfect number because it is the sum of 1, 2, and 3, which are the integers less than 6 that divide evenly into 6. Similarly, 28 is a perfect number because it is the sum of 1, 2, 4, 7, and 14.

Write a predicate function `IsPerfect` that takes an integer n and returns TRUE if n is perfect, and FALSE otherwise. Test your implementation by writing a main program that uses the `IsPerfect` function to check for perfect numbers in the range 1 to 9999 by testing each number in turn. When a perfect number is found, your program should display it on the screen. The first two lines of output should be 6 and 28. Your program should find two other perfect numbers in that range as well.

4. After you have gotten the perfect number program from exercise 3 to work, think carefully about the algorithm you've used. Write a new version of the program that improves the efficiency of the algorithm without sacrificing its correctness.

5. Modify Newton's algorithm as presented in the text so that it calculates cube roots instead of square roots. Express the algorithm in the form of a function `CubeRoot` that takes a `double` and returns another `double`, which is the cube root of the argument. The creative part of this problem is figuring out what numbers you should average to obtain a new guess on each cycle of the loop. If g, for example, lies to one side of the cube root of n, what value can you compute using n and g that would be approximately as close to the root but on the opposite side? If you can find such a value, averaging the two will yield a result that is closer to the actual answer.

6. Mathematicians and other scientists sometimes find unexpected applications for power series approximation. In 1772, the astronomer J. E. Bode proposed a rule for calculating the distance from the sun to each of the planets known at that time. To apply that rule, which subsequently became known as Bode's law, you begin by writing down the sequence

$$b_1 = 1 \quad b_2 = 3 \quad b_3 = 6 \quad b_4 = 12 \quad b_5 = 24 \quad b_6 = 48 \quad \cdots$$

where each subsequent element in the sequence is twice the preceding one. It turns out that an approximate distance to the ith planet can be computed from this series by applying the formula

$$d_i = \frac{4 + b_1}{10}$$

The distance is given in astronomical units; an **astronomical unit** (AU) is the average distance from the sun to the earth, which is approximately 93,000,000 miles. Except for a disconcerting gap between Mars and Jupiter, Bode's law gives reasonable approximations for the distances to the seven planets known in Bode's day:

Mercury	0.5 AU
Venus	0.7 AU
Earth	1.0 AU

Mars	1.6 AU
?	2.8 AU
Jupiter	5.2 AU
Saturn	10.0 AU
Uranus	19.6 AU

Concern about the gap in the sequence led astronomers to discover the asteroid belt, which they decided was left over after the destruction of a planet that had once orbited the sun at distance specified by the missing entry in Bode's table.

Write a program to display the above table, using Bode's formula to calculate the distances.

7. The technique of series approximation can be used to compute approximations of the mathematical constant π. One of the simplest series that involves π is the following:

$$\frac{\pi}{4} \cong 1 - \frac{1}{3} + \frac{1}{5} - \frac{1}{7} + \frac{1}{9} - \frac{1}{11} + \cdots$$

Write a program that calculates an approximation of π consisting of the first 10,000 terms in the series above.

8. Unfortunately, the series used to approximate π in exercise 7 converges extremely slowly. Even after 10,000 terms have been evaluated, the approximation is correct only to four digits. Using this technique to compute π to the limit of floating-point precision would be impractical. The following series converges much more quickly:

$$\frac{\pi}{6} \cong \frac{1}{2} + \left(\frac{1}{2}\right)\frac{1}{3}\left(\frac{1}{2}\right)^3 + \left(\frac{1}{2}\times\frac{3}{4}\right)\frac{1}{5}\left(\frac{1}{2}\right)^5 + \left(\frac{1}{2}\times\frac{3}{4}\times\frac{5}{6}\right)\frac{1}{7}\left(\frac{1}{2}\right)^7 + \cdots$$

Each term can be divided into three parts, as suggested by the parentheses in the formula. Figure out how each part changes from term to term and use this information to write a program that calculates π to the limit of floating-point accuracy. Display your answer with 10 decimal places.

9. You can also approximate π by approximating the area bounded by a circular arc. Consider the quarter circle

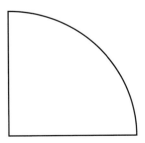

which has a radius r equal to two inches. From the formula for the area of a circle, you can easily determine that the area of the quarter circle should be π

square inches. You can also approximate the area computationally by adding up the areas of a series of rectangles, where each rectangle has a fixed width and the height is chosen so that the circle passes through the midpoint of the top of the rectangle. For example, if you divide the area into 10 rectangles from left to right, you get the following diagram:

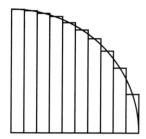

The sum of the areas of the rectangles provides an approximation to the area of the quarter circle. The more rectangles there are, the closer the approximation.

For each rectangle, the width w is a constant derived by dividing the radius by the number of rectangles. The height h, on the other hand, varies depending on the position of the rectangle. If the midpoint of the rectangle in the horizontal direction is given by x, the height of the rectangle can be computed using the distance formula

$$h = \sqrt{r^2 - x^2}$$

The area of each rectangle is then simply $h \times w$.

Write a program to compute the area of the quarter circle by dividing it into 100 rectangles.

10. The mathematical constant e can be computed by expanding the following power series:

$$e \cong 1 + \frac{1}{1!} + \frac{1}{2!} + \frac{1}{3!} + \frac{1}{4!} + \frac{1}{5!} + \frac{1}{6!} + \cdots$$

Write a program that computes the value of e by adding the terms in this series until the program reaches the limit of floating-point precision. Display your answer with 10 significant digits after the decimal point.

PART TWO

Libraries and Modular Development

Overview

If you someday take a job in the software industry, you will find that you write very few programs entirely on your own. In most companies, programmers work as teams to build applications that are much larger than those any person could manage individually. Making it possible for many programmers to work together is a fundamental challenge of modern software engineering. The four chapters in Part Two teach you how to break large programs down into independent modules and how to design those modules so that they can be used as libraries for other applications.

## CHAPTER 7

Libraries and Interfaces: A Simple Graphics Library

Art, it seems to me, should simplify. That, indeed, is very nearly the whole of the higher artistic process; finding what conventions of form and what details one can do without and yet preserve the spirit of the whole.

— Willa Cather, *On the Art of Fiction*, 1920

Objectives

- To understand the meaning of the terms *interface, package, abstraction, implementor,* and *client* as they apply to libraries.

- To recognize that interfaces are represented in C using header files.

- To be able to read the `graphics.h` interface, which provides access to a library for drawing simple pictures on the screen, and to understand the conceptual abstraction used by the graphics library.

- To learn how to draw lines using `MovePen` and `DrawLine` and to draw arcs using `DrawArc`.

- To learn how to extend the basic capabilities of the graphics library by defining new higher-level functions.

- To practice writing large programs using the graphics package.

- To appreciate the importance of general tools and the associated strategy of bottom-up implementation.

Every program you have seen or written in this text has called at least one library function. Even the one-line program `hello.c` calls `printf` to display its message on the screen. In modern programming, it is impossible to write interesting programs without calling library functions, and by this point, you should be reasonably adept at calling them.

So far, the functions you have written have all been part of a single program. You can call them from the main program or from other functions that are part of the same program file, but you have not been able to take your own functions and put them into a library that you can then use for any number of later programs. Before you can do so, you need to learn more about what a library is and how it works. Enormous power comes from being able to design good libraries and use them well. A key part of that power comes from understanding the concept of an *interface,* which is the main topic not only of this chapter but of the next several chapters as well.

To give you a sense of what an interface is and how it works, this chapter concentrates on having you read through an existing interface rather than having you design one from scratch. Before attempting to write novels, authors usually spend many years reading them. In doing so, they learn about the form of the novel and develop their own appreciation of what makes a particular novel good. Here, your job is to learn the basic structure of interfaces, and the best way to do that is to study existing examples. You will have the chance to write your own interfaces beginning in Chapter 8.

This chapter begins by outlining the conceptual structure of interfaces and defining several terms that make it easier to talk about them. It then introduces a simple graphics library that enables you to draw pictures on the screen. That library will make it possible for you to write programs that are much more exciting than those you have seen in the preceding chapters, which makes the graphics library interesting in its own right. As you use the graphics library, however, it's important to keep in mind such issues as how libraries work, what they contain, and how interfaces are used to describe them.

7.1 The concept of an interface

In English, the word *interface* means a common boundary between two distinct entities. The surface of a pond, for example, is the interface between the water and the air. In programming, an interface constitutes a conceptual boundary rather than a physical one: an **interface** is the boundary between the implementation of a library and programs that use that library. Information passes across that boundary whenever functions in that library are called. The interface mediates and gives structure to the exchange of information between the library and its users. Conceptually, a programming interface also represents a shared understanding about the nature of that boundary, providing both creators and users of a library with the critical information they need to know.

Consider, for example, the math library introduced in Chapter 5. The math library defines several functions, such as sqrt. Programs that use the math library can call sqrt to calculate a square root without having to specify the actual steps involved. Those steps are part of the implementation of the square root function, which was written by the programmers who created the math library itself. Chapter 6 presented two possible strategies—Newton's method and Taylor series expansion—for implementing the sqrt function. The library implementors might have used one of those strategies or any other algorithm that computes the correct result.

Knowing how to call the sqrt function and knowing how to implement it are both important skills. It is critical to realize, however, that those two skills—calling a function and implementing one—are to a large extent unrelated. Successful programmers often use functions that they wouldn't know how to write. Conversely, programmers who implement a library function cannot anticipate all the potential uses for that function.

To emphasize the difference in perspective between programmers who implement a library and those who use it, computer scientists have adopted specific terms to refer to programmers working in each of these capacities. Naturally enough, a programmer who implements a library is called an **implementor.** Because the word *user* means someone who runs a program rather than someone who writes part of one, a programmer who calls functions provided by a library is called a **client** of that library.[1]

Even though clients and implementors have different perspectives on the library, both must understand certain aspects of that library's design. As a client, you don't need to know the details of its operation, but you do need to know exactly how to call it. As an implementor, on the other hand, you are not directly concerned with how client programmers will use your library. Even so, you must make it possible for them to do so by providing the information they need to call the functions it contains. For each function in the library, the client must know the following:

- Its name
- The arguments it requires and the types of those arguments
- The type of result it returns

That this information is precisely what a function prototype provides is by no means a coincidence. In C, the prototype for a function and its implementation are separated because they convey information to different audiences. The client and the implementor must agree on the function prototype, which means that it is part of the interface. By contrast, only the implementor is concerned with the function implementation. The act of making a function available to clients by including its prototype in the interface is called **exporting** that function.

---

[1] In computer science, the term *client* sometimes refers to code that uses a library and sometimes to the programmer who writes that code. If there is a possibility for confusion, I will refer to code that uses a library as *client code,* although I will also follow the standard convention and use *client* in such cases, as long as the intent is clear.

The relationship between the client and implementor is illustrated in the following diagram:

client	interface	implementation
Responsible for: •how a function is used	Both sides agree on: •the function prototype	Responsible for: •how a function works

Interfaces and header files

In computer science, an interface is a conceptual entity. It consists of an understanding between the programmer who implements a library and the programmer who uses it, spelling out the information that is required by both sides. When you write a C program, however, you must have some way to represent the conceptual interface as part of the actual program. In C, an interface is traditionally represented by a header file. You have worked with header files ever since Chapter 2 and have encountered several different ones, including `stdio.h`, `math.h`, and `genlib.h`. Each of these header files specifies the interface to the underlying library.

The distinction between the abstract concept of an interface and the actual header file that represents it may seem subtle at first. In many ways, the distinction is the same as that between an algorithm and a program that implements it. The algorithm is an abstract strategy; the program is the concrete realization of that algorithm. Similarly, C uses header files to provide a concrete realization of an interface.

The same distinction between a general concept and its programming manifestation also comes up in the definition of two other terms that are often used in discussions of interfaces. In computer science, you will often hear the term *package* used to describe the software that defines a library. If you were assigned to develop a library, part of your job would consist of producing a `.h` file to serve as the library interface and one or more `.c` files that together provide an implementation. Those files constitute the **package.** To get a full understanding of a library, however, you must look beyond the software. Libraries embody a specific conceptual approach that transcends the package itself. The conceptual basis of a library is called an **abstraction.**

The relationship between an abstraction and a package is best illustrated by an example. When you write your programs, you use the `printf` function in the `stdio.h` interface for all output operations. For input, you use functions like `GetInteger`, `GetReal`, and `GetLine`, which are made available through the `simpio.h` interface. The `stdio.h` interface provides functions for accepting user input, but they turn out to be more difficult for beginning programmers to use. The two libraries embody different approaches to input operations: the `stdio.h` interface emphasizes power and flexibility while the `simpio.h` interface emphasizes simplicity of structure and ease of use. The approach used in each of these interfaces is part of the abstraction. The associated packages implement those abstractions and make them real, in the sense that they can then be used by programmers.

The contents of header files are discussed in detail in Chapter 8. The best way to get a general impression of how header files are used to represent an interface, however, is to look at an example. The following section walks you through the graphics.h header file, which specifies the interface to a simple abstraction for drawing pictures on the screen.

7.2 An introduction to the graphics library

Compared with computer games or commercial word-processing systems, the programs you have worked with so far seem relatively tame. Until now, all programs in this text have displayed their output on the computer screen as numbers and strings formatted by the printf function. Modern computer programs typically use the screen in a much more creative way that involves pictures and fancy graphical displays—features that make using the computer both easier and more exciting.

Although graphical displays may make life easier for the user, incorporating them into a program usually makes life more difficult for the programmer. Considered in its entirety, generating even a simple line drawing on the screen is an enormously complex programming problem—well beyond the scope of this text. Luckily, there is no need to look at the problem in its entirety. If you have access to a graphics library, you can ignore the underlying complexity and concentrate instead on high-level operations that cause lines and other graphical features to appear on the screen. The details are hidden on the implementation side of the interface boundary.

To use the graphics library, you must specify its interface by writing the appropriate #include line at the top of your program, which in this case is

```
#include "graphics.h"
```

The underlying model for graphics.h

Before you can appreciate the procedures and functions available in the graphics.h interface, you first need to understand the underlying abstraction. How do you specify positions on the screen? What units should you use for length? These questions are important for understanding the graphical model, which is a central part of the conceptual abstraction.

The graphical capabilities of the display screen you are using depend on the computing hardware you have available. The graphics.h interface was designed to be as general as possible, and this generality makes it difficult to describe precisely how the graphical display will be presented on any given system. Typically, when you start up the graphics package, a new rectangular window called the **graphics window** is created on the screen and used as the drawing surface. Whenever you call procedures and functions in the graphics library, the results are displayed in the graphics window.

To specify points within the graphics window, the graphics library uses an approach that should be familiar from high-school geometry or algebra. All drawing in the graphics window takes place on a conceptual grid as illustrated in

Figure 7-1. As in traditional geometry, points are identified by specifying their position relative to the **origin,** which is the point at the lower left corner of the graphics window. The horizontal and vertical lines that emanate from the origin along the edges of the graphics window are called the **axes;** the x-axis runs along the bottom of the window and the y-axis runs up the left side. Every point within the graphics window is identified by a pair of values, usually written as (x, y), that specifies the position of that point along the x and y axes. These values are called the **coordinates** of the point. Coordinates are measured in inches relative to the origin, which is the point (0, 0). From there, x values increase as you move to the right, and y values increase as you move up.

Coordinates in the graphics library come in two forms:

- **Absolute coordinates** specify a point in the window by giving its coordinates with respect to the origin. For example, the solid dot in Figure 7-1 is at absolute coordinates (2.0, 1.5).
- **Relative coordinates** specify a position in the window by indicating how far that point is along each axis from the last position specified. For example, the open dot in Figure 7-1 has absolute coordinates (2.5, 1.5). If, however, you express its coordinates relative to the solid dot, this point is shifted by the relative coordinates (0.5, 0.0). If you wanted to connect these dots with a line, the standard approach would be to specify the first point in absolute coordinates, but then to specify the connecting line in the relative mode.

The best mental model to use for the drawing process is to think of a pen positioned over a piece of transparent graph paper covering the screen. You can move the pen to any location on the screen by specifying the absolute coordinates. Once

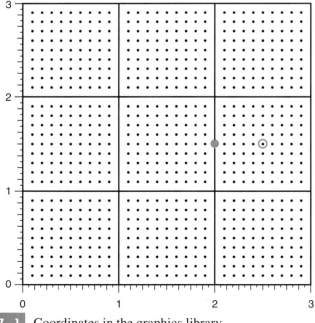

FIGURE 7-1 Coordinates in the graphics library

there, you can draw a straight line by moving the pen relative to its current location with the pen continuously touching the graph paper. From there, you can draw another line beginning from where the last one ended.[2]

The functions in the `graphics.h` interface

The `graphics.h` interface exports only a small number of functions and procedures for drawing. To draw complicated pictures, you would certainly want more capabilities, but the simplicity of this interface makes it possible to present the entire graphics package in one chapter. You can easily understand it all. The graphics library contains the following functions:

`InitGraphics()`	Initializes the graphics package
`MovePen(x, y)`	Moves the pen to an absolute position
`DrawLine(dx, dy)`	Draws a line using relative coordinates
`DrawArc(r, start, sweep)`	Draws an arc specified by a radius and two angles
`GetWindowWidth()`	Returns the width of the graphics window
`GetWindowHeight()`	Returns the height of the graphics window
`GetCurrentX()`	Returns the current x-coordinate of the pen
`GetCurrentY()`	Returns the current y-coordinate of the pen

These functions provide the capabilities you need to begin drawing simple pictures in the graphics window. To understand how to use them, however, you need to read the documentation for each, which is provided by the interface.

The interface for the graphics library is contained in the header file `graphics.h`, shown in Figure 7-2. The header file runs on for several pages, and it is important that you not try to understand it thoroughly all at once. You can read through the initial comments and peruse the file to get a sense of its structure, but it is usually best to use the interface mainly as a reference guide. As new functions are introduced in the text, you should look up the corresponding entries in the interface to see if they make sense.

The `graphics.h` interface contains a few stylized lines that are part of every interface. After the initial comments are the lines

```
#ifndef _graphics_h
#define _graphics_h
```

The very last line in the interface is

```
#endif
```

The purpose of these lines is discussed in Chapter 8, which explains how to write an interface. For the moment, however, you can ignore these lines. Although they turn out to be important to the compiler, they are not at all important to your understanding of how the interface works.

---

[2] My friends who are artists tell me that they tend to think of a figure like

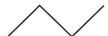

as a single line, because it is unbroken. In this text, we will always use the term *line* to mean a segment of a *straight* line. Thus, the figure in the preceding diagram is actually composed of three lines connected end to end.

FIGURE 7-2 graphics.h interface

```
/*
 * File: graphics.h
 * ----------------
 * This interface provides access to a simple library of
 * functions that make it possible to draw lines and arcs
 * on the screen.  This interface presents a portable
 * abstraction that can be used with a variety of window
 * systems implemented on different hardware platforms.
 */

#ifndef _graphics_h
#define _graphics_h

/*
 * Overview
 * --------
 * This library provides several functions for drawing lines
 * and circular arcs in a region of the screen that is
 * defined as the "graphics window."  Once drawn, these
 * lines and arcs stay in their position, which means that
 * the package can only be used for static pictures and not
 * for animation.
 *
 * Individual points within the window are specified by
 * giving their x and y coordinates.  These coordinates are
 * real numbers measured in inches, with the origin in the
 * lower left corner, as it is in traditional mathematics.
 *
 * The calls available in the package are listed below.  More
 * complete descriptions are included with each function
 * description.
 *
 *    InitGraphics();
 *    MovePen(x, y);
 *    DrawLine(dx, dy);
 *    DrawArc(r, start, sweep);
 *    width = GetWindowWidth();
 *    height = GetWindowHeight();
 *    x = GetCurrentX();
 *    y = GetCurrentY();
 */

/*
 * Function: InitGraphics
 * Usage: InitGraphics();
 * ----------------------
```

```
 * This procedure creates the graphics window on the screen.
 * The call to InitGraphics must precede any calls to other
 * functions in this package and must also precede any printf
 * output.  In most cases, the InitGraphics call is the first
 * statement in the function main.
 */

void InitGraphics(void);

/*
 * Function: MovePen
 * Usage: MovePen(x, y);
 * ----------------------
 * This procedure moves the current point to the position
 * (x, y), without drawing a line.  The model is that of
 * the pen being lifted off the graphics window surface and
 * then moved to its new position.
 */

void MovePen(double x, double y);

/*
 * Function: DrawLine
 * Usage: DrawLine(dx, dy);
 * ------------------------
 * This procedure draws a line extending from the current
 * point by moving the pen dx inches in the x direction
 * and dy inches in the y direction.  The final position
 * becomes the new current point.
 */

void DrawLine(double dx, double dy);

/*
 * Function: DrawArc
 * Usage: DrawArc(r, start, sweep);
 * --------------------------------
 * This procedure draws a circular arc, which always begins
 * at the current point.  The arc itself has radius r, and
 * starts at the angle specified by the parameter start,
 * relative to the center of the circle.  This angle is
 * measured in degrees counterclockwise from the 3 o'clock
 * position along the x-axis, as in traditional mathematics.
 * For example, if start is 0, the arc begins at the 3 o'clock
 * position; if start is 90, the arc begins at the 12 o'clock
 * position; and so on.  The fraction of the circle drawn is
 * specified by the parameter sweep, which is also measured in
 * degrees.  If sweep is 360, DrawArc draws a complete circle;
```

```
 *  if sweep is 90, it draws a quarter of a circle.  If the value
 *  of sweep is positive, the arc is drawn counterclockwise from
 *  the current point.  If sweep is negative, the arc is drawn
 *  clockwise from the current point.  The current point at the
 *  end of the DrawArc operation is the final position of the pen
 *  along the arc.
 *
 *  Examples:
 *    DrawArc(r, 0, 360)    Draws a circle to the left of the
 *                          current point.
 *    DrawArc(r, 90, 180)   Draws the left half of a semicircle
 *                          starting from the 12 o'clock position.
 *    DrawArc(r, 0, 90)     Draws a quarter circle from the 3
 *                          o'clock to the 12 o'clock position.
 *    DrawArc(r, 0, -90)    Draws a quarter circle from the 3
 *                          o'clock to the 6 o'clock position.
 *    DrawArc(r, -90, -90)  Draws a quarter circle from the 6
 *                          o'clock to the 9 o'clock position.
 */

void DrawArc(double r, double start, double sweep);

/*
 * Functions: GetWindowWidth, GetWindowHeight
 * Usage: width = GetWindowWidth();
 *        height = GetWindowHeight();
 * --------------------------------------------
 * These functions return the width and height of the graphics
 * window, in inches.
 */

double GetWindowWidth(void);
double GetWindowHeight(void);

/*
 * Functions: GetCurrentX, GetCurrentY
 * Usage: x = GetCurrentX();
 *        y = GetCurrentY();
 * -----------------------------------
 * These functions return the current x and y positions.
 */

double GetCurrentX(void);
double GetCurrentY(void);

#endif
```

The remainder of the interface consists only of comments and function proto-types. Of these, the comments account for more than 90 percent of the header file. Even though the compiler ignores the comments, they are in many ways the most important part of the interface. The real audience for the interface is not the com-piler but the programmer who is trying to write client code. The purpose of the comments is to help programmers understand the abstraction as a whole and use the facilities provided by the interface.

Initializing the package

The first procedure in the `graphics.h` interface is `InitGraphics`. As the com-ments in the interface indicate, this procedure initializes the graphics library and must be called before any other function in the package and before `printf` is used to display any output on the screen. It is common for a library package to require some initialization. When you use an interface, it is a good policy to read through it to see if it requires any initializing operations.

Drawing straight lines

The functions `MovePen` and `DrawLine` are the principal line-drawing tools the graphics library offers. As a first illustration, let's draw a single straight line that extends one inch upward from the point (0.5, 0.5). The first step in any main pro-gram that uses the graphics library is always

```
InitGraphics();
```

To draw the line, you start by moving the pen to the point (0.5, 0.5):

```
MovePen(0.5, 0.5);
```

From there, all you have to do is draw a line in which the *x*-coordinate does not change at all and the *y*-coordinate moves one inch up the screen:

```
DrawLine(0.0, 1.0);
```

The complete program is shown in Figure 7-3.

Running the program draws the following picture in the graphics window:

COMMON PITFALLS

Make sure the first line in any program that uses the graphics library is a call to the function `InitGraphics`. As a more general rule, you should remember that libraries often need ini-tialization of some sort. You should therefore check each interface to see whether any initial-ization is required.

FIGURE 7-3 oneline.c

```
/*
 * File: oneline.c
 * ---------------
 * This program draws a single straight line.
 */

#include <stdio.h>
#include "genlib.h"
#include "graphics.h"

main()
{
    InitGraphics();
    MovePen(0.5, 0.5);
    DrawLine(0.0, 1.0);
}
```

If you want to draw a square instead of a straight line, you can simply add three more calls to DrawLine to the program, so that the main program looks like this:

```
main()
{
    InitGraphics();
    MovePen(0.5, 0.5);
    DrawLine(0.0, 1.0);
    DrawLine(1.0, 0.0);
    DrawLine(0.0, -1.0);
    DrawLine(-1.0, 0.0);
}
```

which results in this picture:

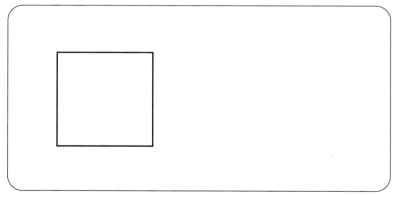

Note that each line begins where the last line ended. This behavior is consistent with the conceptual abstraction of a pen moving around on the surface of the graphics window.

Drawing circles and arcs

The only other drawing function the graphics library provides is `DrawArc`, which you use to create an arc consisting of some fraction of a circle. The prototype for `DrawArc` is

```
void DrawArc(double r, double start, double sweep);
```

Unlike many of the procedure prototypes you have encountered so far, however, the prototype alone is not sufficient for you to understand exactly what this function does. For a complete understanding, you need to look at the comments in the interface as well, which appear in Figure 7-4.

FIGURE 7-4   Interface entry for **DrawArc**

```
/*
 * Function: DrawArc
 * Usage: DrawArc(r, start, sweep);
 * -------------------------------
 * This procedure draws a circular arc, which always begins
 * at the current point.  The arc itself has radius r, and
 * starts at the angle specified by the parameter start,
 * relative to the center of the circle.  This angle is
 * measured in degrees counterclockwise from the 3 o'clock
 * position along the x-axis, as in traditional mathematics.
 * For example, if start is 0, the arc begins at the 3 o'clock
 * position; if start is 90, the arc begins at the 12 o'clock
 * position; and so on.  The fraction of the circle drawn is
 * specified by the parameter sweep, which is also measured in
 * degrees.  If sweep is 360, DrawArc draws a complete circle;
 * if sweep is 90, it draws a quarter of a circle.  If the value
 * of sweep is positive, the arc is drawn counterclockwise from
 * the current point.  If sweep is negative, the arc is drawn
 * clockwise from the current point.  The current point at the
 * end of the DrawArc operation is the final position of the pen
 * along the arc.
 *
 * Examples:
 *    DrawArc(r, 0, 360)     Draws a circle to the left of the
 *                           current point.
 *    DrawArc(r, 90, 180)    Draws the left half of a semicircle
 *                           starting from the 12 o'clock position.
 *    DrawArc(r, 0, 90)      Draws a quarter circle from the 3
 *                           o'clock to the 12 o'clock position.
 *    DrawArc(r, 0, -90)     Draws a quarter circle from the 3
 *                           o'clock to the 6 o'clock position.
 *    DrawArc(r, -90, -90)   Draws a quarter circle from the 6
 *                           o'clock to the 9 o'clock position.
 */

void DrawArc(double r, double start, double sweep);
```

The first sentence in the comments for DrawArc reveals an important piece of information: the arc begins at the current position of the pen. This fact means you have to call MovePen to position the pen at the beginning of the arc you wish to draw, just as you do when you begin drawing a line. The comments also give critically important information about what the angles mean and how they are measured. As a client, you need to know this information to use the function successfully. The comments end by offering five examples that illustrate the use of DrawArc. Such examples can be extremely helpful because it is almost always easier to call a function when you have an example to use as a model.

Here, for instance, the documentation suggests that you should be able to draw a complete circle to the left of the current point by using the call

```
DrawArc(r, 0, 360);
```

The arc has radius r and begins at the angle represented by 0 degrees, which is the 3 o'clock position. It extends for 360 degrees, thus creating a complete circle. The starting position on the arc is the current position of the pen when the call is made. Relative to the circle that is drawn, this position is the rightmost point, and the entire circle lies to the left.

Based on this discussion, you should easily be able to write a program that draws a circle with a half-inch radius, centered at the point (1, 1). All you have to do is move the pen to the starting point at the right edge of the circle and then call DrawArc. The main program is

```
main()
{
    InitGraphics();
    MovePen(1.5, 1.0);
    DrawArc(0.5, 0, 360);
}
```

which produces the following display:

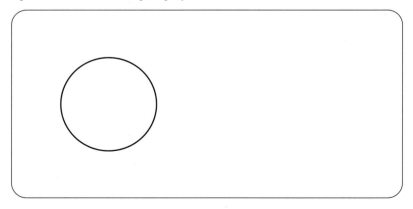

To get more of a feeling for how DrawArc works, you can try the other examples given in the documentation. For example, replacing the DrawArc call in the program by the statement

```
DrawArc(0.5, 90, 180);
```

produces this figure:

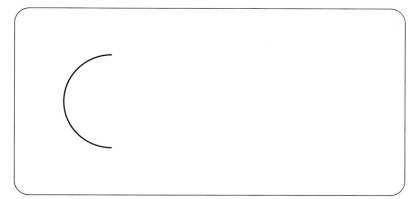

Obtaining information about the graphics window

The last four functions exported by the `graphics.h` interface do not actually affect the graphics window but instead return information about it. The functions `GetWindowWidth` and `GetWindowHeight` return the dimensions of the graphics window, measured in inches. For example, using the statements

```
MovePen(0, 0);
DrawLine(GetWindowWidth(), GetWindowHeight());
```

results in a diagonal line that extends across the entire graphics window.

These functions also enable you to find the coordinates of the center of the screen, which you can use to center a drawing. The x-coordinate of the center is half of the screen width and the y-coordinate is half of the screen height. You can therefore move the pen to the center of the screen by using the statement

```
MovePen(GetWindowWidth() / 2, GetWindowHeight() / 2);
```

The functions `GetCurrentX` and `GetCurrentY` return the x- and y-coordinates of the current pen position. These functions are used primarily in writing higher-level functions and are discussed further in the section on "Switching between absolute and relative coordinates" later in this chapter.

 ## 7.3 Building your own tools

The tools introduced in the last section are more useful than you might at first realize. Not only do you have some experience in drawing lines and arcs; you also have begun to put those tools together into program fragments that perform more sophisticated functions. For example, you learned how to put four lines together to make a rectangular box and how to use the `DrawArc` function to make complete circles. But because drawing boxes and circles are common operations, it would be tedious if you had to go through all the steps involved for each box or circle you wanted to draw. It would be more convenient if the designers of the library had simply given you additional tools for drawing boxes and circles. However, whether such functions are explicitly part of the `graphics.h` interface doesn't actually matter. Because C gives you the ability to define your own functions, you can create these tools yourself.

Defining `DrawBox`

To illustrate this process, suppose you want to define a procedure `DrawBox` that draws a rectangle oriented along the coordinate axes. The first step in the process of writing `DrawBox` is to define its prototype. Doing so is an exercise in design. You know the name of the procedure, but you also have to think about what arguments to include. A useful strategy for figuring out what arguments are required is simply to ask yourself what information the implementation needs. You can't just give it the programming equivalent of the English command: "Draw a rectangle." The implementation needs to know how big a rectangle and where to put it on the screen. The traditional way for the implementation to get this information is to have the client supply it in the form of arguments.

Even so, there is more than one way to design the `DrawBox` procedure. One possible design for `DrawBox` would be to use only two arguments—width and height—to specify the dimensions of the box. To indicate the position of the box, you would call `MovePen`, after which the box would be drawn relative to that position. Thus, to draw a box at position (x, y), you would write

```
MovePen(x, y);
DrawBox(width, height);
```

This example is not the final design.

Another alternative would be to design `DrawBox` to take four arguments—x, y, width, and height—thereby combining the act of setting the position and that of setting the dimensions, as follows:

```
DrawBox(x, y, width, height);
```

Because the second form is usually more convenient for the caller, it probably makes more sense to adopt the second approach, but either design would certainly work.

In addition to determining how many arguments are required, you must also specify the interpretation of the first two arguments. What does it mean to draw a box at position (x, y)? A box does not have an obvious starting point. Where is the point (x, y) relative to the rectangle? One possibility that is convenient for some applications is to implement `DrawBox` so that the point (x, y) specifies the center of the box. A more traditional strategy, however, is to define the origin of the box to be its lower left corner, just as the lower left corner of the graphics window is the origin of the entire coordinate system. The point (x, y) then indicates the position of the origin. No matter how you choose to define the position (x, y) in relation to the box, the main thing you need to do is make sure that the documentation for the function makes your design decision clear.

Thus one possibility for the `DrawBox` prototype is

```
void DrawBox(double x, double y, double width, double height);
```

where x and y specify the origin of the box and width and height specify its dimensions. Since this procedure is one of your creations and not part of a library, you need to define the implementation as well. The implementation consists simply of the steps necessary to draw the four lines of the figure, expressed in terms of the parameter values. You have already drawn one box in this chapter; all you need to do now is convert the explicit coordinates to the more general, parameter-based form

```
void DrawBox(double x, double y, double width, double height)
{
    MovePen(x, y);
    DrawLine(0, height);
    DrawLine(width, 0);
    DrawLine(0, -height);
    DrawLine(-width, 0);
}
```

The implementation moves to the origin point for the box and then draws the four line segments necessary to complete the box.

Now that you have this procedure, you can change the implementation of the program to draw a box on the screen so that it uses your new tool. The resulting program, drawbox.c, appears in Figure 7-5.

The design decision to use the lower left corner as the origin for DrawBox does not prevent you from writing other functions that use a different origin. For example, you could also define a function DrawCenteredBox whose first two arguments specified the center of the box rather than its corner. If you have already defined DrawBox, this new implementation is quite simple to write:

```
void DrawCenteredBox(double x, double y,
                     double width, double height)
{
    DrawBox(x - width / 2, y - height / 2, width, height);
}
```

It is important, however, to be as consistent as you can in your design choices. Using a single model makes it much easier for you, or for anyone else reading your programs, to understand exactly what is going on. In this chapter, functions that draw a figure with respect to some position other than the lower left corner specifically indicate the new origin in the function name, as in DrawCenteredBox.

Defining DrawCenteredCircle

It would also be useful to define a new function to draw complete circles. Because circles have no corners, it makes the most sense to define a function DrawCenteredCircle, which draws the circle relative to its center. This function needs three arguments: the x- and y-coordinates of the center and the radius r. The prototype for DrawCenteredCircle is therefore

```
void DrawCenteredCircle(double x, double y, double r);
```

and its implementation is

```
void DrawCenteredCircle(double x, double y, double r)
{
    MovePen(x + r, y);
    DrawArc(r, 0, 360);
}
```

FIGURE 7-5 drawbox.c

```
/*
 * File: drawbox.c
 * ---------------
 * This program draws a box on the screen.
 */

#include <stdio.h>

#include "genlib.h"
#include "graphics.h"

/* Function prototypes */

void DrawBox(double x, double y, double width, double height);

/* Main program */

main()
{
    InitGraphics();
    DrawBox(0.5, 0.5, 1.0, 1.0);
}

/*
 * Function: DrawBox
 * Usage: DrawBox(x, y, width, height)
 * -----------------------------------
 * This function draws a rectangle of the given width and
 * height with its lower left corner at (x, y).
 */

void DrawBox(double x, double y, double width, double height)
{
    MovePen(x, y);
    DrawLine(0, height);
    DrawLine(width, 0);
    DrawLine(0, -height);
    DrawLine(-width, 0);
}
```

Although you could use DrawArc directly, it is likely that DrawCenteredCircle is better tailored to your needs. For one thing, complete circles are quite common in graphical figures and occur more often than partial arcs. For another, using a higher-level function frees you from having to remember exactly how DrawArc interprets angles, which you don't have to think about when drawing a complete circle. DrawCenteredCircle provides convenience and simplification, both of which are valuable commodities in programming.

Switching between absolute and relative coordinates

The `MovePen` procedure uses absolute coordinates to specify the beginning of a line, which is then drawn by `DrawLine` using relative coordinates. For some applications, it helps to be able to move the pen to a new position relative to its previous position without drawing a line. Conversely, it is sometimes useful to be able to draw a line to a particular absolute coordinate.

The functions `GetCurrentX` and `GetCurrentY` make it easy to write a relative version of `MovePen` and an absolute version of `DrawLine`. The new functions are called `AdjustPen` and `DrawLineTo`, and their implementations are shown in Figure 7-6.

Like `DrawBox` and `DrawCenteredCircle`, these functions are not actually part of the graphics library. If you want to use them in your program, you must copy their definitions.

FIGURE 7-6 Functions AdjustPen and DrawLineTo

```
/*
 * Function: AdjustPen
 * Usage: AdjustPen(dx, dy);
 * ------------------------
 * This procedure adjusts the current point by moving it
 * dx inches from its current x coordinate and dy inches
 * from its current y coordinate.  As with MovePen, no
 * line is actually drawn.
 */

void AdjustPen(double dx, double dy)
{
    MovePen(GetCurrentX() + dx, GetCurrentY() + dy);
}


/*
 * Function: DrawLineTo
 * Usage: DrawLineTo(x, y);
 * ------------------------
 * This function is like DrawLine, except that it uses the
 * absolute coordinates of the endpoint rather than the relative
 * displacement from the current point.
 */

void DrawLineTo(double x, double y)
{
    DrawLine(x - GetCurrentX(), y - GetCurrentY());
}
```

The advantages of defining procedures

As is always the case with procedures, the real advantage of such higher-level tools as DrawBox and DrawCenteredCircle is not that you can use them in a single instance. The big payoff comes from the fact that, once you have defined a new procedure, you can use it over and over again. It is this ability to reuse steps you have written that makes procedures so useful. For example, suppose that you wanted to draw a line of squares across the graphics window, and not just the single square generated by the drawbox.c program. You could call DrawBox several times in a row, or even put it inside a for loop that drew one box in each cycle.

■ 7.4 Solving a larger problem

To develop your understanding of the functions in the graphics library, you need to focus your attention on a larger problem. Suppose you have decided to draw a picture of your dream house, using a level of detail that one might find in an elementary-school art class. A house you might draw is shown in the following diagram:

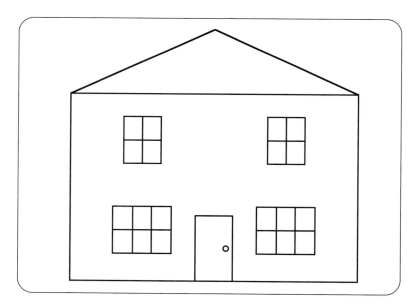

Although the picture has many individual parts, it consists of only two fundamental graphical elements: (1) the straight line, used for the house frame, the door, and the window panes and (2) the circle, used only for the doorknob. If you put these lines and circles together in the right sizes and positions, you can create the complete picture. Moreover, almost all the straight lines are arranged to form boxes, so you can make the most of your new set of tools.

Before you start writing the actual program, however, notice that this specific house has many attributes that define its shape. For example, the house is 3.5 inches wide. The distance from the ground to the attic is 2.5 inches, with another 1.0 inch to the peak of the roof. The door is a rectangle measuring 0.4 inches by 0.7 inches. Each window pane is also a rectangle with dimensions 0.2 by 0.25 inches. Rather than clutter your program with all these numbers, it is useful to give these quantities names, which you can then use in the program. The house diagram shown in the text uses the following constants:

```
#define   HouseHeight          2.0
#define   HouseWidth           3.0
#define   AtticHeight          0.7

#define   DoorWidth            0.4
#define   DoorHeight           0.7
#define   DoorknobRadius       0.03
#define   DoorknobInset        0.07

#define   PaneHeight           0.25
#define   PaneWidth            0.2

#define   FirstFloorWindows    0.3
#define   SecondFloorWindows   1.25
```

The values are real numbers representing inches, and the names describe their physical meaning in the context of the picture. In the program, the fact that these values are represented using symbolic names makes it easy to change the dimensions if, for example, you wanted a house that was a little wider or had larger windows.

Using stepwise refinement

You are now ready to start the implementation. As discussed in Chapter 5, the best way to approach a large programming problem is to use the strategy of stepwise refinement to break the entire problem down into a set of simpler ones. To apply that strategy to the problem of diagramming the house, you start at the most general level of detail: you want to draw a house. You give that operation a name, such as DrawHouse, and define it as a procedure. Implementing the DrawHouse procedure becomes your first subproblem. To complete the implementation, you then decompose the entire problem into smaller pieces: drawing the outline, the door, and the windows. Each of these operations then becomes a subproblem at the next level in the decomposition. You carry on this strategy until all the subproblems are reduced to simple operations that fit the tools you have.

As with the DrawBox procedure, however, you need to determine whether the DrawHouse procedure requires any arguments. The dimensions of the house were specified as constants in the preceding section. You also need to say where to put the house, so it seems appropriate for the DrawHouse procedure to take an x- and a y-coordinate, specifying at what position in the graphics window you want the house to appear. For consistency with DrawBox, it makes sense for these values to specify the coordinates of the lower left corner of the house. Thus the prototype for the DrawHouse procedure would be

```
void DrawHouse(double x, double y);
```

Calling this procedure instructs the computer to draw a house whose lower left corner is the point (x, y).

Having defined the prototype, you can now go back and complete the main program. All you really need to do is figure out where the picture of the house should appear on the screen. For example, suppose that you want the house to be centered in the graphics window. As discussed in the section on "Obtaining information about the graphics window" earlier in this chapter, you can use the functions GetWindowWidth and GetWindowHeight to find the coordinates of the window's center. For example, if you declare the variables cx and cy, you can set them to the coordinates of the center by writing

```
cx = GetWindowWidth() / 2;
cy = GetWindowHeight() / 2;
```

As you have defined DrawHouse, however, the diagram itself is drawn relative to the lower left corner and not the center. How can you relate these two positions?

You know that the house is HouseWidth inches wide. Thus the left edge of the house must be half that distance from the center. It follows that if you position the left edge of the house at the coordinate

```
cx - HouseWidth / 2
```

the center of the house will end up at the center of the screen. You can repeat the same argument for the y-coordinate. The only difference is that the total height of the house is the sum of the heights of the rectangular structure and the roof. The lower left corner of the house must therefore have the y-coordinate

```
cy - (HouseHeight + AtticHeight) / 2
```

Now that you have the coordinates of the lower left corner of the house, you can finish the implementation of main as follows:

```
main()
{
    double cx, cy;

    InitGraphics();
    cx = GetWindowWidth() / 2;
    cy = GetWindowHeight() / 2;
    DrawHouse(cx - HouseWidth / 2,
              cy - (HouseHeight + AtticHeight) / 2);
}
```

This definition completes the highest level of the decomposition.

Implementing the `DrawHouse` procedure

At this point, you need to turn your attention to the implementation of DrawHouse. Thinking in terms of stepwise refinement, you should already have an idea of what the fundamental operations are. In skeletal form, the DrawHouse procedure looks like this:

```
void DrawHouse(double x, double y)
{
    DrawOutline(. . .);
    DrawDoor(. . .);
    DrawWindows(. . .);
}
```

You simply need to fill in the arguments. The procedures DrawOutline, DrawDoor, and DrawWindows cannot access the values of the local variables x and y in DrawHouse, so you must pass the coordinate information along to each of the procedures. Choosing exactly what values to pass, however, requires some thought. The outline starts at the same corner as the house, so the x and y values there are probably the same. For the door, you might want to compute the coordinates of the door itself and then pass those coordinates to DrawDoor. Because there are several windows drawn relative to the house frame, the DrawWindows function should probably take the house coordinates as arguments, although it will compute more specific coordinates for each of the windows as part of its implementation. If you implement the DrawHouse procedure as suggested, it will come out looking like this:

```
void DrawHouse(double x, double y)
{
    DrawOutline(x, y);
    DrawDoor(x + (HouseWidth - DoorWidth) / 2, y);
    DrawWindows(x, y);
}
```

Looking for common patterns

When you approach large problems, stepwise refinement is only one of several strategies you can use to your advantage. Another extremely useful strategy involves trying to find common elements within the different parts of a large problem so that you can apply a single solution technique to all of them. In essence, this approach consists of determining what tools would be best for the job. For example, if you could solve several parts of a problem easily using one procedure that performed a particular operation, it might be worth creating that procedure.

If you think about the problem of drawing the house from this perspective, there are several tools you might want, some of which you have already written. For example, the outline of the house is a box, as are the door frame and the windows, so the DrawBox tool should prove very handy. The doorknob is a circle, which suggests the use of DrawCenteredCircle. But you should also think about other tools that would help. The roof of the house is a triangle. Even though there is only one triangle in the picture, writing a DrawTriangle procedure might be worthwhile, particularly since you would then have it available for use in other programs. It is even more important, however, to notice the regular structure of the windows and consider the possibility of writing a more general procedure that can draw each of the different sets of windows.

To design a tool that is appropriate for the windows, it pays to generalize the problem as much as you can. The more general your tools are, the easier it is to apply them to a wide variety of circumstances. One way to ensure that the tools you build are widely applicable is to step back from the specific characteristics of the current problem and try to visualize the necessary operations at a higher, more abstract level. In the context of the house, the picture

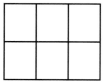

depicts a window with several panes. When you focus on this figure by itself, however, what you see is simply a rectangular grid composed of two rows, each of which contains three boxes. If you had a procedure DrawGrid that drew a rectangular grid, you could use that procedure to draw each set of windows.

What arguments does DrawGrid require? To achieve the necessary generality, you have to make sure that the DrawGrid procedure does not refer to the particular context of the house. Because using the constants PaneWidth and PaneHeight would make the procedure specific to the house picture, it is better to have the caller pass the width and height of each box within the grid as arguments. The caller knows that it is drawing a window and can supply PaneWidth and PaneHeight for this specific application. The procedure itself is just drawing boxes. Besides the height and width of each box within the grid, DrawGrid also needs to know the coordinate position of the grid as a whole. To be consistent with the other tools, DrawGrid should interpret these coordinates as representing the lower left corner of the grid. Finally, the procedure must know the number of columns and rows in the grid. Thus, the prototype for DrawGrid should look like this:

```
void DrawGrid(double x, double y, double width, double height,
              int columns, int rows);
```

Given that you already have the function DrawBox, the implementation of DrawGrid is reasonably straightforward. The implementation consists of a pair of nested for loops that calls DrawBox for each column within each row, as follows:

```
/*
 * Function: DrawGrid
 * Usage: DrawGrid(x, y, width, height, columns, rows);
 * ----------------------------------------------------
 * DrawGrid draws rectangles arranged in a two-dimensional
 * grid.  As always, (x, y) specifies the lower left corner
 * of the figure.
 */
```

```
void DrawGrid(double x, double y, double width, double height,
              int columns, int rows)
{
    int i, j;

    for (i = 0; i < columns; i++) {
        for (j = 0; j < rows; j++) {
            DrawBox(x + i * width, y + j * height,
                    width, height);
        }
    }
}
```

Given the implementation of DrawGrid, you can construct each of the window patterns just by calling DrawGrid with the appropriate arguments.

Even though it is usually best to *design* a problem from the top down, it is often best to *implement* it from the bottom up. Implementing the low-level tools first makes it much easier to debug the individual pieces of your program, which is usually easier than trying to debug all of it at once. This strategy is called **bottom-up implementation.**

Finishing the decomposition

Given the new DrawGrid tool, the rest of the program to draw the house is a straightforward example of stepwise refinement. The complete program, house.c, appears in Figure 7-7.

FIGURE 7-7 house.c

```
/*
 * File: house.c
 * -------------
 * This program draws a simple frame house.
 */

#include <stdio.h>

#include "genlib.h"
#include "graphics.h"

/*
 * Constants
 * ---------
 * The following constants control the sizes of the
 * various elements in the display.
 */
```

```
#define HouseHeight       2.0
#define HouseWidth        3.0
#define AtticHeight       0.7

#define DoorWidth         0.4
#define DoorHeight        0.7
#define DoorknobRadius    0.03
#define DoorknobInset     0.07

#define PaneHeight        0.25
#define PaneWidth         0.2

#define FirstFloorWindows  0.3
#define SecondFloorWindows 1.25

/* Function prototypes */

void DrawHouse(double x, double y);
void DrawOutline(double x, double y);
void DrawWindows(double x, double y);
void DrawDoor(double x, double y);
void DrawBox(double x, double y, double width, double height);
void DrawTriangle(double x, double y, double base, double height);
void DrawCenteredCircle(double x, double y, double r);
void DrawGrid(double x, double y, double width, double height,
              int columns, int rows);

/* Main program */

main()
{
    double cx, cy;

    InitGraphics();
    cx = GetWindowWidth() / 2;
    cy = GetWindowHeight() / 2;
    DrawHouse(cx - HouseWidth / 2,
              cy - (HouseHeight + AtticHeight) / 2);
}

/*
 * Function: DrawHouse
 * Usage: DrawHouse(x, y);
 * ------------------------
 * This function draws a house diagram with the lower left corner
 * at (x, y).  This level of the function merely divides up
 * the work.
 */
```

```
void DrawHouse(double x, double y)
{
    DrawOutline(x, y);
    DrawDoor(x + (HouseWidth - DoorWidth) / 2, y);
    DrawWindows(x, y);
}

/*
 * Function: DrawOutline
 * Usage: DrawOutline(x, y);
 * ------------------------
 * This function draws the outline for the house, using (x, y)
 * as the origin.  The outline consists of a box with a triangle
 * on top.
 */

void DrawOutline(double x, double y)
{
    DrawBox(x, y, HouseWidth, HouseHeight);
    DrawTriangle(x, y + HouseHeight, HouseWidth, AtticHeight);
}

/*
 * Function: DrawDoor
 * Usage: DrawDoor(x, y);
 * ----------------------
 * This function draws a door, with its doorknob.  As usual,
 * (x, y) specifies the lower left corner of the door.
 */

void DrawDoor(double x, double y)
{
    DrawBox(x, y, DoorWidth, DoorHeight);
    DrawCenteredCircle(x + DoorWidth - DoorknobInset,
                       y + DoorHeight / 2, DoorknobRadius);
}

/*
 * Function: DrawWindows
 * Usage: DrawWindows(x, y);
 * -------------------------
 * This function draws all the windows for the house,
 * taking advantage of the fact that the windows are all
 * arranged in two-dimensional grids of equal-sized panes.
 * By calling the function DrawGrid, this implementation
 * can create all of the window structures using a single
 * tool.
 */
```

```
void DrawWindows(double x, double y)
{
    double xleft, xright;

    xleft = x + HouseWidth * 0.25;
    xright = x + HouseWidth * 0.75;
    DrawGrid(xleft - PaneWidth * 1.5, y + FirstFloorWindows,
            PaneWidth, PaneHeight, 3, 2);
    DrawGrid(xright - PaneWidth * 1.5, y + FirstFloorWindows,
            PaneWidth, PaneHeight, 3, 2);
    DrawGrid(xleft - PaneWidth, y + SecondFloorWindows,
            PaneWidth, PaneHeight, 2, 2);
    DrawGrid(xright - PaneWidth, y + SecondFloorWindows,
            PaneWidth, PaneHeight, 2, 2);
}

/*
 * Function: DrawBox
 * Usage: DrawBox(x, y, width, height)
 * ----------------------------------
 * This function draws a rectangle of the given width and
 * height with its lower left corner at (x, y).
 */

void DrawBox(double x, double y, double width, double height)
{
    MovePen(x, y);
    DrawLine(0, height);
    DrawLine(width, 0);
    DrawLine(0, -height);
    DrawLine(-width, 0);
}

/*
 * Function: DrawTriangle
 * Usage: DrawTriangle(x, y, base, height)
 * ---------------------------------------
 * This function draws an isosceles triangle (i.e., one with
 * two equal sides) with a horizontal base.  The coordinate of
 * the left endpoint of the base is (x, y), and the triangle
 * has the indicated base length and height.  If height is
 * positive, the triangle points upward.  If height is negative,
 * the triangle points downward.
 */
```

```
void DrawTriangle(double x, double y, double base, double height)
{
    MovePen(x, y);
    DrawLine(base, 0);
    DrawLine(-base / 2, height);
    DrawLine(-base / 2, -height);
}

/*
 * Function: DrawCenteredCircle
 * Usage: DrawCenteredCircle(x, y, r);
 * ----------------------------------
 * This function draws a circle of radius r with its
 * center at (x, y).
 */

void DrawCenteredCircle(double x, double y, double r)
{
    MovePen(x + r, y);
    DrawArc(r, 0, 360);
}

/*
 * Function: DrawGrid
 * Usage: DrawGrid(x, y, width, height, columns, rows);
 * ----------------------------------------------------
 * DrawGrid draws rectangles arranged in a two-dimensional
 * grid.  As always, (x, y) specifies the lower left corner
 * of the figure.
 */

void DrawGrid(double x, double y, double width, double height,
              int columns, int rows)
{
    int i, j;

    for (i = 0; i < columns; i++) {
        for (j = 0; j < rows; j++) {
            DrawBox(x + i * width, y + j * height,
                    width, height);
        }
    }
}
```

SUMMARY

In this chapter, you have started to explore the concept of an *interface,* which is one of the most powerful ideas in modern programming. An interface is the point of connection between the implementor of a library abstraction and its clients. The interface specifies the information that both sides need to know. You will learn more about interfaces—along with strategies for designing them—in Chapter 8.

This chapter also presents a particular interface—graphics.h—to serve as a general example of how interfaces work. The graphics.h interface makes it possible for you to draw simple pictures by positioning lines and arcs on the screen. Along with the functions provided by the interface itself, you have also learned how to write additional high-level tools, such as DrawBox, DrawCenteredCircle, and DrawGrid, that extend the power of the graphics library.

Important points introduced in this chapter include:

- The code used to represent a library is collectively called a *package.* The package is the programming manifestation of an *abstraction,* which is the underlying conceptual basis for the library.
- The functions in a library are written by *implementors* and are called by *clients.* The point at which clients and implementors come together is called the *interface.*
- Interfaces in C are represented using *header files.* Header files used as interfaces contain extensive documentation as well as the prototypes for the functions *exported* by the library.
- The graphics library makes it possible for you to draw pictures on the screen. The facilities in the library are described in the graphics.h interface, which appears in Figure 7-2.
- Pictures drawn using the graphics library consist of lines and arcs that appear in the *graphics window.* Coordinates in the library are specified in inches relative to the *origin,* which is the lower left corner of the graphics window. The model used for the library is that of a pen moving across the screen.
- Before using any of the other functions in the graphics library, you must first call InitGraphics to initialize the package.
- To draw a line segment, you first call MovePen to position the pen at the starting point and then call DrawLine to draw the actual line. The arguments to MovePen are specified as *absolute coordinates,* indicating a particular position in the graphics window. The arguments to DrawLine are *relative coordinates,* which indicate how far the pen moves from its previous position. Once you have drawn one line, you then can draw additional lines, each of which begins where the last one ended. To draw a line in a new position, you must again call MovePen to position the pen at the new starting point.
- To draw a circular arc, you first call MovePen to position the pen at a point on the circle and then call DrawArc. The arguments to DrawArc are the radius of the circle, the angle at which the arc begins, and the number of degrees in the arc.

- You can extend the capabilities of the library by defining new functions, such as DrawBox and DrawCenteredCircle.
- Stepwise refinement is a critically important tool for solving large graphics programs, just as it is for other types of programming.
- Another useful strategy for working with large programs is to think about general tools that would be applicable to the current problem. If you then build those tools, you can more easily solve the current problem as well as others that involve similar operations. When you write the program itself, it is usually best to build these tools first so that you can test your program in pieces as you go. This approach is called *bottom-up implementation.*

REVIEW QUESTIONS

1. True or false: Everything you need to know about interfaces has been covered in this chapter.

2. Define the following terms: *interface, package, abstraction, implementor, client.*

3. What is the difference in perspective between the implementor and the client?

4. How are interfaces represented in C?

5. What goes into a C header file?

6. Why are comments particularly important in header files?

7. How are coordinates measured in the graphics library? What is meant by the term *origin,* and where is it in the graphics window?

8. Describe the difference between absolute and relative coordinates.

9. What are the eight functions exported by the graphics library?

10. When you use the graphics library, what statement should appear at the beginning of the main program?

11. What function in the graphics library do you use to change the position of the pen?

12. What statements would you write to draw a line from the origin to the point (2, 1)?

13. What does it mean if the third argument to DrawArc is negative?

14. Describe the arcs produced by each of the following calls to DrawArc:
    a. DrawArc(1.0, 0, 270);
    b. DrawArc(1.0, 135, -90);
    c. DrawArc(1.0, 180, -45);
    d. DrawArc(1.0, -90, 180);

15. On a piece of graph paper, sketch an approximation of the shape that would be produced by the following statements:

```
MovePen(1.0, 1.0);
DrawArc(4.0, -15, 2 * 15);
DrawArc(4.0, 180 - 15, 2 * 15);
```

16. How do you obtain the coordinates of the center of the graphics window?

17. What are the advantages of implementing new procedures like `DrawBox` and `DrawCenteredCircle`?

18. When you design a function for use as a tool, why is it useful to step outside the specific problem domain and consider the problem more abstractly?

19. What is meant by bottom-up implementation? What are its advantages?

PROGRAMMING EXERCISES

1. Write a function `DrawCrossedBox` that takes the same arguments as `DrawBox` but also draws lines along the diagonals of the rectangle. For example, the call

```
DrawCrossedBox(0.5, 0.5, 1.0, 0.5);
```

should produce the figure with the lower left corner of the rectangle at the point (0.5, 0.5).

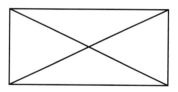

2. Write a program that draws a pyramid consisting of bricks arranged in horizontal rows, so that the number of bricks in each row decreases by one as you move up the pyramid, as shown in the following diagram:

Your implementation should use the constant `NBricksInBase` to specify the number of bricks in the bottom row and the constants `BrickWidth` and `BrickHeight` to specify the dimensions of each brick.

3. One way to draw a heart-shaped figure is by drawing two semicircles on top of a square that is positioned so that its sides run diagonally, as illustrated by the following diagram:

Write a program that uses this construction to draw a heart on the screen. Your program should display the heart without drawing the interior lines that form the top of the square, so the output looks like this:

4. In the 1960s, this symbol

became universally identified as the *peace symbol,* and it still shows up from time to time as a motif for T-shirts or jewelry. The peace symbol took its form from the letters N and D—the initial letters in *nuclear disarmament*—as expressed in the international semaphore code:

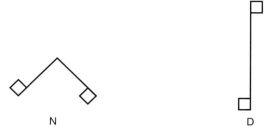

N   D

The peace symbol is formed by superimposing the lines in these two diagrams (without the flags) and enclosing them in a circle.

Implement a function `DrawPeaceSymbol` with the prototype

```
void DrawPeaceSymbol(double x, double y, double r);
```

that draws a peace symbol centered at the point (x, y) with a circle of radius r. Write a main program to test your function.

5. The sample runs in this text are represented by enclosing the output from the computer inside a box with rounded corners. Implement a function `DrawRoundedBox` to draw such boxes using the graphics library. The function should take exactly the same arguments as `DrawBox` but should replace the corners with quarter circles of a constant radius given by

```
#define CornerRadius 0.2
```

For example, calling `DrawRoundedBox` with a width of 1.0 inch and a height of 0.6 inch should produce this figure:

Make certain that your function behaves in a reasonable way if the height or width is less than `CornerRadius`.

6. Write a program to draw your initials on the graphics window. For example, if I wrote this program, I would want the output to be

You'll need to think about the best decomposition to use in writing the program. Imagine that you've been asked to design a more general letter-drawing library. How would you want the functions in that library to behave in order to make using them as simple as possible for your clients?

7. Write a program that draws a picture of the Halloween pumpkin shown in the following diagram:

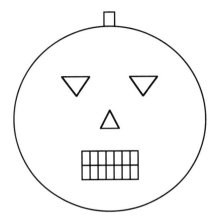

As in the `house.c` program shown in Figure 7-7, your picture should be controlled by several constants:

```
#define   HeadRadius        1.0
#define   StemWidth         0.1
#define   StemHeight        0.15
#define   EyeWidth          0.3
#define   EyeHeight         0.2
#define   NoseWidth         0.2
#define   NoseHeight        0.2
#define   NTeethPerRow      7
#define   ToothWidth        0.083333
#define   ToothHeight       0.15
```

These values are the ones used to produce the pumpkin shown in the diagram, and you should be able to figure out what each constant means by looking at the picture. Your program must be written so that changing any of these constants changes the picture in the appropriate way. For example, if you change `NTeethPerRow` to 4, the new diagram should have only four teeth in each row, but the mouth should still be centered horizontally. The two eyes and the mouth of the pumpkin face should be drawn halfway from the center to the edge of the circle in the appropriate direction, so that changing `HeadRadius` also changes the positions at which these features are drawn. The center of the circle representing the pumpkin should appear at the center of the screen.

8. If you wanted a house to go along with the Halloween pumpkin you designed in exercise 7, you might want to draw a diagram of the House of Usher, which Edgar Allen Poe describes as follows:

> I looked upon the scene before me . . . upon the bleak walls—upon
> the vacant eye-like windows . . . with an utter desperation of soul . . .

From Poe's description, you might imagine a house that looks something like this:

Write a program that draws the house illustrated in the diagram, using the following constants to specify the various dimensions:

```
#define HouseWidth          1.5
#define HouseHeight         2.0
#define HouseArch           1.0

#define TowerWidth          0.4
#define TowerHeight         2.3
#define TowerArch           0.6

#define DoorWidth           0.3
#define DoorHeight          0.5
#define DoorArch            0.25

#define WindowLevel         1.4
#define WindowSize          0.3
```

The constants whose names end in `Arch` specify the height of the triangular portion on top of the rectangular base. The windows are assumed to be square and therefore have only the single dimension `WindowSize`.

9. Write a program that draws the following stylized picture of the Lincoln Memorial in Washington, D.C.:

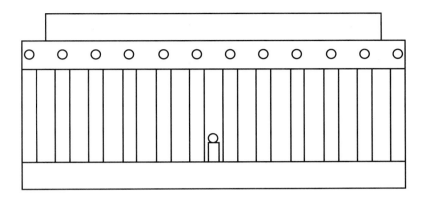

As in exercises 7 and 8, your program should use the following constants to define the characteristics of the picture:

```
#define MemorialWidth          4.0
#define PedestalHeight         0.3

#define NumberOfColumns        12
#define ColumnWidth            0.15
#define ColumnHeight           1.0
#define ColumnCircleRadius     0.05

#define LowerRoofHeight        0.3
#define UpperRoofWidth         3.5
#define UpperRoofHeight        0.3

#define StatueWidth            0.1
#define StatueHeight           0.2
```

Note that `NumberOfColumns` is one of the constants that define the picture. In designing your program, you should be sure that it is possible to change the value of `NumberOfColumns` and still have the columns come out equally spaced across the width of the memorial.

10. Write a function `DrawShadedBox` that draws a box whose interior is shaded by closely spaced diagonal lines throughout the entire figure. The function should take a fifth parameter (after the four used in `DrawBox`) that species the distance between each of the shading lines, measured along the edges of the box rather than diagonally. The shading separation parameter should be an integer measured in **points,** a unit of measure favored by printers and typesetters that is

equal to 1/72 of an inch. For example, the function call

```
DrawShadedBox(1.0, 1.0, 2.0, 0.75, 5);
```

should produce the following output:

11. Use the DrawShadedBox function from exercise 10 as part of a main program to draw a checkerboard, for which the edge length of each square is 0.25 inches and the shading separation for the dark squares is 3 points. The program should result in the following figure:

CHAPTER 8

Designing Interfaces: A Random Number Library

And such a wall as I would have you think
That had in it a crannied hole, or chink
Through which the lovers, Pyramus and Thisbe
Did whisper often, very secretly

— Shakespeare, *A Midsummer Night's Dream,* 1595-1596

Objectives

- To appreciate the principal criteria used to evaluate the design of an interface.

- To discover how programs can simulate random behavior through the use of pseudo-random numbers.

- To understand the behavior of the library function `rand`.

- To learn how you can use arithmetic operations to change the range of the pseudo-random number sequence.

- To recognize the common types of interface entries.

- To learn the syntactic rules and conventions required to write an interface header file.

- To be able to use the facilities provided by the `random.h` interface.

In Chapter 7, you were introduced to the concept of an interface. Moreover, working with the `graphics.h` interface gave you a chance to think about what goes into an interface and how to use one in your programming. But to understand interfaces fully, you must also learn how to implement them. This chapter gives you a chance to design a new interface together with its underlying implementation.

Depending on how broadly you view the problem, writing an interface can be either very simple or extremely challenging. If you consider only C's syntax and structure, there are not many new rules to learn. You already know how to write comments and function prototypes, which are the principal components of an interface. As is true with algorithms, however, the challenge comes not in *coding* the interface but in *designing* it. The important question is not so much how to write an interface but rather how to write a good one.

Designing a good interface is a subtle problem that requires you to balance many competing design criteria. This chapter examines those criteria and illustrates their application. To make the illustrations concrete, this chapter also walks you through the development of a library package that provides access to a simple random number abstraction.

8.1 Interface design

Programming is hard because programs reflect the complexity of the problems they solve. As long as we use computers to solve problems of ever-increasing sophistication, the process of programming will need to become more sophisticated as well.

Writing a program to solve a large or difficult problem forces you to manage an enormous amount of complexity. There are algorithms to design, special cases to consider, user requirements to meet, and innumerable details to get right. To make programming manageable, you must reduce the complexity of the programming process as much as possible.

In Chapter 5, you learned how to use functions and procedures to reduce some of the complexity. Interfaces offer a similar reduction in programming complexity but at a higher level of detail. A function gives its caller access to a set of steps that together implement a single operation. An interface gives its client access to a set of functions that together implement a programming abstraction. The extent to which the interface simplifies the programming process, however, depends largely on how well it is designed.

To design an effective interface, you must balance several criteria. In general, you should try to develop interfaces that are

- *Unified.* A single interface should define a consistent abstraction with a clear unifying theme. If a function does not fit within that theme, it should be defined in a separate interface.
- *Simple.* To the extent that the underlying implementation is itself complex, the interface must seek to hide that complexity from the client.
- *Sufficient.* When clients use an abstraction, the interface must provide sufficient functionality to meet their needs. If some critical operation is missing from an interface, clients may decide to abandon it and develop their own,

more powerful abstraction. As important as simplicity is, the designer must avoid simplifying an interface to the point that it becomes useless.

■ *General.* A well-designed interface should be flexible enough to meet the needs of many different clients. An interface that performs a narrowly defined set of operations for one client is not as useful as one that can be used in many different situations.

■ *Stable.* The functions defined in an interface should continue to have precisely the same structure and effect, even if the underlying implementation changes. Making changes in the behavior of an interface forces clients to change their programs, which compromises the value of interface.

The sections that follow discuss each of these criteria in detail.

The importance of a unifying theme

Unity gives strength.

— Aesop, *The Bundle of Sticks,* sixth century B.C.

A central feature of a well-designed interface is that it presents a unified and consistent abstraction. In part, this criterion implies that the functions within a library should be chosen so that they reflect a coherent theme. For example, the math library consists of mathematical functions, the standard I/O library provides functions to perform input and output, and the graphics library provides functions for drawing pictures on the screen. Each function exported by these interfaces fits the purpose of that interface. For example, you would not expect to find sqrt in the graphics.h interface, even though graphical applications will often call sqrt to compute the length of a diagonal line. The sqrt function fits much more naturally into the framework of the math library.

The principle of a unifying theme also influences the design of the functions within a library interface. The functions within an interface should behave in as consistent a way as possible. Differences in the ways its functions work make using an interface much harder for the client. For example, all the functions in the graphics library use coordinates specified in inches and angles specified in degrees. If the implementor of the library had decided to add a function that required a different unit of measurement, clients would have to remember what units to use for each function. Similarly, the functions DrawLine and DrawArc in the graphics library were each designed so that drawing begins at the current position of the pen. Doing so means that the underlying conceptual model has a consistent structure that makes it easier to understand the library and its operation.

Simplicity and the principle of information hiding

Embrace simplicity.

— Lao-tzu, *The Way of Lao-tzu,* ca. 550 B.C.

Because a primary goal of using interfaces is to reduce the complexity of the programming process, it makes sense that simplicity is a desirable criterion in the design of an interface. In general, an interface should be as easy to use as possible. The underlying implementation may perform extremely intricate operations, but the client should nonetheless be able to think about those operations in a simple, more abstract way.

To a certain extent, an interface acts as a reference guide to a particular library abstraction. When you want to know how to use the math library, you go to the `math.h` interface to find out how to do so. The interface contains precisely the information that you, as a client, need to know—and no more. For clients, getting too much information can be as bad as getting too little, because additional detail is likely to make the interface more difficult to understand. Often, the real value of an interface lies not in the information it *reveals* but rather in the information it *hides*.

When you design an interface, you should try to protect the client from as many of the complicating details of the implementation as possible. In that respect, it is perhaps best to think of an interface not primarily as a communication channel between the client and the implementation, but instead as a wall that divides them.

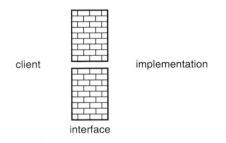

client   implementation

interface

Like the wall that divided the lovers Pyramus and Thisbe in Greek mythology, the wall representing an interface has a small chink that allows the client and the implementation to communicate. The main purpose of the wall, however, is to keep the two sides apart. Because we conceive of it as lying at the border of the abstraction represented by the library, an interface is sometimes called an **abstraction boundary.** Ideally, all the complexity involved in the realization of a library lies on the implementation side of the wall. The interface is successful if it keeps that complexity away from the client side. Keeping details confined to the implementation domain is called **information hiding.**

The principle of information hiding has important practical implications for interface design. When you write an interface, you should be sure you don't reveal details of the implementation, even in the commentary. Especially if you are writing an interface and an implementation at the same time, you may be tempted to document in your interface all the clever ideas you used to write the implementation. Try to resist that temptation. The interface is written for the benefit of the client and should contain only what the client needs to know.

Similarly, you should design the functions in an interface so that they are as simple as possible. If you can reduce the number of arguments or find a way to eliminate confusing special cases, it will be easier for the client to understand how to use those functions. Moreover, it is usually good practice to limit the total number of functions exported by interface, so that the client does not become lost in a mass of functions, unable to make sense of the whole.

Meeting the needs of your clients

Everything should be as simple as possible, but no simpler.

— attributed to Albert Einstein

Simplicity is only part of the story. You can easily make an interface simple just by throwing away any parts of it that are hard or complicated. There is a good chance you will also make the interface useless. Sometimes clients need to perform tasks that have some inherent complexity. Denying your clients the tools they require just to make the interface simpler is not an effective strategy. Your interface must provide sufficient functionality to serve the clients' needs. Learning to strike the right balance between simplicity and completeness in interface design is one of the fundamental challenges in programming.

In many cases, the clients of an interface are concerned not only with whether a particular function is available but also with the efficiency of the underlying implementation. For example, if a programmer is developing a system for air-traffic control and needs to call functions provided by a library interface, those functions must return the correct answer quickly. Late answers may be just as devastating as wrong answers.

For the most part, efficiency is a concern for the implementation rather than the interface. Even so, you will often find it valuable to think about implementation strategies while you are designing the interface itself. Suppose, for example, that you are faced with a choice of two designs. If you determine that one of them would be much easier to implement efficiently, it makes sense—assuming there are no compelling reasons to the contrary—to choose that design.

The advantages of general tools

Give us the tools and we will finish the job.

— Winston Churchill, radio address, 1941

An interface that is perfectly adapted to a particular client's needs may not be useful to others. A good library abstraction serves the needs of many different clients. To do so, it must be general enough to solve a wide range of problems and not be limited to one highly specific purpose. By choosing a design that offers your clients flexibility in how they use the abstraction, you can create interfaces that are widely used.

The desire to ensure that an interface remains general has an important practical implication. When you are writing a program, you will often discover that you need a particular tool. If you decide that the tool is important enough to go into a library, you then need to change your mode of thought. When you design the interface for that library, you have to forget about the application that caused you to want the tool in the first place and instead design such a tool for the most general possible audience.

You encountered the need for this shift in perspective in the section on "Looking for common patterns" in Chapter 7. From the perspective of a client, you needed a function to draw windows for a house. To build the tool, however, you had to think more generally. The result was the function `DrawGrid`, which can be used in many different situations.

The value of stability

> People change and forget to tell each other. Too bad—causes so many mistakes.
>
> — Lillian Hellman, *Toys in the Attic,* 1959

Interfaces have another property that makes them critically important to programming: they tend to be stable over long periods of time. Stable interfaces can dramatically simplify the problem of maintaining large programming systems by establishing clear boundaries of responsibility. As long as the interface does not change, both implementors and clients are relatively free to make changes on their own side of the abstraction boundary.

For example, suppose that you are the implementor of the math library. In the course of your work, you discover a clever new algorithm for calculating the `sqrt` function that cuts in half the time required to calculate a square root. If you can say to your clients that you have a new implementation of `sqrt` that works just as it did before, only faster, they will probably be pleased. If, on the other hand, you were to say that the name of the function had changed or that its use involved certain new restrictions, your clients would be justifiably annoyed. To use your "improved" implementation of square root, they would be forced to change their programs. Changing programs is a time-consuming, error-prone activity, and many clients would happily give up the extra efficiency for the convenience of being able to leave their programs alone.

Interfaces, however, simplify the task of program maintenance only if they remain stable. Programs change frequently as new algorithms are discovered or as the requirements of applications change. Throughout such evolution, however, the interfaces must remain as constant as possible. In a well-designed system, changing the details of an implementation is a straightforward process. The complexity involved in making that change is localized on the implementation side of the abstraction boundary. On the other hand, changing an interface often produces a global upheaval that requires changing every program that depends on it. Thus, interface changes should be undertaken very rarely and then only with the active participation of clients.

Some interface changes, however, are more drastic than others. For example, adding an entirely new function to an interface is usually a relatively straightforward process, since no clients already depend on that function. Changing an interface in such a way that existing programs will continue to run without modification is called **extending** the interface. If you find that you need to make evolutionary changes over the lifetime of an interface, it is usually best to make those changes by extension.

 ## 8.2 Generating random numbers by computer

To illustrate the foregoing principles of interface design, the rest of this chapter focuses on the problem of how to write programs that make seemingly random choices. Being able to simulate random behavior is necessary, for example, if you want to write a computer game that involves flipping a coin or rolling a die, but is also useful in more practical contexts.

Getting programs to behave in a random way involves a certain amount of complexity. For the benefit of client programmers, you want to hide that complexity behind an interface. In this chapter, you will have the opportunity to focus your attention on that interface from each of the possible perspectives—those of the interface designer, the implementor, and the client.

Deterministic versus nondeterministic behavior

Until now, all programs described in this text have behaved **deterministically,** which means that their actions are completely predictable given any set of input values. The behavior of such programs is repeatable. If a program produces one result when you run it today, it will produce the same result tomorrow.

In some programming applications, such as games or simulations, it is important that the behavior of your programs not be so predictable. For example, a computer game that always had the same outcome would be boring. In order to build a program that behaves randomly, you need some mechanism for representing a random process, such as flipping a coin or tossing a die, in the context of your programs. Programs that simulate such random events are called **nondeterministic** programs.

Random versus pseudo-random numbers

Partly because early computers were used primarily for numerical applications, the idea of generating randomness using a computer is often expressed in terms of being able to generate a **random number** in a particular range. From a theoretical perspective, a number is random if there is no way to determine in advance what value it will have among a set of equally probable possibilities. For example, rolling a die generates a random number between 1 and 6. If the die is fair, there is no way to predict which number will come up. The six possible values are equally likely.

Although the idea of a random number makes intuitive sense, it is a difficult notion to represent inside a computer. Computers operate by following a sequence of instructions in memory and therefore function in a deterministic mode. How is it possible to generate unpredictable results by following a deterministic set of rules? If a number is generated by a deterministic process, any user should be able to work through that same set of rules and anticipate the computer's response.

Yet computers do in fact use a deterministic procedure to generate what we call random numbers. This strategy works because, even though the user could, in theory, follow the same set of rules and anticipate the computer's response, no one actually bothers to do so. In most practical applications, it doesn't matter if the numbers are truly random; all that matters is that the numbers *appear* to be random. For numbers to appear random, they should (1) behave like random numbers from a statistical point of view and (2) be sufficiently difficult to predict in advance that no user would bother. "Random" numbers generated by an algorithmic process inside a computer are referred to as **pseudo-random numbers** to underscore the fact that no truly random activity is involved.

Generating pseudo-random numbers in ANSI C

The ANSI C library includes a function rand that produces pseudo-random numbers as part of the stdlib.h interface. The prototype for rand as given in the interface is

```
int rand(void);
```

which indicates that rand takes no arguments and returns an integer that is a pseudo-random value—a different result is returned on each call to rand. The result of rand is guaranteed to be nonnegative and no larger than the constant RAND_MAX, which is also defined in the stdlib.h interface. Thus, each time rand is called, it returns a different integer between 0 and RAND_MAX, inclusive.

The value of RAND_MAX depends on the computer system. In the typical Macintosh environment, RAND_MAX is 32,767. On a typical Unix workstation, it is 2,147,483,647. When you write programs that work with random numbers, you should not make any assumptions about the precise value of RAND_MAX. Instead, your programs should be prepared to use whatever value of RAND_MAX the system defines. If you are careful in doing so, you can take a program that works on one system and recompile it so that it works on another.

Running the program randtest.c given in Figure 8-1 shows how rand behaves.

On the computer in my office, randtest.c generates the following output:

```
On this computer, RAND_MAX = 32767.
Here are the results of 10 calls to rand:
      16838
       5758
      10113
      17515
      31051
       5627
      23010
       7419
      16212
       4086
```

FIGURE 8-1   randtest.c

```
/*
 * File: randtest.c
 * ----------------
 * This program tests the ANSI rand function.
 */

#include <stdio.h>
#include <stdlib.h>
#include "genlib.h"

/*
 * Constants
 * ---------
 * NTrials -- Number of trials
 */

#define NTrials 10

/* Main program */

main()
{
    int i, r;

    printf("On this computer, RAND_MAX = %d.\n", RAND_MAX);
    printf("Here are the results of %d calls to rand:\n", NTrials);
    for (i = 0; i < NTrials; i++) {
        r = rand();
        printf("%10d\n", r);
    }
}
```

You can see that the program is generating numbers, all of which are positive and none of which is greater than 32,767, which the sample run shows as the value of RAND_MAX for this computer system. Because these are pseudo-random numbers, you know that there must be some pattern, but it is unlikely that you can discern one. From your point of view, the numbers appear to be random, because you don't know what the underlying pattern is.

Changing the range of random numbers

The rand library function gives you a mechanism for generating pseudo-random numbers, but it rarely gives you precisely the range of values you need to fit a particular application. It generates numbers that are uniformly distributed over the range between 0 and RAND_MAX. Depending on your application, you are likely to want is a number that falls in some other range, usually much smaller. For example, if you are trying to simulate flipping a coin, you need to convert this large range of random number possibilities into a range containing only two outcomes: heads and tails. Similarly, if you are trying to represent rolling a die, then you need to convert the pseudo-random numbers returned by rand into numbers between 1 and 6, inclusive.

To make this sort of conversion, you need to reinterpret each random number produced by rand so that it covers a different range. The rand function generates numbers that lie somewhere on the number line between 0 and RAND_MAX:

```
0                                                                    RAND_MAX
```

If you want to simulate a coin toss, you can divide this line up so that half of it represents heads and the other half represents tails:

```
              heads                              tails
```

You could easily use this insight to develop the cointest.c program shown in Figure 8-2, which simulates tossing a coin.

This program prints out either the string "Heads" or the string "Tails", with each outcome occurring approximately 50 percent of the time. If you test the program, you get the following sample run:

```
Tails
Heads
Heads
Tails
Tails
Heads
Tails
Heads
Heads
Heads
```

**COMMON
PITFALLS**

When converting the
result of rand to a
more restricted range of
integers, do not try to
use the remainder opera-
tor. The only random
property that you are
allowed to count on when
using rand is the posi-
tion of the result along
the number line.

There is a reasonable mixture of heads and tails, and you can discern no easily detectable pattern.

In thinking about how to convert the result of rand into two possibilities, many new programmers may be tempted to adopt what seems initially like a simpler approach—using the remainder operator. If you divide the result of rand by 2 and take the remainder, the result is either 0 or 1. In a program, you could define 0 to

FIGURE 8-2   cointest.c

```
/*
 * File: cointest.c
 * ----------------
 * This program simulates flipping a coin.
 */

#include <stdio.h>
#include <stdlib.h>
#include "genlib.h"

/*
 * Constants
 * ---------
 * NTrials -- Number of trials
 */

#define NTrials 10

/* Main program */

main()
{
    int i;

    for (i = 0; i < NTrials; i++) {
        if (rand() <= RAND_MAX / 2) {
            printf("Heads\n");
        } else {
            printf("Tails\n");
        }
    }
}
```

be heads and 1 to be tails. This strategy is dangerous because there is no guarantee that the result of rand will be randomly distributed between even and odd numbers. The only guarantee is that the magnitude of the result will be randomly distributed along the number line between 0 and RAND_MAX.

One common implementation of rand provides a vivid illustration of how serious an error this approach to generating random numbers can be. On many computer systems, the rand function is implemented in such a way that the result alternates between even and odd values. The results are still randomly scattered on the number line in terms of how far along the line they fall. Even so, a program that uses the remainder operator to simulate a coin flip ends up generating heads and tails in a strictly alternating pattern.

What about simulating a die roll? If you use the strategy of the `cointest.c` example, all you need to do is overlay the outcomes

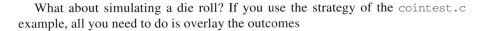

on the number line

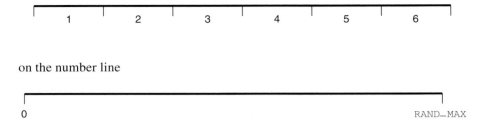

Suppose you tried to handle this task in a brute-force way by following the structure of the `cointest.c` example. The result of doing so is shown in Figure 8-3.

Unfortunately, this implementation of the `RollDie` function has a few serious problems. Because they are the sort of problems you might run into in your own coding, they are worth considering closely.

The first problem in the code is that you have made an assumption that was easy and natural to make although nonetheless unwarranted in the context.[1] The program was supposed to express the following English idea:

[1] In his book, *Zen and the Art of Motorcycle Maintenance,* Robert Pirsig calls this sort of error—one in which a seemingly reasonable assumption leads to false conclusions—a *gumption trap*. Gumption traps come up often in programming, and Pirsig's book offers at least as many useful insights to debugging programs as it does to repairing motorcycles.

FIGURE 8-3 First attempt at RollDie

```
int RollDie(void)
{
    if (rand() < RAND_MAX / 6) {
        return (1);
    } else if (rand() < RAND_MAX * 2 / 6) {
        return (2);
    } else if (rand() < RAND_MAX * 3 / 6) {
        return (3);
    } else if (rand() < RAND_MAX * 4 / 6) {
        return (4);
    } else if (rand() < RAND_MAX * 5 / 6) {
        return (5);
    } else {
        return (6);
    }
}
```

This implementation contains several errors.

- If the random number generated is less than 1/6 of the maximum, return the value 1.
- Otherwise, if the number is less than 2/6 of the maximum, return the value 2.
- Otherwise, if the number is less than 3/6 of the maximum, return the value 3, and so on.

The problem is that your code doesn't quite capture this idea. By repeatedly calling the function rand, you will generate a *new* random number in each of the if statements. The structure of the function depends on the assumption that the random number remains the same each time. To see that this is in fact the case, look at the buggy implementation of RollDie and try to understand under what conditions it will return the answer 2. In order for the function to return 2, the first if statement must come out FALSE and the second one must come out TRUE. The condition in the first if statement is FALSE five times out of six. The second if statement is written so that it returns TRUE one third of the time, because the call to rand returns an entirely new random value. In statistics, the probability of two independent events occurring is the product of the individual probabilities, so the probability that RollDie returns 2 is

$$\frac{5}{6} \times \frac{1}{3} = \frac{5}{18}$$

Five chances out of 18 is almost twice as large as one chance in six, meaning that the RollDie function is much more likely to return 2 than it should be. To solve at least this one problem, you need to declare a variable to hold the result of the call to rand and then test that variable in each line, as shown in Figure 8-4.

COMMON PITFALLS

When you call a function that produces a pseudo-random number, it is important to remember that the function will generate a different value each time it is called. If you want to keep track of a particular value, you must store the result of the function in a variable.

FIGURE 8-4   Second attempt at RollDie

```
int RollDie(void)
{
    int r;

    r = rand();
    if (r < RAND_MAX / 6) {
        return (1);
    } else if (r < RAND_MAX * 2 / 6) {
        return (2);
    } else if (r < RAND_MAX * 3 / 6) {
        return (3);
    } else if (r < RAND_MAX * 4 / 6) {
        return (4);
    } else if (r < RAND_MAX * 5 / 6) {
        return (5);
    } else {
        return (6);
    }
}
```

This implementation is still incorrect.

Unfortunately, this implementation is still buggy. The second problem, however, is more subtle. On most systems, RAND_MAX is given the value it has for a reason. The usual value chosen for RAND_MAX is not merely the maximum possible result for the rand function, but also the largest positive value that the system can represent using type int. This limitation causes a serious problem in the proposed implementation of RollDie, because the program is written in such a way that intermediate results may be larger than the maximum integer size. Even though the final result of

```
RAND_MAX * 2 / 6
```

fits in a value of type int, C's rules of precedence indicate that RAND_MAX is first multiplied by 2 and then divided by 6. Generating an integer outside of the allowable range is called an **arithmetic overflow**. If such an overflow occurs, the program will not produce the intended answer. You can fix this problem by writing

```
RAND_MAX / 6 * 2
```

There is, however, a better approach.

The real problem with the RollDie implementation is that the procedure is much too complicated. The code tests for each of the six possible outcomes as a separate case. What you need is some mathematical insight that will allow you to eliminate the special cases altogether.

Look once more at the geometric problem. What you need to do is to convert the number line

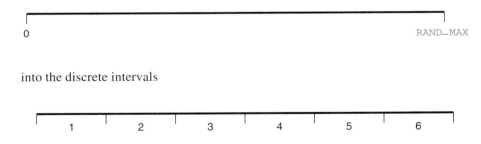

into the discrete intervals

This time, rather than using if statements, it makes more sense to use arithmetic operations to accomplish the task. Before deciding how arithmetic operations apply to this situation, however, it is useful to generalize the problem so that your solution technique can serve a wider variety of applications.

Generalizing the problem

To simulate rolling a die, you generate a random integer between 1 and 6. If you want a program to "pick a card, any card," you want it to choose a number between 1 and 52. To model a European roulette wheel, you would want it to pick a number between 0 and 36. In general, what you need is not a function that chooses a number between 0 and RAND_MAX but one that chooses a random integer between two limits that you supply. The function you need might be defined using the following prototype:

```
int RandomInteger(int low, int high);
```

In other words, if you give this function two integers, it will return a random integer that lies between those endpoints, including each endpoint in the range. Thus, to simulate a roll of a die, you would call

```
RandomInteger(1, 6)
```

and, for a spin of the European roulette wheel, you would call

```
RandomInteger(0, 36)
```

Such a general tool has many uses, and it will be to your advantage to put this tool in a library so that you can use it again and again.

You already know how to generate a random number in the interval 0 to RAND_MAX. To convert this to a random number in a more restricted range, you can use the following four-step process:

1. *Normalize* the integer result from rand by converting it into a floating-point number d in the range $0 \leq d < 1$.
2. *Scale* the value d by multiplying it by the size of the desired range, so that it spans the correct number of integers.
3. *Truncate* the number back to an integer by throwing away any fraction. This step gives you a random integer with a lower bound of 0.
4. *Translate* the integer so that the range begins at the desired lower bound.

To normalize the value, you first need to convert your result to a double and then divide it by the number of elements in the range. The numbers run from 0 to RAND_MAX, inclusive, so that the number of possible outcomes is RAND_MAX plus 1 (there are RAND_MAX values between 1 and RAND_MAX, and you also need to account for the value 0).

As noted in the section on "Assignment statements" in Chapter 2, you can use a type cast to specify an explicit conversion from one type to another. Type casts are written by enclosing the name of the desired new type in parentheses and writing it before the value to be converted. In this case, for example, you can convert the result of rand into a number d between 0 and 1 by writing:

```
d = (double) rand() / ((double) RAND_MAX + 1);
```

The numerator in this fraction must be less than the denominator so that the end result will always be strictly less than 1. Therefore, at the end of this process, you have a random real number that is at least 0 but always strictly less than 1. In mathematics, a range of real numbers that can be equal to one endpoint but not the other is called a **half-open interval**. In diagrams, the endpoint that is not included in the range is indicated using an open circle. Thus the range of possibilities for the variable d is diagrammed as follows:

0   1

The next step is to scale this value so that the range stretches to cover the correct number of integers. For example, to simulate the die roll, you need to multiply the value by 6, so that the new scaled range looks like this:

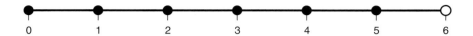

Note that there are six integers covered by the range: the integers 0, 1, 2, 3, 4, and 5. The value 6 itself lies outside of the range of possibilities, since the value d can never be as large as 1.

In the general case, you want to multiply the normalized random number by the number of elements in the range, which is given by the expression

```
(high - low + 1)
```

The "extra" 1 in this expression is necessary because the range is inclusive and therefore contains both endpoints. Subtraction gives the distance between two integers, which is one less than the number of integers contained in the inclusive range. There are six outcomes for a die roll—1, 2, 3, 4, 5, and 6—but 6 minus 1 is only 5. To compute the number of outcomes, you need to subtract the smallest value from the largest and then add 1.

Next, you truncate the real number back to an integer. In C, if you convert a `double` to an `int` using a type cast, the conversion is done by throwing away any fractional part. Thus, if you take a real number that you know to be greater than or equal to 0 but strictly less than 6, you will get one of the integers 0, 1, 2, 3, 4, or 5.

The last step in the process is to translate the result so that it lies in the desired range. You have the correct number of integer outcomes; the only problem is that they start at 0. To obtain the correct set of possibilities, you simply add the value of the lower bound.

You can put all of these steps together and write the implementation of the function `RandomInteger` as follows:

```
int RandomInteger(int low, int high)
{
    int k;
    double d;

    d = (double) rand() / ((double) RAND_MAX + 1);
    k = (int) (d * (high - low + 1));
    return (low + k);
}
```

8.3 Saving tools in libraries

The `RandomInteger` function is useful enough that you should put it in a library. The first step in this process is to create an interface. Once you complete the interface, you then write a corresponding implementation in a separate file. In most cases, the files used for an interface and its implementation have the same name except for the file type. Thus, if the interface is named `random.h`, you would ordinarily use `random.c` as the name of the implementation file.

The contents of an interface

The basic structure of an interface is illustrated by the `graphics.h` example introduced in Chapter 7. Like all the interfaces introduced in this text, `graphics.h` consists primarily of comments written for the benefit of clients who use that library. These comments are a critical part of the interface and should never be neglected when you are designing one.

A single definition exported by an interface to its clients is called an **interface entry.** Interface entries come in several different forms, of which the following are the most common:

- *Function prototypes.* An interface must contain the prototype of every function it makes available to the client.
- *Constant definitions.* An interface will often use `#define` to define a constant that the client will need to know. For example, the `stdlib.h` interface defines the constant `RAND_MAX` to tell its clients the maximum value returned by the `rand` function.
- *Type definitions.* Although you do not yet know how to define new types yourself, it is useful to know that interfaces often define new types for use by clients. For example, the `genlib.h` interface defines the types `bool` and `string`. Defining types in an interface is an extremely important technique in modern programming. You will see several examples of interfaces that export types beginning in Chapter 9.

In addition to these entries and their associated comments, every interface you write should contain three lines that are used to help the compiler keep track of the interfaces it has read. After the initial comments, but before any of the actual entries, every interface should contain the lines

```
#ifndef _name_h
#define _name_h
```

where *name* is the name of the interface file. The last line of the interface must be

```
#endif
```

In complicated programs, a single interface may be included many times through a variety of paths. So that the compiler will not read through the same interface each time, the line

```
#ifndef _name_h
```

causes the compiler to skip all of the text up to the `#endif` line if the symbol *_name_h* has been previously defined. On the first

---

S Y N T A X **for an interface file**

```
#ifndef _name_h
#define _name_h
any required #include lines
interface entries
#endif
```

where:
  name is the name of the library
  the *#include lines* section is used only if the interface itself requires other libraries and consists of standard `#include` lines
  interface entries represents the function prototypes, constants, and types exported by the library
Comments should appear throughout the interface to provide clients with the information they need to use the library.

time through the interface it hasn't, so the compiler goes on reading. Immediately thereafter, however, the compiler encounters the line

```
#define _name_h
```

which defines the symbol _name_h. If the compiler should later start to read the same interface, _name_h will already have been defined, and the compiler knows that it can ignore the entire contents of the interface.

Whether or not you understand precisely how this technique works, the rule is clear. Whenever you write an interface, you must include the #ifndef, #define, and #endif lines, as shown in the syntax box. This sort of stylized pattern that is included every time you write a particular type of file is often called **boilerplate.** These lines are the boilerplate for interfaces. You don't really need to understand them; you just need to make sure that they are always there.

In addition to the boilerplate, an interface will sometimes need to include other interfaces using the same #include lines that you have already used in your own programs. The rules for when such lines are required are discussed in the section on "Including header files in an interface" later in this chapter.

Writing the `random.h` interface

If you apply the rules from the preceding section to the problem of writing the random.h interface, you should realize that your first responsibility is to write an initial comment explaining what the library provides and who might use it. After the comment, you must include the boilerplate for interfaces, which in this case is

```
#ifndef _random_h
#define _random_h
```

The next thing to write in the random.h interface is a comment about the RandomInteger procedure:

```
/*
 * Function: RandomInteger
 * Usage: n = RandomInteger(low, high);
 * ------------------------------------
 * This function returns a random integer in the range
 * low to high, inclusive.
 */
```

This comment provides the client with the information necessary to use the function. The usage line, for example, illustrates a sample call to the function, which is often particularly helpful to the client. The comment also contains an English description of what the function does but no discussion of how the function does it.

The next component of the interface is the prototype for the function itself:

```
int RandomInteger(int low, int high);
```

This line is the only one in the interface that has any real significance to the compiler; the others are either comments or boilerplate.

The last line in the interface is simply the #endif line that is part of the boilerplate for interfaces.

The portion of the `random.h` interface discussed so far appears in Figure 8-5. As noted in the caption, the interface in Figure 8-5 is only a preliminary version. Later in the chapter, new functions are added to this interface that extend its capabilities.

The `random.c` implementation

The implementation for the `random.h` interface goes in a separate file, `random.c`. For the interface as it now exists, the corresponding implementation file is shown in Figure 8-6.

The implementation begins with an initial comment, which is simply a reference to the interface. The next section lists the `#include` files required for the compilation. You always want `stdio.h` and `genlib.h`, and you need `stdlib.h` so that you have access to the function `rand`. Finally, every implementation needs to include its own interface so the compiler can check the prototypes against the actual definitions.

After the `#include` lines, the next section consists of the implementations of the functions exported by the interface, along with any comments that would be useful to the programmers who may need to maintain this program in the future.

Like all other forms of expository writing, comments must be written so that they take account of their audience. When you write comments, you must put yourself in the role of the reader so that you can understand what information that reader will want to see. Comments in the .c file have a different audience than their counterparts in the .h file. The comments in the implementation are written for another implementor who may have to modify the implementation in some

---

FIGURE 8-5   Preliminary version of **random.h**

```
/*
 * File: random.h
 * --------------
 * This file contains a preliminary version of a library
 * interface to produce pseudo-random numbers.
 */

#ifndef _random_h
#define _random_h

/*
 * Function: RandomInteger
 * Usage: n = RandomInteger(low, high);
 * ------------------------------------
 * This function returns a random integer in the range
 * low to high, inclusive.
 */

int RandomInteger(int low, int high);

#endif
```

FIGURE 8-6 Preliminary version of random.c

```
/*
 * File: random.c
 * --------------
 * This file implements the preliminary random.h interface.
 */

#include <stdio.h>
#include <stdlib.h>

#include "genlib.h"
#include "random.h"

/*
 * Function: RandomInteger
 * -----------------------
 * This function first obtains a random integer in
 * the range [0..RAND_MAX] by applying four steps:
 * (1) Generate a real number between 0 and 1.
 * (2) Scale it to the appropriate range size.
 * (3) Truncate the value to an integer.
 * (4) Translate it to the appropriate starting point.
 */

int RandomInteger(int low, int high)
{
    int k;
    double d;

    d = (double) rand() / ((double) RAND_MAX + 1);
    k = (int) (d * (high - low + 1));
    return (low + k);
}
```

---

way. They therefore must explain how the implementation works and provide any details that later maintainers would want to know. Comments in the interface, on the other hand, are written for the client. A client should never have to read the comments inside the implementation. The comments in the interface should be sufficient.

Constructing a client program

You can test the random.c implementation by writing the program dicetest.c shown in Figure 8-7. The main program makes use of your new random number library, so you need to include the line

```
#include "random.h"
```

in the dicetest.c file so that it can use the RandomInteger function.

FIGURE 8-7 dicetest.c

```
/*
 * File: dicetest.c
 * ----------------
 * This program simulates rolling a die.
 */

#include <stdio.h>
#include "genlib.h"
#include "random.h"

/*
 * Constants
 * ---------
 * NTrials -- Number of trials
 */

#define NTrials 10

/* Function prototypes */

int RollDie(void);

/* Main program */

main()
{
    int i;

    for (i = 0; i < NTrials; i++) {
        printf("%d\n", RollDie());
    }
}

/*
 * Function: RollDie
 * Usage: die = RollDie();
 * -----------------------
 * This function generates and returns a random integer in the
 * range 1 to 6, representing the roll of a six-sided die.
 */

int RollDie(void)
{
    return (RandomInteger(1, 6));
}
```

Let's quickly test the program to make sure that it works. Running the program gives the following result:

```
4
2
2
4
6
2
5
2
3
1
```

Once again, the numbers are all in the correct range and appear random. The number 2 comes up more often than the others, but it is statistically possible that the number 2 will come up four times by pure chance. Even so, you might want to investigate by running the program again. This time it gives:

```
4
2
2
4
6
2
5
2
3
1
```

The disturbing observation is not simply that the number 2 came up just as many times on this second run. The entire result is exactly the same. In fact, every time you run this program, you get precisely the same result. This behavior on the part of your test program does not bode well for the prospect of writing interesting computer games.

Initializing the random number generator

The fact that the `dicetest.c` program produces the same sequence of numbers each time is not because of any bug in the implementation of `RandomInteger`. This behavior comes instead from the definition of the `rand` function in the standard ANSI libraries. Unless the caller takes specific action to change the standard mode of operation, the `rand` function always returns the same sequence of values on every execution of a program that calls it. Thus, every program presented so far in this chapter will have exactly the same effect each time it is run.

At first glance, you may find it hard to see any reason why `rand` might behave as it does, particularly since the `rand` function exists to simulate a nondeterministic process. As the `stdlib.h` interface is defined, the behavior of `rand` is entirely deterministic. There is, however, an extremely good reason to define `rand` in this way: programs that behave deterministically are easier to debug.

To illustrate this fact, suppose you have just written a program to play an intricate game, such as Monopoly. As is always the case with newly written programs, the odds are good your program has a few bugs. In a complex program, bugs can be relatively obscure, in the sense that they only occur in rare situations. Suppose that you've been playing the game and find that the program starts behaving in a bizarre way, but you weren't alert enough to pay attention to all the relevant symptoms. You would like to run the program again and watch more carefully this time.

If the program is running in a nondeterministic way, a second run of the program will behave differently from the first. Bugs that showed up the first time may not occur on the second pass. In general, it is extremely difficult to reproduce the conditions that cause a program to fail if the program is behaving in a truly random fashion. If, on the other hand, the program is operating deterministically, it will do the same thing each time it is run. This behavior makes it possible for you to recreate a problem. During the debugging phase, the `rand` function is doing the right thing by returning the same sequence of values every time.

Even if the system definition of `rand` has advantages for debugging, it is still important to be able to change that behavior once the program is working. Understanding how to make this change, however, requires knowing a little more about the implementation of `rand`.

The ANSI libraries generate pseudo-random numbers by keeping track of the last number generated. Each time `rand` is called, it takes the last number and performs a series of calculations using that number to produce the next one. Because you don't know what those calculations are, it is best to think of the entire operation as a black box where old numbers go in on one side and new pseudo-random numbers pop out on the other.

The `randtest.c` program described in the section on "Generating pseudo-random numbers in ANSI C" earlier in this chapter provides an illustration of the internal operation of `rand`. On the computer in my office, the first 10 calls to `rand` generate the numbers shown in this sample run:

```
On this computer, RAND_MAX = 32767.
Here are the results of 10 calls to rand:
    16838
     5758
    10113
    17515
    31051
     5627
    23010
     7419
    16212
     4086
```

The first call to `rand` produces the number 16838. The next call corresponds to putting 16838 into one end of the black box representing the internal implementation and having 5758 pop out on the other side:

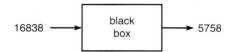

Similarly, on the next call to `rand`, the implementation puts 5758 into the black box, which returns 10113:

This same process is repeated on each call to `rand`. The computation inside the black box is designed so that (1) the numbers are uniformly distributed over the legal range, and (2) the sequence goes on for a long time before it begins to repeat.

But what about the first call to `rand`—the one that returns 16838? The implementation must have a starting point. There must be an integer, *s*, that goes into the black box and produces 16838:

This initial value—the value that is used to get the entire process started—is called a **seed** for the random number generator. The ANSI library implementation sets the initial seed to a constant value every time a program is started so that it always produces the same sequence. You can change the sequence by setting the seed to a different value. To do so, you need to call the function `srand`, which takes the new seed as an argument. To make sure the value of the new seed changes for each run of the program, the standard approach is to use the value of the internal system clock as the initial seed. Because the time keeps changing, the random number sequence will change as well.

You can retrieve the current value of the system clock by calling the function `time`, which is defined in the ANSI library interface `time.h`, and then converting the result to an integer. This technique allows you to write the following statement, which has the effect of initializing the pseudo-random number generator to some unpredictable point:

```
srand((int) time(NULL));
```

Although it requires only a single line, the operation to set the random seed to an unpredictable value based on the system clock is relatively obscure. If this line were to appear in the client program, the client would have to understand the concept of a random number seed, the `time` function, and the meaning of the mysterious constant `NULL`. To make things simpler for the client, it would be much better to give this operation a simple name like `Randomize` and add it to the random number library. If you make this change, all the client needs to do is call

```
Randomize();
```

which is certainly easier to explain.

The implementation of `Randomize` is simply

```
void Randomize(void)
{
    srand((int) time(NULL));
}
```

 ## 8.4 **Evaluating the design of the** `random.h` **interface**

As part of the process of designing an interface, you should keep in mind the general principles guiding such design. In the case of the evolving `random.h` interface, for example, it is important to consider how well the current interface meets the five basic criteria outlined earlier in this chapter:

- *Is it unified?* The two functions, `RandomInteger` and `Randomize`, both fit under the unifying theme of providing access to a random number abstraction. Thus, the interface is unified.

- *Is it simple?* Although you have not had much opportunity to use the functions and see if they are in fact simple to use, the `dicetest.c` program gives some evidence that they are. Moreover, it is clear that the interface hides considerable complexity. Calling `RandomInteger` frees the client from having to worry about the internal steps of normalization, scaling, truncation, and translation, since all those operations are performed by the implementation. Similarly, the `Randomize` function protects the client from all the internal details of seeding the random number generator. Thus, the interface certainly provides some measure of simplification.

- *Is it sufficient?* This question is always difficult to answer because it raises the companion question: sufficient for what? Though you probably cannot anticipate the needs of all clients, it is a good idea to try. The current version of the package is useful for clients who need random integers, but some clients would require other operations, such as some means of simulating random real numbers over a continuous range. The possibility suggests that some further design work may be required to meet this need.

- *Is it general?* The issue of generality is closely linked with that of sufficiency, but also includes the question of whether the interface design unconsciously incorporates any assumptions that are really in the domain of a particular client, thereby reducing its utility to others. For example, if the interface were defined to include functions that simulated a die roll, as opposed to allowing the client to build such functions on top of

RandomInteger, that interface would likely be too narrow in its design. As it stands, however, the functions in the interface seem to meet the criterion of generality.

- *Is it stable?* The issue of stability is not so much a question for the design phase as for the long-term maintenance cycle of the package as a whole. The important question at this point is whether the interface design promotes long-term stability in some way. In general, an interface that satisfies the other requirements can probably remain stable, although preserving such stability requires good discipline on the part of those who are in charge of maintaining the library.

Thus, the only pending concern is that the random.h interface does not provide all the functions that clients are likely to need. In particular, the analysis of the design in the preceding section suggests that providing random real numbers would increase the utility of the random number library for some clients. It is therefore worth defining an additional function, presumably called RandomReal to go along with RandomInteger, that provides the necessary capability.

Generating random real numbers

As it happens, you have already used the rand function to generate a random real number as part of the implementation of RandomInteger. The first step in the process of generating a random integer was to generate a random floating-point number between 0 and 1. To implement the RandomReal function, one approach would be to do the same calculation and return the result. Such a design, however, violates to some extent the unifying principles that give the library consistency. Designed with that approach, RandomReal would take no arguments and return a floating-point value in a preset range. The RandomInteger function behaves differently. It takes two arguments and returns a value in the range defined by those inputs. For consistency, it is probably best that RandomReal have the same basic design. If it does, clients who know how RandomInteger works can correctly predict the structure of RandomReal. Thus, RandomReal should have the following prototype:

```
double RandomReal(double low, double high);
```

The implementation essentially consists of the first two lines of the implementation of RandomInteger, except that the scaling factor is now the actual distance between the endpoints instead of the number of integers contained in that range. Thus the implementation of RandomReal is

```
double RandomReal(double low, double high)
{
    double d;

    d = (double) rand() / ((double) RAND_MAX + 1);
    return (low + d * (high - low));
}
```

Simulating a probabilistic event

In addition to random real numbers, there is another type of random variable that might be useful to include in a general abstraction for simulating random behavior. Suppose you are writing a program in which you want a certain event to occur with random probability. For example, suppose that your program is intended to model an assembly line on which there is a defect that occurs, on average, in 1 out of every 1000 parts that travel down the line. In terms of the simulation, another way to think about this situation is that each part has a 1 in 1000 chance of being defective. In mathematics and statistics, probabilities are represented as numbers between 0 and 1, so the probability of a defect in this example is .001 (1/1000).

In this example, the outcome has only two possibilities: either there is a defect or there isn't. The fact that there are two outcomes that represent the presence or absence of a condition suggests that it would be appropriate to represent the situation using a Boolean value. The value TRUE is used to signify that a defect has been detected, which should occur with probability .001.

In situations of this sort, it is helpful to have a predicate function that returns TRUE with some specified probability. If you had access to such a function, which might be named RandomChance, you could represent the assembly line example using the following code:

```
if (RandomChance(.001)) {
    printf("A defect has occurred.\n");
}
```

As a second example, you could use RandomChance to simulate flipping a coin:

```
if (RandomChance(.5)) {
    printf("heads\n");
} else {
    printf("tails\n");
}
```

The advantage of this implementation over the one presented in the section on "Changing the range of random numbers" earlier in this chapter is that this one does not require the client to understand the operation of the rand function itself. The client can instead rely only on the functions defined in the higher-level random.h interface. The existence of the rand function can then be considered as a detail of concern only in the implementation.

The prototype and implementation for the RandomChance function are each very simple. The prototype, which becomes part of the interface, is

```
bool RandomChance(double p);
```

You can easily write the implementation in terms of RandomReal like this:

```
bool RandomChance(double p)
{
    return (RandomReal(0, 1) < p);
}
```

Including header files in an interface

Adding `RandomChance` to the `random.h` interface, however, brings up an important issue. `RandomChance` is a predicate function and therefore returns a result of type `bool`. As noted in the section on "Boolean data" in Chapter 4, the type `bool` is not actually a part of C but is instead defined in the `genlib.h` interface. For the compiler to interpret correctly the prototype for `RandomChance` when it reads through the `random.h` interface, it needs access to the definition of `bool` in `genlib.h`.

To provide the compiler with the information it requires, you need to include the `genlib.h` header file as part of the interface. Thus, right after the boilerplate lines

```
#ifndef _random_h
#define _random_h
```

the `random.h` header file must include the line

```
#include "genlib.h"
```

which instructs the compiler to read the definitions in `genlib.h`. The compiler will therefore have read the definition for `bool` by the time it reaches the prototype for `RandomChance` later in the file.

Each interface must include only those header files that are required to compile the interface itself and not the corresponding implementation. For example, the implementation file `random.c` needs access to `stdlib.h` and `time.h` in order to use functions like `rand`, `srand`, and `time`. These functions, however, appear only in the implementation, not in the interface. Thus, the `random.h` interface does not need to include these header files even though the `random.c` implementation does. By contrast, the type `bool` appears explicitly in the `random.h` interface, which means that the interface must include `genlib.h`.

Completing the implementation of the random-number package

All that remains to complete the definition of the `random.h` interface and the corresponding `random.c` implementation is to add the new functions defined in the last few sections to the preliminary versions of these files given in Figures 8-5 and 8-6, along with enough commentary to allow clients to understand the interface. Because all the sections of code have been shown individually, the complete versions of the interface and implementation do not appear in this chapter but in Appendix B.

■■■ 8.5 Using the random-number package

Now that you have a random-number package, you can use it as often as you want. Whenever you decide to write a new computer game or any other application that involves random numbers, you'll have a set of tools you can use without having to remember the underlying details. All you need to do to use the random number library is to include the header file `random.h` in your program and make sure the library is available when you compile and run the program.

To illustrate the use of the package, a program called `craps.c` is shown in Figure 8-8. This program simulates the casino game of craps, which is played as

COMMON PITFALLS

Each interface must include any header files that are necessary for the compiler to understand the interface itself. An interface does not, however, include header files that are only required by the underlying implementation. Those header files are included only in the .c file that implements the interface.

craps.c

```
/*
 * File: craps.c
 * -------------
 * This program plays the dice game called craps.  For a discussion
 * of the rules of craps, please see the GiveInstructions function.
 */

#include <stdio.h>
#include "genlib.h"
#include "random.h"
#include "simpio.h"
#include "strlib.h"

/* Function prototypes */

void GiveInstructions(void);
void PlayCrapsGame(void);
int RollTwoDice(void);
bool GetYesOrNo(string prompt);

/* Main program */

main()
{
    Randomize();
    if (GetYesOrNo("Would you like instructions? ")) {
        GiveInstructions();
    }
    while (TRUE) {
        PlayCrapsGame();
        if (!GetYesOrNo("Would you like to play again? ")) break;
    }
}

/*
 * Function: GiveInstructions
 * Usage: GiveInstructions();
 * --------------------------
 * This function welcomes the player to the game and gives
 * instructions on the rules to craps.
 */

void GiveInstructions(void)
{
    printf("Welcome to the craps table!\n\n");
    printf("To play craps, you start by rolling a pair of dice\n");
    printf("and looking at the total.  If the total is 2, 3, or\n");
```

```
        printf("12, that's called 'crapping out' and you lose.  If\n");
        printf("you roll a 7 or an 11, that's called a 'natural' and\n");
        printf("you win.  If you roll any other number, that number\n");
        printf("becomes your 'point' and you keep on rolling until\n");
        printf("you roll your point again (in which case you win)\n");
        printf("or a 7 (in which case you lose).\n");
}


/*
 * Function: PlayCrapsGame
 * Usage: PlayCrapsGame();
 * -----------------------
 * This function plays one game of craps.
 */

void PlayCrapsGame(void)
{
    int total, point;

    printf("\nHere we go!\n");
    total = RollTwoDice();
    if (total == 7 || total == 11) {
        printf("That's a natural.  You win.\n");
    } else if (total == 2 || total == 3 || total == 12) {
        printf("That's craps.  You lose.\n");
    } else {
        point = total;
        printf("Your point is %d.\n", point);
        while (TRUE) {
            total = RollTwoDice();
            if (total == point) {
                printf("You made your point.  You win.\n");
                break;
            } else if (total == 7) {
                printf("That's a seven.  You lose.\n");
                break;
            }
        }
    }
}


/*
 * Function: RollTwoDice
 * Usage: total = RollTwoDice();
 * -----------------------------
 * This function rolls two dice and returns their sum.  As part
 * of the implementation, the result is displayed on the screen.
 */
```

```
int RollTwoDice(void)
{
    int d1, d2, total;

    printf("Rolling the dice . . .\n");
    d1 = RandomInteger(1, 6);
    d2 = RandomInteger(1, 6);
    total = d1 + d2;
    printf("You rolled %d and %d -- that's %d.\n", d1, d2, total);
    return (total);
}

/*
 * Function: GetYesOrNo
 * Usage: if (GetYesOrNo(prompt)) . . .
 * ------------------------------------
 * This function asks the user the question indicated by prompt
 * and waits for a yes/no response.  If the user answers "yes"
 * or "no", the program returns TRUE or FALSE accordingly.
 * If the user gives any other response, the program asks
 * the question again.
 */

bool GetYesOrNo(string prompt)
{
    string answer;

    while (TRUE) {
        printf("%s", prompt);
        answer = GetLine();
        if (StringEqual(answer, "yes")) return (TRUE);
        if (StringEqual(answer, "no")) return (FALSE);
        printf("Please answer yes or no.\n");
    }
}
```

follows. You start by rolling two six-sided dice and looking at the total. The game then breaks down into the following cases based on that first roll:

- You rolled a 2, 3, or 12. Rolling these numbers on your first roll is called *crapping out* and means that you lose.
- You rolled a 7 or an 11. When either of these numbers comes up on your first roll, it is called a *natural,* and you win.
- You rolled one of the other numbers (4, 5, 6, 8, 9, or 10). In this case, the number you rolled is called your *point,* and you continue to roll the dice until either you roll your point a second time, in which case you win, or you roll a 7, in which case you lose. If you roll any other number (including 2, 3, 11, and 12, which are no longer treated specially), you just keep on rolling until your point or a 7 appears.

The program itself is a straightforward translation of the English rules into C code. As you look through the `craps.c` program, you should notice the following features:

- The program includes the interface `random.h` so it can use the functions in that library. Moreover, the program uses only the functions in that library and never calls `rand` (or `srand` or `time`) directly. The random number sequence is initialized by calling `Randomize`, and each die roll is generated by a call to `RandomInteger`.

- The program is broken up into units that successively indicate greater detail. This decomposition helps to highlight the program structure and makes it possible for you to understand how the pieces fit together.

- The problem of rolling two dice comes up at several points in the program, so the combined action of simulating the roll of two dice, displaying the result, and remembering the total is encapsulated into the function `RollTwoDice`, which can be used in other contexts as well.

SUMMARY

In this chapter, you have had the chance to consider the process of writing an interface and its corresponding implementation. At one level, you have learned about the syntactic structure of an interface and the components it contains. You have also learned several more general principles of interface design—principles that will prove extremely important as you begin to solve larger tasks. Finally, you had the opportunity to see those design principles as they were applied to the construction of the `random.h` interface.

Important points introduced in this chapter include:

- The challenge of constructing an interface lies in the *design* of the interface rather than its *coding*.

- A well-designed interface must be *unified, simple, sufficient, general,* and *stable.* Since these criteria sometimes conflict with each other, you must learn to strike an appropriate balance in your interface design.

- All the functions defined in an interface should fit a unifying theme and be as consistent as possible in their behavior.

- A main purpose of an interface is to keep the complexity of the implementation away from its clients. This principle is called *information hiding.*

- The abstraction represented by an interface must be powerful enough to satisfy the needs of its clients.

- An interface that is designed to be general enables many different clients to use the same library package.

- Clients must be able to rely on the stability of the interfaces they use. Changing an interface is a serious matter and not one to be undertaken lightly. On the other hand, maintaining a stable interface allows the implementor considerable freedom to change the underlying implementation.

- Programs can simulate random behavior by using an algorithmic process to generate a sequence of numbers that appears to be random. The numbers in such a sequence are called *pseudo-random numbers.*
- The ANSI library defines a function `rand` that returns a pseudo-random number between 0 and `RAND_MAX`.
- You can change the range of the pseudo-random numbers by applying simple arithmetic operations.
- The definitions exported by an interface are called *interface entries.* The most common interface entries are *function prototypes, constant definitions,* and *type definitions.* The interface should also contain comments for each entry so that the client can understand how to use that entry.
- To ensure that the compiler reads an interface only once, every interface should include these lines before the first interface entry:

```
#ifndef _name_h
#define _name_h
```

and this line at the end of the interface file:

```
#endif
```

- Unless you take special action, the `rand` function generates the same sequence of random numbers every time the program is run. To generate an unpredictable sequence, you must change the initial random-number *seed.* When you are using the `random.h` interface, the easiest way to set the seed is by calling the function `Randomize`.
- Each interface must include any header files that are necessary for the compiler to understand the interface itself. An interface should not include header files that are required only by the underlying implementation.
- If you want to work with pseudo-random numbers in your programs, you should use the `random.h` interface, which exports the functions `Randomize`, `RandomInteger`, `RandomReal`, and `RandomChance`. Using this interface is much simpler than working directly with `rand`.

REVIEW QUESTIONS

1. True or false: The hardest thing about writing an interface is following all of C's syntactic rules.

2. What are the five criteria for good interface design listed in this chapter?

3. What is an abstraction boundary?

4. Why is it important for an interface to be stable?

5. What is meant by the term *pseudo-random number?*

6. On most computers, how is the value of RAND_MAX chosen?

7. What four steps are necessary to convert the result of rand into an integer value with a different range?

8. How would you use RandomInteger to generate a pseudo-random number between 1 and 100?

9. By executing each of the statements by hand, determine whether RandomInteger works with negative arguments. What are the possible results of calling the function RandomInteger(-5, 5)?

10. Could you use the multiple assignment statement

```
d1 = d2 = RandomInteger(1, 6);
```

to simulate the process of rolling two dice?

11. What are the three most common interface entries?

12. If you were defining an interface named magic.h, what would the interface boilerplate look like? What is the purpose of these lines?

13. True or false: The rand function ordinarily generates the same sequence of random numbers every time a program is run.

14. What is meant by the term *seed* in the context of random numbers?

15. What suggestion does this chapter offer for debugging a program involving random numbers?

16. What functions are defined in the final version of the random.h interface? In what context would you use each function?

PROGRAMMING EXERCISES

1. Run the randtest.c program on your computer system. What is the value of RAND_MAX on your machine?

2. Write a program that displays a random even number between 2 and 100.

3. Write a program that displays a random seven-digit phone number. The output should adhere to the following rules, which apply in the United States:

   ▪ The output contains a hyphen between the third and fourth digit, as in 555-1968.
   ▪ Neither of the first two digits is 0 or 1. This rule has actually been dropped in many parts of the United States, but you should nevertheless apply it for the

purpose of this problem. Thus your program might generate the number 781-9902 but not the number 718-9902.

4. Write a program that displays the name of a card randomly chosen from a complete deck of 52 playing cards. Each card consists of a *rank* (ace, 2, 3, 4, 5, 6, 7, 8, 9, 10, jack, queen, king) and a *suit* (clubs, diamonds, hearts, spades). Your program should display the complete name of the card, as shown in the following sample run:

```
Queen of Spades
```

5.
>   Heads. . . .
>   Heads. . . .
>   Heads. . . .
>   A weaker man might be moved to re-examine his faith, if in nothing
>   else at least in the law of probability.
>
>   — *Rosencrantz and Guildenstern Are Dead*, Tom Stoppard, 1967

Write a program that simulates flipping a coin repeatedly and continues until three *consecutive* heads are tossed. At that point, your program should display the total number of coin flips that were made. The following is one possible sample run of the program:

```
tails
heads
heads
tails
tails
heads
tails
heads
heads
heads
It took 10 flips to get heads 3 consecutive times.
```

6. Although it is often easiest to think of random numbers in the context of games of chance, they have other, more practical uses in computer science and mathematics. For example, you can use random numbers to generate a rough approximation of the constant π by writing a simple program that simulates a dart

board. Imagine that you have a dart board hanging on your wall. It consists of a circle painted on a square backdrop, as in the following diagram:

What happens if you throw a whole bunch of darts completely randomly, ignoring any darts that miss the board altogether? Some of the darts will fall inside the painted circle, but some will be outside the circle in the white corners of the square. Because you threw the darts randomly, the ratio of the number of darts that landed inside the circle to the total number of darts hitting the square should be approximately equal to the ratio between the two areas. The ratio of the areas is independent of the actual size of the dart board, as illustrated by the following formula:

$$\frac{\text{darts falling inside the circle}}{\text{darts falling inside the square}} \cong \frac{\text{area of the circle}}{\text{area of the square}} = \frac{\pi r^2}{4 r^2} = \frac{\pi}{4}$$

To simulate this process in a program, imagine that the dart board is drawn on the standard coordinate plane introduced in the section on "The underlying model for `graphics.h`" in Chapter 7, with its center at the origin and a radius of 1 unit. The process of throwing a dart randomly at the square can be modeled by generating two random numbers, x and y, each of which lies between −1 and 1. This (x,y) point always lies somewhere inside the square. The point (x,y) lies inside the circle if

$$\sqrt{x^2 + y^2} < 1$$

This condition, however, can be simplified considerably by squaring each side of the inequality, which gives the following more efficient test:

$$x^2 + y^2 < 1$$

If you perform this simulation many times and compute the fraction of darts that fall within the circle, the result will be somewhere in the neighborhood of $\pi/4$.

   Write a program that simulates throwing 10,000 darts and then uses the simulation technique described in this exercise to generate and display an approximate value of π. Don't worry if your answer is correct only in the first few digits. The strategy used in this problem is not particularly accurate, even though it occasionally proves useful as a technique for making rough approximations. In mathematics, this technique is called *Monte Carlo integration,* after the capital city of Monaco.

7. Albert Einstein said that "I shall never believe that God plays dice with the world." Despite Einstein's metaphysical objections, the current models of physics, and particularly of quantum theory, are based on the idea that nature does indeed involve random processes. A radioactive atom, for example, does not decay for any specific reason that we mortals understand. Instead, that atom has a random probability of decaying within a period of time. Sometimes it does, sometimes it doesn't, and there is no way to know for sure.

   Because physicists consider radioactive decay a random process, it is not surprising that random numbers can be used to simulate that process. Suppose you start with a collection of atoms, each of which has a certain probability of decaying in any unit of time. You can then approximate the decay process by taking each atom in turn and deciding randomly whether it decays, considering the probability.

   Write a program that simulates the decay of a sample that contains 10,000 atoms of radioactive material, where each atom has a 50 percent chance of decaying in a year. The output of your program should be a table showing the year and the number of atoms remaining, such as the table shown in this sample run:

```
Year       Atoms left
----       ----------
   0          10000
   1           4969
   2           2464
   3           1207
   4            627
   5            311
   6            166
   7             89
   8             40
   9             21
  10              8
  11              4
  12              1
  13              0
```

As the numbers indicate, roughly half the atoms in the sample decay each year. In physics, the conventional way to express this observation is to say that the sample has a *half-life* of one year.

8. As computers become more common in schools, it is important to find ways to use the machines to aid in the teaching process. This need has led to the development of an educational software industry that has produced many programs that help teach concepts to children.

   As an example of an educational application, write a program that poses a series of simple arithmetic problems for a student to answer, as illustrated by the following sample run:

```
Welcome to Math Quiz!
What is 14 + 2? 16↵
That's the answer!
What is 17 - 15? 17↵
That's incorrect.  Try a different answer: 15↵
That's incorrect.  Try a different answer: 3↵
No, the answer is 2.
What is 20 - 16? 4↵
That's the answer!
What is 9 + 4? 11↵
That's incorrect.  Try a different answer: 13↵
That's the answer!
What is 11 - 1? 10↵
That's the answer!
```

Your program should meet these requirements:

- It should ask a series of five questions. As with any such limit, the number of questions should be coded as a #define constant so that it can easily be changed.
- Each question should consist of a single addition or subtraction problem involving just two numbers, such as "What is 2 + 3?" or "What is 11 − 7?". The type of problem—addition or subtraction—should be chosen randomly for each question.
- To make sure the problems are appropriate for students in the first or second grade, none of the numbers involved, including the answer, should be less than 1 or greater than 20. This restriction means that your program should never ask questions like "What is 11 + 13?" or "What is 4 − 7?" because the answers are outside the legal range. Within these constraints, your program should choose the numbers randomly.
- The program should give the student three chances to answer each question. If the student gives the correct answer, your program should indicate that fact in some properly congratulatory way and go on to the next question. If the student does not get the answer in three tries, the program should give the answer and go on to another problem.

9. Even though the program in exercise 8 was designed to offer encouragement when the student responds correctly, the monotonous repetition of a sentence like "That's the answer!" has the opposite effect after a while. To add variety to the interaction, modify your solution to exercise 8 so that it randomly chooses among four or five different messages when the student gets the right answer, as illustrated in this sample run:

```
Welcome to Math Quiz!
What is 14 + 2? 16↵
Correct!
What is 17 - 15? 2↵
You got it. The answer is 2.
What is 20 - 16? 4↵
You got it. The answer is 4.
What is 9 + 4? 13↵
Correct!
What is 11 - 1? 10↵
That's the answer!
```

10. Using the graphics library presented in Chapter 7, write a program that draws a set of 10 circles with different sizes and positions. Each circle should have a randomly chosen radius between 0.05 and 0.5 inches and should be positioned at a random location in the drawing window, subject to the condition that the entire circle must fit inside the window without extending past the edge. The following sample run shows one possible outcome:

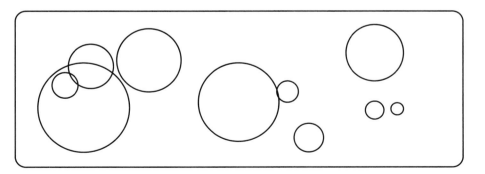

11. Imagine that you live in a well-planned city laid out so that its streets and avenues form blocks that are precisely square, as in this diagram:

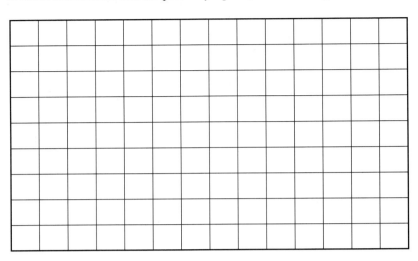

Suppose your office is located at the northeast corner of the map and you want to walk to your home in the southwest corner. Even if you don't want to back-track or go out of your way, there are still many possible routes for getting home. At each intersection, you can choose randomly to go west or south. When you reach the southern or western edge of the map, you can just head home along that roadway. For example, the colored line in the following diagram shows one random route:

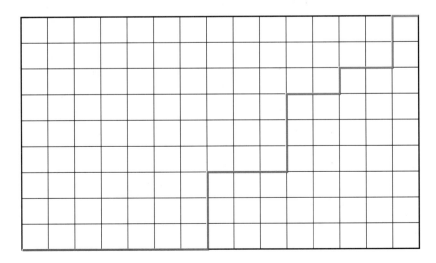

Write a program that uses the graphics library to trace out a random path through the city. You should start by moving the pen to the intersection in the upper right corner. From there, you draw a line either horizontally or vertically to get yourself to the next intersection, choosing the direction at random. Continue this process until you get home, making sure you don't run off the map.

Your program should not try to draw the entire map; it is enough just to show the path. If you want more practice using the graphics library, however, you could try to draw the entire figure shown in the example showing the random path. To make the heavy line for the random path, you need to draw two straight lines, one on each side of the actual grid lines.

12. In casinos from Monte Carlo to Las Vegas, one of the most common gambling devices is the slot machine—the "one-armed bandit." A typical slot machine has three wheels that spin around behind a narrow window. Each wheel is marked with the following symbols: CHERRY, LEMON, ORANGE, PLUM, BELL, and BAR. The window, however, allows you to see only one symbol on each wheel at a time. For example, the window might show the following configuration:

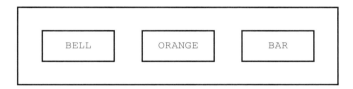

If you put a silver dollar into a slot machine and pull the handle on its side, the wheels spin around and eventually come to rest in some new configuration. If the configuration matches one of a set of winning patterns printed on the front of the slot machine, you get back some money. If not, you're out a dollar. The following table shows a typical set of winning patterns, along with their associated payoffs:

BAR	BAR	BAR	pays	$250
BELL	BELL	BELL/BAR	pays	$20
PLUM	PLUM	PLUM/BAR	pays	$14
ORANGE	ORANGE	ORANGE/BAR	pays	$10
CHERRY	CHERRY	CHERRY	pays	$7
CHERRY	CHERRY	—	pays	$5
CHERRY	—	—	pays	$2

The notation BELL/BAR means that either a BELL or a BAR can appear in that position, and the dash means that any symbol at all can appear. Thus, getting a CHERRY in the first position is automatically good for two dollars, no matter what appears on the other wheels. Note that there is never any payoff for the LEMON symbol, even if you happen to line them up three of them.

Write a program that simulates playing a slot machine. Your program should provide the user with an initial stake of $50 and then let the user play until either the money runs out or the user decides to quit. During each round, your program should take away a dollar, simulate the spinning of the wheels, evaluate the result, and pay the user any appropriate winnings. For example, a user might be lucky enough to see the following sample run:

```
Would you like instructions? no↵
You have $50.  Would you like to play? yes↵
PLUM    LEMON  LEMON  -- You lose
You have $49.  Would you like to play? yes↵
PLUM    BAR    LEMON  -- You lose
You have $48.  Would you like to play? yes↵
BELL    LEMON  ORANGE -- You lose
You have $47.  Would you like to play? yes↵
CHERRY CHERRY ORANGE -- You win $5
You have $51.  Would you like to play? yes↵
LEMON   ORANGE BAR    -- You lose
You have $50.  Would you like to play? yes↵
PLUM    BELL   PLUM   -- You lose
You have $49.  Would you like to play? yes↵
BELL    BELL   BELL   -- You win $20
You have $68.  Would you like to play? yes↵
CHERRY PLUM   LEMON  -- You win $2
You have $69.  Would you like to play? yes↵
ORANGE BAR    PLUM   -- You lose
You have $68.  Would you like to play? yes↵
ORANGE PLUM   BELL   -- You lose
You have $67.  Would you like to play? yes↵
BAR    BAR    BAR    -- You win $250
You have $316.  Would you like to play? no↵
```

Even though doing so is not realistic (and would make the slot machine unprofitable for the casino), you should assume that each of the six symbols is equally likely on each wheel.

13. Chapter 7 defined several general functions for creating graphical figures that are useful enough to put into a separate library. These include DrawBox, DrawCenteredBox, DrawCenteredCircle, DrawTriangle, and DrawGrid. Define a new interface gfigures.h that exports those five functions, and write the corresponding gfigures.c file to implement that interface. Rewrite the house.c program (Figure 7-7) so that it uses your new interface.

14. The calendar.c program in Chapter 5 includes several functions that are general enough to consider including in a library. It is easy to imagine, for example, that clients other than the calendar program itself would want to call the functions MonthName, MonthDays, FirstDayOfMonth, and IsLeapYear. Create a new interface caltools.h that exports those four functions along with the constant names for the days of the week. Then create a separate file caltools.c that contains the implementations of those functions. Rewrite the calendar.c program (Figure 5-6) so that it uses your new interface.

CHAPTER 9

Strings and Characters

Surely you don't think numbers are as important as words.

— King Azaz to the Mathemagician, *The Phantom Tollbooth,* Norton Juster, 1961.

Objectives

- To understand the principles of enumeration and integer encoding as strategies for defining new data types.

- To be able to define and manipulate enumeration types in C.

- To understand how computer systems represent the data type `char` and how to manipulate objects of that type.

- To learn how to use the functions in the `ctype.h` interface

- To understand the concept of an abstract type.

- To be able to use the functions in the `strlib.h` interface to perform string operations.

Until now, most of the programming examples you have seen in this book have used numbers as their basic data type. As Juster's Mathemagician would insist, numbers are certainly important, but there are many other kinds of data in the world. These days, computers work less with numeric data than with **text data,** that is, any information composed of individual characters that appear on the keyboard and the screen. The ability of modern computers to process text data has led to the development of word processing systems, on-line reference libraries, electronic mail, and a wide variety of other useful applications.

The concept of text data was introduced informally in Chapter 2, beginning with the first line of code in this book, which includes the string

```
"Hello, world.\n"
```

Since then, you have learned how to read a string value using `GetLine`, display a string using `printf`, and compare two strings using `StringEqual`. These operations, however, represent only a tiny fraction of the operations you can perform on strings. To unlock the full power of text data, you need to know how to manipulate strings in more sophisticated ways. In this chapter, you'll learn how to use a library of string operations that will enable you to write creative and exciting programs involving text data.

Because a string is composed of individual characters, it is important for you to understand how characters work and how they are represented inside the computer. Thus, this chapter focuses on the data type `char` as well as the data type `string`. Before examining the details of either type, however, you need to understand data representation from a more general perspective.

9.1 The principle of enumeration

As the use of computing technology grows, more and more information is stored electronically. To store information within a computer, it is necessary to represent the data in a form the machine can use. The representation of a particular item depends on its data type. Integers have one representation inside the computer; floating-point numbers have a different one. Even though you do not know exactly what those representations look like, you have relied on the fact that the computer is able to store numbers in its internal memory. There are, however, many types of useful data other than numbers, so computers must be able to represent nonnumeric data as well.

To gain insight into the nature of nonnumeric data, think for a moment about the information that you yourself provide to institutions and agencies over the course of a year. For example, if you live in the United States, you supply data to the Internal Revenue Service with your annual tax return. Much of that information is numeric—your salary, deductions, taxes, withholdings, and the like. Some consists of text data, such as your name, address, and occupation. But other items on your tax return cannot easily be classified into either of these forms. For example, one of the questions is

Filing status (check one):

☐ single
☐ married filing joint return
☐ married filing separate return
☐ head of household
☐ qualifying widow(er)

As with every other entry on the form, your answer represents data. Your response, however, is neither numeric data nor text data. The best way to describe the data type would be simply to call it *filing status data*—an entirely new data type whose domain consists of five values: *single, married filing joint return, married filing separate return, head of household,* and *qualifying widow(er).*

You can easily imagine many other data types that have a similar structure. For example, other forms might ask you for your sex, ethnicity, or status as a student. In each case, you would choose a response from a list of possibilities that constitutes the domain of a distinct conceptual type. The process of listing all the elements in the domain of a type is called **enumeration.** A type defined by listing all of its elements is called an **enumeration type.**

Because the title of this chapter is "Strings and Characters," discussing enumeration types might seem like a digression. As it happens, though, characters are similar in structure to enumeration types. Understanding how enumeration types work will help you appreciate how characters work.

At this point, however, enumeration types are an abstract concept. To understand how they apply to programming, you need to learn how the computer represents such values internally. You must also learn how to use enumeration types in the context of a C program. The next two sections address these issues.

Representing enumeration types inside the machine

If the Internal Revenue Service decides to review your tax return, the first step in the process is to enter the data from your return into a computer system. To store that data, the computer must have a way of representing each of the different data items, including your filing status. If you were developing a strategy for recording a taxpayer's filing status, what would you do?

The insight you need to solve this problem comes from building on the capabilities you know computers have. Computers are good at working with numbers. That's how they're built. As part of their basic hardware operation, they can store, add, subtract, compare, and do all sorts of other things with numbers. The fact that computers are good at manipulating numbers suggests a solution to the problem of representing an enumeration type. To represent a finite set of values of any type, all you have to do is give each value a number. For example, given the list of allowable filing status values, you could simply count them off, letting *single* be 1, *married filing joint return* be 2, *married filing separate return* be 3, and so on. (In fact, these numeric codes are listed directly on the tax form.) Assigning an integer to each of the different possibilities means that you can use that integer to represent the corresponding filing status.

Thus, all you have to do to define a representation for any enumeration type is to number its elements. The process of assigning an integer to each element of an enumeration type is called **integer encoding**—the integer acts as a coded representation of the original value.

Representing enumeration types as integers

C programmers use several strategies to represent enumeration types in C. One approach is to use the type `int` explicitly and then to use the `#define` facility to introduce new constant names. In fact, you have already seen an example of using integers to represent an enumeration type. The `calendar.c` program in Figure 5-6 keeps track of the days of the week. To define each weekday, the program assigns a number to each day: Sunday is 0, Monday is 1, Tuesday is 2, and so forth. Those numbers are then defined as constants using C's `#define` facility, as follows:

```
#define   Sunday      0
#define   Monday      1
#define   Tuesday     2
#define   Wednesday   3
#define   Thursday    4
#define   Friday      5
#define   Saturday    6
```

To use this strategy to represent enumeration types, you must specify the integer encoding explicitly. If you want to introduce a variable to store a value of that type, you simply declare it to be of type `int`.

You can apply this strategy to the problem of representing the filing status on a tax return by defining the following constants:

```
#define   Single                         1
#define   MarriedFilingJointReturn       2
#define   MarriedFilingSeparateReturn    3
#define   HeadOfHousehold                4
#define   QualifyingSurvivingSpouse      5
```

The name of the last constant has changed from what appears on the tax form to conform to C's rules for names, which disallow parentheses.

Once you have defined the constants, you can declare a variable of type `int` to represent the filing status:

```
int filingStatus;
```

Defining new enumeration types

While the approach described in the preceding section is common in C programs, it does not take full advantage of the facilities the language offers. Instead of using the type `int` to represent nonnumeric values, it is possible in C to define an actual type name to represent an enumeration type. Inside the machine, the two strategies produce exactly the same result: every element of the enumeration type is represented by an integer code. From the programmer's point of view, however, defining separate enumeration types has these advantages:

- The compiler is able to choose the integer codes, thereby freeing the programmer from this responsibility.
- The fact that there is a separate type name often makes the program easier to read because declarations can use a meaningful type name instead of the general-purpose designation `int`.
- On many computer systems, programs that use explicitly defined enumeration types are easier to debug because the compiler can provide the debugging system with additional information about how that type behaves.

C provides more than one syntactic form for introducing a new enumeration type. In this text, all new enumeration types are defined using the syntax shown in the box on the right. The definition starts with the keyword `typedef`, which is used to introduce new type names. In this context, the keyword `typedef` is followed by the keyword `enum`, which indicates that the new type is an enumeration type. The names for each of the elements of the enumeration are then listed inside a pair of curly braces, followed by the name of the type and a semicolon. (The `typedef` keyword is used in other type definitions as well as illustrated in Chapter 16.)

S Y N T A X **for defining an enumeration type**

```
typedef enum {
      list of elements
} type name ;
```

where:
list of elements is a list of names used to refer to the individual values that comprise the enumeration type. The elements in the list are separated by commas. Each element may also be followed by an equal sign and an integer constant that specifies a particular internal representation.
type name indicates the name of the new enumerated type.

Using this method, you can define the weekday names in the `calendar.c` program by introducing the following enumeration type:

```
typedef enum {
   Sunday, Monday, Tuesday, Wednesday, Thursday, Friday, Saturday
} weekdayT;
```

This definition introduces a new type named `weekdayT` that joins the other types available in the language, such as `int` and `bool`. The capital `T` at the end of the name emphasizes that the name `weekdayT` refers to a type and not a variable. In this text, the names of all defined types—other than `bool` and `string`, which are considered part of the fundamental collection of types—will end with a capital `T`. This stylistic convention helps make programs readable.

The declarations of variables used to refer to days of the week in the `calendar.c` program need to be changed so that they use the type `weekdayT` instead of the type `int`. (You have the opportunity to do so in exercise 2.) As mentioned earlier in this section, an advantage of using enumeration types in a program is that the type names can convey useful information. Declaring a variable to be type int leads anyone reading the program to believe that the variable is going to hold integers; the fact that the integer corresponds to some day of the week is completely lost. Declaring a variable to be of type weekdayT immediately tells the reader the type of value that variable contains.

The definition of weekdayT also defines the seven constants that correspond to the days of the week. These constants are similar to those that were introduced using #define and in fact have the same internal representations. Whenever you define a new enumeration type, the elements are assigned consecutive integer values starting with 0. Thus, in the weekdayT example, Sunday still has the value 0, Monday the value 1, and so forth, just as before.

The C compiler also allows you to specify explicitly the internal representation for the elements of an enumeration type as part of the definition. For example, it might be essential to the Internal Revenue Service that the internal codes used to represent filing status have precisely the values that are printed on the tax form. After all, they presumably have years of data in storage for which the filing status is encoded with *single* equal to 1, and so on. In defining the filing status type, you would need to specify the values of the constants, as follows:

```
typedef enum {
    Single = 1,
    MarriedFilingJointReturn = 2,
    MarriedFilingSeparateReturn = 3,
    HeadOfHousehold = 4,
    QualifyingSurvivingSpouse = 5
} filingStatusT;
```

You can, however, shorten this definition somewhat. If no equal sign appears, the C compiler assigns consecutive values to each element in turn. Thus writing

```
typedef enum {
    Single = 1,
    MarriedFilingJointReturn,
    MarriedFilingSeparateReturn,
    HeadOfHousehold,
    QualifyingSurvivingSpouse
} filingStatusT;
```

has precisely the same effect as the preceding definition. The name Single is explicitly assigned the value 1, and the rest of the names are numbered consecutively from there.

You can use enumerations for all sorts of values. For example, you can define the colors of the rainbow by writing

```
typedef enum { Red, Orange, Yellow, Green, Blue, Violet } colorT;
```

or the four principal directions on a compass with

```
typedef enum { North, East, South, West } directionT;
```

Each of these definitions introduces a new type name and a set of constants that are elements of that type.

In fact, the definition of `bool` in `genlib.h` is simply an enumeration type:[1]

```
typedef enum { FALSE, TRUE } bool;
```

Operations on enumeration types

C compilers automatically convert values belonging to an enumeration type to integers whenever the values are used in an expression. Because every enumeration constant is represented by an integer value, all computation involving enumeration types simply uses the underlying integer codes. For example, if you declare the variable `weekday` to be of type `weekdayT`, you can still write the expression

```
weekday = (weekday + 1) % 7;
```

just as it appears in the `calendar.c` program. The variable weekday has some internal integer value between 0 and 6. This statement adds 1 to that integer and then ensures that the result stays between 0 and 6 by dividing by 7 and taking the remainder. All arithmetic for enumeration types works the same way it does for integers.

In C, however, you need to be careful when working with enumeration types, because the compiler does not check to see that the result of a computation is a valid member of a particular enumeration type. For example, if you had erroneously written the statement

```
weekday = weekday + 1;
```

you would run into trouble if `weekday` happened to have the value `Saturday`. The computer would take the value 6 representing `Saturday`, add 1 to it, and store the value 7 back in the variable `weekday`, even though 7 is not a legal element of the type `weekdayT`. C compilers could generate extra code to check for this condition and report the error, but very few do. Of course, if you represent `weekday` as an integer instead, leaving out the remainder operator would still be an error, so choosing to use an enumeration type is not the cause of the problem.

Scalar types

Types, such as enumeration types, that behave like integers are called **scalar types.** In C, scalar types are automatically converted to integers whenever you use them in an expression. Moreover, you can use scalar types in any context in which an integer might appear. For example, a variable of an enumeration type can be

---

[1] In a C expression representing a Boolean condition, the integer 0 indicates that the condition is false, and *any* nonzero value is interpreted to mean that the condition is true, although the integer 1 is designated as the "official" value of the constant TRUE. C programmers often rely on the fact that C interprets nonzero integers as true conditions, although the programs in this text do not. By limiting yourself to using explicit Boolean values in conditional contexts, you will develop good programming habits that will make your programs easier to read and debug.

used as the control expression in a `switch` statement. Assuming that `directionT` is defined as

```
typedef enum { North, East, South, West } directionT;
```

the following function returns the direction opposite to that indicated by its argument:

```
directionT OppositeDirection(directionT dir)
{
    switch (dir) {
      case North: return (South);
      case East:  return (West);
      case South: return (North);
      case West:  return (East);
      default:    Error("Illegal direction value");
    }
}
```

Thus, calling `OppositeDirection(North)` returns `South`.

 ## 9.2 Characters

Characters form the basis for all text data processing. Although strings certainly occur more often in programs than single characters, characters are the fundamental type—the "atoms" used to construct all other forms of text data. Understanding how characters work is therefore critical to understanding all other aspects of text processing. In a sense, characters constitute a built-in enumeration type, although the term *enumeration type* is usually reserved for types specified using the `enum` keyword. By all accounts, however, characters are a scalar type, as defined at the end of the preceding section, and are therefore part of the same general type class as the user-defined enumeration types.

The data type `char`

In C, single characters are represented using the data type `char`, which is one of the predefined data types. Like all the basic types introduced in Chapter 2, the type `char` consists of a domain of legal values and a set of operations for manipulating those values. Informally, the domain of the data type `char` is the set of symbols that can be displayed on the screen or typed on the keyboard. These symbols—the letters, digits, punctuation marks, spacebar, Return key, and so forth—are the building blocks for all text data. Because `char` is a scalar type, the set of operations available for characters is the same as that for integers. Understanding what those operations mean in the character domain, however, requires looking more closely at how characters are represented inside the machine.

The ASCII code

Single characters are represented inside the machine just like any other scalar type. Conceptually, the central idea is that you can assign every character a number by writing them all down in a list and then counting them off one at a time. The code used to represent a particular character is called its **character code.** For example, you could let the integer 1 represent the letter *A*, the integer 2 represent the letter *B*, and so on. After you got to the point of letting 26 represent the letter *Z*, you could then keep going and number each of the lowercase letters, digits, punctuation marks, and other characters with the integers 27, 28, 29, and so on.

Even though it is technically possible to design a computer in which the number 1 represents the letter *A*, it would certainly be a mistake to do so. In today's world, information is often shared between different computers: you might copy a program from one machine to another on a floppy disk or arrange to have your computer communicate directly with others over a national or international network. To make that kind of communication possible, computers must be able to "talk to each other" in a common language. An essential feature of that common language is that the computers use the same codes to represent characters, so that the letter *A* on one machine does not come out as a *Z* on another.

In the early days of computing, different computers actually used different character codes. The letter *A* might have a particular integer representation on one machine but an entirely different representation on a computer made by some other manufacturer. Even the set of available characters was subject to change. One computer, for example, might have the character ¢ on its keyboard, while another computer would not be able to represent that character at all. Computer communication was plagued by all the difficulties that people speaking different languages encounter.

Over time, however, the enormous advantage that comes from enabling computers to communicate effectively has led most computer manufacturers to adopt a single standard for character representation—a coding system for characters called **ASCII,** which stands for the *American Standard Code for Information Interchange.* Table 9-1 shows the ASCII code used to represent each character.

TABLE 9-1   ASCII codes

	0	1	2	3	4	5	6	7	8	9
0	\000	\001	\002	\003	\004	\005	\006	\a	\b	\t
10	\n	\v	\f	\r	\016	\017	\020	\021	\022	\023
20	\024	\025	\026	\027	\030	\031	\032	\033	\034	\035
30	\036	\037	*space*	!	"	#	$	%	&	'
40	(	)	*	+	,	–	.	/	0	1
50	2	3	4	5	6	7	8	9	:	;
60	<	=	>	?	@	A	B	C	D	E
70	F	G	H	I	J	K	L	M	N	O
80	P	Q	R	S	T	U	V	W	X	Y
90	Z	[	\	]	^	_	`	a	b	c
100	d	e	f	g	h	i	j	k	l	m
110	n	o	p	q	r	s	t	u	v	w
120	x	y	z	{			}	~	\177		

Although Table 9-1 contains several entries that appear on the keyboard, there are several less familiar entries represented by a backward slash (\), usually called a *backslash,* followed by a single letter or a sequence of digits. These entries, called *special characters,* are discussed in a separate section later in this chapter.

You can calculate the ASCII code for any character in Table 9-1 by adding the row and column number associated with that entry. For example, the letter *A* near the center of the chart is in the row labeled 60 and the column labeled 5. The ASCII code for the letter *A* is therefore 60 + 5, or 65. You can use the table to find the code for any character in this same way. In most cases, however, you will not need to do so. Although it is important to know that characters are represented internally using a numeric code, it is not generally useful to know what numeric value corresponds to a particular character. When you type the letter *A,* the hardware logic built into the keyboard automatically translates that character into the ASCII code 65, which is then sent to the computer. Similarly, when the computer sends the ASCII code 65 to the screen, the letter *A* appears.

Character constants

When you want to refer to a specific character in a C program, the standard approach is to specify a **character constant,** which is written by enclosing the desired character in single quotation marks. For example, to indicate the ASCII code for the letter *A,* all you have to write is 'A'. The C compiler knows that this notation means to use the ASCII character code for the letter *A,* which happens to be 65. Similarly, you can indicate the space character by writing ' ' or the digit 9 by writing '9'. Note that the constant '9' refers to a *character* and should not be confused with the *integer* value 9. As an integer, the value '9' is the value for that character given in the ASCII table, which is 57.

**COMMON
PITFALLS**

Avoid using integer constants to refer to ASCII characters within a program. All character constants should be indicated by enclosing the character in single quotation marks, as in 'A' or '*'.

As long as your computer uses the ASCII character set, you could replace the character constant 'A' with the integer 65. The program would work in exactly the same way but would be much harder to read. You need to keep in mind that some other programmer will eventually come along and have to make sense out of what you've written. Unless that programmer has memorized the ASCII table, seeing the integer 65 written as part of the program won't immediately conjure up an image of the letter *A.* On the other hand, the character constant 'A' conveys that meaning directly.

This text includes Table 9-1 to give you a more concrete understanding of how characters are represented inside the machine. As soon as you have that idea in mind, you should forget about the specific character codes and concentrate instead only on the character itself.

Important properties of the ASCII coding scheme

Even though it is important not to think about specific character codes, the following two structural properties of the ASCII table are worth remembering:

1. The codes for the characters representing the digits 0 through 9 are consecutive. Even though you do not need to know exactly what code corresponds to the digit character '0', you know that the code for the digit '1' is the next

larger integer. Similarly, if you add 9 to the code for '0', you get the code for the character '9'.

2. The letters in the alphabet are divided into two separate ranges: one for the uppercase letters *(A–Z)* and one for the lowercase letters *(a–z)*. Within each range, however, the ASCII values are consecutive, so that you can count through the letters one at a time in order of their ASCII code.[2]

Each of these properties will be useful in programs at various points later in this text.

Special characters

Most of the characters in Table 9-1 are the familiar ones that can be displayed on the screen. These characters are called **printing characters.** The ASCII table, however, also includes various **special characters,** which are used to perform a particular action.

You have been using one of these special characters—the newline character indicated by the two-character sequence \n—ever since Chapter 2. The newline character, which appears in a large majority of printf calls, is used to position the cursor at the beginning of the next line on the screen. In addition to the newline character, there are several other special characters with predefined functions. Special characters are indicated in programs by using a backslash followed by a letter or numeric value. The combination of the backslash and the characters that follow it is called an **escape sequence.** Table 9-2 lists the predefined escape sequences.

---

[2] The second property is in fact not guaranteed by ANSI C, even though it is almost always true. There are still computer systems that use character coding systems in which the letters are not consecutive, but it is unusual to program in C on those computers. Because making the assumption that the letters form a consecutive set simplifies certain programming problems considerably, the programs in this text assume that the character set in fact has this property.

TABLE 9-2

Escape sequences for special characters

Escape sequence	Function
\a	Audible alert (beeps or rings a bell)
\b	Backspace
\f	Formfeed (starts a new page)
\n	Newline (moves to the beginning of the next line)
\r	Return (returns to the beginning of the current line without advancing)
\t	Tab (moves horizontally to the next tab stop)
\v	Vertical tab (moves vertically to the next tab stop)
\0	Null character (the character whose ASCII code is 0)
\\	The character \ itself
\'	The character ' (requires the backslash only in character constants)
\"	The character " (requires the backslash only in string constants)
\ddd	The character whose ASCII code is the octal number *ddd*

You can include special characters in character constants by writing the escape sequence as part of the constant. Although each escape sequence consists of several characters, each sequence is translated into a single ASCII code inside the machine. The codes for the special characters are included in Table 9-1. For example, the newline character is represented internally by the integer 10.

When the compiler sees the backslash character, it expects it to be the first character in an escape sequence. If you want to represent the backslash character itself, you have to use two consecutive backslashes inside single quotation marks like this: `'\\'`. Similarly, the single quotation mark, when used as a character constant, must also be preceded by a backslash: `'\''`.

Special characters can also be used in string constants, as you have seen in the case of the newline character. The fact that a double quotation mark is used to indicate the end of a string means that the double quotation mark must be marked as a special character if it is part of a string. For example, if you write a program containing the `printf` line

```
printf("\"Bother,\" said Pooh.\n");
```

the output is

```
"Bother," said Pooh.
```

Many of the special characters in ASCII do not have explicit names and are instead represented in programs using their internal numeric codes. The only wrinkle in this process is that the numeric codes for special characters are indicated using base 8 notation, which is usually called **octal notation.** In octal notation, every digit position is worth 8 times as much as the next digit to its right. For example, the character constant `'\177'` represents the character whose ASCII code is the octal number 177. (This character is the code that corresponds to pressing the Delete key, which is labeled Rubout on some keyboards.) Numerically, the octal value 177 corresponds to the integer

$$1 \times 64 + 7 \times 8 + 7$$

which works out to be the decimal number 127.

Most of the special characters in the ASCII coding system are rarely used in practice. For most programming applications, the only special characters you will need to know are the newline character (`'\n'`), the tab character (`'\t'`), and the null character (`'\0'`), which is discussed in Chapter 14.

Character arithmetic

In C, character values can be manipulated as if they were integers; no special conversions are required. The result is defined according to the internal ASCII codes. For example, the character `'A'`, which is represented internally using the ASCII code 65, is treated as the integer 65 whenever it is used in an arithmetic context.

Because integers and characters can be freely converted back and forth, you can easily define a function `RandomLetter` that returns a randomly chosen uppercase letter. Given the `RandomInteger` function exported by the `random.h` interface from Chapter 8, the implementation is simply

```
char RandomLetter(void)
{
    return (RandomInteger('A', 'Z'));
}
```

Even though it is legal to apply any arithmetic operation to values of type `char`, not all operations are meaningful in that domain. For example, it is legal to multiply `'A'` by `'B'` as part of a program. To determine the result, the computer takes the internal codes, 65 and 66, and multiplies them to get 4290. The problem is that this integer means nothing as a character and is in fact outside the ASCII character range. Only a few of the arithmetic operations are likely to be useful when applied to characters. The operations that generally make sense are:

- *Adding an integer to a character.* If `c` is a character and `n` is an integer, the expression `c + n` represents the character code that comes `n` characters after `c` in the coding sequence. For example, the expression `'0' + n` computes the character code of the nth digit, if `n` is between 0 and 9. Thus `'0' + 5` computes the character code for `'5'`. Similarly, the expression `'A' + n - 1` computes the character code of the nth letter in the alphabet, assuming that `n` is between 1 and 26.

- *Subtracting an integer from a character.* The expression `c - n` represents the code of the character that comes `n` characters before `c` in the coding sequence. For example, the expression `'Z' - 2` computes the character code for `'X'`.

- *Subtracting one character from another.* If `c1` and `c2` are both characters, the expression `c1 - c2` represents the distance between those characters in coding sequence. For example, if you look back to Table 9-1 and compute the ASCII values of each character, you can determine that `'a' - 'A'` is 32. More importantly, the distance between a lowercase character and its uppercase counterpart is constant, so that `'z' - 'Z'` is also 32.

- *Comparing two characters against each other.* Comparing two character values using any of the relational operators is a common operation, often used to determine alphabetical ordering. For example, the expression `c1 < c2` is TRUE if `c1` comes before `c2` in the ASCII table.

To see how these operations apply to practical problems, consider how the computer executes a function like `GetInteger`. When a user types a number, such as 102, the computer receives the individual keystrokes as characters and must therefore work with the input values `'1'`, `'0'`, and `'2'`. Because the `GetInteger` function must return an integer, it needs to translate the character into the integers they represent. To do so, `GetInteger` takes advantage of the fact that the digits are consecutive in the ASCII sequence. For example, suppose that `GetInteger` has just read a character from the keyboard and stored it in the variable `ch`. It can convert the character to its numeric form by evaluating the expression

```
ch - '0'
```

Assuming that `ch` contains a digit character, the difference between its ASCII code and the ASCII code for the digit `'0'` must correspond to the decimal value of that digit. Suppose, for example, that the variable `ch` contains the character `'9'`. If you consult the ASCII table, you can determine that the character `'9'` has the internal code 57. The digit `'0'` has the ASCII code 48, and $57 - 48$ is 9. The key point is that the function makes no assumption that `'0'` has the ASCII code 48, which means that the same function would work even if the computer used a different character set. The only assumption is that the codes for the digits form a consecutive sequence.

But how can `GetInteger` determine whether the character `ch` is in fact a digit? Once again, it can take advantage of the fact that the digits are consecutive in the ASCII table. The statement

```
if (ch >= '0' && ch <= '9') . . .
```

distinguishes the digit characters from the rest of the ASCII set. Similarly, the statement

```
if (ch >= 'A' && ch <= 'Z') . . .
```

identifies the uppercase letters, and

```
if (ch >= 'a' && ch <= 'z') . . .
```

identifies the lowercase letters.

The `ctype.h` interface

As it happens, however, you won't usually encounter the `if` statements used at the end of the preceding section in a typical C program. The operations for checking whether a character is a digit or a letter are so common that the designers of C put them in a library. The interface to that library is `ctype.h`, which exports several functions for determining the type of a character. As with any interface, you gain access to these functions by including the line

```
#include <ctype.h>
```

The `ctype.h` interface declares several predicate functions for determining the type of a character, of which the following are the most important:

`islower(ch)`	Returns TRUE if the character `ch` is a lowercase letter
`isupper(ch)`	Returns TRUE if `ch` is an uppercase letter
`isalpha(ch)`	Returns TRUE if `ch` is a letter (either upper- or lowercase)
`isdigit(ch)`	Returns TRUE if `ch` is a digit
`isalnum(ch)`	Returns TRUE if `ch` is **alphanumeric**, which means that it is either a letter or a digit
`ispunct(ch)`	Returns TRUE if `ch` is a punctuation symbol
`isspace(ch)`	Returns TRUE if `ch` is one of the characters `' '` (the space character), `'\t'`, `'\n'`, `'\f'`, or `'\v'`, all of which appear as blank space on the screen

In addition, `ctype.h` defines these two extremely useful conversion functions:

tolower(ch)   If ch is an uppercase letter, returns its lowercase equivalent; otherwise returns ch unchanged

toupper(ch)   If ch is a lowercase letter, returns its uppercase equivalent; otherwise returns ch unchanged

Although tolower and toupper are already available through the ctype.h interface, you can appreciate their operation more if you try to implement them from scratch. Once again, you can ignore the actual ASCII codes involved and rely only on the continuity assumptions. If ch contains a character code for an uppercase letter, you can convert it to its lowercase form by adding the constant difference in value that separates the uppercase and lowercase characters. Rather than write that difference as an explicit constant, however, the program is easier to read if you express it using character arithmetic as 'a' - 'A'. Thus, you could implement the tolower function as follows:

```
char tolower(char ch)
{
    if (ch >= 'A' && ch <= 'Z') {
        return (ch + ('a' - 'A'));
    } else {
        return (ch);
    }
}
```

The function toupper has a similar implementation.

Even though the functions defined in the ctype.h interface are easy to implement, it is good programming practice to use the library functions instead of writing your own. There are three principal reasons for doing so.

1. Because the library functions are standard, programs you write will be easier for other programmers to read. Assuming those programmers are at all experienced in C, they will recognize the functions in the ctype.h interface and know exactly what they mean.
2. It is easier to rely on library functions for correctness than on your own. Because the ANSI C libraries are used by millions of client programmers, there is considerable pressure on the implementors to get the functions right. If you rewrite library functions yourself, the chance of introducing a bug is much larger.
3. The library implementations of functions are often more efficient than those you would write yourself. In the ctype.h interface, for example, the library mechanism runs much faster than the implementations given in this section, often by a factor of three or four. How these more efficient implementations work is beyond the scope of this chapter, but the important point is that you can take advantage of that added efficiency by using the library forms.

Control statements involving characters

Because char is a scalar type, you can use it in all the statement forms in which integers appear. For example, if ch is declared to be of type char, you can use the following `for` header line to execute a loop 26 times, once for each uppercase letter in the alphabet:

```
for (ch = 'A'; ch <= 'Z'; ch++)
```

Similarly, you can use a character as the control expression in a `switch` statement. For example, the following predicate function returns TRUE if its argument is a vowel:

```
bool IsVowel(char ch)
{
    switch (tolower(ch)) {
      case 'a': case 'e': case 'i': case 'o': case 'u':
        return (TRUE);
      default:
        return (FALSE);
    }
}
```

Note that the implementation uses the `tolower` function to recognize vowels in both their uppercase and lowercase forms.

Character input and output

Traditionally, character input and output is performed using the functions `getchar` and `putchar` in the standard I/O library. This text discusses these functions in Chapter 15 along with the other functions the `stdio.h` interface provides. Until then, the programs in this text read character data by calling `GetLine` to read an entire line and then selecting the individual characters in that line, as discussed in the section on "Selecting characters from a string" later in this chapter. To display a single character on the screen, you can use the `printf` function with the format code `%c`. For example, the following main program uses the `IsVowel` predicate from the preceding section to list the English vowels in their uppercase form:

```
main()
{
    char ch;

    printf("The English vowels are:");
    for (ch = 'A'; ch <= 'Z'; ch++) {
        if (IsVowel(ch)) printf(" %c", ch);
    }
    printf("\n");
}
```

■ 9.3 Strings as abstract data

The real power of using characters comes from the fact that you can string them together, one after another, to form a sequence of characters called a *string*. As noted in the introduction to this chapter, you already know how to perform several string operations. You can read a string from the user by calling `GetLine`, display a string on the screen by calling `printf`, and determine whether two strings are precisely equal by calling `StringEqual`. As you will discover, however, there is a lot more you need to learn about strings in order to unlock the enormous power they bring to programming. To understand strings in their entirety, you must consider them from several different perspectives at differing levels of detail.

As you have found many times in this text, you can approach programming from both a reductionistic and a holistic perspective. When you concern yourself with the internal details of data representation, you are taking the reductionistic view. From this perspective, your job is to understand how characters are stored in the computer's memory, how a sequence of those characters can be stored to form a string, and how, for example, a 200-character string can fit inside the same variable that holds a 2-character string. These are all interesting questions, and you will discover the answers in due course. When you consider strings from the holistic perspective, however, your job is to understand how to manipulate a string as a single logical unit. By focusing on the abstract behavior of strings, you can learn how to use them effectively without getting bogged down in details.

Ideally, it would be best to interleave the holistic and reductionistic perspectives so that you could use each perspective to shed light on the other. Understanding the internal structure of strings, however, requires that you first become familiar with several of the more advanced topics covered in this text, such as arrays and pointers. Trying to master all these ideas at the same time is just too difficult. Focusing too early on the representation of strings means that the abstract perspective—how strings are used and why they're there—tends to get lost.

To make sure that you can comprehend strings holistically, this text adopts a multistage approach. In this chapter, you will learn about the abstract behavior of strings by using a string library that hides most of the underlying complexity. As you go through the rest of the text, you will discover more of the details about how strings are represented, eventually reaching a point when you can write the entire string library yourself. Beyond making it possible to learn about strings gradually, this approach also provides another example of effective interface design and the principle of information hiding.

Layered abstractions

Although this chapter concentrates on strings from an abstract perspective, it is useful to know what other perspectives exist and how those perspectives are related. As is the case with most abstract concepts in programming, the high-level approach taken in this chapter is made possible through a series of string abstractions at varying levels of detail. The different abstractions form a hierarchy, with the most primitive facilities at the base. Each new abstraction is built on top of the preceding one and provides a more sophisticated view of the string concept.

An abstraction that is constructed in several hierarchical stages is called a **layered abstraction.** The structure of the layered abstraction used to represent strings is shown in the following diagram:

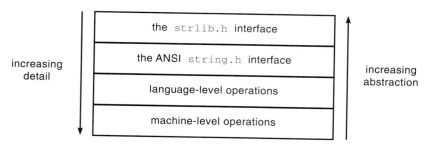

The hardware devices that perform input and output automatically translate between ASCII codes and the symbols that appear on the screen or the keyboard. As discussed earlier in this chapter, the computer can manipulate individual characters by applying arithmetic operations to the integer codes used to represent them. These facilities constitute the machine-level operations available for strings and form the lowest level of the hierarchy.

On top of the basic capabilities provided by the hardware, programming languages also usually include some support for string manipulation. The built-in operations available for strings form the second layer in the hierarchy. In many languages, these facilities are quite powerful, making it possible to perform complex string manipulation directly at the language level. ANSI C, however, provides almost no support for strings within the language itself. The only direct language support for strings is the ability to define string constants, which were introduced in the section on "Constants" in Chapter 2. All other string operations are provided by libraries. Even the type name string is not included as part of the language and is defined instead as an extension in the genlib.h interface.

In ANSI C, most of the string operations that programmers use in practice are supplied through the string.h interface. This library provides a powerful set of string operations, but the conceptual abstraction used in the string.h interface will be beyond your reach until after you have learned the material in Chapters 11 and 13. Moreover, certain common operations are difficult to perform using the string.h interface. For example, when you use the functions in string.h, you cannot easily return string values from functions or even assign a string value directly to a variable. Because using the string.h interface is the standard approach to string manipulation in ANSI C, you must learn how to use it eventually. By delaying that introduction of the string.h interface until Chapter 14, this book makes sure that you have all the background you need before you try to make sense of the conceptual abstraction used in that package.

To give you a chance to work with strings using a conceptually simpler model, this text introduces another string library, which is accessible through the strlib.h interface. Like genlib.h and stdio.h, the strlib.h interface is an extension to the standard ANSI C library. Therefore, to include it in your program, you must use quotation marks:

```
#include "strlib.h"
```

The `strlib.h` interface, which forms the highest layer in the abstraction hierarchy, makes it relatively easy to work with strings.

The concept of an abstract type

The principal advantage of the `strlib.h` interface is that it makes it possible to work with strings as an *abstract type*. Although the definition will be refined in Chapter 17, in which abstract types are a central theme, it is sufficient for now to think of an **abstract type** as a type defined only by its *behavior* and not in terms of its *representation*.

The behavior of an abstract type is defined by the operations that can be performed on objects of that type. The legal operations for a particular abstract type are called its **primitive operations** and are defined as functions in an interface associated with the type. Details of those operations and the underlying representation of the type are hidden away in the implementation of that interface. Whenever a client wants to manipulate values of an abstract type, the client must use the functions provided by the interface.

In the context of strings, what are the primitive operations that you might want to perform? To begin with, you already know how to

- Specify a string constant in a program
- Read in a string from the user by using `GetLine`
- Display a string on the screen by using `printf`
- Determine whether two strings are exactly equal by using `StringEqual`

What else might you want to do? When working with strings, you might, for example, want to perform any of the following operations:

- Find out how long a string is
- Select the first character—or, more generally, the ith character—within a string
- Combine two strings to form a longer string
- Convert a single character into a one-character string
- Extract some piece of a string to form a shorter one
- Compare two strings to see which comes first in alphabetical order
- Determine whether a string contains a particular character or set of characters

There are other operations you might consider, but this list offers an interesting and useful start. Each of these operations is provided by a function in the `strlib.h` interface. This interface gives you the tools you need to use strings without requiring you to comprehend the details of the underlying representation. The fact that you do not need to understand those details is the essence of data abstraction.

9.4 The `strlib.h` interface

In Chapters 7 and 8, you learned to read and write header files that represent interfaces to libraries. The entire `strlib.h` header file appears in Appendix B. As an exercise in reading header files, you can look at the comments in the interface and figure out precisely what each of the functions does. The next several sections, however, offer more detailed descriptions of those functions in more goal-oriented terms. Instead of focusing on what each function does, the rest of this chapter concentrates on the abstract operations you might want to perform, describing the functions you need to accomplish those operations.

Until now, each new function has been introduced by giving its complete prototype and then describing its operation. Beginning in this chapter, new functions are often introduced in the text somewhat less formally, using what is sometimes called an **implicit prototype,** which is simply a sample call to the function with descriptive names for the parameters. In your programs, you must continue to provide the complete prototype showing the types of each parameter. Using implicit prototypes in the text, however, often makes it easier to see at a glance how to use the function. For example, the implicit prototype for the RandomInteger function in Chapter 8 would be RandomInteger(low, high). Beginning with this chapter, most new functions are introduced using the implicit prototype form, after which the text explains the effect of the function in terms of the parameter names. This style of description is common in other reference material about C.

Determining the length of a string

When writing programs to manipulate strings, you often need to know how many characters a particular string contains. The total number of characters a string contains—counting all letters, digits, spaces, punctuation marks, and special characters—is called the **length** of the string.

Using the strlib.h interface, you can obtain the length of a string s by calling the function StringLength(s). For example, the first string you encountered in this book was the string

```
"Hello, world.\n"
```

This string has length 14—five characters in the word Hello, five more in world, two punctuation marks (a comma and a period), one space, and one newline character. Thus the function call

```
StringLength("Hello, world.\n")
```

returns the value 14.

The following program reads in a single line of text from the user and reports its length:

```
main()
{
    string str;

    printf("This program tests the StringLength function.\n");
    printf("Enter a string: ");
    str = GetLine();
    printf("The length is %d.\n", StringLength(str));
}
```

Selecting characters from a string

In C, positions within a string are numbered starting from 0. For example, the individual characters in the string `"Hello there!"` are numbered as in the following diagram:

The position number written underneath each character in the string is called its **index** within the string.

To enable you to select a particular character in a string given its index, the `strlib.h` interface provides a function called `IthChar` that takes two arguments—a string and an integer representing the index—and returns a character. For example, if the variable `str` contains the string `"Hello there!"`, calling `IthChar(str, 0)` returns the character `'H'`. Similarly, calling `IthChar(str, 5)` returns `' '`, which is the space character. Be sure to remember that C numbers characters starting with 0, not 1. It is easy to forget this rule and assume that `IthChar(str, 5)` will return the fifth character in the string. `IthChar(str, 5)` returns the character at index position 5, which is the *sixth* character as you would number character positions in English.

Given the library function, `IthChar`, you can define a new function `LastChar(str)` that returns the last character in `str` as follows:

```
char LastChar(string str)
{
    return (IthChar(str, StringLength(str) - 1));
}
```

For example, calling `LastChar` on the string `"Hello there!"` returns the exclamation point character `'!'`.

Concatenation

Another useful function for working with strings is the `Concat` function, which takes two strings and connects them, end to end, with no intervening characters. In programming, this operation is called **concatenation.** For example, the value of

```
Concat("Hello", "there")
```

is the 10-character string `"Hellothere"`.

If you want to put a space between two words represented as string values, you have to perform an additional concatenation. The `Concat` function takes only two arguments at a time. To concatenate three or more string values, you have to make several calls to `Concat`, each of which combines two pieces. For example, if the variable `word1` contains `"Hello"` and the variable `word2` contains `"there"`, you have to make nested calls to `Concat` in order to generate the 11-character string `"Hello there"`, as illustrated by the following expression:

COMMON PITFALLS

The `Concat` function always takes two arguments. If you need to concatenate more than two strings, you must use nested calls to `Concat`. The innermost call combines two strings, the next call adds another string onto the result, and so forth.

```
Concat(Concat(word1, " "), word2)
```

You can also use `Concat` to define a function `ConcatNCopies(n, str)`, which returns a string consisting of n repeated copies of `str` concatenated together end to end. For example, calling the function `ConcatNCopies(10, "*")` returns a string consisting of 10 asterisks. A simple implementation of `ConcatNCopies` is

```
string ConcatNCopies(int n, string str)
{
    string result;
    int i;

    result = "";
    for (i = 0; i < n; i++) {
        result = Concat(result, str);
    }
    return (result);
}
```

In a way, the implementation strategy used in this example is similar to that used in the `Factorial` function presented in the section on "Functions involving internal control structures" in Chapter 5. In both cases, the function uses a local variable to keep track of the partially computed result during each cycle of a `for` loop. In the `ConcatNCopies` function, each cycle in the `for` loop concatenates the value of `str` onto the end of the previous value of `result`. Because each cycle adds one copy of `str` to the end of `result`, the final value of `result` after n cycles must consist of n copies of that string.

In each of the two functions—`Factorial` and `ConcatNCopies`—the initialization of the variable used to hold the result is worthy of some note. In the `Factorial` function, the variable `product` is initialized to 1, so that multiplying it by each successive value of `i` properly keeps track of the result as the computation proceeds. In the case of `ConcatNCopies`, the corresponding statement initializes the string variable `result` so that it grows through concatenation. After the first cycle of the loop, the variable `result` must consist of one copy of the string `str`. Prior to the first cycle, therefore, `result` must contain zero copies of the string, which means it has no characters at all. The string with no characters at all is called the **empty string** and is written in C using adjacent double quotes: `""`. Whenever you need to construct a new string by concatenating successive parts onto an existing string variable, you should initialize that variable to the empty string.

Converting characters to strings

When using the `Concat` function, you often run into situations in which you want to add a character to an existing string. The `Concat` function seems like the right conceptual tool but doesn't quite fit the situation. The `Concat` function requires both of its arguments to be strings. In many cases, what you have is a string and a character. To solve this problem, the `strlib.h` library includes the function `CharToString(ch)`. This function takes a single character `ch` and returns a string consisting only of that character. After converting a single character into a string, you can then concatenate it with another string.

To get a sense of how to apply this technique, suppose you have been asked to write a function `ReverseString(str)` that returns a new string composed of the characters in `str` arranged in reverse order, so that `ReverseString("ABC")` returns `"CBA"`. To implement this function, you can go through the original string character by character using a `for` loop and put a new string together using concatenation. If you proceed from left to right and add each character of the original string to the *front* of the new one, the new string will come out in reverse order. The following implementation of `ReverseString` illustrates this strategy:

```
string ReverseString(string str)
{
    string result;
    int i;

    result = "";
    for (i = 0; i < StringLength(str); i++) {
        result = Concat(CharToString(IthChar(str, i)), result);
    }
    return (result);
}
```

Note that each character must be converted to a string before it is concatenated to the beginning of the variable `result`.

Extracting parts of a string

Concatenation makes longer strings from shorter pieces. You often need to do the reverse: separate a string into the shorter pieces it contains. A string that is part of a longer string is called a **substring.** The `strlib.h` library provides a function `SubString(s, p1, p2)`, the effect of which is to extract the characters in `s` lying between positions `p1` and `p2`, inclusive. Thus the function call

```
SubString("Hello there!", 1, 3)
```

returns the string `"ell"`. As you know, numbering in C begins at 0, so the character at index position 1 is the character `'e'`.

As an example of the use of `SubString`, the function `SecondHalf(s)` returns the substring consisting of the last half of the characters in `s`, including the middle character if the length of the string is odd:

```
string SecondHalf(string str)
{
    int len;

    len = StringLength(str);
    return (SubString(str, len / 2, len - 1));
}
```

The `SubString` function handles certain special cases as follows:

1. If p1 is negative, it is set to 0 so that it indicates the first character in the string.
2. If p2 is greater than StringLength(s) − 1, it is set to StringLength(s) − 1 so that it indicates the last character.
3. If p1 ends up being greater than p2, SubString returns the empty string.

Although the reasons for these design choices will probably not become clear until you have more experience with strings, these rules make string programming easier by requiring you to test for fewer special cases when you call SubString.

Comparing one string with another

Since Chapter 5, you have been able to use the StringEqual function to compare two strings for equality. On many occasions, you will also find it useful to determine how two strings relate to each other in alphabetical order. The strlib.h interface provides the function StringCompare for this purpose. The StringCompare function takes two strings, s1 and s2, and returns an integer whose sign indicates their relationship, as follows:

- If s1 precedes s2 in alphabetical order, StringCompare returns a negative integer.
- If s1 follows s2 in alphabetical order, StringCompare returns a positive integer.
- If the two strings are exactly the same, StringCompare returns 0.

Thus, if you want to determine whether s1 comes before s2 in alphabetical order, you need to write

```
if (StringCompare(s1, s2) < 0) . . .
```

Although the StringCompare function returns an integer, it is not legal to make any assumptions about the value of that integer except that it has the correct sign. On some systems, the values returned by StringCompare will always be −1, 0, or 1. On others, the value is some seemingly arbitrary integer with the correct sign.

The "alphabetical order" computers use is different from the order that dictionaries use in certain respects. When StringCompare compares two strings, it compares them using the numeric ordering imposed by the underlying character codes. This order is called **lexicographic order** and differs from traditional alphabetical order in several respects. For example, in an alphabetical index, you will find the entry for *aardvark* before the entry for *Achilles,* because traditional alphabetical ordering does not consider uppercase and lowercase letters separately. If the StringCompare function is called with the arguments "aardvark" and "Achilles", the function simply compares the ASCII codes. In ASCII, the lowercase character 'a' comes after an uppercase 'A'. In lexicographic order, the string "Achilles" comes first. Thus the function call

```
StringCompare("aardvark", "Achilles")
```

returns a positive integer.

When you call StringCompare, it compares the strings starting with the first character in each. If those characters are different, StringCompare considers how the two character values relate to each other in the ASCII sequence and returns an integer that indicates that result. If the first characters match, `StringCompare` goes on to look at the second characters, continuing this process until a difference is detected. If `StringCompare` runs out of characters in one of the two strings, that string is automatically considered to precede the longer one, just as in traditional alphabetical ordering. For example,

```
StringCompare("abc", "abcdefg")
```

returns a negative integer. Only if the two strings match all the way down the line and end at the same place does `StringCompare` return the value 0.

In C, the biggest problem that arises in using `StringCompare` or `StringEqual` is not figuring out what the functions do. That part is simple. What's hard is remembering to use them in the first place. It is easy to make a mental slip and try to use one of the relational operators instead. If you want to know whether `s1` comes before `s2`, the temptation is strong—even for experienced programmers— to write down what you're thinking and express the condition as

```
if (s1 < s2) . . .                          This doesn't work!
```

> **COMMON PITFALLS**
>
> When comparing string values, remember to use `StringEqual` and `StringCompare`, *not the relational operators.* The C compiler will not detect this error, but the program will give completely unpredictable results.

Expressions of this form do not have the intended effect. Worse still, the compiler doesn't even tell you that you've made a mistake, because the expression you wrote means something to the compiler—it just doesn't mean what you wanted it to. In fact, the Boolean value returned when a relational operator is applied to two strings turns out to be completely independent of their values. You will be able to understand what such an expression means after you complete Chapter 14. For now, just keep in mind that using the relational operators to compare strings almost certainly creates a bug. Avoiding this mistake in the first place will save you a lot of debugging time.

Searching within a string

From time to time, you will find it useful to search a string to see whether it contains a particular character or substring. The `strlib.h` interface provides two functions, `FindChar` and `FindString`, for doing so. The prototype for `FindChar` is

```
int FindChar(char ch, string text, int start);
```

The function searches through the string `text`, starting at the character index specified by `start`, looking for the first occurrence of the character `ch`. If the character is found, `FindChar` returns the index position of that character. If the character does not appear before the end of the text string, `FindChar` returns the value −1. The following examples illustrate the operation (remember that the index numbering begins at 0):

```
FindChar('l', "Hello there", 0) returns 2
FindChar('l', "Hello there", 3) returns 3
FindChar('l', "Hello there", 4) returns −1
```

As with string comparison, the functions for searching a string consider uppercase and lowercase characters to be different. Thus, the call

```
FindChar('h', "Hello there", 0)
```

returns 7 because the first occurrence of the lowercase *h* appears at index position 7. The uppercase *H* at index position 0 is ignored.

You can use `FindChar` to implement a function that generates an **acronym,** which is a new word formed by combining, in order, the initial letters of a series of words. For example, the word *scuba* is an acronym formed from the first letters in *self contained underwater breathing apparatus.* The function `Acronym` takes a string composed of separate words and return its acronym. Thus, calling the function

```
Acronym("self contained underwater breathing apparatus")
```

returns `"scuba"`.

Provided that the words are separated by a single space and that no extraneous characters appear, the implementation of `Acronym` can simply take the very first letter and then go into a loop searching for each space. Whenever it finds one, it can concatenate the next character onto the end of the string variable used to hold the result. When no more spaces appear in the string, the acronym is complete. This strategy can be translated into a C implementation as follows:

```
string Acronym(string str)
{
    string acronym;
    int pos;

    acronym = CharToString(IthChar(str, 0));
    pos = 0;
    while (TRUE) {
        pos = FindChar(' ', str, pos + 1);
        if (pos == -1) break;
        acronym = Concat(acronym,
                    CharToString(IthChar(str, pos + 1)));
    }
    return (acronym);
}
```

The function `FindString(str, text, start)` works like `FindChar`, except that the first argument is a string. The function searches through the string `text` looking for the string `str`, starting at position `start`. If a match is found, `FindString` returns the index position of the beginning of the match. For example,

```
FindString("there", "Hello there", 0)
```

returns the value 6. If no match is found, `FindString` returns −1, just as `FindChar` does.

For example, the function `ReplaceFirst(str, pattern, replacement)` searches through the string `str` and replaces the first instance of the string `pattern` with the value of the `replacement` string, returning the entire new string as the value of the function. If the `pattern` string does not appear, the original string is returned unchanged. The program `repfirst.c`, shown in Figure 9-1, contains an implementation of the `ReplaceFirst` function, along with a test program.

The following is a sample run of the `repfirst.c` program:

```
This program edits a string by replacing the first
instance of a pattern substring by a new string.
Enter the string to be edited:
This is a test of the ReplaceFirst function.↵
Enter the pattern string: a↵
Enter the replacement string: a successful↵
This is a successful test of the ReplaceFirst function.
```

Case conversion

The `strlib.h` library includes two functions, `ConvertToUpperCase(s)` and `ConvertToLowerCase(s)`, that convert the case of any alphabetic characters to the indicated case. For example, calling the function

```
ConvertToUpperCase("Hello, world.")
```

returns the string `"HELLO, WORLD."` Note that any nonalphabetic characters appearing in the string—such as the comma, space, and period in this example—are unaffected.

Like all functions in the `strlib.h` interface, `ConvertToUpperCase` and `ConvertToLowerCase` do not change any characters in their argument, but instead return an entirely new string as the result of the function. Thus, to change the value stored in the string variable `word` so that all letters within it appear in lowercase, you need to use an assignment statement, such as

```
word = ConvertToLowerCase(word);
```

If you simply call

```
ConvertToLowerCase(word);
```
                                        This statement leaves word unchanged.

without making the assignment, the characters in word will not be affected.

You can implement the `ConvertToLowerCase` function using `IthChar` and `Concat` as follows:

```
string ConvertToLowerCase(string str)
{
    string result;
    char ch;
    int i;

    result = "";
    for (i = 0; i < StringLength(str); i++) {
        ch = IthChar(str, i);
        result = Concat(result, CharToString(tolower(ch)));
    }
    return (result);
}
```

FIGURE 9-1 repfirst.c

```
/*
 * File: repfirst.c
 * ----------------
 * This file implements and tests the function ReplaceFirst.
 */

#include <stdio.h>
#include "genlib.h"
#include "strlib.h"
#include "simpio.h"

/* Function prototypes */

string ReplaceFirst(string str, string pattern, string replacement);

/* Main program */

main()
{
    string str, pattern, replacement;

    printf("This program edits a string by replacing the first\n");
    printf("instance of a pattern substring by a new string.\n");
    printf("Enter the string to be edited:\n");
    str = GetLine();
    printf("Enter the pattern string: ");
    pattern = GetLine();
    printf("Enter the replacement string: ");
    replacement = GetLine();
    str = ReplaceFirst(str, pattern, replacement);
    printf("%s\n", str);
}

/*
 * Function: ReplaceFirst
 * Usage: newstr = ReplaceFirst(str, pattern, replacement);
 * --------------------------------------------------------
 * This function searches through the string str and replaces the
 * first instance of the pattern with the specified replacement.
 * If the pattern string does not appear, str is returned unchanged.
 */
```

```
string ReplaceFirst(string str, string pattern, string replacement)
{
    string head, tail;
    int pos;

    pos = FindString(pattern, str, 0);
    if (pos == -1) return (str);
    head = SubString(str, 0, pos - 1);
    tail = SubString(str, pos + StringLength(pattern),
                          StringLength(str) - 1);
    return (Concat(Concat(head, replacement), tail));
}
```

Numeric conversion

The `strlib.h` interface exports two functions, `IntegerToString` and `RealToString`, that convert a number into its representation as a string of characters. The function `IntegerToString(n)` converts the integer n into a string of digits, preceded by a minus sign if n is negative. For example, calling `IntegerToString(123)` returns the string `"123"`; calling `IntegerToString(-4)` returns the string `"-4"`. The `RealToString(d)` function converts the floating-point number d into the string that would be displayed by `printf` using the `%G` format code, which sometimes produces a number in scientific notation form. For example, calling `RealToString(3.14)` returns `"3.14"`, but calling `RealToString(0.00000000015)` returns `"1.5E-10"`.

The functions `IntegerToString` and `RealToString` are useful if you want to manipulate the text representation of a number as a sequence of characters. For example, you can use `IntegerToString` to write a function `ProtectedIntegerField(n, places)` that generates a string that includes the text representation of the integer n preceded by enough asterisks so that the entire string is at least as long as the value given by `places`. The implementation of `ProtectedIntegerField`, which uses the previously defined `ConcatNCopies` function, is as follows:

```
string ProtectedIntegerField(int n, int places)
{
    string numstr, fill;

    numstr = IntegerToString(n);
    fill = ConcatNCopies(places - StringLength(numstr), "*");
    return (Concat(fill, numstr));
}
```

This function would be useful in a check-writing application. For instance, if the `printf` call

```
printf("$%s.00\n", ProtectedIntegerField(123, 8));
```

appeared in a program, it would generate the sample run

```
$*****123.00
```

The asterisks make it more difficult for someone to alter the value.

The `strlib.h` interface also exports the functions `StringToInteger` and `StringToReal`. These functions convert strings that represent numeric values back into numbers. For example, calling `StringToInteger("42")` returns the integer 42. Similarly, calling `StringToReal("3.14159")` returns the floating-point number 3.14159. If the argument to either function is not a valid numeric string, an error is reported. Both are useful primarily for input operations. As an example, the following implementation of `addlist.c` uses a blank line as its sentinel value:

```
main()
{
    int total;
    string line;

    printf("This program adds a list of numbers.\n");
    printf("Signal end of list with a blank line.\n");
    total = 0;
    while (TRUE) {
        printf(" ? ");
        line = GetLine();
        if (StringEqual(line, "")) break;
        total += StringToInteger(line);
    }
    printf("The total is %d\n", total);
}
```

Because `GetInteger` cannot read a blank line as data, using a blank line as a sentinel was not an option when `addlist.c` was introduced in Chapter 3. If the program instead reads the input using `GetLine`, the blank line shows up as the empty string. If the line read in from the user is not a blank line, the characters on that line are converted to an integer and added to the running total.

Efficiency and the `strlib.h` library

All the function implementations in this chapter were written for clarity rather than efficiency. As you will discover when you study the internal details of the various string libraries in Chapter 14, many of these implementations are extremely inefficient—so much so that they would not be appropriate for serious applications work. They are, however, concise, effective, and easy to understand. By working with the functions in this form, you can gain a sense of how strings work conceptually.

This knowledge will help enormously when you look at the implementation of the `strlib.h` interface and discover how it works.

Summary

With this chapter, you have begun the process of understanding how to work with *text data.* In C, the most common form of text data is a *string,* which is an ordered collection of individual characters. Individual characters are represented in C using the data type `char`, which is part of a larger class of data called *scalar types.* Scalar types also include the *enumeration types,* which were presented in this chapter as well. Working with characters is fundamental to string processing because characters are the "atoms" from which all strings are built.

In this chapter, you learned how to manipulate strings as an *abstract type.* The internal representation of an abstract type is hidden. The client can use values of that type only by calling functions defined in an interface. In the case of strings, the interface that provides access to the string operations is `strlib.h`, which forms the highest level of a *layered abstraction.* By learning to manipulate strings as abstract types, you can develop a good sense of how to use them in exciting and sophisticated ways, even though the underlying structure remains hidden from view.

Because strings are fundamental to modern programming, however, it is essential for you to explore them from many different perspectives. You will learn more about strings and their representation in Chapters 11, 13, and 14.

Important points raised in this chapter include:

- Types whose conceptual values are not numbers can usually be represented inside the computer by numbering the elements in the domain of the type and then using those numbers as codes for the original values. Types defined by counting off their elements are called *enumeration types.*
- C makes it possible to define new enumeration types using the keywords `typedef` and `enum`.
- Enumeration types are a subclass of *scalar types,* which are those types that behave exactly like integers. Explicit conversions between scalar types and integers are not required in C.
- Characters are represented internally as integers according to a predefined *character code.* Although some computers use different character coding systems, most modern computers use the ASCII coding system shown in Table 9-1.
- The data type `char` used to represent single characters is a scalar type. Character values can therefore be manipulated using the standard operations of arithmetic.
- The `ctype.h` interface contains several functions for classifying individual characters, as well as functions to change the case of a single characters.
- The `strlib.h` interface makes it possible to work with strings as an *abstract type.*
- The `strlib.h` interface defines several functions for manipulating strings. These functions are summarized in Table 9-3.

Function call	Return value
StringLength(s)	length of s
IthChar(s, i)	i^{th} character in s
Concat(s1, s2)	s1 and s2 concatenated end to end
CharToString(ch)	one-character string containing ch
SubString(s, p1, p2)	substring of s from p1 to p2
StringEqual(s1, s2)	TRUE if s1 and s2 are equal
StringCompare(s1, s2)	integer indicating a string comparison
FindChar(ch, text, start)	index of the first occurrence of ch in text after start or −1 if not found
FindString(s, text, start)	index of the first occurrence of s in text after start or −1 if not found
ConvertToLowerCase(s)	copy of s with all letters in lowercase
ConvertToUpperCase(s)	copy of s with all letters in uppercase
IntegerToString(n)	string representation of the integer n
StringToInteger(s)	integer symbolized by the string s
RealToString(d)	%G format representation of d as a string
StringToReal(s)	floating-point value symbolized by the string s

TABLE 9-3

String operations provided by strlib.h

REVIEW QUESTIONS

1. What is an enumeration type?

2. What are the two options presented in this chapter for representing enumeration types in C?

3. How would you define a new enumeration type outcomeT consisting of the three constants Lose, Draw, and Win?

4. How would you modify the definition of outcomeT from the preceding question if it were important that Lose be represented internally as −1, Draw as 0, and Win as 1?

5. Given the definition

        typedef enum { North, East, South, West } directionT;

   what are the internal numeric representations of the four constants?

6. What does *ASCII* stand for?

7. By consulting Table 9-1, determine the ASCII values of the characters '$', '@', '\a', and 'x'.

8. What groups of characters can you assume are consecutive in the ASCII table?

9. Of the special characters listed in Table 9-2, which one is used most often in C programs?

10. What are the four most useful arithmetic operations to apply to character values?

11. The implementation of `RandomInteger` presented in Chapter 8 is

```
int RandomInteger(int low, int high)
{
    int k;
    double d;

    d = (double) rand() / ((double) RAND_MAX + 1);
    k = (int) (d * (high - low + 1));
    return (low + k);
}
```

When the `RandomLetter` function calls `RandomInteger('A', 'Z')`, the values `low` and `high` represent characters, even though their type is `int`. Work through the steps in the implementation and verify that the operations performed on all values that represent characters are indeed in the class of operations you listed in response to the preceding question.

12. What is the result of calling `isdigit(5)`? What is the result of calling `isdigit('5')`?

13. What is the result of calling `toupper('5')`?

14. True or false: It is legal to use character constants as case expressions within a `switch` statement.

15. What is a layered abstraction?

16. True or false: An abstract type is defined in terms of its behavior rather than its representation.

17. What is the result of calling each of the following functions?
   a. `StringLength("ABCDE")`
   b. `StringLength("")`
   c. `StringLength("\a")`
   d. `IthChar("ABC", 2)`
   e. `Concat("12", ".00")`
   f. `CharToString('2')`
   g. `SubString("ABCDE", 0, 3)`
   h. `SubString("ABCDE", 4, 1)`
   i. `SubString("ABCDE", 3, 9)`
   j. `SubString("ABCDE", 3, 3)`

18. What functions from `strlib.h` are useful if you want to add a new character to the end of an existing string?

19. What is the most important caution to keep in mind when comparing strings?

20. What is the result of calling each of the following functions? (For calls to `StringCompare`, simply indicate the sign of the result.)
    a. `StringEqual("ABCDE", "abcde")`
    b. `StringCompare("ABCDE", "ABCDE")`
    c. `StringCompare("ABCDE", "ABC")`
    d. `StringCompare("ABCDE", "abcde")`
    e. `FindChar('a', "Abracadabra", 0)`
    f. `FindString("ra", "Abracadabra", 3)`
    g. `FindString("is", "This is a test.", 0)`
    h. `FindString("This is a test", "test", 0)`

21. What is the result of calling each of the following functions?
    a. `ConvertToLowerCase("Catch-22")`
    b. `StringToInteger(SubString("Catch-22", 5, 7))`
    c. `RealToString(3.140)`
    d. `Concat(IntegerToString(4 / 3), " pi")`

PROGRAMMING EXERCISES

1. Define the function `LeftFrom(dir)`, which takes a value of type `directionT` representing a compass point and returns the compass point that lies 90 degrees to the left. Write a test program for your function that displays the result of calling `LeftFrom` on every compass point, as shown:

```
This program tests the LeftFrom function.
LeftFrom(North) = West
LeftFrom(East)  = North
LeftFrom(South) = East
LeftFrom(West)  = South
```

2. Exercise 14 in Chapter 8 asked you to reimplement the `calendar.c` program from Chapter 5 in the form of a `calendar.c` main program and a separate `caltools.c` file. As in the original implementation, the `caltools.c` file uses integers directly to indicate the names of the months and the days of the week.

   Reimplement the two-file solution from Chapter 8, exercise 14, so that your new version uses two enumeration types—`weekdayT` and `monthT`—to refer to weekdays and months. You should add the enumeration type definitions to the `caltools.h` interface, but you will also need to edit the `calendar.c` and `caltools.c` files to reflect those changes. In your solution, you should make sure that every variable used to hold a weekday or a month is declared as the appropriate enumeration type rather than as an integer.

3. Implement the function `IsConsonant(ch)`, which returns `TRUE` if ch is a consonant, that is, any letter except one of the five vowels: `'a'`, `'e'`, `'i'`, `'o'`, and `'u'`. Like `IsVowel`, your function should recognize consonants of both cases. Write a test program that displays all the uppercase consonants, as follows:

```
The English consonants are:
  B C D F G H J K L M N P Q R S T V W X Y Z
```

4. Write a function `RandomWord` that returns a randomly constructed "word" consisting of randomly chosen letters. The number of letters in the word should also be chosen randomly by picking a number between the values of the `#define` constants `MinLetters` and `MaxLetters`. Write a main program that tests your function by displaying five random words. The following is a sample run that uses the values 2 and 8 for `MinLetters` and `MaxLetters`:

```
This program generates 5 random words.
EINYE
FMDCKH
ZNTQ
UVDQIJX
KPUYW
```

5. In the crossword game called Scrabble, points are assigned to each letter in the alphabet as follows.

Points	Letters
1	A, E, I, L, N, O, R, S, T, U
2	D, G
3	B, C, M, P
4	F, H, V, W, Y
5	K
8	J, X
10	Q, Z

For example, the Scrabble word `"FARM"` is worth 9 points: 4 for the *F*, 1 each for the *A* and the *R*, and 3 for the *M*. Write a function `ScrabbleScore` that takes a word as its argument and returns the score the word would earn if played on the Scrabble board, not counting any of the other bonuses that occur in the game. You should ignore any characters other than uppercase letters in computing the score. In particular, lowercase letters are assumed to represent blank tiles, which can stand for any letter but which have a score of 0.

Write a main program to test your `ScrabbleScore` function. A possible sample run for such a test program is

```
This program tests the ScrabbleScore function.
Enter words, ending with a blank line.
Word: XI↵
The basic score for 'XI' is 9.
Word: HORN↵
The basic score for 'HORN' is 7.
Word: SCRABBLE↵
The basic score for 'SCRABBLE' is 14.
Word: QUIzZICAL↵
The basic score for 'QUIzZICAL' is 28.
Word:
```

6. Implement a function `Capitalize(str)` that returns a string in which the initial character is capitalized (if it is a letter) and all other letters are converted so that they appear in lowercase form. Characters other than letters are not affected. For example, `Capitalize("BOOLEAN")` and `Capitalize("boolean")` should each return the string `"Boolean"`.

7. Implement a predicate function `EqualIgnoringCase(s1, s2)`, which returns TRUE if the strings `s1` and `s2` are the same, not counting differences in the case of a letter. For example, `EqualIgnoringCase("CAT", "cat")` should return TRUE.

8. One of the simplest types of codes used to make it harder for someone to read a message is a **letter-substitution cipher,** in which each letter in the original message is replaced by some different letter in the coded version of that message. A particularly simple type of letter-substitution cipher is a **cyclic cipher,** in which each letter is replaced by its counterpart a fixed distance ahead in the alphabet. The word *cyclic* refers to the fact that if the operation of moving ahead in the alphabet would take you past Z, you simply circle back to the beginning and start over again with A.

As an example, the following sample run shows how each letter in the alphabet is changed by shifting it ahead four places. The A becomes E, the B becomes F, the Z becomes D (because it cycles back to the beginning), and so on:

```
This program encodes a message using a cyclic cipher.
Enter the numeric key: 4↵
Enter a message: ABCDEFGHIJKLMNOPQRSTUVWXYZ↵
Encoded message: EFGHIJKLMNOPQRSTUVWXYZABCD
```

To solve this problem, you should first define a function `EncodeString` with the prototype

```
string EncodeString(string str, int key);
```

The function returns the new string formed by shifting every letter in `str` forward the number of letters indicated by `key`, cycling back to the beginning of the alphabet if necessary. After you have implemented `EncodeString`, write a test program that duplicates the examples shown in the following sample run:

```
This program encodes a message using a cyclic cipher.
Enter the numeric key: 13↵
Enter a message: This is a secret message.↵
Encoded message: Guvf vf n frperg zrffntr.
```

Note that the coding operation applies only to letters; any other character is included unchanged in the output. Moreover, the case of letters is unaffected: lowercase letters come out as lowercase, and uppercase letters come out as uppercase.

Write your program so that a negative value of `key` means that letters are shifted toward the beginning of the alphabet instead of toward the end, as illustrated by the following sample run:

```
This program encodes a message using a cyclic cipher.
Enter the numeric key: -1↵
Enter a message: IBM 9000.↵
Encoded message: HAL 9000.
```

9. A **palindrome** is a word that reads identically backward and forward, such as *level* or *noon*. Write a predicate function `IsPalindrome(str)` that returns TRUE if the string `str` is a palindrome. In addition, design and write a test program that calls `IsPalindrome` to demonstrate that it works. In writing the program, concentrate on how to solve the problem simply rather than how to make your solution more efficient.

10. The concept of a palindrome introduced in exercise 9 is often extended to full sentences by ignoring punctuation and differences in the case of letters. For example, the sentence

   Madam, I'm Adam.

is a sentence palindrome, because if you only look at the letters and ignore any distinction between uppercase and lowercase letters, it reads identically backward and forward. Write a predicate function `IsSentencePalindrome(str)` that returns TRUE if the string `str` fits this definition of a sentence palindrome. For example, you should be able to use your function to write a main program capable of producing the following sample run:

```
This program checks for palindromes.
Indicate the end of the input with a blank line.
Enter a string: Madam, I'm Adam.⏎
That is a palindrome.
Enter a string: A man, a plan, a canal: Panama!⏎
That is a palindrome.
Enter a string: Not a palindrome.⏎
That is not a palindrome.
Enter a string:
```

11. Write a function `DateString(day, month, year)` that returns a string consisting of the day of the month, a hyphen, the first three letters in the name of the month, another hyphen, and the last two digits of the year. For example, calling the function

    ```
    DateString(22, 11, 1963)
    ```

    should return the string `"22-Nov-63"`.

12. If the designers of the string library described in this chapter had not defined the searching functions, you could implement those functions using the other functions available in the library. Without calling either `FindChar` or `FindString` directly, implement a function `MyFindString` that behaves in exactly the same way that `FindString` does.

13. Modify the function `ReplaceFirst` defined in the section on "Searching within a string" earlier in this chapter into a `ReplaceAll` function that replaces *all* instances of the pattern string with the replacement, rather than just the first. For example, calling

    ```
    ReplaceAll("beebee", "e", "o")
    ```

    should return the string `"booboo"`.

14. Write a function `RegularPluralForm(word)` that returns the plural of `word` formed by following these standard English rules:
    a. If the word ends in *s, x, z, ch,* or *sh,* add *es* to the word.
    b. If the word ends in *y* and the *y* is preceded by a consonant, change the *y* to *ies.*
    c. In all other cases, add just an *s.*

    Write a test program and design a set of test cases to verify that your program works.

## CHAPTER 10

Modular Development

It is particularly important, it seems to me, in an era of ever increasing departmentalization and specialization, to make the attempt occasionally to see wholes and to understand what lies behind the exterior manifestations.

— Jessamyn West, *The Quaker Reader,* 1962

Objectives

- To appreciate the importance of dividing a single program into separate modules.

- To understand the need to preserve state information between calls to functions in a module.

- To be able to use global variables to represent state information that must be maintained across function calls.

- To recognize the dangers associated with overusing global variables.

- To be able to use the `static` keyword to keep functions and global variables private to a single module.

So far, most of this text has focused on short programs designed to illustrate a specific aspect of the C language. Concentrating on individual statement forms or other details of the language makes sense when you are first learning to program. Doing so enables you to consider each concept in isolation and learn how it works without being overwhelmed by the complexity inherent in a large program. The real challenge, however, is to master this complexity. To do so, you must practice writing large programs that combine the individual concepts and tools.

The most important technique for managing large programs is the strategy of stepwise refinement that you learned in Chapter 5: when you are faced with a big problem that seems to require a complex solution, you break the problem down into smaller ones that are easier to solve.

The strategy of decomposing a large problem into smaller pieces applies at many levels of the programming process. The `calendar.c` example in Chapter 5 illustrated this technique in the context of a single source file. As programs get longer, however, it becomes hard to manage so many functions in a single source file. Just as it can be difficult to understand a 50-line function all at once, it can be hard to understand a program composed of 50 different functions. In either case, imposing some additional structure is helpful. When faced with a 50-line function, your best strategy is to divide it up into smaller functions that call each other to complete the task. When faced with a 50-function program, your best strategy is to divide that program into several smaller source files, each of which contains a set of related functions. The smaller source files that each constitute a piece of the entire program are called **modules.** Each individual module is simpler than the program as a whole. Moreover, if you are careful in your design, you can use the same module as part of many different applications.

When you divide a program into modules, it is important to choose a decomposition strategy that limits the extent to which the modules depend on each other.

program.c

```
main()
{
    ProcA();
    ProcB();
}

void ProcA(void)
{
    . . .
}

void ProcB(void)
{
    . . .
}
```

FIGURE 10-1 Program structured as a single module

The module containing the function main is called the **main module** and occupies the highest level in the decompositional hierarchy. Each of the other modules represents a separate abstraction whose operations are defined in an interface.

To illustrate the principle, imagine that you have written the file program.c shown in Figure 10-1. The program consists of a single source file that contains a main program and two procedures, ProcA and ProcB.

You can break this source file down into a main module for the function main and two subsidiary modules, the first for ProcA and the second for ProcB, as illustrated in Figure 10-2.

The main module now contains only part of the code for the complete program. The implementations of the functions ProcA and ProcB are in separate modules. Before the program can be run, the code for each of these modules must be linked to form a single executable program. The task of linking program pieces together is part of the standard process of program execution, illustrated in Figure 1-2.

In a sense, each of the subsidiary modules acts as a library for the main module. As with any library, each of these modules must have an interface that provides the compiler with the necessary information about the functions that module contains. These interfaces are shown in Figure 10-2 as the header files module1.h and module2.h.

```
main.c
    #include "module1.h"
    #include "module2.h"

    main()
    {
        ProcA();
        ProcB();
    }
```

```
module1.h
    void ProcA(void);
```

```
module2.h
    void ProcB(void);
```

```
module1.c
    #include "module1.h"

    void ProcA(void)
    {
        . . .
    }
```

```
module2.c
    #include "module2.h"

    void ProcB(void)
    {
        . . .
    }
```

FIGURE 10-2 Program divided into separate modules

The example in Figure 10-2 is a simplified example of modular decomposition. Breaking up a program into modules that contain only a single function, as in this example, carries decomposition to an extreme. In more typical applications, each module includes several related functions that form an easily identified component of the application as a whole.

10.1 Pig Latin—a case study in modular development

The technique of breaking up a program into modules is called **modular development.** To illustrate this technique, this chapter solves a problem in which modular decomposition offers clear advantages. The problem is to write a program that reads in a line of text from the terminal and translates each word in that line from English into Pig Latin.

Pig Latin is an invented language formed by transforming each English word according to the following simple rules:

1. If the word begins with a consonant, you form its Pig Latin equivalent by moving the initial consonant string (that is, all the letters up to the first vowel) from the beginning of the word to the end and then adding the suffix *ay.*
2. If the word begins with a vowel, you just add the suffix *way.*

For example, suppose the word is *scram.* Because the word begins with a consonant, you divide it into two parts: one consisting of the letters before the first vowel and one consisting of that vowel and the remaining letters:

You then interchange these two parts and add *ay* at the end, as follows:

creating the Pig Latin word *amscray.* For a word that begins with a vowel, such as *apple,* you simply add *way* to the end, which leaves you with *appleway.*

Applying top-down design

Since the problem is to translate an entire line of English text into Pig Latin, the program should be able to produce sample runs like this one:

```
Enter a line: this is pig latin.↵
isthay isway igpay atinlay.
```

You can start designing a solution to the Pig Latin problem without deciding immediately whether you need to separate the program into modules. Often, the fact that a program requires a particular modular decomposition becomes apparent only after you have explored various solution strategies. Usually, the best approach is to begin by applying top-down design, as described in the section on "Stepwise refinement" in Chapter 5.

With top-down design, you start at the level of the main program and work your way down through a series of functions, each of which solves a successively simpler part of the entire problem. At the initial stage, you define the function `main` as a sequence of high-level steps that have yet to be implemented. Although it is often possible to code the steps directly as function calls, it is usually easier to write them in English first. For example, as long as you are designing your program on paper, you can write a rough draft of the Pig Latin program as follows:

```
main()
{
     Read in a line of text from the user.
     Translate the line of text into Pig Latin.
}
```

In this example, the function header line and the braces are part of C's standard syntax, but the statements themselves are written as English sentences that describe what the program will do. Programs that consist of a mixture of English and C are said to be written in **pseudocode.**

Using pseudocode

Although it makes no sense to the compiler, pseudocode is useful for you as a programmer because it enables you to keep track of the stepwise refinement process. After you write out the complete program as a sequence of English steps, you can go back through the pseudocode statements and substitute the actual C code necessary to implement them. In this case, for example, it is easy to translate the first pseudocode statement into C because it matches the idiom for reading a string that you have been using since Chapter 2. After you fill in the details of the operation required to read in a line of text from the user, the pseudocode version of the program looks like this:

```
main()
{
     string line;

     printf("Enter a line: ");
     line = GetLine();
     Translate the line of text into Pig Latin.
}
```

The result is still pseudocode, but you have made progress. The remaining English statement is harder to code, so the best strategy is to apply stepwise refinement, replacing the line of pseudocode with a new function that has the effect of the English sentence. In this case, you want a function that will "translate the line of text into Pig Latin," which you might choose to name `TranslateLine`. Using that name, you can complete the implementation of `main` as follows:

```
main()
{
    string line;

    printf("Enter a line: ");
    line = GetLine();
    TranslateLine(line);
}
```

At this level of detail, the program is satisfyingly simple: you display a prompt, read in a line, and then call `TranslateLine` to complete the job. Though you haven't yet written `TranslateLine`, you can say something about its behavior from the caller's point of view. In fact, you have enough information to specify a description and prototype for `TranslateLine`:

```
/*
 * Function: TranslateLine
 * Usage: TranslateLine(line);
 * --------------------------
 * This function takes a line of text and translates
 * the words in the line to Pig Latin, displaying the
 * translation as it goes.
 */

void TranslateLine(string line);
```

Implementing `TranslateLine`

After reaching this point, you are ready to begin implementing `TranslateLine`. At this level, the problem is still so complex that you need to decompose it further. As is often true in programming, there are many strategies for doing so, some of which work better than others. In most cases, however, no particular strategy for decomposition is clearly the "correct" one. You will usually need to consider several ways of subdividing the problem and see which strategy works best.

Let's return to the case at hand. In implementing `TranslateLine`, you need to solve the problem of how to divide a string into words, translate each word into Pig Latin, and display each Pig Latin word on the screen. This statement of the problem suggests the following conceptual decomposition:

```
void TranslateLine(string line)
{
    Divide the line into words.
    Translate each word into Pig Latin.
    Display each translated word.
    Display a newline character to complete the output line.
}
```

This decomposition is reasonable in theory but leads to certain practical problems. In the first step, dividing the line into words, how would you store the result? A function to implement that concept would have to return not a single word but a list of words. Once you complete Chapter 11, you will have the tools you need to manipulate lists of words, but for now you must make do with the tools you have. If you think carefully about the problem, you will discover that you don't need to keep track of all the words at once. As soon as you find one word, you can translate and display it right away. Once that word is displayed, you can forget it and go on to the next. This observation suggests a second strategy:

```
void TranslateLine(string line)
{
    while (there are any words left on the line) {
        Get the next word.
        Translate that word into Pig Latin.
        Display the translated word.
    }
    Display a newline character to complete the output line.
}
```

There are several details missing from the pseudocode version of the strategy, but the overall idea seems to make sense and avoids the problem of having to keep track of an entire list of words.

Taking spaces and punctuation into account

The strategy used in the pseudocode version of `TranslateLine` has a small problem. Suppose, for example, that the user enters the following input line when the program is run:

```
Enter a line: this is pig latin.↵
```

If you conceive of the input as being the four words `"this"`, `"is"`, `"pig"`, and `"latin"`, the output of the program, assuming that all the English steps work exactly as they are supposed to, would be

```
Enter a line: this is pig latin.↵
isthayiswayigpayatinlay
```

This output is not really what you want. All the words run together because the spaces and punctuation marks have disappeared. The pseudocode version of `TranslateLine` doesn't take spacing and punctuation into account. On the other hand, neither did the original English statement of the problem. The problem was incompletely specified.

One of the realities of programming is that English descriptions of problems are usually incompletely specified. As a programmer, you will often trip over some detail that the framer of the problem either overlooked or considered too obvious to mention. In some cases, the omission is serious enough that you have to discuss it with the person who assigned you the programming task. In many cases, however, you will have to choose for yourself a policy that seems reasonable.

Deciding what seems reasonable, however, can sometimes be tricky. In this case, you might decide to print a space between each word in the output, ignoring any other punctuation. This strategy is simple and might be reasonable in this context. On the other hand, it is probably not the best strategy. Punctuation helps make output readable. Because the punctuation marks and spaces convey meaning, it would be better to display them in precisely the same places where they appear in the input. Thus you probably want the output to look like this:

```
Enter a line: this is pig latin.↵
isthay isway igpay atinlay.
```

There are many ways to redesign the program so that punctuation marks appear correctly in the output. One approach, for example, is to change the main loop so that it goes through the string character by character instead of word by word. If you use this strategy, the pseudocode for the implementation has the following structure:

```
void TranslateLine(string line)
{
    for (i = 0; i < StringLength(line); i++) {
        if (the iᵗʰ character in the line is some kind of separator) {
            Display that character.
        } else if (the iᵗʰ character is the end of a word) {
            Extract the word as a substring.
            Translate the word to Pig Latin.
            Display the translated word.
        }
    }
    Display a newline character to complete the output line.
}
```

With some amount of effort, you can get this strategy to work. (You have the opportunity to do so in exercise 2.) Nonetheless, such a strategy has certain drawbacks. One is that the program structure has become more complicated. The original pseudocode design was shorter, in part because it allowed you to work with the string in larger units.

A more serious problem, however, shows up in the decomposition. The version of the pseudocode presented in the preceding section contains the English statement

Get the next word.

That statement has disappeared in the most recent version. If you think like a programmer, you will recognize that the operation "get the next word" is a useful general tool, one that has application far beyond a simple Pig Latin program. Many problems require you to break up text into words. If you can develop a general function for performing this operation, you will have a tremendous head start toward solving those problems.

On the other hand, simply being able to get the next word does not solve the punctuation problem. To be useful in the current application, the function that returns the next word must be able to return the spaces and punctuation marks as well, so the output line can include them.

Refining the definition of a word

What you need to do at this point is refine your notion of what constitutes a word. If you look at the input line

    this is pig latin.

you might simply see it as the four words, *this, is, pig,* and *latin.* Alternatively, you can also choose to think about the line as being composed of eight separate pieces, as follows:

interpreting the spaces and punctuation marks, like the words, as distinct entities. In computer science, a sequence of characters that acts as a coherent unit is called a **token.** In the preceding diagram, each of the boxed units constitutes a token.

Considering spaces and punctuation characters as separate tokens allows you to modify the TranslateLine strategy so these characters are displayed as well. The revised pseudocode strategy is

```
void TranslateLine(string line)
{
    while (there are any tokens left on the line) {
        Get the next token.
        if (the token is a regular English word) {
            Replace the token by its Pig Latin translation.
        }
        Display the token.
    }
    Display a newline character to complete the output line.
}
```

The strategy is still quite simple. Moreover, the individual operations of getting a token and testing to see whether tokens remain on the line are likely to be useful in a variety of applications.

The idea of dividing a line into separate tokens comes up quite often in computer science. For example, when the C compiler translates one of your programs into machine code, the first step in the process is to break up the input file into the individual tokens used in C: variable names, numbers, operators, and so on. This process of dividing the input into tokens is called **lexical analysis** or, less formally, **token scanning.**

Designing the token scanner

To complete the implementation of TranslateLine using the new strategy, you must first design a token scanner that can divide up the input line. Moreover, keeping in mind its potential as a general tool, you want a token scanner you can apply to many problems other than translating strings to Pig Latin. Thus, it makes sense to design the token scanner as a separate module. Initially, the design process requires thinking about how you should organize the scanner module and, in particular, what functions it should contain.

In the latest pseudocode version of TranslateLine, shown in the preceding section, the scanner module comes into play at two different points. First, the scanner must provide a function to return the next token from the line. Second, the scanner must let the client know when the last token has been scanned. Because you are designing the interface, you get to choose the function names. For the function responsible for returning the next token, GetNextToken seems like a reasonable choice. To report that all tokens have been scanned, one option is to define a predicate function called AtEndOfLine, which returns TRUE after the last token has been read.

At this point, however, you face an interesting question: what arguments do these functions take? At first glance, it seems as if the caller must pass the input line to GetNextToken because the tokens come from that line. On the other hand, the idea of calling GetNextToken(line) raises a conceptual dilemma. If GetNextToken acts the way functions usually do, GetNextToken(line) will return the same result every time because the value of line isn't changing.

To illustrate the problem, let's suppose that you want to divide the string "Hello there" into the three tokens it contains: the word "Hello", the space that follows it, and the word "there". In addition, suppose you have stored the string "Hellothere" in the variable line using the following assignment statement:

```
line = "Hello there";
```

If GetNextToken takes line as its argument, it is easy to imagine obtaining the first word by calling GetNextToken(line). The problem is how to get the next token. If you again call GetNextToken(line), the variable line still contains the entire string "Hello there". Since this function call occurs in exactly the same form as the first one, it will presumably return the same value.

To fix this problem, you must design the scanner module to keep track of how much progress it has made in dividing up the line. After GetNextToken returns a token from the line, it must remember that it has scanned that token so it can return a different result the next time it is called. Information that must be retained between calls to functions within a module is called its **internal state.**

When a module maintains internal state, the interface to that module usually exports a function that initializes the state information. In the case of the scanner module, for example, it makes sense to provide a function InitScanner(line) so that clients can tell the scanner to return tokens starting at the beginning of the string line. To get those tokens, clients simply call GetNextToken with no arguments. The information about which token should be returned is part of the internal state maintained by the scanner module. The first call to GetNextToken returns the first token, the next call returns the second token, and so on until all the tokens have been read. At that point, the function AtEndOfLine, which also requires no arguments, will return TRUE.

You can use the functions InitScanner, GetNextToken, and AtEndOfLine to flesh out the implementation of TranslateLine, as follows:

```
void TranslateLine(string line)
{
    string token;

    InitScanner(line);
    while (!AtEndOfLine()) {
        token = GetNextToken();
        if (the token is a legal word) {
            Replace the token by its Pig Latin translation.
        }
        Display the token.
    }
    Display a newline character to complete the output line.
}
```

The function still has a few unfinished pieces, but the loop structure itself is now complete. The implementation first tells the scanner to extract tokens from the variable line by calling InitScanner. It then enters a loop in which it calls GetNextToken to retrieve each new token in turn, until all the tokens have been read.

Completing the TranslateLine implementation

Before fleshing out the design of the scanner interface and learning how to implement it, you might want to tidy things up at this level by completing the implementation of TranslateLine, which is still in pseudocode form. If you continue with the strategy of stepwise refinement, you can finish the implementation by replacing the remaining English statements with calls to functions. In this example, the functions are either simple calls to printf or calls to new functions that you will then implement at the next level of the refinement. In either case, the function calls themselves are a straightforward translation of their English counterparts. The completed implementation of TranslateLine is therefore

```
void TranslateLine(string line)
{
    string token;

    InitScanner(line);
    while (!AtEndOfLine()) {
        token = GetNextToken();
        if (IsLegalWord(token)) token = TranslateWord(token);
        printf("%s", token);
    }
    printf("\n");
}
```

The code is now complete at this level of the decomposition. The solution, however, is expressed in terms of two functions that remain unimplemented: IsLegalWord and TranslateWord.

The predicate function IsLegalWord determines whether the token returned by GetNextToken is a word that should be translated into Pig Latin or whether it is simply part of the punctuation. The rules of Pig Latin make sense only if a word consists entirely of letters. It therefore seems reasonable to have IsLegalWord(token) return TRUE if every character in token is a letter. By now, you should be familiar enough with strings to implement this function immediately, like this:

```
bool IsLegalWord(string token)
{
    int i;

    for (i = 0; i < StringLength(token); i++) {
        if (!isalpha(IthChar(token, i))) return (FALSE);
    }
    return (TRUE);
}
```

The process of translating a single word is only slightly harder. In pseudocode, the structure of TranslateWord mirrors the rules for Pig Latin:

```
string TranslateWord(string word)
{
    Find the position of the first vowel.
    if (the vowel appears at the beginning of the word) {
        Return the word concatenated with "way".
    } else {
        Extract the initial substring up to the vowel and call it the "head."
        Extract the substring from that position onward and call it the "tail."
        Return the tail, concatenated with the head, concatenated with "ay".
    }
}
```

FIGURE 10-3 scanner.h

```
/*
 * File: scanner.h
 * ---------------
 * This file is the interface to a package that divides
 * a line into individual "tokens".  A token is defined
 * to be either
 *
 * 1. a string of consecutive letters and digits representing
 *    a word, or
 *
 * 2. a one-character string representing a separator
 *    character, such as a space or a punctuation mark.
 *
 * To use this package, you must first call
 *
 *        InitScanner(line);
 *
 * where line is the string (typically a line returned by
 * GetLine) that is to be divided into tokens.  To retrieve
 * each token in turn, you call
 *
 *        token = GetNextToken();
 *
 * When the last token has been read, the predicate function
 * AtEndOfLine returns TRUE, so that the loop structure
 *
 *        while (!AtEndOfLine()) {
 *            token = GetNextToken();
 *            . . . process the token . . .
 *        }
 *
 * serves as an idiom for processing each token on the line.
 *
 * Further details for each function are given in the
 * individual descriptions below.
 */

#ifndef _scanner_h
#define _scanner_h

#include "genlib.h"
```

```
/*
 * Function: InitScanner
 * Usage: InitScanner(line);
 * -------------------------
 * This function initializes the scanner and sets it up so that
 * it reads tokens from line.  After InitScanner has been called,
 * the first call to GetNextToken will return the first token
 * on the line, the next call will return the second token,
 * and so on.
 */

void InitScanner(string line);

/*
 * Function: GetNextToken
 * Usage: word = GetNextToken();
 * -----------------------------
 * This function returns the next token on the line.
 */

string GetNextToken(void);

/*
 * Function: AtEndOfLine
 * Usage: if (AtEndOfLine()) . . .
 * -------------------------------
 * This function returns TRUE when the scanner has reached
 * the end of the line.
 */

bool AtEndOfLine(void);

#endif
```

Even though you have not yet learned how to maintain internal state in a C program, you have seen several examples of library packages that maintain state information. In the graphics library, for example, every line starts where the last one left off. The current point in the graphics library is part of its state and is retained between calls to the graphics library. Similarly, the random number function rand defined in the stdlib.h remembers the previous random number so that it can generate the next one. In each case, the modules that implement these libraries preserve the values of some variables from call to call.

Global variables

In Chapter 5, you learned about the mechanics of the function-calling process. Whenever a function is called, the variables it declares are created in a separate region of memory called a *stack frame.* In Chapter 5, stack frames are diagrammed as index cards. You saw that calling a function is equivalent to creating a new index card and placing it on top of the pile of cards that represent other active functions. Returning from a function is equivalent to throwing away its index card and continuing in the context of the caller.

The variables declared inside a function, called *local variables,* exist only in the context of a stack frame. When a function returns, the local variables in its stack frame disappear completely. The index card representing the stack frame is thrown away, and the values of those variables are lost. If a module needs to maintain its internal state between function calls, it cannot use local variables to do so. It must use *global variables.*

A local variable is one that you declare in the context of a function. The names of the parameters and the names of variables declared at the beginning of the block that constitutes the function body can be referenced only inside that function. Variable declarations, however, may also appear outside of any function definition. Variables declared in this way are called **global variables.** The declarations look exactly the same as those for local variables, except that they occur at the top level of the file. For example, in the code fragment

```
int g;

void MyProcedure()
{
    int i;

    . . .
}
```

the variable g is a global variable, and the variable i is a local variable. The local variable i is valid only within the function MyProcedure. The global variable g, on the other hand, can be used in any function that follows its declaration in the module. The portion of the program in which a variable can be used is called its **scope.** Thus, the scope of a local variable is the function in which it is defined. The scope of a global variable is the entire remainder of the source file in which it appears.

Unlike local variables, global variables are stored in memory in such a way that their values are not affected by function calls. In terms of the index card analogy, global variables are stored on a separate card that is always available, as if it had been glued to the desk top and never covered up by the stack containing the local variables. Every function in the module can see the variables on that card. Moreover, the values of those variables are not lost when a function returns. A global variable keeps the same value until you assign it a new one.

The dangers of using global variables

Many new programmers find the idea of global variables attractive. After all, because global variables can be seen from any part of the program, you don't need to pass them as arguments to individual functions. However, programmers quickly learn that using global variables tends to make their programs much harder to read.

Oddly enough, the properties that seem like advantages to the novice are precisely the ones that most concern the more experienced programmer. A new programmer likes the idea that global variables can be manipulated from any function in a source file. For an experienced programmer, this fact signals danger. Suppose, for example, that you are hunting for a bug in a program that fails because a variable is somehow getting set to the wrong value. If the variable is a global one, the problem could be absolutely anywhere in the source file since every function in the module can manipulate that variable. Local variables are much more constrained. If a local variable has the wrong value, the programmer can focus on a single function when looking for the bug.

To avoid such problems, global variables are used infrequently in well-structured programs. Their principal advantage is that they make it possible for a module, such as the scanner module, to maintain internal state. Since global variables maintain their value between function calls, they are ideal for this purpose. Thus, in the scanner module, you could use global variables to keep track of the line passed to `InitScanner` and the current position in that line.

Keeping variables private to a module

The fact that global variables are visible everywhere in a single module is only part of the problem with using them. Unless you make an explicit declaration to the contrary, the C compiler assumes that it is appropriate for other modules to see global variables as well. Thus, when you declare a global variable, the set of functions that might change its value is not even limited to a single module. The variable can be referenced by any module in the entire program.

In a well-structured program, individual modules exchange data through function calls that pass arguments from one module to another. In most cases—particularly when you are first developing your programming habits—it is best to ensure that each global variable is never referenced by more than one module. To avoid the possibility that two modules will reference the same global variable, you should eliminate the danger entirely by writing the keyword `static` at the beginning of the declaration, as in

```
static int cpos;
```

This declaration defines `cpos` as a global integer, visible from anywhere in the module in which is defined. The name `cpos`, however, is not made available to other modules and is thus entirely private to the one in which it appears. In this book, all global variables will be declared to be `static`.

In C, the word *static* refers to how a particular variable is stored, which is discussed in Chapter 11. For most practical purposes, however, it is better to think of the word *static* as a synonym for *private,* which more closely describes its purpose

COMMON PITFALLS

In writing a program, it is usually best to avoid the use of global variables since they make the program harder to understand and debug. The principal situation in which global variables are necessary is when a module must maintain internal state between function calls.

in this context. By declaring variables using the keyword `static`, you keep them private to your abstraction.

Initializing global variables

In the `scanner.h` interface, the global variables are initialized by calling the function `InitScanner`. Using an initialization function to assign values to the global variables that represent the internal state of a module is called **dynamic initialization.** The key feature of dynamic initialization is that it occurs when the program is run. The client program calls the initialization function for a module, which then uses assignment statements to give initial values to the global state variables.

In C, global variables can also be given initial values *before* the program starts to run. As discussed in the section on "Programming languages and compilation" in Chapter 1, the compiler produces object files that contain the instructions necessary to execute the program using the computer's own internal language. In addition to these instructions, object files may also contain data values that specify the initial contents of a global variable. Because this type of initialization occurs prior to the execution of the program, it is called **static initialization.**

To specify static initialization of a global variable, you include in its declaration an equal sign after the variable name, followed by the initial value, which must be a constant.[1] For example, the declaration

```
static int startingValue = 1;
```

not only declares the variable `startingValue` to be a global integer variable that is private to this module but also guarantees that the contents of the variable will be 1 when the program starts to run.

In this text, most of the interfaces that maintain internal state use dynamic initialization and include a function to perform it explicitly, like the `InitScanner` function in the `scanner.h` interface. There are, however, two cases in which static initialization is a better choice:

1. *If the value of a variable is constant throughout the lifetime of the program.* This condition occurs rarely in the case of simple variables but will become important when you start to use more complicated data structures in Chapter 11.
2. *If a variable usually has a particular initial value that only a few clients might want to change.* In cases of this sort, the best strategy is usually to set the standard option using static initialization and then provide a function in the interface that allows clients to change the value if necessary.

The second condition is best illustrated by example. Let's suppose that a client of the scanner module asked you to change the scanner interface so that all tokens containing alphabetic characters were returned in upper case. Thus, after calling

```
InitScanner("Hello there");
```

---

[1] In certain cases, the same syntax for initialization can be applied to local variables as well. If you initialize a local variable, the effect is the same as performing an assignment and can just as easily be written as such. To simplify the discussion of initialization, this text does not use initializers for local variables.

your client would like the tokens to be `"HELLO"`, `" "`, and `"THERE"`. This behavior would not make sense for all your clients. On the other hand, it would probably be useful for some of them.

How could you satisfy the request of this client without making your other clients unhappy? The functionality is easy enough to provide. All you need to do is call the function `ConvertToUpperCase` before you return from `GetNextToken`. On the other hand, you only want to do so if the client has requested this behavior. To keep track of whether the client wants uppercase tokens, you could declare a global Boolean variable as follows:

```
static bool uppercaseFlag;
```

If `uppercaseFlag` has the value `TRUE`, the scanner returns tokens entirely in upper case; if it is `FALSE`, the scanner behaves as it did originally.

How should you initialize `uppercaseFlag`? And how should you design the interface to allow clients to change the value of that flag? These questions raise important issues of interface design.

One approach would be to use dynamic initialization. With this design, the client would select the behavior by passing an additional Boolean argument to `InitScanner` that would serve as the setting of the `uppercaseFlag` option. Calling

```
InitScanner("Hello there", TRUE);
```

would indicate that the client wanted uppercase tokens returned. Conversely, calling

```
InitScanner("Hello there", FALSE);
```

would indicate that the client wanted the traditional behavior of the scanner, with tokens returned using a mixture of uppercase and lowercase letters, exactly as those characters appeared on the input line.

This approach, however, has two serious drawbacks. First, it is extremely difficult for a reader of the program to know what the `TRUE` and `FALSE` arguments mean in the call to `InitScanner`. To decipher the purpose of these arguments, any client would have to read the comments in the interface. Second, the new design changes an existing interface and therefore violates the stability condition. If the scanner interface has clients, those clients would have to change their programs.

A much better strategy that avoids both of these problems is to extend the scanner interface rather than change it. All the old functions work precisely as they have before. To provide the option of returning uppercase tokens, you can add a new function called `ReturnUppercaseTokens` that takes a Boolean value and uses it as the setting for `uppercaseFlag`. Thus, by calling

```
ReturnUppercaseTokens(TRUE);
```

the client could select the new style of behavior in which all tokens are returned in upper case.

The key point to notice is that if `ReturnUppercaseTokens` is never called, the module must continue to work as it did previously. After all, none of the existing programs that use the old `scanner.h` interface call `ReturnUppercaseTokens`; that function did not even exist when those clients were written. The variable `uppercaseFlag` therefore must have `FALSE` as its initial value even if no calls are made to set it explicitly. To make sure it has the proper value, you need to use static initialization by writing

```
static bool uppercaseFlag = FALSE;
```

Exercise 8 in this chapter gives you the opportunity to complete the implementation of the `ReturnUppercaseTokens` extension.

Values that are used within a program unless a client specifically takes action to change them are called **default values.** In a typical module, global variables that specify options the client might set are initialized statically to their default values. Clients that need to change those values do so by calling a function provided in the interface.

Private functions

In addition to its use with global variables, the keyword `static` can also be used to indicate that a function is private to a particular module. When you define an interface, the functions exported by the interface are not private. The whole point of the interface is to allow these functions to be called from other modules. In many cases, a module will include functions that are called only within the module in which they appear. To indicate that a particular function is restricted to a particular module, you can use the keyword `static` at the beginning of both the function prototype and its implementation. Doing so makes it impossible for clients to call these functions, which in turn makes the abstraction boundary between the interface and the client much more solid.

Declaring functions to be `static` also has advantages in the context of large programs that are being developed by several programmers. If a function or a global variable is not declared to be `static`, its name cannot be used anywhere else in the collection of modules that make up the program as a whole. The possibility that names in different functions might interfere with each other means that the developers of independent modules must either (1) communicate with each other to ensure that they do not use the same names or (2) make all the names they introduce private to their own module by using the `static` keyword.

The following rule is an excellent guideline for modular development:

STATIC DECLARATION RULE	All functions other than `main` and those explicitly exported by an interface should be declared as `static`.

From here on, all programs in this book follow the Static Declaration Rule.

 ## 10.3 Implementing the scanner abstraction

As soon as you understand that the internal state of a module can be stored using global variables, the actual process of implementing the scanner abstraction is not at all difficult. The scanner module must keep track of the line passed to

InitScanner and also the current position in the line, which is presumably an integer index. Computer scientists often use the term **buffer** to refer to an internal storage area, so the private copy of the line might be stored in a string variable called buffer and the current position in an integer variable called cpos. It is also convenient to keep track of the length of the buffer string, so that the functions do not have to recalculate the length of the string each time. The variable for this purpose is again an integer and might be named buflen.

Each of these variables should be declared to be global within the scanner module but private to it in the sense that no other module has access to these variables. Thus, the global variables required for the scanner module are

```
static string buffer;
static int buflen;
static int cpos;
```

Once you have declared these variables, the implementation of InitScanner simply initializes them to their correct values, like this:

```
void InitScanner(string line)
{
    buffer = line;
    buflen = StringLength(buffer);
    cpos = 0;
}
```

The line passed by the caller is stored in the variable buffer to keep track of the line within the scanner module, the variable buflen is set to the length of the buffer, and the variable cpos is set to 0 to indicate that the scanner is at the beginning of the line.

The implementation of GetNextToken follows precisely from the definition of the function as given in the interface. The function begins by looking at the next character in the line. If that character is a letter or digit, the function searches to find an unbroken string of such characters and returns the entire string. If the current character is not a letter or digit, the function returns a one-character string containing that character. The implementation of GetNextToken is therefore

```
string GetNextToken(void)
{
    char ch;
    int start;

    if (cpos >= buflen) Error("No more tokens");
    ch = IthChar(buffer, cpos);
    if (isalnum(ch)) {
        start = cpos;
        while (cpos < buflen && isalnum(IthChar(buffer, cpos))) {
            cpos++;
        }
        return (SubString(buffer, start, cpos - 1));
    } else {
        cpos++;
        return (CharToString(ch));
    }
}
```

The token stream is complete when the index cpos reaches the end of the string, so the implementation of AtEndOfLine is simply

```
bool AtEndOfLine(void)
{
    return (cpos >= buflen);
}
```

The complete text of the scanner.c module appears in Figure 10-4, followed by the piglatin.c module in Figure 10-5.

FIGURE 10-4 scanner.c

```
/*
 * File: scanner.c
 * ---------------
 * This file implements the scanner.h interface.
 */

#include <stdio.h>
#include <ctype.h>

#include "genlib.h"
#include "strlib.h"
#include "scanner.h"

/*
 * Private variables
 * -----------------
 * buffer  -- Private copy of the string passed to InitScanner
 * buflen  -- Length of the buffer, saved for efficiency
 * cpos    -- Current character position in the buffer
 */

static string buffer;
static int buflen;
static int cpos;

/*
 * Function: InitScanner
 * ---------------------
 * All this function has to do is initialize the private
 * variables used in the package.
 */
```

```
void InitScanner(string line)
{
    buffer = line;
    buflen = StringLength(buffer);
    cpos = 0;
}

/*
 * Function: GetNextToken
 * ----------------------
 * The implementation of GetNextToken follows its behavioral
 * description as given in the interface: if the next character
 * is alphanumeric (i.e., a letter or digit), the function
 * searches to find an unbroken string of such characters and
 * returns the entire string.  If the current character is not
 * a letter or digit, a one-character string containing that
 * character is returned.
 */

string GetNextToken(void)
{
    char ch;
    int start;

    if (cpos >= buflen) Error("No more tokens");
    ch = IthChar(buffer, cpos);
    if (isalnum(ch)) {
        start = cpos;
        while (cpos < buflen && isalnum(IthChar(buffer, cpos))) {
            cpos++;
        }
        return (SubString(buffer, start, cpos - 1));
    } else {
        cpos++;
        return (CharToString(ch));
    }
}

/*
 * Function: AtEndOfLine
 * ---------------------
 * This implementation compares the current buffer position
 * against the saved length.
 */

bool AtEndOfLine(void)
{
    return (cpos >= buflen);
}
```

FIGURE 10-5   piglatin.c

```
/*
 * File: piglatin.c
 * ----------------
 * This program translates a line of text from English
 * to Pig Latin.  The rules for forming Pig Latin words
 * are as follows:
 *
 * o  If the word begins with a vowel, add "way" to the
 *    end of the word.
 *
 * o  If the word begins with a consonant, extract the set
 *    of consonants up to the first vowel, move that set
 *    of consonants to the end of the word, and add "ay".
 */

#include <stdio.h>
#include <ctype.h>

#include "genlib.h"
#include "strlib.h"
#include "simpio.h"
#include "scanner.h"

/* Private function prototypes */

static void TranslateLine(string line);
static string TranslateWord(string word);
static bool IsLegalWord(string token);
static int FindFirstVowel(string word);
static bool IsVowel(char ch);

/* Main program */

main()
{
    string line;

    printf("Enter a line: ");
    line = GetLine();
    TranslateLine(line);
}

/*
 * Function: TranslateLine
 * Usage: TranslateLine(line);
 * ---------------------------
 * This function takes a line of text and translates
```

```
 * the words in the line to Pig Latin, displaying the
 * translation as it goes.
 */

static void TranslateLine(string line)
{
    string token;

    InitScanner(line);
    while (!AtEndOfLine()) {
        token = GetNextToken();
        if (IsLegalWord(token)) token = TranslateWord(token);
        printf("%s", token);
    }
    printf("\n");
}

/*
 * Function: TranslateWord
 * Usage: word = TranslateWord(word)
 * ---------------------------------
 * This function translates a word from English to Pig Latin
 * and returns the translated word.
 */

static string TranslateWord(string word)
{
    int vp;
    string head, tail;

    vp = FindFirstVowel(word);
    if (vp == -1) {
        return (word);
    } else if (vp == 0) {
        return (Concat(word, "way"));
    } else {
        head = SubString(word, 0, vp - 1);
        tail = SubString(word, vp, StringLength(word) - 1);
        return (Concat(tail, Concat(head, "ay")));
    }
}

/*
 * Function: IsLegalWord
 * Usage: if (IsLegalWord(token)) ...
 * ----------------------------------
 * IsLegalWord returns TRUE if every character in the argument
 * token is alphabetic.
 */
```

```
static bool IsLegalWord(string token)
{
    int i;

    for (i = 0; i < StringLength(token); i++) {
        if (!isalpha(IthChar(token, i))) return (FALSE);
    }
    return (TRUE);
}

/*
 * Function: FindFirstVowel
 * Usage: k = FindFirstVowel(word);
 * --------------------------------
 * FindFirstVowel returns the index position of the first vowel
 * in word.  If word does not contain a vowel, FindFirstVowel
 * returns -1.
 */

static int FindFirstVowel(string word)
{
    int i;

    for (i = 0; i < StringLength(word); i++) {
        if (IsVowel(IthChar(word, i))) return (i);
    }
    return (-1);
}

/*
 * Function: IsVowel
 * Usage: if (IsVowel(ch)) . . .
 * -----------------------------
 * IsVowel returns TRUE if ch is a vowel.  This function
 * recognizes vowels in either upper or lower case.
 */

static bool IsVowel(char ch)
{
    switch (tolower(ch)) {
      case 'a': case 'e': case 'i': case 'o': case 'u':
        return (TRUE);
      default:
        return (FALSE);
    }
}
```

Summary

In this chapter, you have learned several new techniques that make it easier to divide a single application into separate modules that together constitute the program as a whole. In particular, you have learned how to represent internal state within a module, which makes it possible for the functions in the module to have an effect that persists between function calls.

Important points introduced in this chapter include:

- Large programs can be simplified by dividing them into separate *modules*. Each module is written as a separate source file. The module containing the function `main` is the *main module*.
- An effective modular decomposition for a program often becomes apparent as you attempt to solve the problem through top-down design.
- In designing a function, it is often best to write the individual steps in a combination of English and C, which is called *pseudocode*.
- Modules often need to maintain *internal state* that persists between individual function calls.
- Internal state must be stored using *global variables*. Global variables are accessible from all functions in a module. Unlike local variables, global variables do not disappear when a function returns.
- Using global variables can make programs more difficult to read and debug. To avoid these problems, you should only use global variables when they are needed to maintain the internal state of a module.
- All variables used to record internal state should be declared as private to the module in which they appear. You do this by using the `static` keyword at the beginning of the variable declaration.
- Unless a function is exported by an interface, you should use the `static` keyword to declare that function as private to the current module.

REVIEW QUESTIONS

1. True or false: Each module corresponds to a separate source file.

2. How do you determine which of several modules is the main module?

3. True or false: You should always choose the modular decomposition of a program before you begin to apply top-down design.

4. What is meant by the term *pseudocode*?

5. What should you do when you discover that a problem is incompletely specified?

6. What is a token?

7. What are the principal differences between local and global variables?

8. Looking at a program, how can you determine which variables are local and which are global?

9. What is the scope of a local variable? Of a global variable?

10. Why is it dangerous to overuse global variables?

11. What is the function of the keyword `static`?

12. What is the difference between static and dynamic initialization? When is static initialization most useful?

PROGRAMMING EXERCISES

1. A couple of centuries ago, abbreviations were formed differently than they are today. Rather than comprising just the leading characters in a word, an old-style abbreviation consists instead of the leading consonants (or just the first letter if the word begins with a vowel), followed by the very last letter in the word. This style is preserved in the traditional abbreviations (not the two-letter postal abbreviation) of many state names, such as

Connecticut	Ct.	Maine	Me.
Florida	Fla.	Pennsylvania	Pa.
Iowa	Ia.	Vermont	Vt.

Write a function `OldStyleAbbreviation` that takes a string as argument and returns a string consisting of an old-style abbreviation formed by connecting in sequence the following pieces:
   a. The initial consonant string, up to the first vowel. If the original string begins with a vowel, use that vowel instead (see the Iowa example).
   b. The last letter in the word.
   c. A period.

2. Rewrite the Pig Latin program so that it uses the algorithmic strategy of going through the line character by character rather than word by word. The pseudocode version of this strategy is given in this chapter in the section on "Taking spaces and punctuation into account."

3. The input used to test the Pig Latin program in this chapter was written entirely in lower case. If the input instead included capitalized words, the output would

be somewhat messy, since the capital letters would show up in the middle of words, as shown in the following sample run:

```
Enter a line: This is Pig Latin.↵
isThay isway igPay atinLay.
```

Modify the Pig Latin program so that any word that begins with a capital letter in the English line still begins with a capital letter in Pig Latin. Thus, after making your changes in the program, the output should look like this:

```
Enter a line: This is Pig Latin.↵
Isthay isway Igpay Atinlay.
```

4. The English word *trash* has the interesting property that its Pig Latin translation, *ashtray,* happens to be another English word. There are about 20 such words in English. You could try to find them yourself as a sort of word game, but it would be more reliable to use the computer to search for the entire set.

   Suppose that you had access to an interface `worddict.h` that exported the following functions:

`InitDictionary()`	Initializes the dictionary package
`GetNextDictionaryEntry()`	Returns the next word in the dictionary
`AtEndOfDictionary()`	Returns TRUE after reading the last word
`IsEnglishWord(word)`	Returns TRUE if word is in the dictionary

   Use the `worddict.h` interface to write a main program that lists all the English words for which the Pig Latin translation is also an English word.

5. Write a program that counts the number of words in input text entered by the user. The input may consist of several lines, with the end of the data indicated by a blank line. A word should be counted only if it consists entirely of letters. One possible sample run of the program is

```
This program counts the number of words in a paragraph.
End the paragraph with a blank line.

We hold these truths to be self-evident, that all
men and women are created equal.↵
                -- Seneca Falls Declaration, 1848↵

Number of words: 19
```

6. Write a function `LongestWord(line)` that returns the longest word in `line`. Test your function with a main program that can duplicate this sample run:

```
Enter a line:
All mimsy were the borogoves.⏎
The longest word is "borogoves".
```

7. Write a function `ReverseSentence(line)` that divides `line` into words and returns a string consisting of the same words in reverse order. Your function should discard all the original punctuation and separate each word in the result with a single space. For example, a main program that reads in a line and then displays the result of calling `ReverseSentence` might produce the following output:

```
Enter a line: double, double toil and trouble:⏎
trouble and toil double double
```

8. Extend the `scanner.h` interface so that it includes the `ReturnUppercaseTokens` function described in the section on "Initializing global variables." Write a test program that tests your scanner by reading in a line of data and then displaying each of the tokens, one per line, as illustrated by this sample run:

```
Enter a line: Hello there⏎
The tokens are:
    "HELLO"
    " "
    "THERE"
```

Make sure the `piglatin.c` program can use the extended scanner module without any internal changes.

9. In a C program, spaces and tabs are used only to separate individual tokens and have no other significance. If you were writing a token scanner for a C compiler, it would be useful for it to discard tokens that consist entirely of white space. Design an extension to the `scanner.h` interface that allows the client to specify that spaces, tabs, and any other character for which the `isspace` function in `ctype.h` returns `TRUE` should be ignored. Make sure that your design does not affect any existing clients of the `scanner.h` interface.

10. Write a program `calc.c` that implements a simple arithmetic calculator. Input to the calculator consists of lines composed of integer constants separated by the five arithmetic operators used in C: `+`, `-`, `*`, `/`, and `%`. For each line of input,

your program should display the result of applying the operators to the surrounding terms. To read the individual values and operators, you should use the scanner module as extended in exercise 9, so that spacing is ignored. Your program should exit when the user enters a blank line.

To reduce the complexity of the problem, your calculator should ignore C's rules of precedence and instead apply the operators in left-to-right order. Thus, in your calculator program, the expression

```
2 + 3 * 4
```

has the value 20 and not 14, as it would in C.

The following is a sample run of the `calc.c` program:

```
This program implements a simple calculator.
When the > prompt appears, enter an expression
consisting of integer constants and the operators
+, -, *, /, and %. To stop, enter a blank line.
> 2 + 2↵
4
> 1 + 2 + 3 + 4 + 5↵
15
> 10 % 4↵
2
> 4+9-2*16+1/3*6-67+8*2-3+26-1/34+3/7+2-5↵
0
>
```

11. In some programming applications, it is useful to be able to generate a series of names that form a sequential pattern. For example, if you were writing a program to number diagrams in a document, having a function that returned the sequence of strings `"Figure 1"`, `"Figure 2"`, `"Figure 3"`, and so on, would be very handy. Similarly, a program designed to label points in a geometric diagram could use a function that returned the sequence `"P1"`, `"P2"`, `"P3"`, and so forth.

If you think about this problem from a broader perspective, the tool that would be most useful is a label generator module containing a function that returns the next label in a consecutive sequence, where each label is composed of a prefix string (`"Figure "` or `"P"` in the examples from the preceding paragraph) and an integer used as a sequence number.

Design an interface `labelseq.h` that provides an abstraction for generating these sequences of labels. Your interface should export a function `GetNextLabel` that takes no arguments and returns the next label in the sequence. If no explicit initialization is performed, the labels should use the string `"Label"` as the prefix and begin with sequence number 1. Clients, however, should be able to change these defaults by calling `SetLabelPrefix(prefix)` and

`SetLabelNumber(nextNumber)` to set the prefix and sequence number, respectively, for the next label. Implement the interface by writing the corresponding `labelseq.c` file.

Write a test program for the `labelseq` package that reads in a prefix and a starting sequence number and then displays the next five labels returned by `GetNextLabel`, as illustrated by the following sample run:

```
This program tests the labelseq abstraction.
Prefix to use for labels: P↵
Starting number: 0↵
P0
P1
P2
P3
P4
```

12. When text is displayed on the printed page or a computer screen, it usually must be adjusted to fit within fixed margins. Output that is too wide must be broken up and displayed on several lines. If the text is composed of words, the divisions between the lines are made at the spaces between the word boundaries. As long as an entire word fits on the current line without extending past the right margin, it is placed there. If a word would extend past the right margin, the spaces before it are converted to a newline character, and the word is placed at the beginning of the next line. Subsequent words are then added to the newly created line until that line fills up as well. This process is called **filling** and can be repeated as long as there is any text to display.

The need to fill lines of output comes up in many different applications. Because filling is a general problem, the idea of writing a library package to perform filling operations has considerable appeal. An interface to such a package is shown in Figure 10-6.

Implement the `fill.h` interface by writing the corresponding `fill.c` module. To test your implementation, write a program that displays the prime numbers between 1 and 200 using as few lines as possible for the output. The following sample run shows the output when using a fill margin of 55 characters:

```
The primes between 0 and 200 are: 2, 3, 5, 7, 11, 13,
17, 19, 23, 29, 31, 37, 41, 43, 47, 53, 59, 61, 67, 71,
73, 79, 83, 89, 97, 101, 103, 107, 109, 113, 127, 131,
137, 139, 149, 151, 157, 163, 167, 173, 179, 181, 191,
193, 197, 199.
```

FIGURE 10-6   fill.h

```
/*
 * fill.h
 * ------
 * This file is the interface to an abstraction that enables
 * you to display filled output.  To use the package, you first
 * call SetFillMargin to set an output margin and then make
 * calls to PrintFilledString to display the output.  These
 * functions are described in more detail below.
 */

#ifndef _fill_h
#define _fill_h

#include "genlib.h"

/*
 * Function: SetFillMargin
 * Usage: SetFillMargin(margin);
 * ---------------------------------
 * This function sets the fill margin to the value given by the
 * margin parameter.  When strings are displayed using the
 * function PrintFilledString, the output will be broken up
 * into separate lines so that no lines extend past the margin.
 * If no margin is set explicitly, the package uses 65 for the
 * fill margin as a default.
 */

void SetFillMargin(int margin);

/*
 * Function: PrintFilledString
 * Usage: PrintFilledString(str);
 * --------------------------------
 * The string str is displayed on the screen, starting from
 * where the last string left off.  Spaces and newline characters
 * in the string are treated specially.  If a space character
 * appears in an argument, the function may choose to divide
 * the string at that point by moving to the next line.
 * Such division occurs when the next word would not fit
 * within the margin established by SetFillMargin.  A newline
 * character in the string forces the cursor to advance to the
 * beginning of the next line.
 */

void PrintFilledString(string str);

#endif
```

## PART THREE

Compound Data Types

Overview

Although you know that programs manipulate data, the earlier parts of this text have focused on the control structures that perform the manipulation, not the underlying data. In Chapters 11 through 17, you will see that, like control structures, data structures are central to programming. By learning to assemble data into larger structures, you can extend your programming capabilities considerably and write programs that are both more useful and more exciting.

## CHAPTER 11

Arrays

Little boxes on a hillside, little boxes made of ticky-tacky
Little boxes, little boxes, little boxes all the same
There's a green one and a pink one and a blue one and a yellow one
And they're all made out of ticky-tacky and they all look just the same

— Malvina Reynolds, "Little Boxes," 1962

Objectives

- To appreciate the importance of array data to programming.

- To be able to declare and manipulate simple arrays.

- To understand how data values are stored in memory.

- To recognize how the process of passing arrays as function parameters differs from the process of passing simple variables.

- To learn how to apply static initialization to arrays.

- To understand the structure of multidimensional arrays.

Up to now, the examples in this book have focused on the use of increasingly sophisticated algorithms to manipulate simple data. As the algorithms become more detailed, the programs used to implement them increase in size and complexity. To reduce the algorithmic complexity, programmers use the general strategy of stepwise refinement to break a large program down into smaller, more easily managed functions. When those smaller functions become too complicated, they are then divided into still smaller functions. The complete solution has the form of a hierarchy in which high-level functions make calls to lower-level functions, which in turn call even lower-level functions, until the functions are simple enough to implement directly without making further calls.

Beginning in this chapter, you will discover that data types also form a hierarchy. You can use the simple data types you have encountered in the earlier chapters to define more complicated types, which can then be used to define types of still greater complexity, to whatever level the program requires. The principal advantage of defining these new types is that doing so enables you to combine many independent data values and think of them as a single unified collection. By considering a collection of data as a single entity, you can reduce the conceptual complexity of your programs significantly.

Just as the control statements and function calls in a program define its algorithmic control structure, the hierarchy of type definitions comprises its **data structure.** These two ideas—control structure and data structure—together constitute the foundations of modern programming. In 1976, Niklaus Wirth, the inventor of the programming language Pascal, expressed this principle in the title of a programming text, which he wrote in the form of an equation:

Algorithms + Data Structures = Programs

Each half of the left side of this equation is critical to programming. At this point, you know something about algorithms. To become a full-fledged programmer, you must also learn about data structures.

C provides several different mechanisms for defining new data types based on existing ones. In this chapter, you will have a chance to learn about *arrays,* which are the most common compound structure in programming. The other major mechanisms for creating new types—*pointers* and *records*—are discussed in Chapters 13 and 16, respectively.

11.1 Introduction to arrays

An **array** is a collection of individual data values with two distinguishing characteristics:

1. *An array is ordered.* You must be able to count off the individual components of an array in order: here is the first, here is the second, and so on.
2. *An array is homogeneous.* Every value stored in an array must be of the same type. Thus, you can define an array of integers or an array of floating-point numbers but not an array in which the two types are mixed.

From an intuitive point of view, it is best to think of an array as a sequence of boxes, one box for each data value in the array. Each of the values in an array is called an **element.** For example, the following diagram represents an array with five elements:

In C, each array has two fundamental properties:

- The **element type,** which is the type of value that may be stored in the elements of the array
- The **array size,** which is the number of elements the array contains

Whenever you create a new array in your program, you must specify both the element type and the array size.

Array declaration

Like any other variable in C, an array must be declared before it is used. The general form for an array declaration is shown in the syntax box to the right. For example, the declaration

```
int intArray[10];
```

declares an array named intArray with 10 elements, each of which is of type int. You can represent this declaration pictorially by drawing a row of 10 boxes and giving the entire collection the name intArray:

> **SYNTAX** for array declarations
>
> *elementtype arrayname* [*size*] ;
>
> where:
> *elementtype* is the type of each element in the array
> *array-name* is the name of the variable being declared as an array
> *size* is the number of elements that are allocated as part of the array

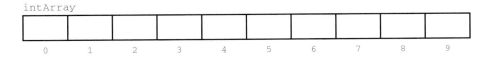

Each element in the array is identified by a numeric value called its **index.** In C, the index numbers for an array always begin with 0 and run up to the array size minus one. Thus, in an array with 10 elements, the index numbers are 0, 1, 2, 3, 4, 5, 6, 7, 8, and 9, as the preceding diagram shows.

In most cases, you should specify the size of the array using a symbolic constant instead of an explicit integer. Using a symbolic constant makes it easier for programmers who will maintain your program in the future to change the array size. For example, instead of writing the declaration

```
int intArray[10];
```

it would be preferable to define the size as a constant

```
#define NElements 10
```

and then to write the declaration as

```
int intArray[NElements];
```

As is the case with any variable, you use the name of an array to indicate to other readers of the program what sort of value is being stored. For example, suppose that you wanted to define an array that was capable of holding the scores for a sporting event, such as gymnastics or figure skating, in which scores are assigned by a panel of judges. Each judge rates the performance on a scale from 0 to 10, with 10 being the highest. Because a score may include a decimal fraction, as in 9.9, each element of the array must be of type `double`, which is the standard floating-point type. Thus the declaration

```
double scores[NJudges];
```

declares an array named `scores` with one element of type `double` to hold each judge's score. If, for example, there are five judges, and the constant `NJudges` is therefore defined as

```
#define NJudges 5
```

the declaration of `scores` introduces an array with five elements, as shown in the following diagram:

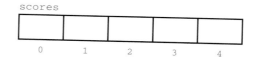

When you declare an array, the values of its elements are initially undefined. Thus, just as you discovered with simple variables, you cannot rely on the contents of any element unless you initialize it explicitly. To do so, you need a mechanism that makes it possible to assign a value to each of the individual elements.

Array selection

To refer to a specific element within an array, you need to specify both the array name and the index corresponding to the position of that element within the array. The process of identifying a particular element within an array is called **selection** and is indicated in C by writing the name of the array and following it with the index written in square brackets. The result is a **selection expression,** which has the following form:

array-name[*index*]

Within a program, a selection expression acts just like a simple variable. You can use it in an expression, and, in particular, you can assign a value to it. Thus, if the first judge (judge #0, since C counts array elements beginning at zero) awarded the contestant a score of 9.2, you could store that score in the array by writing the assignment statement

```
scores[0] = 9.2;
```

The effect of this assignment can be diagrammed as follows:

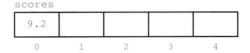

You could then go ahead and assign scores for each of the other four judges using, for example, the statements

```
scores[1] = 9.9;
scores[2] = 9.7;
scores[3] = 9.0;
scores[4] = 9.5;
```

Executing these statements results in the following picture:

```
scores
┌───────┬───────┬───────┬───────┬───────┐
│  9.2  │  9.9  │  9.7  │  9.0  │  9.5  │
└───────┴───────┴───────┴───────┴───────┘
    0       1       2       3       4
```

In working with arrays, it is essential to understand the distinction between the *index* of an array element and the *value* of that element. For instance, the first box in the array has index 0, and its value is 9.2. It is also important to remember that you can change the values in an array but never the index numbers.

The real power of array selection comes from the fact that the index value need not be constant, but can be any expression that evaluates to an integer or any other scalar type. In many cases, the selection expression is the index variable of a `for` loop, which makes it easy to perform an operation on each element of the array in turn. For example, you can set each element in the `scores` array to 0.0 with the following statement:

```
for (i = 0; i < NJudges; i++) {
    scores[i] = 0.0;
}
```

Example of a simple array

The program `gymjudge.c` given in Figure 11-1 provides a simple example of array manipulation. This program asks the user to enter the score for each judge and then displays the average score.

FIGURE 11-1 gymjudge.c

```
/*
 * File: gymjudge.c
 * ----------------
 * This program averages a set of five gymnastic scores.
 */

#include <stdio.h>
#include "genlib.h"
#include "simpio.h"

/*
 * Constants
 * ---------
 * NJudges -- Number of judges
 */

#define NJudges 5

/* Main program */

main()
{
    double gymnasticScores[NJudges];
    double total, average;
    int i;

    printf("Please enter a score for each judge.\n");
    for (i = 0; i < NJudges; i++) {
        printf("Score for judge #%d:   ", i);
        gymnasticScores[i] = GetReal();
    }
    total = 0;
    for (i = 0; i < NJudges; i++) {
        total += gymnasticScores[i];
    }
    average = total / NJudges;
    printf("The average score is %.2f\n", average);
}
```

Running the `gymjudge.c` program with the data used in the examples in the preceding section produces the following sample run:

```
Please enter a score for each judge.
Score for judge #0:   9.2↵
Score for judge #1:   9.9↵
Score for judge #2:   9.7↵
Score for judge #3:   9.0↵
Score for judge #4:   9.5↵
The average score is 9.46
```

Changing the index range

In C, the first element in every array is at index position 0. In many applications, however, this design may cause confusion for the user. To a nontechnical person using the gymjudge.c program, the fact that it asks about judge #0 is likely to be disconcerting. In the real world, we tend to number elements in a list beginning at 1. It would therefore be more natural for the program to ask the user to enter the scores for judges numbered from 1 to 5 instead.

There are two standard approaches for solving this problem:

1. Use the indices 0 to 4 internally, but add 1 to each index value when requesting data from the user or displaying data on the screen. If you adopt this approach, the only part of the gymjudge.c program that needs to change is the printf statement that displays the prompt for each input value, which becomes

   ```
   printf("Score for judge #%d:   ", i + 1);
   ```

2. Declare the array with an extra element so that its indices run from 0 to 5, and then ignore element 0 entirely. Using this approach, the main program becomes

   ```
   main()
   {
       double gymnasticScores[NJudges + 1];
       double total, average;
       int i;

       printf("Please enter a score for each judge.\n");
       for (i = 1; i <= NJudges; i++) {
           printf("Score for judge #%d:   ", i);
           gymnasticScores[i] = GetReal();
       }
       total = 0;
       for (i = 1; i <= NJudges; i++) {
           total += gymnasticScores[i];
       }
       average = total / NJudges;
       printf("The average score is %.2f\n", average);
   }
   ```

   Note that the declaration of the scores array uses the expression NJudges + 1 to specify the array size. The array size in a declaration can be an expression, but only if all the terms in the expression are constant.

The advantage of the first approach is that the internal array indices still begin with 0, which often makes it easier to use existing functions that depend on that assumption. The disadvantage is that the program requires two different sets of indices: an external set for the user and an internal set for the programmer. Even though the user sees a consistent and familiar index pattern, having to think about both sets of indices can complicate the programming process. The advantage of the second approach is that the internal indices match those you use to communicate with the user.

11.2 Internal representation of data

Although the `gymjudge.c` program in Figure 11-1 is sufficient to solve a specific problem, it is too simple to illustrate several of the most important issues that arise when using arrays. The most significant weakness of the `gymjudge.c` example is that it is written as a single function using none of the techniques of decomposition that you have learned in the earlier chapters. In order to write more sophisticated programs that use arrays, you will need to learn how to pass an array as an argument from one function to another.

Before you can appreciate the details of how array data can be communicated between two functions, however, you must first gain a deeper understanding of how C uses memory to represent data. In C, passing an array as an argument to a function is not quite the same as passing a simple variable. If you understand how arrays are represented inside the computer, C's approach to arrays makes a certain amount of sense. If you don't understand the internal representation, C's approach makes no sense at all.

In order to develop a mental model of how data is stored inside a computer, you need to look more closely at how the memory system operates in a typical machine. The fact that the computer has a memory system came up in the section on "The components of a typical computer" in Chapter 1, but you have not yet had a chance to learn how that memory works.

Bits, bytes, and words

At the most primitive level, all data values inside the computer are stored in the form of fundamental units of information called *bits*. A **bit** records precisely one value, which can be in either of two possible states. If you think of the circuitry inside the machine as if it were a tiny light switch, you might label those states as *on* and *off*. Historically, the word *bit* is a contraction of *binary digit*, and it is therefore more common to label those states using the symbols 0 and 1, which are the two digits used in the binary number system on which computer arithmetic is based.

Since a single bit holds so little information, the bits themselves do not provide a particularly convenient mechanism for storing data. To make it easier to store such traditional types of information as numbers or characters, individual bits are collected together into larger units that are then treated as integral units of storage. The smallest such combined unit is called a **byte** and is large enough to hold a single character, which typically requires eight individual bits.[1] On most machines, bytes are assembled into larger structures called **words,** where a word is usually defined to be the size required to hold an integer value. Some machines use two-byte words (16 bits), some use four-byte words (32 bits), and some use less conventional sizes. The amount of memory available to a particular computer varies over a wide range. Memory sizes are usually measured in kilobytes (KB) or megabytes (MB). In most sciences, the prefixes *kilo* and *mega* stand for 1000 and 1,000,000,

---

[1] Even though a byte consists of eight bits on almost all modern computers, the rules for ANSI C do not require that bytes be precisely this long. The only rule is that objects of type `char` are defined to occupy one byte of information. Thus, a byte must be large enough to hold any character code.

respectively. In the world of computers, however, the decimal system does not match the internal structure of the machine, and these prefixes are taken to represent the power of two closest to their traditional values. Thus, in programming, these prefixes have the following meanings:

$$\text{kilo (K)} \quad = 2^{10} = \quad\quad 1{,}024$$
$$\text{mega (M)} = 2^{20} = \ 1{,}048{,}576$$

A 64KB computer—a tiny machine by modern standards—would therefore have 64×1024 or 65,536 bytes of memory. Similarly, an 8MB workstation would have $8 \times 1{,}048{,}576$ or 8,388,608 bytes of memory.

Memory addresses

Within the memory system, every byte is identified by a numeric **address.** Typically, the first byte in the computer is numbered 0, the second is numbered 1, and so on, up to the number of bytes in the machine. For example, you can diagram the memory of a 64KB computer as follows:

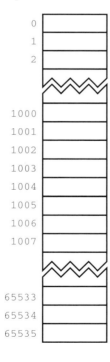

Each byte of memory can hold one character of information. For example, if you were to declare the character variable ch, the compiler would reserve one byte of storage for that variable as part of the current function frame. Suppose that this byte happened to be at address 1000. If the program then executed the statement

```
ch = 'A';
```

the internal representation of the character `'A'` would be stored in location 1000. Since the ASCII code for `'A'` is 65, the resulting memory configuration would look like this:

```
        ┌────────────┐
1000    │     65     │
1001    │            │
1002    │            │
1003    │            │
1004    │            │
1005    │            │
1006    │            │
1007    │            │
        └────────────┘
```

In most programming applications, you will have no way of predicting the actual address at which a particular variable is stored. In the preceding diagram, the variable ch is assigned to address 1000, but this choice is entirely arbitrary. Whenever your program makes a function call, the variables within the function are assigned to memory locations, but you have no way of predicting the addresses of those variables in advance. Even so, you may find it useful to draw pictures of memory and label the individual locations with addresses beginning at a particular starting point. These addresses—even though you choose them yourself—can help you to visualize what is happening inside the memory of the computer as your program runs.

Values that are larger than a single character are stored in consecutive bytes of memory. For example, if an integer takes up two bytes on a particular computer, that integer requires two consecutive bytes of memory and might therefore be stored in the shaded area in the following diagram:

```
        ┌────────────┐
1000    │▓▓▓▓▓▓▓▓▓▓▓▓│
1001    │▓▓▓▓▓▓▓▓▓▓▓▓│
1002    │            │
1003    │            │
1004    │            │
1005    │            │
1006    │            │
1007    │            │
        └────────────┘
```

Data values requiring multiple bytes are identified by the address of the first byte, so that the integer represented by the shaded area is the word stored at address 1000.

As a second example, values of type `double` typically require eight bytes of memory, so that a variable of type `double` stored at address 1000 would take up all the bytes between addresses 1000 and 1007, inclusive:

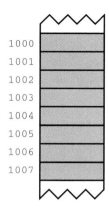

The `sizeof` operator

Except for the type `char`, which is defined to be one byte in length on all computer systems, the number of bytes required to store a value of a particular type may differ from machine to machine. For example, variables of type `int` take up two bytes on some microcomputers but usually require four bytes on larger machines. Similarly, although eight bytes is a reasonably common size for a value of type `double`, some computers represent a `double` using a different number of bytes. In general, the designer of the C compiler for a particular computer chooses the size that is most efficient for that machine.

When you write a C program, you can determine how much memory will be assigned to a particular variable by using the `sizeof` operator. The `sizeof` operator takes a single operand, which must be a type name enclosed in parentheses or an expression. If the operand is a type, the `sizeof` operator returns the number of bytes required to store a value of that type; if the operand is an expression, `sizeof` returns the number of bytes required to store the value of that expression. For example, the expression

```
sizeof(int)
```

returns the number of bytes required to store a value of type `int`. The expression

```
sizeof x
```

returns the number of bytes required to store the variable x.

Allocation of memory to variables

Whenever you declare a variable in a program, the compiler must reserve memory space to hold its value. The process of reserving memory space is called **allocation.** Global variables are allocated when the program begins execution and remain at the same addresses until the program exits. Local variables are allocated only when a function is called. The variables themselves are allocated in a region of memory assigned to that function, which is called its **frame.** As long as a function is running, its local variables remain at the same address within that frame. When the function returns, the frame is discarded along with all its variables, making it available for use by some other function.

If you declare a simple variable, the compiler reserves the number of bytes corresponding to the size of that object—the same number the `sizeof` operator would return. If you declare an array variable, the compiler reserves consecutive memory locations to hold all the values that comprise the array, one right after another. Depending on the element type, each element of the array may fit into a single memory byte, or it may require several bytes. For example, the declaration

```
char charArray[20];
```

reserves exactly 20 bytes of storage because characters are defined to occupy exactly one byte each.

Data types that require more storage will take up more than one byte per element. For example, assuming that `NJudges` is defined to be 5 and that each value of type `double` requires eight bytes of memory, the array `scores` declared by writing the line

```
double scores[NJudges];
```

would require

$$8 \text{ bytes/element} \times 5 \text{ elements} = 40 \text{ bytes}$$

To reserve storage for the entire array, the compiler would therefore need to allocate 40 bytes as part of the current frame. If the frame began at address 1000 in memory, the elements of the array would be laid out as shown in Figure 11-2. Element 0 of the array is stored in the eight bytes between 1000 and 1007, element 1 is stored in the eight bytes between 1008 and 1015, and so on.

When the C compiler encounters a selection expression, such as

```
scores[i]
```

it calculates the appropriate memory address by multiplying the index by the size of each element in bytes and adding the resulting value to the initial address of the array. In Figure 11-2, the element size is 8, and the initial address of the array is 1000. Thus, if `i` is 2, the location of element `scores[i]` is given by

$$2 \times 8 + 1000$$

The address is 1016, which matches the address for `scores[2]`, as the diagram shows. In this calculation, the initial address of the array (i.e., 1000) is called the **base address** of the array, and the adjustment necessary to find the correct element (i.e., the 2×8 or 16) is called the **offset.**

References to elements outside the array bound

The array `scores` diagrammed in Figure 11-2 has five legal index values: 0, 1, 2, 3, and 4. What happens if you try to select an element in the array whose index

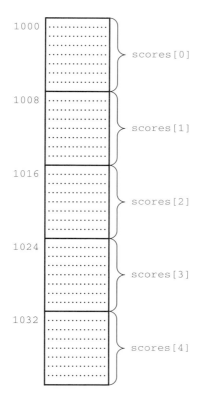

FIGURE 11-2 Memory layout for **scores** array

falls outside this range? For example, suppose that you were to evaluate the expression

```
scores[i]
```

when i happened to have the value 5. Since there is no element 5 in the array, the result is meaningless. What does C do in this case?

If you are fortunate enough to be using one of the very few C compilers that protect unwary programmers from such mistakes, you will get an error message when you run the program indicating that an array index is out of bounds. It is far more likely, however, that the program blithely goes ahead without catching the error at all. On most systems, programs evaluate a selection expression by taking the base address of the array and then adding the offset, which is itself calculated by multiplying the element number by the size of the element type. Thus, in this example, C would try to select the value stored at address

$$5 \times 8 + 1000 = 1040$$

The problem is that you have no idea what is stored in address 1040. It might be some other variable in the program or possibly a part of the program itself. In any case, the contents of address 1040 have nothing to do with the scores array, and referencing an out-of-range element is certainly an error—even though it may not be detected as such by the computer. Your program might crash or deliver entirely meaningless results, giving no concrete indication of the precise source of the problem.

When a program seems to be misbehaving in some inexplicable way, you should be suspicious of the array selections. One helpful technique in debugging such programs is to print out the value of the index before referencing an element of an array. For example, if you were to add the line

```
printf("i = %d\n", i);
```

before the line that evaluates scores[i], you could monitor the behavior of your program as it reached this line. If the output indicated that i was equal to 5 or −23 or some other value outside the legal index range, you would know where to start looking for the problem. Once you had discovered and repaired the problem, you could then remove the printf call.

In some cases, however, it is safest to include an explicit conditional test to see if an array subscript is out of bounds. Before evaluating scores[i], you might want to include the following statement:

```
if (i < 0 || i >= NJudges) {
    Error("Index i (value %d) is out of bounds", i);
}
```

If you include this statement, your program will generate an error message if i is out of bounds, alerting you to a bug that might otherwise go undetected.

On the other hand, writing conditional tests of this sort for every subscript operation would make your program much longer and more complicated. In general, you should use such tests when there is a reasonable chance that the subscript might in fact be out of bounds. For example, there would be no point in checking the value of i inside a for loop with the following control line:

```
for (i = 0; i < NJudges; i++)
```

The for loop itself ensures that the value of i remains in bounds. However, if you are using an index value that was passed in as a parameter, it pays to be more suspicious. In such cases, you have less control over the value of the index because its source is in some other part of the program. In a large program, someone else may have written that part, and you have no way of knowing whether that programmer was as careful as you are. In such cases, testing the values you receive as parameters can save considerable debugging time.

11.3 Passing arrays as parameters

As you know from Chapter 5, the key to writing a large program is breaking it down into many functions, each of which is small enough for you to comprehend it as a unit. The individual functions communicate by passing parameters from one function to another. If a large program involves arrays, decomposing that program will often require functions to pass entire arrays as parameters. In C, the operation of passing an array as a parameter is closely tied to the internal representation of arrays in memory and can therefore seem mysterious. Having become acquainted with that internal representation, you are now ready to learn how array parameters work and how to use them effectively.

The issues involved in using arrays as parameters are best illustrated in the context of a simple example. Let's suppose that you have been asked to write a program reverse.c that performs these steps:

1. Reads in a list of integers until 0 is entered as a sentinel value
2. Reverses the elements in that list
3. Displays the list in reverse order

The following sample run illustrates the operation of the program:

```
? 1↵
? 2↵
? 3↵
? 4↵
? 5↵
? 0↵
5
4
3
2
1
```

To illustrate the process of passing arrays as parameters, it is important to decompose this program into three functions that correspond to the three phases of the program operation: reading the input values and storing them in an array, reversing the elements of the array, and displaying the results. Using this decomposition, the main program would have a structure something like this:

```
main()
{
    int list[NElements];

    GetIntegerArray(list);
    ReverseIntegerArray(list);
    PrintIntegerArray(list);
}
```

This program is only a rough outline of the list reversal program. The final version has a different argument structure.

This general design, however, raises two important issues:

1. As written, the number of items in the array is specified by the constant NElements. But the specification of the problem requires that the number of elements be indicated by having the user enter the sentinel value 0 after the last data value.

2. The functions `GetIntegerArray` and `ReverseIntegerArray` are only useful if they change the values in their argument arrays. However, up to now, the functions you have seen in this text have been unable to change the values of their arguments at all. If arrays acted the same way simple variables do, the entire design of the program would have to be changed.

Each of these issues is discussed in detail in the sections that follow.

Generalizing the number of elements

According to the specification, the `reverse.c` program does not fix the number of list elements in advance but instead allows the user to enter any number of values, indicating the end of the list with a predefined sentinel value. While this design is convenient for the user, it creates a problem for the programmer writing the code. Because the array variable `list` is declared in the main program, the compiler must allocate memory for it as soon as the program begins. At this point, the user has not yet entered any data, so there is no way to know precisely how large the array should be. Even so, the compiler requires you to specify the size. Moreover, the size you specify in the declaration of the array must be a constant whose value can be determined at the time of compilation. The problem is therefore to find a way to achieve the effect of an array that can hold a varying number of elements even though arrays in fact have a fixed size.

The usual strategy for solving this problem is to declare an array that is larger than you need and use only part of it. Thus, instead of declaring the array based on the *actual* number of elements—which you often do not know in advance—you define a constant indicating the *maximum* number of elements and use that constant in the declaration of the array. For example, in the main program for `reverse.c`, you could declare the variable `list` using

```
int list[MaxElements];
```

You choose as the value of `MaxElements` a number larger than those you would ever expect to encounter in practice. For example, if you were writing `reverse.c` for use with lists of 100 elements or so, you would choose some larger value for `MaxElements`. And because it often makes sense to provide room for growth, you might choose a somewhat larger value for `MaxElements`, such as 250. On any given use of the program, the actual number of elements in the list would be smaller than this bound. For example, your program might end up using only the first 75 elements in the array, leaving the others unused. For simple applications like this one, you are not in danger of running out of memory on a modern computer, and you don't need to worry about whether you are "wasting memory." If memory usage turns out to be important, you can allocate the array memory explicitly, as discussed in the section on "Dynamic arrays" in Chapter 13.

Once you choose to allocate `MaxElements` elements for the array, you must confront the problem that the functions using that array need to know how many elements are actually in use. To provide this information, your program needs to maintain a separate variable to keep track of the number of elements in use at any particular time. For example, you could declare the variable n in the main program and use it to indicate the number of valid array elements, which will usually be less than `MaxElements`. The size of the array specified in the declaration—in this case indicated by the constant `MaxElements`—is called the **allocated size** of the array. The number of elements actually in use—represented here by the variable `n`—is called the **effective size** of the array.

If a function takes an existing array, it needs to know the effective size. For example, the function `PrintIntegerArray` must take the effective size of that array as a parameter so it knows how many elements to display. The call to `PrintIntegerArray` in the main program must therefore include `n` in the list of arguments along with the array `list`, as follows:

```
PrintIntegerArray(list, n);
```

Because the call to `PrintIntegerArray` passes two arguments, its prototype must declare two matching parameters: an array of integers containing the data and an integer representing the effective size. In C, an array parameter specification looks exactly like an array declaration, except that the array size is optional. Although it is legal to write the prototype for `PrintIntegerArray` as

```
void PrintIntegerArray(int array[MaxElements], int n);
```

it is much more common to eliminate the upper bound from the parameter specification and instead write

```
void PrintIntegerArray(int array[], int n);
```

This style of specification makes it more explicit that `PrintIntegerArray` can take an integer array of any allocated size. You specify the actual number of elements to print by passing the effective size as the parameter `n`.

As with any function, the names of the formal parameters declared in the prototype may be different from the names of the actual arguments. The association of arguments with parameters is established on the basis of their position in the argument list: the first argument is associated with the first parameter, and so forth. In this example, the array is called `list` in the main program and `array` in each of the subsidiary functions. Choosing different names makes it easier for you to distinguish references to the array in the main program from those in the other functions.

Because `ReverseIntegerArray` also needs access to the array data and the effective size, it must take the same arguments that `PrintIntegerArray` does. Its prototype therefore looks like this:

```
void ReverseIntegerArray(int array[], int n);
```

The function `GetIntegerArray`, however, has a different structure. It is impossible for the main program to pass the effective size of the array to `GetIntegerArray`; at the time `GetIntegerArray` is called, the main program does not know the effective size. `GetIntegerArray` must determine the effective size itself by counting the values as the user enters them, until the user enters the sentinel. At that point, `GetIntegerArray` must tell the main program how many values the user entered and must therefore be a function that returns an integer.

Even though `GetIntegerArray` does not need to take the effective size as an argument, it does need to know the allocated size. If the user types in more data than the array can hold, it is important for `GetIntegerArray` to report an error. In addition, `GetIntegerArray` is more general if it also takes the sentinel value as a parameter, which makes it possible to use the same function to read lists of input data that use different sentinel values. Thus, the prototype for `GetIntegerArray` should look like this:

```
int GetIntegerArray(int array[], int max, int sentinel);
```

The mechanics of array parameter transmission

Before you try to implement any of these functions, however, it is important to resolve the remaining issue concerning array parameters. When a function is called with a simple variable, the function receives a copy of the calling argument. Because it works only with a copy and not with the original value, a function cannot change the value of the calling arguments. When a function is called with an array argument, however, the relationship between the argument and the corresponding parameter changes.

To understand how arrays are passed from one function to another, you need to consider the underlying representation of those arrays in memory. Assuming that `MaxElements` is defined to be 250, the declaration

```
int list[MaxElements];
```

asks the compiler to reserve space for an array of 250 integers in the frame for `main`. Although it is not possible to know exactly what addresses will be used inside the machine, let's suppose that the memory assigned to the array `list` begins at address 1000 and continues for the next 250 integer-sized words. If integers take up two bytes of memory on the computer you're using, the values in the array `list` would be stored in bytes 1000 to 1499, inclusive:

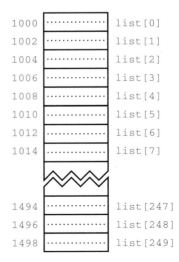

When you write a function that accepts an array argument, you usually want the function to work directly with the values in the memory locations corresponding to that array. C does precisely that. Whenever any array is passed to a function, only the base address of the array is recorded in the local frame. If you select an element of the local array declared within the function, the operation of adding the offset to the base address ends up generating an address within the calling array. The ultimate effect is that the formal array parameter declared in a function header ends up being a synonym for the argument array in the caller and not a copy of it.

To understand the details of the array operation, it helps to think about what happens when the main program calls `ReverseIntegerArray`. If the array contains the five values 1, 2, 3, 4, and 5, the initial configuration of the frame for `ReverseIntegerArray` looks like this:

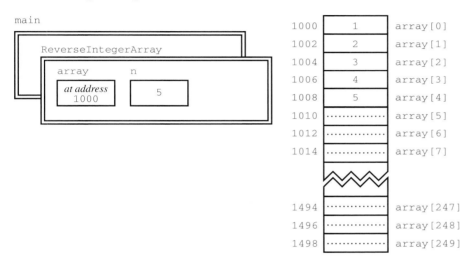

If `ReverseIntegerArray` does its job, it will reverse the order of the first `n` elements in the array whose base address is 1000, resulting in the following state:

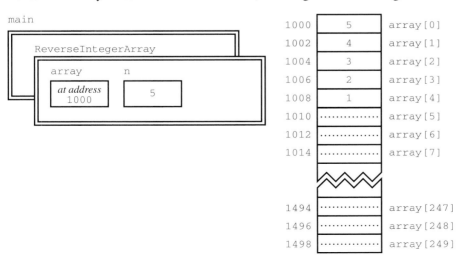

When `ReverseIntegerArray` returns, its frame disappears, but the changes made to the contents of the five memory words starting at 1000 are permanent, since these addresses are not part of that frame.

Although the way C treats array parameters makes it easier for functions to manipulate array data, it is critical to remember that C treats simple variables in an entirely different way. If array parameters were treated like all other parameters, calling

```
ReverseIntegerArray(list, n);
```

would create an entirely new array in the frame for `ReverseIntegerArray` and would copy all 250 elements of the array `list` into the corresponding local variable `array`. That approach would make it impossible for the `ReverseIntegerArray` function to affect the values in `list`, thereby rendering the function useless. Even for functions like `PrintIntegerArray` that do not need to change the values of their array parameters, the way C treats array parameters increases the efficiency of the program because it eliminates the need to copy the entire array, which can take a considerable amount of execution time if the array is large.[2]

Because in C the behavior of array parameters is different from that of other parameters, it is worth thinking of the difference in terms of the following rule:

A R R A Y	If you call a function that takes an array as a formal para-
P A R A M E T E R	meter, the array storage used for the parameter is shared
R U L E	with that of the actual argument. Changing the value of an
	element of the parameter array therefore changes the value
	of the corresponding element in the argument array.

Implementing `PrintIntegerArray` and `GetIntegerArray`

To complete the `reverse.c` program, you need to implement each of the functions called by the main program. Although you can choose to write such functions in any order, it often makes sense to start with the easiest one, which in this case is certainly `PrintIntegerArray`. This function has the task of going through and displaying each of the elements in the array on a separate line. To go through the elements, all you need is a `for` loop that begins at 0 and continues until it has processed all the active elements. The upper bound of the `for` loop is the effective size n. The implementation of `PrintIntegerArray` is therefore

---

[2] When a function accepts an array parameter but does not change the elements of the array, ANSI C allows you to document that fact by preceding the parameter declaration with the keyword `const`, as in

```
void PrintIntegerArray(const int array[], int n);
```

The keyword `const` lets the compiler know, along with any clients, that the function will not change the value of any array elements. Unfortunately, C compilers implement `const` with varying degrees of success. On some systems, the keyword is ignored; on others, programs written using it cannot always be compiled successfully. Because such problems occur even with some widely used compilers, this text does not use the `const` keyword.

```
static void PrintIntegerArray(int array[], int n)
{
    int i;

    for (i = 0; i < n; i++) {
        printf("%d\n", array[i]);
    }
}
```

The implementation of `GetIntegerArray` is slightly more complicated, mostly because you need to check to make sure the user does not enter more data than the array can hold. Because C provides no protection against writing past the end of the array, such checking is critically important. If you fail to check and the user enters too much data, the data can easily overwrite other important information and cause your program to fail in mysterious ways. The following implementation of `GetIntegerArray` incorporates the test for too much data:

```
static int GetIntegerArray(int array[], int max, int sentinel)
{
    int n, value;

    n = 0;
    while (TRUE) {
        printf(" ? ");
        value = GetInteger();
        if (value == sentinel) break;
        if (n == max) Error("Too many input items for array");
        array[n] = value;
        n++;
    }
    return (n);
}
```

As soon as you have implemented `GetIntegerArray` and `PrintIntegerArray`, it probably makes sense to test them before going on to write `ReverseIntegerArray`. For example, you could take these two functions and compile them with the following main program:

```
main()
{
    int list[MaxElements], n;

    n = GetIntegerArray(list, MaxElements, Sentinel);
    PrintIntegerArray(list, n);
}
```

From the user's point of view, this program does not do anything particularly interesting: it simply reads in a list of integers and displays that list in exactly the same order. From your perspective as a programmer, however, this program accomplishes a great deal. If it works, you know that `GetIntegerArray` and

PrintIntegerArray are working, which means that you have less to worry about when you write ReverseIntegerArray. Testing a program in stages is an important programming strategy that you should try to take advantage of wherever possible.

Implementing ReverseIntegerArray

As soon as you have tested your implementations of the functions GetIntegerArray and PrintIntegerArray, you are ready to turn to ReverseIntegerArray itself. The basic algorithm is simple: to reverse an array, you need to exchange the first element with the last one, the second element with the next-to-last one, and so on until all the elements have been exchanged. Because arrays are numbered beginning at 0, the last element in an array of n items is at index n - 1, the next-to-last element is at index n - 2, and so forth. In fact, given any integer index i, the array element that occurs i elements from the end is always at index position

```
n - i - 1
```

Thus, in order to reverse the elements of array, all you need to do is swap the values in array[i] and array[n - i - 1] for each index value i from the beginning of the array up to the center, which falls at index position n / 2. As soon as you reach the center, the elements in the second half of the array will already have their correct values because each cycle of the for loop correctly repositions two array elements—one in each half. In pseudocode, the implementation of ReverseIntegerArray is therefore

```
static void ReverseIntegerArray(int array[], int n)
{
    int i;

    for (i = 0; i < n / 2; i++) {
        Swap the values in array[i] and array[n - i - 1]
    }
}
```

The operation of swapping two values in an array is useful even beyond the bounds of this example. For this reason, it makes sense to define that operation as a separate function and to replace the remaining pseudocode in ReverseIntegerArray with a single function call.

   Although it is tempting to try, the function call that exchanges the two elements cannot be written as

```
Swap(array[i], array[n - i - i]);                This design can't work.
```

In this call, the arguments to Swap are individual array elements. Array elements act like simple variables and are therefore copied to the corresponding formal parameters. The Swap function could easily interchange the local copies of these values but could not make permanent assignments to the calling arguments.

To avoid this problem, you can simply pass the entire array to the function that performs the swap operation, along with the two indices that indicate the positions that should be exchanged. For example, the call

```
SwapIntegerElements(array, i, n - i - 1);
```

exchanges the elements at index positions i and n – i – 1 of array, which is precisely what you need to replace the pseudocode in ReverseIntegerArray.

Implementing SwapIntegerElements

Implementing SwapIntegerElements is a little more complicated than it first appears. You cannot simply assign one element to another because the original value of the destination would then be lost. The easiest way to handle the problem is to use a local variable to hold one of the values temporarily. If you hold onto the value of one of the elements, you are then free to assign the other value directly, after which you can copy the first value from the temporary variable.

Suppose you want to exchange the values in array at positions 0 and 4. The strategy requires three separate steps.

1. Store the value in array[0] in the temporary variable, as illustrated in the following diagram:

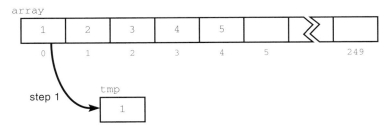

2. Copy the value from array[4] into array[0], leaving the following configuration:

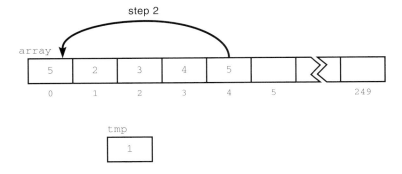

Because the old value of array[0] has previously been stored in tmp, no information is lost.

3. Assign the value in `tmp` to `array[4]`, as shown in this diagram:

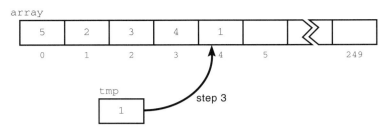

This three-step strategy is used as the basis for the following implementation of `SwapIntegerElements`:

```
static void SwapIntegerElements(int array[], int p1, int p2)
{
    int tmp;

    tmp = array[p1];
    array[p1] = array[p2];
    array[p2] = tmp;
}
```

This function fills in the last missing piece of the `reverse.c` program, which appears in its complete form in Figure 11-3.

▮▮▮▮ 11.4 Using arrays for tabulation

The data structure of a program is typically designed to reflect the organization of data in the real-world domain of the application. If you are writing a program to solve a problem that involves a list of values, you should probably use an array to represent that list in the program. For example, in the `gymjudge.c` program shown in Figure 11-1, the problem involves a list of scores—one for each of five judges. Because the individual scores form a list in the conceptual domain of the application, it is not surprising that an array is used to represent the data in the program. The array elements have a direct correspondence to the individual data items in the list. Thus, `scores[0]` corresponds to the score for judge #0, `scores[1]` to the score for judge #1, and so on.

In general, whenever an application involves data that can be represented in the form of a list like

$$a_0, a_1, a_2, a_3, a_4, \ldots, a_{N-1}$$

an array is the natural choice for the underlying representation. It is also quite common for programmers to refer to the index of an array element as a **subscript,** reflecting the fact that arrays are used to hold data that would typically be written with subscripts in mathematics.

There are, however, important uses of arrays in which the relationship between the data in the application domain and the data in the program takes a different form. Instead of storing the data values in successive elements of an array, for

FIGURE 11-3   reverse.c

```
/*
 * File: reverse.c
 * ----------------
 * This program reads in an array of integers, reverses the
 * elements of the array, and then displays the elements in
 * their reversed order.
 */

#include <stdio.h>
#include "genlib.h"
#include "simpio.h"

/*
 * Constants
 * ---------
 * MaxElements -- Maximum number of elements
 * Sentinel    -- Value used to terminate input
 */

#define MaxElements 250
#define Sentinel        0

/* Private function prototypes */

static int GetIntegerArray(int array[], int max, int sentinel);
static void PrintIntegerArray(int array[], int n);
static void ReverseIntegerArray(int array[], int n);
static void SwapIntegerElements(int array[], int p1, int p2);
static void GiveInstructions(void);

/* Main program */

main()
{
    int list[MaxElements], n;

    GiveInstructions();
    n = GetIntegerArray(list, MaxElements, Sentinel);
    ReverseIntegerArray(list, n);
    PrintIntegerArray(list, n);
}
```

▶

```
/*
 * Function: GetIntegerArray
 * Usage: n = GetIntegerArray(array, max, sentinel);
 * -------------------------------------------------
 * This function reads elements into an integer array by
 * reading values, one per line, from the keyboard.  The end
 * of the input data is indicated by the parameter sentinel.
 * The caller is responsible for declaring the array and
 * passing it as a parameter, along with its allocated
 * size.  The value returned is the number of elements
 * actually entered and therefore gives the effective size
 * of the array, which is typically less than the allocated
 * size given by max.  If the user types in more than max
 * elements, GetIntegerArray generates an error.
 */

static int GetIntegerArray(int array[], int max, int sentinel)
{
    int n, value;

    n = 0;
    while (TRUE) {
        printf(" ? ");
        value = GetInteger();
        if (value == sentinel) break;
        if (n == max) Error("Too many input items for array");
        array[n] = value;
        n++;
    }
    return (n);
}


/*
 * Function: PrintIntegerArray
 * Usage: PrintIntegerArray(array, n);
 * -----------------------------------
 * This function displays the first n values in array,
 * one per line, on the console.
 */

static void PrintIntegerArray(int array[], int n)
{
    int i;

    for (i = 0; i < n; i++) {
        printf("%d\n", array[i]);
    }
}
```

```
/*
 * Function: ReverseIntegerArray
 * Usage: ReverseIntegerArray(array, n);
 * -------------------------------------
 * This function reverses the elements of array, which has n as
 * its effective size.  The procedure operates by going through
 * the first half of the array and swapping each element with
 * its counterpart at the end of the array.
 */

static void ReverseIntegerArray(int array[], int n)
{
    int i;

    for (i = 0; i < n / 2; i++) {
        SwapIntegerElements(array, i, n - i - 1);
    }
}


/*
 * Function: SwapIntegerElements
 * Usage: SwapIntegerElements(array, p1, p2);
 * ------------------------------------------
 * This function swaps the elements in array at index
 * positions p1 and p2.
 */

static void SwapIntegerElements(int array[], int p1, int p2)
{
    int tmp;

    tmp = array[p1];
    array[p1] = array[p2];
    array[p2] = tmp;
}


/*
 * Function: GiveInstructions
 * Usage: GiveInstructions();
 * --------------------------
 * This function gives instructions for the array reversal program.
 */

static void GiveInstructions(void)
{
    printf("Enter numbers, one per line, ending with the\n");
    printf("sentinel value %d.  The program will then\n", Sentinel);
    printf("display those values in reverse order.\n");
}
```

some applications it makes more sense to use the data to generate array indices. Those indices are then used to select elements in an array that records some statistical property of the data as a whole.

Understanding how this approach works and appreciating how it differs from more traditional uses of arrays requires looking at a concrete example. Suppose you want to write a program that reads lines of text from the user and keeps track of how often each of the 26 letters appears. When the user types a blank line to signal the end of the input, the program should display a table indicating how many times each letter appears in the input data. The operation of the program is illustrated by the following sample run:

```
This program counts letter frequencies.
Enter a blank line to signal end of input.
Peter Piper picked a peck⏎
of pickled peppers.⏎
⏎
A      1
C      3
D      2
E      8
F      1
I      3
K      3
L      1
O      1
P      9
R      3
S      1
T      1
```

In order to generate the letter-frequency table, the program has to search each line of text character by character. Every time a letter appears, the program must update a running count that keeps track of how often that letter has appeared so far in the input. The interesting part of the problem lies in designing the data structure necessary to maintain a count for each of the 26 letters.

It is possible to solve this problem without arrays by defining 26 separate variables—nA, nB, nC, and so forth up to nZ—and then using a switch statement to check all 26 cases:

```
switch (toupper(ch)) {
   case 'A': nA++; break;
   case 'B': nB++; break;
   case 'C': nC++; break;
   . . .
   case 'Z': nZ++; break;
}
```

This process results in a long, repetitive program. A better approach is to combine the 26 individual variables into an array and then use the character code to select the appropriate element within the array. Each element contains an integer representing the current count of the letter that corresponds to that index in the array. If you call the array `letterCounts`, you can declare it by writing

```
int letterCounts[NLetters];
```

where `NLetters` is defined to be the constant 26. This declaration allocates space for an integer array with 26 elements, as shown in this diagram:

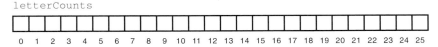

Each time a letter character appears in the input, you need to increment the corresponding element in `letterCounts`. Finding the element to increment is simply a matter of converting the character into an integer in the range 0 to 25 by using character arithmetic. The conversion process is accomplished by the function `LetterIndex`, which has the following implementation:

```
int LetterIndex(char ch)
{
    if (isalpha(ch)) {
        return (toupper(ch) - 'A');
    } else {
        return (-1);
    }
}
```

The `LetterIndex` function returns a value between 0 and 25 if `ch` is a letter in either upper or lower case. If `ch` is not a letter, `LetterIndex` returns −1. Thus, to record each character, all you need to do is

- Convert the character to an index by calling `LetterIndex`
- If the index value is not −1, increment the `letterCounts` array element at that index position

You can easily translate these steps into C, as shown in the following implementation of the function `RecordLetter`:

```
void RecordLetter(char ch, int letterCounts[])
{
    int index;

    index = LetterIndex(ch);
    if (index != -1) letterCounts[index]++;
}
```

It is essential for `RecordLetter` to check that the value returned by `LetterIndex` is not −1. If you fail to include this check, the program will increment the integer in location `letterCounts[-1]`. Even though this element does not in fact exist, most compilers will generate code that examines the integer word immediately preceding the start of the array, as indicated by the colored box in the following diagram:

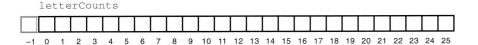

letterCounts

−1 0 1 2 3 4 5 6 7 8 9 10 11 12 13 14 15 16 17 18 19 20 21 22 23 24 25

Because the location in memory that immediately precedes the `letterCounts` array might hold some other data the program needs, changing that location could easily lead to erroneous results and might cause the program to crash.

Before you can count the individual characters, you must ensure that each element of the array is initialized to 0 at the beginning of the program. This phase of the program operation is accomplished by the function `ClearIntegerArray`, which is likely to prove useful in other applications as well. The code for `ClearIntegerArray` is

```
static void ClearIntegerArray(int array[], int n)
{
    int i;

    for (i = 0; i < n; i++) {
        array[i] = 0;
    }
}
```

The function `DisplayLetterCounts` generates the frequency table at the end of the program and has the following implementation:

```
void DisplayLetterCounts(const int letterCounts[])
{
    char ch;
    int num;

    for (ch = 'A'; ch <= 'Z'; ch++) {
        num = letterCounts[LetterIndex(ch)];
        if (num != 0) printf("%c  %4d\n", ch, num);
    }
}
```

It's important to note that the `for` loop counts from `'A'` to `'Z'` rather than from 0 to 25. Because we use indices that correspond to our conception of the problem, the resulting `for` loop becomes much easier to understand. You should also note that it is unnecessary in this case to check for a −1 result from `LetterIndex` because the structure of `DisplayLetterCounts` ensures that the out-of-range condition cannot occur.

The rest of the program, shown in Figure 11-4, consists of the code necessary to scan the input character by character.

▮▮▮ 11.5 Static initialization of arrays

Array variables can be declared to be either local or global like any other variable. To avoid the pitfalls associated with using global variables, arrays should be declared as local unless there is a compelling reason to the contrary. The reasons

FIGURE 11-4   countlet.c

```
/*
 * File: countlet.c
 * ----------------
 * This program counts the occurrences of individual letters
 * that appear in text read in from the user.  This program
 * might be useful as a tool in solving cryptograms.
 */

#include <stdio.h>
#include <ctype.h>
#include "simpio.h"
#include "strlib.h"
#include "genlib.h"

/*
 * Constants
 * ---------
 * MaxLines -- Maximum number of input lines
 * NLetters -- Number of letters
 */

#define MaxLines 100
#define NLetters  26

/* Private function declarations */

static void CountLetters(int letterCounts[]);
static void CountLettersInString(string str, int letterCounts[]);
static void RecordLetter(char ch, int letterCounts[]);
static void DisplayLetterCounts(const int letterCounts[]);
static int LetterIndex(char ch);
static void ClearIntegerArray(int array[], int n);

/* Main program */

main()
{
    int letterCounts[NLetters];

    printf("This program counts letter frequencies.\n");
    printf("Enter a blank line to signal end of input.\n");
    ClearIntegerArray(letterCounts, NLetters);
    CountLetters(letterCounts);
    DisplayLetterCounts(letterCounts);
}
```

```
/*
 * Function: CountLetters
 * Usage: CountLetters(letterCounts);
 * ---------------------------------
 * This function updates the values in the letterCounts array
 * by scanning through a series of strings read in from the
 * user.  A blank line is used to signal the end of the input
 * text.
 */

static void CountLetters(int letterCounts[])
{
    string line;

    while (TRUE) {
        line = GetLine();
        if (StringLength(line) == 0) break;
        CountLettersInString(line, letterCounts);
    }
}

/*
 * Function: CountLettersInString
 * Usage: CountLettersInString(str, letterCounts);
 * -----------------------------------------------
 * This function updates the values in the letterCounts array for
 * each character in the string str.
 */

static void CountLettersInString(string str, int letterCounts[])
{
    int i;

    for (i = 0; i < StringLength(str); i++) {
        RecordLetter(IthChar(str, i), letterCounts);
    }
}

/*
 * Function: RecordLetter
 * Usage: RecordLetter(ch, letterCounts);
 * --------------------------------------
 * This function records the fact that the character ch has
 * been seen by incrementing the appropriate element in the
 * letterCounts array.  Non-letters are ignored.
 */
```

```
void RecordLetter(char ch, int letterCounts[])
{
    int index;

    index = LetterIndex(ch);
    if (index != -1) letterCounts[index]++;
}


/*
 * Function: DisplayLetterCounts
 * Usage: DisplayLetterCounts(letterCounts);
 * ----------------------------------------
 * This function displays the letter frequency table, leaving
 * out any letters that did not occur.
 */

void DisplayLetterCounts(const int letterCounts[])
{
    char ch;
    int num;

    for (ch = 'A'; ch <= 'Z'; ch++) {
        num = letterCounts[LetterIndex(ch)];
        if (num != 0) printf("%c  %4d\n", ch, num);
    }
}


/*
 * Function: LetterIndex
 * Usage: index = LetterIndex(ch);
 * -------------------------------
 * This function converts a character into the appropriate index
 * for use with the letterCounts array.  In this implementation,
 * LetterIndex converts characters in either case to an integer
 * in the range 0 to 25.  If ch is not a valid letter, LetterIndex
 * returns -1.  Clients should check for a -1 return value unless
 * they are able to guarantee that the argument is a letter.
 */

int LetterIndex(char ch)
{
    if (isalpha(ch)) {
        return (toupper(ch) - 'A');
    } else {
        return (-1);
    }
}
```

```
/*
 * Function: ClearIntegerArray
 * Usage: ClearIntegerArray(array, n);
 * ---------------------------------
 * This function sets the first n elements in the array to 0.
 */

static void ClearIntegerArray(int array[], int n)
{
    int i;

    for (i = 0; i < n; i++) {
        array[i] = 0;
    }
}
```

for choosing to use global declaration are outlined in the discussion of global variables in Chapter 10. Moreover, global arrays used in a program module should usually be declared as static variables to avoid having them exported to other modules.

If an array is declared to be a static global variable, its individual elements can be assigned initial values before the program begins to run. This process is an example of static initialization, which was introduced in the section on "Initializing global variables" in Chapter 10. In the case of an array variable, the equal sign specifying the initial value is followed by a list of the initial values for each element, enclosed in curly braces. For example, the declaration

```
static int digits[10] = { 0, 1, 2, 3, 4, 5, 6, 7, 8, 9 };
```

introduces a global array called `digits` in which each of the 10 elements is initialized to its own index number.

Automatic determination of array size

When initializers are provided for an array, it is legal to omit the array size from the declaration. Thus, you could also write the declaration for the array `digits` as

```
static int digits[] = { 0, 1, 2, 3, 4, 5, 6, 7, 8, 9 };
```

When the compiler encounters a declaration of this form, it counts the number of initializers and reserves exactly that many elements for the array.

In the `digits` example, there is little advantage in leaving out the array bound. You know that there are 10 digits and that new digits are not going to be added to this list. For arrays whose initial values may need to change over the life cycle of the program, having the compiler compute the array size from the initializers is useful for program maintenance because it frees the programmer from having to maintain the element count as the program evolves.

For example, imagine you're writing a program that requires an array containing the names of all U.S. cities with populations of over 1,000,000. Taking data from the 1990 census, you could declare that array as follows:

```
static string bigCities[] = {
    "New York",
    "Los Angeles",
    "Chicago",
    "Houston",
    "Philadelphia",
    "San Diego",
    "Detroit",
    "Dallas",
};
```

When the figures are in from the 2000 census, it is likely that Phoenix and San Antonio will have joined this list. If they do, you could then simply add their names to the initializer list. The compiler will then expand the array size to accomodate the new values.

Note that the last initializer for the `bigCities` array is followed by a comma. This comma is optional, but it is good programming practice to include it. Doing so allows you to add new cities without having to change the existing entries in the initializer list.

Determining the size of an initialized array

If you write a program that uses the `bigCities` array, you will probably need to know how many cities the list contains. The compiler has this number because it counted the initializers. The question is how to make that information available to the program.

In C, there is a standard idiom for determining the number of elements in an array whose size is established by static initialization. Given any array `a`, the number of elements in `a` can be computed using the expression

```
sizeof a / sizeof a[0]
```

In English, this expression takes the size of the entire array and divides it by the size of the initial element in the array. Because all elements of an array are the same size, the result is the number of elements in the array, regardless of the element type. Thus you could initialize a variable `nBigCities` to hold the number of cities in the `bigCities` array by writing

```
static int nBigCities = sizeof bigCities / sizeof bigCities[0];
```

Initialized arrays and scalar types

According to the definition given in Chapter 9, a scalar type can be used in any context in which an integer can appear. It is therefore possible to use values of any scalar type as array indices. This fact increases the power of scalar types and often simplifies their use.

As an example, initialized arrays make it very easy to convert values of an enumeration type into their corresponding names—an operation that is not directly supported by C. For instance, if you want to display Boolean values using the names FALSE and TRUE, you can do so by declaring the array `booleanNames` as

```
static string booleanNames = { "FALSE", "TRUE" };
```

and then using a `printf` statement such as

```
printf("flag = %s\n", booleanNames[flag]);
```

Because the type `bool` is defined in `genlib.h` using

```
typedef enum { FALSE, TRUE } bool;
```

the constant `FALSE` has the internal value 0 and `TRUE` has the internal value 1. Using these values as indices into the `booleanNames` array generates the name string corresponding to the appropriate Boolean value. The same strategy works with any consecutive enumeration type.

11.6 Multidimensional arrays

In C, the elements of an array can be of any type. In particular, the elements of an array can themselves be arrays. Arrays of arrays are called **multidimensional arrays.** The most common form of multidimensional array is the two-dimensional array, which is most often used to represent data in which the individual entries form a rectangular structure marked off into rows and columns. This type of two dimensional structure is called a **matrix.** Arrays of three or more dimensions are also legal in C but occur much less frequently.

As an example of a two-dimensional array, suppose you wanted to represent a game of tic-tac-toe as part of a program. As you probably know, tic-tac-toe is played on a board consisting of three rows and three columns, as follows:

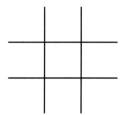

Players take turns placing the letters *X* and *O* in the empty squares, trying to line up three identical symbols horizontally, vertically, or diagonally.

To represent the tic-tac-toe board, the most sensible strategy is to use a two-dimensional array with three rows and three columns. Although you could also define an enumeration type to represent the three possible contents of each square—empty, *X,* and *O*—it is probably simpler in this case to use `char` as the element type and to represent the three legal states for each square using the characters `' '`, `'X'`, and `'O'`. The declaration for the tic-tac-toe board would then be written as

```
char board[3][3];
```

Given this declaration, you could then refer to the characters representing the individual squares on the board by supplying two separate indices, one specifying the row number and a another specifying the column number. In this representation, each number varies over the range 0 to 2, and the individual positions in the board have the following names:

board[0][0]	board[0][1]	board[0][2]
board[1][0]	board[1][1]	board[1][2]
board[2][0]	board[2][1]	board[2][2]

Internally, C represents the variable board as an array of three elements, each of which is an array of three characters. The memory allocated to board consists of nine bytes arranged in the following form:

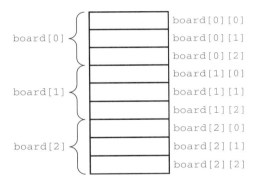

In the two-dimensional diagram of the board array, the first index is assumed to indicate the row number. This choice, however, is arbitrary because the two-dimensional geometry of the matrix is entirely conceptual; in memory, these values form a one-dimensional list. If you wanted the first index to indicate the column and the second to indicate the row, the only functions you would need to change would be those that depend on the conceptual geometry, such as a function that displays the current state of the board. In terms of the internal arrangement, however, it is always true that the first index value varies least rapidly as the array elements are positioned in memory. Thus all the elements of board[0] appear in memory before any elements of board[1].

Passing multidimensional arrays to functions

Multidimensional arrays are passed between functions just as single-dimensional arrays are. The parameter declaration in the function header looks like the original declaration of the variable and includes the index information. For example, the following function displays the current state of the board array:

```
static void DisplayBoard(char board[3][3])
{
    int row, column;

    for (row = 0; row < 3; row++) {
        if (row != 0) printf("---+---+---\n");
        for (column = 0; column < 3; column++) {
            if (column != 0) printf("|");
            printf(" %c ", board[row][column]);
        }
        printf("\n");
    }
}
```

Much of the code in `DisplayBoard` is used to format the output so that the board appears in the following easy-to-read form:

```
 X | O | X
---+---+---
   | X | O
---+---+---
 X |   | O
```

When a function accepts a multidimensional array as a parameter, C requires that you specify the size of each index in the array except for the first, which is optional. Thus, the function header for `DisplayBoard` could have been written as

```
static void DisplayBoard(char board[][3])
```

The program would then have worked in exactly the same way because the base address of the array and the size of the second index are sufficient for C to determine the address of every element in `board`, no matter how many rows it contains. However, leaving out the first index makes the declaration unsymmetrical, and it is therefore more common to include the array bounds for each index in the declaration of a multidimensional array parameter.

Initializing multidimensional arrays

You can use static initialization with multidimensional arrays just like single-dimensional arrays. To emphasize the overall structure, the values used to initialize each internal array are usually enclosed in additional set of curly braces. For example, the declaration

```
static double identityMatrix[3][3] = {
    { 1.0, 0.0, 0.0 },
    { 0.0, 1.0, 0.0 },
    { 0.0, 0.0, 1.0 }
};
```

declares a 3×3 matrix of floating-point numbers and initializes it to contain the following values:

1.0	0.0	0.0
0.0	1.0	0.0
0.0	0.0	1.0

This particular matrix comes up frequently in mathematical applications and is called the **identity matrix.**

As in the case of parameters, the declaration of a statically initialized multidimensional array must specify all index bounds except possibly the first, which can be determined by counting the initializers. As was true with parameters, however, it is usually best to specify all of the index bounds explicitly when you declare a multidimensional array.

Additional examples of how static initialization can be used with multidimensional arrays appear in Chapter 12.

SUMMARY

In this chapter, you have learned about two distinct but related concepts: the internal representation of data in memory and the particular data structure called the *array*. The fundamental points to remember about memory and data representation are:

- Each variable is stored somewhere in memory and therefore has an address.
- Once allocated, the address of a variable never changes, even though its contents may change.
- Depending on the type of data it holds, a variable will require different amounts of memory. Moreover, the amount of memory required to hold a value of a particular type varies from machine to machine. Within a program compiled for a specific machine, you can use the `sizeof` operator to determine the number of bytes required to hold any data value.

In terms of arrays, the important points discussed in this chapter include:

- Arrays are used to represent collections of data that are both *ordered* and *homogeneous*. Each component of the array is called an *element* and is identified by a numeric *index*. In C, all arrays begin with index number 0.
- When you declare an array variable, you have to specify the array size, which must be constant. For applications that need to work with varying amounts of data, the typical approach is to allocate enough space in the

arrays to hold the maximum number of values and to use only a part of that storage. The maximum number of elements is called the *allocated size* of the array; the number of elements actually in use is called the *effective size.*

- The process of referring to an individual element in an array is called *selection* and is indicated by writing an expression in square brackets after the name of the array.

- In memory, the elements of an array are stored in consecutive memory locations. The first address in the array is called its *base address,* and the adjustment required to select a particular element is called the *offset* of that element.

- Whenever you pass an array as an argument to a function, the corresponding formal parameter is initialized to hold the base address of the calling array. Within the function, all references to elements of the formal parameter array refer to the corresponding elements of the calling array. An array parameter is therefore shared with its calling argument, even though any other parameter type is merely a copy.

- When you use an array as a formal parameter, you can omit the array size from the declaration. In such cases, it is usually necessary to pass the effective size of the array as a separate parameter.

- The index of an array can be of any scalar type, including integers, characters, or enumerations.

- You can apply static initialization to global arrays by including a list of initializers enclosed in curly braces, one for each element of the array.

- Arrays can be declared with more than one index, in which case they are called *multidimensional arrays*. In C, multidimensional arrays are treated as arrays of arrays. The first index value selects an element of the outermost array, the second index value selects an element from that array, and so on.

REVIEW QUESTIONS

1. What are the two characteristic properties of an array?

2. Define the following terms: *element, index, element type, array size, selection.*

3. Write array declarations for the following array variables:
   a. An array `realArray` consisting of 100 floating-point values
   b. An array `inUse` consisting of 16 Boolean values
   c. An array `lines` that can hold up to 1000 strings

Remember that the upper bounds for these arrays should be defined as constants to make them easier to change.

4. Write the variable declaration and `for` loop necessary to create and initialize the following integer array:

squares

0	1	4	9	16	25	36	49	64	81	100
0	1	2	3	4	5	6	7	8	9	10

5. What are the two approaches outlined in this chapter for representing an array in which the natural index values begin at 1 instead of at 0? What are the trade-offs between these two approaches?

6. Define the following terms: *bit, byte, word, address.*

7. How can you determine the number of bytes required to represent a data value in C?

8. How many bytes are required to hold an array of 20 characters?

9. Write a C expression that computes the number of bytes needed to represent an array containing `NElements` values of type `double`.

10. What happens on most machines if you try to select an array element outside the allocated bounds of that array?

11. What is the difference between allocated size and effective size?

12. In your own words, state the Array Parameter Rule. From the programmer's point of view, what is the central difference between the operation of passing an array as a parameter and that of passing a simple variable?

13. Given your understanding of how arrays are allocated in memory, explain briefly why the Array Parameter Rule applies.

14. True or false: When you declare an array parameter in a function, the array size is optional.

15. What is the role of the variable `tmp` in the `SwapIntegerElements` function?

16. In Review Question 4, you initialized the contents of the array

squares

0	1	4	9	16	25	36	49	64	81	100
0	1	2	3	4	5	6	7	8	9	10

using dynamic initialization. Rewrite the declaration so that `squares` is a statically initialized global array.

17. What is the idiom introduced in this chapter for determining the number of elements in an array whose size is set by static initialization?

18. In the discussion of enumeration types in Chapter 9, the type `directionT` was defined as follows:

    ```
    typedef enum { North, East, South, West } directionT;
    ```

    Given a variable `dir` of type `directionT`, show how you could use a statically initialized array to display the name of that direction on the screen.

19. What is a multidimensional array?

20. Assuming that the base address for the array is 1000 and that values of type `int` require two bytes of memory, draw a diagram that shows the address of each element in the array declared as follows:

    ```
    int rectangular[2][3];
    ```

21. What variable declaration would you use to record the state of a chessboard, which consists of an 8 × 8 array of squares, each of which may contain any one of the following symbols:

K	white king	k	black king
Q	white queen	q	black queen
R	white rook	r	black rook
B	white bishop	b	black bishop
N	white knight	n	black knight
P	white pawn	p	black pawn
–	empty square		

    How could you initialize this array statically so that it holds the standard starting position for a chess game:

r	n	b	q	k	b	n	r
p	p	p	p	p	p	p	p
–	–	–	–	–	–	–	–
–	–	–	–	–	–	–	–
–	–	–	–	–	–	–	–
–	–	–	–	–	–	–	–
P	P	P	P	P	P	P	P
R	N	B	Q	K	B	N	R

PROGRAMMING EXERCISES

1. Write a program that uses the `sizeof` operator to display the number of bytes required to store a value of each of the basic types. The results of this program

for the machine I used to generate this text appear in the following sample run:

```
Values of type char require 1 byte.
Values of type int require 2 bytes.
Values of type short require 2 bytes.
Values of type long require 4 bytes.
Values of type float require 4 bytes.
Values of type double require 12 bytes.
```

Because the size varies among different computer systems, the results you get are likely be different from those shown.

2. Because individual judges may have some bias, it is common practice to throw out the highest and lowest score before computing the average. Write a program that reads in scores from a panel of seven judges and then computes the average of the five scores that remain after discarding the highest and lowest.

3. In statistics, a collection of data values is usually referred to as a **distribution.** A primary purpose of statistical analysis is to find ways to compress the complete set of data into summary statistics that express properties of the distribution as a whole. The most common statistical measure is the **mean,** which is simply the traditional average. For the distribution $x_1, x_2, \ldots, x_n$, the mean is usually represented by the symbol $\bar{x}$.

   Write a function `Mean(array, n)` that returns the mean of an array of type `double` whose effective size is n. Test your function by incorporating it into the `gymjudge.c` program in Figure 11-1.

4. Another common statistical measure is the **standard deviation,** which provides an indication of how much the individual values in the distribution differ from the mean. To calculate the standard deviation whose elements are $x_1, x_2, \ldots, x_n$ you need to perform the following steps:

   a. Calculate the mean of the distribution as in exercise 3.
   b. Go through the individual data items in the distribution and calculate the square of the difference between each data value and the mean. Add all these values to a running total.
   c. Take the total from step b and divide it by the number of data items.[3]
   d. Calculate the square root of the resulting quantity, which represents the standard deviation.

   In mathematical form, the standard deviation (σ) is given by the following formula:

$$\sigma = \sqrt{\frac{\sum_{i=1}^{n}(\bar{x} - x_i)^2}{n}}$$

---

[3] The procedure given here is used by statisticians to compute the standard deviation of a complete data distribution. If you want to calculate the standard deviation based instead on a sample of the distribution, you need to divide by $n-1$.

The Greek letter sigma (Σ) represents a summation of the quantity that follows, which in this case is the square of the difference between the mean and each individual data point.

Write a function `StandardDeviation(array, n)` that takes an array of floating-point values and the effective size of that array and returns the standard deviation of the data distribution contained in the array.

5. In the third century B.C., the Greek astronomer Eratosthenes developed an algorithm for finding all the prime numbers up to some upper limit N. To apply the algorithm, you start by writing down a list of the integers between 2 and N. For example, if N were 20, you would begin by writing down the following list:

$$2 \quad 3 \quad 4 \quad 5 \quad 6 \quad 7 \quad 8 \quad 9 \quad 10 \quad 11 \quad 12 \quad 13 \quad 14 \quad 15 \quad 16 \quad 17 \quad 18 \quad 19 \quad 20$$

You then begin by circling the first number in the list, indicating that you have found a prime. You then go through the rest of the list and cross off every multiple of the value you have just circled, since none of those multiples can be prime. Thus, after executing the first step of the algorithm, you will have circled the number 2 and crossed off every multiple of two, as follows:

② 3 ✗ 5 ✗ 7 ✗ 9 ✗ 11 ✗ 13 ✗ 15 ✗ 17 ✗ 19 ✗

From here, you simply repeat the process by circling the first number in the list that is neither crossed off nor circled, and then crossing off its multiples. In this example, you would circle 3 as a prime and cross off all multiples of 3 in the rest of the list, which would result in the following state:

②③✗ 5 ✗ 7 ✗✗✗ 11 ✗ 13 ✗✗✗ 17 ✗ 19 ✗

Eventually, every number in the list will either be circled or crossed out, as shown in this diagram:

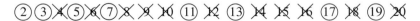

The circled numbers are the primes; the crossed-out numbers are composites. This algorithm for generating a list of primes is called the *sieve of Eratosthenes*.

Write a program that uses the sieve of Eratosthenes to generate a list of the primes between 2 and 1000.

6. In May of 1844, Samuel F. B. Morse sent the message "What hath God wrought!" by telegraph from Washington to Baltimore, heralding the beginning

of the age of electronic communication. To make it possible to communicate information using only the presence or absence of a single tone, Morse designed a coding system in which letters and other symbols are represented as coded sequences of short and long tones, traditionally called *dots* and *dashes*. In Morse code, the 26 letters of the alphabet are represented by the following codes:

A	·—	J	·———	S	···
B	—···	K	—·—	T	—
C	—·—·	L	·—··	U	··—
D	—··	M	——	V	···—
E	·	N	—·	W	·——
F	··—·	O	———	X	—··—
G	——·	P	·——·	Y	—·——
H	····	Q	——·—	Z	——··
I	··	R	·—·		

You can easily store these codes in a program by declaring an array with 26 elements and storing the sequence of characters corresponding to each letter in the appropriate array entry.

Write a program that reads in a string from the user and translates each letter in the string to its equivalent in Morse code, using periods to represent dots and hyphens to represent dashes. Separate words in the output by replacing each space in the input with a newline character, but ignore all other punctuation characters. Your program should be able to generate the following sample run:

```
This program translates a line into Morse code.
Enter English text: What hath God wrought⏎
.-- .... .- -
.... .- - ....
--. --- -..
.-- .-. --- ..- --. .... -
```

7. A *histogram* is a graphical way of displaying data by dividing the data into separate ranges and then indicating how many data values fall into each range. For example, given the set of exam scores

    100, 95, 47, 88, 86, 92, 75, 89, 81, 70, 55, 80

a traditional histogram would have the following form:

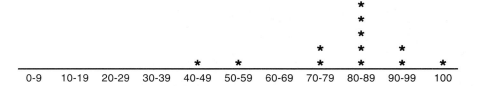

The asterisks in the histogram indicate one score in the 40s, one score in the 50s, five scores in the 80s, and so forth.

When you generate histograms using a computer, however, it is usually much easier to display them sideways on the page, as in this sample run:

```
 0-9   |
10-19  |
20-29  |
30-39  |
40-49  | *
50-59  | *
60-69  |
70-79  | **
80-89  | *****
90-99  | **
100    | *
```

Write a program that reads in an array of integers using `GetIntegerArray` and then displays a histogram of those numbers, divided into the ranges 0–9, 10–19, 20–29, and so forth, up to the range containing only the value 100. Your program should generate output that looks as much like the sample run as possible.

8. Rewrite your solution to exercise 7 by defining a separate `hist.h` interface that provides clients with a more general facility for generating histograms of integer data. The package should allow the client to specify the minimum and maximum values as well as the size of each histogram range; you might choose to provide other options as well.

9. When you are trying to represent the behavior of some quantity that varies over time, one of the usual tools is the **line graph**, in which a set of data values are plotted on an *x-y* grid with each pair of adjacent points connected by a straight-line. For example, given the following set of 10 points:

$$(0.0, 0.67)$$
$$(0.4, 0.68)$$
$$(0.8, 0.71)$$
$$(1.2, 0.86)$$
$$(1.6, 0.86)$$

(2.0, 1.04)
(2.4, 1.30)
(2.8, 1.81)
(3.2, 1.46)
(3.6, 1.86)

the line graph that represents them looks like this:

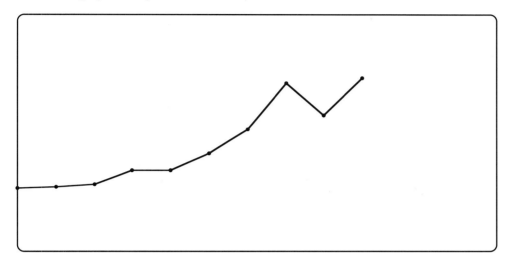

Write a function `DrawLineGraph` that generates a line graph given an array of x-coordinate values, a second array of the corresponding y-coordinate values, and the number of data points.

10. The mechanism depicted in the following diagram—which has sometimes been marketed by toy stores as a "probability board"—can be used to demonstrate important properties of random processes.

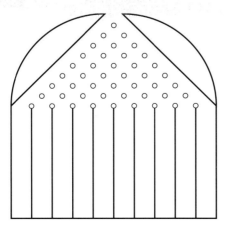

The mechanism works as follows. You start by dropping a marble in the hole at the top. The marble falls down and hits the uppermost peg, indicated by the small circle in the diagram. The marble bounces off the peg and falls, with equal probability, to the left or right. Whichever way it goes, it then hits a peg on the second level and bounces again, one direction or the other. The process continues until the marble passes all the pegs and drops into one of the channels at the bottom. For example, the colored line in the following diagram shows one possible path for the marble:

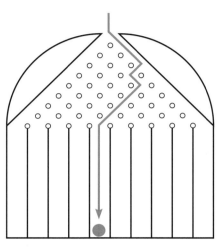

Write a program to simulate the operation of dropping 50 marbles into a probability board with 10 channels along the bottom, as in the diagram. Your program should display its results pictorially using the graphics library described in Chapter 7. As each marble lands, the program should draw a circle at the appropriate place on the screen.

The following screen image shows one possible sample run:

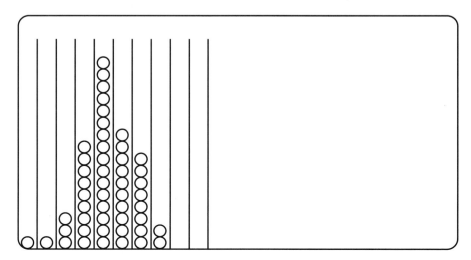

Note that the marbles tend to cluster in the center channels. The reason for this behavior is that there are many more ways in which a marble can reach the center columns than the ones on the ends. For example, to reach the leftmost column, the marble must have bounced to the left nine times in a row. In contrast, there are many paths from the top to the two center columns because the order of the left and right bounces can be reordered without affecting where the marble ends up. In general, the likelihood that a random process will end up in a particular state depends on the number of ways of reaching that state.

11. Using the declaration of the tic-tac-toe board given in the section on "Multidimensional arrays" earlier in this chapter, write a predicate function `IsWinningPosition(board, player)` that returns `TRUE` if the specified player, which is either the character `'X'` or the character `'O'`, has won the tic-tac-toe game. A winning position is one in which three identical symbols are lined up horizontally, vertically, or diagonally. Test your function by writing a main program that reads in the current contents of the board array and then reports whether either player has won the game, as illustrated by this following sample run:

```
This program tests the IsWinningPosition function.
Enter the state of the board, row by row.

XOX⏎
-XO⏎
X-O⏎

X has won
```

12. The initial state of a checkers game is shown in the following diagram:

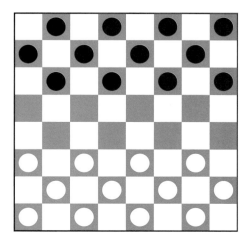

The dark squares in the bottom three rows are occupied by red checkers (which appear in white in the diagram); the dark squares in the top three rows contain black checkers. The two center rows are unoccupied.

If you want to store the state of a checkerboard in a computer program, you need a two-dimensional array indexed by rows and columns. The elements of the array could be of various different types, but a reasonable approach—as illustrated by the tic-tac-toe example—is to use characters. For example, you could use the letter *r* to represent a red checker and the letter *b* to represent a black checker. Empty squares could be represented as spaces or hyphens depending on whether the color of the square was light or dark.

Implement a function `InitCheckerboard` that initializes a checkerboard array so that it corresponds to the starting position of a checkers game. Implement a second function `DisplayCheckerboard` that displays the current state of a checkerboard on the screen, as follows:

```
    b   b   b   b
  b   b   b   b
    b   b   b   b
  -   -   -   -
    -   -   -   -
  r   r   r   r
    r   r   r   r
  r   r   r   r
```

CHAPTER 12

Searching and Sorting

Had I been present at the creation, I would have given some useful hints for the better ordering of the universe.

— Alfonso the Wise, thirteenth century

Objectives

- To be able to implement and use the linear search and binary search algorithms to find data in an array.
- To appreciate the differences in efficiency between these algorithms.
- To understand the implementation of a simple sorting algorithm called *selection sort*.
- To recognize how the efficiency of the selection sort algorithm depends on the number of data items.

In Chapter 11, you had the opportunity to learn about most of the fundamental array operations and to see how arrays are used in a variety of applications. There are, however, two important array operations Chapter 11 omits so that they can be covered more thoroughly in a chapter of their own. These operations are:

- **Searching,** which is the process of finding a particular element in an array
- **Sorting,** which is the process of rearranging the elements in an array so that they are stored in some well-defined order

Because searching and sorting are closely related to arrays, this chapter is in a sense a continuation of the array discussion. This chapter, however, has another central theme that links it not just to Chapter 11 but also to the discussion of algorithms in Chapter 6. Because there are many different strategies for searching and sorting—with vastly different levels of efficiency—these operations raise interesting algorithmic issues.

 12.1 Searching

In earlier chapters, you have already encountered functions that perform searches, although they have not appeared in the context of arrays. For example, the function `FindFirstVowel` that appears as part of the `piglatin.c` program (Figure 10-5) searches a string to find the first vowel. The implementation

```
int FindFirstVowel(string word)
{
    int i;

    for (i = 0; i < StringLength(word); i++) {
        if (IsVowel(IthChar(word, i))) return (i);
    }
    return (-1);
}
```

adopts a simple and straightforward algorithmic approach to the searching problem. Starting at the beginning of the string, the function looks at each character of the string in turn. If that character is a vowel, `FindFirstVowel` returns the index of that character in the original string. If it goes all the way through the string without finding any vowels, `FindFirstVowel` returns −1 to inform the client that no vowels appear.

Searching in an integer array

You can easily apply the same strategy to searching for a specific data item within an array. For example, the function `FindIntegerInArray` looks for the integer `key` in an array of integers whose effective size is `n`:

```
int FindIntegerInArray(int key, int array[], int n)
{
    int i;

    for (i = 0; i < n; i++) {
        if (key == array[i]) return (i);
    }
    return (-1);
}
```

Using a structure that resembles that of FindFirstVowel, the for loop in
FindIntegerInArray looks at the first n elements of array in turn. If one of those
elements matches the value of the parameter key, the function returns the array
index at which the match is found. If the for loop goes all the way through the
array without finding the desired value, FindIntegerInArray returns −1.

You can use FindIntegerInArray to write a program findcoin.c that displays the name of a U.S. coin, given its value, as shown in Figure 12-1.

FIGURE 12-1   findcoin.c

```
/*
 * File: findcoin.c
 * ----------------
 * This program uses a search operation to report the names of
 * legal U.S. coins.
 */

#include <stdio.h>
#include <ctype.h>
#include "simpio.h"
#include "genlib.h"

/*
 * Global variables
 * ----------------
 * coinNames  -- Array containing the corresponding coin names
 * coinValues -- Array containing the value of each coin
 * nCoins     -- Number of distinct coins
 */

static string coinNames[] = {
    "penny",
    "nickel",
    "dime",
    "quarter",
    "half-dollar",
};
```

```
static int coinValues[] = { 1, 5, 10, 25, 50 };

static int nCoins = sizeof coinValues / sizeof coinValues[0];

/* Private function declarations */

static int FindIntegerInArray(int key, int array[], int n);

/* Main program */

main()
{
    int value, index;

    printf("This program looks up names of U.S. coins.\n");
    printf("Enter coin value: ");
    value = GetInteger();
    index = FindIntegerInArray(value, coinValues, nCoins);
    if (index == -1) {
        printf("There is no such coin.\n");
    } else {
        printf("That's called a %s.\n", coinNames[index]);
    }
}

/*
 * Function: FindIntegerInArray
 * Usage: index = FindIntegerInArray(key, array, n);
 * ----------------------------------------------------
 * This function returns the index of the first element in the
 * specified array of integers that matches the value key.  If
 * key does not appear in the first n elements of the array,
 * FindIntegerInArray returns -1.
 */

static int FindIntegerInArray(int key, int array[], int n)
{
    int i;

    for (i = 0; i < n; i++) {
        if (key == array[i]) return (i);
    }
    return (-1);
}
```

The `FindIntegerInArray` function returns the index of the coin value in the array `coinValues`. If the coin is one of the five standard coins minted in the United States, the resulting index is then used to select the corresponding element from the array `coinNames`, which gives the name of that coin. The two arrays are related by the fact that the values in corresponding index positions refer to the same coin, as illustrated by the following diagram:

Arrays that use corresponding index positions to store related data values are called **parallel arrays.**

A more sophisticated example of searching

As a prelude to a discussion of different algorithms for searching, this section introduces a more sophisticated searching application that will make it easier to describe the issues that arise. Suppose that you wanted to represent the following mileage table[1] in a program:

	Atlanta	Boston	Chicago	Denver	Detroit	Houston	Los Angeles	Miami	New York	Philadelphia	San Francisco	Seattle
Atlanta		1108	708	1430	732	791	2191	663	854	748	2483	2625
Boston	1108		994	1998	799	1830	3017	1520	222	315	3128	3016
Chicago	708	994		1021	279	1091	2048	1397	809	785	2173	2052
Denver	1430	1998	1021		1283	1034	1031	2107	1794	1739	1255	1341
Detroit	732	799	279	1283		1276	2288	1385	649	609	2399	2327
Houston	791	1830	1091	1034	1276		1541	1190	1610	1511	1911	2369
Los Angeles	2191	3017	2048	1031	2288	1541		2716	2794	2703	387	1134
Miami	663	1520	1397	2107	1385	1190	2716		1334	1230	3093	3303
New York	854	222	809	1794	649	1610	2794	1334		101	2930	2841
Philadelphia	748	315	785	1739	609	1511	2703	1230	101		2902	2816
San Francisco	2483	3128	2173	1255	2399	1911	387	3093	2930	2902		810
Seattle	2625	3016	2052	1341	2327	2369	1134	3303	2841	2816	810	

[1] Data source: *Rand McNally Road Atlas 1994,* New York: Rand McNally.

The individual entries in the table itself form a two-dimensional array with 12 rows and 12 columns. Each individual entry in the matrix is an integer that indicates the number of miles between the cities corresponding to that row and column. The following declaration introduces a global variable called `mileageTable` and uses static initialization to fill it with the data shown in the mileage chart:

```
#define NCities 12

static int mileageTable[NCities][NCities] = {
    {    0,1108, 708,1430, 732, 791,2191, 663, 854, 748,2483,2625},
    {1108,    0, 994,1998, 799,1830,3017,1520, 222, 315,3128,3016},
    { 708, 994,    0,1021, 279,1091,2048,1397, 809, 785,2173,2052},
    {1430,1998,1021,    0,1283,1034,1031,2107,1794,1739,1255,1341},
    { 732, 799, 279,1283,    0,1276,2288,1385, 649, 609,2399,2327},
    { 791,1830,1091,1034,1276,    0,1541,1190,1610,1511,1911,2369},
    {2191,3017,2048,1031,2288,1541,    0,2716,2794,2703, 387,1134},
    { 663,1520,1397,2107,1385,1190,2716,    0,1334,1230,3093,3303},
    { 854, 222, 809,1794, 649,1610,2794,1334,    0, 101,2930,2841},
    { 748, 315, 785,1739, 609,1511,2703,1230, 101,    0,2902,2816},
    {2483,3128,2173,1255,2399,1911, 387,3093,2930,2902,    0, 810},
    {2625,3016,2052,1341,2327,2369,1134,3303,2841,2816, 810,    0},
};
```

Because the city names in this chart are the same for both the rows and columns, they can be stored in a single array called `cityTable`, which you can declare and initialize as follows:

```
static string cityTable[NCities] = {
    "Atlanta",
    "Boston",
    "Chicago",
    "Denver",
    "Detroit",
    "Houston",
    "Los Angeles",
    "Miami",
    "New York",
    "Philadelphia",
    "San Francisco",
    "Seattle",
};
```

Now that you have the data, the next question to consider is how to write a program that reads in the names of two cities and displays the distance between them, as illustrated by the following sample run:

```
This program looks up intercity mileage.
Enter name of city #1: San Francisco⏎
Enter name of city #2: Boston⏎
Distance between San Francisco and Boston: 3128 miles.
```

All your program has to do is execute the following steps:

1. Read in the names of the two cities as strings.
2. Find the index positions at which the city names occur in the `cityTable` array.
3. Use the index positions to select the result from `mileageTable`.

Assuming that you can implement a function `FindStringInArray` that searches through an array of strings, the rest of the program is straightforward:

```
main()
{
    int city1, city2;

    printf("This program looks up intercity mileage.\n");
    city1 = GetCity("Enter name of city #1: ");
    city2 = GetCity("Enter name of city #2: ");
    printf("Distance between %s", cityTable[city1]);
    printf(" and %s:", cityTable[city2]);
    printf(" %d miles.\n", mileageTable[city1][city2]);
}

static int GetCity(string prompt)
{
    string cityName;
    int index;

    while (TRUE) {
        printf("%s", prompt);
        cityName = GetLine();
        index = FindStringInArray(cityName, cityTable, NCities);
        if (index >= 0) break;
        printf("Unknown city name -- try again.\n");
    }
    return (index);
}
```

Linear search

The only piece missing from the program is the code for `FindStringInArray`. If you follow the logic used to implement `FindIntegerInArray`, you only need to change the argument types and use `StringEqual` to compare the string values within the loop. The resulting code, with its comments, appears in Figure 12-2.

The algorithm used in `FindStringInArray` (and in the earlier `FindIntegerInArray` function as well) is called the **linear search algorithm.** Using this algorithm, the search starts at the beginning of the array and goes straight down the line of elements until it finds a match or reaches the end of the array.

FIGURE 12-2 FindStringInArray

```
/*
 * Function: FindStringInArray
 * Usage: index = FindStringInArray(key, array, n);
 * --------------------------------------------------
 * This function returns the index of the first element in the
 * specified array of strings that matches the value key.  If
 * key does not appear in the first n elements of the array,
 * FindStringInArray returns -1.
 */

static int FindStringInArray(string key, string array[], int n)
{
    int i;

    for (i = 0; i < n; i++) {
        if (StringEqual(key, array[i])) return (i);
    }
    return (-1);
}
```

To search an array of 12 city names, looking at every element takes very little time on a modern computer system. But what if the array instead had thousands or even millions of elements? At some point, if the array became large enough, you would begin to notice a delay as the computer searched through every value. But is searching every value really necessary? It's worth stopping to think for a moment about this question.

Suppose that someone asked *you* to find the distance between San Francisco and Boston in the mileage table. To find the entry for San Francisco, would you start at the top of the page and work your way down? Probably not. Because the list of cities is in alphabetic order, you know that San Francisco must come somewhere near the end of the list and that Boston is somewhere near the top. The odds are good that your eyes would find these values very quickly without ever looking at most of the names in the list.

Binary search

To take advantage of the fact that the `cityTable` array is already in alphabetic order, you need to use a different algorithm. To illustrate the process as concretely as possible, let's suppose that you are looking for San Francisco in an array with the following values:

```
          cityTable
```

0	Atlanta
1	Boston
2	Chicago
3	Denver
4	Detroit
5	Houston
6	Los Angeles
7	Miami
8	New York
9	Philadelphia
10	San Francisco
11	Seattle

Instead of starting at the top of the array as in linear search, what happens if you start by picking an element somewhere near the center? The index of the center element can be computed by averaging the endpoints of the index range and is therefore

$$\frac{0+11}{2}$$

When evaluated using integer arithmetic, this expression has the value 5.

The city name stored in `cityArray[5]` is Houston. Given that you're looking for San Francisco, what do you know at this point? You haven't found San Francisco yet, so you have to keep looking. On the other hand, you know that San Francisco must come after Houston because the array is in alphabetic order. Thus, you can immediately eliminate all the city names in index positions 0 through 5, which leaves you in the following position:

cityTable

0	~~Atlanta~~
1	~~Boston~~
2	~~Chicago~~
3	~~Denver~~
4	~~Detroit~~
5	~~Houston~~
6	Los Angeles
7	Miami
8	New York
9	Philadelphia
10	San Francisco
11	Seattle

In one step, you've managed to cross out half the possibilities. The really good news, however, is that you can now do the same thing all over again. You know that San Francisco—if it exists in the list at all—must lie between positions 6 and 11 of cityTable. The center of that range can therefore be computed by evaluating

$$\frac{6+11}{2}$$

using integer arithmetic, which produces the value 8. San Francisco comes later in the alphabet than New York does, so you can now cross off three more positions.

cityTable

0	~~Atlanta~~
1	~~Boston~~
2	~~Chicago~~
3	~~Denver~~
4	~~Detroit~~
5	~~Houston~~
6	~~Los Angeles~~
7	~~Miami~~
8	~~New York~~
9	Philadelphia
10	San Francisco
11	Seattle

When you look at the center of the remaining range, you find San Francisco at index position 11, thereby completing the entire search operation in only three steps.

This algorithm—looking at the center element in a sorted array and then determining which half to search on that basis—is called **binary search.** To implement this algorithm, all you need to do is keep track of two indices that mark the endpoints of the index range within which the search is limited. In the function, these indices are stored in the variables `lh` and `rh`, which represent the left-hand (lower) index and right-hand (upper) index, respectively. Initially, these index bounds cover the entire array, but move closer together as possibilities are eliminated. If the index values ever cross, the key value does not exist in the array.

The code for the function `FindStringInSortedArray`, which uses the binary search algorithm, appears in Figure 12-3.

Relative efficiency of the search algorithms

The discussion in the previous section suggests that the binary search algorithm is more efficient that the linear search algorithm. Even so, it is hard to appreciate just how much better binary search is without being able to compare the performance of the two algorithms using some quantitative measure. For searching, a convenient measure that provides a good indication of algorithmic performance is the number of times `StringEqual` or `StringCompare` is called to compare the key against some element in the array.

Suppose that you execute the linear search algorithm on an array containing N elements. How many times will the function call `StringEqual`? The answer depends of course on where the key value shows up in the list. In the worst case—which occurs when the key is in the last position or does not appear at all—`FindStringInArray` will call `StringEqual` N times, once for each element in the array.

What about the binary search algorithm that was used in the implementation of `FindStringInSortedArray`? After the first call to `StringCompare`, the algorithm can immediately eliminate half of the array elements, leaving only $N/2$ elements to search. After the second call, it can rule out half of those elements, leaving $N/4$ elements. Each time, the number of possibilities is halved. Eventually, after you divide an integer N in half enough times, you will eventually end up with 1, at which point there is only a single comparison left to be made. The number of steps required to reach this point is the number of times you can divide N by 2 before you get 1, which is represented by k in the following formula:

$$\underbrace{N/2/2/\ldots/2/2}_{k \text{ times}} = 1$$

Multiplying by all those 2s gives the equivalent equation

$$N = 2^k$$

If you remember logarithms from high-school algebra, you can express the value of k as

$$k = \log_2 N$$

FIGURE 12-3 FindStringInSortedArray

```
/*
 * Function: FindStringInSortedArray
 * Usage: index = FindStringInSortedArray(key, array, n);
 * --------------------------------------------------------
 * This function returns the index of an element that matches key
 * in the specified array of strings, which must be sorted in
 * lexicographic order.  If key appears more than once in the
 * array, the function can return any index at which it appears.
 * If key does not appear at all in the first n elements
 * of the array, FindStringInSortedArray returns -1.
 *
 * This implementation uses the "binary search" algorithm.  At
 * each stage, the function computes the midpoint of the remaining
 * range and compares the element at that index position to the
 * key.  If there is a match, the function returns the index.
 * If the key is less than the string at that index position, the
 * function searches in the first half of the array; if the key is
 * larger, the function searches in the second half of the array.
 */

int FindStringInSortedArray(string key,
                            string array[],
                            int n)
{
    int lh, rh, mid, cmp;

    lh = 0;
    rh = n - 1;
    while (lh <= rh) {
        mid = (lh + rh) / 2;
        cmp = StringCompare(key, array[mid]);
        if (cmp == 0) return (mid);
        if (cmp < 0) {
            rh = mid - 1;
        } else {
            lh = mid + 1;
        }
    }
    return (-1);
}
```

Thus, to search an array of N elements requires N comparisons if you use linear search and $\log_2 N$ comparisons if you use binary search.

Expressing the relative efficiency of these algorithms in mathematical form is useful as a means of making quantitative predictions about efficiency. For most people, however, such formulas do not convey a real sense of how these algorithms compare. For that, you need to look at some numbers. The following table shows the closest integer to $\log_2 N$ for various values of N.

N	$\log_2 N$
10	3
100	7
1000	10
1,000,000	20
1,000,000,000	30

Reflecting on what the values in this table mean, you can see that, for small arrays, both strategies work reasonably well. On the other hand, if you have an array with 1,000,000,000 elements, linear search requires 1,000,000,000 comparisons to search that array in the worst case, whereas the binary search algorithm gets the job done using at most 30 comparisons. Clearly, this reduction in the number of required comparisons represents an overwhelming increase in algorithmic efficiency.

The only problem is that the binary search algorithm requires that the array elements be listed in sorted order. If they are not, you may have to resort to linear searching. Alternatively, you can ensure that the array elements are in the correct order by sorting the array yourself. Sorting an array is a slightly more challenging problem than searching one and is the subject of the remainder of this chapter.

12.2 Sorting

In most commercial applications, computers are used for extremely simple operations such as adding a sequence of numbers or calculating an average—precisely the sort of problem you learned to solve in the earlier chapters. However, several important operations required for commercial programming are more sophisticated. Of these, the most important is **sorting,** the process of arranging a list of values (usually represented as an array) into some well-defined order. For example, you might rank a list of numbers from lowest to highest based on their numeric value. Alternatively, you might choose to alphabetize a list of names. These two operations turn out to be quite similar. Despite differences in detail (one uses numbers and the other uses strings), the problem to be solved is precisely the same: given a list and a mechanism for comparing two elements in that list, how can you rearrange the elements of the list so that the elements are properly ordered?

Sorting an integer array

Let's consider, for example, the problem of sorting an array of integers. Suppose that you have been presented with an array of integers in some random order, such as the following:

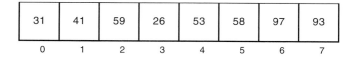

What you need to do at this point is to define a new function, which you could call SortIntegerArray, that would rearrange the elements of this array so that they run from lowest to highest, as follows:

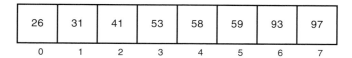

Because SortIntegerArray should be as general as possible, it should take as parameters both the name of the array and the effective size. Its prototype is therefore

```
void SortIntegerArray(int array[], int n);
```

which is similar in structure to the ReverseIntegerArray function introduced in Chapter 11. In fact, this function is general enough that it makes sense to export it through an interface so that other modules can use it as a library. Such an interface, called sort.h, is shown in Figure 12-4.

Writing the corresponding sort.c implementation, however, is trickier than it might seem, particularly if you are interested in finding an efficient strategy for sorting the data. As is the case with many problems in computer science, there are many different algorithms you can use. In an advanced computer science course, you might well spend several weeks studying various different algorithms for sorting, each of which has particular advantages or disadvantages. At this point in your study of computer science, however, it is best to begin with one algorithm for sorting that you can understand in detail.

The selection sort algorithm

Of the many possible sorting algorithms, one of the easiest to explain is the **selection sort** algorithm. When you apply the selection sort algorithm, you put the array into its final order one element at a time. In the first step, you find the smallest element in the entire list and put it where it belongs—at the beginning. In the second step, you find the smallest remaining element and put it in the second position. If you continue this process for the entire array, the final result is in sorted order.

To get a sense of the selection sort approach, watch what happens if you start with the following array of numbers:

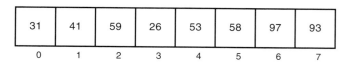

FIGURE 12-4 sort.h

```
/*
 * File: sort.h
 * ------------
 * This file provides an interface to a simple procedure
 * for sorting an integer array into increasing order.
 */

#ifndef _sort_h
#define _sort_h

/*
 * Function: SortIntegerArray
 * Usage: SortIntegerArray(array, n);
 * ----------------------------------
 * This function sorts the first n elements in array into
 * increasing numerical order.  In order to use this procedure,
 * you must declare the array in the calling program and pass
 * the effective number of elements as the parameter n.
 * In most cases, the array will have a larger allocated
 * size.
 */

void SortIntegerArray(int array[], int n);

#endif
```

Because the smallest element is the value 26 in position 3, you move this element into position 0. As with the reverse.c program shown in Figure 11-3, you don't want to lose track of the value that was originally in position 0, so the easiest thing to do is exchange the values in positions 0 and 3. Doing so leaves the array in the following state:

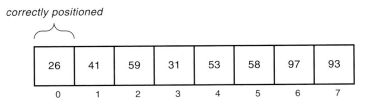

correctly positioned

After the exchange, position 0 is correctly filled with the smallest value.

From this point, you can proceed with the rest of the list. The next step is to use the same strategy to correctly fill the second position in the array. The smallest value (except for the value 26 already placed correctly) is the 31, which is now in position 3. If you exchange this value with the one at index position 1, you reach the following state, with the correct values in the first two elements:

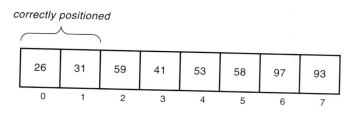

On the next cycle, you switch the next smallest value (which turns out to be 41) into position 2:

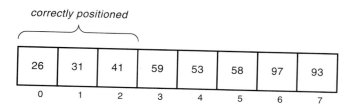

If you continue on in this way, you can correctly fill up index positions 3, 4, and so on until the array is completely sorted.

To keep track of which element you are trying to fill at each step in the algorithm, you can imagine that you use your left hand to point to each of the index positions in turn. For each left-hand position, you then use your right hand to identify the smallest element remaining in the rest of the array. Once you find it, you can just take the values to which your hands point and exchange them. In the implementation, your left and right hands are replaced by variables—`lh` and `rh`—that hold the index number of the appropriate element in the array.

You can turn this intuitive outline into pseudocode as follows:

```
for (each index position lh in the array) {
       Let rh be the index position of the smallest value between lh and the end of the
    list
       Swap the elements at index positions lh and rh
    }
```

Replacing the pseudocode with the correct C statements is straightforward, mostly because two of the operations are familiar: the `for` loop control line is a standard idiom, and you can accomplish the swap operation at the end of the loop by calling the `SwapIntegerElements` function defined as part of the `reverse.c` program in Figure 11-3. The one remaining step is the one that finds the smallest value. Following the discipline of stepwise refinement, you can define a new function to perform this operation and complete the coding of the `SortIntegerArray` procedure as follows:

```
void SortIntegerArray(int array[], int n)
{
    int lh, rh;

    for (lh = 0; lh < n; lh++) {
        rh = FindSmallestInteger(array, lh, n-1);
        SwapIntegerElements(array, lh, rh);
    }
}
```

The `FindSmallestInteger` function takes three arguments: the array and two index numbers indicating the range within the array in which to find the smallest value. The function returns the index—not the value—of the smallest element of the array between the specified index positions. Thus, the prototype for `FindSmallestInteger` looks like this:

```
int FindSmallestInteger(int array[], int low, int high);
```

To implement `FindSmallestInteger`, the simplest approach is to go through the list, keeping track at each loop cycle of the index of smallest value so far. When you reach the end of the list, the smallest value so far will be the smallest value in the list as a whole. This suggests the following code, in which the variable `spos` keeps track of the index position of the smallest value so far:

```
int FindSmallestInteger(int array[], int low, int high)
{
    int i, spos;

    spos = low;
    for (i = low; i <= high; i++) {
        if (array[i] < array[spos]) spos = i;
    }
    return (spos);
}
```

At the beginning of the scan, the first value you consider is automatically the smallest value so far. Thus, you can initialize `spos` to the starting index position, which is given by the parameter `low`. As you look at each position in turn, you have to see if the current value is smaller than your previous candidate for the smallest value. If it is, the old value can no longer be the smallest in the entire list, and you need to correct the value of `spos` to indicate the new position, which will retain its value until you find an even smaller value.

The function `SwapIntegerElements` is precisely the same function as in the `ReverseIntegerArray` implementation from Chapter 11, and there is no reason to rewrite it. Whenever you write a function that implements some generally useful operation, it is wise to keep that function around so that it is available for future use. Successful programmers always try to reuse existing code as much as possible because doing so saves the trouble of writing and debugging those parts of the program from scratch.

Copying the code for `SwapIntegerElements` completes the code for the entire selection sort algorithm. The complete code for the `sort.c` implementation appears in Figure 12-5.

Evaluating the efficiency of selection sort

The selection sort algorithm has several positive qualities. For one thing, it is relatively easy to understand. For another, it gets the job done. There are, however, sorting algorithms that are far more efficient. Unfortunately, the most efficient ones require techniques beyond your current level of programming knowledge. For this reason, the text defers discussion of more efficient sorting algorithms until Chapter 17.

Even though you cannot yet substantially improve the efficiency of selection sort, you are nonetheless in a position to consider how efficient it is. One interesting question is how long it takes to execute selection sort on a given set of input data. There are two ways you can approach this question.

1. You can run the program and measure how long it takes. Because programs run very quickly on modern computers and often finish their work in a fraction of a second, you might not be able to measure the elapsed time with a stopwatch, but you can accomplish the same result by using the computer's internal clock.
2. You can think more generally about the operation of the program and try to develop a qualitative sense of how it behaves.

Measuring the running time of a program

To determine how long it takes to run a program, the most common approach is to use the system libraries to keep track of the amount of computing time required. The ANSI interface `time.h` exports a procedure called `clock` that returns the amount of time the processing unit of the computer has used in executing the program. The result type of the `clock` function is a machine-dependent clock unit, but you can convert those clock units into seconds using the following expression:

```
(double) clock() / CLOCKS_PER_SEC
```

If you record the starting and finishing times in the variables `start` and `finish`, you can use the following code to compute the time required to perform a calculation:

```
double start, finish, elapsed;

start = (double) clock() / CLOCKS_PER_SEC;
. . . Perform some calculation . . .
finish = (double) clock() / CLOCKS_PER_SEC;
elapsed = finish - start
```

You can apply this technique to calculate the running time for the selection sort algorithm implemented in Figure 12-5. The time required to call `SortIntegerArray` on arrays of different sizes is shown in Table 12-1. In the table, *N* indicates the number of array elements and the *running time* column

FIGURE 12-5   sort.c

```
/*
 * File: sort.c
 * ------------
 * This file implements the sort.h interface using the selection
 * sort algorithm.
 */

#include <stdio.h>
#include "genlib.h"
#include "sort.h"

/* Private function prototypes */

static int FindSmallestInteger(int array[], int low, int high);
static void SwapIntegerElements(int array[], int p1, int p2);

/*
 * Function: SortIntegerArray
 * --------------------------
 * This implementation uses an algorithm called selection sort,
 * which can be described in English as follows.  With your left
 * hand, point at each element in the array in turn, starting at
 * index 0.  At each step in the cycle:
 *
 * (1)  Find the smallest element in the range between your left
 *        hand and the end of the array, and point at that element
 *        with your right hand.
 *
 * (2)  Move that element into its correct index position by
 *        switching the elements indicated by your left and right
 *        hands.
 */

void SortIntegerArray(int array[], int n)
{
    int lh, rh;

    for (lh = 0; lh < n; lh++) {
        rh = FindSmallestInteger(array, lh, n-1);
        SwapIntegerElements(array, lh, rh);
    }
}
```

```
/*
 * Function: FindSmallestInteger
 * Usage: index = FindSmallestInteger(array, low, high);
 * ------------------------------------------------------
 * This function returns the index of the smallest value in the
 * specified array of integers, searching only between the index
 * positions low and high, inclusive.  It operates by keeping track
 * of the index of the smallest so far in the variable spos.  If the
 * index range is empty, the function returns low.
 */

static int FindSmallestInteger(int array[], int low, int high)
{
    int i, spos;

    spos = low;
    for (i = low; i <= high; i++) {
        if (array[i] < array[spos]) spos = i;
    }
    return (spos);
}


/*
 * Function: SwapIntegerElements
 * Usage: SwapIntegerElements(array, p1, p2);
 * ------------------------------------------
 * This function swaps the elements in array at index
 * positions p1 and p2.
 */

static void SwapIntegerElements(int array[], int p1, int p2)
{
    int tmp;

    tmp = array[p1];
    array[p1] = array[p2];
    array[p2] = tmp;
}
```

shows the average time in milliseconds (thousandths of a second) required to sort an array of that size using selection sort.

The table reveals some highly interesting results. For small values of *N*, selection sort runs reasonably quickly. As *N* gets larger, however, the selection sorting algorithm slows down precipitously. If the array contains 30 values, for example, SortIntegerArray can sort the array in a thousandth of a second. By the time you reach 800 items, selection sort takes more than half a second. Commercial applications often require sorting 10,000 or 100,000 values or more. With arrays on that scale, selection sort becomes prohibitively slow.

N	Running time
10	0.13
20	0.33
30	1.00
40	1.47
50	2.40
100	9.67
200	37.33
400	146.67
800	596.67

TABLE 12-1

Running times for the selection sort algorithm in milliseconds

Analyzing the selection sort algorithm

To understand why these timing numbers come out as they do, it is important to think about how the algorithm works. Consider the timing data for selection sort in Table 12-1. When N is 50, the algorithm requires 2.4 milliseconds to run. When N doubles to 100, however, the algorithm requires 9.67 milliseconds, almost four times as long. The rest of the table shows the same progression. Whenever you double the number of data items, the time required goes up by a factor of four. Algorithms of this sort are said to be **quadratic,** because their running time grows as the square of the size of the input.

The fact that selection sort is a quadratic algorithm is not surprising if you think about how it works. In sorting a list of eight numbers, the selection sort implementation of `SortIntegerArray` executes the outer `for` loop eight times. The first cycle finds the smallest value out of a group of eight numbers, the next cycle finds the smallest value out of the remaining seven numbers, and so on. The number of operations the program executes is proportional to the number of values it must check, which in this specific case is

$$8 + 7 + 6 + 5 + 4 + 3 + 2 + 1$$

More generally, given N elements, the time required to execute the selection sort algorithm is proportional to the following sum:

$$N + N - 1 + N - 2 + \ldots + 3 + 2 + 1$$

The sum of the first N integers can be expressed more compactly by applying the following mathematical formula

$$N + N - 1 + N - 2 + \ldots + 3 + 2 + 1 = \frac{N^2 + N}{2}$$

The quadratic behavior comes from the appearance of the N^2 term.

The process of applying mathematical techniques to predict algorithmic efficiency is called **analysis of algorithms,** which is discussed further in Chapter 17.

If you go on in computer science, you will learn how to analyze the performance of algorithms in much more detail. This knowledge will prove to be a powerful tool for evaluating which algorithm is best suited for a particular application.

SUMMARY

With this chapter, you have had the opportunity to learn about two of the most important operations on arrays—*searching* and *sorting*—each of which is an interesting algorithmic problem in its own right. The important points covered in this chapter include:

- The *linear search algorithm* operates by looking at each element of an array in sequential order until the desired element is found. Linear search is a reasonable strategy for small arrays but becomes inefficient as the size of the array increases.
- The *binary search algorithm* is much more efficient than linear search but requires that the elements of the array be in sorted order.
- Sorting algorithms vary considerably in their efficiency. For arrays containing a small number of elements, simple algorithms such as *selection sort* are perfectly adequate. For larger arrays, however, such algorithms cease to be cost-effective.

REVIEW QUESTIONS

1. Define the terms *searching* and *sorting*.

2. What changes would you have to make to the `FindIntegerInArray` function to change it to a `FindRealInArray` function that found a matching value in an array of floating-point numbers?

3. What are parallel arrays?

4. Describe the linear search and binary search algorithms in simple English.

5. True or false: If the number of data items is large enough, the binary search algorithm can be millions of times faster than the linear search algorithm.

6. What condition must be true before the binary search algorithm can be applied?

7. Describe the steps that are involved in the selection sort algorithm.

8. The `for` loop control line in the selection sort implementation of `SortIntegerArray` was written as

```
for (i = 0; i < n; i++)
```

Would the function still work if you changed this line to

```
for (i = 0; i < n - 1; i++)
```

9. What expression can you use to determine how many seconds of processor time have been consumed by your program?

10. What does it mean to say that an algorithm is quadratic?

PROGRAMMING EXERCISES

1. A **resistor** is a common component in electronic circuitry that restricts the flow of electrical current. The extent to which a resistor opposes the current flow is called its **resistance,** which is traditionally measured in ohms (Ω). As the resistance increases, current flows less freely.

    The resistance is usually indicated on the resistor itself using a color code. The resistor is a small ceramic cylinder with a wire extending from each end. Three colored bands encircle the body of the cylinder, as shown in this diagram:

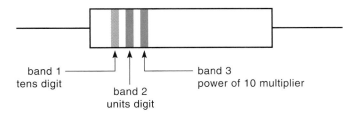

The colors of the bands correspond to digits as follows:

0	black	5	green
1	brown	6	blue
2	red	7	violet
3	orange	8	gray
4	yellow	9	white

The first two bands indicate the first two digits of the resistance; the third band indicates a power of ten by which the first two digits are multiplied. For example, the color-code sequence yellow-violet-orange (4-7-3) corresponds to

$$47 \times 10^3$$

or 47,000Ω.

Write a program that reads in the colors of the three bands on a resistor and writes out the corresponding resistance, as illustrated by the following sample run:

```
This program interprets the resistor color code.
Color of first band: Yellow↵
Color of second band: Violet↵
Color of third band: Orange↵
Resistance = 47000 ohms.
```

2. Write a program `guessnum.c` that plays a number-guessing game with its user, who is presumably an elementary-school child. The child thinks of a number and then answers a series of questions from the computer until it correctly guesses the number. The following sample run shows what happens when the child's number is 17:

```
Think of a number between 1 and 100 and I'll
guess it.
Is it 50? no↵
Is it less than 50? yes↵
Is it 25? no↵
Is it less than 25? yes↵
Is it 12? no↵
Is it less than 12? no↵
Is it 18? no↵
Is it less than 18? yes↵
Is it 15? no↵
Is it less than 15? no↵
Is it 16? no↵
Is it less than 16? no↵
Is it 17? yes↵
I guessed the number!
```

3. Write a predicate function `IsSorted(array, n)` that takes an integer array and its effective size as parameters and returns `TRUE` if the array is sorted in nondecreasing order.

4. Extend the `sort.h` and `sort.c` files given in Figures 12-4 and 12-5 so that, in addition to exporting the `SortIntegerArray` function, the interface also exports a function `Alphabetize` that sorts an array of strings into lexicographic order.

5. In Chapter 11, exercises 3 and 4 asked you to write programs to compute two common statistical measures: the mean and the standard deviation. Another common statistical measure is the **median,** the data value that occupies the central element position in a distribution whose values have been sorted from

lowest to highest. If the distribution contains an even number of values and therefore has no central element, the standard convention is to average the two values that fall closest to the midpoint.

Write a function `Median(array, n)` that returns the median of an array of floating-point values. Your implementation may not assume that the array is in sorted order but may change the order of elements as it runs.

6. Besides the mean and the median, the third statistical measure designed to indicate the most representative element of a distribution is the **mode,** the value that occurs most often in the array. For example, in the array

65	84	95	75	82	79	82	72	84	94	86	90	84

the mode is the value 84, because it appears three times. The only other value that appears more than once is 82, which only appears twice.

Write a function `Mode(array, n)` that returns the mode of an array composed of integer values. If there are several values that occur equally often and outnumber any of the other values (such distributions are called **multimodal**), your function may return any of those values as the mode. As in exercise 5, your implementation may not assume that the array is in sorted order but may change the order of elements if doing so makes the solution easier to write.

7. Write a function `RemoveZeroElements(array, n)` that goes through an array of integers and eliminates any elements whose value is 0. Because this operation changes the effective size of the array, `RemoveZeroElements` should return the new effective size as a result. For example, suppose that `scores` contains an array of scores on an optional exam and that `nScores` indicates the effective size of the array, as shown:

scores

65	0	95	0	0	79	82	0	84	94	86	90	0

nScores

13

At this point, the statement

```
nScores = RemoveZeroElements(scores, nScores);
```

should remove the 0 scores, compressing the array into the following configuration:

scores

65	95	79	82	84	94	86	90	?	?	?	?	?

nScores

8

8. Write a function RemoveDuplicates(array, n) that removes all duplicate values from a sorted array of integers, leaving only a single copy of each value. As in exercise 7, RemoveDuplicates should return the effective size of the new array. Suppose, for example, that the array scores contains the following data values:

scores

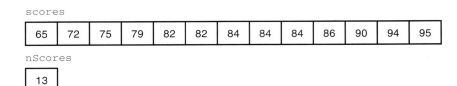

nScores

| 13 |

The statement

```
nScores = RemoveDuplicates(scores, nScores);
```

should then remove the duplicate scores, leaving the following configuration:

scores

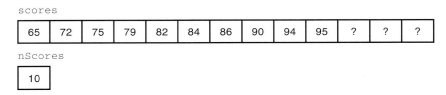

nScores

| 10 |

9. Many algorithmic problems are related to sorting in their solution structure. For example, you can shuffle an array by "sorting" it according to a random key value. One way to do this is to begin with the selection sort algorithm and then replace the step that finds the position of smallest value with one that selects a random position. The result is a shuffling algorithm in which each possible output configuration is equally likely.

   Write a program shuffle.c that displays the integers between 1 and 52 in a randomly sorted order.

10. One of the most famous algorithmic problems taught at the introductory level is the Dutch National Flag problem, first proposed by Edsger Dijkstra. Suppose that you have an array with n elements, each of which is a character—'R', 'W', or 'B'—representing one of the colors in the Dutch flag. Initially, these values might be jumbled in the array, as shown in the following configuration:

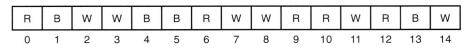

   Your job is to rearrange these characters so that they appear in the same order as they do in the Dutch flag: all the reds, followed by all the whites, followed by all the blues.

Try to infer the algorithm by studying the following sample run of a program to solve this problem, which displays the sequence of the colors each time it interchanges two positions:

```
Initial state:
R B W W B B R W W R R W R B W
Swapping positions 1 and 14
R W W W B B R W W R R W R B B
Swapping positions 4 and 13
R W W W B B R W W R R W R B B
Swapping positions 4 and 12
R W W W R B R W W R R W B B B
Swapping positions 1 and 4
R R W W W B R W W R R W B B B
Swapping positions 5 and 11
R R W W W W R W W R R B B B B
Swapping positions 2 and 6
R R R W W W W W W R R B B B B
Swapping positions 3 and 9
R R R W W W W W W R B B B B
Swapping positions 4 and 10
R R R R W W W W W W B B B B
```

Write a program that implements the algorithm on a randomly constructed initial state.

11. There are several other sorting algorithms besides selection sort that make sense at your level of programming knowledge. Unfortunately, those algorithms do not offer any advantages over selection sort in terms of their algorithm performance. Even so, coding these algorithms gives you more practice using arrays.

For example, you can sort an integer array from lowest to highest by applying the following procedure. Start by going through the array, looking at adjacent pairs of values. If the values forming the pair are correctly ordered, do nothing; if the values are out of order, swap them. In either case, move on to the next pair of values. The pairs overlap as you move through the list so that the second element in one pair becomes the first element of the next pair. Repeat this operation until you make a complete pass in which you do not need to exchange any integers. This algorithm is called **bubble sort,** because the values seem to "bubble up" to their eventual positions.

Reimplement the SortIntegerArray function using the bubble sort algorithm.

12. Another sorting algorithm—**insertion sort**—operates as follows. You go through each element in the array in turn, as with the selection sort algorithm. At each step in the process, however, your goal is not to find the smallest value remaining value and switch it into its correct position, but rather to ensure that the values you've covered so far in the array are correctly ordered with respect

to each other. Although those values may shift as more elements are processed, they form an ordered sequence in and of themselves.

For example, if you consider again the data used in the selection sort discussion, the first cycle of the insertion sort algorithm requires no work because an array of one element is always sorted:

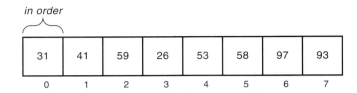

The next two cycles of the main loop also require no rearrangement of the array, because the sequence 31-41-59 forms an ordered subarray.

The first significant operation occurs on the next cycle, when you need to fit 26 into this sequence. To find where 26 should go, you need to move backward through the earlier elements, which you know are in order with respect to each other, looking for the position where 26 belongs. At each step, you need to shift the other elements over one position to make room for the 26, which winds up in position 0. Thus, the configuration after the fourth cycle is

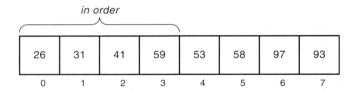

On each subsequent step, you again insert the next element in the array into its proper position in the initial subarray, which is always sorted at the end of each step.

The insertion sort algorithm is particularly efficient if the array is already more or less in the correct order. It therefore makes sense to use insertion sort to restore order to a large array in which only a few elements are out of sequence.

Reimplement the `SortIntegerArray` function using the insertion sort algorithm.

CHAPTER 13

Pointers

Orlando ran her eyes through it and then, using the first finger of her right hand as pointer, read out the following facts as being most germane to the matter.

— Virginia Woolf, *Orlando*, 1928

Objectives

- To appreciate the importance of being able to use addresses as data values.

- To be able to use the pointer operators & and *.

- To be able to use call by reference to share data between a function and its caller.

- To recognize the relationship between pointers and arrays.

- To understand in detail how to use the ++ and -- operators.

- To be able to apply dynamic allocation to reserve new storage as a program runs.

This chapter introduces the concept of a **pointer**—a data item whose value is the address in memory of some other value. In many high-level programming languages, pointers are used sparingly because those languages provide other mechanisms that eliminate much of the need for pointers. In C, which was designed to give programmers as much access as possible to the facilities provided by the hardware itself, the pointer concept is pervasive. Thus, it is impossible to understand C programs without understanding something about how pointers work. Moreover, if you want to become an effective C programmer, you will have to go further and learn how to use pointers effectively in applications.

In C, pointers serve several purposes, of which the following are the most important:

- *Pointers allow you to refer to a large data structure in a compact way.* Data structures in a program can become arbitrarily large. No matter how large they grow, however, the data structures still reside somewhere in the computer's memory and therefore have an address. Pointers allow you to use the address as a shorthand for the complete value. Because a memory address is internally represented as an integer, this strategy offers considerable space savings when the data structures themselves are large. This principle comes up repeatedly in the rest of this text, particularly in Chapters 14 and 16.
- *Pointers facilitate sharing data between different parts of a program.* If you pass the address of some data value from one function to another, both functions have access to the same data. This application of pointers is explained in the section on "Passing parameters by reference" later in this chapter.
- *Pointers make it possible to reserve new memory during program execution.* Up to now, the only memory that you have been able to use in your programs has been the memory assigned to variables that you have declared explicitly. In many applications, it is convenient to acquire new memory as the program runs and to refer to that memory using pointers. This strategy is discussed in the section on "Dynamic allocation" later in this chapter.
- *Pointers can be used to record relationships among data items.* In advanced programming applications, pointers are used extensively to model connections between individual data values. For example, programmers often indicate that one data item follows another in a conceptual sequence by including a pointer to the second item in the internal representation of the first. This topic is considered briefly in Chapter 17, although a complete discussion of this application of pointers lies beyond the scope of this text.

As with most programming concepts, mastering the use of pointers requires that you consider them from both the reductionistic and the holistic perspectives. This chapter begins on the reductionistic level by reviewing the fundamentals of memory addressing, which were introduced in Chapter 11, using that framework as a context for discussing the mechanics of pointers. Thereafter, the chapter proceeds to investigate some of the basic applications of pointers. The examples in this chapter, however, are intended primarily to reinforce your understanding of the underlying details. Because pointers are a substantial topic—too large to cover entirely in one chapter—some of the holistic presentation of pointers is deferred to later chapters, which build on the framework presented here.

 ## 13.1 Using addresses as data values

As you discovered in Chapter 11, simple variables are not the only repository for data in a program. Data can also exist in more complicated data structures, such as arrays. In C, any expression that refers to an internal memory location capable of storing data is called an **lvalue** (pronounced "ell-value"). The *l* at the beginning of *lvalue* comes from the observation that lvalues can appear on the left side of an assignment statement in C. For example, simple variables are lvalues because you can write a statement like

```
x = 1.0;
```

Similarly, selection expressions are lvalues because you can assign them values directly, as in

```
intarray[2] = 17;
```

Many values in C, however, are not lvalues. For example, constants are not lvalues because a constant cannot be changed. Similarly, arithmetic expressions return results that are values but not lvalues because it is illegal to assign a value to the result of an arithmetic expression.

The concept of an lvalue makes it possible to recast the three principles outlined in the summary of Chapter 11 in a more general way:

1. Every lvalue is stored somewhere in memory and therefore has an address.
2. Once it has been declared, the address of an lvalue never changes, even though the contents of the lvalue may change.
3. Depending on the type of data they contain, different lvalues require different amounts of memory.

To pave the way for a discussion of pointers, it is useful to add a fourth principle to this list:

4. The address of an lvalue is itself data that can be manipulated and stored in memory.

This last point may seem rather unexciting at first, but its implications for programming turn out to be profound. As an illustration, consider the declaration

```
int i;
```

This declaration reserves storage somewhere in memory for the integer i. For example, if integers require four bytes on the computer running the program, the variable i might be assigned to locations 1000 through 1003, as indicated by the shaded area in this diagram:[1]

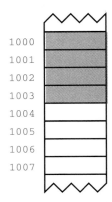

According to the fourth principle, the address 1000 associated with the variable i is a data value in its own right. The value 1000 is just an integer, after all, and can be stored in memory as such. That it happens to represent the address of another value is important to the programming process, but does not affect how the value 1000 is represented internally. It fits into memory just like any other integer. For example, it is possible to store the address of the variable i in the next memory word, which consists of the range of bytes between addresses 1004 and 1007. At this point, you do not yet know how to write C code to store that address, but the result of doing so is illustrated in the following diagram:

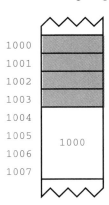

The value 1000 shown in address 1004 can then be used to refer to the value of the variable i stored in the shaded region. To emphasize relationships such as that

---

[1] In Chapter 11, the diagrams assume that integers require two bytes; this chapter assumes that they require four. The change in representation is intended to remind you that the space required to store an integer can vary from one computer to another. Making an assumption about the size of any object limits the extent to which your programs can be made to work on other machines.

between the address in location 1004 and the variable i at location 1000, programmers often draw arrows on their box diagrams of memory, like this:

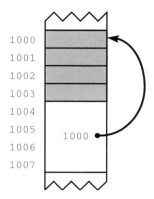

Of course, there are no arrows inside the computer. The word at address 1004 simply contains a sequence of bits that corresponds to the numeric value 1000. That same sequence of bits can be used as an integer or as an address depending on how you have declared that variable in your program. If you have declared the variable as a pointer, you can interpret the value 1000 stored in location 1004 as the address of the variable i in memory and then use that pointer to retrieve or manipulate i's value.

13.2 Pointer manipulation in C

C includes facilities for manipulating pointers, just as it includes facilities for manipulating integers. You can store address values in pointer variables or pass them as parameters to functions, just like any other data type. Before you begin to do so, however, it is important to consider some of the mechanical details that govern the use of pointers in C.

Declaring pointer variables in C

As with all other variables in C, you must declare pointer variables before you use them. To declare a pointer variable, you need to use the declaration syntax shown in the syntax box to the right. For example, the declaration

```
int *p;
```

declares the variable p to be of the conceptual type pointer-to-int. Similarly, the declaration

```
char *cptr;
```

declares the variable `cptr` to be of type pointer-to-`char`. These two types— pointer-to-`int` and pointer-to-`char`—are distinct in C, even though each of them is represented internally as an address. To use the data at that address, the compiler needs to know how to interpret it and therefore requires that the type of the underlying value be specified explicitly. The type of the value to which a pointer points is called the **base type** of that pointer. Thus, the type pointer-to-`int` has `int` as its base type.

It is important to note that the asterisk used to indicate that a variable is a pointer belongs syntactically with the variable name and not with the base type. If you use the same declaration to declare two pointers of the same type, you need to mark each of the variables with an asterisk, as in

```
int *p1, *p2;
```

The declaration

```
int *p1, p2;
```

declares `p1` as a pointer to an integer but declares `p2` as an integer variable.

The fundamental pointer operations

C defines two operators that manipulate pointer values:

    `&`   Address-of
    `*`   Value-pointed-to

The `&` operator takes as its operand an expression that corresponds to some value stored in memory, which is usually a variable or an array reference. The operand is written after the `&` and must be an lvalue. Given a particular lvalue, the `&` operator returns the memory address in which that lvalue is stored.

The `*` operator takes a value of any pointer type and returns the lvalue to which it points. This operation is called **dereferencing** the pointer. The `*` operation produces an lvalue, which means that you can assign a value to a dereferenced pointer.

The easiest way to illustrate these operators is by example. Consider the declarations

```
int x, y;
int *p1, *p2;
```

These declarations allocate memory for four words, two of type `int` and two of type pointer-to-`int`. For concreteness, let's suppose that these values are stored in the machine addresses indicated by the following diagram:

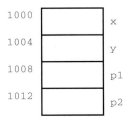

COMMON PITFALLS

New programmers sometimes forget that the `*` used in the declaration of the pointer must appear before each pointer variable. For example, the declaration

```
char *cp, c;
```

declares `cp` to be of type pointer-to-`char` but `c` to be of type `char`.

You can assign values to x and y using assignment statements, just as you always have. For example, executing the assignment statements

```
x = -42;
y = 163;
```

results in the following memory state:

```
1000  ┌─────────┬──┐
      │   -42   │ x│
1004  ├─────────┼──┤
      │   163   │ y│
1008  ├─────────┼──┤
      │         │p1│
1012  ├─────────┼──┤
      │         │p2│
      └─────────┴──┘
```

To initialize the pointer variables p1 and p2, you need to assign values that represent the addresses of some integer objects. In C, the operator that produces addresses is the & operator, which you can use to assign the addresses of x and y to p1 and p2, respectively:

```
p1 = &x;
p2 = &y;
```

These assignments leave memory in the following state:

```
1000  ┌─────────┬──┐
      │   -42   │ x│
1004  ├─────────┼──┤
      │   163   │ y│
1008  ├─────────┼──┤
      │  1000   │p1│
1012  ├─────────┼──┤
      │  1004   │p2│
      └─────────┴──┘
```

Once again, the pointer values in p1 and p2 have the intuitive effect of "pointing" to the variables to which they refer. You can diagram this relationship using arrows, as follows:

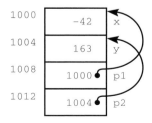

To move from a pointer to the value it points to, you use the * operator. For example, the expression

```
*p1
```

indicates the value in the memory location to which p1 points. Moreover, since p1 is declared as a pointer to an integer, the compiler knows that the expression *p1 must refer to an integer. Thus, given the configuration of memory illustrated in the diagram, *p1 turns out to be another name for the variable x.

Like the simple variable name x, the expression *p1 is an lvalue, and you can assign new values to it. Executing the assignment statement

```
*p1 = 17;
```

changes the value in the variable x because that is where p1 points. After you make this assignment, the memory configuration is

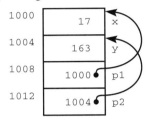

You can see that the value of p1 itself is unaffected by this assignment. It continues to hold the value 1000 and therefore still points to the variable x.

It is also possible to assign new values to the pointer variables themselves. For instance, the statement

```
p1 = p2;
```

instructs the computer to take the value contained in the variable p2 and copy it into the variable p1. The value contained in p2 is the pointer value 1004. If you copy this value into p1, both p1 and p2 point to the variable y, as the following diagram shows:

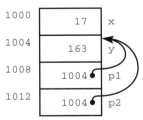

In terms of the operations that occur inside the machine, copying a pointer is exactly the same as copying an integer. The value of the pointer is simply copied unchanged to the destination. From the conceptual perspective of the diagram, the effect of copying a pointer is to replace the destination pointer with a new arrow that points to the same location as the old one. Thus, the effect of the assignment

```
p1 = p2;
```

is to change the arrow leading out of p1 so that it points to the same memory address as the arrow originating at p2.

It is important to be able to distinguish the assignment of a *pointer* from that of a *value*. Pointer assignment, such as

```
p1 = p2;
```

makes `p1` and `p2` point to the same location. Value assignment, which is represented by the statement

```
*p1 = *p2;
```

copies the values from the memory location addressed by `p2` into the location addressed by `p1`.

The special pointer `NULL`

In pointer applications—particularly those that extend beyond the scope of this text—it is useful to be able to store in a pointer variable a special value indicating that the variable does not in fact point to any valid data, at least for the present. C defines a special constant called `NULL` for this purpose.[2] The constant `NULL` can be assigned to any pointer variable and is represented internally as the address value 0.

If a pointer variable has the value `NULL`, it is important not to dereference that variable with the `*` operator. The intent of the `NULL` value is to indicate that the pointer does not point to valid data, so the idea of trying to find the data associated with a `NULL` pointer does not really make sense. Unfortunately, most compilers do not produce programs that explicitly check for this error. If you dereference `NULL`, the usual approach is for the computer to look and see what value is stored in address 0. If you happen to change that value by performing value assignment through a `NULL` pointer, the program can easily crash, giving no clue as to the nature of the problem. The same is true for pointer variables whose values have not yet been initialized.

The uses of the `NULL` pointer will be introduced as they become relevant to a particular application. For now, the important thing to remember is that this constant exists.

COMMON PITFALLS

Be careful not to dereference pointers that are not initialized or whose value is `NULL`. Doing so can result in references to memory locations that are not part of the program, which may in turn cause the program to crash.

▇▇ 13.3 Passing parameters by reference

To get a sense of how pointer variables are used in practice, it is helpful to look at one of the most common applications of pointers in C—the technique of passing pointers to a function to allow that function to manipulate data in its caller. In C, whenever you pass a simple variable from one function to another, the function gets a copy of the calling value. Assigning a new value to the parameter as part of the function changes the local copy but has no effect on the calling argument. For

---

[2] The constant `NULL` is actually defined in the `stdlib.h` header file, which is automatically included whenever a program includes the `stdio.h` header file. Because all programs in this book include `stdio.h`, you can proceed as if `NULL` were a built-in constant in C.

example, if you tried to implement a function that initialized a variable to zero using the following strategy

```
void SetToZero(int var)
{
    var = 0;
}
```

This program is buggy and in fact has no effect.

the function would have no effect whatever. If you called

```
SetToZero(x);
```

the parameter `var` would be initialized to a copy of whatever value was stored in `x`. The assignment statement

```
var = 0;
```

inside the function sets the local copy to 0 but leaves `x` unchanged in the calling program.

One approach to fixing this problem is to pass the function a pointer to a variable instead of the variable itself. Although adopting this strategy changes the structure of the function, making this change is necessary for the function to work at all. The new coding is

```
void SetToZero(int *ip)
{
    *ip = 0;
}
```

To use this function, the caller must supply a pointer to an integer variable. To set `x` to 0, for example, you would need to make the following call:

```
SetToZero(&x);
```

Leaving out the `&` would be an error because `x` does not have the required type: `SetToZero` requires a pointer to an integer and not the integer itself.

For the purpose of illustration, assume that `SetToZero` is called from the main program and that the frame for `main` includes an integer variable named `x`. Before the main program calls `SetToZero`, the frame for `main` looks like this:

Although frame diagrams do not typically include addresses, it is important to realize that the variable `x` lives somewhere in memory. For example, if the variable

is stored in address 1000, the concrete representation within memory is a frame that includes the word at that address, as illustrated in this diagram:

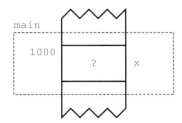

When main calls SetToZero using the statement

```
SetToZero(&x);
```

a new frame is created for the SetToZero function. Its parameter is the variable ip, which is a pointer to an integer. Making the call initializes ip to the value of the calling argument, which is &x—the address of x. Thus, the frame for SetToZero looks like this:

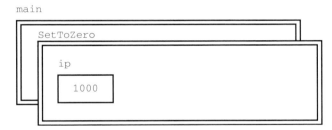

This frame also lives somewhere in memory, so the memory diagram might be[3]

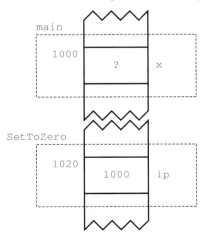

---

[3] There is no way to predict what addresses are actually assigned to these frames, or even the relative orientation of the two frames. On most modern machines, the frame for SetToZero would appear at a lower memory address than the frame for main, but understanding the memory structure does not depend on any such assumption.

The statement

```
*ip = 0;
```

has the effect of setting the value of the integer word addressed by `ip` to 0 as shown:

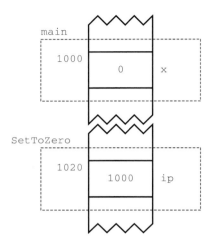

When the `SetToZero` function returns, the change made to address 1000 remains in effect, so that the frame for `main` now looks like this:

The use of pointers as parameters makes it possible for functions to change values in the frame of their caller. In C, you must indicate explicitly your intention to allow such changes by declaring the parameter value as a pointer type and then passing addresses as arguments. In many other languages, this mechanism is part of the language definition and is referred to as **call by reference.** While the C approach is somewhat less convenient and takes more time to learn, it does have some advantages. The most important advantage is that the syntax of the function call itself indicates whether the values of the argument variables can be changed during the execution of the function. For example, without knowing anything at all about the function `Mystery`, you know that the value of a variable x is not changed by the call

```
Mystery(x);
```

If `Mystery` is to change the value of x, the function would have to be redefined to take a pointer parameter, and the call would then appear as

```
    Mystery(&x);
```

This rule makes it easier to predict the effects of a function call.

Designing a `SwapInteger` function

To illustrate how using call by reference affects the design of a program, let's return to the selection sort algorithm presented in Figure 12-5. The `SortIntegerArray` procedure itself is implemented as follows:

```
void SortIntegerArray(int array[], int n)
{
    int lh, rh;

    for (lh = 0; lh < n; lh++) {
        rh = FindSmallestInteger(array, lh, n-1);
        SwapIntegerElements(array, lh, rh);
    }
}
```

On each cycle of the `for` loop, the procedure identifies the index of the smallest value remaining in the list and then exchanges that value with the element at index position `lh`. The last statement in the `for` loop accomplishes the exchange operation by making the following function call:

```
    SwapIntegerElements(array, lh, rh);
```

At first glance, this function call seems poorly designed. What you would like to do at this point is exchange two integers. It seems as if the code would convey the essential idea more clearly if you could make the following call instead:

```
    SwapInteger(array[lh], array[rh]);          This can't work.
```

Unfortunately, as indicated in Chapter 11 when the `SwapIntegerElements` function was introduced, it is impossible to define a function like `SwapInteger` in C because that function would have to change the values of its calling arguments.

You can, however, use call by reference to accomplish the same effect. If you pass the addresses of the arguments to `SwapInteger` rather than their values, it then becomes possible to implement the function like this:

```
static void SwapInteger(int *p1, int *p2)
{
    int tmp;

    tmp = *p1;
    *p1 = *p2;
    *p2 = tmp;
}
```

The `SwapInteger` function takes pointers to two integers and exchanges the values in the memory cells to which those pointers point.

Using call by reference to return multiple results

The most common situation for using call by reference arises when a function needs to return more than one value to the calling program. A single result can easily be returned as the value of the function itself. If you need to return more than one result from a function, the return value is no longer appropriate. The standard approach to solving the problem is to turn that function into a procedure and pass values back and forth through the argument list.

For instance, let's suppose that you want to write a function that converts a time given in minutes into the appropriate number of hours and minutes. For example, 235 minutes is equal to 3 hours and 55 minutes. As a function, this calculation takes in a single value representing the total time in minutes and "returns" two values: the number of hours and the number of leftover minutes, which is always in the range 0 to 59. Because this operation has two results, you might choose to code it as a procedure that uses call by reference. That implementation appears, along with a test program, in Figure 13-1.

In Figure 13-1, the procedure ConvertTimeToHM takes three arguments. The first argument (time) provides input data for the function; the second two (pHours and pMinutes) permit the function to deliver its results to the calling program. In the calling program, these last two arguments must specify the addresses into which the data should be stored, so the call is

```
ConvertTimeToHM(time, &hours, &minutes);
```

FIGURE 13-1 hours.c

```
/*
 * File: hours.c
 * ------------
 * This program converts a time given in minutes into
 * separate values representing hours and minutes.  The
 * program is written as an illustration of C's mechanism
 * for simulating call by reference.
 */

#include <stdio.h>
#include "genlib.h"
#include "simpio.h"

/* Constants */

#define MinutesPerHour 60

/* Function prototypes */

static void ConvertTimeToHM(int time, int *pHours, int *pMinutes);
```

```
/* Test program */

main()
{
    int time, hours, minutes;

    printf("Test program to convert time values\n");
    printf("Enter a time duration in minutes: ");
    time = GetInteger();
    ConvertTimeToHM(time, &hours, &minutes);
    printf("HH:MM format: %d:%02d\n", hours, minutes);
}


/*
 * Function: ConvertTimeToHM
 * Usage: ConvertTimeToHM(time, &hours, &minutes);
 * ---------------------------------------------------
 * This function converts a time value given in minutes into
 * an integral number of hours and the remaining number of minutes.
 * Note that the last two arguments must be passed using their
 * addresses so that the function can correctly set those values.
 */

static void ConvertTimeToHM(int time, int *pHours, int *pMinutes)
{
    *pHours = time / MinutesPerHour;
    *pMinutes = time % MinutesPerHour;
}
```

Inside the implementation, these values are represented as pointers to the actual variables. Thus, in order to compute the number of hours, the appropriate assignment statement is

```
    *pHours = time / MinutesPerHour;
```

You need the * operator to ensure that the result is stored in the variable to which pHours points.

The danger of overusing call by reference

Although the call-by-reference strategy has valuable applications, it is easy to overuse this approach. In most cases—particularly after you have learned how to use records, as described in Chapter 16—you can redesign your programs so that all results are returned as the values of functions. Value-returning functions are usually easier to use than procedures, primarily because function calls can be nested. You can pass the result of one function as a parameter to another, continuing this process to whatever level the application requires. When you use procedures, you must call them one after another as separate statements. Any values that must be communicated from one procedure to the next must be stored in a variable and conveyed through the parameter list.

Consider, for example, how you might rewrite the `hours.c` program in Figure 13-1 to eliminate the need for call by reference. In place of the procedure `ConvertTimeToHM`, you could define two separate functions: an `Hours` function to return the integral number of hours and a `Minutes` function to return the extra minutes. One of the main advantages of this approach is that none of the functions have to use pointers at all. For example, the `Hours` function is simply

```
int Hours(int time)
{
    return (time / MinutesPerHour);
}
```

and the main program can be simplified to

```
main()
{
    int time;

    printf("Test program to convert time values\n");
    printf("Enter a time duration in minutes: ");
    time = GetInteger();
    printf("HH:MM format: %d:%02d\n", Hours(time), Minutes(time));
}
```

Two of the local variables (`hours` and `minutes`) have disappeared from the program because it is possible to use the results of the functions directly without assigning them to variables first.

13.4 Pointers and arrays

So far, the examples in this chapter have limited their use of pointers to those contexts in which the pointer holds the address of a simple variable. Actually, a pointer can refer to any lvalue. In particular, array elements are lvalues and therefore have addresses. For example, as you know from Chapter 11, the array declaration

```
double list[3];
```

reserves three consecutive units of memory, each of which is large enough to hold a value of type `double`. Assuming that a `double` is eight bytes long, the memory diagram for this array would look like the following:

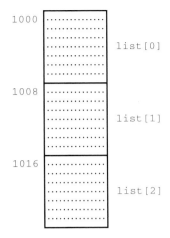

Each of the three elements in the array has an address, which can be derived using the & operator. For example, the expression

    &list[1]

has the pointer value 1008 because the element list[1] is stored at that address. Moreover, the index value need not be constant. The selection expression

    list[i]

is an lvalue, and it is therefore legal to write

    &list[i]

which indicates the address of the ith element in list.

Because the address of the ith element in list depends on the value of the variable i, the C compiler cannot compute this address when compiling the program. To determine the address, the compiler generates instructions that take the base address of the array and add the appropriate offset, which is computed by multiplying the value of i by the size of each array element in bytes. Thus, the numeric calculation necessary to find the address of list[i] is given by the formula

$$1000 + i \times 8$$

If i is 2, for example, the result of the address calculation is 1016, which matches the address shown in the diagram for list[2]. Because the process of calculating the address of an array element is entirely automatic, you don't have to worry about the details when writing your programs.

Pointer arithmetic

When the operators + and – were introduced in Chapter 2, you probably didn't give them a great deal of thought. After all, you have been using these operators since elementary school. When the operands to + and – are numbers, the result is determined by simple arithmetic. In C, you can also apply these operators to pointers. The results are similar to the familiar arithmetic operations in certain respects but different in others. The process of applying addition and subtraction to pointer values is called **pointer arithmetic.**

The fundamental insight necessary to understand how pointer arithmetic works is encapsulated in the following rule.

POINTER ARITHMETIC RULE

If `p` is a pointer to the initial element in an array `arr`, and `k` is an integer, the following identity always holds:

`p + k`   *is defined to be*   `&arr[k]`

In other words, if you add an integer `k` to a pointer value, the result is the address of the array element at index `k` for an array beginning at the original pointer address.

To illustrate the Pointer Arithmetic Rule, let's suppose that a function contains these variable declarations:

```
double list[3];
double *p;
```

Each of these variables is given space in the frame for this function. For the array variable `list`, the compiler allocates space for the three elements in the array, each of which is large enough to hold a `double`. For `p`, the compiler allocates enough space for a pointer, which will be used to hold the address of some lvalue of type `double`. If the frame begins at location 1000, the memory allocation looks like this:

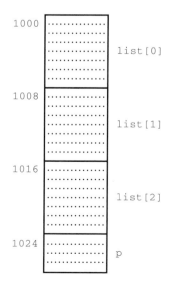

Since no values have been assigned to any of these variables, you have no way of determining their initial contents. However, you can assign values to them. For

example, you can use the following assignment statements to store arbitrary values
in each of the array elements:

```
list[0] = 1.0;
list[1] = 1.1;
list[2] = 1.2;
```

and initialize the pointer variable p to the beginning of the array by executing the
assignment statement

```
p = &list[0];
```

After these assignments, the memory cells hold the following values:

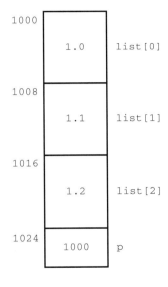

In this diagram, p now points to the initial address in the array `list`. If you add
an integer k to the pointer p, the result is the address corresponding to the array
element at index position k. For example, if a program contained the expression

```
p + 2
```

the result of evaluating this expression would be a new pointer value that references `list[2]`. Thus, in the preceding diagram, in which p points to address 1000,
p + 2 points to the address of the element that appears two elements later in the
array, which is at address 1016. It's important to note that pointer addition is not
equivalent to traditional addition because the arithmetic must take into account the
size of the base type. In this example, for each unit that is added to a pointer value,
the internal numeric value must be increased by eight to take account of the fact
that each `double` requires eight bytes.

The C compiler interprets subtraction of an integer from a pointer in a similar
way. The expression

```
p - k
```

in which p is a pointer and k is an integer, computes the address of an array element located k elements before the address currently indicated by p. Thus, if you had set p to the address of list[1] using

```
p = &list[1];
```

the addresses corresponding to p - 1 and p + 1 would be the addresses of list[0] and list[2], respectively.

From your perspective as a programmer, it is important to realize that pointer arithmetic is defined so that the size of the base type is automatically taken into account. Given any pointer p and integer k, the expression

```
p + k
```

always means the pointer k elements farther along in the array past the current setting of p, no matter how much memory the elements require. The size is only relevant for understanding how the computer performs this calculation internally.

The arithmetic operations *, /, and % make no sense for pointers and cannot be used with pointer operands. Moreover, the uses of + and - are limited. In C, you can add or subtract an integer offset from a pointer, but you cannot, for example, add two pointers together. The only other arithmetic operation defined for pointers is subtracting one pointer from another. The expression

```
p1 - p2
```

where both p1 and p2 are pointers, is defined to return the number of array elements between the current values of p2 and p1. For example, if p1 points at list[2] and p2 points at list[0], as indicated in the following diagram:

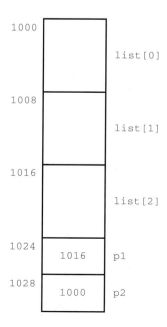

the expression

```
p1 - p2
```

has the value 2 since there are two elements between the current pointer values. Another way to think about this definition is to notice that pointer subtraction is defined such that the value assigned to the integer variable k by the assignment

```
k = p1 - p2;
```

is precisely the value necessary to make the following relationship hold:

```
p1 == p2 + k
```

New capabilities of the ++ and -- operators

Before delving further into the mysteries of pointers, it makes sense to take a new look at the increment and decrement operators, ++ and --, which were introduced in Chapter 3. Up to now, the programs in this text have executed these operators only for the effect on their operands—they either add or subtract 1 from the lvalue to which they are applied.

As it happens, these operators are much more complex than the previous examples would suggest. First of all, each of these operators can be written in either of two ways. The operator can come after the operand to which it applies, as in the familiar

```
x++
```

or before the operand, as in

```
++x
```

The first form, in which the operator follows the operand, is called the **postfix** form, the second, the **prefix** form.

If all you do is execute the ++ operator in isolation—as you do if it acts as a separate statement or as the increment operator in a for loop—the prefix and postfix operators have precisely the same effect. The difference comes only if you use these operators as part of a larger expression. Like all operators, the ++ operator returns a value, but the value depends on where the operator is written relative to the operand. The two cases are as follows:

x++ Calculates the value of x first and then increments it. The value returned to the surrounding expression is the original value *before* the increment operation is performed.

++x Increments the value of x first and then uses the new value as the value of the ++ operation as a whole.

The -- operator behaves similarly, except that the value is decremented rather than incremented.

For example, if you were to execute the following program:

```
main()
{
    int x, y;

    x = 5;
    y = ++x;
    printf("x = %d, y = %d\n", x, y);
}
```

the output would look like this:

```
x = 6, y = 6
```

If, on the other hand, the program had been written as

```
main()
{
    int x, y;

    x = 5;
    y = x++;
    printf("x = %d, y = %d\n", x, y);
}
```

the final result would be

```
x = 6, y = 5
```

The statement

```
y = x++;
```

does increment x so that it has the value 6, but the value assigned to y is the value prior to the increment operation, which is 5.

You may wonder why would anyone use such an arcane feature. The ++ and -- operators are certainly not essential. Moreover, there are not many circumstances in which programs that embed these operators in larger expressions are demonstrably better than those that use a simpler approach. On the other hand, ++ and -- are firmly entrenched in the historical tradition shared by C programmers. They are idioms, and programmers use them frequently. Because these operators are so common, you need to understand them so that you can make sense of existing code.

As an example, let's suppose that you wanted to set the first n elements of an array arr to 0. The straightforward approach is to use the for statement

```
for (i = 0; i < n; i++) arr[i] = 0;
```

Some programmers, however, might notice that the increment operation can be combined with the selection operation and instead write

```
for (i = 0; i < N; ) arr[i++] = 0;
```

This example requires the i++ form rather than ++i. You want to increment i, but you also want to select the elements in the array numbered 0, 1, 2, and so forth. Thus, you need the old value of i before it is incremented as the selection expression.

On some machines—most notably the PDP-11 machine on which C was designed—the second coding is ever so slightly more efficient than the first. Even so, the difference in efficiency is certainly not sufficient to warrant making the change, since the latter coding violates the spirit of the for loop. The header of a for loop should tell you exactly what you need to know in order to understand the behavior of the index variable on each cycle of the loop.

Using the ++ operator as part of an expression can also lead to ambiguity. Suppose, for example, that you wanted to set every element in arr to its own index number, so that, at the end, arr[0] contained 0, arr[1] contained 1, and so on. The overly clever programmer might write

```
for (i = 0; i < n;   ) arr[i] = i++;        This statement is ambiguous.
```

reasoning that arr[i] will be set to i and that i is then incremented to prepare for the next loop cycle. This interpretation, however, is not guaranteed in C. Given an expression involving a binary operator, a C program can evaluate the operands to that operator in either order, and usually chooses the order that is most convenient for the machine. Our overly clever programmer is assuming that the program first calculates the address of arr[i], then calculates i++, and finally goes on to assign the value of i++ (which is the old value of i) to the address it computed earlier. However, the program may very well compute the value of i++ first and then go on to compute the value of arr[i]. The value returned as the result of the expression i++ is still the old value of i, but by the time the computer tries to figure out what box arr[i] refers to, i has already been incremented. Thus, the program will try to assign the value 0 to the box numbered 1.

One way to avoid this kind of ambiguity is to make sure that any variable you use in conjunction with ++ or -- does not appear anywhere else in the expression. The body of the preceding for statement violates this principle because i appears both on the left and right sides of the assignment. The best way to avoid this kind of ambiguity is to restrict the increment and decrement operators to their stand-alone form and avoid using their value in an expression.

Incrementing and decrementing pointers

This expanded understanding of ++ and --, coupled with the earlier definition of pointer arithmetic, makes it possible to explain one of the most common idiomatic constructions in C, which is the expression:

```
*p++
```

The first question you need to resolve in determining what this expression might mean is what the order of operations is. Both the * operator and the ++ operator compete here for the operand p. Depending on the precedence and associativity rules of the language, the expression could be equivalent to either

> **COMMON PITFALLS**
>
> Whenever you work with the ++ and -- operators, be careful to avoid writing ambiguous expressions in which the order of evaluation would produce different results on different machines. As a general rule, a variable that is incremented or decremented using these operators should not appear again in the same expression.

```
(*p)++
```

or

```
*(p++)
```

As it happens, unary operators in C are evaluated in right-to-left order. Thus, the ++ takes precedence over the *, so the second interpretation is correct. But you still need to determine what the expression means.

The postfix ++ operator, as you have seen before, increments the value of p and then returns the value that p had prior to the increment operation. Since p is a pointer, you need to define the increment operation in terms of pointer arithmetic. Thus, in evaluating p+1, you know that the resulting value should point to the next element in the array. If p originally pointed to arr[0], for example, the increment operation would cause it to point to arr[1]. Thus, the expression

```
*p++
```

has the following meaning in English:

> Dereference the pointer p and return as an lvalue the object to which it currently points. As a side effect, increment the value of p so that, if the original lvalue was an element within an array, the new value of p points to the next element in that array.

To see why this operator might be useful, however, it is necessary to consider in more detail how pointers and arrays relate to one another.

The relationship between pointers and arrays

Of the unusual characteristics of C, one of the most interesting is that the name of an array is treated as being synonymous with a pointer to the initial element in that array. This concept is most easily illustrated by example.

The declaration

```
int intlist[5];
```

allocates space for an array of five integers, which is assigned storage somewhere inside the computer's memory, as illustrated in the following diagram:

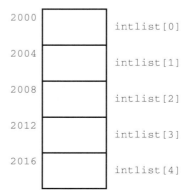

The addresses that appear to the left of the boxes are arbitrary; in this diagram, the initial address is shown as 2000, but it could just as easily have been any other address.

The name `intlist` represents an array but can also be used directly as a pointer value. When it is used as a pointer, `intlist` is defined to be the address of the initial element in the array. For any array `arr`, the following identity always holds in C:

> `arr`   *is defined to be identical to*   `&arr[0]`

Given any array name, you can assign its address to any pointer variable directly. The most common example of this equivalence occurs when an array is passed from one function to another. The called function typically declares the array using the syntax illustrated by the `Sort` prototype from Chapter 12:

```
void SortIntegerArray(int array[], int n);
```

If you were to call `Sort` with the array `intlist` defined above, the value passed to the formal parameter `array` within `Sort` would be the address of the first element in `intlist`. The `Sort` function would work exactly the same way if the prototype had been written as

```
void SortIntegerArray(int *array, int n);
```

In this case, the first argument is declared as a pointer, but the effect is the same. The address of the first element in `intlist` is copied into the formal parameter `array` and manipulated using pointer arithmetic. Inside the machine, the declarations are equivalent and the same operations can be applied in either case.

As a general rule, you should declare parameters in the way that reflects their usage. If you intend to use a parameter as an array and select elements from it, you should declare that parameter as an array. If you intend to use the parameter as a pointer and dereference it, you should declare it as a pointer.

The crucial difference between arrays and pointers in C comes into play when variables are originally declared, not when those values are passed as parameters. The fundamental distinction between the declaration

```
int array[5];
```

and the declaration

```
int *p;
```

is one of memory allocation. The first declaration reserves five consecutive words of memory capable of holding the array elements. The second declaration reserves only a single word, which is large enough only to hold a machine address.

The implication of this difference is extremely important to you as a programmer. If you declare an array, you have storage to work with; if you declare a pointer variable, that variable is not associated with any storage until you initialize it explicitly.

Given your current level of understanding, the only way to use a pointer as an array is to initialize the pointer by assigning the base address of the array to the pointer variable. If, after making the preceding declarations, you were to write

```
p = array;
```

the pointer variable p would then point to the same addresses used for array, and you could use the two names interchangeably.

The technique of setting a pointer to the address of an existing array is rather limited. After all, if you already have an array name, you might as well use it. Assigning that name to a pointer does not really do you any good. The real advantage of using a pointer as an array comes from the fact that you can initialize that pointer to new memory that has not previously been declared, which allows you to create new arrays as the program runs. This important programming technique is described in the next section.

13.5 Dynamic allocation

Up to this point in the text, you have seen two mechanisms for assigning memory to variables. When you declare a global variable, the compiler allocates memory space for that variable that persists throughout the entire program. This style of allocation is called **static allocation** because the variables are assigned to fixed locations in memory. When you declare a local variable inside a function, the space for that variable is allocated on the system stack. Calling the function assigns memory to the variable, which is then freed when the function returns. This style of allocation is called **automatic allocation**. There is also a third way of allocating memory that permits you to acquire new memory when you need it and to free it explicitly when it is no longer needed. The process of acquiring new storage while the program is running is called **dynamic allocation**.

When a program is loaded into memory, it usually occupies only a fraction of the available storage. In most systems, you can allocate some of the unused storage to the program whenever it needs more memory. For example, if you need space for a new array while the program is running, you can reserve part of the unallocated memory, leaving the rest for subsequent allocations. The pool of unallocated memory available to a program is called the **heap**.

As part of the library interface stdlib.h, the ANSI C environment provides functions for allocating new memory from the heap. The most important function is called malloc, which has the effect of allocating a block of memory of a given size. The size of the block to be allocated is given in bytes (as you recall, a byte is the memory unit large enough to hold a character value). For example, if you want to allocate 10 bytes of memory, you call

```
malloc(10)
```

which returns a pointer to a block of storage 10 bytes in size. In order to use the newly allocated storage, you must store the result of malloc in a pointer variable, after which you can use that pointer variable just like an array.

The type void *

Before giving examples of the use of malloc, however, it is important to bring up a potentially thorny issue. In C, pointers have types. If you declare a variable ip by writing

```
int *ip;
```

that variable has the conceptual type pointer-to-`int`. The declaration

```
char *cp;
```

introduces a variable `cp` whose type is pointer-to-`char`. In ANSI C, these types are distinct, and the compiler will issue a warning message if you try to assign one of those pointers to the other.

The idea that pointers have types raises the interesting question of what type `malloc` returns. The `malloc` function is used to allocate new storage for any type of value that the caller desires and must therefore return a "general" pointer of an as-yet-unspecified type. In C, the general pointer type is indicated as if were a pointer to the nonexistent type `void`, which is also used to indicate functions that return no values or empty parameter lists. If you declare a pointer to be of type pointer-to-`void`, as in

```
void *vp;
```

you can store a pointer value of any type in that variable but you are not allowed to use the `*` operator to dereference `vp`. The compiler has no idea what base type to use for `vp`, and there is thus no meaningful way to talk about the value to which `vp` points.

The type `void *` is nonetheless useful because it allows functions—`malloc`, in particular—to return general pointers whose actual types the caller can establish later. The `malloc` function returns a pointer value of type `void *`, which means that its prototype is:[4]

```
void *malloc(int nBytes);
```

Note that the result type of this function prototype is declared in much the same way that a pointer variable is. The `*` indicating that the result is a pointer is syntactically associated with the function name and not with the base type, even though the conceptual association works the other way around. C's syntax for functions that return pointer values can be confusing until you get used to it.

ANSI C performs automatic conversions between the type pointer-to-`void` and pointer types that specify an explicit base type. For example, if you declare the character pointer `cp` as

```
char *cp;
```

you can assign the result of `malloc` to it directly, using the statement

```
cp = malloc(10);
```

Partly for historical reasons and partly because doing so makes the conversion between pointer types explicit, many programmers write this statement using a type cast to convert the result of `malloc` to a character pointer before making the assignment, as follows:

COMMON PITFALLS

Be sure you can differentiate the procedure prototype

```
void f(. . .);
```

from the function prototype

```
void *f(. . .);
```

which declares a function returning a general pointer.

---

[4] The argument type to `malloc` is actually the type `size_t`, which is defined in the `stddef.h` header file. On some machines, the type `int` may not be large enough to represent the size of a large block of memory. In any event, the argument is conceptually an integer.

```
cp = (char *) malloc(10);
```

Whether or not the explicit type cast is used, this statement has the effect of allocating 10 bytes of new memory space and storing the address of the first byte in `cp`.

Dynamic arrays

From a conceptual perspective, an assignment of the form

```
cp = (char *) malloc(10);
```

creates the following configuration in memory:

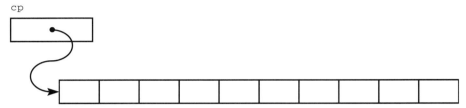

The variable `cp` points to a set of 10 consecutive bytes that have been allocated in the heap. Because pointers and arrays are freely interchangeable in C, the variable now acts exactly as if it had been declared as an array of 10 characters.

Arrays that you allocate on the heap and reference using a pointer variable are called **dynamic arrays** and play a significant role in modern programming. In general, allocating a dynamic array consists of the following steps:

1. Declare a pointer variable to hold the base of the array.
2. Call `malloc` to allocate memory for each element of the array. Because different data types require different amounts of memory, the `malloc` call must request a byte count equal to the number of elements in the array multiplied by the size in bytes of each element.
3. Assign the result of `malloc` to the pointer variable.

For example, to allocate a new integer array of 10 elements and then assign that storage to the variable `arr`, you must first declare `arr` using

```
int *arr;
```

and then allocate its storage by writing

```
arr = malloc(10 * sizeof(int));
```

The principal differences between declared arrays and dynamic arrays are that

- The memory associated with a declared array is allocated automatically as part of the declaration process; when the frame for the function declaring the array is created, all the elements of that array are allocated as part of the frame. In the case of a dynamic array, the actual memory is not allocated until you call the `malloc` function.

- The size of a declared array must be a constant in the program. Because their memory comes from the heap, dynamic arrays can be of any size. Moreover, you can determine the size of the array according to the amount of data. If you know you need an array with precisely *N* elements, you can reserve just the right amount of storage.

Detecting errors in `malloc`

Since all computer memory systems are finite in size, the heap will eventually run out of space. When this occurs, `malloc` returns the pointer `NULL` to indicate its failure to allocate a block of the requested size. As a conscientious programmer, you should check for this possibility on every call to `malloc`. Thus, after allocating a dynamic array, you need to write something like

```
arr = malloc(10 * sizeof(int));
if (arr == NULL) Error("No memory available");
```

Since dynamic allocation tends to be used frequently in a wide class of programs, error checking—as important as it is—can become extremely tedious. It also has a tendency to obscure the structure of the algorithm by cluttering the code with error messages. When you run out of memory, there is usually nothing you can do about it; having the program display an error message and halt is often the only reasonable option. Thus, it probably makes sense to take the call to `malloc` and embed it within a new abstraction layer that includes the out-of-memory test.

The `genlib.h` interface exports a function `GetBlock` that combines the action of `malloc` with the test for the `NULL` result. If `GetBlock` detects the out-of-memory condition, it simply calls the `Error` function. Thus, if you replace the preceding two lines of code with

```
arr = GetBlock(10 * sizeof(int));
```

the implementation of the `GetBlock` function combines the operations of allocating memory and testing for errors. Because `GetBlock` tidies up the memory allocation operations and makes the programs that use it easier to read, this text generally uses `GetBlock` instead of `malloc`. Conceptually, the two functions perform exactly the same job.

To simplify the process of allocating dynamic arrays still further, the `genlib.h` library also defines the function `NewArray`, which takes the number of elements and the base type and returns a pointer to a dynamic array of the specified size. Thus, to allocate a dynamic array of 50 strings, you would call `NewArray(50, string)`.

Freeing memory

One way to help ensure that you don't run out of memory is to free any storage you have allocated when you are finished using it. The standard ANSI libraries provide a function `free`, which returns to the heap memory that was previously allocated using `malloc`. If, for example, you determine that you are completely finished using the storage allocated for `arr`, you can free that storage for later reuse by calling

```
free(arr);
```

Because this text uses `GetBlock` to perform dynamic allocation, however, it makes more sense to present a unified abstraction that includes compatibly named mechanisms for allocating and freeing storage. For this purpose, the `genlib.h` interface also includes a `FreeBlock` function, which is identical in operation to `free`.

As it turns out, knowing when to free a piece of memory is not such an easy task. The central problem is that the operations of allocating and freeing memory are most naturally situated on opposite sides of the interface boundary between an implementation and its client. The implementation knows when to allocate memory and returns pointers to the client. The implementation, however, does not know when the client is finished with the allocated object, so freeing the storage has to remain the client's responsibility, even though the client may not understand enough about the object's structure to do so.

Given the size of most memories today, you can often allocate whatever memory you need without ever bothering to free it again. Such a strategy works for almost all programs that do not need to run for any significant amount of time. The problem of limited memory only becomes consequential when you design an application that needs to run for a long period of time, such as the operating system on which all the other facilities of the system depend. In these applications, it is important to free memory when you no longer need it.

Some languages support a system for dynamic allocation that actively goes through memory to see what parts of it are in use, freeing any storage that is no longer needed. This strategy is called **garbage collection.** Garbage-collecting allocators exist for C, and it is likely that their use will increase in coming years. If it does, the policy of ignoring deallocation will become reasonable even in long-running applications because you will be able to rely on the garbage collector to perform the deallocation operations automatically.

For the most part, this text assumes that your applications fall into the class of problems for which allocating memory whenever you need it is a workable strategy. This assumption will simplify your lives considerably and make it easier for you to concentrate on algorithmic details.

SUMMARY

This chapter has introduced you to the concept of a *pointer,* which is defined to be the address of a data value in the computer's memory. Pointers are useful because they

- Allow you to represent large data structures compactly.
- Provide a facility for sharing data between different components of a program.
- Make it possible to reserve new memory during program execution.
- Offer a powerful mechanism for recording relationships among data items.

Although this chapter has illustrated some of these benefits, the examples in Chapters 14 and 16 give you further insight into why pointers are valuable in programming.

Important points introduced in this chapter include:

- An *lvalue* is any expression in C that refers to a memory location and therefore has an address.
- The address of an lvalue is called a *pointer* and can be manipulated as data by a program.
- Like other variables, pointer variables must be declared before they are used.
- The fundamental operators on pointers are & and *. The & operator takes an lvalue and returns a pointer to it; the * operator takes a pointer and returns the lvalue to which it points. The operation of moving from a pointer to the lvalue to which it points is called *dereferencing* the pointer.
- *Pointer assignment* makes two pointers indicate the same location. *Value assignment* copies the value from the address specified by one pointer into the address specified by another.
- A special pointer value called NULL is used to indicate that a pointer does not currently point to any data.
- Pointers can be used to allow a function to share data with its caller. This process is termed *call by reference*.
- In C, pointers and arrays are closely associated. You can use pointers as if they were arrays and vice versa. The relationship between pointers and arrays also makes it possible to give sensible meanings to the arithmetic operators + and – in the pointer domain.
- The operators ++ and -- can be written either before or after the operand to which they apply. The ++x form first increments x and then returns the incremented value. The x++ form increments x but returns the value x had before the increment was performed.
- The type void * is used to indicate a general pointer type that is compatible with all other pointer types.
- While a program is running, you can allocate new memory dynamically from a pool of unused storage called the *heap*. The ANSI function malloc is used to allocate heap memory, which is then available for use. When that memory is no longer needed, the program can return it to the heap by calling the function free. In the programs in this book, *dynamic allocation* is typically performed by the functions GetBlock and FreeBlock. These functions are identical to malloc and free except that they handle the out-of-memory error internally.
- You can use dynamic allocation to allocate arrays whose size is determined when the program runs, not when it is compiled. Such arrays are called *dynamic arrays*.

REVIEW QUESTIONS

1. Define the terms *pointer* and *lvalue*.

2. What are the four uses of pointers outlined in the introduction to this chapter?

3. What declaration would you use to declare a variable named `flagp` as a pointer to a Boolean value?

4. What are the types of the variables introduced by the declaration

   ```
   double * p1, p2;
   ```

5. Explain the difference between pointer assignment and value assignment.

6. Assuming that variables of type `double` require eight bytes of memory and that a pointer requires four, draw a memory diagram showing a portion of the stack frame that contains the following declarations:

   ```
   double d1;
   double d2;
   double *dp1;
   double *dp2;
   ```

   In your diagram, trace through the operation of these statements:

   ```
   dp1 = &d1;
   dp2 = &d2;
   *dp1 = 3.14159;
   d2 = 2.71828;
   dp1 = dp2;
   *dp1 -= d2;
   ```

7. True or false: For any variable x, the expression `*&x` is essentially a synonym for x.

8. True or false: For any variable x, the expression `&*x` is essentially a synonym for x.

9. What is the internal representation of the constant `NULL`?

10. What happens if you try to dereference a `NULL` pointer?

11. What does the phrase *call by reference* mean?

12. Without knowing anything about the function `ApplySpecialOperation`, determine which of the integer variables x and y could possibly be affected by the call

    ```
    ApplySpecialOperation(&x, y);
    ```

13. In what circumstances are you likely to use call by reference?

14. Assuming that `intArray` is declared as

    ```
    int intArray[10];
    ```

    and that `j` is an integer variable, describe the steps the computer would take to determine the value of the following expression:

    ```
    &intArray[j + 3];
    ```

15. If `arr` is declared to be an array, describe the distinction between the expressions

    ```
    arr[2]
    ```

and

```
arr + 2
```

16. Assume that variables of type `double` take up eight bytes on the computer system you are using. If the base address of the array `doubleArray` is 1000, what is the address value of `doubleArray + 5`?

17. Suppose that the values of the integer variables x and y are 2 and 5, respectively. In each of the following cases, determine the value of the expression and show the effect of executing that expression on the values of x and y. (In answering this question, treat each of the expressions as independent rather than cumulative. In other words, you should assume that x and y have the values 2 and 5 prior to each calculation.)

    a.   `x++`
    b.   `--x`
    c.   `x++ + ++y`
    d.   `y += x--`

18. Give an example of an expression involving the `++` operator for which the results would differ depending on the interpretation used by the machine.

19. True or false: If p is a pointer variable, the expression p++ adds 1 to the internal representation of p.

20. Which operator, `*` or `++`, is applied first in the expression

```
*p++
```

In general, what rule does C use to determine the precedence of unary operators?

21. True or false: Because C treats arrays as pointers to their initial element, declaring an array variable is identical internally to declaring that same variable as a pointer.

22. What is the heap?

23. Describe the effect of the `malloc` function from your perspective as a client.

24. What is the purpose of the type `void *`?

25. How would you allocate a dynamic array called `flags` consisting of 100 Boolean values?

26. What is the difference between the `malloc` function and the `GetBlock` function exported by `genlib.h`?

27. What is the purpose of the function `free` (or the identical `genlib.h` function `FreeBlock`)?

28. What is meant by the term *garbage collection?*

PROGRAMMING EXERCISES

1. In C, you can use `printf` to display the internal value of a pointer by using a type cast to convert the pointer to a `long` and then displaying the resulting value with the `printf` format code `%lu`. For example, if `ip` is a pointer, you can display its internal numeric representation using the statement

   ```
   printf("ip = %lu\n", (long) ip);
   ```

   Write a program that displays the addresses for the global variables

   ```
   static int globalCount;
   static double globalArray[100];
   static char *globalPointer;
   ```

   and the following local variables declared within the function `main`:

   ```
   int count;
   double array[100];
   char *cp;
   ```

   What do the results tell you about where in memory these variables are allocated on your computer?

2. Write a function `GetDate` with the prototype

   ```
   void GetDate(int *dp, int *mp, int *yp);
   ```

   that reads in a date from the user in the form

   dd-mmm-yy

   where *dd* is a one- or two-digit day, *mmm* is a three-letter abbreviation for a month, and *yy* is a two-digit year. Your implementation should take apart the components of the date and give them back to the caller in numeric form by assigning values to the three arguments, each of which is passed by reference.

   Test your function with a simple main program that is capable of generating this sample run:

   ```
   Enter a date as dd-mmm-yy: 28-Aug-63↵
   Day = 28
   Month = 8
   Year = 63
   ```

3. Design a function prototype that would allow a single function to find and return simultaneously both the lowest and highest values in an array of type

double. Implement and test your function as shown in the following sample run:

```
Enter the elements of the array, one per line.
Use -1 to signal the end of the list.
? 67↵
? 78↵
? 75↵
? 70↵
? 71↵
? 80↵
? 69↵
? 86↵
? 65↵
? 54↵
? 76↵
? 78↵
? 70↵
? 68↵
? 77↵
? -1↵
The range of values is 54-86
```

4. Rewrite the selection sort implementation presented in Figure 12-5 so that all of the array references are changed into pointer references. When you finish, the square bracket characters [and] should not appear in your source file. Even so, the SortIntegerArray function should behave exactly as it did before.

5. Write a function IndexArray(n) that returns a pointer to a dynamically allocated integer array with n elements, each of which is initialized to its own index. For example, assuming that ip is declared as

```
int *ip;
```

the statement

```
ip = IndexArray(10);
```

should produce the following memory configuration:

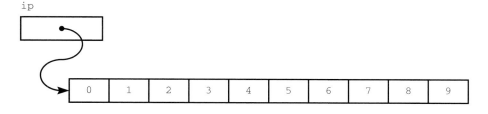

6. Write a function `Tabulate(array, n)` that takes an array of integers and its effective size and writes out a tabulation showing the number of times each element appears. For example, given the input array

91	93	98	92	92	95	93	92	91	95	99	92	98

your program should produce this tabulation:

```
91: 2
92: 4
93: 2
95: 2
98: 2
99: 1
```

The difference between this problem and a more traditional histogram problem lies in the fact that you don't know the range of input values in advance. Here, the input values lie between 91 and 99. For a different set of input data, the values might lie between 600 and 625.

Because of this constraint, you cannot declare a counting array at the beginning of the function and know that all the values in the data array will correspond to index positions in the counting array. In this case, you should solve the problem by first calculating the range of the data and then allocating an array that contains the appropriate number of elements so that one index position corresponds to each of the possible data items in that range.

7. Suppose that the C libraries did not provide a `malloc` function for dynamic allocation. To a certain extent, you could achieve the same result by allocating a large global array at the beginning of a program and giving out pieces of that array to clients who need to use additional storage.

Design and implement an interface `myalloc.h` that exports a function `MyGetBlock` to simulate the dynamic allocation process. Calling `MyGetBlock(nBytes)` should return a pointer to a block of memory that is `nBytes` long. Each new memory block is taken from the large global array, beginning wherever the last block left off. Make sure that your implementation includes any static initialization necessary for the first call to `MyGetBlock` to succeed.

Consider the memory you allocate to be assigned for the lifetime of the program. Designing an allocation facility that allows clients to free memory is beyond the scope of this text.

8. Write a program that reads simple data declarations and responds with the amount of memory that would be allocated to that variable. For example, the

following sample run shows the output of the program for two possible input lines:

```
Enter variable declarations, ending with a blank line.
int x, y;↵
x requires 2 bytes
y requires 2 bytes
char c, *cptr, carray[80];↵
c requires 1 byte
cptr requires 4 bytes
carray requires 80 bytes
```

Each input line should consist of
   a. A type name, which must be one of the following: char, int, short, long, float, or double. (You can obtain the sizes of these types by using the sizeof operator.)
   b. One or more individual declaration specifications (as outlined below) separated by commas.
   c. A semicolon marking the end of the line.

Your program should exit if it reads a blank input line.

The individual declaration specifications must consist of a variable name, which can be modified in either or both of the following ways:

   ▪ Preceded by an asterisk, to indicate a pointer variable
   ▪ Followed by an integer enclosed in brackets, to indicate an array

Although multiple levels of pointers or multidimensional arrays are legal in C, your program should limit declarations to a single asterisk and subscript for each variable.

Your program will be much easier to write if you use the scanner module from Chapter 10.

C H A P T E R   1 4

Strings Revisited

. . . Untune that string
And, hark! what discord follows;

— Shakespeare, *Troilus and Cressida*

Objectives

- To understand the underlying representation of string data.

- To appreciate the differences between string variables declared as arrays and those declared as pointers.

- To be able to use the functions in the ANSI string library.

- To recognize how you can implement the `strlib.h` interface using the `string.h` functions.

You have been using strings ever since Chapter 2 and have been able to perform high-level string operations since Chapter 9. So far, however, the programs in this text have used `string` only as an abstract type. As an abstract type, a value of type `string` acts as a complete and indivisible entity. You pass strings to functions, return them as results, and assign one string to another. If you want to select a character from a string or perform a more complex string operation, you must call one of the functions exported by the `strlib.h` interface.

As with any interface, one of the principal goals of `strlib.h` is to hide unnecessary detail from the client. However, because string manipulation is an important aspect of many programming applications, you must learn to work with strings at a lower level of detail. To get a complete picture of how strings work, it is essential for you to look beyond the abstraction barrier and consider the underlying representation.

14.1 Conceptual representations of the type `string`

To use strings effectively in C, you must be able to think about them in three ways:

1. As an array of characters
2. As a pointer to an individual character
3. As a complete entity with conceptual integrity as a whole

These three views are not conflicting but complementary. Each view describes one perspective on reality. Given a string stored within the computer, you can choose to think about it in any of these three ways. The string itself does not change because you choose to regard it differently. The only thing that changes is your conception of how that string is represented.

Strings as arrays

Internally, strings are represented as arrays of characters. Whenever a string is stored in memory, the characters within it are assigned to consecutive bytes. For example, when the compiler sees the string constant `"Hello"` in a program, it stores the characters that make up the string in consecutive bytes of memory.

Storing the characters themselves, however, is not sufficient to represent all the important information about a string. Programs that manipulate string values must have some way to determine where each string ends. If the compiler were to store the characters for the string constant `"there"` immediately after the characters in the string constant `"Hello"`, memory would look like this:

1000	H
1001	e
1002	l
1003	l
1004	o
1005	t
1006	h
1007	e
1008	r
1009	e

This diagram does not correctly reflect the way strings are stored in memory.

The problem with this representation is that the two strings run together. If strings were stored in this fashion, there would be no way to tell where one string ended and the next began.

To avoid this problem, the C compiler always stores a null character in the byte that immediately follows the last character of a string. As noted in the section on "Special characters" in Chapter 9, the null character is written as `\0` in string and character constants and has 0 as its ASCII code. In a string, the null character serves as a sentinel marking the end. Thus, if the string constants `"Hello"` and `"there"` appear in a program, the C compiler reserves six bytes of memory space for each string and initializes memory as follows:

1000	H
1001	e
1002	l
1003	l
1004	o
1005	\0
1006	t
1007	h
1008	e
1009	r
1010	e
1011	\0

In C, you can use any character array to hold string data. For example, you can declare the array `carray` and initialize it to hold the string `"Hello"` with the following code:

```
char carray[6];

carray[0] = 'H';
carray[1] = 'e';
carray[2] = 'l';
carray[3] = 'l';
carray[4] = 'o';
carray[5] = '\0';
```

Because a string is an array, it is possible to choose the ith character from a string str using the notation for array selection, as follows:

```
str[i]
```

Just as with any array, index numbers in a string begin at 0. Thus, if str contains the string "Hello", then str[0] has the value 'H', str[1] has the value 'e', and so on. Selecting characters from a string is therefore similar to calling the IthChar function from the strlib library.

If you use array notation to do string processing, you need to learn a new set of idioms. The standard idiom for processing every character in a string looks like this:[1]

```
for (i = 0; str[i] != '\0'; i++) {
    . . . body of loop that manipulates str[i] . . .
}
```

On each loop cycle, the selection expression str[i] refers to the ith character in the string. Because the purpose of the loop is to process every character, the loop continues until str[i] selects the null character marking the end of the string. This for loop is therefore equivalent in function to the following idiom, introduced in Chapter 9, for the same purpose:

```
for (i = 0; i < StringLength(str); i++) {
    . . . body of loop that manipulates IthChar(str, i) . . .
}
```

The array selection form is considerably more efficient than the version that uses the functions from the strlib.h interface. For one thing, using array selection avoids the cost of calling the IthChar function. Moreover, using

```
i < StringLength(str)
```

as the test condition in the for loop control line means that the program must recompute the length on every cycle of the loop, even though the length of the string does not usually change. By checking for the sentinel character, the program can avoid these redundant calculations.

---

[1] As you will discover if you read existing C code, many C programmers use an idiom for processing strings that is even more compact than the example. Because C treats the value zero as FALSE and any nonzero value as TRUE, many C programmers leave the comparison out of the for loop control line, as follows:

```
for (i = 0; str[i]; i++)
```

Even though you will often encounter this shorthand form in existing C programs and therefore need to recognize it, this text always includes the comparison explicitly to emphasize the conceptual distinction between Boolean and integer data.

To see how the two styles compare, you can reimplement the `FindFirstVowel` function introduced in the Pig Latin example in Figure 10-5 without using any functions from the `strlib.h` interface. The original implementation from Chapter 10 appears in Figure 14-1.

If you write the same function using array notation, the implementation is that shown in Figure 14-2.

Algorithmically, the two implementations are identical. They differ only in the details of coding: how the end of the string is detected and how individual characters are selected.

Strings as pointers

As with any array in C, a character array can also be interpreted as a pointer to its first element. Moreover, given a pointer to a string value, you can use pointer arithmetic to refer to individual characters within that string. Thus, `FindFirstVowel` can also be coded as shown in Figure 14-3.

In this case, the `for` loop control line

```
for (cp = word; *cp != '\0'; cp++)
```

begins by initializing the pointer variable `cp` to the base address of `word` and advances it along the string until it points to the null character at the end. Inside the `for` loop, the function checks each character to see if it is a vowel. As soon as it

FIGURE 14-1 Implementation of **FindFirstVowel** using abstract strings

```
int FindFirstVowel(string word)
{
    int i;

    for (i = 0; i < StringLength(word); i++) {
        if (IsVowel(IthChar(word, i))) return (i);
    }
    return (-1);
}
```

FIGURE 14-2 Array-based implementation of **FindFirstVowel**

```
int FindFirstVowel(char word[])
{
    int i;

    for (i = 0; word[i] != '\0'; i++) {
        if (IsVowel(word[i])) return (i);
    }
    return (-1);
}
```

FIGURE 14-3 Pointer-based implementation of FindFirstVowel

```
int FindFirstVowel(char *word)
{
    char *cp;

    for (cp = word; *cp != '\0'; cp++) {
        if (IsVowel(*cp)) return (cp - word);
    }
    return (-1);
}
```

---

finds one, the function calculates the index of that character by subtracting the base address of the array from the current value of cp. For example, if FindFirstVowel were called on the string "scram", the function would find the first vowel in the following position:

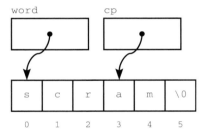

The result returned by the function is the difference between these two pointers, defined in terms of element positions. Because cp points to word[3], the expression cp - word returns 3, which is the index of the first vowel.

Strings as an abstract type

Even though this chapter focuses on the underlying representation of strings, it is still valuable to think of strings abstractly. If you need to refer to the individual characters in a string, you need to pay attention to its representation. In many cases, however, it is possible to think of a string as a unified whole. Doing so makes the program easier to comprehend because you need not be concerned with as many details. Up to now, this text has encouraged you to think about strings only from this holistic perspective.

The genlib.h library defines a type named string primarily to emphasize that strings make sense as a conceptually distinct type. The definition in genlib.h is

```
typedef char *string;
```

which makes string identical to the type char *. The two types mean exactly the same thing to the compiler. The two type names, however, send different messages to human readers. If you declare a variable to be of type `char *`, you reveal its underlying representation as a pointer. On the other hand, if you declare the same variable to be of type `string`, you focus the reader's attention on the string as a whole.

String parameters

From the caller's point of view, each of the three versions of `FindFirstVowel` presented in Figures 14-1 through 14-3 works in exactly the same way. The caller provides a string value, and `FindFirstVowel` returns an integer corresponding to the position of the first vowel. The implementations, however, treat those strings differently, as reflected by the different prototypes. The original version presented in Figure 14-1 treats the string as an abstract whole and refers to individual characters only through the functions defined in `strlib.h`. The function emphasizes the abstract character of its formal parameter by declaring it to be of the abstract type `string`, as illustrated by its header line

```
int FindFirstVowel(string word)
```

The implementation given in Figure 14-2 views `word` as an array of characters. Inside the `for` loop, it selects individual characters using array subscript notation. Because this implementation of the function uses array notation, its formal parameter is declared as a character array, as follows:

```
int FindFirstVowel(char word[])
```

The implementation presented in Figure 14-3 treats its argument as a pointer, declaring it as such with the following function header line:

```
int FindFirstVowel(char *word)
```

As far as the C compiler is concerned, the parameter declarations in the three function headers are identical and can be used interchangeably. The value in choosing a particular representation lies in the additional information it gives the reader. In general, you should declare formal parameters to match the style in which those parameters are used. If you think of a string as an array of characters and select individual characters using square brackets, you should declare the string as an array. If you think of the string as a pointer and use * to dereference it, you should declare the string as a pointer. If you think of the string as a complete entity that is more important than its component parts, the best approach is to declare it using the type `string`.

String variables

Despite the fact that arrays and pointers can often be used interchangeably in C, it is essential to recognize that declaring a variable as an array is not the same as declaring it as a pointer, unless that variable is a formal parameter as described in the preceding section. For all other types of variables, your choice of declaration style determines how memory is allocated.

If you declare an array by writing the line

```
char carray[MaxChars];
```

space is allocated for `carray` in the frame of the current function. You have `MaxChars` bytes that you can use for character storage, as shown in this conceptual diagram:

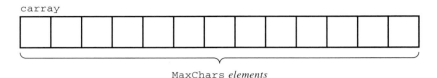

carray

MaxChars *elements*

Because the storage is allocated explicitly, you can assign values directly to the elements of `carray`. You can also pass the `carray` array to some other function, which is then free to manipulate that storage.

If you instead declare a variable `cptr` using the declaration

```
char *cptr;
```

or, equivalently, as

```
string cptr;
```

no character memory is assigned at all. The variable `cptr` is simply a pointer variable:

cptr

Because this variable has not been explicitly initialized, its contents are undetermined. It might contain 0 or 42 or any other random value left over from the last time that location was used. Suppose that `cptr` just happens to contain 1729, as shown:

cptr

1729

If you change the contents of `cptr[0]`, you will change the value stored in address 1729. Unfortunately, address 1729 might be used for a variable or a part of your program. Making such assignments can easily corrupt critical data and cause your program to crash.

Before you can use `cptr`, you must provide the necessary character memory by assigning it a pointer value that corresponds to the address of some usable region of memory. One approach you can take is to assign to `cptr` the address of an existing array. For example, if you execute the statement

```
cptr = carray;
```

COMMON PITFALLS

When you declare a pointer variable, be sure that you initialize it so that it points to real locations in memory. Failure to initialize pointers is a common source of errors. These errors are hard to detect because the compiler cannot catch them. The best approach is to avoid them altogether.

the resulting conceptual picture looks like this:

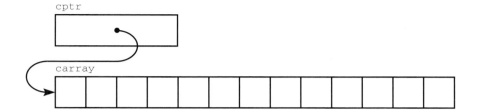

At this point, `cptr` and `carray` are synonymous.

A more common strategy for obtaining memory is to use `GetBlock` or `malloc` to allocate that memory dynamically. The memory diagram of the statement

```
cptr = GetBlock(MaxChars);
```

is nearly identical to the preceding one. The only difference is that the character storage is allocated dynamically from the heap and therefore looks like this:

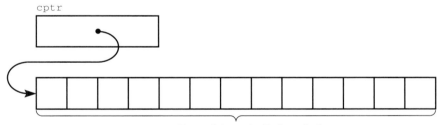

memory allocated dynamically from the heap

After this assignment, you can use `cptr` as if it were a character array. It now has memory associated with it, and you can safely refer to those individual elements as long as you do not reference elements outside the boundaries of the allocated region of storage.

Differences between pointer and array variables

In C, if you declare a pointer variable, it acts much like any other variable. Conceptually, it represents a named box that holds the address of some other value. As with any other variable, you give a pointer variable a new value by writing an assignment statement. For example, once you have declared the pointer variable `cptr` by writing

```
char *cptr;
```

you can assign a value to the `cptr` box by writing a statement such as

```
cptr = NULL;
```

This statement assigns the value on the right-hand side to the memory cell that corresponds to the `cptr` variable. In this respect, pointer variables act just like variables of the basic types.

If you declare an array, on the other hand, the situation is quite different. Conceptually speaking, an array declaration reserves many boxes, one for each element in the array. The name of the array corresponds to the entire collection of boxes and not to any single box. As such, the name of an array is not a simple variable and cannot be used like one. In particular, the name of an array is not an lvalue in C and cannot appear on the left-hand side of an assignment operation.

The fact that arrays are not lvalues has important implications in terms of string manipulation. If you allocate string storage by declaring an array variable such as

```
char carray[6];
```

it is illegal to write an assignment statement like

```
carray = "hello";                          This statement is illegal.
```

Because the variable `carray` is not an lvalue, you cannot assign a value to it.

There is no such restriction if you declare a string as a pointer. For example, after making the declaration

```
char *cptr;
```

it is perfectly legal to write

```
cptr = "world";
```

The compiler puts the characters for `"world"` somewhere in memory, and the assignment statement stores the address of the first character of the string in `cptr`. For example, if the compiler placed the characters for `"world"` in memory locations beginning at 500, the effect of executing the assignment to `cptr` could be diagrammed as follows:

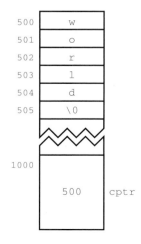

The variable `cptr` is simply updated to point to a new position.

A similar restriction applies when you call a function. Even though a function can accept an array as a parameter, it is not legal in C for a function to return an array. Functions can, however, return pointers, which allows you to achieve much the same effect. If you have used dynamic allocation within a function to create storage for an array, you can return a pointer to that storage as the value of the function, assign the result to a pointer variable, and then use that pointer variable as if it were an array.

As an example, the `CharToString` function in the `strlib` library can be implemented as follows:

```
string CharToString(char ch)
{
    char *cptr;

    cptr = GetBlock(2);
    cptr[0] = ch;
    cptr[1] = '\0';
    return (cptr);
}
```

The first statement allocates two bytes of memory from the heap: one for the character and one for the null character that must appear at the end of every string. The next two statements assign the correct values to those two bytes. The final statement returns the pointer to the newly allocated storage as the value of the function. It is then legal for a client to write a statement such as

```
star = CharToString('*');
```

assuming that `star` is declared as a character pointer or, equivalently, as the abstract type `string`.

It is important to realize that this approach works only if you allocate the array storage dynamically. If you try to return a pointer to an array declared within a function, your program will fail. The problem is that the memory assigned to an array declared as a local variable is deallocated when that function returns.

To understand the problem, imagine that you had tried to implement `CharToString` using the following incorrect approach:

```
string CharToString(char ch)
{
    char carray[2];

    carray[0] = ch;
    carray[1] = '\0';
    return (carray);
}
```

This implementation is in error because it returns a pointer to memory declared within this function's frame.

The contents of the array variable `carray` are correct at the moment the function returns. The problem is that the memory for `carray` is allocated in the stack frame

COMMON PITFALLS

When you return a pointer as the result of a function, make sure that the storage addressed by that pointer is not part of the current stack frame. Memory in the current frame will be deallocated when the function returns and is thus not available to clients.

for `CharToString`. When `CharToString` returns, all the memory in its stack frame is deallocated and made available for use by other functions. The client program that received the result of the buggy implementation of `CharToString` therefore has a pointer to memory whose contents will mysteriously change when another function uses that same memory at a later point.

Deciding on a strategy for string representation

Whenever you use a string in a program, you must decide how to declare the variable that holds that string. Should you declare it as an array and reserve the space for the individual characters as part of the declaration? Or should you declare it as a pointer and then allocate space for the characters as the program runs? To a large extent, the answer depends on the tools you use to manipulate the string. Different library abstractions incorporate different models of string behavior that determine which declaration style makes sense for use with the particular package. If a library abstraction takes care of string allocation for you—as the `strlib` library introduced in Chapter 9 does—you should use the pointer style of declaration. On the other hand, if you are working with a library that expects its clients to allocate their own string storage—as the ANSI string library described in the next section does—you have to ensure that memory is available before you call the functions in that library. In most cases, the easiest way to ensure that string storage exists is to declare your string variables as arrays. Both approaches are reasonable. The key to using strings successfully is to make sure that your declaration style matches the discipline of the library you are using.

14.2 The ANSI string library

So far, your use of strings has been limited to the operations defined in `strlib.h`, so that you could work with strings before learning about their internal representation as arrays. Commercially produced C programs do not have access to this library and instead rely on the `string.h` interface, which is defined as part of the ANSI standard. The functions in `string.h`, though harder to use than those in `strlib.h`, are essential for practical work.

The relationship between the `strlib.h` and `string.h` interfaces was discussed in Chapter 9, which introduced the concept of a layered abstraction. To review, the abstraction hierarchy for strings looks like this:

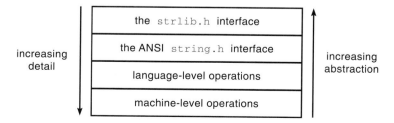

The `strlib.h` interface presents the most abstract view of string data, in the sense that as much detail as possible is hidden from the client. The `string.h` interface occupies the next level in the abstraction hierarchy and provides the basis for the implementation of `strlib.h`.

The `string.h` interface exports a large number of functions, many of which are useful only in certain relatively specialized applications. The most important functions exported by `string.h` are shown in Table 14-1.

At first glance, the functions in the ANSI string library look similar to those exported by `strlib.h`. Both libraries include functions to find the length of a string, to compare one string against another, to concatenate two strings, and to search a string for a particular character or substring. Some of these functions are identical in their operation. For example, the `strlen` and `strcmp` functions are exactly the same as the `StringLength` and `StringCompare` functions you have used since Chapter 9. However, even though the functions in the two libraries perform similar tasks, learning how to use the `string.h` interface requires more than learning a set of new function names. The `string.h` interface is based on a fundamentally different model of how strings work that requires you to think about strings in a new way.

The biggest difference between the two string libraries lies in how memory for the characters in a string is allocated. In the case of the `strlib.h` interface, the functions themselves allocate whatever memory is required. As a client, you don't have to worry about the details of that allocation, which is what makes the `strlib.h` interface easy to use. The functions in the `string.h` interface shift the burden of memory allocation to the client. Whenever memory is required for a new string, the client is responsible for providing that memory. To do so, the client usually declares a character array large enough to hold the result and passes it as an argument to the library function. The implementation then writes the new string data into the memory provided by the caller.

Function call	Operation
`strcpy(dst, src)`	Copies characters from `src` into `dst`
`strncpy(dst, src, n)`	Copies at most `n` characters from `src` into `dst`
`strcat(dst, src)`	Appends characters from `src` to the end of `dst`
`strncpy(dst, src, n)`	Appends at most `n` characters from `src` to `dst`
`strlen(s)`	Returns the length of `s`
`strcmp(s1, s2)`	Returns an integer indicating the result of the comparison
`strncmp(s1, s2, n)`	Like `strcmp` but compares at most `n` characters
`strchr(s, ch)`	Returns a pointer to the first instance of `ch` in `s` (or `NULL`)
`strrchr(s, ch)`	Returns a pointer to the last instance of `ch` in `s` (or `NULL`)
`strstr(s1, s2)`	Returns a pointer to the first instance of `s2` in `s1` (or `NULL`)

TABLE 14-1

Common functions exported by `string.h`

The `strcpy` function

The function `strcpy` in the `string.h` interface provides the simplest illustration of how functions in that library return new string values to their caller. The `strcpy` function copies characters from a string called the *source* into another string called the *destination.* To be consistent with the assignment operator, in which copying proceeds from right to left, `strcpy` takes its destination argument first and has the following prototype:[2]

```
void strcpy(string dst, string src);
```

The `strcpy` function is useful if you want to manipulate a string while retaining its original value. For example, suppose that the string variable `line` contains a line of text read in from the user and that your application requires you to make some editing substitutions to the characters in `line`. Using array selection to change the elements of `line` directly would destroy the original contents of `line`, which you may need for some other purpose later. To avoid changing `line`, you can copy the individual characters to another array and manipulate them there.

An array used to hold an intermediate copy of data is called a **buffer.** What you need in this situation is a character buffer into which you can copy the data from `line`. When you work with the ANSI string library, the usual approach is to allocate such buffers explicitly by declaring a character array with enough space to hold the largest string you expect to encounter in that application. Thus, if the constant `MaxLine` contains the length of the longest anticipated input line, you can declare the buffer by writing

```
char buffer[MaxLine+1];
```

where the `+1` leaves room for the null character at the end of a string that is exactly `MaxLine` characters long.

It's important to remember that you cannot copy the characters from `line` into `buffer` by writing an assignment statement like

```
buffer = line;                          This statement is illegal.
```

Because arrays are not lvalues in C, they cannot appear on the left side of an assignment statement. To copy the characters, you need to call the `strcpy` function as follows:

```
strcpy(buffer, line);
```

This call copies the characters from `line` into `buffer` until the null character is found at the end of the source string. The `strcpy` function always copies the null character to the destination string along with the rest of the characters to ensure that the new string is properly terminated.

---

[2] As it is defined in the library, the `strcpy` function actually returns the address of the destination array, although most clients ignore this value. For simplicity of presentation, this text defines the `strcpy` function as if it were a procedure with no result.

You can implement the `strcpy` function using either arrays or pointers. In the array formulation, the implementation would look something like this:

```
void strcpy(char dst[], char src[])
{
    int i;

    for (i = 0; src[i] != '\0'; i++) {
        dst[i] = src[i];
    }
    dst[i] = '\0';
}
```

Although this implementation of the code is fairly easy to read, it is not the version that an experienced programmer would most likely generate. C programmers quickly become used to thinking about strings as pointers and are encouraged by traditional practice to write most string-processing functions using pointer manipulation. The traditional implementation of `strcpy` is shown below:

```
void strcpy(char *dst, char *src)
{
    while (*dst++ = *src++);
}
```

All the work for this function is done in the test for the `while` statement, which has a body consisting only of a semicolon. The semicolon by itself constitutes the **null statement**—a legal statement form in C that has no effect. The test first copies a character from the source string into the destination buffer, updating each of the pointers to contain the address of the next character. Because C interprets any nonzero value as being equivalent to TRUE, the `while` loop in the `strcpy` implementation continues as long as the result assigned is not 0. The loop therefore terminates only when the null character is copied at the end of the string.

To become a successful C programmer, you must be able to read code that is as dense as the preceding example. You will encounter similar code when you read existing programs and must therefore know what it means. When you write your own code, however, your should strive to make it as readable as you can. Dense coding styles that rely heavily on shorthand operators tend to work against this goal.

When you use `strcpy`, it is your responsibility as a client to allocate enough space to hold the destination string and the terminating null character. If the `strcpy` function tries to write more characters to the destination array than you allocated for it, your program can fail in mysterious ways that can be difficult to track down. For example, suppose that you have written a program that executes a call to `strcpy` in which the source string is larger than the destination array, as follows:

```
char carray[6];

strcpy(carray, "A long string");
```

Executing this program copies correctly the first six characters of `"A long string"` into `carray`. Unfortunately, the program goes on to copy the rest of the

COMMON PITFALLS

When you call `strcpy`, be sure that the first argument specifies a character array large enough to hold the entire string value you are copying, including the terminating null character. If you cannot guarantee that the necessary space is available, you should include explicit code to catch this error.

characters into the bytes that come immediately after `carray` in memory. Thus, after the call to `strcpy`, memory looks like this:

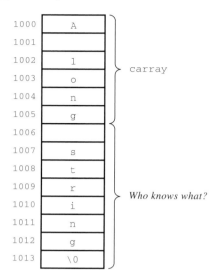

The bytes between addresses 1006 and 1013 presumably hold other variables or parts of the program itself, so changing them is almost certain to cause the program to fail. Writing data past the end of an array used as a buffer is a common programming error and is called **buffer overflow.**

An equally serious problem occurs if the destination string is a pointer variable that has not been properly initialized. Suppose, for example, that you have declared a string variable `str` using

```
string str;
```

You could not copy a string into that variable by using `strcpy`. If you tried to write

```
strcpy(str, "A long string");         This doesn't work.
```

without first initializing the variable `str` to point to a character array, the characters from `"A long string"` would be copied into some unpredictable region of memory.

As a programmer, it is your responsibility to make sure that these errors do not happen. If you think the string space you have allocated to the destination might not be sufficient, you have an obligation to check the length of the data before you copy it using `strcpy`. Thus, before using `strcpy` to copy the contents of `line` into `buffer`, you should make sure that buffer overflow cannot occur by testing the length of the line, as follows:

```
if (strlen(line) > MaxLine) Error("Input line too long");
strcpy(buffer, line);
```

Failure to check for buffer overflow can have dire consequences. In 1988, a gradu-ate student at Cornell University released a program that spread like a virus through computers connected to a worldwide network called the Internet. This program, which became known as the *Internet worm*, took advantage of the fact that a system utility program used on many Internet computers failed to check whether character storage in an internal buffer had been exhausted by the input data. By providing enough input data to use up the allocated storage, the Internet worm was able to overwrite the system program itself and cause it to execute commands on its behalf.

The strncpy function

To make it easier to avoid buffer overflow when you use the strcpy function, the ANSI string library includes an alternative form of strcpy called strncpy. The strncpy function allows the client to specify a length limit and has the following prototype:

```
void strncpy(string dst, string src, int n);
```

Like strcpy, strncpy copies characters from the string specified by src into the character array specified by dst. The difference is that strncpy will copy a maxi-mum of n characters from src, stopping earlier if a null character is encountered. By allowing you to specify the maximum string size, strncpy makes it possible to guard against writing data past the end of a character array. For example, if you have declared the character array buffer by writing

```
char buffer[MaxLine+1];
```

you can safely copy string data from line into buffer using the function call

```
strncpy(buffer, src, MaxLine);
```

Because the call to strncpy guarantees that at most MaxLine characters will be copied, it is no longer possible for the function call to overwrite data appearing after the end of buffer.

Unfortunately, the usefulness of the strncpy function is limited by the following design flaws:

- When strncpy(dst, src, n) returns, the destination array will be terminated with a null character only if the length of the source string is less than n. If src contains exactly n characters, the call copies those characters to the dst array but does not store a null character at the end. To ensure that the destination string is properly terminated, you must allocate an extra element to dst and explicitly initialize dst[n] to the null character.
- Calling the function strncpy(dst, src, n) writes null characters in every character position of dst until it fills up n positions. Thus, if MaxLine were 1000, calling strncpy(buffer, line, MaxLine) would assign new values to the first 1000 characters of buffer, even if line were extremely short. Having to fill the rest of the destination array with null characters substantially reduces the efficiency of strncpy.

The `strcat` and `strncat` functions

The ANSI string library includes functions for string concatenation, but these functions are used quite differently from the `Concat` function in the `strlib.h` interface. The `Concat` function returns a brand new string and does not change either of its arguments. In contrast, the corresponding function in the ANSI library, `strcat(s1, s2)`, works with the string storage supplied by the client and appends the characters in `s2` to the end of the string `s1`.

The `strcat` function is used frequently to assemble a larger string from smaller pieces. Thinking back to the Pig Latin program in Figure 10-5, you could use `strcpy` and `strcat` together to reassemble the components of a Pig Latin word. For example, suppose that the variables `head` and `tail` contain the strings `"src"` and `"am"`, respectively. You could put these strings together to form the string `"amscray"` using the following code:

```
char pigword[MaxWord+1];

strcpy(pigword, tail);
strcat(pigword, head);
strcat(pigword, "ay");
```

Note that the first component of the new string is copied into `pigword` using `strcpy`, not `strcat`. When `pigword` is declared, you have no way of knowing the initial contents of its elements, and you cannot assume that it contains the empty string. By calling

```
strcpy(pigword, tail);
```

you ensure that the characters in `tail` are copied to the beginning of the `pigword` array, which at this point has the following configuration:

pigword

When you call

```
strcat(pigword, head);
```

the `strcat` function finds the end of the current contents of `pigword` and starts copying the contents of `head` there, which results in the following state:

pigword

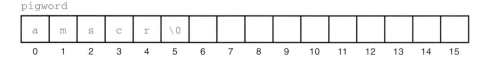

In the final step, calling

```
strcat(pigword, "ay");
```

completes the Pig Latin word, as follows:

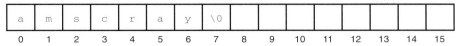

As with `strcpy`, you must use care with the `strcat` function to avoid concatenating more characters than the buffer can accommodate. The string library includes a function `strncat` that helps to a certain extent, but less than you might imagine. Calling `strncat(s1, s2, n)` copies at most `n` characters from `s2` to the end of `s1`. Unfortunately, to determine what value you should use for `n`, you need to check the current length of `s1` so that you know how much room remains in the buffer.

The `strlen`, `strcmp`, and `strncmp` functions

The `strlen` and `strcmp` functions exported by `string.h` are identical to the functions `StringLength` and `StringCompare`, which were introduced in Chapter 9. When you work with the ANSI libraries, you can use `strlen` and `strcmp` just as you have used their counterparts up to now.

The `string.h` interface, however, contains no direct counterpart to the `StringEqual` function. To test whether two strings are equal, C programmers simply call `strcmp` and check to see whether the result is 0. When programs compare the result to 0 explicitly, this approach does not cause much confusion. Programs become difficult to read if programmers start to rely on the fact that C interprets the integer 0 as equivalent to FALSE and all other integers as equivalent to TRUE. For example, you will sometimes see `if` statements such as

```
if (strcmp(s1, s2)) {
    . . . statements . . .
}
```

which executes the body of the `if` statement when s1 and s2 are *different*.

The following implementation of the `FindStringInArray` function given in Figure 12-2 offers an even more cryptic example of dense coding styles:

```
int FindStringInArray(string key, string array[], int n)
{
    int i;

    for (i = 0; i < n && strcmp(key, array[i]); i++);
    if (i < n) return (i);
    return (-1);
}
```

The `for` loop continues as long as `i` is less than `n` and the key does not match the current array entry. When the `for` loop exits, there are two possibilities: either the elements in the array have been exhausted or the loop has terminated with a match at index i. Because the `for` control line includes all the required work, the body of the loop is simply a semicolon.

The `string.h` interface exports another string comparison function that is occasionally quite useful: `strncmp`. Calling `strncmp(s1, s2, n)` is similar to calling `strcmp(s1, s2)` except that the implementation considers at most n characters from the two strings. If the first n characters of the strings are the same, `strncmp` returns 0 even if the strings differ at some later point.

The `strchr`, `strrchr`, and `strstr` functions

The `string.h` interface exports several functions for searching a string. The function `strchr(s, ch)` serves the same purpose as `FindChar(ch, s, 0)`. The main difference between the two is that `strchr` returns a *pointer* to the matching character while `FindChar` returns the *index* of that character. If the character is not found, `strchr` returns `NULL`. The function `strrchr(s, ch)` works much like `strchr` except that it searches backward from the end of the string to find the *last* instance of ch rather than the first. The `string.h` interface also includes the function `strstr(s1, s2)`, which searches for the first occurrence of the string s2 in s1 and is therefore analogous to `FindString`.

An application of the ANSI string functions

If you go on to take a job in the computer industry, the programs you encounter will not ordinarily make use of higher-level string libraries such as `strlib.h`. You will instead find yourself using the functions in the `string.h` interface or, just as often, working directly with the underlying representation of strings.

This section presents a simple example of string programming that does not use any of the `strlib.h` functions. The problem is to convert a name written in conventional order, like this:

First Middle Last

into inverted order, as follows:

Last, First Middle

Inverted order is useful if you want to arrange a list of names alphabetically.

Your goal in this example is to write a function `InvertName` that converts a name from conventional order into the last-name-first form. If its design is to conform to the usual discipline for working with strings in the ANSI library, `InvertName` must take two arguments, one that contains the original name and one that provides space for the inverted result. To maintain symmetry with `strcpy`, it makes sense to list the result argument first, as shown in the following prototype:

```
static void InvertName(char result[], char name[]);
```

The implementation of `InvertName` is easy to write using the functions in the `string.h` interface. Figure 14-4 shows one possible implementation together with a test program that reads in names and prints out their inverted form, as illustrated by the following sample run:

```
This program converts a name in standard order
into inverted order with the last name first.
Indicate the end of input with a blank line.
Name: Charles Babbage⏎
Babbage, Charles
Name: Augusta Ada Byron⏎
Byron, Augusta Ada
Name: J. Presper Eckert⏎
Eckert, J. Presper
Name: Euclid⏎
Euclid
Name: ⏎
```

14.3 Implementing the `strlib` library

To complete the discussion of the abstraction hierarchy used to represent strings at varying levels of detail, the rest of this chapter examines the implementation of the `strlib.h` interface. As indicated earlier in the chapter, the principal purpose of `strlib.h` is to hide complexity from the client by taking care of allocation details. When using this library, clients no longer have to allocate character arrays of fixed sizes or worry about whether they are exceeding the space bounds. All strings are represented as pointers to character memory acquired from the heap through dynamic allocation.

Implementing the pass-through functions

Of the functions exported by `strlib.h`, the simplest ones to implement are those that are identical to functions in `string.h`: `StringLength` and `StringCompare`. The inclusion in `strlib.h` of functions that are the same as those in a standard library may seem somewhat wasteful. Instead of having you work with `StringLength` and `StringCompare`, this text could have introduced `strlen` and `strcmp` initially, thereby giving you a head start on learning about the standard interface.

As it happens, the technique of exporting functions from one interface that simply rename functions in a lower-level interface is a common practice. Such functions are called **pass-through functions.** The point of providing a pass-through function—as opposed to having clients use its lower-level counterpart—is to reduce the conceptual complexity for the client. If you had to use some facilities from `strlib.h` and others from `string.h`, you would need to include both library

---

FIGURE 14-4   invert.c

```
/*
 * File: invert.c
 * --------------
 * This file implements a function InvertName(result, name)
 * that takes a name in standard order (first middle last) and
 * returns a new string in inverted order (last, first middle),
 * which makes it easier to alphabetize the names. The test
 * program reads in names and prints out their inverted form,
 * stopping when a blank line is entered.
 */

#include <stdio.h>
#include <string.h>
#include "genlib.h"
#include "simpio.h"

/*
 * Constant
 * --------
 * MaxName -- Maximum number of characters in a name
 */

#define MaxName 40

/* Private function prototypes */

static void InvertName(char result[], char name[]);

/* Main program */

main()
{
    char *standardName;
    char invertedName[MaxName+1];

    printf("This program converts a name in standard order\n");
    printf("into inverted order with the last name first.\n");
    printf("Indicate the end of input with a blank line.\n");
    while (TRUE) {
        printf("Name: ");
        standardName = GetLine();
        if (strlen(standardName) == 0) break;
        InvertName(invertedName, standardName);
        printf("%s\n", invertedName);
    }
}
```

```
/*
 * Function: InvertName
 * Usage: InvertName(result, name);
 * --------------------------------
 * This function inverts a name from its standard order
 *
 *      First Middle Last
 *
 * into inverted order, which is
 *
 *      Last, First Middle
 *
 * The client must supply an output array called result in which
 * the inverted name will be stored.  That array must contain
 * at least MaxName character positions, plus one for a
 * terminating null character.  If storing the inverted name
 * would exceed that limit, the function generates an error.
 * The output is always one character longer than the input
 * because of the comma, so it is possible to determine the
 * output length immediately.
 *
 * The last name is assumed to consist of all characters in the
 * name string following the last space character.  If there are
 * no space characters in the word, the entire name is copied to
 * the destination array unchanged.
 */

static void InvertName(char result[], char name[])
{
    int len;
    char *sptr;

    len = strlen(name);
    sptr = strrchr(name, ' ');
    if (sptr != NULL) len++;
    if (len > MaxName) Error("Name too long");
    if (sptr == NULL) {
        strcpy(result, name);
    } else {
        strcpy(result, sptr + 1);
        strcat(result, ", ");
        strncat(result, name, sptr - name);
        result[len] = '\0';
    }
}
```

interfaces in your programs. More importantly, you would have to understand both of those interfaces and the functions they provide. Defining strlib.h so that it is complete in itself frees you from having to learn anything about the lower-level interface until you are ready to do so.

Implementing pass-through functions is extremely easy. The strlib.c versions of StringLength and StringCompare are simply

```
int StringLength(string s)
{
    return (strlen(s));
}

int StringCompare(string s1, string s2)
{
    return (strcmp(s1, s2));
}
```

Implementing the strlib allocation functions

The main feature of most functions in the strlib.h interface is that they allocate memory dynamically for any new strings they create. To centralize this phase of the operation, the strlib.c implementation defines a private function CreateString(len) that allocates memory for a string of size len, taking account of the fact that strings require an extra byte for the '\0' character at the end. The implementation of CreateString, like most of the package, is straightforward:

```
static string CreateString(int len)
{
    return ((string) GetBlock(len + 1));
}
```

Once you have this function, you can use it to write all the functions in strlib that need to allocate memory. For example, consider the following implementation of CharToString, which allocates a string consisting of a single character:

```
string CharToString(char ch)
{
    string result;

    result = CreateString(1);
    result[0] = ch;
    result[1] = '\0';
    return (result);
}
```

The function dynamically allocates space to hold a one-character string and then initializes that memory by assigning both the specified character and the terminating null.

Let's look at a more substantial function, such as Concat. One approach is to code all the copying explicitly. Again, the implementation begins by allocating space for the combined string and then copies the characters from each string in turn, as follows:

```
string Concat(string s1, string s2)
{
    string s;
    int len1, len2, i;

    len1 = strlen(s1);
    len2 = strlen(s2);
    s = CreateString(len1 + len2);
    for (i = 0; i < len1; i++) s[i] = s1[i];
    for (i = 0; i < len2; i++) s[i + len1] = s2[i];
    s[len1 + len2] = '\0';
    return (s);
}
```

Although this implementation works, it does not take advantage of the functions in the lower-level libraries. The functions in the ANSI string library are usually engineered so that they are as efficient as possible given the hardware characteristics of the computer on which they run. If you use those functions in your implementation, the resulting code will often be more efficient than an implementation that performs the character operations explicitly. Thus, it makes sense to use `strcpy` as part of the implementation, which then looks like this:

```
string Concat(string s1, string s2)
{
    string s;
    int len1, len2;

    len1 = strlen(s1);
    len2 = strlen(s2);
    s = CreateString(len1 + len2);
    strcpy(s, s1);
    strcpy(s + len1, s2);
    return (s);
}
```

In many ways, this coding is even simpler than the earlier one, but it does include the somewhat cryptic line

```
strcpy(s + len1, s2);
```

To understand this line, you need to remember that adding a pointer and an integer advances the pointer by the indicated number of elements. In this example, since you're working with characters, the destination address is simply the address of an array that begins `len1` characters after `s`, which is precisely where the copy of `s2` belongs. Calling `strcpy(s + len1, s2)` at this point has the same effect as calling `strcat(s, s2)`. The `strcpy` form is more efficient because it avoids having to search for the end of `s`.

You can use the same techniques to implement most functions in the `strlib.h` interface. Representative examples of these implementation problems are included in the programming exercises.

SUMMARY

In this chapter, you have learned to think about strings in new ways. Up to this point, the details of string manipulation have been hidden by the `strlib.h` interface, which has allowed you to work with strings as an abstract type. Looking beyond the abstraction barrier to the underlying representation of strings as character arrays, you have had a chance to see how strings are implemented. This perspective gives you more flexibility in working with strings and makes it easier for you to understand existing C code.

Along with the discussion of string representation, you have also learned to use the ANSI `string.h` interface, which provides a set of standard tools for working with strings. Although the functions in this interface are similar to those exported by `strlib.h`, the two libraries differ markedly in their use of memory. When you call functions in `strlib.h`, the implementation automatically allocates any memory required to hold the result. If you call functions in `string.h`, you must allocate space for the result explicitly.

Important points raised in this chapter include:

- Strings may be regarded in three complementary ways: as an array of characters, as a pointer to a character, and as an abstract entity with conceptual integrity as a whole.
- In C, a string is represented internally as an array of characters terminated by a null character.
- Because any array in C can also be interpreted as a pointer to its first element, you can manipulate string values by using pointer operations.
- Declaring a variable to be an array of characters does not have the same effect as declaring it to be a pointer to a character. Array declaration reserves space for the specified number of elements; pointer declaration reserves only enough space for the pointer. A string declared as a pointer must be initialized before you can select its component characters.
- Like any array, a character array is not an lvalue in C and cannot appear on the left-hand side of an assignment. It is also illegal for a function to return a character array, although you can often achieve a similar effect by having a function return a character pointer.
- The `string.h` interface contains several standard functions for manipulating strings. As a client of `string.h`, you must take responsibility for allocating enough memory space to hold the result.
- The `strlib.h` interface has a straightforward implementation that uses a combination of dynamic allocation and the `string.h` functions.

REVIEW QUESTIONS

1. This chapter asks you to think about strings from three different perspectives. What are they?

2. In terms of the underlying representation, how do you determine the end of a string?

3. What idiom can you use to process each character in a string that you view as an array of characters? How does the idiom change if you instead regard the string as a pointer to a character?

4. True or false: Declaring a parameter to be a character array has the same effect as declaring it to be a pointer.

5. True or false: Declaring a local variable to be a character array has the same effect as declaring it to be a pointer.

6. What restrictions does C place on the use of array variables?

7. Why is it an error to return a pointer to a local array as the value of a function?

8. What is the principal difference between the abstraction models presented by the `string.h` and `strlib.h` interfaces?

9. If you call `strcpy(s1, s2)`, which argument is the source and which is the destination?

10. Before you call `strcpy`, what responsibility do you assume as client?

11. What is meant by the term *buffer overflow?*

12. What two factors limit the utility of the function `strncpy`?

13. When you are using the ANSI string library, how do you accomplish the effect of the `StringEqual` function?

14. What two functions in `strlib.h` are implemented as pass-through functions? Why was it important to include these functions in the interface?

15. Why is it better to use the function `strcpy` in the implementation of `Concat` than to write the `for` loops explicitly?

PROGRAMMING EXERCISES

1. The simplest function in the string library is `strlen`, which calculates the length of a string by finding the null character marking its end. Write an implementation of `strlen` that treats its argument as an array of characters.

2. Rewrite your answer to exercise 1 so that the implementation of `strlen` works with its argument as a pointer to a character and uses only pointer manipulation to look at each character in the string.

3. Write an implementation of the function `strcmp` that works directly with the underlying representation of its argument and calls no other functions. For extra practice, implement this function in two forms: one using only array operations and the other using only pointer operations.

4. The section entitled "Searching within a string" in Chapter 9 defines a function `Acronym(s)` that returns a new word formed by combining the initial letters of each word in the string `s`, which is assumed to consist of a series of words separated by a single space. In its design, the `Acronym` function fits the `strlib.h` model because it allocates and returns a new string. To fit the discipline of the `string.h` interface, such a function must deliver its result by writing data into a character buffer supplied by the caller. Design and implement a function to compute acronyms that uses this strategy. Your implementation should not include `strlib.h` or use any of its functions.

5. Write a function `ReverseString(carray)` that reverses the characters in its argument. For example, if `carray` originally contains the data

carray

A	B	C	D	\0											

calling `ReverseString(carray)` should reverse the characters so that the contents of the array become

carray

D	C	B	A	\0											

6. Rewrite the cipher program described in exercise 8 of Chapter 9 so that it uses the ANSI string library rather than `strlib.h`.

7. Using only functions from the `string.h` interface, implement the function `SubString(s, p1, p2)` from the `strlib` library, which returns the substring of `s` beginning at position `p1` and ending at position `p2`. Make sure that your function correctly applies the following rules:
   a. If `p1` is negative, it is set to 0 so that it indicates the first character in the string.
   b. If `p2` is greater than `strlen(s) − 1`, it is set to `strlen(s) − 1` so that it indicates the last character.
   c. If `p1` ends up being greater than `p2`, `SubString` returns the empty string.

8. Using only functions from the `string.h` interface, implement the function `FindString(s, text, start)`, which returns the index position of the first occurrence of `s` in `text` after position `start` or returns −1 if no such match occurs.

9. Using only functions from `string.h` and `ctype.h`, implement the function `ConvertToUpperCase(s)`, which returns a copy of `s` in which all alphabetic characters have been converted to upper case.

10. Redesign the `scanner.h` interface presented in Figure 10-3 so that it uses a string-handling discipline consistent with the ANSI string library. Reimplement the interface without using any functions from `strlib.h`.

11. Using the revised `scanner.h` interface from exercise 10, reimplement the Pig Latin program given in Figure 10-5 without using any functions from `strlib.h`. Your program may continue to read the input line using `GetLine`, which is defined in `simpio.h`.

12. Use the ANSI string library to write a program that plays the game of hangman. In hangman, the computer begins by selecting a secret word at random from a list of possibilities. It then prints out a row of dashes—one for each letter in the secret word—and asks the user to guess a letter. If the user guesses a letter that appears in the word, the word is redisplayed with all instances of that letter shown in the correct positions, along with any letters guessed correctly on previous turns. If the letter does not appear in the word, the player is charged with an incorrect guess. The player keeps guessing letters until either (1) the player has correctly guessed all the letters in the word or (2) the player has made eight incorrect guesses. A sample run of the hangman program is shown in Figure 14-5.

FIGURE 14-5   Sample run of the hangman program

```
Let's play hangman! I will pick a secret word.
On each turn, you guess a letter. If the letter
is in the secret word, I will show you where it
appears. If you make an incorrect guess, part
of your body gets strung up on the scaffold.
The object is to guess the word before you are
hanged.
The word now looks like this: ----
You have 8 guesses left.
Your guess: A↵
There are no A's in the word.
The word now looks like this: ----
You have 7 guesses left.
Your guess: E↵
There are no E's in the word.
The word now looks like this: ----
You have 6 guesses left.
Your guess: I↵
```

```
There are no I's in the word.
The word now looks like this: ----
You have 5 guesses left.
Your guess: O↵
There are no O's in the word.
The word now looks like this: ----
You have 4 guesses left.
Your guess: U↵
That guess is correct.
The word now looks like this: -U--
You have 4 guesses left.
Your guess: S↵
There are no S's in the word.
The word now looks like this: -U--
You have 3 guesses left.
Your guess: N↵
That guess is correct.
The word now looks like this: -UN-
You have 3 guesses left.
Your guess: K↵
That guess is correct.
The word now looks like this: -UNK
You have 3 guesses left.
Your guess: H↵
There are no H's in the word.
The word now looks like this: -UNK
You have 2 guesses left.
Your guess: B↵
There are no B's in the word.
The word now looks like this: -UNK
You have only one guess left.
Your guess: J↵
That guess is correct.
You guessed the word: JUNK
You win.
```

As it is usually played, incorrect guesses are recorded by drawing an evolving picture of the user being hanged on a scaffold. For each incorrect guess, a new part of a stick-figure body—first the head, then the body, then each arm, each leg, and finally each foot—is added to the scaffold until the hanging is complete. For example, the following diagrams show the drawing after the first incorrect guess (just the head), after the third incorrect guess (the head, body, and left arm), and at the tragic end of a losing game.

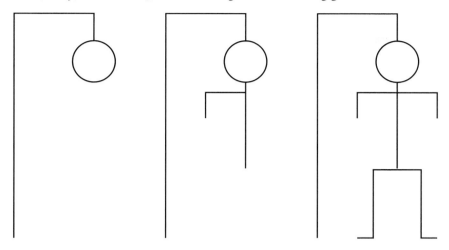

If you feel up to an additional challenge, use the graphics library described in Chapter 7 to display the current picture after each turn.

CHAPTER 15

Files

Everybody gets so much information all day that they lose their
common sense.

— Gertrude Stein, untitled essay, 1946

Objectives

- To understand the concept of a text file and how such files provide permanent storage.

- To be able to open and close files using the functions `fopen` and `fclose`.

- To learn how to process files in character mode using the functions `getc` and `putc`.

- To be able to process files in line mode using the functions `fgets` and `fputs`.

- To understand the structure and operation of the `scanf` family of functions.

Programs use variables to store information: input data, calculated results, and any intermediate values generated along the way. Such information, however, is ephemeral. When the program stops running, the values of those variables are lost. For many applications, it is important to be able to store data in some more permanent fashion.

Whenever you want to store information on the computer for longer than the running time of a program, the usual approach is to collect the data into a logically cohesive whole and store it on a permanent storage medium as a *file,* a concept that was introduced in Chapter 1. Ordinarily, a file is stored on a disk, either a removable floppy disk or a hard disk built into the machine. Occasionally, files are stored in another medium, such as a magnetic tape or a CD, but the basic principles and modes of operation are the same. The important point is that the permanent data objects you store on the computer—documents, games, executable programs, source code, and the like—are all stored in the form of files.

■■■■ 15.1 Text files

On most systems, files come in a variety of types. For example, in the programming domain, you work with source files, object files, and executable files, each of which has a distinct representation. When you use a file to store data for use by a program, that file usually consists of text and is therefore called a **text file.** You can think of a text file as a sequence of characters stored in a permanent medium and identified by a file name. The name of the file and the characters it contains have the same relationship as the name of a variable and its contents.

For example, suppose you had decided to collect a set of quotations from Shakespeare and store each quotation in a separate file. Your collection might begin by storing the following quotation from *Hamlet* in a file named `hamlet.txt`:

```
To be, or not to be: that is the question.
Whether 'tis nobler in the mind to suffer
The slings and arrows of outrageous fortune,
Or to take arms against a sea of troubles,
And by opposing end them?
```

As a second quotation, you might choose to store the following lines from *Romeo and Juliet* in the file `juliet.txt`:

```
What's in a name?
That which we call a rose
By any other name would smell as sweet.
```

When you look at a file, it often makes sense to regard it as a two-dimensional structure—a sequence of lines composed of individual characters. For example, suppose that you have added to your collection of quotations a new file `witches.txt` containing the following lines from *Macbeth*:

```
Double, double toil and trouble:
Fire burn and cauldron bubble.
```

It is easiest to think of `witches.txt` as consisting of two lines. Internally, however, text files are represented as a one-dimensional sequence of characters. In addition to the printing characters you can see, files also contain the end-of-line character `'\n'`, which you have used ever since Chapter 2. Thus, the `witches.txt` file is perhaps more correctly viewed as having the following form:

```
Double, double toil and trouble:\nFire burn and cauldron bubble.\n
```

In many respects, text files are similar to strings. A text file consists of an ordered collection of characters, just as a string does. Moreover, they both have a definite endpoint. In strings, the end of the data is indicated with a null character. A text file ends with a special end-of-file marker indicating that no more characters occur after that point. For example, the file `witches.txt` ends after the `\n` character following the word *bubble*. When you read characters from a file, you need to be able to detect this end-of-file marker so that you know when there are no more characters to read.

On the other hand, strings and files differ in several important respects. Of these, the most important difference is the permanence of the data. A string is stored temporarily in the computer's memory during the time that a program runs; a file is stored on a long-term storage device and continues to exist until it is explicitly deleted or overwritten. But there is also a difference in the way you use data in strings and files. A string is an array of characters. You can select characters in any order by specifying the appropriate index. In the context of a program, a file is usually read or written in a sequential fashion. When a program reads an existing file, it starts at the beginning and reads characters until it reaches the end. When a program creates a new file, it starts by writing the first character and continues in order with each subsequent character.

15.2 Using files in C

In ANSI C, basic file operations are provided as part of the standard I/O library interface `stdio.h`. You have used the standard I/O library since Chapter 2 but have had relatively little opportunity to investigate the facilities it contains. The real power of the standard I/O library is that it permits you to specify file operations in a portable way that is nonetheless convenient and efficient.

To use a file in a C program, you

1. Declare a variable of type `FILE *`.
2. Associate the variable with an actual file by calling the `fopen` function. This operation is called **opening** the file. Opening a file requires you to specify the name of the file and to indicate whether that file is used for input or output.
3. Call the appropriate functions in `stdio.h` to perform the necessary I/O operations. For an input file, these functions read data from the file into your program; for an output file, the functions transfer data from the program to the file.
4. Indicate that the file operations are complete by calling `fclose`. This operation, called **closing** the file, breaks the association between a `FILE *` variable and the actual file.

The next four sections consider each of these steps in turn.

Declaring a `FILE *` variable

The standard I/O library defines a type called `FILE`, which is used to store the information needed by the system to manage file processing activity. Because the structure of file systems differs from machine to machine, the underlying representation of the type `FILE` also differs. The main purpose of `stdio.h` is to make it possible to ignore those differences. From your perspective as a programmer, you don't need to know anything about the underlying details. All you need to do to manipulate a file is keep track of a pointer to a `FILE` structure—however it is defined for a particular machine—trusting in the local implementation of `stdio.h` to manage the relevant details.

As with any pointer, you declare a `FILE *` variable in C by writing a line like

```
FILE *infile;
```

The variable `infile` is therefore of type pointer-to-`FILE`.

You must declare a separate `FILE *` variable for each of the files that may be open simultaneously. For example, if your application requires you to read information from one file, process it, and then write the processed data to a second file, you will need to declare two `FILE *` variables. If you choose to call these variables `infile` and `outfile`, the appropriate declaration would be

```
FILE *infile, *outfile;
```

When you later call a function to read data from the input file, you need to include the variable `infile` as an argument to the function. Similarly, calls to functions used to write output data need to specify the variable `outfile`. The `FILE *` parameter tells the function what file is involved.

Opening a file

When you first declare a `FILE *` variable, it is not yet associated with an actual file. To make that association, you must call the function `fopen`, which has the following form:

file pointer variable = `fopen`(*file name*, *mode*);

The first argument to `fopen` is a string specifying the name of the file using the naming conventions of the local system. The second argument is a string specifying the mode of data transfer, which is ordinarily one of the following:

"r"   The file is open for *reading*. The file pointer variable returned by `fopen` can be used only in input operations. The file must already exist.

"w"   The file is open for *writing*. The resulting file pointer variable can be used only for output operations. If the file does not yet exist, a new file is created with the specified name. If there is already a file with that name, its contents are erased.

"a"   The file is open for *appending*. This mode is similar to "w" mode in that the resulting file pointer is available for output operations. The only difference occurs if the specified file already exists, in which case any new information written to the file appears at the end of the existing data.

For example, if you wanted to open the file `juliet.txt` for input and associate it with the variable `infile`, you would write

```
infile = fopen("juliet.txt", "r");
```

This statement establishes the association of the variable `infile` with the file `juliet.txt` and makes it possible for you to begin reading data.

It is, of course, possible for this operation to fail. For example, there might not be a file named `juliet.txt`. If the requested input file is missing or if other errors are detected, the `fopen` call returns the pointer value `NULL` to indicate that an error has occurred. As a programmer, you have a responsibility to check for this error and report it to the user. One approach is to report the failure by calling the `Error` function, as follows:

```
infile = fopen("juliet.txt", "r");
if (infile == NULL) Error("Can't open the file juliet.txt");
```

Not being able to find an input file is particularly likely when the program reads that file name from the user because the user can easily make typographical errors. Rather than have the whole program stop, it is usually better to give the user another chance to enter a valid name, as the following code does:

```
while (TRUE) {
    printf("Input file name: ");
    filename = GetLine();
    infile = fopen(filename, "r");
    if (infile != NULL) break;
    printf("Can't open the file %s. Try again.\n", filename);
}
```

Performing I/O operations

Once you have opened a file, the next step is to read or write the actual data. To do so, you can choose any of several strategies, depending on the application. At the simplest level, you can read or write files character by character using the functions getc and putc. In many cases, however, it is more convenient to process files line by line. For that purpose, the stdio.h interface provides the functions fgets and fputs, but it is often simpler to use the function ReadLine from simpio.h, which solves a number of problems that arise when using the ANSI standard functions. At a still higher level, you can choose to read and write formatted data using fscanf and fprintf. Doing so allows you to intermix numeric data with strings and other data types. The functions mentioned in this paragraph are described later in the chapter. The discussion is organized so that functions that use the same basic discipline are considered together.

Closing files

No matter which strategy you choose for the I/O operations, you should be sure to close any files you open. Closing a file is accomplished by calling the function fclose with the appropriate file pointer. Thus, to close the files corresponding to the variables infile and outfile, you would write

```
fclose(infile);
fclose(outfile);
```

Even though exiting from a program automatically closes any open files, it is good to get into the habit of closing files explicitly because

- It will be much easier for readers of your program to determine precisely when a file is in use and when that file is no longer needed.
- It will be easier to incorporate your code into a larger program that may open and close on its own.

Standard files

The standard I/O library defines three special identifiers—stdin, stdout, and stderr—that act as FILE * constants and are available to all programs. These constants are referred to as **standard files.** The constant stdin designates the standard input file, which is the source for user input. The constant stdout indicates standard output and represents the device on which output data is written to the user. The constant stderr represents the standard error file and is used to report any error messages the user should see. Typically, the standard files all refer to the computer console. When you read data from stdin, the input comes from the keyboard; when you write data to stdout or stderr, the output appears on the screen. Some systems, however, make it easy to change these associations so that standard input comes from a file or so that standard output is assigned to some other file or device.

Even if the system you are using does not provide the ability to change the assignment of the standard files, their existence is nonetheless useful because it means that any of the functions described in this chapter can be used directly with the console. By using the names stdin, stdout, and stderr, you can read or write characters, lines, or formatted data.

15.3 Character I/O

The simplest approach to file processing is to go through files character by character. The `stdio.c` interface defines a function `getc(infile)` that reads the next character in a file and returns it to its caller. It also defines a function `getchar()` that reads from the standard input file and is therefore equivalent to `getc(stdin)`.

The idea of `getc` seems simple enough, but there is a confusing aspect in its design. If you look at the formal definition of `getc`, its prototype looks like this:

```
int getc(FILE *infile);
```

At first glance, the result type seems odd. The prototype indicates that `getc` returns an integer, even though the function conceptually returns a character.

The reason for this design decision is that returning a character would make it impossible for a program to detect the end-of-file mark. There are only 256 possible character codes, and a data file might contain any of those values. There is no value—or at least no value of type `char`—that you could use as a sentinel to indicate the end-of-file condition. By extending the definition so that `getc` returns an integer, the implementation can return a value outside the range of legal character codes to indicate the end-of-file condition. That value is given the symbolic name of `EOF` in `stdio.h` and usually has the value −1, although you should never depend on the fact that `EOF` has a particular internal value.

To write a single character, you use the function `putc(ch, outfile)`, which writes its first argument to the specified output file. The `stdio.c` interface also includes a function `putchar(ch)`, which is defined to be the same as `putc(ch, stdout)`.

As an example of the use of `getc` and `putc`, you can copy one file to another using the `copyfile.c` program shown in Figure 15-1.

The `while` loop in `CopyFile` is highly idiomatic and deserves some consideration. The test expression for the `while` loop uses embedded assignment to combine the operations of reading in a character and testing for the end-of-file condition. When the program evaluates the `while` condition, it begins by evaluating the subexpression

```
ch = getc(infile)
```

which reads a character and assigns it to `ch`. Before executing the loop body, the program then goes on to make sure the result of the assignment is not `EOF`. The parentheses around the assignment are required; without them, the expression would incorrectly assign to `ch` the result of comparing the character against `EOF`. The effect of the loop is thus the same as the longer expression

```
while (TRUE) {
    ch = getc(infile);
    if (ch == EOF) break;
    putc(ch, outfile);
}
```

In most C programs you will encounter, this loop is written in its abbreviated form.

COMMON PITFALLS

Remember that `getc` returns an `int`, not a `char`. If you use a variable of type `char` to store the result of `getc`, your program will be unable to detect the end-of-file condition.

FIGURE 15-1 copyfile.c

```
/*
 * File: copyfile.c
 * ----------------
 * This program copies one file to another using character I/O.
 */

#include <stdio.h>
#include "genlib.h"
#include "simpio.h"

/* Private function prototypes */

static void CopyFile(FILE *infile, FILE *outfile);
static FILE *OpenUserFile(string prompt, string mode);

/* Main program */

main()
{
    FILE *infile, *outfile;

    printf("This program copies one file to another.\n");
    infile = OpenUserFile("Old file: ", "r");
    outfile = OpenUserFile("New file: ", "w");
    CopyFile(infile, outfile);
    fclose(infile);
    fclose(outfile);
}

/*
 * Function: CopyFile
 * Usage: CopyFile(infile, outfile);
 * ---------------------------------
 * This function copies the contents of infile to outfile. The
 * client is responsible for opening these files before calling
 * CopyFile and for closing them afterward.
 */

static void CopyFile(FILE *infile, FILE *outfile)
{
    int ch;

    while ((ch = getc(infile)) != EOF) {
        putc(ch, outfile);
    }
}
```

```
/*
 * Function: OpenUserFile
 * Usage: fileptr = OpenUserFile(prompt, mode);
 * ------------------------------------------------
 * This function prompts the user for a file name using the
 * prompt string supplied by the user and then attempts to
 * open that file with the specified mode. If the file is
 * opened successfully, OpenUserFile returns the appropriate
 * file pointer. If the open operation fails, the user is
 * informed of the failure and given an opportunity to enter
 * another file name.
 */

static FILE *OpenUserFile(string prompt, string mode)
{
    string filename;
    FILE *result;

    while (TRUE) {
        printf("%s", prompt);
        filename = GetLine();
        result = fopen(filename, mode);
        if (result != NULL) break;
        printf("Can't open the file \"%s\"\n", filename);
    }
    return (result);
}
```

Updating a file

The copyfile.c program shown in Figure 15-1 makes an exact duplicate of a file
with a different name. Instead of making a duplicate copy, you can easily use the
same basic structure to write a program that transforms the characters as they go
by. For example, the following loop copies data from infile to outfile, converting all characters to upper case:

```
while ((ch = getc(infile)) != EOF) {
    putc(toupper(ch), outfile);
}
```

If you used this loop as the body of the CopyFile procedure in Figure 15-1, the
resulting program would take one file and generate an uppercase copy as a separate file.

In many cases, however, you don't really want a second file. What you want to
do is modify an existing one. The process of changing an existing file is called

updating the file and is not as simple as it might seem. On most systems, it is not legal to open a file for output if that file is already open for input. Depending on how files are implemented on a particular system, the call to `fopen` may fail or end up destroying the original contents of the file.

The most common way to update a file is to write the new data into a temporary file and then replace the original file with the temporary one after you have written the entire contents of the updated file. Thus, if you wanted to write a program to change all the characters in a file to upper case, that program would execute the following steps:

1. Open the original file for input.
2. Open a temporary file for output with a different name.
3. Copy the input file to the temporary file, substituting uppercase characters for any lowercase characters encountered.
4. Close both files.
5. Delete the original file.
6. Rename the temporary file so that it once again has the original name.

Suppose, for example, that you wanted to update the file `witches.txt` by converting all its characters to upper case. At the beginning, all you have is the original file `witches.txt`, as shown:

witches.txt

```
Double, double toil and trouble:
Fire burn and cauldron bubble.
```

The next step is to create a temporary file and open it for output. Initially, the temporary file is empty, as indicated in the following diagram:

witches.txt   tempfile

```
Double, double toil and trouble:
Fire burn and cauldron bubble.
```

Because the two files are separate, it is easy to copy the data from one file to another, transforming characters as you go, which leads to the following state:

witches.txt   tempfile

```
Double, double toil and trouble:      DOUBLE, DOUBLE TOIL AND TROUBLE:
Fire burn and cauldron bubble.        FIRE BURN AND CAULDRON BUBBLE.
```

At this point, `tempfile` has the desired final contents. If you delete the old file named `witches.txt` and then rename `tempfile` as a new `witches.txt` file, you are left with a single file that contains exactly what it's supposed to, as follows:

witches.txt

```
DOUBLE, DOUBLE TOIL AND TROUBLE:
FIRE BURN AND CAULDRON BUBBLE.
```

To write the code necessary to implement this strategy, you need to use three new functions from the `stdio.h` interface—`tmpnam`, `remove`, and `rename`—each of which is described in the remainder of this section.

Although you are certainly free to choose your own name for a temporary file, the `stdio.h` interface includes a function called `tmpnam` that generates temporary file names. The conventions for naming files differ from machine to machine. Calling the function `tmpnam(NULL)` returns a string whose value is a temporary file name suitable for use on that machine.[1] Thus, you can create and open a new temporary file using the following code:

```
temp = tmpnam(NULL);
outfile = fopen(temp, "w");
```

To delete a file, all you have to do is call the function `remove`(*name*), where *name* is the name of the file. Renaming a file is just as simple and is accomplished by calling `rename`(*old name*, *new name*). Like many functions in the ANSI libraries, `remove` and `rename` each return 0 if they are successful and a nonzero value if they fail. Although you will certainly encounter code in which these functions are used as if they were procedures, it is safer to test their return value to make sure that the operation has succeeded.

These three functions give you everything you need to write the program `ucfile.c` shown in Figure 15-2, which converts a file to upper case.

Rereading characters in the input file

On many occasions when you are reading data from an input file, you will find yourself in the problematic position of not knowing that you should stop reading characters until you have already read more than you need. For example, suppose that you were reading characters from a file looking for a number composed of decimal digits. As long as you read digit characters from the file, you should go on and read the next character. Thus, the loop that reads characters until you get a non-digit might look like this (using the `isdigit` function from `ctype.h`):

```
while (isdigit(ch = getc(infile)))  . . .
```

But what happens when you are finished? You only know that you are done with the number when you read the first non-digit. That non-digit signals the end of the

---

[1] When it is called with `NULL` as its argument, the `tmpnam` function returns a pointer to memory that is private to the implementation of the standard I/O library. As a result, it is not safe to use `tmpnam` to generate a second temporary file name before you have finished with the first. If you need to do so, you can copy the result of `tmpnam` into new memory using `CopyString` or `strcpy`.

FIGURE 15-2   ucfile.c

```
/*
 * File: ucfile.c
 * --------------
 * This program updates the contents of a file by converting all
 * letters to upper case.
 */

#include <stdio.h>
#include <ctype.h>
#include "genlib.h"
#include "simpio.h"

/* Private function prototypes */

static void UpperCaseCopy(FILE *infile, FILE *outfile);

/* Main program */

main()
{
    string filename, temp;
    FILE *infile, *outfile;

    printf("This program converts a file to upper case.\n");
    while (TRUE) {
        printf("File name: ");
        filename = GetLine();
        infile = fopen(filename, "r");
        if (infile != NULL) break;
        printf("File %s not found -- try again.\n", filename);
    }
    temp = tmpnam(NULL);
    outfile = fopen(temp, "w");
    if (outfile == NULL) Error("Can't open temporary file");
    UpperCaseCopy(infile, outfile);
    fclose(infile);
    fclose(outfile);
    if (remove(filename) != 0 || rename(temp, filename) != 0) {
        Error("Unable to rename temporary file");
    }
}
```

```
/*
 * Function: UpperCaseCopy
 * Usage: UpperCaseCopy(infile, outfile);
 * -------------------------------------
 * This function copies the contents of infile to outfile,
 * converting alphabetic characters to upper case as it does so.
 * The client is responsible for opening and closing the files.
 */

static void UpperCaseCopy(FILE *infile, FILE *outfile)
{
    int ch;

    while ((ch = getc(infile)) != EOF) {
        putc(toupper(ch), outfile);
    }
}
```

loop but may well be part of the next value you're trying to read from that file. By calling getc, you have already read that character into the variable ch and taken it out of the input stream.

What you would like to do at this point is to say something akin to "Whoops! I didn't really mean to read in that character. Here, just put it back in the file stream and forget that I ever saw it." C provides a function, ungetc(ch, infile), that does exactly that. The effect of this call is to "push" the character ch back into the input stream so that it is returned on the next call to getc. However, the C libraries only guarantee the ability to push back one character into the input file, so you should not rely on being able to read several characters ahead and then push them all back. Fortunately, being able to push back one character is sufficient in the vast majority of cases.

To appreciate how the ungetc function can be useful, suppose you wanted to write a program that copies a program from one file to another, removing all comments as it does so. As you know, a comment in C begins with the character sequence /* and ends with the sequence */. A program to remove them must copy characters until it detects the initial /* sequence and then read characters without copying them until it detects the */ at the end.

The only aspect of this problem that poses any difficulty at all is the fact that the comment markers are two characters long. If you are copying the file a character at a time, what do you do when you encounter a slash? It might be the beginning of a comment, in which case you should not copy it to the output file. On the other hand, it might be the division operator. The only way to determine which of these cases applies is to look at the next character. If it is an asterisk, you need to ignore both characters and make note of the fact that a comment is in progress. If it not, however, the easiest thing to do is to push the character back into the input stream and copy it on the next cycle. The CopyRemovingComments function shown in Figure 15-3 implements this strategy.

FIGURE 15-3 CopyRemovingComments

```
static void CopyRemovingComments(FILE *infile, FILE *outfile)
{
    int ch, nch;
    bool commentFlag;

    commentFlag = FALSE;
    while ((ch = getc(infile)) != EOF) {
        if (commentFlag) {
            if (ch == '*') {
                nch = getc(infile);
                if (nch == '/') {
                    commentFlag = FALSE;
                } else {
                    ungetc(nch, infile);
                }
            }
        } else {
            if (ch == '/') {
                nch = getc(infile);
                if (nch == '*') {
                    commentFlag = TRUE;
                } else {
                    ungetc(nch, infile);
                }
            }
            if (!commentFlag) putc(ch, outfile);
        }
    }
}
```

15.4 Line-oriented I/O

Because files are usually subdivided into individual lines, it is often useful to read
an entire line of data at a time. The function in `stdio.h` that performs this operation is called `fgets` and has the following prototype:

```
string fgets(char buffer[], int bufSize, FILE *infile);
```

The effect of this function is to copy the next line of the file into the character
array `buffer`. Ordinarily, `fgets` stops after reading the first newline character but
returns earlier if the size of the buffer, as specified by the parameter `bufSize`,
would otherwise be exceeded. Thus, the last character in `buffer` before the terminating null character will be a newline unless the line from the file is too long to fit
in the buffer. Irrespective of whether it reads the entire line or a part of it, `fgets`
ordinarily returns a pointer to the character array given as the first argument. If
`fgets` is called at the end of the file, it returns NULL.

The corresponding function for output is called `fputs` and has the prototype

```
void fputs(string str, FILE *outfile);
```

Calling `fputs` copies characters from the string to the output file until the end of the string is reached.

You can also use `fgets` and `fputs` to implement the `CopyFile` function introduced in the section on "Character I/O" earlier in this chapter, as follows:

```
static void CopyFile(FILE *infile, FILE *outfile)
{
    char buffer[MaxLine];

    while (fgets(buffer, MaxLine, infile) != NULL) {
        fputs(buffer, outfile);
    }
}
```

When you use `fgets`, you must supply a buffer for the input line. In the `CopyFile` example, the array is allocated explicitly in the current frame by the declaration

```
char buffer[MaxLine];
```

It is important to remember that the memory space for this buffer will be deallocated when the function returns. If you want to store the characters in the line more permanently, you need to copy the data into memory that persists after the call. In some cases, that memory may consist of a global character array or an array passed down from a calling function, but it is often easier to allocate the memory dynamically from the heap.

You also need to allocate new memory if you use the same temporary buffer for more than one `fgets` call. Assignment alone is not sufficient. For example, the following code appears to read two lines from an input file, storing the data in the string variables `line1` and `line2`:

```
void ReadTwoLines(FILE *infile)
{
    string line1, line2;
    char buffer[MaxLine];

    fgets(buffer, MaxLine, infile);
    line1 = buffer;
    fgets(buffer, MaxLine, infile);
    line2 = buffer;
    . . .  rest of program  . . .
}
```

This code leaves `line1` and `line2` with the same contents.

The problem is that the variable `buffer`, though conceptually a string in many respects, occupies specific locations in memory, and the assignment

```
line1 = buffer;
```

COMMON PITFALLS

If you use the same buffer to read multiple lines from the same file, you must remember to copy the data out of the buffer into some other storage before going on to the next line. If you do not, the contents of the previous line will be overwritten.

only copies the address of `buffer` into the variable `line1`. When the program goes on to reuse this space to read the second line, the same memory is used to hold that second string. The variables `line1` and `line2` end up pointing to the same memory and therefore contain the same string.

One solution to this problem is to use the function `CopyString` from the `strlib` library to copy each of these strings into its own memory in the heap, like this:

```
void ReadTwoLines(FILE *infile)
{
    string line1, line2;
    char buffer[MaxLine];

    fgets(buffer, MaxLine, infile);
    line1 = CopyString(buffer);
    fgets(buffer, MaxLine, infile);
    line2 = CopyString(buffer);
    .  .  .  rest of program  .  .  .
}
```

Another solution is to use the `ReadLine` function defined in `simpio.h`, which also avoids the following problems associated with `fgets`:

- There is no easy way to know how big the buffer limit should be. Some files contain very long lines, and it is difficult to pick a buffer size that works for all files.
- It is hard to tell whether the buffer limit has been exceeded. Specifying a maximum size in the `fgets` call means that data will not be written past the end of the allocated buffer, but it is still useful to know if the `fgets` call has read a complete line. The only way to do so when using `fgets` is to look through the characters in the buffer to see if they include a newline character.
- The fact that `fgets` stores the newline character is usually an annoyance. In most applications, the newline character serves only as a sentinel marking the end of the line; it is not actually part of the data. Using `fgets` means that you have to take the extra steps necessary to remove the newline character from the buffer.

The `ReadLine` function is similar in operation to the `GetLine` function introduced in Chapter 2. The only difference is that the input data comes from a data file supplied as an argument. `ReadLine` offers the following advantages over `fgets`:

- `ReadLine` allocates its own heap memory as needed, making it impossible to overflow the buffer.
- `ReadLine` removes the newline used to signal the end of the line, so that the data returned consists simply of the characters on the line.
- Each string returned by `ReadLine` is stored in its own memory, so that no confusion can occur as to whether a string needs to be copied before it is stored.

The `ReadLine` function returns `NULL` when it encounters the end-of-file marker.

15.5 Formatted I/O

Of all the facilities provided by the standard I/O library, none are more emblematic of C than the formatted I/O functions `printf` and `scanf`. You have used `printf` since Chapter 2 but have only scratched the surface of what you can do with it. The next few sections provide more background on the `printf`/`scanf` family of functions and are included so you can use these functions more effectively in your own code and make sense of other programs that use them.

The three forms of `printf`

The `printf` function comes in three different forms:

```
printf(control string, . . .);
fprintf(output stream, control string, . . .);
sprintf(character array, control string, . . .);
```

The `printf` form always writes its output to standard output. The `fprintf` function is identical, except that it takes a `FILE` pointer argument as its first argument and writes its output to that file. The `sprintf` form takes a character array as its first argument and writes the characters that would have been displayed by a `printf` call into that array. It is the responsibility of the caller to ensure that there is sufficient space in the array to contain the output data.

Other than the destination to which the output is directed, all three of the `printf` forms work in the same way: they take a string called the *control string* and copy it, character by character, to the indicated destination. If the string contains a percent sign (`%`), that character is treated as the beginning of a *format code*, which is replaced by a string representation of the next available argument in the `printf` call. The nature of the formatting is indicated by the letter that comes at the end of the format code, which may also include modifiers that specify field width, precision, and alignment. The most common `printf` options are described in the section on "Formatted output" in Chapter 3.

The `scanf` functions

The `scanf` functions provide an input counterpart to `printf` that is intended to make it easier for programs to read in values of the various basic types. Presumably, the designers of the C library once had the idea that `printf` and `scanf` would be symmetric mechanisms. Unfortunately, partly because of the rules of C and partly because one uses different conversions in the input direction, `printf` and `scanf` have a number of asymmetries that make their use confusing.

The most important asymmetry between `printf` and `scanf` comes from the fact that `printf` needs to be able to *take* multiple values from its caller whereas `scanf` needs to *return* multiple values to its caller. The operation of returning multiple values is not well supported in C and requires extensive use of pointers. Leaving out the address-of operator (`&`) in calls to `scanf` is a common error in C programs that use this facility—an error made all the more serious by the fact that the compiler cannot recognize the omission as an error. The compiler accepts the incorrect `scanf` call, but then the program fails mysteriously later on.

Like `printf`, `scanf` comes in three different forms:

```
scanf(control string, . . .)
fscanf(input stream, control string, . . .)
sscanf(character string, control string, . . .)
```

The first reads values from standard input, the second from the `FILE` pointer indicated by the input stream parameter, and the third from the specified character string. Each of these forms reads characters from the source and converts them according to the specifications in the control string. The data values themselves are stored in memory provided by the caller through additional arguments.

Because `scanf` must return information to its caller, the arguments after the control string must use call by reference, as described in Chapter 13. Each of the arguments after the control string must therefore be a pointer. In most cases, you simply include the address-of operator (`&`) in front of a variable name to convert that variable to its address, but it is important to remember that the names of character arrays are already pointers and therefore do not require the `&`.

The control string for `scanf` consists of three different classes of characters:

**COMMON
PITFALLS**

Remember that each argument to `scanf` following the control string must be a pointer. For simple variables, the argument is preceded by an ampersand (`&`) to indicate that you are taking its address. If the argument is a character array, however, the array name is automatically interpreted as a pointer, and the `&` is not used.

- Characters that appear as blank space, which cause `scanf` to skip ahead to the next nonblank character. Such characters are called **white-space characters** in C and consist of those characters for which the `isspace` predicate function in the `ctype.h` interface returns `TRUE`. The most common white-space characters are the space, tab, and newline characters. In the `scanf` control string, any amount of white space matches any amount of white space in the input.
- A percent sign followed by a conversion specification.
- Any other character, which must match the next character in the input. This facility allows the program to check for required punctuation, such as a comma between two numbers, and so forth.

Conversion specifications are structurally similar to their `printf` analogues, but the set of available options is different. A conversion specification for `scanf` is composed of the following options, listed in the order in which you must specify them:

- An optional assignment-suppression flag indicated by an asterisk (`*`), which specifies that the value from the input should be discarded rather than stored through one of the argument pointers.
- An optional numeric field width indicating the maximum number of characters to be read for the field.
- An optional size specification consisting of either the letter `h`, which indicates an integer value of type `short`, or the letter `l`, which indicates either an integer value of type `long` or a floating-point value of type `double`.
- A conversion specification letter, which is ordinarily one of those shown in Table 15-1.

All forms of `scanf` return the number of conversions successfully performed, not counting those that were suppressed using the `*` specification. If the end-of-file condition is detected before any conversions occur, `scanf` returns the value `EOF`.

Code	Interpretation
%d	The next value from the input is scanned as a decimal integer. That integer value is then stored in the memory cell addressed by the next pointer argument. It is crucial that the size of the variable match the size indicated by the specification.
%f %e %g	The next input value is scanned as a floating point value and stored in the memory cell indicated by the next pointer in the argument list. If the target of the pointer type is `float`, the conversion specification should be %f. If the target of the pointer type is `double`, the conversion specification must be %lf. The %e and %g codes are identical to %f and are included for symmetry with `printf`.
%c	The next character is read and stored at the address indicated by the next argument, which must be a character pointer. In contrast to the other specifications, the %c specification does not skip white-space characters before conversion.
%s	Characters are read from the input and stored in successive elements of the character array indicated by the next argument. The caller must ensure that enough space has been allocated in the array to accommodate the value being read. Input is terminated by the first white-space character.
%[...] %[^...]	The conversion specification may consist of a set of characters enclosed in square brackets. In this case, a string is read up to the first character that is not in the bracketed set. The string is stored at the address specified by the next argument to `scanf`, which must be a character array. If the set of characters begins with a circumflex (^), the characters that follow are instead interpreted as those that are *not* permitted in the input. For example, the specification %[0123456789] reads in the next sequence of digits as a string; the specification %[^.!?] reads a string of characters up to the next end-of-sentence mark (period, exclamation point, or question mark).
%%	No conversion is done; a percent sign must follow in the input.

TABLE 15-1

Conversion specifications for `scanf`

Reading strings with `scanf`

Table 15-1 includes several conversion characters—the forms `"%s"`, `"%[...]"`, and `"%[^...]"`—that are used to read string values. With each of these conversion specifications, the caller is responsible for allocating sufficient space to hold the data. The `scanf` argument used to receive the string should therefore be a character array declared by the caller. For example, in order to read in a string bounded by white space, you must first declare an array to hold that string, using a declaration such as

```
#define MaxWord 25

char word[MaxWord];
```

Once space for the result has been set aside, your program can then read a string with the statement

```
fscanf(infile, "%s", word);
```

Note that there is no `&` character before the variable name. The `fscanf` function requires that all of its arguments be pointers to the space into which the values are stored. The name of an array is already a pointer to its first element, so you do not use the `&` operator.

One major problem with this example is that you could easily overflow the available space. If you fail to allocate enough memory, `fscanf` keeps writing into the next several memory locations, destroying whatever values were there. To guard against this type of buffer overflow, you can specify a field width to indicate the maximum number of data characters you are willing to read in:

```
fscanf(infile, "%24s", word);
```

This call stores only the first 24 characters into the array, thereby ensuring that no space is overwritten beyond the array. Because `MaxWord` is defined to be 25, you also have room to store the final `'\0'` character marking the end of the string.[2]

The `"%[...]"` and `"%[^...]"` conversion options can be particularly useful in reading formatted input. For example, in order to read an entry of the form

name: *value*

where *name* is a string and *value* is an integer, you could use the following call to `fscanf`:

```
fscanf(infile, "%[^:]: %d", name, &value);
```

Unfortunately, you cannot use this statement repeatedly to read several input lines in the same form. The problem is that, after the program reads the integer corresponding to *value*, the newline that terminates the number remains in the input stream, where it will be read as part of the next word. Adding a newline character at the end of the control string, as in

```
fscanf(infile, "%[^:]: %d\n", name, &value);
```

often solves the problem, but not for the reason that you might expect. The inclusion of the newline character does not force `fscanf` to match a newline character

---

[2] You can avoid using the constant 24 in the `scanf` control string, although doing so is rather clumsy and can make the program harder to read. To make this constant depend on the value of `MaxWord`, you need to generate the `scanf` control string by calling `sprintf` as follows:

```
char controlString[MaxControlString];

sprintf(controlString, "%%%ds", MaxWord - 1);
fscanf(infile, controlString, word);
```

When `fscanf` is called, the character array `controlString` contains the string `"%24s"`.

at that point in the input. Instead, the newline is treated as a white-space character, which causes scanf to read past any white-space characters in the input file. If you assume that a newline character always occurs immediately after the number, everything is fine. If, on the other hand, you want your program to test for the possibility of an improperly formatted input file, you have to use a different approach.

A safer solution is to read an additional character in the fscanf call and then to test it to make sure it's a newline, as shown in this loop:

```
while (TRUE) {
    nscan = fscanf(infile, "%[^:]: %d%c",
                               name, &value, &termch);
    if (nscan == EOF) break;
    if (nscan != 3 || termch != '\n') Error("Bad input line");
}
```

When you use this strategy, the code also checks to make sure the fscanf call reads exactly three items: the name, the value, and the terminating character.

If you need to know how much of the file has been read when an error occurs, it is often best to read an entire line using fgets and then call sscanf to convert the fields in the resulting string, as follows:

```
while (fgets(line, MaxLine, infile) != NULL) {
    nscan = sscanf(line, "%[^:]: %d%c",
                               name, &value, &termch);
    if (nscan != 3 || termch != '\n') Error("Bad input line");
}
```

An example of formatted I/O

To appreciate how scanf works, it is essential to work through examples of its use and practice writing similar applications of your own. For example, suppose that you wanted to read the data contained in the file elements.dat, which lists the following information for each of the chemical elements:

- *The element name,* which is never more than 15 characters long
- *The chemical symbol,* which is never more than two characters long
- *The atomic number,* which is an integer indicating the number of protons in the nucleus
- *The atomic weight,* which is a floating-point number (this value specifies the relative weight of this element averaged over the naturally occurring isotopes, but the details are unimportant for the example).

The first 10 lines of the file would then look like this:

```
Hydrogen, H, 1, 1.008
Helium, He, 2, 4.003
Lithium, Li, 3, 6.939
Beryllium, Be, 4, 9.012
Boron, B, 5, 10.811
Carbon, C, 6, 12.011
Nitrogen, N, 7, 14.007
Oxygen, O, 8, 15.999
Fluorine, F, 9, 18.998
Neon, Ne, 10, 20.183
```

Now let's suppose you want to read in the data from this file and display it in the following tabular form:

```
        Element (symbol)      Atomic Weight
    -------------------------------------
     1. Hydrogen (H)              1.008
     2. Helium (He)               4.003
     3. Lithium (Li)              6.939
     4. Beryllium (Be)            9.012
     5. Boron (B)                10.811
     6. Carbon (C)               12.011
     7. Nitrogen (N)             14.007
     8. Oxygen (O)               15.999
     9. Fluorine (F)             18.998
    10. Neon (Ne)                20.183
```

In the output, the atomic number appears first, followed by the name and symbol together in a fixed-width field, followed in turn by the atomic weight.

Your first task is to design a control string for `fscanf` that correctly reads in the data for a single line from the file. The input line begins with the element name, which is a string terminated by a comma. The easiest way to read this field is to use the conversion specification `%15[^,]` to read a string consisting of any characters up to the first appearance of a comma. The field width of 15 ensures that the `elementName` buffer does not overflow. After the specification for the element name, the control string contains a comma to match its counterpart in the input, followed by a space to skip over any spaces that follow the comma. The symbol field is read using the specification `%2[^,]`, which is just like the first specification except for the smaller field width. The last two fields on the line are of type `int` and `double`, respectively. To scan these fields, the control string must contain the specifications `%d` and `%1f`. The conversion specification used to read the atomic weight must include the letter `l` because the corresponding variable is a `double` rather than a `float`. At the end of the line, it is useful to read the character after the atomic weight to make sure it is a newline. Thus, the complete `fscanf` call is

```
nscan = fscanf(infile, "%15[^,], %2[^,], %d, %lf%c",
                      elementName, elementSymbol,
                      &atomicNumber, &atomicWeight,
                      &termch);
```

The first two variables in the `fscanf` call are character arrays and are already treated as addresses. The `atomicNumber`, `atomicWeight`, and `termch` variables are not arrays and must therefore be preceded by an `&` to obtain their addresses.

The formatted I/O functions are also useful in generating the output table. In the table, the element name and its corresponding symbol are displayed together in a single field. To align the atomic weight column correctly, you have to make sure that the field combining the name and symbol maintains a constant width. You can do so explicitly by computing the width of each string using `strlen` and then writing out the appropriate number of spaces. Alternatively, you can combine the fields together into a single string using `sprintf` and then use the standard field width facilities of `printf` to generate the correct output. This approach is illustrated by the `elements.c` program shown in Figure 15-4.

FIGURE 15-4   elements.c

```
/*
 * File: elements.c
 * ----------------
 * This program copies the information from the elements.dat
 * file into a table formatted into fixed-width columns. The
 * data values in the file are read using fscanf.
 */

#include <stdio.h>
#include "genlib.h"
#include "simpio.h"

/*
 * Constants
 * ---------
 * ElementsFile   -- Name of the elements data file
 * MaxElementName -- Maximum length of element name
 * MaxSymbolName  -- Maximum length of element symbol
 */

#define ElementsFile   "elements.dat"
#define MaxElementName 15
#define MaxSymbolName   2
```

```
/* Main program */

main()
{
    FILE *infile;
    char elementName[MaxElementName+1];
    char elementSymbol[MaxSymbolName+1];
    char namebuf[MaxElementName+MaxSymbolName+4];
    int atomicNumber;
    double atomicWeight;
    char termch;
    int nscan;

    infile = fopen(ElementsFile, "r");
    if (infile == NULL) Error("Can't open %s", ElementsFile);
    printf("    Element (symbol)    Atomic Weight\n");
    printf("-------------------------------------\n");
    while (TRUE) {
        nscan = fscanf(infile, "%15[^,], %2[^,], %d, %lf%c",
                               elementName, elementSymbol,
                               &atomicNumber, &atomicWeight,
                               &termch);
        if (nscan == EOF) break;
        if (nscan != 5 || termch != '\n') {
            Error("Improper file format");
        }
        sprintf(namebuf, "%s (%s)", elementName, elementSymbol);
        printf("%3d. %-20s %8.3f\n", atomicNumber, namebuf,
                               atomicWeight);
    }
}
```

Limitations on the use of `scanf`

The principal advantage of scanf is that it provides a convenient way to read input data written in a consistent format. By choosing the right conversion specifications, you can often read and interpret many data items in a single function call. Particularly if you are writing code to test an application and need to read some test data, scanf provides just the right tool. In such cases, you have generated the test data and know exactly how it is formatted.

The scanf function, however, is less useful when the input comes from a source that you do not directly control. If the input data might contain errors, your program must test the input to make sure it is in the correct form. If you are using scanf, however, it is often impossible to check input data as thoroughly as you should. As a result, scanf is not used extensively in commercial C programs, for which such error-checking is critical. P. J. Plauger, who chaired the committee to standardize the ANSI C libraries, issues the following warning:[3]

> You will find that the scan conversion specifications are not as complete as the print conversion specifications. Too often, you want to exercise control over an input scan. Or you may find it impossible to determine where a scan failed well enough to recover properly from the failure. . . . Be prepared . . . to give up on the scan functions beyond a point. Their usefulness, over the years, has proved to be limited.

SUMMARY

When you want to store information that persists after a program completes its execution, you must store it in a *file* on a secondary storage device that supports permanent storage, such as a disk. The most common type of file used in programming consists of character data and is called a *text file*. Text files can be used for input or output and are usually processed sequentially.

The `stdio.h` interface provides several functions for input/output operations that allow you to choose among several different strategies. For example, you can process files character by character, line by line, or as collections of formatted fields.

Important points considered in this chapter include:

- To use a text file within a program, you must first declare a variable of type `FILE *` to hold whatever information the system needs to keep track of the operations on that file.
- You establish the link between the `FILE *` variable by calling `fopen` and later break that connection by calling `fclose`.
- The `stdio.h` interface defines three *standard files*—`stdin`, `stdout`, and `stderr`—that make it possible to apply any of the I/O functions to the console itself.
- If you choose to process a file one character at a time, the fundamental operations are the functions `getc` and `putc`. The standard I/O library also defines a function `ungetc`, which allows you to push a character back into the input stream.
- If you choose to process a file a line at a time, you can call the functions `fgets` and `fputs` defined in `stdio.h` as long as you are careful about memory allocation. It is often more convenient, however, to use the `ReadLine` function from `simpio.h`, which performs any necessary memory allocation automatically.

---

[3] P. J. Plauger, *The Standard C Library,* Englewood Cliffs, NJ: Prentice Hall, 1992, p. 268.

- The printf function has an input counterpart called scanf that allows you to read formatted data. The functions fprintf and fscanf allow you to perform formatted I/O operations on files, and the functions sprintf and sscanf provide an equivalent facility for working with character buffers.

REVIEW QUESTIONS

1. Which representation more closely corresponds to the internal representation of a text file: (a) a two-dimensional array consisting of a sequence of lines or (b) a one-dimensional sequence of characters?

2. What is meant by the phrase *opening a file?*

3. What is the purpose of the type FILE *? Is understanding the underlying structure of this type important to most programmers?

4. The second argument to fopen is usually one of the following strings: "r", "w", or "a". What is the significance of this argument and what do each of these values mean?

5. How does the fopen function report failure to its caller?

6. When a program exits, all open files are automatically closed. Why should you bother to close files explicitly?

7. The stdio.h interface automatically defines three standard files. What are their names? What purpose does each one serve?

8. True or false: The function getc returns a value of type char.

9. When you are using the getc function, how do you detect the end of a file?

10. What steps are involved in the process of updating a file?

11. If you call the function rename(f1, f2), does the name of the file f1 change to become f2 or is it the other way round?

12. What is the purpose of the function ungetc?

13. The function fgets takes three arguments. What are they?

14. What are the major differences between fgets and ReadLine?

15. The formatted printing function comes in three forms: printf, fprintf, and sprintf. What are the differences?

16. True or false: Every argument to scanf after the control string must be a pointer.

17. True or false: Every argument to `scanf` after the control string must be preceded with an ampersand (`&`).

18. How are white-space characters defined?

19. What does it mean if a white-space character appears in a `scanf` control string?

20. If the variable `i` is declared as an `int` and the variable `d` as a `double`, what is wrong with the following `scanf` call:

```
scanf("%d, %f", &i, &d);
```

21. What is the effect of the `scanf` specification `"%10[^,:]"`?

22. True or false: Over the years, the `scanf` function has proven to be an extremely valuable feature of the standard I/O library.

PROGRAMMING EXERCISES

1. Write a program `wc.c` that reads a file and reports how many lines, words, and characters appear in it. For the purposes of this program, a word consists of a consecutive sequence of any characters except white-space characters. For example, if the file `lear.txt` contains the following passage from *King Lear*,

```
Poor naked wretches, wheresoe'er you are,
That bide the pelting of this pitiless storm,
How shall your houseless heads and unfed sides,
Your loop'd and window'd raggedness, defend you
From seasons such as these? O, I have ta'en
Too little care of this!
```

your program should be able to generate the following sample run:

```
File:   lear.txt↵
Lines:    6
Words:   43
Chars:  254
```

2. On occasion, publishers find it useful to evaluate layouts and stylistic designs without being distracted by the actual words. To do so, they sometimes typeset sample pages in such a way that all of the original letters are replaced by random letters. The resulting text has the spacing and punctuation structure of the original, but no longer conveys any meaning that might get in the way of the design. The publishing term for text that has been replaced in this way is *greek,*

presumably after the old saying "It's all Greek to me," which is itself adapted from a line from *Julius Caesar.*

Write a program `greek.c` that reads characters from an input file and displays them on the console after making the appropriate random substitutions. Any uppercase character in the input should be replaced by a random uppercase character and every lowercase character by a random lowercase one. Nonalphabetic characters are displayed without change. For example, if the input file `troilus.dat` contains the text from *Troilus and Cressida,*

```
Ay, Greek; and that shall be divulged well
In characters as red as Mars his heart
Inflamed with Venus:
```

your program should generate output that looks something like this:

```
Hb, Jwyqt; cwq ocgs lsosn jo hdricyoc lino
Dm bzongsmdrv uj qew ya Okor umj ioyvq
Ipqpqnpj vrvy Snszv:
```

3. Some files use tab characters to align data into columns. Doing so, however, can cause problems for certain applications that are unable to work directly with tabs. For these applications, it is useful to have access to a program that replaces tabs in an input file with the number of spaces required to reach the next tab stop. In programming, tab stops are usually set at every eight columns. For example, suppose that the input file contains a line of the form

```
abc ——————| nopqr ——| xyz
```

where the ——| symbol represents the space taken up by a tab, which differs depending on its position in the line. If the tab stops are set every eight spaces, the first tab character must be replaced by five spaces and the second one by three.

Write a program `untabify.c` that reads a file name from the user and updates the file so that all the tabs are replaced by enough spaces to reach the next tab stop.

4. Because text files consist only of ASCII characters, they do not allow you to represent a document with multiple fonts and styles. To get around the limitations of ASCII, people have developed a variety of conventions to represent certain typographical styles. For example, people sometimes use asterisks in ASCII files to mark a region of text that should be underlined. For example, to

note that *The C Programming Language* is a title and not just an otherwise ordinary collection of words, a text file might contain the following line:

```
*The C Programming Language* by Kernighan and Ritchie
```

Even if they lack more advanced typographical features, such as italics, most printers can underline text by using the backspace character (indicated as `'\b'` in C). If you print an underscore character (`'_'`), followed by a backspace, followed by some other character, what appears on the page is an underlined character.

Write a program that reads characters from one file to another, converting text enclosed within asterisks into underlined character sequences. When your program encounters the first asterisk, it should start underlining characters; it should stop underlining when it reaches the next one. From there on, it should continue in the same fashion, turning underlining on and off, until the end-of-file is reached. Your program must also handle the following two special conditions:
a. As required by most style guides, all characters in an underlined passage, including spaces and punctuation, should be underlined. If, however, you read in a newline (because a title is split onto more than one line as shown in the example below), the newline character should not be underlined.
b. If the asterisk that would ordinarily start the underlining process is followed immediately by a white-space character, the asterisk is considered to be a regular asterisk. In this case, the asterisk should appear unchanged without triggering the underlining process.

As an example, suppose the file kandr.txt has the following contents:

```
According to the table on page 53 of *The C
Programming Language* by Kernighan and Ritchie,
the operator * has a *higher* precedence than +,
and the precedence of * is equal to that of /.
```

Given this input file, your program should produce an output file that looks like this when printed:

```
According to the table on page 53 of The C
Programming Language by Kernighan and Ritchie,
the operator * has a higher precedence than +,
and the precedence of * is equal to that of /.
```

5. Particularly now that computer memories tend to be reasonably large, it is often easiest to read in the contents of a file all at once and then to begin processing its data. Write a function with the prototype

```
string *ReadFile(FILE *infile)
```

that reads the entire contents of `infile` and returns it in the form of a dynamic array of strings, one for each line of the file, followed by an extra element containing the value `NULL` to mark the end of the file. For example, suppose that the file `prospero.txt` contains the following lines from *The Tempest:*

```
What seest thou else
In the dark backward and abysm of time?
If thou remember'st aught ere thou camest here,
How thou camest here thou mayst.
```

If you open `prospero.txt` for input as `infile` and call `ReadFile(infile)`, the function returns a pointer to a dynamic string array, as this diagram shows:

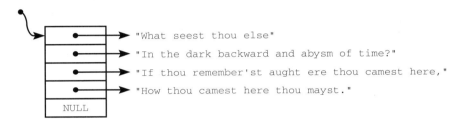

The most interesting question in the design of the `ReadFile` implementation is how much space to allocate for the dynamic array. The problem is that you don't know how many lines will be in the file before you start to read them. To solve this problem, the most general approach is to allocate an array of some arbitrary initial size and then allocate additional space later on if more space is needed. If you do need to allocate more space, you will have to perform the following steps:

a. Allocate a new dynamic array larger than the old one.
b. Copy the previously stored elements from the old array to the new one.
c. Free the old array.
d. Assign the new array pointer to the variable used to refer to the array.

Put the implementation of `ReadLine` in a separate `readline.c` file and design a `readline.h` interface that gives clients access to it. Use the `readline.h` interface to write a main program that displays the lines in a file in reverse order. For example, given the `prospero.txt` file as input, the output of the program should be

```
How thou camest here thou mayst.
If thou remember'st aught ere thou camest here,
In the dark backward and abysm of time?
What seest thou else
```

6. In the 1960s, entertainer Steve Allen often played a game called *Madlibs* as part of his comedy routine. Allen would ask the audience to supply words that fit specific categories—a verb, an adjective, or a plural noun, for example—and then use these words to fill in blanks in a previously prepared text that he would then read back to the audience.

To illustrate the process, suppose that the hidden text consists of the following lines from *Hamlet* with certain key words removed, as shown:

> To (a verb) or not to (the same verb) : that is the question.
> Whether 'tis nobler in the mind to suffer
> The slings and arrows of (an adjective) fortune,
> Or to take arms against a sea of (a plural noun),
> And by opposing end them?

The audience fills in the blanks with words of the appropriate type without knowing what the original text is. Depending on what words are chosen, the result can be funny, although the adjective *silly* probably applies more often.

In this exercise, your task is to write a program that plays Madlibs with the user. The text for the story comes from a text file that includes occasional placeholders enclosed in angle brackets. For example, the input file hamlet.mad that contains Hamlet's soliloquy would look like this:

```
To <verb>, or not to <same verb>: that is the question.
Whether 'tis nobler in the mind to suffer
The slings and arrows of <adjective> fortune,
Or to take arms against a sea of <plural noun>,
And by opposing end them?
```

Your program must read this file and display it on the console, giving the user the chance to fill in the blanks. The following sample run illustrates a possible session with the program:

```
Input file: hamlet.mad↵
   verb: program↵
   same verb: program↵
   adjective: random↵
   plural noun: bugs↵

To program, or not to program: that is the question.
Whether 'tis nobler in the mind to suffer
The slings and arrows of random fortune,
Or to take arms against a sea of bugs,
And by opposing end them?
```

Note that the user must provide all the substitutions before any of the text is displayed. This design complicates the program structure slightly because it is impossible to display the output text as you go. The simplest strategy is to write the output to a temporary file first and then copy the contents of the temporary file back to the screen.

7. Write a program that reads a file and keeps track of the number of times each word appears in that file. When your program finishes reading the file, it should generate an alphabetical table showing each word and the number of times it appears. For example, if the input file `malvolio.txt` contains the following lines from *Twelfth Night:*

```
Some are born great, some achieve greatness,
and some have greatness thrust upon them.
```

the program should generate the following table:

```
Word frequency table:
achieve      1
and          1
are          1
born         1
great        1
greatness    2
have         1
some         3
them         1
thrust       1
upon         1
```

Note that the program converts all characters in each word to lower case so that *Some* and *some* are not treated as different words.

In designing your solution, think carefully about modular decomposition. What modules would be helpful? In particular, are there any existing modules already used for other applications that you can also apply to this problem?

8. Write a program that transforms a file containing a list of computer equipment you would like to buy into a nicely formatted order form. The input file consists of several lines, each of which contains the following fields:

- *A part number,* which consists of up to six characters, extending from the beginning of the line to the first blank space.

- *A product name*, which consists of up to 20 characters. This field begins after the part number and continues to the first slash character (/), which must appear in every input line.
- *The number of units*, which is an integer.
- *The unit price,* which is a floating-point value separated from the number of units by a commercial at-sign (@).

Additional white space may occur between any of the fields, but each line must include all four of the data fields and the required separators. The format of the input file is illustrated by the file order.dat, as follows:

```
NC271X Notebook computer / 1 @ 1729.00
LP552 Laser printer / 1 @ 1499.00
TC552V Toner cartridge / 2 @ 99.00
DS420 3.5" diskettes / 10 @ 2.99
CC542 Carrying case / 1 @ 27.99
```

Your program should read the input file and redisplay each of the fields in a fixed-width column. In addition, your program should display the total price for each line item (the number of units times the unit price) as well as the grand total for the entire order. Given the data above, the output of your program should look like this:

```
Order file: order.dat↵
NC271X    Notebook computer    1 @ 1729.00 = 1729.00
LP552     Laser printer        1 @ 1499.00 = 1499.00
TC552V    Toner cartridge      2 @   99.00 =  198.00
DS420     3.5" diskettes      10 @    2.99 =   29.90
CC542     Carrying case        1 @   27.99 =   27.99
-----------------------------------------------------
TOTAL                                         3483.89
```

9. Using the graphics library from Chapter 7, write a program that displays polygons on the screen. The coordinates for the vertices of a polygon are stored in a data file, one coordinate per line. Each coordinate consists of two floating-point numbers enclosed in parentheses and separated by a comma. The input file may contain vertex coordinates for several different polygons; each polygon is separated from the preceding one by a blank line in the file. For example, the file

polygon.dat contains the coordinates for a square and a triangle, as follows:

```
(0.5, 0.5)
(1.0, 0.5)
(1.0, 1.0)
(0.5, 1.0)

(2.0, 0.5)
(3.0, 0.5)
(2.0, 1.0)
```

Your program should read the input file and draw the polygons on the screen. Given the input file polygon.dat, the display should look like this:

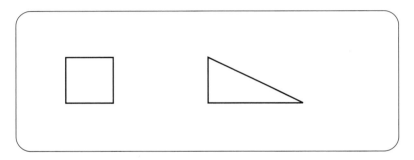

CHAPTER 16

Records

Let's look at the record.

— Al Smith, presidential campaign slogan, 1928

Objectives

- To understand the concept of a record and its importance to programming.

- To recognize the difference between defining a record type and declaring a record variable.

- To be able to manipulate records and pointers to records using the . (dot) and -> operators.

- To be able to allocate new record storage dynamically.

- To understand the process of database design.

When you learned about arrays in Chapter 11, you took the first steps toward understanding an extremely important idea in computer programming: the use of compound data structures to represent complex collections of information. When you declare an array in the context of a program, you are able to combine an arbitrarily large number of data values into a single structure that has conceptual integrity as a whole. If you need to do so, you can select particular elements of that array and manipulate them individually. But you can also treat the array as a unit and manipulate it all at once.

The ability to take individual values and organize them into coherent units is one of the fundamental features of modern programming languages. Procedures and functions allow you to unify many independent operations under a single name. Compound data structures—of which arrays are only one example—offer the same facility in the data domain. In each case, being able to aggregate the tiny pieces of a program into a single, higher-level structure provides both conceptual simplification and a significant increase in your power to express ideas in programming. The power of unification is hardly a recent discovery; it has given rise to social movements and to nations, as reflected in the labor anthem that proclaims "the union makes us strong" and the motto *"E Pluribus Unum"*—"out of many, one"—on the Great Seal of the United States.

Using arrays is a powerful strategy when you are trying to model a real-world collection of data that has two fundamental properties. First, the data must be ordered, in the sense that you can refer to individual elements by some index number. Second, the data must be homogeneous, in the sense that all elements have the same basic type. When the real-world situation you are trying to model consists of a list or collection of similar things, arrays are usually the perfect tool. On the other hand, it is also important to be able to take a collection of unordered, heterogeneous values and think of it as a single unit. In C, such a collection is called a **structure;** in computer science generally, it is usually called a **record.** This text uses the term *record* most of the time, reserving the term *structure* for contexts in which it is important to highlight the specific implementation of records in C.

▌▌▌▌ 16.1 The concept of the data record

To understand the idea of a record, imagine for a moment that you are in charge of the payroll system for a small company. You need to keep track of various pieces of information about each employee. For example, in order to print a paycheck, you need to know the employee's name, job title, Social Security number, salary, withholding status, and perhaps some additional data as well. These pieces of information, taken together, form the employee's data record.

What do employee records look like? It is often easiest to think of records as lines in a table. For example, consider the case of the small firm of Scrooge and Marley, portrayed in Charles Dickens's *A Christmas Carol,* as it might appear in this day of Social Security numbers and withholding allowances. The employee roster contains two records, which might have the following values:

Name	Job title	Soc Sec. #	Salary	# With.
Ebenezer Scrooge	Partner	271-82-8183	250.00	1
Bob Cratchit	Clerk	314-15-9265	15.00	7

Each record is broken up into individual components that provide a specific piece of information about the employee. Each of these components is usually called a **field,** although the term **member** is also used, particularly in the context of C programming. For example, given an employee record, you can talk about the name field or the salary field. Each of the fields is associated with a type, which may be different for different fields. The name and title field are strings, the salary field might well be represented as a floating-point number, and the number of withholding exemptions is presumably an integer. The Social Security number could be represented as either an integer or a string; because Social Security numbers are too big to fit within the limits imposed on integers by many systems, they are represented here as strings.

Even though a record is made up of individual fields, it must have meaning as a coherent whole. In the example of the employee roster, the fields in the first line of the table represent a logically consistent set of data referring to Ebenezer Scrooge; those in the second line refer to Bob Cratchit. The conceptual integrity of each record suggests that the data for that employee should be collected into a compound data structure. Moreover, since the individual fields making up that structure are of different types, arrays are not suited to the task. In cases such as this, you need to define the set of data for each employee as a record.

It makes sense to use a compound data structure whenever you need to represent real-world information that has more than one component but nonetheless has integrity as a whole. If the components are ordered and homogeneous, you should declare the structure as an array. If the components are logically unordered, you should declare it as a record, even if the component types happen to be the same.

 ## 16.2 Using records in C

To create record data in C, you use a two-step process.

1. *Define a new structure type.* Before you declare any variables, you must first define a new structure type. The type definition specifies what fields make up the record, what the names of those fields are, and what type of information the fields contain. This structure type defines a model for all objects that have the new type but does not by itself reserve any storage.
2. *Declare variables of the new type.* Once you have defined the new type, your next step is to declare variables of that type so that you can store actual data values.

These two steps are fundamentally different operations. New programmers often forget that both steps are required. After defining a new type, they imagine that the new type is itself a variable and try to use it as such. The structure type is only a template for use in declaring other variables and has no storage of its own.

Defining a new structure type

Although there are other ways to define structures in C, this text uses the definition form shown in the syntax box on the left. The name of the new type goes on the last line and is preceded by descriptions of the fields that comprise the structure. The fields are defined by writing a set of field declarations that look exactly like variable declarations in a function. For example, the following code defines a new structure type called `employeeT` to represent employee records:

```
typedef struct {
    string name;
    string title;
    string ssnum;
    double salary;
    int withholding;
} employeeT;
```

This definition provides a template for all objects that have the new type `employeeT`. Each such object will have five fields, starting with a `name` field, which is a `string`, and continuing through a `withholding` field, which is an `int`.

Declaring structure variables

Now that you have defined a new type, the next step is to declare variables of that type. For example, given the type `employeeT`, you can declare `emp` to be a variable of that type by writing

```
employeeT emp;
```

If you want to illustrate this variable using a box diagram, you can choose to represent it in either of two ways. If you take a very general view of the situation—which corresponds conceptually to looking at the diagram from a considerable distance—what you see is just a box named `emp`:

emp

If, on the other hand, you step close enough to see the details, you discover that the box labeled emp is composed internally of five individual boxes:

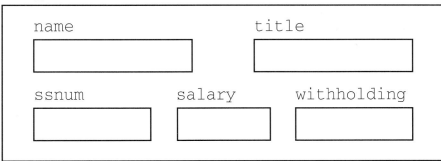

Record selection

Once you have declared the variable emp by writing

```
employeeT emp;
```

you can refer to the record as a whole simply by using its name. At some point, however, you will need to open up the record structure and manipulate its individual fields. To refer to a specific field within a record, you write the name of the complete record, followed by a period, followed by the name of the field. Thus, to refer to the job title of the employee stored in emp, you need to write

```
emp.title
```

When used in this context, the period is invariably called a *dot,* so that you would read this expression aloud as "emp *dot* title." Selecting a field using the dot operator is called **record selection.**

Initializing records

As with any other type of variable, you can initialize the contents of a record variable by assigning values to its components. The dot operator returns an lvalue, which means that you can assign values to a record selection expression. For example, if you were to execute the statements

```
emp.name = "Ebenezer Scrooge";
emp.title = "Partner";
emp.ssnum = "271-82-8183";
emp.salary = 250.00;
emp.withholding = 1;
```

you would create the employee record for Ebenezer Scrooge used in the earlier examples.

If a record variable is declared as a static global variable, you can also initialize its contents statically using the same syntax described for arrays in the section "Static initialization of arrays" in Chapter 11. Initializers for a record are provided in the order in which they appear in the structure definition. Thus, you could declare and initialize a static global record named `manager` that contains the data for Mr. Scrooge, as follows:

```
static employeeT manager = {
    "Ebenezer Scrooge", "Partner", "271-82-8183", 250.00, 1
};
```

Simple records

Although records can be extremely large and complex, it is important to remember that record types can be useful even when they are simple. To appreciate the power of simple record definitions, think back to the structure of the graphics library presented in Chapter 7. When you use this library, you work extensively with *x* and *y* coordinate values. Many of the functions exported by the interface therefore take as arguments both an *x* and a *y* value. This design is certainly easy enough to use. Nevertheless, it is not your only option. At a conceptual level, the functions don't work with individual coordinates as much as they do with *points*. A point consists internally of an *x* and a *y* coordinate but also acts as a coherent entity in its own right. It therefore makes sense to combine the individual coordinates into a record. If you do so, you can then treat the point as a single entity, which makes it easier to use.

To make it possible to represent a point as a single entity, the first step is to define the type `pointT` as a pair of coordinate values, as follows:

```
typedef struct {
    double x, y;
} pointT;
```

You can then write procedures and functions that manipulate `pointT` values. For example, the following function takes two coordinates and combines them into a `pointT` value:

```
pointT CreatePoint(double x, double y)
{
    pointT p;

    p.x = x;
    p.y = y;
    return (p);
}
```

You can use this function to initialize a variable of type `pointT`, as the following code does:

```
pointT origin;

origin = CreatePoint(0, 0);
```

This example illustrates an important difference between records and arrays. In C, a record variable is an lvalue; an array variable is not. When you assign one record to another, both records must be of the same type. The effect of the assignment

```
rec1 = rec2;
```

is that all fields in rec2 are copied to the corresponding fields of rec1.

Records can also be passed as arguments to functions. Consider, for example, the function AddPoint, which is defined as follows:

```
pointT AddPoint(pointT p1, pointT p2)
{
    pointT p;

    p.x = p1.x + p2.x;
    p.y = p1.y + p2.y;
    return (p);
}
```

If you call AddPoint(p1, p2), where p1 and p2 are values of type pointT, the function returns the pointT whose coordinates are obtained by adding together the corresponding coordinates of p1 and p2.

When you call a function that takes a record argument, the value of the record argument is *copied* to the corresponding formal parameter. If a function changes the value of the formal parameter or the value of any of its internal fields, the calling argument retains its original value. This behavior is consistent with the way C treats all parameters except arrays.

 ## 16.3 Combining records and arrays

One of the most important features of a modern programming language is that, once you have a type, you can use it to create new, more sophisticated types. To do so, it is often useful to define arrays of records and records that contain arrays. These new types can in turn be used to create additional types in an ever more complex hierarchy.

For example, the section on "Defining a new structure type" earlier in this chapter introduced a type called employeeT. Once that type has been defined, you can use it to declare an array whose elements are of type employeeT. Just as

```
int scores[10];
```

declares scores to be an array of 10 integers, the declaration

```
employeeT staff[10];
```

declares `staff` to be an array of 10 employees. The employee records for Ebenezer Scrooge and Bob Cratchit fit nicely into such an array, which would fill up the first two elements of `staff` as follows:

staff

0	Ebenezer Scrooge	Partner	271-82-8183	250.00	1
1	Bob Cratchit	Clerk	314-15-9265	15.00	7

You can select the individual components of the `staff` array just as you do with any other array. For example, you can use the expression `staff[1]` to select the entire employee record containing the data for Bob Cratchit:

Bob Cratchit	Clerk	314-15-9265	15.00	7

From this record, you can make further selections by indicating the appropriate field name. For example,

```
staff[1].name
```

selects Bob Cratchit's name:

Bob Cratchit

Depending on the application, selecting the name may be sufficient. On the other hand, there is nothing that prohibits you from making further selections. The value of the `name` field is a string, so you can select its elements. Thus, if you wanted to select the first initial of the employee in position 1 of the `staff` array, you would write the following selection expression:

```
staff[1].name[0]
```

Given the example record above, this expression returns the character `'B'` in the string `"Bob Cratchit"`. In programs that work with complex data structures, you will often see long chains of selection operations, selecting fields from records and elements from arrays, as appropriate.

As with any array, the usual approach to declaring an array of records is to allocate space for some maximum size and then to keep track of the effective size in a separate integer variable. For example, if you define the constant `MaxEmployees` by writing

```
#define MaxEmployees 100
```

you can then declare the variables `staff` and `nEmployees`, as follows:

```
employeeT staff[MaxEmployees];
int nEmployees;
```

Your program can now handle a staff of up to 100 employees, even though at any given time there will typically be fewer employees than this maximum, with the current number stored in the variable nEmployees. Thus, if you wanted to represent just the two records shown above, you would store the relevant data in the first two records and indicate that number in nEmployees:

staff

0	Ebenezer Scrooge	Partner	271-82-8183	250.00	1
1	Bob Cratchit	Clerk	314-15-9265	15.00	7
2					

99					

nEmployees

2

Once you have defined a compound data structure such as the array of employees stored in staff, you can write procedures and functions to manipulate it. For example, the following function lists all the employee names along with their job titles:

```
static void ListEmployees(employeeT staff[], int nEmployees)
{
    int i;

    for (i = 0; i < nEmployees; i++) {
        printf("%s (%s)\n", staff[i].name, staff[i].title);
    }
}
```

If you were to execute this procedure using the values of staff and nEmployees shown in the preceding diagram, your program would generate the sample run

```
Ebenezer Scrooge (Partner)
Bob Cratchit (Clerk)
```

As another example, the following function returns the average salary of all employees:

```
static double AverageSalary(employeeT staff[], int nEmployees)
{
    double total;
    int i;

    total = 0;
    for (i = 0; i < nEmployees; i++) {
        total += staff[i].salary;
    }
    return (total / nEmployees);
}
```

You can easily define other functions that would be useful in the context of an employee database system.

16.4 Pointers to records

Although small records are sometimes used directly in C, variables that hold structured data in C are usually declared to be pointers to records rather than the records themselves. A pointer to a record is usually smaller and more easily manipulated than the record itself. More importantly, if you pass a pointer to a record to a procedure, that procedure can change the contents of the record. If you try to pass the record itself, the record will be copied (just as an integer is copied), and you will then be unable to make any permanent changes. As you discovered in Chapter 11, the fact that C uses pointers to pass array variables means that you can change the components of an array within the context of a function. Similarly, passing a pointer to a record allows functions to manipulate the fields of those records.

To give yourself practice using pointers to records, you can start by declaring pointers to the employeeT record defined earlier in the chapter as

```
typedef struct {
    string name;
    string title;
    string ssnum;
    double salary;
    int withholding;
} employeeT;
```

Given that definition, you can declare a variable of type pointer-to-employeeT by writing

```
employeeT *empptr;
```

which declares the variable empptr as a pointer to an object of type employeeT. When you do so, space is reserved only for the pointer itself. Before using empptr, you still need to provide the actual storage for the fields in the complete record.

Before getting into the question of how to create storage for the record, however, it makes sense to consider an alternative approach. In the foregoing example, you defined a record type representing an employee and then declared a pointer to that type. This style of operation requires you to keep track of two different conceptual types: the type employeeT and the type pointer-to-employeeT. It would be easier on your memory if you could work with a single type that also provides the advantages of working with pointers as opposed to entire records.

Defining a pointer-to-record type

In the preceding section, the type employeeT is defined to be a record, so variables declared as pointers to that type must include the * operator in their declaration. In most cases, you can adopt an alternative declaration strategy. As long as you are willing to refer to any value of the record type by its address, you can define the type `employeeT` to be the pointer rather than the record itself. To do so, you need to make a minor adjustment to the preceding type definition for `employeeT`, as follows:

```
typedef struct {
    string name;
    string title;
    string ssnum;
    double salary;
    int withholding;
} *employeeT;
```

The only difference between this type definition and the previous one is the asterisk before `employeeT`. This definition indicates that the type `employeeT` points to a record of the given description, even though that record type itself has no explicit name.

Once you have established the new type definition, you can declare `employeeT` objects in the same way that you did earlier. The declaration

```
employeeT emp;
```

once again defines the variable `emp` to be of type `employeeT`. The difference is that this type is now a pointer type rather than a record type.

As you read through this chapter, you may at first be confused by the fact that I have chosen to apply the name `employeeT` to two different types, one of which is a record, the other a pointer. I could have chosen to give the two types different names, such as `employeeRec` and `employeePtr`. The problem is that changing the name of the type would obscure an important point. In most applications, you do not want to work with two different types. You want a single type that represents an employee. You want the type `employeeT`. You do, however, have a choice as to how you define the type `employeeT`: you can define it as a record or as a pointer to a record. To decide which of these two representations is better for a particular application, you need to consider these factors:

- *The size of the record type.* Whenever you pass a record to a function or assign it to a record variable, all the fields in the record must be copied. For small records, the copying time is not significantly greater than that required for an integer or any other atomic value. If, on the other hand, the record is large, copying the record can take considerable time. If you work instead with pointers to records, you can avoid making these copies. Thus, the larger a record is, the greater the advantage in using a pointer to refer to it.

- *The cost of memory allocation.* Although using a pointer to a record rather than the record itself can reduce the need for data copying, using pointers forces you to think more carefully about how you allocate memory for the underlying data. The process of allocating memory can complicate the logic of your program.

- *The discipline used by functions that manipulate the type.* When you define a new data type, you will usually define additional functions to manipulate values of that type. If you pass a record as an argument to a function, the function cannot change its value. If you pass a pointer instead, that function has direct access to the underlying data. If you need to be able to change the components of a record from within a function, you must declare the type as a pointer. If you do not need to do so, defining the type as a record provides a measure of safety because you know that no function will be able to overwrite the values passed as arguments.

In the case of the `employeeT` definition, it is probably best to use the pointer definition, primarily because the record is large. As is often the case, however, either choice would work.

Allocating storage for record data

Although you can usually choose either the record or pointer-to-record option when you define a new type, the choice you make determines how the resulting variables are used. If you define the type `employeeT` using

```
typedef struct {
    string name;
    string title;
    string ssnum;
    double salary;
    int withholding;
} *employeeT;
```

and then declare a variable of that type by writing

```
employeeT emp;
```

the compiler reserves space only for the pointer. There is no storage allocated for the actual record itself. Before you can make use of the variable `emp`, you must make sure that the pointer actually points to a usable address in memory.

The easiest way to provide storage for the record is to use dynamic allocation as described in Chapter 13. To determine how much space you need to hold the employee record itself, you can use the `sizeof` operator in the following idiomatic way:

```
emp = (employeeT) GetBlock(sizeof *emp);
```

This statement uses `GetBlock` to request enough storage to hold values of the type to which `emp` points.

Even though the idiom using `GetBlock` and `sizeof` is short and reasonably clear, the operation of allocating space for a new record is so fundamental to record-based programming that it pays to define an even simpler form. For that reason, the `genlib.h` interface defines a function `New` that takes the name of a pointer type as argument and returns a pointer to a newly allocated area of memory large enough to hold the underlying value. Thus, if you write

```
emp = New(employeeT);
```

the system allocates space for an employee record in the heap and returns a pointer to that record.

The effect of this operation can be illustrated as follows. Before you execute the call to New, the variable emp holds a pointer value that is not yet initialized. The variable emp is therefore not associated with any record storage and can be diagrammed as an empty box.

The assignment statement

    emp = New(employeeT);

allocates space for the underlying record and assigns the pointer address to emp, which results in the following diagram:

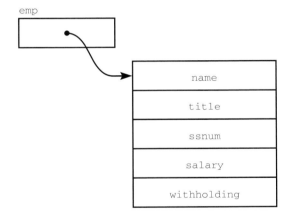

Manipulating pointers to records

Even though you will often think of variables like emp as complete entities, you will at some point need to refer to the individual fields within the record. In a record declared without using pointers, you select an individual field using the dot operator. If you have declared a pointer to the record instead, how can you refer to an individual field?

In seeking an answer, it is easy to be misled by your intuition. Given the declaration

    employeeT emp;

it is *not* appropriate to write, for example

    *emp.salary   This is incorrect.

Contrary to what you might have expected, this statement does not select the salary component of the object to which `emp` points, because the precedence of the operators in the expression does not support that interpretation. The selection operator takes precedence over dereferencing, so the expression has the meaningless interpretation

```
*(emp.salary)
```

rather than the intended

```
(*emp).salary
```

The latter form has the desired effect but is much too cumbersome for everyday use. Pointers to structures are used all the time. Forcing the user to include parentheses in every selection would make records much less convenient.

For this reason, C defines the operator `->` so that it combines the operations of dereference and selection into a single operator. Thus, the conventional way to refer to the employee's salary is to write

```
emp->salary
```

16.5 Building a database of records

Data structures that hold large collections of structured objects are often called **databases**. In the section on "Combining records and arrays" earlier in this chapter, you learned how to store information about employees in a company by using an array of `employeeT` values. The `staff` array, coupled with the number of active elements stored in `nEmployees`, constitutes a simple database.

There is, however, a certain amount of clumsiness in having to pass two variables—the array itself and its effective size—whenever you want to give another function access to the data. It would be better to bundle the effective size together with the data records as a single object. You can do so by defining a new structure type that includes both values. Because the resulting structure contains the entire array of employees and is therefore rather large, it is more efficient to define the new type as a pointer to a record rather than simply as a record. Thus, an appropriate structure for the entire employee database is

```
typedef struct {
    employeeT staff[MaxEmployees];
    int nEmployees;
} *employeeDB;
```

This definition introduces a new type called `employeeDB`. You can then declare a variable of type `employeeDB` by writing the declaration

```
employeeDB db;
```

Creating the employee database

As of yet, the variable `db` consists only of the memory space for the pointer, and there is no storage allocated to it. You still have to provide storage for the components of this record, as well as storage for all the individual employee records within it. To get an idea of what you need, it helps to begin by drawing a picture of the structure you want to create. As in procedural decomposition, it often works best to draw that picture from the top down, refining each level of the structure in turn.

At the highest level of detail, the database is simply a pointer to a record whose contents you do not yet have to understand:

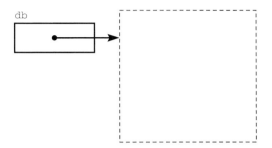

To refine this picture, you need to look at the details of the `employeeDB` record, where you discover that the dotted box can be replaced by a structure containing both an array of `MaxEmployees` elements and the actual number of employees, as shown:

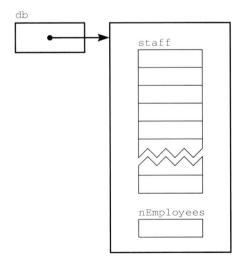

Finally, each of the elements in the `staff` array—according to the most recent definition of the type `employeeT`—is a pointer to a record, so the complete picture will include pointers to individual `employeeT` structures, as shown:

To create this structure, you need to be able to build it up from its parts. For each box in the structure that is referenced by a pointer, there must be a call to the function New to create the storage for that record.

To make this example more concrete, let's suppose you want to write a program that reads in an employee database from the user. For each individual record, the program must request the five pieces of data required about an employee. A blank name field will serve as a sentinel that the database is complete. The individual records must be stored in the database along with the record count.

The operation of reading the database is certainly large enough and sufficiently well-contained that it makes sense to define it as a function. Because the database is a pointer, `ReadEmployeeDatabase` can simply allocate the necessary storage internally and return a pointer to it. Thus, the main program declares the database by writing

```
employeeDB db;
```

and then reads it in by calling

```
db = ReadEmployeeDatabase();
```

The implementation of `ReadEmployeeDatabase` is straightforward, particularly if you use stepwise refinement to break it down into two functions: the function `ReadEmployeeDatabase` itself, which creates the database structure, and a function `ReadOneEmployee`, which reads in the data for a single employee. Because `ReadOneEmployee` is responsible for reading the data from the file, that function must also detect the end-of-file condition and pass that information back to `ReadEmployeeDatabase` by returning a special sentinel value. Because the `ReadOneEmployee` function returns a value of the pointer type `employeeT`, the best choice for the end-of-data sentinel is the pointer value NULL.

The code for the `ReadEmployeeDatabase` function is

```
static employeeDB ReadEmployeeDatabase(void)
{
    employeeDB db;
    employeeT emp;
    int nEmployees;

    db = New(employeeDB);
    nEmployees = 0;
    printf("Enter employee data (use blank name to stop).\n");
    while ((emp = ReadOneEmployee()) != NULL) {
        db->staff[nEmployees] = emp;
        nEmployees++;
    }
    db->nEmployees = nEmployees;
    return (db);
}
```

The `ReadOneEmployee` function allocates space for an employee and fills in its fields, as shown in the following implementation:

```
static employeeT ReadOneEmployee(void)
{
    employeeT emp;
    string name;

    printf("Name: ");
    name = GetLine();
    if (StringLength(name) == 0) return (NULL);
    emp = New(employeeT);
    emp->name = name;
    printf("Title: ");
    emp->title = GetLine();
    printf("SSNum: ");
    emp->ssnum = GetLine();
    printf("Salary: ");
    emp->salary = GetReal();
    printf("Withholding: ");
    emp->withholding = GetInteger();
    return (emp);
}
```

Using the database

Once you have created the database, you can use it as the source of data for programs that generate a report or calculate statistics. For example, you can rewrite the `ListEmployees` procedure introduced earlier to use the new database structure, as follows:

```
static void ListEmployees(employeeDB db)
{
    int i;

    for (i = 0; i < db->nEmployees; i++) {
        printf("%s (%s)\n", db->staff[i]->name,
                            db->staff[i]->title);
    }
}
```

Moreover, because `employeeT` is represented as a pointer, you can also write functions that change the internal data. The following procedure doubles the salary of every employee with five or more withholding allowances:

```
static void GiveRaise(employeeDB db)
{
    int i;

    for (i = 0; i < db->nEmployees; i++) {
        if (db->staff[i]->withholding >= 5) {
            db->staff[i]->salary *= 2;
        }
    }
}
```

■■■■ 16.6 Designing a record-based application

Twenty years or so ago, when computers were just starting to be used as general-purpose tools, there was a movement within the educational community to use computers as part of the teaching process. One of the proposed techniques for doing so is called **programmed instruction,** a process in which a computerized teaching tool asks a series of questions so that previous answers determine the order of subsequent questions. If a student is getting all the right answers, the programmed instruction process skips most of the easy questions and moves quickly on to more challenging topics. For the student who is having trouble, the process moves more slowly, leaving time for repetition and review.

Let's suppose you have been assigned the problem of writing an application that makes it possible to present material in a programmed instruction style. In a nutshell, your program must be able to

- Ask the student a question
- Get an answer from the student
- Move on to the next question, the choice of which depends on the student's response

Such a program will likely be much simpler than a commercial application, but you can easily design a program that illustrates the general principles involved.

The importance of using a database

It is possible to design a programmed instruction application as a set of procedures. Each procedure asks a question, reads in an answer, and then calls another procedure appropriate to the answer the student supplies. Such a program, however, would be difficult to change. Someone who wanted to add questions or design an entirely new course would need to write new procedures. Writing procedures is simple enough for someone who understands programming, but not everyone does. Most programmed instruction courses are designed by teachers in a specific discipline; those teachers are usually not programmers. Forcing them to work in the programming domain limits their ability to use the application.

As the programmer on the project, your goal is to develop an application that presents a programmed instruction course to the student but allows teachers without programming skills to supply the questions, expected answers, and cross-reference information so that your application can present the questions in the appropriate order. To do so, the best approach is to design your application as a general tool that takes all data pertaining to the programmed instruction course from a file. If you adopt this approach, the same program can present many different courses by using different data files.

In designing the application, you need to begin by considering broad questions about the design, such as these:

- What are the overall requirements of the general problem? In particular, you need to understand the set of operations your program must support, apart from any specific domain of instruction.
- How can you represent the data for the programmed instruction course in the context of your program? As part of the design phase, you need to develop an appropriate data structure consisting of some combination of records and arrays.
- What should a course data file look like? As you make this decision, you need to keep in mind that the data file is being edited by nonprogrammers whose expertise is in the specific domain under consideration.
- How do you convert the external representation used in the data file into the internal one?
- How do you write the program that manipulates the database?

The rest of this chapter considers each of these questions in turn.

Framing the problem

At one level, it is easy to outline the operation of the program. When your program runs, its basic operation is to execute the following steps repeatedly:

1. Ask the student the current question. A question consists of one or more lines of text, which you can represent as strings.
2. Request an answer from the student, which can also be represented as a string.

3. Look up the answer in a list of possibilities provided for that question. If the answer appears in the list, consult the data structure to choose what question should become the new current question. If the student's answer does not match any of the possibilities provided by the database, the student should be informed of that fact and given another chance at the same question.

Many details are missing from this outline, but it is a start. Even at this level, the outline provides some insight into the eventual implementation. For example, you know that you need to keep track of what the "current question" is. To do so, it makes sense to number the questions and then store the current question number in a variable.

Writing the program itself turns out to be one of the easier pieces of the task; the harder problems arise in representing the database. For the program to be general and flexible, all the information that pertains to an actual course must be stored in a data file, not built directly into the program. The program's job is to read that data file, store the information in an internal data structure, and then process that structure as outlined earlier in this section. Thus, your next major task is to design the data structures required for the problem so that you have a context for building the program as a whole.

The process of designing the data structures has two distinct components. First, you have to design an *internal* data structure for use by the program. The internal data structure consists of type definitions that combine arrays and records so that the resulting types mirror the organization of the real-world information you seek to represent. Second, you must design an *external* data structure that indicates how the information is stored in the data file. These two processes are closely related, mostly because they each represent the same information. Even so, the two structures are tailored to meet different purposes. The internal structure must be easy for the programmer to use. The external structure must make it easy for someone to write a course, without making it too difficult for the program to manipulate.

Designing the internal representation

The first step in the process is to design a data structure that incorporates the necessary information. As with the `employeeDB` type presented in the section on "Creating the employee database" earlier in the chapter, it helps to design the data structure from the top down, starting with the highest-level structure and then refining it by specifying more and more of the details.

In designing a database, one of the most important concepts is that of **encapsulation,** which is the process of combining related pieces of data into structures that can be treated as complete units. For a large database, the encapsulation process is hierarchical and must be considered at varying levels of detail. At the highest level, you want to think of the entire database as a single variable, which contains all the information you will need. Thus, the following diagram represents the database as a pointer to a structure whose details you will fill in later:

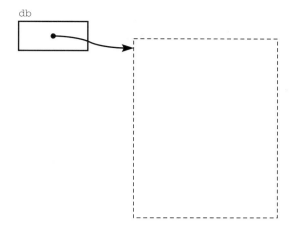

Whenever you need to pass the entire database to a function or a procedure, all you have to do is pass the variable db, which is a small, easily manipulated pointer that gives you access to the other data. It is only when a function or procedure needs to manipulate the individual fields of the database that it has to look inside the structure to see its details.

Given that your current purpose is to design the internal structure, however, you do need to understand what is contained within the dotted box in the diagram above. Intuitively, you know that the database as a whole contains a list of questions, although it may make sense to include other information as well, such as the title of the course. The questions themselves are an array of some as-yet-undefined structure that defines a single question. Thus, the database structure at the current level of decomposition looks like this:

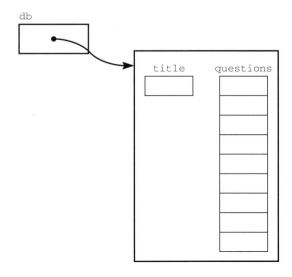

Although you don't yet know the details of the underlying type used to represent a question, you can nonetheless convert this diagram into a data structure definition. You know the types of the other fields and can therefore put together an appropriate record definition, such as

```
typedef struct {
    string title;
    questionT questions[MaxQuestions+1];
} *courseDB;
```

The constant `MaxQuestions` is the largest question number your program will allow. Because array numbering always begins at 0 even though the course will presumably begin with question 1, you need to allocate an extra element in the array so that there is a question numbered `MaxQuestions`.

The definition of `courseDB` makes it possible for you to declare a variable `db` that holds the entire database, as follows:

```
courseDB db;
```

By itself, however, this declaration only reserves storage for the pointer and thus corresponds to the dotted-box picture earlier in this section. When you create the structure in your program, it is necessary to allocate space for the structure by writing

```
db = New(courseDB);
```

At this point, you need to supply some of the missing details. For example, you have not yet provided a definition for the type `questionT` used in the definition of `courseDB`. To write the complete data structure, you need to flesh out this aspect of the design. A question consists of the text of the question, which may include multiple lines, and a list of answers. Both of these structures are arrays. The question text is an array of strings representing the individual lines in the question. The expected answers are stored in an array whose structure is a little more complicated. For now, you can declare the answers as an array of values of type `answerT` and fill in the details on your next refinement step.

Whenever you use an array, you need to provide some mechanism for keeping track of the effective size of the array, which is usually less than the allocated size. There are two possible strategies for recording the effective size:

- You can store a sentinel value after the last data value in the array.
- You can store the number of elements explicitly in an integer variable, which then becomes part of the record.

Deciding which strategy is better for a particular application depends on how the array is used and whether it is possible to choose an appropriate sentinel value.

To illustrate both modes of operation, the sample program uses both strategies in the definition of `questionT`. The lines representing the text of the questions are stored as an array of strings, which are simply pointers to the characters making up the string. For pointer data, the constant `NULL` provides a natural sentinel value. Because the elements of the answers array are of type `answerT`, which you have not yet defined, it is harder to know what a sentinel value would look like. Hence, it seems more appropriate in this case to store the number of answers explicitly as part of the structure.

The structure for an individual question can therefore be diagrammed as follows:

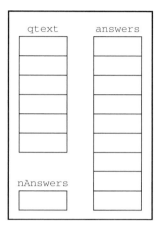

Because this structure is large and because it makes sense to think about a question as a single unit, it is appropriate to declare this structure as a pointer type, as follows:

```
typedef struct {
    string qtext[MaxLinesPerQuestion+1];
    answerT answers[MaxAnswersPerQuestion];
    int nAnswers;
} *questionT;
```

Declaring the structure as a pointer means that you need to call New to allocate space for each question.

The last step in designing the data structure is to define the type answerT. An answer consists of the following pair: the expected answer and the question to which you should move if that answer is given. The expected answer is a string, and the next question can be represented by an integer used to hold the question number. Thus, the answer structure looks like this:

The corresponding structure is a record pairing a string and an integer, as follows:

```
typedef struct {
    string ans;
    int nextq;
} answerT;
```

In this case, the structure is small enough that it makes sense to define it as a record rather than a pointer.

This last definition makes it possible for you to diagram the entire data structure, as follows:

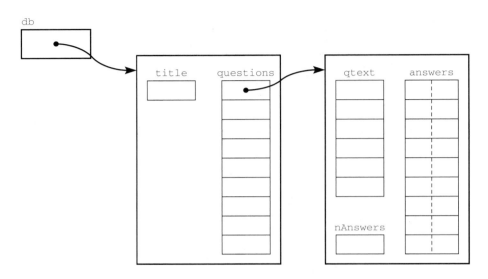

Designing the external structure

Once you have defined the structure used for the internal data, you must then decide how to represent the same information within the data file. Files are simply text, and the organization provided by the data structure hierarchy in C must be expressed in the design of the file format. The file structure design must also make it easy for someone to write and edit, even if that person is not a programmer. Thus, you should choose a representation that is as simple as possible. In this case, it seems easiest to write out each question, one after another, along with its likely answers. So that the computer can tell where the answers to one question stop and the next question begins, you must define some convention for separating the question-and-answer units. A blank line works well in this context, as it does in most file structures. Thus, in individual units separated by blank lines, you have the data for each question and its answers.

But what goes into each question-and-answer unit? First of all, you need the text of the question, which consists of individual lines from the file. You also need some way to indicate the end of the question text, and the easiest way, both for you and for the course writer, is to define a sentinel. In this program, I have arbitrarily chosen a line of five dashes to indicate the end of the question text. Furthermore, you must allow the course writer to specify the answer/next-question pairs. Here, I have chosen to represent both of these values on a single data line consisting of the answer text, followed by a colon, followed by the index of the next question. I could have chosen other formats, but this design seems as if it would be easy for a novice to learn. Thus, the data for an individual question entry in the file looks like this:

```
True or false: The earth revolves around the sun.
-----
true: 3
false: 2
```

The question text consists of a single line, after which there are two acceptable answers. If the user types in `false`, the program should go to question 2; if the user types in `true`, it should move on to question 3.

This example brings up an interesting question. How do you assign question numbers to each of these entries? One approach would be to arrange the questions in the file and number them sequentially. This strategy makes life easy for you as the programmer. The problem is that it makes life difficult for the person writing a course.

To understand why this is so, suppose that the course writer wants to add a new question near the beginning of an existing course. All subsequent questions move down by one, all the question numbers change, and the course writer has to spend a considerable amount of time renumbering all the next-question indicators. A better approach is to let the person who writes the question give it a number. For example, if the sample question about the earth and sun were question #1 in the database, its entry in the file would begin with its question number, as follows:

```
1
True or false: The earth revolves around the sun.
-----
true: 2
false: 3
```

The advantage of allowing the course writer to supply question numbers is that it makes editing the course much easier. Someone who wants to add a new question can just give it a question number that hasn't been used before. None of the other question numbers need to change. The course writer can then insert the new question anywhere in the data file, because there is no longer any reason that the question numbers need to be consecutive.

Coding the program

Once you have defined the internal data structure and the external file format, the process of writing the code for the teaching machine program is surprisingly straightforward, as long as you decompose the entire task into simpler functions using stepwise refinement. The complete program is contained in the file `teach.c` shown in Figure 16-1.

FIGURE 16-1 teach.c

```
/*
 * File: teach.c
 * ------------
 * This program executes a simple programmed instruction course.
 * The course is specified by a data file containing all the
 * course information.  The data structures and the format of
 * the data file are described in Chapter 16.
 */

#include <stdio.h>
#include <string.h>
#include <ctype.h>

#include "genlib.h"
#include "strlib.h"
#include "simpio.h"

/*
 * Constants
 * ---------
 * MaxQuestions          -- Maximum question number
 * MaxLinesPerQuestion   -- Maximum number of lines per question
 * MaxAnswersPerQuestion -- Maximum answers per question
 * EndMarker             -- String marking end of question text
 */

#define MaxQuestions          100
#define MaxLinesPerQuestion    20
#define MaxAnswersPerQuestion  10
#define EndMarker "-----"

/* Data structures */

/*
 * Type: answerT
 * -------------
 * This structure provides space for each possible answer
 * to a question.
 */

typedef struct {
    string ans;
    int nextq;
} answerT;
```

```
/*
 * Type: questionT
 * ---------------
 * This structure provides space for all the information
 * needed to store one of the individual question records.
 * Because this structure is large and it makes sense
 * to refer to it as a single entity, questionT is defined
 * as a pointer type.
 */

typedef struct {
    string qtext[MaxLinesPerQuestion+1];
    answerT answers[MaxAnswersPerQuestion];
    int nAnswers;
} *questionT;

/*
 * Type: courseDB
 * --------------
 * This type is used to define the entire database, which is
 * a pointer to a record containing the title and an array of
 * questions.
 */

typedef struct {
    string title;
    questionT questions[MaxQuestions+1];
} *courseDB;

/* Private function declarations */

static courseDB ReadDataBase(void);
static bool ReadOneQuestion(FILE *infile, courseDB course);
static void ReadQuestionText(FILE *infile, questionT q);
static void ReadAnswers(FILE *infile, questionT q);
static FILE *OpenUserFile(string prompt, string mode);
static void ProcessCourse(courseDB course);
static void AskQuestion(questionT q);
static int FindAnswer(string ans, questionT q);

/* Main program */

main()
{
    courseDB course;

    course = ReadDataBase();
    ProcessCourse(course);
}
```

```
/* Section 1 -- Functions to read the data file */

/*
 * Function: ReadDataBase
 * Usage: ReadDataBase();
 * ---------------------
 * This function asks the user for a file name and reads
 * in the database for the course.  The file is formatted
 * as discussed in the section "Designing the external
 * structure" in Chapter 16.
 */

static courseDB ReadDataBase(void)
{
    FILE *infile;
    courseDB course;

    infile = OpenUserFile("Enter name of course: ", "r");
    course = New(courseDB);
    course->title = ReadLine(infile);
    while (ReadOneQuestion(infile, course));
    fclose(infile);
    return (course);
}


/*
 * Function: ReadOneQuestion
 * Usage: while (ReadOneQuestion(infile, course));
 * -----------------------------------------------
 * This function reads in a single question from infile into the
 * course data structure.  As long as the complete question is
 * read successfully, this function returns TRUE.  When the end
 * of the file is encountered, the function returns FALSE.
 * Thus, the "Usage" line above reads the entire data file.
 */

static bool ReadOneQuestion(FILE *infile, courseDB course)
{
    questionT question;
    string line;
    int qnum;

    line = ReadLine(infile);
    if (line == NULL) return (FALSE);
    qnum = StringToInteger(line);
    if (qnum < 1 || qnum > MaxQuestions) {
        Error("Question number %d out of range", qnum);
    }
```

```
        question = New(questionT);
        ReadQuestionText(infile, question);
        ReadAnswers(infile, question);
        course->questions[qnum] = question;
        return (TRUE);
}


/*
 * Function: ReadQuestionText
 * Usage: ReadQuestionText(infile, question);
 * -------------------------------------------
 * This function reads the text of the question into the
 * question data structure, which must have been allocated
 * by the caller.  The end of the question text is signaled
 * by a line matching the string EndMarker.
 */

static void ReadQuestionText(FILE *infile, questionT q)
{
    string line;
    int nlines;

    nlines = 0;
    while (TRUE) {
        line = ReadLine(infile);
        if (StringEqual(line, EndMarker)) break;
        if (nlines == MaxLinesPerQuestion) {
            Error("Too many lines");
        }
        q->qtext[nlines] = line;
        nlines++;
    }
    q->qtext[nlines] = NULL;
}


/*
 * Function: ReadAnswers
 * Usage: ReadAnswers(infile, question);
 * -------------------------------------
 * This function reads the answer pairs for the question
 * from the input file.  Each answer consists of a string
 * followed by a colon, followed by the number of the next
 * question to be read.  The end of the answer list is
 * signaled by a blank line or the end of the file.
 */
```

```
static void ReadAnswers(FILE *infile, questionT q)
{
    string line, ans;
    int len, cpos, nextq, nAnswers;

    nAnswers = 0;
    while ((line = ReadLine(infile)) != NULL
            && (len = StringLength(line)) != 0) {
        cpos = FindChar(':', line, 0);
        if (cpos == -1) Error("Illegal answer format");
        ans = SubString(line, 0, cpos - 1);
        nextq = StringToInteger(SubString(line, cpos+1, len-1));
        q->answers[nAnswers].ans = ConvertToUpperCase(ans);
        q->answers[nAnswers].nextq = nextq;
        nAnswers++;
    }
    q->nAnswers = nAnswers;
}

/*
 * Function: OpenUserFile
 * Usage: fileptr = OpenUserFile(prompt, mode);
 * -----------------------------------------------
 * This function prompts the user for a file name using the
 * prompt string supplied by the user and then attempts to
 * open that file with the specified mode.  If the file is
 * opened successfully, OpenUserFile returns the appropriate
 * file pointer.  If the open operation fails, the user is
 * informed of the failure and given an opportunity to enter
 * another file name.
 */

static FILE *OpenUserFile(string prompt, string mode)
{
    string filename;
    FILE *result;

    while (TRUE) {
        printf("%s", prompt);
        filename = GetLine();
        result = fopen(filename, mode);
        if (result != NULL) break;
        printf("Can't open the file \"%s\"\n", filename);
    }
    return (result);
}
```

```
/* Section 2 -- Functions to process the course */

/*
 * Function: ProcessCourse
 * Usage: ProcessCourse(course);
 * -----------------------------
 * This function processes the course supplied by the caller.
 * The basic operation consists of a loop that (a) prints out
 * the current question, (b) reads in an answer, (c) looks up
 * the answer in the database, and (d) goes to a new question
 * on the basis of that answer. In this implementation, the
 * variable qnum holds the index of the question and the
 * variable q holds the actual question data structure.  The
 * course always begins with question #1, after which the
 * order is determined by the answers.
 */

static void ProcessCourse(courseDB course)
{
    questionT q;
    int qnum;
    string ans;
    int index;

    printf("%s\n", course->title);
    qnum = 1;
    while (qnum != 0) {
        q = course->questions[qnum];
        AskQuestion(q);
        ans = ConvertToUpperCase(GetLine());
        index = FindAnswer(ans, q);
        if (index == -1) {
            printf("I don't understand that.\n");
        } else {
            qnum = q->answers[index].nextq;
        }
    }
}

/*
 * Function: AskQuestion
 * Usage: AskQuestion(q);
 * ----------------------
 * This function asks the question indicated by the questionT
 * specified by q.  Asking the question consists of displaying
 * each of the lines that comprise the question text.
 */
```

```
static void AskQuestion(questionT q)
{
    int i;

    for (i = 0; q->qtext[i] != NULL; i++) {
        printf("%s\n", q->qtext[i]);
    }
}

/*
 * Function: FindAnswer
 * Usage: FindAnswer(ans, q)
 * -------------------------
 * This function looks up the string ans in the list of answers
 * for question q.  If the answer is found, its index in the
 * answer list is returned.  If not, the function returns -1.
 * The function uses a simple linear search algorithm to look
 * through the array.
 */

static int FindAnswer(string ans, questionT q)
{
    int i;

    for (i = 0; i < q->nAnswers; i++) {
        if (StringEqual(ans, q->answers[i].ans)) return (i);
    }
    return (-1);
}
```

It is worth spending some time going through the teach.c program to make sure that you understand the following points:

1. How the program initializes the internal data structures from the data in the file
2. How the program then uses those data structures to process the individual questions

The value of a data-driven design

The teach.c program in Figure 16-1 takes all its data from the course data file. The questions it asks, the answers it accepts, and even the sequencing of the questions are supplied by the data file, not by the program. Programs that control their entire operation on the basis of information from a database are said to be **data-driven.** Data-driven programs are usually shorter, more flexible, and easier to maintain than programs that incorporate the same information directly into the program design.

To illustrate just how flexible a data-driven system like teach.c can be, it is useful to show the program in operation. According to the initial goals of the project, the teach.c program would be used for a traditional programmed instruction course, such as the file `cs.dat` whose first few questions appear in Figure 16-2. When the `teach.c` program is used in conjunction with this data file, a student might see the sample run also shown in Figure 16-2.

Because it is data-driven, the same program can be used in completely different contexts. For example, Figure 16-3 contains the first few lines from the data file `advent.dat`, which is adapted from the original computer adventure game developed by Willie Crowther in the early 1970s. As the sample run shows, someone who uses the `teach.c` program in conjunction with the file `advent.dat` will perceive the program's purpose very differently than someone who runs it with the `cs.dat` file. Even though the `teach.c` program has not changed at all, the programmed instruction course has become an adventure game. The only difference is the data file.

SUMMARY

As you learned in Chapter 11, arrays make it possible to store ordered collections of homogeneous values. This chapter has introduced the equally important concept of a *record,* which permits you to store unordered, heterogeneous components as a single collection. Arrays are ordinarily used to model a collection of objects in the real world; records are used to model single objects composed of identifiable parts. You can use arrays and records together to form hierarchical structures of arbitrary complexity. A complete structure used to represent a collection of data is called a *database.*

Important points considered in this chapter include:

- A record is composed of individual components called *fields.* In C, a record is often called a *structure* and its components are called *members.*
- Declaring a record is a two-step process. You first define a type that serves as a template for the record, after which you can declare variables of that type.
- Given a record, you select its individual fields using the . (dot) operator.
- In many cases, it makes sense to use pointers to records rather than the records themselves. Using pointers is more efficient in terms of space and makes it possible for functions to modify the underlying record data.
- If you have a pointer to a record, you use the `->` operator to combine the operations of dereference and field selection.
- You can dynamically allocate memory space for a record by calling the function `New` defined in `genlib.h`. The `New` function takes a pointer type and returns the address of a newly allocated object of the underlying type.
- Database design is a complex process that uses stepwise refinement in much the same way that program design does.

FIGURE 16-2   Data file cs.dat and an associated sample run

```
C programming review
1
Would you like help with int or bool type?
-----
int:    2
bool:   10

2
True or false: Integers can have fractional parts.
-----
true:   3
false:  5

3
No.  Floating-point numbers have fractional parts;
integers do not.
True or false: Integers can be negative.
-----
true:   5
false:  4

4
No.  You should go back and review the text.
Would you like to quit?
-----
yes:    0
y:      0
no:     1
n:      1
```

      . . . file continues with additional questions . . .

```
Enter name of course: cs.dat⏎
C programming review
Would you like help with int or bool type?
int⏎
True or false: Integers can have fractional parts.
true⏎
No.  Floating-point numbers have fractional parts;
integers do not.
True or false: Integers can be negative.
false⏎
No.  You should go back and review the text.
Would you like to quit?
yes⏎
```

FIGURE 16-3   Data file **advent.dat** and an associated sample run

```
Welcome to ADVENTURE!
1
You are standing at the end of a road before a
small brick building.  A small stream flows out
of the building and down a gully to the south.
A road runs up a small hill to the west.
-----
south: 2
north: 8
in:    8
west:  9

2
You are in a valley in the forest beside a stream
tumbling along a rocky bed.  The stream is flowing
to the south.
-----
south: 3
down:  3
north: 1

3
At your feet all the water of the stream splashes
down a two-inch slit in the rock.  To the south,
the streambed is bare rock.
-----
north: 2
south: 4
down:  4
```

. . . *file continues with additional rooms* . . .

```
Enter name of course: advent.dat↵
Welcome to ADVENTURE!
You are standing at the end of a road before a
small brick building.  A small stream flows out
of the building and down a gully to the south.
A road runs up a small hill to the west.
south↵
You are in a valley in the forest beside a stream
tumbling along a rocky bed.  The stream is flowing
to the south.
down↵
At your feet all the water of the stream splashes
down a two-inch slit in the rock.  To the south,
the streambed is bare rock.
```

1. Define the terms *record* and *field.* What terms are often used by C programmers to refer to each of these concepts?

2. True or false: The types of each element in an array must be the same.

3. True or false: The types of each field in a record must be different.

4. What steps are necessary to declare a record variable?

5. What operator is used to select a field from a record? If you read the name of that operator aloud, what word do you use for it?

6. True or false: Fields of a record are lvalues in C.

7. True or false: A record is itself an lvalue in C.

8. Suppose that the first two elements of `staff` have been initialized to contain the following values, just as in the chapter:

staff

0	Ebenezer Scrooge	Partner	271-82-8183	250.00	1
1	Bob Cratchit	Clerk	314-15-9265	15.00	7

   Starting with the variable `staff`, how would you select the field corresponding to Bob Cratchit's salary? How would you select Ebenezer Scrooge's first initial?

9. In this chapter, `employeeT` is defined first as a record type and later as a pointer to a record. What syntactic change was necessary to implement the change in representation?

10. What factors should you consider in deciding whether to define a new type as a record or as a pointer to a record?

11. What function exported by `genlib.h` helps to simplify dynamic allocation of records?

12. If the variable `p` is declared as a pointer to a record that contains a field called `cost`, what is wrong with the expression

    ```
    *p.cost
    ```

    as a means of following the pointer from `p` to its value and then selecting the `cost` field? What expression would you write in C to accomplish this dereference-and-select operation?

13. What is a database?

14. When you want to store a database in a file, you must define both an internal and an external representation. Why are both representations necessary? What factors must you consider in the design of each one?

15. In the `teach.c` program, it would certainly be possible for the computer to number the questions automatically as it reads the data file. In the design presented in this chapter, however, the course writer supplies the question numbers as part of the data file. What is the reason for this design decision?

16. What is meant by the term *data-driven design?* What are the advantages of using such an approach?

PROGRAMMING EXERCISES

1. Write a program that generates weekly payroll checks for a company whose employment records are stored in a database of type `employeeDB`, as defined in this chapter. Each employee is paid the salary given in the employee record, after deducting taxes. Your program should compute taxes as follows:

   - Deduct $1 from the salary for each withholding exemption. This figure is the *adjusted income.* (If the result of the calculation is less than 0, use 0 as the adjusted income.)
   - Multiply the adjusted income by the *tax rate,* which you should assume is a flat 25 percent.

   For example, Bob Cratchit has a weekly income of $15. Because he has seven dependents, his adjusted income is $15 − (7 × $1), or $8. Twenty-five percent of $8 is $2, so Mr. Cratchit's net pay is $15 − $2, or $13.

   The checks should include the name of the employee, the net pay, and a note showing the gross pay and taxes, as shown in the following sample run:

```
+------------------------------------------------+
| Scrooge and Marley Ltd.                        |
|                                                |
| Pay to the order of: Ebenezer Scrooge   187.75 |
|                                                |
|                                                |
| 250.00 gross - 62.25 tax           E. Scrooge  |
+------------------------------------------------+



+------------------------------------------------+
| Scrooge and Marley Ltd.                        |
|                                                |
| Pay to the order of: Bob Cratchit        13.00 |
|                                                |
|                                                |
| 15.00 gross - 2.00 tax             E. Scrooge  |
+------------------------------------------------+
```

Your job includes printing the border around the check and formatting the internal information.

2. Suppose that you have been assigned the task of computerizing the card catalog system for a library. As a first step, your supervisor has asked you to develop a prototype capable of storing the following information for each of 1000 books:

   - The title
   - A list of up to five authors
   - The Library of Congress catalog number
   - Up to five subject headings
   - The publisher
   - The year of publication
   - Whether the book is circulating or noncirculating

   Design the data structures that would be necessary to keep all the information required for this prototype library database. Given your definition, it should be possible to write the declaration

   ```
   libraryDB libdata;
   ```

   and have the variable `libdata` contain all the information you would need to keep track of up to 1000 books. Remember that the actual number of books will usually be less than this upper bound.

   Write a procedure `SearchBySubject` that takes as parameters the library database and a subject string. For each book in the library that lists the subject string as one of its subject headings, `SearchBySubject` should display the title, the name of the first author, and the Library of Congress catalog number of the book.

3. Write a function `Midpoint(p1, p2)` that returns the midpoint of the line segment between the points `p1` and `p2`. The argument and the result are each of type `pointT`, which was defined in the text as follows:

   ```
   typedef struct {
       double x, y;
   } pointT;
   ```

4. Design an interface `ptgraph.h` that uses points rather than individual coordinates to specify coordinates and relative displacements. For example, instead of calling `MovePen(x, y)`, clients of `ptgraph.h` might call `MovePenToPoint(pt)`, where the parameter `pt` is a value of type `pointT` as defined in exercise 3. In your interface, you need not redefine any functions that do not take coordinate values as arguments, such as `InitGraphics` or `DrawArc`. Implement the `ptgraph.h` interface as a layered abstraction on top of `graphics.h`.

5. A **rational number** is one that can be expressed as the quotient of two integers. Thus, the number 1.25 is a rational number because it is equal to 5 divided by 4.

Many numbers, such as π or the square root of 2 are not rational, although proving that fact is beyond the mathematical scope of this course. Computation using rational numbers has an important advantage over floating-point arithmetic: unlike floating-point numbers, rational numbers are exact. It would therefore be useful to design a package for manipulating rational numbers, which are not one of C's predefined types.

Design and implement an interface `rational.h` that permits simple operations on rational numbers. At a minimum, your interface should export the following entries:

- The type `rationalT`, which can be used to represent a rational value.
- A function `CreateRational(num, den)`, which returns the rational $\dfrac{num}{den}$.
- A function `AddRational(r1, r2)`, which returns the sum of two rational numbers. The sum of two rational numbers is given by the following formula:

$$\frac{num_1}{den_1} + \frac{num_2}{den_2} = \frac{num_1 \times den_2 + num_2 \times den_1}{den_1 \times den_2}$$

- A function `MultiplyRational(r1, r2)`, which returns the product of two rational numbers. The product of two rational numbers is given by the following formula:

$$\frac{num_1}{den_1} \times \frac{num_2}{den_2} = \frac{num_1 \times num_2}{den_1 \times den_2}$$

- A function `GetRational(r)`, which reads a rational number from the user in the form *num / den*.
- A function `PrintRational(r)`, which displays the number as a fraction on the screen.

All computation using rational numbers should reduce their results to lowest terms. For example, multiplying 1/2 by 2/3 should result in the rational number whose internal representation is 1/3, not 2/6.

Use the `rational.h` interface to write a program that adds a list of rational numbers and displays their sum, as illustrated in the following sample run:

```
This program adds a list of rational numbers.
Signal end of list with a 0.
  ? 1/3↵
  ? 1/6↵
  ? 0↵
The total is 1/2
```

6. In Roman numerals, characters of the alphabet are used to represent integers as shown in this table:

Symbol	Value
I	1
V	5
X	10
L	50
C	100
D	500
M	1000

Each character in a Roman numeral stands for the corresponding value. Ordinarily, the value of the Roman numeral as a whole is the sum of the individual character values given in the table. Thus, the string `"LXXVI"` denotes 50 + 10 + 10 + 5 + 1, or 76. The only exception occurs when a character corresponding to a smaller value precedes a character representing a larger one, in which case the value of the first letter is subtracted from the total, so that the string `"IX"` corresponds to 10 − 1, or 9.

Write a function `RomanToDecimal(roman)` that takes a string representing a Roman numeral and returns the corresponding decimal number. To find the values of each Roman numeral character, your implementation should look up the value in a statically initialized data structure that includes the data in the Roman numeral conversion table. If the argument string contains characters that are not in the table, `RomanToDecimal` should return −1.

7. Suppose that you have been hired as a programmer for a bank to automate the process of converting between different foreign currencies at the prevailing rate of exchange. Every day, the bank receives a data file called `exchange.dat` containing the current exchange rates. The file is composed of lines in the following form:

```
dollar      1.00
yen         0.0078
franc       0.20
mark        0.68
pound       1.96
```

Each line consists of the name of a particular kind of currency, at least one space, and the dollar equivalent of one unit of that currency. Thus, the sample input file tells us that the British pound is worth $1.96 and the German mark is worth 68 cents. (Note that the file includes a line for dollars, for which the exchange rate is always 1.00. The presence of this line means that U.S. dollars need not be treated as a special case.)

Write a program that performs these steps:

a. Read in the `exchange.dat` data file into a suitable internal data structure.

b. Ask the user to enter two currency names: that of the old currency being converted and of the new currency being returned.

c. Ask for a value in the original currency.

d. Display the resulting value in the second currency. The easiest way to compute this value is to convert the original currency to dollars and then convert the dollars to the target currency.

The following sample run illustrates the operation of this program using the data in the `exchange.dat` file:

```
Convert from:  mark↵
Into:  yen↵
How many units of type mark?  200↵
200 mark = 17435.9 yen
```

8. In many applications, it is extremely useful to be able to associate a string with a definition in much the same way that a dictionary does. At one point in the program, you can enter a definition for a particular string; at a later point, you can look up that string to find its definition. More formally, what you need is a package that allows you to associate a value with a particular key (the `Define` operation) and, later, to retrieve any value associated with that key (the `Lookup` operation).

The interface `dict.h` shown in Figure 16-4 provides such a capability. By calling `Define(key, value)`, you make it possible to retrieve that value at a later point by calling `Lookup(key)`. Using arrays of records to represent the data, implement the `dict.h` interface.

9. Although the Madlibs program in exercise 6 of Chapter 15 was originally presented as a game, the same program can be used in more practical contexts, particularly if you use the dictionary facility from exercise 8 to extend the program's capabilities. For example, elected officials could use the program to generate form letters in response to mail from their constituents. All a staff person would need to do is fill in the appropriate blanks in a form stored as a file, as

FIGURE 16-4 dict.h

```
/*
 * File: dict.h
 * ------------
 * This interface exports functions for defining and looking
 * up words in a dictionary. The dictionary is maintained in
 * static storage private to the implementation.
 */

#ifndef _dict_h
#define _dict_h

#include "genlib.h"

/*
 * Function: InitDictionary
 * Usage: InitDictionary();
 * ------------------------
 * This function initializes the dictionary to be empty and must be
 * called before any of the other operations are used.
 */

void InitDictionary(void);

/*
 * Function: Define
 * Usage: Define(word, definition);
 * --------------------------------
 * This function defines the word, using the indicated definition.
 * Any previous definition for word is lost. If defining this
 * word would exceed the capacity of the dictionary, an error is
 * generated.
 */

void Define(string word, string definition);

/*
 * Function: Lookup
 * Usage: str = Lookup(word);
 * --------------------------
 * This function looks up the word in the dictionary and returns
 * its definition. If the word has not been defined, Lookup
 * returns NULL.
 */

string Lookup(string word);

#endif
```

illustrated by the following general-purpose response form stored in
`formlet.txt`:

```
Dear <name>:

Thank you for taking the time to express your interest in
<topic>. Since being elected to Congress,
<topic> has been my top priority.

Because your <message type> means so much to me, I have
taken the time to respond personally. I hear from many
constituents every day, but your <message type> on
<topic> moved me deeply.

Please be assured that I will do all I can to fight the
special interests that oppose us on this critical issue.

                              Sincerely yours,

                              Your Congressperson
```

Note that even though the placeholders `<topic>` and `<message type>` appear
more than once in the file, the program should request a value only once for
each placeholder, as shown in the following sample run:

```
Input file: formlet.txt⏎
   name: Dr. Roberts⏎
   topic: the misuse of computers⏎
   message type: e-mail message⏎

Dear Dr. Roberts:

Thank you for taking the time to express your interest in
the misuse of computers. Since being elected to Congress,
the misuse of computers has been my top priority.

Because your e-mail message means so much to me, I have
taken the time to respond personally. I hear from many
constituents every day, but your e-mail message on
the misuse of computers has moved me deeply.

Please be assured that I will do all I can to fight the
special interests that oppose us on this critical issue.

                              Sincerely yours,

                              Your Congressperson
```

Extend the Madlibs program so that it stores each substitution in a dictionary and replaces it in the text every time it appears.

10. The teach.c program in Figure 16-1 can sometimes produce confusing output because of a flaw in its design. As the course database file in Figure 16-2 illustrates, the feedback that the student gets from the program about an incorrect answer has to be combined with the next question. For example, the text of question 3 in the cs.dat file is

```
No. Floating-point numbers have fractional parts;
integers do not.
True or false: Integers can be negative.
```

The first two lines constitute the response to the previous question; the last line is the next question in the series.

The fact that these two pieces are conjoined leads to certain problems. For example, if the student responds to question 3 with some unrecognized answer, the computer repeats the text of the question. Unfortunately, the text of the question includes the feedback generated in response to the previous answer, which no longer makes sense. Thus, if the student were to respond with the string "maybe", the screen would look like this:

```
True or false: Integers can be negative.
maybe⏎
I don't understand that.
No. Floating-point numbers have fractional parts;
integers do not.
True or false: Integers can be negative.
```

Think about how you might redesign the teach.c program to avoid this problem; then implement and test your new design.

C H A P T E R   1 7

Looking Ahead

There is no justification for present existence other than its expansion into
an indefinitely open future.

— Simone de Beauvoir, *The Second Sex,* 1953

Objectives

- To recognize the power of recursion and be able to apply it in simple cases.

- To be able to define a new abstract type and specify its concrete underlying representation.

- To be able to evaluate the computational complexity of simple algorithms and express that complexity using big-O notation.

After completing the first 16 chapters of this text, you have learned the fundamentals of C programming along with many important concepts from computer science. Computer science, however, is a large and ever-expanding field, and you still have much to learn. This chapter introduces three topics that you must master if you continue your study of computer science:

- *Recursion*
- *Abstract data types*
- *Algorithmic analysis*

Because these topics are central to modern computer science, many schools introduce them in the first programming course. To make sure that this text meets the needs of a wide range of institutions, this chapter offers an overview of each of these topics. Even if you are not required to learn this material for a class, reading through this chapter will help you if you continue in computer science. When you encounter these ideas in a more advanced course, they will not be entirely new, and you will be able to pick them up more quickly.

17.1 Recursion

Most algorithmic strategies used to solve programming problems have counterparts outside the domain of computing. When you perform a task repeatedly, you are using iteration. When you make a decision, you exercise conditional control. Because these operations are familiar, most people learn to use the control statements `for`, `while`, and `if` with relatively little trouble.

Before you can solve many sophisticated programming tasks, however, you will have to come to grips with a powerful problem-solving strategy that has few direct counterparts in the real world. That strategy, called **recursion,** is defined as any solution technique in which large problems are solved by reducing them to smaller problems *of the same form*. The italicized phrase is crucial to the definition, which otherwise describes the strategy of stepwise refinement introduced in Chapter 5. Both strategies involve decomposition. What makes recursion special is that the subproblems in a recursive solution have the same form as the original problem.

If you are like most new programmers, the idea of breaking a problem down into subproblems of the same form does not make much sense when you first hear it. Unlike repetition or conditional testing, recursion is not a concept that comes up in day-to-day life. Because it is unfamiliar, learning how to use recursion can be difficult. To do so, you must develop the intuition necessary to make recursion seem as natural as all the other control structures. For most students of programming, reaching that level of understanding takes considerable time and practice. Even so, learning to use recursion is definitely worth the effort. As a problem-solving tool, recursion is so powerful that it at times seems almost magical. In addition, using recursion often makes it possible to write complex programs in simple and profoundly elegant ways.

A simple illustration of recursion

To gain a better sense of what recursion is, imagine that you have been appointed as the funding coordinator for a large charitable organization that, like many such organizations, is long on volunteers and short on cash. Your job is to raise $1,000,000 in contributions so that the organization can meet its expenses.

If you know someone who is willing to write a check for the entire $1,000,000, your job is easy. On the other hand, you may not be lucky enough to have friends who are generous millionaires. In that case, you must raise the $1,000,000 in smaller amounts. If the average contribution to your organization is $100, you might choose a different tack: call 100,000 friends and ask each of them for $100. But then again, you probably don't have 100,000 friends. So what can you do?

As is often the case when you are faced with a task that exceeds your own capacity, the answer lies in delegating part of the work to others. Your organization has a reasonable supply of volunteers. If you could find 10 dedicated supporters in different parts of the country and appoint them as regional coordinators, each of those 10 people could then take responsibility for raising $100,000.

Raising $100,000 is simpler than raising $1,000,000, but it hardly qualifies as easy. What should your regional coordinators do? If they adopt the same strategy, they will in turn delegate parts of the job. If they each recruit 10 fundraising volunteers, those people will only have to raise $10,000. The delegation process can continue further until the volunteers are able raise the money they need all at once. Because the average contribution is $100, the volunteer fundraisers can probably find a single donor who is willing to give that much, which eliminates the need for further delegation.

If you express this fundraising strategy in pseudocode, it has the following structure:

```
void CollectContributions(int n)
{
    if (n <= 100) {
        Collect the money from a single donor.
    } else {
        Find 10 volunteers.
        Get each volunteer to collect n/10 dollars.
        Combine the money raised by the volunteers.
    }
}
```

The most important thing to notice about this pseudocode translation is that the line

   Get each volunteer to collect n/10 *dollars.*

is simply the original problem reproduced at a smaller scale. The basic character of the task—raise *n* dollars—remains exactly the same; the only difference is that *n* has a smaller value. Moreover, because the problem is the same, you can solve it by calling the original function. Thus, the preceding line of pseudocode would eventually be replaced with the following line:

```
CollectContributions(n / 10);
```

It's important to note that the `CollectContributions` function ends up calling itself if the contribution level is greater than $100. In the context of programming, having a function call itself is the defining characteristic of recursion.

The `Factorial` function

The `CollectContributions` example is useful because it conveys the idea of recursion in an easily understood way. On the other hand, it gives little insight into how recursion is used in practice, mostly because the primitive operations it uses, such as finding 10 volunteers and collecting money, are not easily represented in a C program. To get a more practical sense of the nature of recursion, it is necessary to consider problems that fit more easily into the programming domain.

It is easiest to illustrate recursion in the context of a simple mathematical function, such as the factorial function introduced in Chapter 5. The factorial of an integer n—denoted in mathematics as $n!$—is simply the product of the integers between 1 and n. As you discovered in Chapter 5, you can easily implement the factorial function using a `for` loop, as illustrated by the following implementation, which is taken from Figure 5-4:

```
int Factorial(int n)
{
    int product, i;

    product = 1;
    for (i = 1; i <= n; i++) {
        product *= i;
    }
    return (product);
}
```

This implementation, however, does not take advantage of an important property of factorials. Each factorial is related to the factorial of the next smaller number in the following way:

$$n! = n \times (n-1)!$$

Thus, 4! is $4 \times 3!$, 3! is $3 \times 2!$, and so on. To make sure that this process stops at some point, mathematicians define 0! to be 1. Thus, the conventional mathematical definition of the factorial function looks like this:

$$n! = \begin{cases} 1 & \text{if } n = 0 \\ n \times (n-1)! & \text{otherwise} \end{cases}$$

This definition is recursive because it defines $n!$ in terms of the factorial of $(n-1)!$. The new problem—finding the factorial of $n-1$—has the same form as the original problem, which is the defining characteristic of recursion. You can then use the same process to define $(n - 1)!$ in terms of $(n - 2)!$. Moreover, you can carry this process forward step by step until the solution is expressed in terms of $0!$, which is equal to 1 by definition.

The most exciting aspect of this approach is that you can use it directly as a solution technique. Because C allows functions to call themselves recursively, you can implement the `Factorial` function in the following way, which is a direct translation of the mathematical definition:

```
int Factorial(int n)
{
    if (n == 0) {
        return (1);
    } else {
        return (n * Factorial(n - 1));
    }
}
```

If you work from the mathematical definition, writing the recursive implementation of factorial is straightforward. On the other hand, when you are learning about recursion for the first time, this implementation seems to leave something out. Even though it clearly reflects the mathematical definition, the recursive implementation makes it hard to identify where the actual computational steps occur. When you call `Factorial`, you want the computer to give you the answer. In the recursive implementation, all you see is a formula that transforms one call to `Factorial` into another one. Because the steps in that calculation are not explicit, the fact that the computer gets the right answer sometimes seems magical.

If you follow through the logic that the computer uses to evaluate any function call, however, you discover that no magic is involved. When the computer evaluates a call to the recursive `Factorial` function, it goes through the same process it uses to evaluate any other function call. To illustrate the process, suppose that you have executed the statement

```
fact = Factorial(4);
```

as part of the function `main`. When `main` calls `Factorial`, the computer creates a new frame and copies the argument value into the formal parameter n. The frame for `Factorial` temporarily supersedes the frame for `main`, as shown in the following diagram:

In the diagram, the code for the body of Factorial is shown inside the frame to make it easier to keep track of the current position in the program, which is indicated by an arrow. In the current diagram, the arrow appears at the beginning of the code because all function calls start at the first statement of the function body.

The computer now proceeds to evaluate the body of the function, starting with the if statement. Because n is not equal to 0, control proceeds to the else clause, where the program must evaluate and return the value of the expression

```
n * Factorial(n - 1)
```

Evaluating this expression requires computing the value of Factorial(n - 1), which requires a recursive call. When that call returns, all the program has to do is to multiply the result by n. The current state of the computation can therefore be diagrammed as follows:

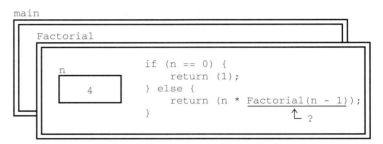

As soon as the call to Factorial(n - 1) returns, the result is substituted for the underlined expression, allowing computation to proceed.

The next step in the computation is therefore to evaluate the call to Factorial(n - 1), which begins by evaluating the argument expression. Because the current value of n is 4, the argument expression n - 1 has the value 3. The computer then creates a new frame for Factorial in which the formal parameter is initialized to this value. Thus, the next frame looks like this:

```
main
  Factorial
    Factorial
                    n           → if (n == 0) {
                                      return (1);
                        3       } else {
                                      return (n * Factorial(n - 1));
                                }
```

There are now two frames labeled Factorial. In the most recent one, the computer is just starting to calculate Factorial(3). In the preceding frame, which the newly created frame hides, the `Factorial` function is awaiting the result of the call to `Factorial(n - 1)`.

The current computation, however, is that required to complete the topmost frame. Once again, `n` is not 0, so that control passes to the `else` clause of the `if` statement, where the computer must evaluate `Factorial(n - 1)`. In this frame, however, `n` is equal to 3, so that the required result is that computed by calling `Factorial(2)`. As before, this process requires the creation of a new stack frame, as shown:

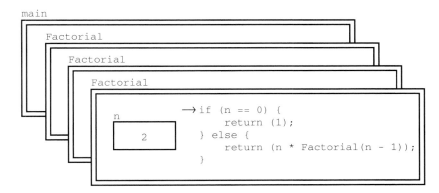

Following the same logic, the program must now call `Factorial(1)`, which in turn calls `Factorial(0)`, thereby creating two new stack frames. The resulting stack configuration looks like this:

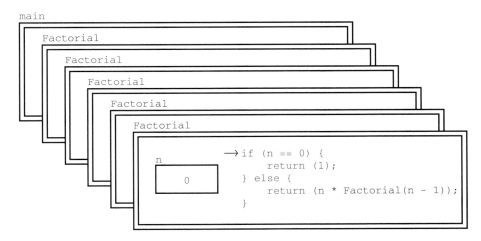

At this point, however, the situation changes. Because the value of n is 0, the function can return its result immediately by executing the statement

```
return (1);
```

The value 1 is returned to the calling frame, which resumes its position on the top of the stack, as shown:

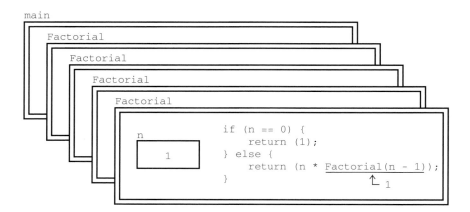

From this point, the computation consists of proceeding back through each of the recursive calls, using the value returned by Factorial at one level to compute the result at the next level. In this frame, for example, the call to Factorial(n - 1) can be replaced by the value 1, so that the result at this level can be expressed as follows:

```
return (n * 1));
```

In this stack frame, n has the value 1, so that the result of this call is simply 1. This result gets propagated back to its caller, which is represented by the top frame in the following diagram:

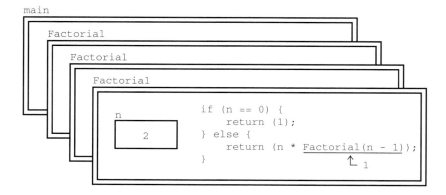

Because n is now 2, evaluating the return statement causes the value 2 to be passed back to the previous level, as follows:

```
main
    Factorial
        Factorial
                           if (n == 0) {
              n                  return (1);
                           } else {
                   3           return (n * Factorial(n - 1));
                           }                         ↳ 2
```

At this stage, the program returns 3×2 to the previous level, so that the frame for the initial call to `Factorial` looks like this:

```
main
    Factorial
                           if (n == 0) {
              n                  return (1);
                           } else {
                   4           return (n * Factorial(n - 1));
                           }                       ↳ 6
```

The final step in the calculation process consists of calculating 4×6 and returning the value 24 to the main program.

The recursive leap of faith

The point of the long `Factorial(4)` example in the preceding section is to show you that the computer treats recursive functions just like all other functions. When you are faced with a recursive function, you can—at least in theory—mimic the operation of the computer and figure out what it will do. By drawing all the frames and keeping track of all the variables, you can duplicate the entire operation and come up with the answer. If you do so, however, you will usually discover that the complexity of the process ends up making the problem much harder to understand.

When you think about a recursive program, you must be able to put these underlying details aside and focus instead on a single level of the operation. At that level, you are allowed to assume that any recursive call automatically gets the right answer as long as the arguments to that call are simpler than the original argument in some respect. For example, to compute `Factorial(n)` with n equal to 4, the recursive implementation must compute the value of the expression

```
n * Factorial(n - 1)
```

By substituting the current value of n into the expression, you know that the result is

```
4 * Factorial(3)
```

Stop right there. Computing Factorial(3) is simpler than computing Factorial(4). Because it is simpler, you are allowed to assume that it works. You know that Factorial(3) is $3 \times 2 \times 1$, or 6. The result of calling Factorial(4) is therefore 4×6, or 24, which is the right answer.

Learning to assume that any simpler recursive call works while you are designing a recursive function is an essential programming strategy called the **recursive leap of faith.** Until you have had extensive experience working with recursive functions, applying the recursive leap of faith will not come easily. After all, when you write a program, the odds are good—even if you are an experienced programmer—that your program won't work the first time. Suspending your disbelief and assuming that it does work violates your own healthy skepticism about the likely correctness of your programs. Even so, you must conquer that psychological barrier. Looking more than one level down in a recursive function inevitably makes the problem harder to solve.

The recursive paradigm

Almost every recursive function you will encounter has the same basic structure as the Factorial function in the preceding section. The body of the typical recursive function has the following paradigmatic form:

```
if (test for simple case) {
    return (simple solution computed without using recursion);
} else {
    return (recursive solution involving a call to the same function);
}
```

The recursive Factorial function fits this paradigm, as does the following function that raises an integer n to the kth power:

```
static int RaiseIntToPower(int n, int k)
{
    if (k == 0) {
        return (1);
    } else {
        return (n * RaiseIntToPower(n, k - 1));
    }
}
```

This implementation of RaiseIntToPower relies on the mathematical property that

$$n^k = \begin{cases} 1 & \text{if } k = 0 \\ n \times n^{k-1} & \text{otherwise} \end{cases}$$

The problems of computing a factorial or raising a number to a power have natural recursive solutions because the problems meet the following conditions:

1. You can identify *simple cases* for which the answer is easily determined.
2. You can apply a *recursive decomposition* to break down more complicated instances of the problem into simpler problems of the same type, which you can then solve by applying the same solution technique.

When a recursive decomposition follows directly from a mathematical definition, as it does in the case of the functions Factorial and RaiseIntToPower, applying recursion is not particularly hard. The situation changes, however, when the problems themselves become more complicated and the recursive decomposition requires some cleverness to find. The next section solves a more complex problem in which the recursive decomposition is more difficult to see.

Generating permutations

A large part of playing many word games is the ability to rearrange a set of letters to form a word. If, for example, you want to write a Scrabble™ program, it would be useful to have a facility for generating all possible arrangements of a particular set of tiles. In word games, such arrangements are generally called **anagrams.** In mathematics, they are known as **permutations.**

Suppose that you want to write a function ListPermutations(s) that displays all permutations of the string s. For example, if you call

```
ListPermutations("ABC");
```

your program should display the six arrangements of "ABC", as follows:

```
ABC
ACB
BAC
BCA
CBA
CAB
```

The order of the output is unimportant, but each of the possible arrangements should appear exactly once.

How would you go about implementing the ListPermutations function? If you are limited to iterative control structures, such as while and for loops, finding a general solution that works for strings of any length is difficult. Thinking about the problem recursively, on the other hand, leads to a relatively simple solution.

As is usually the case with recursive programs, the hard part of the solution process is figuring out how to divide the original problem into simpler instances of the same problem. In this case, to generate all permutations of a string, you need to discover how being able to generate all permutations of a shorter string might contribute to the solution.

To give yourself more of a feel for the problem, consider a concrete case. Suppose that you want to generate all permutations of a five-character string, such as `"ABCDE"`. In your solution, you can apply the recursive leap of faith to generate all permutations of any shorter string. Just assume that the recursive calls work and be done with it. Once again, the critical question is how being able to permute shorter strings helps you to solve the problem of permuting the original five-character string.

The key to solving the permutation problem is recognizing that the permutations of the five-character string `"ABCDE"` consist of the following strings:

- The character `'A'` followed by every possible permutation of `"BCDE"`
- The character `'B'` followed by every possible permutation of `"ACDE"`
- The character `'C'` followed by every possible permutation of `"ABDE"`
- The character `'D'` followed by every possible permutation of `"ABCE"`
- The character `'E'` followed by every possible permutation of `"ABCD"`

More generally, to display all permutations of a string of length n, you can take each of the n characters in turn and display that character followed by every possible permutation of the remaining $n - 1$ characters.

The only problem with the solution strategy as presented is that the recursive subproblem does not have exactly the same form as the original, which is a requirement for a recursive solution. The original problem requires you to display all permutations of a string. The subproblem requires you to display a character from a string followed by all permutations of the remaining letters. To make the recursive solution work, you need to transform the problem slightly so that the recursive subproblems are the same all the way along.

In this case, the best approach is to define a new procedure `PermuteWithFixedPrefix` that generates all permutations of a string with the first k letters fixed. When k is 0, all the letters are free to change, which gives you the original problem. As k increases, the problem becomes simpler. When k is the length of the string, there are no characters to interchange, and the string can be displayed exactly as it appears. The `PermuteWithFixedPrefix` procedure has the following pseudocode form:

```
static void PermuteWithFixedPrefix(string str, int k)
{
    if (k is equal to the length of the string) {
        Display the string.
    } else {
        For each character position i between k and the end of the string  {
            Exchange the characters in positions i and k.
            Generate all permutations with the first k+1 characters fixed.
            Restore the original string by again exchanging positions i and k.
        }
    }
}
```

Translating this function from pseudocode to C is reasonably simple, particularly if you define a function to exchange two characters. In C, PermuteWithFixedPrefix looks like this:

```
static void PermuteWithFixedPrefix(string str, int k)
{
    int i;

    if (k == StringLength(str)) {
        printf("%s\n", str);
    } else {
        for (i = k; i < StringLength(str); i++) {
            ExchangeCharacters(str, k, i);
            PermuteWithFixedPrefix(str, k + 1);
            ExchangeCharacters(str, k, i);
        }
    }
}
```

The program, however, is not quite finished. For one thing, you need to complete the stepwise refinement by defining the function ExchangeCharacters. The implementation of this function is similar to the function SwapIntegerElements introduced in Chapter 11 and has the following form:

```
static void ExchangeCharacters(string str, int p1, int p2)
{
    char tmp;

    tmp = str[p1];
    str[p1] = str[p2];
    str[p2] = tmp;
}
```

A more important problem is that you have yet to define the function ListPermutations, which was the original goal of the exercise. The function PermuteWithFixedPrefix does all the necessary work, but it does not have the desired prototype. When you call PermuteWithFixedPrefix, you need to pass an integer as well as the string. Most clients think only about permuting the characters in a string; there are no integers involved. For the benefit of the client, it therefore makes sense to define ListPermutations with the following implementation:

```
static void ListPermutations(string str)
{
    PermuteWithFixedPrefix(str, 0);
}
```

When you solve problems recursively, you often need to define a recursive function whose prototype is slightly different from that of the original problem. As in the case of `PermuteWithFixedPrefix`, the new function usually has additional arguments that are not required for the problem as a whole. Those arguments track the progress of the recursive algorithm and provide a standard of measurement under which the subproblems become simpler. The function that is made available to clients calls the internal function, passing in the appropriate initial values for the additional arguments, as illustrated by the implementation of `ListPermutations`. A function like `ListPermutations` whose only purpose is to supply additional arguments for a more general function is called a **wrapper.**

Thinking recursively

More than any other aspect of programming, learning to use recursion requires you to think about the programming process holistically. If you adopt the reductionistic approach of tracing through all the steps in a complex recursive decomposition, you end up having to manage a huge amount of detail—detail that is better left to the computer. The process of going through the steps in the calculation of `Factorial(4)` earlier in this chapter takes several pages. In contrast, the holistic idea that

```
Factorial(4) = 4 * Factorial(3)
```

only takes a single line. The difference in the conceptual complexity of these two approaches to recursion is enormous. By maintaining a holistic perspective, you can reduce the complexity of most recursive programs to a point at which you can comprehend the solution. If, on the other hand, your uncertainty about the correctness of your solution forces you down the reductionistic path, the mass of details will almost certainly make it impossible for you to understand the high-level structure of the solution.

Thinking about recursive problems in the right way does not come easily. Learning to use recursion effectively requires practice and more practice. For many students, mastering the concept takes years. But because recursion will turn out to be one of the most powerful techniques in your programming repertoire, that time will be well spent.

 17.2 Abstract data types

As you have discovered in this text, data structures form a hierarchy within a program. The atomic data types—such as `int`, `char`, `double`, and enumerated types— occupy the lowest level in the hierarchy. To represent more complex information, you combine the atomic types to form larger structures. These larger structures can then be assembled into even larger ones in an open-ended process. You build each new level in the hierarchy by using one of the three primitives for type construction: arrays, records, and pointers. Given an existing type, you can define an array of that type, include it as a field of a record, or declare a pointer to it. These three facilities constitute the mortar of the data hierarchy and allow you to build arbitrarily complex structures.

As you learn more about programming, however, you will discover that particular data structures can be extremely useful and are worth studying in their own right. For example, a string is represented internally as an array of characters, which is in turn represented as a pointer to the first address in the array. In this book, you learned about the underlying structure of a string in Chapter 14. But a string also has an abstract behavior that transcends its representation. You learned about its abstract properties in Chapter 9. When you use a string, its representation is often unimportant; what matters most is how it behaves. As you learned when string operations were introduced in Chapter 9, a type defined in terms of its behavior rather than its representation is called an **abstract data type,** which is often abbreviated to **ADT.**

Because an abstract data type is defined in terms of its behavior, the programmer who implements an abstract type is free to change its underlying representation. Typically, an abstract type is exported by an interface along with a collection of functions that define its behavior. The representation is a property of the implementation. As with any abstraction, it is appropriate to change the implementation as long as the interface remains the same.

The queue abstraction

To illustrate the concept of an abstract data type whose underlying representation can change, this section introduces a common data structure that happens to be important in many programming applications. The real-world analogy to the structure is a waiting line such as you might find in a supermarket. When customers finish their shopping, they go to the back of a checkout line and wait for their turn to pay. Each customer eventually reaches the front of the line, at which point the cashier totals up the purchases and collects the money. Once the business has been completed, the customer leaves the line. In programming, a structure that simulates the behavior of a waiting line is called a **queue.**

Let's suppose that you have been assigned the task of designing a queue package that gives your clients access to the fundamental operations required for queues. Your first step is to determine what those fundamental operations are. As a thought experiment, you can go back to the waiting-line analogy to think about what happens. In an environment that uses waiting lines, such as a supermarket, the following operations are important:

- *Create a new waiting line.* The typical supermarket has more than one checkout line. When things get busy, the store often opens a new line. To make your queue package general enough to model the activity of a supermarket, you must allow clients to create new queues dynamically.
- *Eliminate an existing waiting line.* If supermarkets open new checkout lines when business is heavy, they also must be able to close lines when business falls off. In the programming analogue, it must be possible to eliminate a queue and free any memory space associated with it.
- *Add a customer to the end of a waiting line.* A new customer who arrives at a checkout stand enters the line at the rear and waits until the earlier customers

have been served. In programming terminology, adding a new entry to the end of the line is called the **enqueue** operation.

- ▪ *Remove a customer from the front of a waiting line.* After reaching the front of the line and being served by the cashier, the customer leaves the line, and the rest of the people waiting move forward one position. In programming terminology, removing the entry from the front of the line is called the **dequeue** operation.

- ▪ *Determine how many customers are in a line.* For the supermarket management to make decisions about whether to open or close checkout lines, it must be possible to determine how many people are in the existing lines. In the real world, you can just count the customers. Your interface must provide a function that returns this information.

Although there are others you might also consider, these operations are sufficient for many queue applications.

Representing types in the queue abstraction

Before you can design the `queue.h` interface that exports these functions, however, you need to think about the data types involved. These operations work with two different types of data: an individual customer and the waiting line itself. What data type should you use to represent each of these conceptual entities? This question is actually rather subtle and requires you to think carefully about how the queue abstraction will be used. In particular, you need to decide whether each type is part of the queue implementation or part of the client's domain.

Think for a moment about the customer. What is a customer in this model? The answer depends entirely on how the queue is used. If you are simulating lines in a bank, you may want to keep track of different data for each customer than you would if you were simulating a supermarket. For many applications, the word *customer* may be inappropriate. When you send an electronic mail message, most systems put that message in a queue and process it later. Similarly, most systems that support more than one user queue documents for printing. When you want to print out a file, that file gets entered into a queue somewhere in the system. When the printer has finished servicing the requests that came in ahead of yours, it can then begin to print your file. The queue operations are the same, but the information stored in the queue is completely different.

The critical point is that the *client* of the queue package must determine the type of data stored in the waiting line. If the client is an electronic mail system, it needs to queue messages. If the client is a program that prints a file, it needs to queue print requests. If the client is a supermarket simulation, it needs to be able to queue some representation of a supermarket customer. The queue package doesn't really care. As far as the queue package is concerned, its responsibility during an enqueue operation is to enter the data supplied by the client into the queue. When a dequeue operation is performed at a later point, the queue package needs to give exactly the same data back to the client.

Thus, to make your queue package as general as possible, you need to let your client control the type of data stored in the queue. The only problem is that you have to refer to that type in the interface. Unlike some programming languages, C does not include a type specification that matches any type at all. In C, the best you can do is to use the type `void *`, which matches any pointer type. If you use `void *`, clients of your queue package can enqueue and dequeue data of any pointer type. Because it is always possible to allocate new space for nonpointer data and use the resulting address, this restriction is not a problem in practice.

The next question is how to represent the waiting line itself. Unlike the customer, the waiting line is the property of the *implementation*. Your package is responsible for enqueueing new data at the end of the waiting line and dequeueing data from the front. The implementation you write must control the representation of the waiting line so that it can perform these operations. In the interface, you therefore want to define the abstract queue type `queueADT`, leaving the underlying representation under the control of the implementation.

In C, you can define a type in an interface so that its underlying representation remains hidden from clients. To do so, you include in the interface an abstract type definition of the form shown in the syntax box to the right. For example, to define `queueADT` as an abstract type, the interface would include the following definition:

```
typedef struct queueCDT *queueADT;
```

As far as C's syntax is concerned, this line defines the type `queueADT` as a pointer to a structure identified by the name `queueCDT`, which has not yet been defined. Because pointers are always the same size, the C compiler allows you to work with pointers to structures even if it does not know any details about the structure itself. A structure that has not yet been defined is called an **incomplete type.**

In the implementation, you complete the type by writing the structure definition, as shown in the syntax box on the right. The definition includes the name used to identify the incomplete structure, which is called the **structure tag.** The type *name*CDT is the concrete data type associated with the abstract type *name*ADT defined in the interface. Clients of the interface see only the abstract type. Clients can declare variables of the abstract type and then manipulate the values of those variables as if they were atomic types. Because the compiler has no information about the underlying representation, however, clients are not able to dereference the abstract type to see how it is constructed. The implementation, on the other hand, has access to the concrete type as well. Because the compiler now

> **SYNTAX** for abstract type definitions:
>
> ```
> typedef struct nameCDT *nameADT;
> ```
>
> where:
>   *name*ADT is the name of the abstract type
>   *name*CDT is the name of the corresponding
>   concrete type

> **SYNTAX** for concrete type definitions:
>
> ```
> struct nameCDT {
>      field-declarations
> };
> ```
>
> where:
>   *name*CDT is the name of the concrete type
>   *field-declarations* identify the fields in the
>   underlying structure

knows about the underlying structure, functions in the implementation are free to dereference the abstract type pointer in order to see the fields that are part of the concrete type.

Partly because it was not possible to do so in earlier implementations of C, many programmers do not bother to separate the underlying representation of a type from its abstract definition. If you include the concrete definition of a type directly within the interface, the program will still work correctly. In doing so, however, you lose both security and flexibility. If the client is permitted to cross the abstraction boundary and manipulate the internal representation directly, the client can destroy data the implementation needs. Using an abstract type denies the client access to that representation and protects the underlying data. Moreover, by taking the representation completely outside the client's domain, use of the abstract type mechanism makes it easier to modify the underlying representation.

The `queue.h` interface

Having resolved the issue of how to define the relevant data types, you can now go ahead and design the `queue.h` interface, even though you know very little about the underlying implementation. The interface, shown in Figure 17-1, exports the type `queueADT` along with five operations on that type: `NewQueue`, `FreeQueue`, `Enqueue`, `Dequeue`, and `QueueLength`. The behavior of each operation is outlined in the interface.

FIGURE 17-1 queue.h

```
/*
 * File: queue.h
 * -------------
 * This file provides an interface to a simple queue
 * abstraction.
 */

#ifndef _queue_h
#define _queue_h

#include "genlib.h"

/*
 * Type: queueADT
 * --------------
 * This line defines the abstract queue type as a pointer to
 * its concrete counterpart.  Clients have no access to the
 * underlying representation.
 */

typedef struct queueCDT *queueADT;
```

```
/*
 * Function: NewQueue
 * Usage: queue = NewQueue();
 * --------------------------
 * This function allocates and returns an empty queue.
 */

queueADT NewQueue(void);

/*
 * Function: FreeQueue
 * Usage: FreeQueue(queue);
 * ------------------------
 * This function frees the storage associated with queue.
 */

void FreeQueue(queueADT queue);

/*
 * Function: Enqueue
 * Usage: Enqueue(queue, obj);
 * ---------------------------
 * This function adds obj to the end of the queue.
 */

void Enqueue(queueADT queue, void *obj);

/*
 * Function: Dequeue
 * Usage: obj = Dequeue(queue);
 * ----------------------------
 * This function removes the data value at the head of the queue
 * and returns it to the client.  Dequeueing an empty queue is
 * an error.
 */

void *Dequeue(queueADT queue);

/*
 * Function: QueueLength
 * Usage: n = QueueLength(queue);
 * ------------------------------
 * This function returns the number of elements in the queue.
 */

int QueueLength(queueADT queue);

#endif
```

Implementing the queue abstraction

Once you have designed the interface, the next step is to implement the queue package. As part of the implementation, you need to define the underlying representation of the waiting line itself. The most straightforward representation is simply an array coupled with an integer to keep track of the effective size. The concrete type definition is therefore

```
struct queueCDT {
    void *array[MaxQueueSize];
    int len;
};
```

where `MaxQueueSize` is a constant specifying the maximum number of elements that can be stored in a queue.

To implement the `NewQueue` function, all you need to do is allocate the space for the concrete structure and initialize the length of the queue to 0. The implementation looks like this:

```
queueADT NewQueue(void)
{
    queueADT queue;

    queue = New(queueADT);
    queue->len = 0;
    return (queue);
}
```

The `Enqueue` function is also easy to implement. When you enter a new value into the queue, it must be inserted at the end of the line, increasing the queue length by 1. These operations, along with a test to see if the queue capacity has been exceeded, comprise the implementation of `Enqueue`, as follows:

```
void Enqueue(queueADT queue, void *obj)
{
    if (queue->len == MaxQueueSize) {
        Error("Enqueue called on a full queue");
    }
    queue->array[queue->len++] = obj;
}
```

For example, suppose that you have created a new queue by executing the statement

```
queue = NewQueue();
```

The effect of this statement is to create an empty queue with the following structure:

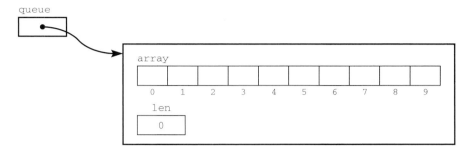

If you then call

```
Enqueue(queue, "A");
```

the string `"A"` (which is a pointer and therefore compatible with the type `void *`) is stored in element 0 of the array. As a side effect, the `++` operator increments the queue length, leaving the queue in the following state:

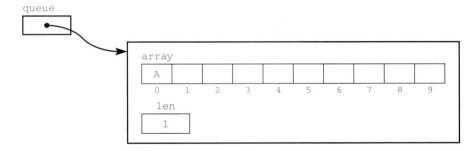

Then if you execute the statements

```
Enqueue(queue, "B");
Enqueue(queue, "C");
```

customers *B* and *C* are inserted into the next two array positions, as follows:

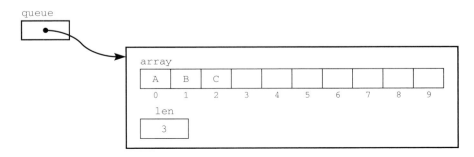

What about the `Dequeue` operation? In the queue shown in the preceding diagram, the `Dequeue` operation should remove *A* from the queue and return it as the value of the `Dequeue` call. Given the current representation, the only way to remove the first element from the queue is to shift each of the other elements one position to the left, so that the queue ends up looking like this:

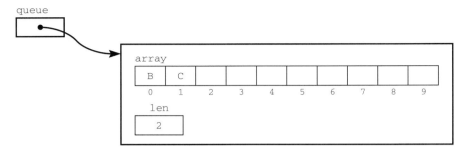

Implementing this strategy leads to the following implementation of `Dequeue`:

```
void *Dequeue(queueADT queue)
{
    void *result;
    int i;

    if (queue->len == 0) Error("Dequeue of empty queue");
    result = queue->array[0];
    for (i = 1; i < queue->len; i++) {
        queue->array[i - 1] = queue->array[i];
    }
    queue->len--;
    return (result);
}
```

The entire implementation of the `queue.h` interface is given in the file `queue.c`, shown in Figure 17-2.

Alternative implementations of the queue abstraction

The implementation of the queue package developed in the preceding section is not the only one you might choose. Although it is quite simple, the implementation has two problems that limit its utility:

1. Calling `Dequeue` is inefficient. Every time `Dequeue` is called, the implementation has to shift all the remaining entries in the queue toward the beginning of the array. For queues that contain a large number of entries, this operation can be time-consuming. If a client wants to use your queue package in an application with tight time constraints, the inefficiency of `Dequeue` may be unacceptable.
2. The queue has a fixed maximum size specified by the constant `MaxQueueSize`. Some clients may be unable to accept this limitation. For those clients, it would be better if the queue could expand dynamically as long as memory was available.

FIGURE 17-2   queue.c

```
/*
 * File: queue.c
 * -------------
 * This file implements the queue.h abstraction using an array.
 */

#include <stdio.h>

#include "genlib.h"
#include "queue.h"

/*
 * Constants:
 * ----------
 * MaxQueueSize -- Maximum number of elements in the queue
 */

#define MaxQueueSize 10

/*
 * Type: queueCDT
 * --------------
 * This type provides the concrete counterpart to the queueADT.
 * The representation used here consists of an array coupled
 * with an integer indicating the effective size.  This
 * representation means that Dequeue must shift the existing
 * elements in the queue.
 */

struct queueCDT {
    void *array[MaxQueueSize];
    int len;
};

/* Exported entries */

/*
 * Functions: NewQueue, FreeQueue
 * ------------------------------
 * NewQueue allocates and initializes the storage for a
 * new queue.  FreeQueue allows the client to free that
 * storage when it is no longer needed.
 */
```

```
queueADT NewQueue(void)
{
    queueADT queue;

    queue = New(queueADT);
    queue->len = 0;
    return (queue);
}

void FreeQueue(queueADT queue)
{
    FreeBlock(queue);
}

/*
 * Function: Enqueue
 * -----------------
 * This function adds a new element to the queue.
 */

void Enqueue(queueADT queue, void *obj)
{
    if (queue->len == MaxQueueSize) {
        Error("Enqueue called on a full queue");
    }
    queue->array[queue->len++] = obj;
}

/*
 * Function: Dequeue
 * -----------------
 * This function removes and returns the data value at the
 * head of the queue.
 */

void *Dequeue(queueADT queue)
{
    void *result;
    int i;

    if (queue->len == 0) Error("Dequeue of empty queue");
    result = queue->array[0];
    for (i = 1; i < queue->len; i++) {
        queue->array[i - 1] = queue->array[i];
    }
    queue->len--;
    return (result);
}
```

```
/*
 * Function: QueueLength
 * ---------------------
 * This function returns the number of elements in the queue.
 */

int QueueLength(queueADT queue)
{
    return (queue->len);
}
```

If you choose a different underlying representation for the queue structure, you can solve both of these problems. Moreover, because the interface defines queueADT as an abstract type, you are free to change the underlying representation of a queue without affecting clients of the interface.

As a first step, think about what you might do to solve the efficiency problem of Dequeue. The source of the inefficiency is the fact that the function must shift all the elements in the array so that the first entry in the queue is always at index position 0. Although doing so makes the implementation of the package simpler, it is not strictly necessary. You could instead have the implementation keep track of two index positions: the index of the first entry in the waiting line and the index into which the next entry will be stored. Programmers call these positions the **head** and **tail** of the queue, respectively. A concrete type definition that includes both of these indices is

```
struct queueCDT {
    void *array[MaxQueueSize];
    int head;
    int tail;
};
```

The tail index indicates the array element in which the next Enqueue operation will store its data and therefore specifies an unused position in the array. The head index indicates the element to be returned by the next Dequeue operation. When the queue is empty, the head index is equal to the tail index, as illustrated by the following diagram:

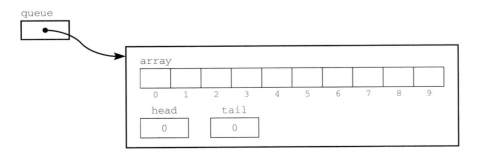

Adding new entries to the queue involves storing the data at the `tail` position and then incrementing `tail`. Thus, executing the statements

```
Enqueue(queue, "A");
Enqueue(queue, "B");
```

starting with an empty queue results in the following configuration:

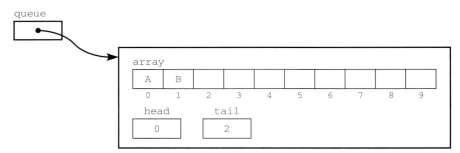

The `Dequeue` function returns the value at the position indexed by `head` and then increments `head` so that it indicates the next position. Thus, if you continue the current example by calling `Dequeue(queue)`, the internal data structure looks like this:

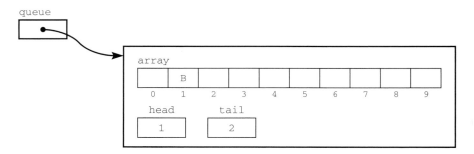

Using this approach eliminates the need to shift any data as part of the `Dequeue` operation. The only problem is that you quickly run out of space at the end of the array. Let's consider the situation in which customers *C, D, E, F, G, H, I,* and *J* are entered into the queue, but there is only enough time to serve *B, C,* and *D*. At this point, customers *E, F, G, H, I,* and *J* are still in the queue, which looks like this:

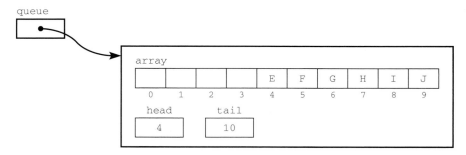

What happens when customer *K* arrives? There are no vacant positions at the end of the array; in fact, the `tail` index currently indicates an element outside the array bound. On the other hand, the array is not "full" in any conceptual sense, because the first four positions are once again free. If you are careful with your use of indices, you can implement the queue package so that calls to `Enqueue` reuse space freed by previous `Dequeue` operations. In the current example, *K* can go in element 0 of the array, leaving the queue in the following state:

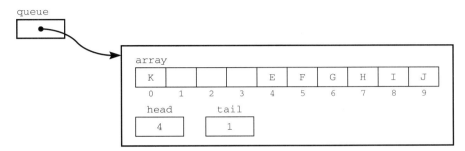

In this design, the end of the array "wraps around" to the beginning, so that the array acts more like a circle than a linear list, as illustrated by the arrow in the following diagram:

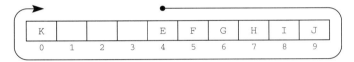

Because the ends of the array are conceptually linked, programmers call this representation a **ring buffer.** Ring buffers are often used in practice to implement queues, and you will have the opportunity to implement this design in exercise 7.

If you go on to more advanced study of computer science, you will discover that queues are often implemented in an entirely different way. Instead of using an array to hold the queue, you can design the queue representation so that each entry includes a pointer to the next entry. For example, the queue containing *A*, *B*, and *C* could be represented as follows:

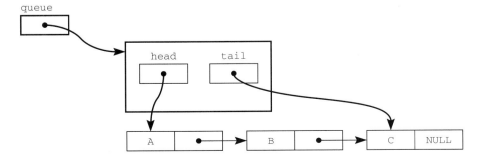

Because each entry of the queue contains a pointer linking it to the next entry, this structure is called a **linked list.** The concrete data type for the queue itself consists of pointers to the first and last elements in the linked list. The implementation of a linked list is beyond the scope of this text but constitutes a major theme of more advanced courses in computer science. The principal advantage of the linked list structure is that it allows the queue to grow dynamically as needed.

17.3 Analysis of algorithms

In evaluating the various queue implementations presented in the preceding section, one of the comparison criteria was *efficiency*. If you think about efficiency as an informal concept, it is easy to accept that one program might be more efficient than another. On the other hand, you have not yet had an opportunity to consider what efficiency means in any detail.

In the examples and exercises presented in this text, you have encountered programs that run very quickly and others that take a significant amount of time. Intuition suggests that programs that run quickly are somehow efficient and those that run slowly are therefore less so. That intuition, however, is misleading. Although running time and efficiency are related concepts, they are not exactly the same because problems differ in their inherent difficulty. An inefficient program to solve an easy problem may take much less time to run than a highly efficient program used to solve a much harder problem. Efficiency must take into account the difficulty of the problem. When you talk about efficiency, it is usually best to consider the *relative* efficiency of different algorithms used to solve the same problem.

If you go on to study more advanced computer science, evaluating the relative efficiency of algorithms will be a major topic that is usually called **analysis of algorithms.** Although a detailed understanding of algorithmic analysis requires some mathematics and a lot of careful thought, it's possible to get a sense of how it works by comparing the performance of a few simple algorithms.

Evaluating algorithmic efficiency

Suppose that you have been given two algorithms for solving the same problem. You want to determine which is more efficient. How would you go about making the comparison?

In some cases, it is feasible to use empirical measurement. If you want to determine which of two algorithms solves a particular problem more quickly, you could simply run each of the programs and see how long each one takes. Assuming that you can measure time accurately at the speed of modern computers, this approach can provide precise timing information for a particular instance of the problem. On the other hand, this approach can also be misleading, particularly when the running time of an algorithm depends on the input data. An algorithm that runs more quickly with one set of input values may turn out to run more slowly for others. Some algorithms work well for a small amount of input data but deteriorate in performance when the amount of data becomes large. In practice, the most valuable insights you can obtain about algorithmic efficiency are those that help you understand how the performance of an algorithm responds to changes in problem size.

For many algorithms, problem size is easy to quantify. For example, the classical algorithms presented in Chapter 6, such as testing primality or finding the greatest common divisor, run more slowly as the numbers involved get larger. In algorithms of this sort, the magnitude of the numbers offers an appropriate measure of problem size. For algorithms that operate on arrays, such as the sorting algorithms in Chapter 12, you can use the number of elements in the array as the problem size. When evaluating algorithmic efficiency, computer scientists use the letter N to represent the size of the problem, no matter how it is calculated. The central question in analysis of algorithms is to determine how the running time of an algorithm changes as a function of N. The relationship between N and the running time of an algorithm as N becomes large is called the **computational complexity** of that algorithm.

Big-O notation

Computer scientists use a special notation to denote the computational complexity of algorithms. That notation is called **big-O notation** (pronounced "big oh") and consists of an oversized letter O, followed by a formula enclosed in parentheses that expresses a proportional measure of running time as a function of problem size. The letter O stands for the word *order* as it is used in the phrase *on the order of*, where it signifies approximation.

A formal definition of big-O notation lies beyond the scope of this text, but you can nonetheless get a feel for how it is used by looking at a few simple examples. As an example, consider the original implementation of the queue package shown in Figure 17-2. The Enqueue operation takes the same amount of time regardless of the problem size, which is most easily defined as the number of items currently in the queue. In computer science, an operation whose time requirements are independent of the size of the problem is said to run in **constant time.** In big-O notation, constant time is denoted by $O(1)$. The notation $O(1)$ means that, as N becomes large, the running time of such a program changes in exactly the same way that 1 changes. Because 1 is a constant, it does not change at all as value of N increases, which is the defining characteristic of a constant-time operation.

The Dequeue operation from Figure 17-2 behaves in a different way. The implementation of Dequeue uses the following for loop to shift each item in the queue toward the beginning of the array:

```
for (i = 1; i < queue->len; i++) {
    queue->array[i - 1] = queue->array[i];
}
```

If the queue contains N items, this for loop executes N cycles. As N increases, the running time of the for loop increases in direct proportion. Moreover, if N is large, the cost of the for loop dominates the cost of all operations outside the loop, which are always executed once no matter how large N is. Thus, in the limit as N

becomes large, the overall running time of the `Dequeue` operation tends to increase just as N does. An operation for which the running time grows in direct proportion to the problem size is said to run in **linear time,** which is indicated in big-O notation as $O(N)$.

The advantage of the ring buffer implementation of the queue package outlined in the section on "Alternative implementations of the queue abstraction" earlier in this chapter is that it reduces the running time of the `Dequeue` operation from linear time to constant time—from $O(N)$ to $O(1)$. If N is large, this reduction represents a significant savings. On the other hand, the savings you realize by making a linear-time algorithm run in constant time are much less dramatic than algorithmic improvements you can achieve when working with more complex algorithms. The rest of this chapter takes a new look at the sorting problem presented in Chapter 12, emphasizing the issue of computational complexity.

Selection sort revisited

In Chapter 12, the algorithm used to implement `SortIntegerArray` is called *selection sort.* Given an array of N items, the selection sort algorithm goes through each element position in the array and finds the value that should occupy that position. To find the appropriate value, the algorithm must search through each of the remaining elements in the array to find the smallest value. Thus, the algorithm takes N steps to fill the first position, $N-1$ steps to fill the second, and so on, so that the total running time is proportional to

$$N + N{-}1 + N{-}2 + \ldots + 3 + 2 + 1$$

As explained in the section on "Analyzing the selection sort algorithm" in Chapter 12, this formula can be simplified to

$$\frac{N^2 + N}{2}$$

When you use big-O notation to estimate the computational complexity of an algorithm, the goal is to provide a *qualitative* insight as to how changes in N affect the algorithmic performance as N becomes large. Because big-O notation is not intended to be a precise quantitative measure, it is appropriate and in fact desirable to simplify the expression inside the parentheses so that it captures the qualitative behavior of the algorithm in the simplest possible form.

You simplify big-O notation by applying the following steps to the formula appearing within the parentheses:

1. *Eliminate any term in the formula that becomes insignificant as N becomes large.* For example, in the selection sort algorithm, as N increases in size, N^2 quickly becomes much larger than N. The running time of selection sort therefore depends much more heavily on the N^2 term. Thus, when you use big-O notation, you are free to ignore N and concentrate on N^2.
2. *Eliminate any constant coefficients.* When you calculate computational complexity your main concern is with the relative running time of the algorithm

for different values of N. If you express the relative time as a ratio, any constant coefficient appearing in both the numerator and the denominator will cancel. A constant coefficient has no effect on the relative running time and can therefore be eliminated when you use big-O notation.

Thus, it would be inappropriate to describe the computational complexity of the selection sort algorithm as

$$O\left(\frac{N^2 + N}{2}\right)$$ This is incorrect.

because this expression includes the term N, which is insignificant with respect to the N^2 term. Nor would you write

$$O\left(\frac{N^2}{2}\right)$$ This is also incorrect.

because you should eliminate the constant factor. The expression used to indicate the complexity of selection sort is simply

$$O\left(N^2\right)$$

Algorithms that exhibit $O(N^2)$ performance are said to run in **quadratic time.** The basic characteristic of quadratic complexity is that, as the size of the problem doubles, the running time increases by a factor of four. As noted in Chapter 12, the fact that selection sort is a quadratic algorithm seriously limits its usefulness as the arrays one needs to sort become large.

Divide-and-conquer strategies

Oddly enough, the very fact that the selection sort algorithm has quadratic performance offers you a certain measure of hope. You know that doubling the size of a quadratic problem has the effect of multiplying its running time by four. This property is what makes selection sort inappropriate for large arrays. The reverse, however, is also true. If you divide the size of a quadratic problem by two, you decrease the running time by that same factor of four. Thus, if you divide a large array in half and use the selection sort algorithm to sort each half, you end up with two sorted subarrays in half the time it would have taken to sort the entire array. (Each of the subarrays requires one quarter of the original time; sorting two such subarrays requires twice as much as that.) If it turns out that sorting two halves of an array simplifies the problem of sorting the complete array, you may be able to reduce the total time substantially. More importantly, once you discover how to improve performance at one level, you can use the same algorithm recursively to sort each of the individual subarrays. Recursive algorithms that divide a problem into roughly equal subproblems and then solve each subproblem recursively are called **divide-and-conquer** algorithms.

In determining whether a divide-and-conquer strategy is applicable to the sorting problem, the crucial question is whether dividing an array into two smaller arrays and then sorting each one helps to solve the general problem. To make this question more concrete, let's go back and think about the array of eight elements used as an example in Chapter 12:

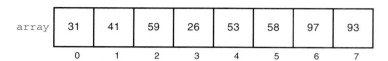

If you divide the array of eight elements into two arrays of length four and then sort each of those smaller arrays—remember that the recursive leap of faith means that you can simply assume that the recursive calls work correctly—you get the following:

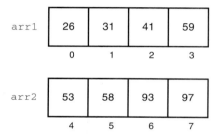

How useful is this decomposition? Remember that your goal is to take the values out of these smaller arrays and put them back, in the correct order, into each position in the original array:

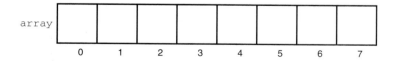

What would you do?

Merging two arrays

As it happens, reconstructing the complete array from the smaller sorted arrays is a much simpler problem than sorting itself. The technique is called **merging** and depends on the fact that the first element in the complete ordering must be either the first element in `arr1` or the first element in `arr2`, whichever is smaller. In this example, the first element in the new array is the 26 in `arr1`. If you put that element into `array[0]` and, in effect, cross it out of `arr1`, you get the following configuration:

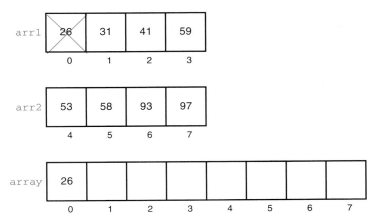

Once again, the next element can only be the first unused element in one of the two smaller arrays. You compare the 31 from `arr1` against the 53 in `arr2` and choose the former:

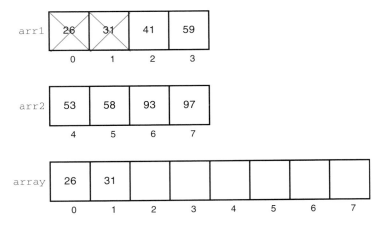

You can continue this process of choosing the smaller value from `arr1` or `arr2` until the entire array is filled.

The merge sort algorithm

The merge operation, combined with recursive decomposition, gives rise to a new sorting algorithm called **merge sort**, which you can implement in a straightforward way. The `SortIntegerArray` function itself first checks the size of the array. If the array has no elements or exactly one element, then that array must already be sorted. This condition therefore defines the simple case. If, instead, the array contains more than one element, you need to execute the following steps:

1. Divide the array into two smaller arrays, each of which is half the size of the original.
2. Sort each of the smaller arrays by making a recursive call to SortIntegerArray.
3. Merge the two small arrays back to fill the original one.

The code for the SortIntegerArray function itself is

```
void SortIntegerArray(int array[], int n)
{
    int i, n1, n2;
    int *arr1, *arr2;

    if (n > 1) {
        n1 = n / 2;
        n2 = n - n1;
        arr1 = NewArray(n1, int);
        arr2 = NewArray(n2, int);
        for (i = 0; i < n1; i++) arr1[i] = array[i];
        for (i = 0; i < n2; i++) arr2[i] = array[n1 + i];
        SortIntegerArray(arr1, n1);
        SortIntegerArray(arr2, n2);
        Merge(array, arr1, n1, arr2, n2);
        FreeBlock(arr1);
        FreeBlock(arr2);
    }
}
```

In this implementation, arr1 and arr2 are the smaller arrays, and their effective sizes are n1 and n2 respectively. All the hard work is done by Merge, which has the following implementation:

```
static void Merge(int array[], int arr1[], int n1,
                                 int arr2[], int n2)
{
    int p, p1, p2;

    p = p1 = p2 = 0;
    while (p1 < n1 && p2 < n2) {
        if (arr1[p1] < arr2[p2]) {
            array[p++] = arr1[p1++];
        } else {
            array[p++] = arr2[p2++];
        }
    }
    while (p1 < n1) array[p++] = arr1[p1++];
    while (p2 < n2) array[p++] = arr2[p2++];
}
```

The `Merge` function takes the destination array, along with the smaller arrays `arr1` and `arr2`, coupled with their effective sizes, `n1` and `n2`. The indices `p1` and `p2` mark the progress through each of the subarrays, and `p` is the index in `array`. On each cycle of the loop, the function selects an element from `arr1` or `arr2`—whichever is smaller—and copies that value into `array`. As soon as the elements in either subarray are exhausted, the function can simply copy the elements from the other array without bothering to test them. In fact, since you know that one of the subarrays is already exhausted when the first `while` loop exits, the function can simply copy the rest of each array to the destination. One of these subarrays will be empty, and the corresponding `while` loop will not be executed at all.

The computational complexity of merge sort

You now have an implementation of the `SortIntegerArray` function that implements the strategy of divide-and-conquer. How efficient is it? You can measure its efficiency by sorting arrays of numbers and timing the result, but it is helpful to start by thinking about the algorithm in terms of its computational complexity.

When you call the merge sort implementation of `SortIntegerArray` on a list of N numbers, the running time can be divided into two components:

1. The amount of time required to execute the operations at the current level of the recursive decomposition
2. The time required to execute the recursive calls

At the top level of the recursive decomposition, the cost of performing the nonrecursive operations is proportional to N. The two `for` loops in `SortIntegerArray` together account for N cycles, and the call to `Merge` has the effect of filling up the original N positions in the array. If you add these operations and ignore the constant factor, you discover that the complexity of any single call to `SortIntegerArray`—not counting the recursive calls within it—requires $O(N)$ operations.

But what about the cost of the recursive operations? To sort an array of size N, you must recursively sort two arrays of size $N / 2$. Each of these operations requires some amount of time. If you apply the same logic, you quickly determine that each of these recursive calls requires time proportional to $N / 2$ at that level, plus whatever time is required by the recursive calls. The same process then continues until you reach the simple case in which the subarrays consist of a single element or no elements at all.

The total time required to solve the problem is the sum of the time required at each level of the recursive decomposition. In general, the decomposition has the structure shown in Figure 17-3. As you move down through the recursive hierarchy, the arrays get smaller, but there are more of them. The amount of work done at each level, however, is always directly proportional to N. Determining the total amount of work is therefore a question of finding out how many levels there will be.

At each level of the hierarchy, the value of N is divided by 2. The total number of levels is equal to the number of times you can divide N by 2 before you get

Sorting an array of size N

N operations

requires sorting two arrays of size N/2

2 x N/2 operations

which requires sorting four arrays of size N/4

4 x N/4 operations

which requires sorting eight arrays of size N/8

8 x N/8 operations

and so on.

FIGURE 17-3   Recursive decomposition of merge sort

down to 1. Rephrasing this question in mathematical terms, you need to find a value of k such that

$$N = 2^k$$

Solving the equation for k gives

$$k = \log_2 N$$

Because the number of levels is $\log_2 N$ and the amount of work done at each level is proportional to N, the total amount of work is proportional to $N \log_2 N$.

Unlike other scientific disciplines, in which logarithms are expressed in terms of powers of 10 (common logarithms) or the mathematical constant e (natural logarithms), computer science almost always uses **binary logarithms,** which are based on powers of 2. Logarithms computed using different bases differ only by a constant factor, and it is therefore traditional to omit the logarithmic base when you talk about computational complexity. Thus, the computational complexity of merge sort is usually written as

$$O(N \log N)$$

Comparing quadratic and N log N performance

But how good is $O(N \log N)$? You can compare its performance to that of $O(N^2)$ by looking at the values of these functions for different values of N, as shown in Table 17-1. The numbers in both columns of the table grow as N becomes larger, but the N^2 column grows much faster than $N \log N$ column does. Sorting algorithms based

TABLE 17-1

Comparison of N^2 and $N \log N$

N	N²	N log N
10	100	33
100	10,000	664
1000	1,000,000	9,965
10,000	100,000,000	132,877

TABLE 17-2

Running times of the sort algorithms (in seconds)

N	Selection sort	Merge sort
10	0.00013	.00094
100	0.00967	.012
1000	1.08	.14
10,000	110.0	1.6

on an $N \log N$ algorithm are therefore useful over a much larger range of array sizes.

It is interesting to try to verify in practice the theoretical results from Table 17-1. Since big-O notation discards constant factors, it may be that selection sort is more efficient for some problem sizes. Running the selection and merge sort algorithms on arrays of varying sizes and measuring the actual running times results in timing data of the kind shown in Table 17-2. Because computers differ in speed, these numbers will vary from machine to machine, but the basic pattern should remain the same.

For 10 items, selection sort is roughly four times faster than merge sort. At 100 items, selection sort is still faster, but only slightly so. By the time you get up to 10,000 items, selection sort is 70 times *slower* than merge sort and takes almost two minutes to run.

These growth factors are what you would expect from the computational complexity. As you multiply the size of the array by 10, the time required for selection sort should go up by a factor of approximately 100, which is what the table shows. For merge sort, increasing the size by a factor of 10 should cause the running time to grow by a factor just a little more 10, which is exactly what you see.

SUMMARY

In this chapter, you have scratched the surface of three topics that are critically important to more advanced work in computer science: *recursion, abstract data types,* and *analysis of algorithms.* A complete treatment of these subjects is beyond the scope of this text, but it is nonetheless useful to begin learning the concepts as early as you can.

Important points covered in this chapter include:

- Recursion is a powerful programming strategy in which complex problems are broken down into simpler problems of the same form.
- In order to use recursion effectively, you must learn to limit your analysis to a single level of the recursive decomposition and to rely on the correctness of all simpler recursive calls. Trusting these simpler calls to work correctly is called the *recursive leap of faith.*
- In C, the body of a recursive function typically has the following form:

```
if (test for simple case) {
    return (simple solution computed without using recursion);
} else {
    return (recursive solution involving a call to the same function);
}
```

- An abstract type can often be implemented in many different ways. As long as the interface does not change, you are free to change the underlying representation of an abstract data type along with the implementation of the functions that manipulate it.
- By using *incomplete types,* you can define an abstract data type so that its underlying representation is hidden from clients.
- The *computational complexity* of algorithms is usually expressed using big-O notation, which indicates how the running time of a program is affected by changes in problem size.
- Reducing the computational complexity of an algorithm can have a profound effect on its efficiency.

REVIEW QUESTIONS

1. Define the term *recursion.*

2. What is the essential difference between recursion and stepwise refinement?

3. What is meant by the term *recursive leap of faith?*

4. What is the first keyword in the body of a typical recursive function?

5. In the implementation of `PermuteWithFixedPrefix`, there are two calls to `ExchangeCharacters`. Is the second call necessary? Why or why not?

6. What is a wrapper? Why are wrappers common in recursive programming?

7. What are the fundamental operations on a queue?

8. Suppose that you want to design an abstract type called `pictureADT` to keep track of graphical structures. Without knowing anything about its underlying representation, how would you define `pictureADT` in the interface so that it is linked to its corresponding concrete type?

9. Does the definition of a concrete type belong in the interface or the implementation?

10. What is a ring buffer? What is the principal advantage of using a ring buffer as the underlying representation of a queue?

11. What modifications are you allowed to make in order to simplify the formula appearing inside the parentheses used with big-O notation?

12. What is the computational complexity of the selection sort algorithm in terms of big-O notation? What is the corresponding complexity of merge sort? Describe the implications of the difference.

13. What is the computational complexity of the binary-search algorithm as implemented in Figure 12-3?

PROGRAMMING EXERCISES

1. Exercise 8 of Chapter 4 introduced you to the Fibonacci series, in which the first two terms are 0 and 1 and every subsequent term is the sum of the two preceding terms. The series therefore begins with

$$
\begin{aligned}
F_0 &= 0 \\
F_1 &= 1 \\
F_2 &= 1 & (F_0 + F_1) \\
F_3 &= 2 & (F_1 + F_2) \\
F_4 &= 3 & (F_2 + F_3) \\
F_5 &= 5 & (F_3 + F_4) \\
F_6 &= 8 & (F_4 + F_5)
\end{aligned}
$$

and continues in the same fashion for all subsequent terms. Write a recursive implementation of the function `Fib(n)` that returns the nth Fibonacci number. Your implementation must depend only on the relationship between the terms in the sequence and may not use any iterative constructs such as `for` and `while`.

2. The mathematical combinations function $C(n, k)$ introduced in Chapter 5 is usually defined in terms of factorials, as follows:

$$
C(n,k) = \frac{n!}{k! \times (n-k)!}
$$

The values of C(*n*, *k*) can also be arranged geometrically to form a triangle in which *n* increases as you move down the triangle and *k* increases as you move from left to right. The resulting structure, called Pascal's Triangle, is arranged like this:

$$C(0, 0)$$
$$C(1, 0) \quad C(1, 1)$$
$$C(2, 0) \quad C(2, 1) \quad C(2, 2)$$
$$C(3, 0) \quad C(3, 1) \quad C(3, 2) \quad C(3, 3)$$
$$C(4, 0) \quad C(4, 1) \quad C(4, 2) \quad C(4, 3) \quad C(4, 4)$$

As noted in Chapter 5, exercise 12, Pascal's Triangle has the interesting property that every entry is the sum of the two entries above it except along the left and right edges where the values are always 1. Consider, for example, the circled entry in the following display of Pascal's Triangle:

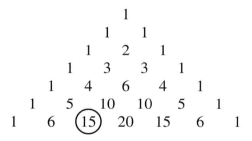

This entry, which corresponds to C(6, 2), is the sum of the two entries—5 and 10—that appear above it to either side. Use this relationship between entries in Pascal's Triangle to write a recursive implementation of the `Combinations` function that uses no loops, no multiplication, and no calls to `Factorial`.

3. Exercise 9 in Chapter 9 introduced the concept of a *palindrome,* which is a string that reads identically backward and forward, such as `"level"` or `"noon"`. For that exercise, you were asked to write a predicate function `IsPalindrome(str)` that tests whether `str` is a palindrome. At the time, you would have used an iterative solution that compared corresponding characters taken from each end of the string, checking to see if they matched.

    The `IsPalindrome` function, however, can also be written recursively. The recursive insight is that long palindromes must contain shorter palindromes in their interior. For example, the string `"level"` consists of the palindrome `"eve"` with an `"l"` at each end. Use this insight to write an implementation of `IsPalindrome` that operates recursively.

4. In almost any computer science course that covers recursion, you will learn about a nineteenth-century puzzle that stands as the archetypal recursive problem. This

puzzle, which goes by the name *Towers of Hanoi,* consists of three towers, one of which contains a set of disks—usually eight in commercial versions of the puzzle—arranged in decreasing order of size as you move from the base of the tower to its top, as illustrated in the following diagram:

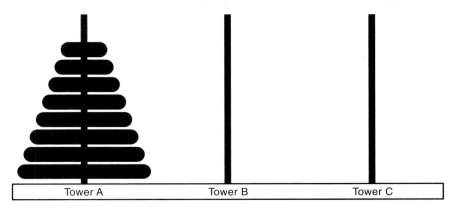

The goal of the puzzle is to move the entire set of disks from Tower A to Tower B, following these rules:

a. You can only move one disk at a time.
b. You can never place a larger disk on top of a smaller disk.

Write a program to display the individual steps required to transfer a tower of *N* disks from Tower A to Tower B. For example, your program should generate the following output when *N* is 3:

```
A -> B
A -> C
B -> C
A -> B
C -> A
C -> B
A -> B
```

The key to solving this problem is finding a decomposition of the problem that allows you to transform the original Tower of Hanoi problem into a simpler problem of the same form.

5. In the late 1970s, a researcher at IBM named Benoit Mandelbrot generated a great deal of excitement by publishing a book on the subject of a delightful mathematical oddity called **fractals,** which are geometrical structures formed by recursive replication of a pattern at many different scales. Mathematicians

have known about fractals for a long time, but there was a strong resurgence of interest in the subject during the 1980s, partly because the development of computers makes it possible to do so much more with fractals than had ever been possible before.

One of the earliest examples of fractal figures is called the *Koch snowflake* after its inventor, Helge von Koch. The Koch snowflake begins with an equilateral triangle

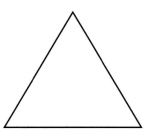

which is called the Koch fractal of order 0. The figure is then revised in stages to generate fractals of successively higher orders. At each stage, every straight line segment in the figure is replaced by one in which the middle third has been replaced by a triangular bump. Thus, if you replace each line segment in the triangle with a line that looks like

you get the Koch fractal of order 1:

If you replace each line segment in this figure with a new line that again includes a triangular wedge, you create the order-2 Koch fractal:

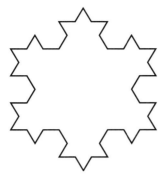

Replacing each of these line segments gives the order-3 fractal shown in the following diagram, which has started to resemble a snowflake:

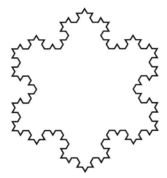

Write a recursive program to draw a Koch fractal snowflake, using the graphics library from Chapter 7 to display the figure on the screen. Your main program should read in the order of the fractal you want to produce along with the edge length of the original order-0 triangle.

In writing this program, it will be helpful to define a procedure DrawPolarLine that draws a line of length *r* in the direction *theta,* measured in degrees counterclockwise from the *x*-axis like the angles for DrawArc, as follows:

```
static void DrawPolarLine(double r, double theta)
{
    double radians;

    radians = theta / 180 * 3.1415926535;
    DrawLine(r * cos(radians), r * sin(radians));
}
```

The name `DrawPolarLine` comes from the mathematical notion of **polar coordinates,** which are coordinates specified in terms of a radius *r* and an angle *theta.*

6. On a standard telephone keypad, the digits are mapped onto the alphabet (minus the letters *Q* and *Z*) as shown in this diagram:

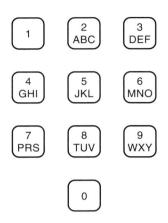

In order to make their phone numbers more memorable, service providers like to find numbers that spell out some word appropriate to their business that makes that phone number easier to remember. Such words that help you remember some other data are called **mnemonics.**

Write a function `ListMnemonics` that generates all possible letter combinations that correspond to a given number, represented as a string of digits. For example, if you call

```
ListMnemonics("723")
```

your program should generate the 27 possible letter combinations corresponding to that prefix, as follows:

```
This program displays mnemonics for a telephone number.
Number: 723↵
PAD   PAE   PAF   PBD   PBE   PBF   PCD   PCE   PCF
RAD   RAE   RAF   RBD   RBE   RBF   RCD   RCE   RCF
SAD   SAE   SAF   SBD   SBE   SBF   SCD   SCE   SCF
```

If the argument passed to `ListMnemonics` contains a 0 or a 1, that position in the output should simply be displayed as that digit, since there are no letters that correspond to it. For example, if you used the function to generate mnemonics for the area code 415, your program should generate the following nine strings:

```
G1J   G1K   G1L
H1J   H1K   H1L
I1J   I1K   I1L
```

7. Complete the implementation of the queue package using a ring buffer described in the section titled "Alternative implementations of the queue abstraction" in this chapter. Remember that your new queue implementation must not require any changes in the queue.h interface.

8. Using a ring buffer to represent a queue improves the efficiency of the Dequeue operation but does not address the problem of queues being limited to a fixed size. One way to solve this problem is to use dynamic arrays in the queue representation. When the client calls NewQueue, the package returns a queue structure that contains space for some default number of elements. If the queue grows beyond that size, the implementation allocates a new array dynamically and copies the old data into it. Reimplement the queue package using this approach.

9. In exercise 8 of Chapter 16, you were asked to implement a dictionary module capable of storing keys and their associated definitions. Given the design suggested in that exercise, however, there can only be one dictionary for the entire program. In some applications, it may be important to support multiple dictionaries used for different purposes.

Redesign the dict.h interface to make the following changes:

a. Define an abstract data type dictionaryADT that can store all the information needed to represent one dictionary.

b. Replace the function InitDictionary with a function NewDictionary that allocates and returns a new dictionaryADT.

c. Export a function FreeDictionary that frees the storage of an existing dictionary.

d. Include an additional argument of type dictionaryADT in the prototypes for Define and Lookup so that these functions know what dictionary they are using.

10. As shown in Table 17-2, selection sort is faster for small arrays than merge sort, although the situation is reversed when the arrays get larger. If you want to design a SortIntegerArray implementation that works well over a wide range of sizes, you can combine the two strategies by using merge sort on large arrays and selection sort on small arrays. Reimplement SortIntegerArray using this strategy. How might you go about choosing the cutoff point separating large arrays from small ones?

APPENDIX A

Summary of C Syntax and Structure

This appendix provides a quick-reference summary of the syntactic rules and structure of ANSI C, as presented in this text. The appendix is not intended as a reference guide to the entire language, although it does include the most important features. To find more information about a particular topic, please refer to the page numbers shown in the margin.

compilation 11 **A.1 An overview of the compilation process**

A C program consists of one or more source files, each of which consists of human-readable text written in a high-level programming language called ANSI C. The C compiler translates each source file into a corresponding object file that contains the actual instructions necessary to execute the program on a particular computer system. The object files—along with additional object files called libraries that implement various common operations—are then linked together to create an executable program.

The process of compiling a source file consists of four phases:

1. *Preprocessing.* During preprocessing, the C compiler transforms the entire text of the source file by applying a set of preliminary operations that include reading in library interfaces and substituting definitions for the names of symbolic constants.
2. *Lexical analysis.* In the lexical analysis phase, the compiler collects the characters in the preprocessed source file to form meaningful units called *tokens.*
3. *Parsing.* This phase consists of checking that the tokens in the source file fit the grammatical rules, or syntax, of the C language. In addition, the parsing phase is responsible for interpreting the meaning, or semantics, of the program.
4. *Code generation.* The final phase of compilation consists of translating the parsed representation of the program into the machine instructions necessary to execute it. Although this phase of the compilation is essential to the process of generating the object file, it has no direct effect on the source file and is therefore less relevant to the programmer.

The first two phases—preprocessing and lexical analysis—are discussed in Sections A.2 and A.3, respectively. Sections A.4 through A.8 focus on the parsing phase and review the syntactic structure of C. Section A.9 reviews the ANSI libraries functions used in the text.

 A.2 The C preprocessor

The preprocessor performs several functions in C, of which only two—defining constants and including interface files—are discussed in detail in this text. They are outlined in the next two subsections.

The #define specification

A source line of the form

    #define name definition

defines the symbol *name* as equivalent to *definition*. Throughout the rest of the source file, the preprocessor looks for any occurrence of *name* that appears as a complete token and replaces it with the characters in *definition*. For example, after encountering the line

    #define Pi 3.14159265

any subsequent occurrence of the name Pi is replaced by 3.14159265.

Substitutions made by the preprocessor are text replacements, and the definition consists of an arbitrary set of characters. This feature allows programmers to include arithmetic operators in constants. For example, after the definitions

    #define MaxStringSize 100
    #define BufferSize   (MaxStringSize + 1)

any subsequent occurrence of the name BufferSize is replaced by the characters

    (100 + 1)

The parentheses around the definition can be extremely important, depending on the context in which the name BufferSize appears. If a program contains the expression

    2 * BufferSize

the preprocessor expands it to

    2 * (100 + 1)

which has the correct value of 202. If the parentheses were omitted from the definition, the multiplication operation would be performed first, leading to the incorrect result of 201.

The #include specification

The #include specification in C appears in the following two forms:

    #include <file name>
    #include "file name"

The two forms are essentially identical in their operation. In either case, the preprocessor looks for a file with the indicated name and replaces the #include line with the entire contents of that file. The only difference between the two forms is that the preprocessor looks in different places to find the file. If the file name is enclosed in angle brackets, the preprocessor looks for that file in a special area reserved for system files, such as the ANSI libraries. If the file name is enclosed in double quotes, the preprocessor first looks for the file in a part of the file system under the control of the user; if the file is not found in the user's area, the preprocessor goes on to check the system files.

The included file is preprocessed just like the original source file and may include constant definitions or additional `#include` lines. In this text, the included file is always an interface, but the preprocessor imposes no such restriction.

Additional features of the preprocessor

The preprocessor has several additional features that are not covered in this text, of which the following are the most important:

- *Pseudo-functions.* The `#define` mechanism includes a facility for passing arguments, which makes it possible for defined symbols to act like functions. This facility is often used to define certain functions in the ANSI library, including `getc` from `stdio.h` and the predicate functions from `ctype.h`, such as `isalpha` and `isdigit`. Preprocessor functions, which are usually called *macros* or *pseudo-functions,* are considerably more efficient than standard C functions but also more restrictive.
- *Conditional compilation.* The preprocessor makes it possible to specify that parts of a source file should be compiled only under certain conditions. In this text, the only use of this facility appears in the boilerplate for interface definitions, but it is also useful for writing more advanced programs that can be more easily transferred from one computer system to another.

More details on using the preprocessor can be found in a C language reference text.

A.3 The lexical structure of C programs

After completing the preprocessing phase, the compiler assembles the individual characters into tokens as outlined in the subsections that follow.

White space

Except in the context of string and character constants, white space characters—most commonly the space, tab, and newline characters—serve to separate other tokens in the source file but are otherwise ignored. Spacing is therefore used to help the human reader understand the structure of the code. Conventionally, each line of a program is indented to mark the control structure. Similarly, blank lines are used to separate different components of the program.

comment 22   Comments

A comment consists of text enclosed between the characters `/*` and `*/`. Comment text can span many source lines, but one comment cannot be nested inside another. Comment text is intended for human readers of the program and is ignored by the compiler.

Identifiers

The names used in a program for variables, functions, types, and so forth are collectively known as *identifiers*. In C, the rules for identifier formation are **variable name 39**

1. The name must start with a letter or the underscore character (_).
2. All other characters in the name must be letters, digits, or the underscore. No spaces or other special characters are permitted in names.
3. The name must not be one of the following keywords:

auto	double	int	struct
break	else	long	switch
case	enum	register	typedef
char	extern	return	union
const	float	short	unsigned
continue	for	signed	void
default	goto	sizeof	volatile
do	if	static	while

Uppercase and lowercase letters appearing in an identifier are considered to be different; for example, the name ABC is not the same as the name abc. Identifiers can be of any length, but C compilers are not required to consider any more than the first 31 characters in determining whether two names are identical. Implementations may impose additional restrictions on identifiers that are shared between modules.

Constants

constant 38

Programs can include constants of the following general types: integer, floating-point, character, and string. The types themselves are discussed in subsequent sections. The formation rules for each type of constant are as follows:

- *Integer.* An integer constant is ordinarily written as a string of digits representing a number in base 10. If the number begins with the digit 0, however, the compiler interprets the value as an octal (base 8) integer. Thus, the constant 040 is taken to be in octal and represents the decimal number 32. If you prefix a numeric constant with the characters 0x, the compiler interprets that number as hexadecimal (base 16). Thus, the constant 0xFF corresponds to the decimal constant 255. You can explicitly indicate that an integer constant is of type long by adding the letter L at the end of the digit string. Thus, the constant 0L is equal to 0, but the value is explicitly of type long. Similarly, if you use the letter U as a suffix, the constant is taken to be unsigned. **integer constant 38**
- *Floating-point.* Floating-point constants in C are written with a decimal point. Thus, if 2.0 appears in a program, the number is represented internally as a floating-point value; if the programmer had written 2, this value would be an integer. Floating-point constants can also be written in scientific notation using the form $x.xxxxE\pm yy$, which stands for $x.xxxx$ times 10 to the yy power. **floating-point constant 38**

character constant
310

- *Character.* You write character constants in C by enclosing the character in single quotes. The value of the character is given by a coding scheme (usually ASCII) that maps each character into a numeric value. In addition to the standard characters, C supports the following escape sequences for indicating special characters:

special character
311

`'\a'`	the alert character (the terminal beeps)
`'\b'`	backspace
`'\f'`	formfeed (starts a new page)
`'\n'`	newline
`'\r'`	return (returns to the beginning of the line without advancing)
`'\t'`	tab
`'\v'`	vertical tab
`'\\'`	the character \ itself
`'\''`	the character ' (the backslash is required only in single characters)
`'\"'`	the character " (the backslash is required only in strings)
`'\ddd'`	the character whose ASCII code is the octal (base 8) number *ddd*.
`'\xdd'`	the character whose ASCII code is the hex (base 16) number *dd*.
`'\0'`	the null character (with zero as its character code)

string constant 38

- *String.* You write string constants by enclosing the characters contained within the string in double quotes. C supports the same escape sequences for strings as for characters. If two or more string constants appear consecutively in a program, the compiler concatenates them together, which makes it possible to break a long string over several lines.

Operators and other punctuation tokens

Punctuation symbols are used to form operators and other tokens required by the syntax of C. Individual operators and related punctuation tokens are described later in this appendix in the section describing the syntactic structure in which those tokens appear.

expression 37

 ## A.4 Expressions

Arithmetic and logical calculations are specified in C in the form of expressions, which consist of individual terms (constants, variables, and function calls) combined together using operators. You can use parentheses to control the grouping of terms. In the absence of parentheses, ANSI C uses precedence and associativity rules to determine which operator is applied first. Whenever two operators compete for the same term, the one that appears higher in Table A-1 is applied first. If the operators are at the same precedence level, the associativity of that class of operators determines whether the left or right operator is applied first.

All the operators in Table A-1 are explained in the text, with the exception of ~, &, |, ^, <<, and >>, which are used to manipulate the individual bits in an integer in applications that require tight programmer control over the underlying representation.

Operator	Associativity
() [] -> .	left
unary operators: − ++ −− ! & * ~ (*type*) sizeof	right
* / %	left
+ −	left
<< >>	left
< <= > >=	left
== !=	left
&	left
^	left
|	left
&&	left
||	left
?:	right
= *op=*	right
,	left

TABLE A-1

Complete precedence table for C operators

=	41
+, −, *, /	43
%	45
op=	62
<, <=, >, >=	75
==, !=	75
&&, ||, !	107
?:	115
sizeof	385
*	458
&	458
++, −−	473
.	561
->	570

A.5 Statements

This section reviews the statement forms available in C.

Simple statements

simple statement
100

The most common statement in C is the simple statement, which consists of an expression followed by a semicolon:

> *expression*;

The null statement

null statement 505

A semicolon by itself constitutes a statement that has no effect. This statement form is called the *null statement* and is most often used as the body of a control structure in which all the important work is done in the header line.

Blocks

block 103

You can combine several statements into a *block* by enclosing them in curly braces:

```
{
     . . . optional declarations . . .

     . . . statements . . .
}
```

You can then use the resulting block as a statement in the context of any of the control statements. As the paradigm shows, the statements in any block may be preceded by declarations of variables. In this text, variable declarations are introduced only in the block that defines the body of a function. Declarations are discussed further in the section on "Functions" later in this appendix.

if statement 112

The if statement

The if statement is used to express simple conditional execution and occurs in two forms:

> if (*expression*) *statement*

and

> if (*expression*) *statement₁* else *statement₂*

switch statement 117

The switch statement

The switch statement is used in contexts in which the value of an expression specifies one of several independent cases. The statement has the form

```
switch (e) {
  case c₁:
    statements
    break;
  case c₂:
    statements
    break;
  . . . more case clauses . . .
  default:
    statements
    break;
}
```

case 118
default 118

Any number of case clauses can appear, but the values used in each case clause must be constants of some scalar type. The default clause is optional but recommended; if no default clause exists and the value on the switch line does not match any of the case constants, the program simply exits from the switch statement without performing any actions.

The break statements occurring within the switch statement are not required by the syntax of C. When a break statement is executed, control passes immediately to the statement following the entire switch statement. If the break statement (or any other statement that changes the control flow, such as a return statement) does not appear, control passes directly into the next case clause. Failure to include a break statement in every clause of a switch statement is a common source of programming errors.

The `while` statement

while **statement**
119

The `while` statement is used to repeat a set of statements until a particular condition arises. The general form of the `while` statement is

```
while (conditional-expression) {
    statements
}
```

For situations in which the exit test falls most naturally in the middle of the loop, this text suggests using the `break` statement to solve the resulting loop-and-a-half problem, as follows:

loop-and-a-half
problem 123

```
while (TRUE) {
    prepare for test
    if (conditional-expression) break;
    do calculation
}
```

The `for` statement

for **statement** 125

The `for` statement is principally used to specify a loop in which an index variable is updated on each cycle through the loop. The general form is

```
for (init; test; step) {
    statements
}
```

and is equivalent to the `while` statement

```
init;
while (test) {
    statements
    step;
}
```

The `break` statement

break **statement**
123

The `break` statement is simply

```
break;
```

When the `break` statement is executed, control exits immediately from the nearest enclosing `switch`, `while`, `for`, or `do` statement.

The `return` statement

return **statement**
142

The `return` statement has two forms. For procedures, you write the statement as

```
return;
```

For functions that return a value, the `return` keyword is followed by an expression, as follows:

```
return expression;
```

Many C programmers enclose the expression in parentheses, although there is no formal requirement to do so.

Executing either form of the `return` statement causes the current function to return immediately to its caller, passing back the value of the expression, if any, to its caller as the value of the function.

Control statements not covered in the text

There are three control statements—`do`, `continue`, and `goto`—that this text does not cover even though they are part of the ANSI standard. The effect of these statements can be accomplished through combinations of the other control statements, so they are not essential to programming in C. More importantly, these control forms are easy to abuse in the sense that undisciplined use of them tends to complicate the structure of a program. The next three paragraphs outline each of these statements in turn so that you will understand them if you encounter them in practice.

The `do` statement is similar to `while` except that the test is performed at the end rather than the beginning of the loop. The general form of the `do` statement is:

```
do {
    statements
} while (conditional-expression);
```

This statement is useful in some situations, although it is usually preferable to use `while`. Programs that use the `do` statement are prone to error because the body of a `do` loop is always executed at least once even if the conditional expression is initially `FALSE`.

The `continue` statement has the form

```
continue;
```

and causes the program to begin the next cycle of the nearest enclosing loop immediately. Although it is often quite convenient, the `continue` statement can reduce the readability of a program, particularly when used in complicated loop structures.

The lowest level of control available in C is the `goto` statement, which has the following general form:

```
goto label;
```

The identifier *label* specifies a particular statement in the current function, which is marked using the identifier *label* followed by a colon, as follows:

```
label: statement
```

The `goto` statement causes control to pass directly to the labeled statement. The undisciplined use of `goto` statements can quickly destroy the structure of a program and make it extremely difficult to read or maintain. This text does not use the `goto` statement and encourages you to show the same discretion.

A.6 Functions

function 137

All executable statements in a C program occur within the body of a function. When the computer executes a program, it begins by calling the function `main`. The function `main` typically calls other functions, each of which solves a part of the problem; these functions in turn call other functions that subdivide the problem further. The process of breaking a problem down into simpler and simpler parts is called *stepwise refinement.*

stepwise refinement 165

Function definitions

function definition 141

A function definition has the following syntactic form:

result-type name (*argument-specifiers*)
{
   . . . *optional declarations* . . .

   . . . *body* . . .
}

In this paradigm, *result-type* is the type of value returned by the function, *name* is the function name, and *argument-specifiers* is a list of parameter declarations separated by commas. The *optional declarations* section includes declarations for local variables used in the function, and *body* consists of the statements required to implement the function.

Function prototypes

function prototype 140

Before you use a function in a C program, you should declare it by specifying its prototype.[1] A prototype has exactly the same form as a function definition, except that the entire body is replaced by a semicolon. The names of the parameter variables are optional in a prototype, although supplying those names usually helps the reader.

Functions and interfaces

interface 222

In this text, all communication between modules is accomplished through function calls. To make functions in one module available to outside callers, the best approach is to define an interface for that module, which is represented as a header file in C. Each interface exports a set of interface entries, which are usually of the following types:

interface entry 275

- Function prototypes
- Constant definitions
- Type definitions

---

[1] To maintain compatibility with earlier versions of C, the compiler assumes certain properties of a function prototype if it is not explictly supplied. In your own code, you should follow the example of this text and define prototypes for every function.

Other modules that use the facilities provided by an interface must include its header file; such modules are called *clients* of the interface.

Private functions

In addition to the functions that are exported to clients through an interface, most modules also define functions that are used only within that module. To maintain the integrity of the interface boundary, it is best to declare these functions as private to the implementation module by preceding their definition with the keyword static.

A.7 Declarations

Most data values in a C program are stored in variables. In C, you must declare each variable before you use it. The act of declaring a variable establishes the association between its name and the type of value it can hold. Declaration also specifies the lifetime and scope of the variable.

Basic declaration syntax

The standard syntax for declaring a variable is

   type name;

where *type* indicates the data type and *name* is an identifier specifying the variable name. Several variables of the same type can be declared on a single line by listing the variable names, separated by commas, as follows:

   type name$_1$, name$_2$, . . . , name$_n$;

For array and pointer variables, however, the declaration syntax includes an indication that a particular name fits into that type class. The syntax for array and pointer declarations is described in Section A.8 where those types are introduced.

Local variables

Most variables are declared at the beginning of the block that constitutes a function body. Such declarations introduce local variables. The scope of a local variable is the function in which it appears. Other functions have no direct access to these variables. The lifetime of a local variable is the time during which that function is active. When the function is called, space for each local variable is allocated in a stack frame assigned to that particular function call. When the function returns, all local variables disappear.

Global variables

If a declaration appears outside any function definition, that declaration introduces a global variable. The scope of a global variable is the entire rest of the module in which it is declared; its lifetime continues throughout the entire execution of a program. Global variables are therefore able to store values that persist after the current function returns. In this text, all global variables are marked with the keyword `static` to ensure that their use is limited to a single module.

Static initialization

Global variables can be initialized to contain specific data values at the time execution begins. To initialize an atomic variable, the required syntax is

type *name* = *initializer*;

For variables of a compound type that have multiple components, you can initialize the entire collection by enclosing a list of initializers within curly braces. If the compound type contains several nested levels of data structure, you can use additional sets of curly braces to specify the interior structures.

▊ A.8 Data types

Every value in C is associated with a data type, which is characterized by a domain of values and a set of operations. These data types fall into two classes: atomic types, which have no internal components, and compound types, which contain values of other types.

Atomic types

The following atomic types are defined in C:

- *Integers.* The basic integer type is `int`, which corresponds to a signed integer. The number of bits used to represent the integer differs from machine to machine, which in turn affects how large a number fits in a value of type `int`. All ANSI-compatible compilers must allow at least 16 bits for type `int`, which means that their range must extend, at a minimum, from −32,768 to 32,767. So that the compiler can allocate more or less space for an integer, the type `int` can be modified by the qualifiers `long` and `short`. In addition, the integer types `int`, `short`, and `long` can be independently modified by the qualifier `signed` or `unsigned` to indicate whether negative values are permitted. When qualifiers are used, the type name `int` is usually omitted.

- *Floating-point numbers.* C defines three floating-point types: `float`, `double`, and `long double`. The precision and storage requirements for these types depends on the compiler and the underlying hardware. For most applications, using type `double` is sufficient.

- *Characters.* The type `char` is used to represent individual characters. Because values of type `char` are defined to require one byte of storage, characters are the fundamental unit for expressing the size of data values.

- *Enumeration types.* In addition to the built-in atomic types, C allows you to define enumeration types whose values are a finite collection of named constants. The standard syntax used in this text to introduce a new enumeration type is

```
typedef enum { list of elements } type name;
```

The `genlib.h` interface uses enumeration types to define the type `bool`, as follows:

```
typedef enum { FALSE, TRUE } bool;
```

Each enumeration constant is assigned an integer value beginning at 0. Thus, in the `bool` example, FALSE is represented internally as 0 and TRUE as 1.

Arrays

An array is an ordered, homogenous collection of values stored in consecutive memory locations. The standard syntax for declaring an array is

element type name [*size*] ;

In this paradigm, *element type* indicates what type of value is stored in each element of the array, *name* is the name of the array variable, and *size* indicates the number of elements to allocate. If you are unsure of how many data values must be stored in an array, the usual approach is to use a value for *size* that is larger than your application is likely to need and then use only part of the allocated space. If you do so, you also need to declare an integer to keep track of how many active elements the array contains at any given time. That integer specifies the *effective* *size* of the array, as opposed to its *allocated size*.

In an array, each element is identified by a numeric index. In C, index values for an array always begin at 0. To select a specific element from an array, you use a selection expression such as `array[i]`, in which the name of the array is followed by an expression enclosed in square brackets that indicates the desired index number.

Pointers

A pointer is the address of a data value. To declare a variable that can point to values of a specific target type, C uses the following declaration form:

*target type *name* ;

Syntactically, the asterisk is associated with the variable name and not with the type; if you use the same declaration to introduce multiple pointer variables, you must mark each one with an asterisk.

The fundamental operators on pointers are `&` and `*`. The `&` operator takes an lvalue and returns a pointer to it; the `*` operator takes a pointer and returns the lvalue to which it points. The operation of moving from a pointer to the lvalue to which it points is called *dereferencing* the pointer.

The pointer value NULL is used to represent a pointer that does not point to any data. The internal representation of NULL is guaranteed to be 0.

To support applications in which the target type of a pointer may not be known, C defines the pointer type `void *` as the most general pointer type. Pointers of type `void *` can be copied, compared, or converted to any specific pointer type, but they cannot be dereferenced.

In C, pointers and arrays are closely related. Whenever the name of an array appears in a C program, that expression is interpreted as a pointer to the initial element in the array. For this reason, passing an array as an argument to a function has the effect of copying only the pointer rather than the entire array. The implication of this design is that the elements of an array declared as a formal parameter are shared with those of the calling array argument. The fact that arrays are defined in terms of pointers also means that arrays can be referenced using either array or pointer notation. The selection expression a[i] is defined to be equivalent to the pointer expression *(a + i). Note that the pointer calculation cannot use simple addition but must instead take account of the size of the value. The C compiler automatically produces the code necessary to perform the required scaling.

pointer arithmetic 469

Records

record 558

In computer science, a collection of heterogeneous objects is called a *record*. The individual components of a record are called *fields*. This text uses the traditional computer-science terms for these concepts, although the terms *structure* and *member* are often used in the C programming community.

Declaring a record variable is a two-step process. The first step is to define the record type; the second is to declare variables as instances of that type. This text uses the following syntax to define a new record type:

```
typedef struct {
     field declarations
} new type name;
```

In this paradigm, *field declarations* are standard variable declarations that define the fields of the record, and *new type name* indicates the name of the new record type. You can define the type to be a pointer to a record instead by including an asterisk before *new type name*.

To select a field from a record, you use the . (dot) operator, which takes a record as its left operand and a field name as its right operand. To select a field given a pointer to a record, you use the -> operator to combine the operations of dereferencing the pointer and selecting the fields.

. 561

-> 570

The typedef mechanism

typedef 305

The keyword typedef is used to introduce names for new types in C. To use it, the first step is to write a declaration for a variable of the type you want to name. That declaration introduces a variable name. If you precede the declaration with the keyword typedef, that name is instead defined as a new type. For example, the declaration

```
int *intptr;
```

defines intptr to be a *variable* of type pointer-to-int. If you instead write

```
typedef int *intptr;
```

the name `intptr` is defined to be the *type* pointer-to-`int`. This mechanism is used in the `genlib.h` library to define the type `string`, as follows:

```
typedef char *string;
```

▉▉▉ A.9 ANSI libraries

The sections that follow describe the ANSI library functions used in this text, organized according to interface.

`stdio.h` **525**   ### The standard I/O library (`stdio.h`)

The standard I/O library provides a standard set of functions for manipulating files and performing input/output operations. The `stdio.h` interface is usually included in every `.c` file.

`fopen` **526**   ### FILE *fopen(string filename, string mode);

This function opens a file and returns a pointer associated with the file. The name of the file is given by the string `filename`. The `mode` string specifies the type of data transmission and is usually one of the following values:

`"r"`	Open file for reading. The file must previously exist.
`"w"`	Open file for writing. If the file exists, all previous contents are erased.
`"a"`	Open file for appending. If the file exists, new output appears at the end.

If any errors occur (such as opening a file for reading that does not exist), `fopen` returns `NULL`.

`fclose` **528**   ### void fclose(FILE *fp);

This function takes a file pointer originally generated by `fopen` and closes it.

`getc` **529**
`getchar` **529**   ### int getc(FILE *infile);
int getchar(void);

The `getc` function reads and returns the next character from `infile`. The value returned is an integer (rather than a character) so that the result type can include the special value `EOF` used to indicate the end of the file. The `getchar` function works the same way except that it always reads its input from the standard input file.

`ungetc` **535**   ### int ungetc(char ch, FILE *infile);

This function pushes the character `ch` back into the file stream indicated by `infile` so that `ch` is read again by the next function that reads characters from the file. Only a single character may be pushed back in this way.

```
void putc(char ch, FILE *outfile);
int putchar(void);
```

putc **529**
putchar **529**

The putc function writes the single character ch to the output file specified by outfile. The putchar function is similar except that it always writes the character to the standard output file.

```
int fgets(char buffer[], int max, FILE *infile);
```

fgets **536**

This function reads a line of text from the input file and stores it into buffer, which must be a character array allocated by the client. At most max characters are read using this function, allowing the client to prevent buffer overflow. The newline character terminating the line is stored as part of the buffer.

```
int fputs(string s, FILE *outfile);
```

fputs **537**

This function writes the string s to the file outfile.

```
void printf(string msg, . . .);
void fprintf(FILE *outfile, string msg, . . .);
void sprintf(char buffer[], string msg, . . .);
```

printf **80**
fprintf **539**
sprintf **539**

The printf function displays the message msg on the standard output device, which is usually the terminal screen; the fprintf and sprintf functions are similar to printf, except that the output is directed to outfile or buffer, as appropriate. In any of the three forms, the characters in msg are copied to the output stream. If a percent sign (%) appears in msg, it indicates that a value is to be substituted in that position. The value is taken from the next unused argument position, so that the substitutions appear in the same order in the string msg as the values appear in the argument list. The characters following the percent sign specify a format code that controls how the value is displayed. An extensive discussion of format codes appears in Chapter 3.

format code **82**

```
int scanf(string format, . . .);
int fscanf(FILE *infile, string format, . . .);
int sscanf(string s, string format, . . .);
```

scanf **540**
fscanf **540**
sscanf **540**

The scanf family of functions provides the standard mechanism used to read data in the ANSI libraries; this text tends to use the simpler interface provided by the library simpio.h. The scanf function itself reads from standard input; the other two forms read data from the file infile or the string s, as appropriate. The format argument specifies a control string that specifies the type and conversion style of the value to be read. The value is stored into the variable given as subsequent arguments to scanf, which must be preceded (except in the case of character arrays, which are already pointer types) by an ampersand (&). The scanf functions return the number of values successfully converted unless they are called at the end of the input file, in which case they return the constant EOF.

remove **664**

```
int remove(string filename);
```

This function deletes the file specified by filename. The function returns 0 if the deletion operation succeeds and some nonzero value if it fails.

rename **664**

```
int rename(string oldname, string newname);
```

This function renames an existing file. The function returns 0 if the renaming operation succeeds and some nonzero value if it fails.

tmpname **664**

```
string tmpname(char *namebuf);
```

This function generates a temporary file name. If the namebuf argument is not NULL, it must point to a character array of sufficient size to hold the temporary file name; if namebuf is NULL, the temporary name is stored in statically allocated memory within the stdio implementation. In either case, the tmpname function returns the newly generated name.

stdlib.h **145**

The standard system library (stdlib.h)

The stdlib.h interface defines several general functions that do not fit well into other classifications.

abs **145**

```
int abs(int n);
```

This function returns the absolute value of n.

rand **266**

```
int rand(void);
```

This function returns a random number in the range 0 to RAND_MAX.

srand **282**

```
void srand(int seed);
```

This function sets the random number seed to the specified value.

malloc **478**

```
void *malloc(int nBytes);
```

The malloc function allocates a block of memory large enough to hold the indicated number of bytes (characters) and returns a pointer to the first address in that block. If no memory is available, malloc returns NULL.

free **481**

```
void free(void *p);
```

This function frees the memory associated with the pointer p, which must have been allocated using malloc.

math.h **139**

The math library (math.h)

The math.h interface exports several mathematical functions. Even though the text uses only a few of these, this section lists the most common mathematical functions.

```
double fabs(double x);
```
fabs 181

This function returns the absolute value of a real number x.

```
double floor(double x);
```

This function returns the floating-point representation of the largest integer less than or equal to x.

```
double ceil(double x);
```

This function returns the floating-point representation of the smallest integer greater than or equal to x.

```
double fmod(double x, double y);
```

This function returns the floating-point remainder of x / y.

```
double sqrt(double x);
```
sqrt 139

This function returns the square root of x.

```
double pow(double x, double y);
```

This function returns x^y.

```
double exp(double x);
```

This function returns e^x.

```
double log(double x);
```

This function returns the natural logarithm of x.

```
double sin(double theta);
```
sin 139

This function returns the trigonometric sine of the angle theta, expressed in radians.

```
double cos(double theta);
```
cos 139

This function returns the trigonometric cosine of the angle theta, expressed in radians.

```
double atan(double x);
```

This function returns the trigonometric arctangent of the value x. The result is an angle expressed in radians between $-\pi/2$ and $+\pi/2$.

```
double atan2(double x, y);
```

This function returns the angle formed between the x-axis and the line extending from the origin through the point (x, y). As with the other trigonometric functions, the angle is expressed in radians.

ctype.h 314   The character type library (ctype.h)

This interface exports a set of extremely efficient functions for classifying differ-ent character types.[2]

```
bool isalpha(char ch);
bool isupper(char ch);
bool islower(char ch);
bool isdigit(char ch);
bool isalnum(char ch);
bool ispunct(char ch);
bool isspace(char ch);
```

These functions return TRUE if the character ch is in the specified class, as follows:

isalpha	Alphabetic characters
isupper	Uppercase alphabetic characters
islower	Lowercase alphabetic characters
isdigit	Decimal digits
isalnum	The union of alphabetic characters and digits
ispunct	Punctuation characters
isspace	White-space characters

tolower 315   char toupper(char ch);
toupper 315   char tolower(char ch);

If ch is a letter, these functions return that character converted to the specified case; if not, these functions return the value of ch unchanged. The argument and result type of these functions is int.

string.h 502   The ANSI string library (string.h)

This interface exports a collection of string functions. In contrast to the functions in the strlib.h interface described in Appendix B, these functions require clients to perform their own memory allocation.

strlen 509   int strlen(string str);

This function returns the length of the string, where the length is defined as the number of characters in the string up to but not including the terminating null char-acter.

strcmp 509   int strcmp(string s1, string s2);
strncmp 510   int strncmp(string s1, string s2, int n);

The strcmp function compares the two strings s1 and s2 by comparing each char-acter in the string in turn. If s1 comes before s2 in the ASCII ordering sequence, strcmp returns a negative number. If s1 comes after s2, strcmp returns a positive

---

[2] Most of the functions in the ctype.h interface are actually defined to use type int so that these func-tions can be called on the constant EOF. The prototypes shown here use type char to enhance readability.

number. If the two strings are the same, strcmp returns 0. The strncmp function is the same, except that the function compares at most the first n characters of the two strings.

```
string strcpy(char dst[], string src);
string strncpy(char dst[], string src, int n);
```

The strcpy function copies the characters from the original string src into the character array specified by dst. A null character is written at the end of the destination string so that it is properly terminated. It is the client's responsibility to ensure that enough space is allocated for the string and the terminating null character. The function returns the address of the destination string, although clients usually ignore this result. The strncpy is similar, except that it copies a maximum of n characters.

```
string strcat(char dst[], string src);
string strncat(char dst[], string src, int n);
```

The strcat function copies the characters from the string src to the end of the string stored in the character array specified by dst. The strncat version copies at most n characters.

```
char *strchr(string str, char ch);
```

This function searches for the first occurrence of the character ch in the string str. If the character is found, strchr returns a pointer to that character. If the character ch does not appear in str, strchr returns NULL.

```
char *strrchr(string str, char ch);
```

This function is similar to strchr, except that function looks for the *last* occurrence of the ch in str.

```
char *strstr(string s1, string s2);
```

This function searches for the first occurrence of the string s2 in the string s1. If the string is found, strstr returns a pointer to the first character position at which the match occurred. If s2 does not appear in s1, strstr returns NULL.

APPENDIX B

Library Sources

This appendix contains the interfaces and implementations for the extended libraries used in this text. These libraries are designed to be portable and may be used with any compiler that conforms to the ANSI standard.

The source code for these libraries—along with the code for all the program examples used in this text—is available from Addison-Wesley through anonymous FTP (file transfer protocol). To retrieve the source code, you need to execute the following steps:

1. Find a computer system that has access to the Internet.
2. Use the `ftp` program to connect to the host `aw.com`.
3. Login with the user name `anonymous`. When the system asks you for a password, enter your e-mail address.
4. Connect to the directory `aw.computer.science/Roberts.CS1.C` (the capitalization is important).
5. Retrieve files from this directory or its subdirectories, according to what sources you need. For more information, please consult the README file in the `Roberts.CS1.C` directory.
6. Disconnect from `aw.com` and quit the `ftp` program.

The commands necessary to perform each of these functions depend to some extent on the `ftp` program you are using. If you are having difficulty following these instructions, please ask your local system consultants for assistance. If you have no access to the Internet, please write to

> The Art & Science of C
> Computer Science: Higher Ed Editorial
> Addison-Wesley Publishing Company
> One Jacob Way
> Reading, MA 01867
> U.S.A.

FIGURE B-1 genlib.h

```
/*
 * File: genlib.h
 * --------------
 * This file contains several definitions that form the
 * core of a general-purpose ANSI C library developed by Eric
 * Roberts.  The goal of this library is to provide a basic
 * set of tools and conventions that increase the readability
 * of C programs, particularly as they are used in a teaching
 * environment.
 *
 * The basic definitions provided by genlib.h are:
 *
 *     1.  Declarations for several new "primitive" types
 *         (most importantly bool and string) that are
 *         used throughout the other libraries and
 *         applications as fundamental types.
 *
 *     2.  A new set of functions for memory allocation.
 *
 *     3.  A function for error handling.
 */

#ifndef _genlib_h
#define _genlib_h

#include <stdio.h>
#include <stdlib.h>
#include <stddef.h>

/* Section 1 -- Define new "primitive" types */

/*
 * Type: bool
 * ----------
 * This type has two values, FALSE and TRUE, which are equal to 0
 * and 1, respectively.  Most of the advantage of defining this type
 * comes from readability because it allows the programmer to
 * provide documentation that a variable will take on only one of
 * these two values.  Designing a portable representation, however,
 * is surprisingly hard, because many libraries and some compilers
 * define these names.  The definitions are usually compatible but
 * may still be flagged as errors.
 */
```

```
#ifdef THINK_C
   typedef int bool;
#else
#  ifdef TRUE
#    ifndef bool
#      define bool int
#    endif
#  else
#    ifdef bool
#      define FALSE 0
#      define TRUE 1
#    else
       typedef enum {FALSE, TRUE} bool;
#    endif
#  endif
#endif

/*
 * Type: string
 * ------------
 * The type string is identical to the type char *, which is
 * traditionally used in C programs.  The main point of defining a
 * new type is to improve program readability.   At the abstraction
 * levels at which the type string is used, it is usually not
 * important to take the string apart into its component characters.
 * Declaring it as a string emphasizes this atomicity.
 */

typedef char *string;

/*
 * Constant: UNDEFINED
 * -------------------
 * Besides NULL, the only other constant of pointer type is
 * UNDEFINED, which is used in certain packages as a special
 * sentinel to indicate an undefined pointer value.  In many
 * such contexts, NULL is a legitimate data value and is
 * therefore inappropriate as a sentinel.
 */

#define UNDEFINED ((void *) undefined_object)

extern char undefined_object[];
```

```
/* Section 2 -- Memory allocation */

/*
 * General notes:
 * --------------
 * These functions provide a common interface for memory
 * allocation.  All functions in the library that allocate
 * memory do so using GetBlock and FreeBlock.  Even though
 * the ANSI standard defines malloc and free for the same
 * purpose, using GetBlock and FreeBlock provides greater
 * compatibility with non-ANSI implementations, automatic
 * out-of-memory error detection, and the possibility of
 * substituting a garbage-collecting allocator.
 */

/*
 * Function: GetBlock
 * Usage: ptr = (type) GetBlock(nbytes);
 * -------------------------------------
 * GetBlock allocates a block of memory of the given size.  If
 * no memory is available, GetBlock generates an error.
 */

void *GetBlock(size_t nbytes);

/*
 * Function: FreeBlock
 * Usage: FreeBlock(ptr);
 * ----------------------
 * FreeBlock frees the memory associated with ptr, which must
 * have been allocated using GetBlock, New, or NewArray.
 */

void FreeBlock(void *ptr);

/*
 * Macro: New
 * Usage: p = New(pointer-type);
 * -----------------------------
 * The New pseudofunction allocates enough space to hold an
 * object of the type to which pointer-type points and returns
 * a pointer to the newly allocated pointer.  Note that
 * "New" is different from the "new" operator used in C++;
 * the former takes a pointer type and the latter takes the
 * target type.
 */

#define New(type) ((type) GetBlock(sizeof *((type) NULL)))
```

```
/*
 * Macro: NewArray
 * Usage: p = NewArray(n, element-type);
 * ---------------------------------------
 * NewArray allocates enough space to hold an array of n
 * values of the specified element type.
 */

#define NewArray(n, type) ((type *) GetBlock((n)*sizeof(type)))

/* Section 3 -- Basic error handling */

/*
 * Function: Error
 * Usage: Error(msg, ...)
 * ----------------------
 * Error generates an error string, expanding % constructions
 * appearing in the error message string just as printf does.
 * After printing the error message, the program terminates.
 */

void Error(string msg, ...);

#endif
```

FIGURE B-2 genlib.c

```
/*
 * File: genlib.c
 * --------------
 * This file implements the general C library package.  See the
 * interface description in genlib.h for details.
 */

#include <stdio.h>
#include <stddef.h>
#include <string.h>
#include <stdarg.h>

#include "genlib.h"

/*
 * Constants:
 * ----------
 * ErrorExitStatus -- Status value used in exit call
 */

#define ErrorExitStatus 1
```

```
/* Section 1 -- Define new "primitive" types */

/*
 * Constant: UNDEFINED
 * -------------------
 * This entry defines the target of the UNDEFINED constant.
 */

char undefined_object[] = "UNDEFINED";

/* Section 2 -- Memory allocation */

void *GetBlock(size_t nbytes)
{
    void *result;

    result = malloc(nbytes);
    if (result == NULL) Error("No memory available");
    return (result);
}

void FreeBlock(void *ptr)
{
    free(ptr);
}

/* Section 3 -- Basic error handling */

void Error(string msg, ...)
{
    va_list args;

    va_start(args, msg);
    fprintf(stderr, "Error: ");
    vfprintf(stderr, msg, args);
    fprintf(stderr, "\n");
    va_end(args);
    exit(ErrorExitStatus);
}
```

FIGURE B-3 simpio.h

```
/*
 * File: simpio.h
 * --------------
 * This interface provides access to a simple package of
 * functions that simplify the reading of input data.
 */

#ifndef _simpio_h
#define _simpio_h

#include "genlib.h"

/*
 * Function: GetInteger
 * Usage: i = GetInteger();
 * ------------------------
 * GetInteger reads a line of text from standard input and scans
 * it as an integer.  The integer value is returned.  If an
 * integer cannot be scanned or if more characters follow the
 * number, the user is given a chance to retry.
 */

int GetInteger(void);

/*
 * Function: GetLong
 * Usage: l = GetLong();
 * ---------------------
 * GetLong reads a line of text from standard input and scans
 * it as a long integer.  The value is returned as a long.
 * If an integer cannot be scanned or if more characters follow
 * the number, the user is given a chance to retry.
 */

long GetLong(void);

/*
 * Function: GetReal
 * Usage: x = GetReal();
 * ---------------------
 * GetReal reads a line of text from standard input and scans
 * it as a double.  If the number cannot be scanned or if extra
 * characters follow after the number ends, the user is given
 * a chance to reenter the value.
 */

double GetReal(void);
```

```
/*
 * Function: GetLine
 * Usage: s = GetLine();
 * --------------------
 * GetLine reads a line of text from standard input and returns
 * the line as a string.  The newline character that terminates
 * the input is not stored as part of the string.
 */

string GetLine(void);

/*
 * Function: ReadLine
 * Usage: s = ReadLine(infile);
 * ----------------------------
 * ReadLine reads a line of text from the input file and
 * returns the line as a string.  The newline character
 * that terminates the input is not stored as part of the
 * string.  The ReadLine function returns NULL if infile
 * is at the end-of-file position.
 */

string ReadLine(FILE *infile);

#endif
```

FIGURE B-4 **simpio.c**

```
/*
 * File: simpio.c
 * --------------
 * This file implements the simpio.h interface.
 */

#include <stdio.h>
#include <string.h>
#include "genlib.h"
#include "strlib.h"
#include "simpio.h"
```

```
/*
 * Constants:
 * ----------
 * InitialBufferSize -- Initial buffer size for ReadLine
 */

#define InitialBufferSize 120

/* Exported entries */

/*
 * Functions: GetInteger, GetLong, GetReal
 * ----------------------------------------
 * These functions first read a line and then call sscanf to
 * translate the number.  Reading an entire line is essential to
 * good error recovery, because the characters after the point of
 * error would otherwise remain in the input buffer and confuse
 * subsequent input operations.  The sscanf line allows white space
 * before and after the number but no other extraneous characters.
 */

int GetInteger(void)
{
    string line;
    int value;
    char termch;

    while (TRUE) {
        line = GetLine();
        switch (sscanf(line, " %d %c", &value, &termch)) {
          case 1:
            FreeBlock(line);
            return (value);
          case 2:
            printf("Unexpected character: '%c'\n", termch);
            break;
          default:
            printf("Please enter an integer\n");
            break;
        }
        FreeBlock(line);
        printf("Retry: ");
    }
}
```

```c
long GetLong(void)
{
    string line;
    long value;
    char termch;

    while (TRUE) {
        line = GetLine();
        switch (sscanf(line, " %ld %c", &value, &termch)) {
          case 1:
            FreeBlock(line);
            return (value);
          case 2:
            printf("Unexpected character: '%c'\n", termch);
            break;
          default:
            printf("Please enter an integer\n");
            break;
        }
        FreeBlock(line);
        printf("Retry: ");
    }
}

double GetReal(void)
{
    string line;
    double value;
    char termch;

    while (TRUE) {
        line = GetLine();
        switch (sscanf(line, " %lf %c", &value, &termch)) {
          case 1:
            FreeBlock(line);
            return (value);
          case 2:
            printf("Unexpected character: '%c'\n", termch);
            break;
          default:
            printf("Please enter a real number\n");
            break;
        }
        FreeBlock(line);
        printf("Retry: ");
    }
}
```

```
/*
 * Function: GetLine
 * -----------------
 * This function is a simple wrapper; all the work is done by
 * ReadLine.
 */

string GetLine(void)
{
    return (ReadLine(stdin));
}

/*
 * Function: ReadLine
 * ------------------
 * This function operates by reading characters from the file
 * into a dynamically allocated buffer.  If the buffer becomes
 * full before the end of the line is reached, a new buffer
 * twice the size of the previous one.
 */

string ReadLine(FILE *infile)
{
    string line, nline;
    int n, ch, size;

    n = 0;
    size = InitialBufferSize;
    line = GetBlock(size + 1);
    while ((ch = getc(infile)) != '\n' && ch != EOF) {
        if (n == size) {
            size *= 2;
            nline = (string) GetBlock(size + 1);
            strncpy(nline, line, n);
            FreeBlock(line);
            line = nline;
        }
        line[n++] = ch;
    }
    if (n == 0 && ch == EOF) {
        FreeBlock(line);
        return (NULL);
    }
    line[n] = '\0';
    nline = (string) GetBlock(n + 1);
    strcpy(nline, line);
    FreeBlock(line);
    return (nline);
}
```

FIGURE B-5   strlib.h

```
/*
 * File: strlib.h
 * --------------
 * The strlib.h file defines the interface for a simple
 * string library.  In the context of this package, strings
 * are considered to be an abstract data type, which means
 * that the client relies only on the operations defined for
 * the type and not on the underlying representation.
 */

/*
 * Cautionary note:
 * ----------------
 * Although this interface provides an extremely convenient
 * abstraction for working with strings, it is not appropriate
 * for all applications.  In this interface, the functions that
 * return string values (such as Concat and SubString) do so
 * by allocating new memory.  Over time, a program that uses
 * this package will consume increasing amounts of memory
 * and eventually exhaust the available supply.  If you are
 * writing a program that runs for a short time and stops,
 * the fact that the package consumes memory is not a problem.
 * If, however, you are writing an application that must run
 * for an extended period of time, using this package requires
 * that you make some provision for freeing any allocated
 * storage.
 */

#ifndef _strlib_h
#define _strlib_h

#include "genlib.h"

/* Section 1 -- Basic string operations */

/*
 * Function: Concat
 * Usage: s = Concat(s1, s2);
 * --------------------------
 * This function concatenates two strings by joining them end
 * to end.  For example, Concat("ABC", "DE") returns the string
 * "ABCDE".
 */

string Concat(string s1, string s2);
```

```
/*
 * Function: IthChar
 * Usage: ch = IthChar(s, i);
 * --------------------------
 * This function returns the character at position i in the
 * string s.  It is included in the library to make the type
 * string a true abstract type in the sense that all of the
 * necessary operations can be invoked using functions. Calling
 * IthChar(s, i) is like selecting s[i], except that IthChar
 * checks to see if i is within the range of legal index
 * positions, which extend from 0 to StringLength(s).
 * IthChar(s, StringLength(s)) returns the null character
 * at the end of the string.
 */

char IthChar(string s, int i);

/*
 * Function: SubString
 * Usage: t = SubString(s, p1, p2);
 * --------------------------------
 * SubString returns a copy of the substring of s consisting
 * of the characters between index positions p1 and p2,
 * inclusive.  The following special cases apply:
 *
 * 1. If p1 is less than 0, it is assumed to be 0.
 * 2. If p2 is greater than the index of the last string
 *    position, which is StringLength(s) - 1, then p2 is
 *    set equal to StringLength(s) - 1.
 * 3. If p2 < p1, SubString returns the empty string.
 */

string SubString(string s, int p1, int p2);

/*
 * Function: CharToString
 * Usage: s = CharToString(ch);
 * ----------------------------
 * This function takes a single character and returns a
 * one-character string consisting of that character.  The
 * CharToString function is useful, for example, if you
 * need to concatenate a string and a character.  Since
 * Concat requires two strings, you must first convert
 * the character into a string.
 */

string CharToString(char ch);
```

```
/*
 * Function: StringLength
 * Usage: len = StringLength(s);
 * ------------------------------
 * This function returns the length of s.
 */

int StringLength(string s);

/*
 * Function: CopyString
 * Usage: newstr = CopyString(s);
 * ------------------------------
 * CopyString copies the string s into dynamically allocated
 * storage and returns the new string.  This function is not
 * ordinarily required if this package is used on its own,
 * but is often necessary when you are working with more than
 * one string package.
 */

string CopyString(string s);

/* Section 2 -- String comparison functions */

/*
 * Function: StringEqual
 * Usage: if (StringEqual(s1, s2)) ...
 * -----------------------------------
 * This function returns TRUE if the strings s1 and s2 are
 * equal.  For the strings to be considered equal, every
 * character in one string must precisely match the
 * corresponding character in the other.  Uppercase and
 * lowercase characters are considered to be different.
 */

bool StringEqual(string s1, string s2);

/*
 * Function: StringCompare
 * Usage: if (StringCompare(s1, s2) < 0) ...
 * -----------------------------------------
 * This function returns a number less than 0 if string s1
 * comes before s2 in alphabetical order, 0 if they are equal,
 * and a number greater than 0 if s1 comes after s2.  The
 * ordering is determined by the internal representation used
 * for characters, which is usually ASCII.
 */

int StringCompare(string s1, string s2);
```

```
/* Section 3 -- Search functions */

/*
 * Function: FindChar
 * Usage: p = FindChar(ch, text, start);
 * -------------------------------------
 * Beginning at position start in the string text, this
 * function searches for the character ch and returns the
 * first index at which it appears or -1 if no match is
 * found.
 */

int FindChar(char ch, string text, int start);

/*
 * Function: FindString
 * Usage: p = FindString(str, text, start);
 * ----------------------------------------
 * Beginning at position start in the string text, this
 * function searches for the string str and returns the
 * first index at which it appears or -1 if no match is
 * found.
 */

int FindString(string str, string text, int start);

/* Section 4 -- Case-conversion functions */

/*
 * Function: ConvertToLowerCase
 * Usage: s = ConvertToLowerCase(s);
 * ---------------------------------
 * This function returns a new string with all
 * alphabetic characters converted to lower case.
 */

string ConvertToLowerCase(string s);

/*
 * Function: ConvertToUpperCase
 * Usage: s = ConvertToUpperCase(s);
 * ---------------------------------
 * This function returns a new string with all
 * alphabetic characters converted to upper case.
 */

string ConvertToUpperCase(string s);
```

```
/* Section 5 -- Functions for converting numbers to strings */

/*
 * Function: IntegerToString
 * Usage: s = IntegerToString(n);
 * -------------------------------
 * This function converts an integer into the corresponding
 * string of digits.  For example, IntegerToString(123)
 * returns "123" as a string.
 */

string IntegerToString(int n);

/*
 * Function: StringToInteger
 * Usage: n = StringToInteger(s);
 * -------------------------------
 * This function converts a string of digits into an integer.
 * If the string is not a legal integer or contains extraneous
 * characters, StringToInteger signals an error condition.
 */

int StringToInteger(string s);

/*
 * Function: RealToString
 * Usage: s = RealToString(d);
 * ----------------------------
 * This function converts a floating-point number into the
 * corresponding string form.  For example, calling
 * RealToString(23.45) returns "23.45".  The conversion is
 * the same as that used for "%G" format in printf.
 */

string RealToString(double d);

/*
 * Function: StringToReal
 * Usage: d = StringToReal(s);
 * ----------------------------
 * This function converts a string representing a real number
 * into its corresponding value.  If the string is not a
 * legal floating-point number or if it contains extraneous
 * characters, StringToReal signals an error condition.
 */

double StringToReal(string s);

#endif
```

FIGURE B-6 strlib.c

```
/*
 * File: strlib.c
 * --------------
 * This file implements the strlib interface.
 */

/*
 * General implementation notes:
 * -----------------------------
 * This module implements the strlib library by mapping all
 * functions into the appropriate calls to the ANSI <string.h>
 * interface.  The implementations of the individual functions
 * are all quite simple and do not require individual comments.
 * For descriptions of the behavior of each function, see the
 * interface.
 */

#include <stdio.h>
#include <string.h>
#include <ctype.h>

#include "genlib.h"
#include "strlib.h"

/*
 * Constant: MaxDigits
 * -------------------
 * This constant must be larger than the maximum
 * number of digits that can appear in a number.
 */

#define MaxDigits 30

/* Private function prototypes */

static string CreateString(int len);
```

```
/* Section 1 -- Basic string operations */

string Concat(string s1, string s2)
{
    string s;
    int len1, len2;

    if (s1 == NULL || s2 == NULL) {
        Error("NULL string passed to Concat");
    }
    len1 = strlen(s1);
    len2 = strlen(s2);
    s = CreateString(len1 + len2);
    strcpy(s, s1);
    strcpy(s + len1, s2);
    return (s);
}

char IthChar(string s, int i)
{
    int len;

    if (s == NULL) Error("NULL string passed to IthChar");
    len = strlen(s);
    if (i < 0 || i > len) {
        Error("Index outside of string range in IthChar");
    }
    return (s[i]);
}

string SubString(string s, int p1, int p2)
{
    int len;
    string result;

    if (s == NULL) Error("NULL string passed to SubString");
    len = strlen(s);
    if (p1 < 0) p1 = 0;
    if (p2 >= len) p2 = len - 1;
    len = p2 - p1 + 1;
    if (len < 0) len = 0;
    result = CreateString(len);
    strncpy(result, s + p1, len);
    result[len] = '\0';
    return (result);
}
```

```
string CharToString(char ch)
{
    string result;

    result = CreateString(1);
    result[0] = ch;
    result[1] = '\0';
    return (result);
}

int StringLength(string s)
{
    if (s == NULL) Error("NULL string passed to StringLength");
    return (strlen(s));
}

string CopyString(string s)
{
    string newstr;

    if (s == NULL) Error("NULL string passed to CopyString");
    newstr = CreateString(strlen(s));
    strcpy(newstr, s);
    return (newstr);
}

/* Section 2 -- String comparison functions */

bool StringEqual(string s1, string s2)
{
    if (s1 == NULL || s2 == NULL) {
        Error("NULL string passed to StringEqual");
    }
    return (strcmp(s1, s2) == 0);
}

int StringCompare(string s1, string s2)
{
    if (s1 == NULL || s2 == NULL) {
        Error("NULL string passed to StringCompare");
    }
    return (strcmp(s1, s2));
}
```

```
/* Section 3 -- Search functions */

int FindChar(char ch, string text, int start)
{
    char *cptr;

    if (text == NULL) Error("NULL string passed to FindChar");
    if (start < 0) start = 0;
    if (start > strlen(text)) return (-1);
    cptr = strchr(text + start, ch);
    if (cptr == NULL) return (-1);
    return ((int) (cptr - text));
}

int FindString(string str, string text, int start)
{
    char *cptr;

    if (str == NULL) Error("NULL pattern string in FindString");
    if (text == NULL) Error("NULL text string in FindString");
    if (start < 0) start = 0;
    if (start > strlen(text)) return (-1);
    cptr = strstr(text + start, str);
    if (cptr == NULL) return (-1);
    return ((int) (cptr - text));
}

/* Section 4 -- Case-conversion functions */

string ConvertToLowerCase(string s)
{
    string result;
    int i;

    if (s == NULL) {
        Error("NULL string passed to ConvertToLowerCase");
    }
    result = CreateString(strlen(s));
    for (i = 0; s[i] != '\0'; i++) result[i] = tolower(s[i]);
    result[i] = '\0';
    return (result);
}
```

```
string ConvertToUpperCase(string s)
{
    string result;
    int i;

    if (s == NULL) {
        Error("NULL string passed to ConvertToUpperCase");
    }
    result = CreateString(strlen(s));
    for (i = 0; s[i] != '\0'; i++) result[i] = toupper(s[i]);
    result[i] = '\0';
    return (result);
}

/* Section 5 -- Functions for converting numbers to strings */

string IntegerToString(int n)
{
    char buffer[MaxDigits];

    sprintf(buffer, "%d", n);
    return (CopyString(buffer));
}

int StringToInteger(string s)
{
    int result;
    char dummy;

    if (s == NULL) {
        Error("NULL string passed to StringToInteger");
    }
    if (sscanf(s, " %d %c", &result, &dummy) != 1) {
        Error("StringToInteger called on illegal number %s", s);
    }
    return (result);
}
```

```
string RealToString(double d)
{
    char buffer[MaxDigits];

    sprintf(buffer, "%G", d);
    return (CopyString(buffer));
}

double StringToReal(string s)
{
    double result;
    char dummy;

    if (s == NULL) Error("NULL string passed to StringToReal");
    if (sscanf(s, " %lg %c", &result, &dummy) != 1) {
        Error("StringToReal called on illegal number %s", s);
    }
    return (result);
}

/* Private functions */

/*
 * Function: CreateString
 * Usage: s = CreateString(len);
 * -----------------------------
 * This function dynamically allocates space for a string of
 * len characters, leaving room for the null character at the
 * end.
 */

static string CreateString(int len)
{
    return ((string) GetBlock(len + 1));
}
```

FIGURE B-7 random.h

```
/*
 * File: random.h
 * --------------
 * Library package to produce pseudo-random numbers.
 */

#ifndef _random_h
#define _random_h

#include "genlib.h"

/*
 * Function: Randomize
 * Usage: Randomize();
 * --------------------
 * This function sets the random seed so that the random sequence
 * is unpredictable.  During the debugging phase, it is best not
 * to call this function, so that program behavior is repeatable.
 */

void Randomize(void);

/*
 * Function: RandomInteger
 * Usage: n = RandomInteger(low, high);
 * ------------------------------------
 * This function returns a random integer in the range low to high,
 * inclusive.
 */

int RandomInteger(int low, int high);

/*
 * Function: RandomReal
 * Usage: d = RandomReal(low, high);
 * ---------------------------------
 * This function returns a random real number in the half-open
 * interval [low .. high), meaning that the result is always
 * greater than or equal to low but strictly less than high.
 */

double RandomReal(double low, double high);
```

```
/*
 * Function: RandomChance
 * Usage: if (RandomChance(p)) . . .
 * -----------------------------------
 * The RandomChance function returns TRUE with the probability
 * indicated by p, which should be a floating-point number between
 * 0 (meaning never) and 1 (meaning always).  For example, calling
 * RandomChance(.30) returns TRUE 30 percent of the time.
 */

bool RandomChance(double p);

#endif
```

FIGURE B-8 random.c

```
/*
 * File: random.c
 * --------------
 * Implements the random.h interface.
 */

#include <stdio.h>
#include <stdlib.h>
#include <time.h>

#include "genlib.h"
#include "random.h"

/*
 * Function: Randomize
 * -------------------
 * This function operates by setting the random number
 * seed to the current time.  The srand function is
 * provided by the <stdlib.h> library and requires an
 * integer argument.  The time function is provided
 * by <time.h>.
 */

void Randomize(void)
{
    srand((int) time(NULL));
}
```

```
/*
 * Function: RandomInteger
 * -----------------------
 * This function first obtains a random integer in
 * the range [0..RAND_MAX] by applying four steps:
 * (1) Generate a real number between 0 and 1.
 * (2) Scale it to the appropriate range size.
 * (3) Truncate the value to an integer.
 * (4) Translate it to the appropriate starting point.
 */

int RandomInteger(int low, int high)
{
    int k;
    double d;

    d = (double) rand() / ((double) RAND_MAX + 1);
    k = (int) (d * (high - low + 1));
    return (low + k);
}

/*
 * Function: RandomReal
 * --------------------
 * The implementation of RandomReal is similar to that
 * of RandomInteger, without the truncation step.
 */

double RandomReal(double low, double high)
{
    double d;

    d = (double) rand() / ((double) RAND_MAX + 1);
    return (low + d * (high - low));
}

/*
 * Function: RandomChance
 * ----------------------
 * This function uses RandomReal to generate a number
 * between 0 and 100, which it then compares to p.
 */

bool RandomChance(double p)
{
    return (RandomReal(0, 1) < p);
}
```

INDEX